HOW

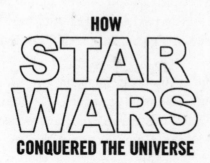

CONQUERED THE UNIVERSE

Chris Taylor is the deputy editor of *Mashable*,
the world's largest social media and technology
news website. He has covered the intersection
of business and culture for two decades as a
writer and editor for *Time, Business 2.0, Fortune
Small Business*, and *Fast Company*. A graduate
of Merton College, Oxford and the Columbia
University Graduate School of Journalism,
he lives in Berkeley, California.

"This is a wildly entertaining book, and if it's not the definitive history of the making of *Star Wars*, I don't know what is. But it's more than that: it tells a rollicking good story about storytelling itself, about the intersection between art and commerce, and paints surely the most complete and deeply felt portrait of George Lucas to date."
—**Dave Eggers, author of** *The Circle*

"George Lucas didn't only create an iconic film franchise, but also a mind-virus that's infected the imaginations of billions of people around the world. Chris Taylor delivers an exuberant forensic analysis of the phenomenon in *How Star Wars Conquered the Universe*—a must-read for any fan, film buff, or student of modern culture."
—**Brad Stone, author of** *The Everything Store:*
Jeff Bezos and the Age of Amazon

"Chris Taylor's colorful biography of *Star Wars*, the franchise that shaped modern culture, is more than just a geek's delight. It is a creativity manual—and shows how the relationship between films and fans can stimulate innovation."
—**Walter Isaacson, author of Steve Jobs official biography**

"It's impossible to overstate the cultural, social and even political impact of *Star Wars*. It started as a balm for a people racked by moral confusion, a juvenile bolt hole for a nation with shattered self-esteem, but the blast wave of enthusiasm and love it inspired was to engulf the planet. Culturally speaking it is, quite simply, the Force. Chris Taylor's affectionate and hugely entertaining book tracks the phenomenon from inception to dominance and with a wry smile, asks us to 'look at the size of that thing!'"
—**Simon Pegg, actor and** *Star Wars* **fan**

"Chris Taylor's *How Star Wars Conquered the Universe* is the definitive guide to the first forty years of the *Star Wars* galaxy. Part biography, part history, part fanboy gossip, *How Star Wars Conquered the Universe* is an accessible, fun read for any lover of *Star Wars*."
—**Ian Doescher, author of the** *William Shakespeare's*
Star Wars **trilogy**

"Smart. Eloquent. Definitive. This is the book you're looking for."
—Lev Grossman, author of the *New York Times* bestselling
Magicians trilogy

"Whether they read the novelization of the first *Star Wars* before the film
came out, like me, or were blown away by *Revenge of the Sith*, anyone touched
by the most enduring space fantasy mythology of the past
two generations will thrill to Taylor's passionate telling of the saga
behind the saga: How a lonely tinkerer from a backwater town
changed the world via interplanetary heroism. To *Star Wars*
obsessives and those wanting to understand modern pop
culture: this is absolutely the book you are looking for."
—Brian Doherty, author of *This Is Burning Man*

"Finally, fans get the full history! The Force is strong with Chris Taylor,
who gives us enough stories and juicy details to impress even
Darth Vader. This book belongs in every *Star Wars* collection."
—Bonnie Burton, author of *The Star Wars Craft Book*
and *You Can Draw: Star Wars*

"Taylor brings a genuine love of pop and nerd culture to this comprehensive
retrospective on one of the 20th century's most popular film series... Taylor
has compiled an impressive collection of background research and insider
info that any fan would be glad to own."
—*Publishers Weekly*

"It's impossible to imagine a *Star Wars* fan who wouldn't love this book...
It really is hard to imagine a book about *Star Wars* being any more
comprehensive than this one. It's full of information and insight and analysis,
and it's so engagingly written that it's a pure joy to read... There are plenty of
books about *Star Wars*, but very few of them are essential reading. This one
goes directly to the top of the pile."
—*Booklist* (starred review)

"A smart, engaging book... welcome reading for fans of *Star Wars*—or, for
that matter, of *THX 1138*."
—*Kirkus Reviews*

HOW
STAR
WARS
CONQUERED THE UNIVERSE

The Past, Present, and Future of
a Multibillion Dollar Franchise

CHRIS TAYLOR

HEAD
ZEUS

For Jess, The True Chosen One

First published in the USA in 2014 by Basic Books,
a Member of the Perseus Books Group

First published in the UK in 2014 by Head of Zeus Ltd

ISBN (E) 9781784970451   ISBN (TPB) 9781784970598

Designed by Pauline Brown

Printed and bound by
Griffin Press

Head of Zeus Ltd
Clerkenwell House
45–47 Clerkenwell Green
London ECIR OHT

WWW.HEADOFZEUS.COM

CONTENTS

Contents

INTRODUCTION: A NAVAJO HOPE

George James Sr. was eighty-eight years old when I met him in July 2013, but in the crimson of a setting desert sun he seemed almost timeless. He wore a white Stetson and had leathery skin, a thin build, and deep-set, coal black eyes; he stooped a little from the shrapnel that has been in his back since 1945. James is Tohtsohnnii, part of the Big Water Clan of the Navajo people, and was born where he still lives, in the mountains near Tsaile, Arizona. When he was seventeen, James was drafted and became that rarest of World War II veterans: a Code Talker. He was one of five Code Talkers who stormed the beaches of Iwo Jima and transmitted more than eight hundred vital messages back and forth between the island and the offshore command post in their native language. Their code was virtually unbreakable because there were then fewer than thirty nonnative speakers of Navajo in the entire world. For an encore, the 165-pound James helped save an unconscious fellow private's life by carrying his 200-pound frame across the black sands of Iwo and into a foxhole. His calmness under fire helped determine the course of the horrific battle, and arguably the war. "Were it not for the Navajo," said a major in George's division, "the Marines would never have taken Iwo Jima."

James's wartime story was enough to make my jaw hit the floor when I met him. But there was something else about him that was almost as incredible. George James was the first person I'd met, in a year of searching, who seemed to genuinely not know the first thing about the movie we were about to watch: something called *Star Wars*.

"When I heard the title, I thought, 'The stars are at war?'" James said, and shrugged. "I don't go to the movies."

There haven't been any movie theaters here in Window Rock, Arizona, the sun-bleached capital of the Navajo nation, since the last one closed in 2005. Window Rock is a one-stoplight town with a McDonald's, a dollar store, a couple of hotels, the eponymous natural stone arch, and a statue honoring the Code Talkers. There are plenty of screens here, but they're all personal: teens thumb through smartphones in parking lots; there are iPads and TVs and Wi-Fi in Window Rock just as in any twenty-first-century western town. But there's no large public screen where the people—they're called Diné (pronounced "dee-nay"), Navajo, or just the People—can get together and share a projected dream.

But for one night in 2013, that changed. On July 3, the first movie ever dubbed into a Native American tongue was screened at the rodeo grounds on a giant screen bolted to the side of a ten-wheeler truck. Just outside of town, on Highway 49, sat the only poster advertising this historic event, on a wilderness billboard that for a time became the hottest roadside attraction on the Arizona–New Mexico border. "*Star Wars Episode IV: A New Hope* translated into the Navajo language," it said, alongside a 1977 poster for the movie.

I must have seen that *Star Wars* poster a million times, but on this highway from Gallup, out of my element and surrounded by brush-covered mesas, I could almost make myself see it through fresh eyes. The kid in white robes appears to be holding some sort of flashlight to the sky; a young woman in strange hair buns holds a gun and poses by his side. Behind them looms a giant gas-mask face with dead eyes and a Samurai helmet. What a strange dream this movie must be.

Just inside town is the Navajo Nation Museum, which spent the past three years persuading Lucasfilm to collaborate on this adaptation of *Star Wars*. I had to wonder why they persisted so long instead of choosing another translation project—and then I walked into the office of the museum director, Manuelito Wheeler, and saw a shelf full of Boba Fett figurines taking pride of place. Manny, as he is known, is a big bear of a guy with a stoic expression and silver flecks in his black ponytail hair. A more relaxed and unpretentious museum director you could never hope to meet. He called me "dude" from our first phone call. He told me he'd loved the original trilogy ever since he caught it on VHS in his late twenties. He can more than hold his own in the traditional geek bonding ritual of quoting *Star Wars* lines. (When I was running late for a subsequent meeting with him, we texted each other Death Star trench-run dialogue: "Stay on target." "I can't maneuver!" "Stay on target.")

Wheeler could wax lyrical about the purpose of the screening, which the museum had conceived of as a way to nurture and preserve the Navajo language, but he also understood that in order for that campaign to be most effective, these matters needed to be approached the same way that *Star Wars* itself begs to be approached: with exuberance and lightness.

Not that the need to preserve the Navajo language is not dire. The people's mother tongue, also known as Diné, is dying. Fewer than half of the three hundred thousand People of the Nation can speak it at all; fewer than one hundred thousand are fluent. Fewer than one in ten can read Diné. Back in George James's day, kids were taught English in reservation schools and spoke Diné at home. These days, Diné is taught in schools, but kids of the twenty-first century don't care to learn it. Why bother, when English fills their smartphones, tablets, and TVs? "We're know-it-alls now," Wheeler sighed. "We need to reinvent ourselves."

What the next generation of Diné needed, he figured, was exactly what George Lucas felt the youth of the 1970s needed: adventure, thrills, good vs. bad, a fairy tale utterly divorced in space and time from the here-and-now, yet also grounded in familiar themes and myths. The story Lucas labored over for years was in many senses a product of its time and the eras that had preceded it, but the dream he captured on celluloid turned out to be utterly malleable and exportable. *Star Wars* might just have the power to make Diné cool again.

But isn't this just a form of American cultural imperialism, in which Native people are surrendering to the forces of Hollywood? Wheeler has two words for that notion: "C'mon, dude." *Star Wars* is not Hollywood. It is the brainchild of a staunchly independent, Hollywood-hating filmmaker in Marin County who recruited a bunch of young countercultural visual effects guys in a Van Nuys warehouse. The villain of this fairy tale, the Empire, was inspired by the US military in Vietnam; the Ewoks by the Viet Cong; the Emperor by President Nixon. The fairy tale was charmingly benign enough to mask that fact, and now every culture around the planet, whether embattled or entitled, sees itself in the Rebel Alliance. But the subversive story was there from the moment Lucas sat down to write his first draft. "*Star Wars* has got a very, very elaborate social, emotional, political context that it rests in," Lucas said in 2012. "But of course, nobody was aware of that."

And there's another reason for the Navajo to embrace *Star Wars* more than most cultures. "There's something spiritual going on here," Wheeler says. He points out that Joseph Campbell, the giant of global mythology, steeped himself in Navajo culture. That was the subject of Campbell's first book, *Where the Two Came to Their Father* (1943), published three years before *The Hero with a Thousand Faces*. If George Lucas was as influenced by that book as he claims, Manny says, "then *Star Wars* in Navajo brings it full circle."

I asked Wheeler what the elders—seniors are highly esteemed in Diné culture—would think of the movie. He raised a finger, pulled out his iPhone, and showed me pictures from the cast and crew screening, a more intimate affair to which he had invited a hundred elders. He swiped through pictures of old women in bright azure and red dresses. "It's a matriarchal culture," he said, "so when Princess Leia comes on the screen and is this powerful figure, they get it." Wheeler grinned and pointed to his grandmother. "And she really digs Obi-Wan."

I was thrilled for Wheeler's grandmother, but my disappointment was palpable. He wasn't to know, but by inviting the elders to the private screening for the cast, he had all but torpedoed my last real hope of finding someone, anyone, who was a true *Star Wars* innocent.

The road that had taken me to Window Rock began just before the thirty-fifth birthday of *Star Wars* in 2012. During a meeting to plan coverage of this milestone at *Mashable*, the website where I work, it was discovered that one of our own—features writer Christine Erickson—had somehow never seen *Star Wars*. Our immediate reaction: How had she survived this long? All her life, Christine had heard incomprehensible phrases like "May the Force be with you" and "These are not the droids you're looking for." Recalled Christine: "I used to have to just ask people what they were talking about." Her friends' reaction always fell on a spectrum "somewhere between scoffing and laughing."

A familiarity with *Star Wars*—or at least the 1977 film of the franchise, which has spawned enough sequels, prequels, TV adaptations, and other spin-offs to boggle the mind and to justify the book you now hold in your hands—is the sine qua non of our modern media-drenched global culture. Shame and scorn is the very least that anyone like Christine can expect. "I've had people say to me, 'We can't be friends anymore,'" says Natalia Kochan, a graduate student who somehow managed to miss the movie despite attending George Lucas's alma mater, the University of Southern California.

I began to notice how *Star Wars*–saturated modern life is; references crop up in the oddest places. I went to a yoga class; the teacher's short hand for the technique of ujjayi breathing was "just breathe like Darth Vader." I went to Facebook for a press briefing on the algorithm that governs what stories we see in our news feeds; the executive explained it by showing how Yoda would see different posts from Luke Skywalker compared to the posts Darth Vader and Princess Leia would see on their feeds, because of the different familial relationships. Nobody in the room batted an eyelid. *Star Wars* had become the one movie series for which it is always perfectly acceptable in modern society to discuss spoilers. (Vader, by the way, is Luke Skywalker's dad.)

Perhaps this is to be expected at Facebook HQ; its founder, Mark Zuckerberg, was enough of a nerd to have had his bar mitzvah *Star Wars*–themed. But you need only peruse those news feeds to see how frequently *Star Wars* memes and references permeate social media. At the time of this writing, the original movie has been "liked" by 268 million Facebook users.

Or if you want to be more old-school about it, just turn on the TV. It almost doesn't matter which channel. *30 Rock, Archer, Big Bang Theory, Bones, Community, The Daily Show, Everybody Loves Raymond, Family Guy, Friends, The Goldbergs, House, Ink Master, Just Shoot Me, King of the Hill, Lost, MythBusters, NewsRadio, The Office, The Simpsons, Saturday Night Live, South Park, Scrubs, That 70s Show*—all these shows and more have casually tossed around *Star Wars* references, written *Star Wars*–based plotlines, or produced special *Star Wars* episodes. The popular nine-year-old sitcom *How I Met Your Mother* spoke for whole generations in its obsession with the original *Star Wars* trilogy. The show's hero learns never to date a woman who hasn't seen it; the show's lothario keeps a Stormtrooper costume center stage in his apartment. There was a time between the trilogies when *Star Wars* lived on the geeky fringes of society. No longer. Now, it seems, society is telling us that *Star Wars* gets you laid and mated.

Star Wars is every bit as important elsewhere in the world as it is in America. In the United Kingdom, there's a popular TV and radio reality show on which guests are asked to perform some activity that they have to shamefully admit they've never done; the title is *Never Seen "Star Wars."* Japan is particularly *Star Wars* crazy; in Tokyo I met an American who'd moved to the country to be with his boyfriend and was still met, years later, with near-constant mockery by the boyfriend's traditional Japanese parents—not for his sexual orientation, but because the poor guy had never seen *Star Wars*. "They keep quoting lines of dialogue at me," he complained.

We at *Mashable* couldn't allow this state of ignorance and shame to continue for one of our own. Plans were made for a live blog. We'd show Christine the original movie. She'd tweet about it; we'd all chime in. The Twitter hash tag for the event was "#starwarsvirgin." *Mashable*'s community was abuzz. What is *Star Wars* like through fresh eyes? Would Christine be blown away? Could we capture the elusive spirit of 1977, just for a moment?

Well, not exactly. Christine got wrapped up in the action, to be sure, but— well, so much of it seemed oddly familiar. Every big-budget special effects movie since *Star Wars* has employed elements from the original film—so many that they are now all recognizable tropes. (For example, the "used universe"— that style of making technology and futuristic costumes look real and dirty and lived-in—was a *Star Wars* innovation. Practically every science fiction movie since the early 1980s has borrowed it, from *Blade Runner* and *Mad Max* on down.) Nor have *Star Wars* virgins been sheltered from the world of advertising, which contains a burgeoning number of *Star Wars* homages. Verizon produced a Halloween ad in 2013 in which entire families dress as *Star Wars* characters, and the fact goes unmentioned, because doesn't everyone? Christine's response on seeing the droids R2-D2 and C-3PO for the first time: "Oh, so that's where the smartphone comes from." (Verizon and Google license the name "Droid" from Lucasfilm.) She recognized R2-D2 as a Pepsi cooler that used to live by the bleachers at high school. Darth Vader? Christine knew that costume: it was the one worn by that kid in the 2011 Volkswagen Super Bowl commercial. And yes, even she knew Vader was Luke's dad already.

Every supposed *Star Wars* virgin has actually picked up an extraordinary number of spoilers in their lives—this was my hypothesis. I decided to test it in a larger experiment. For May the Fourth—*Star Wars* Day, an event first suggested by a British MP's pun on "May the Force" in 1979, but really came into its own as a holiday for the first time in 2013—*Mashable* asked Lucasfilm and the petition website *Change.org* to collaborate on a screening of the original movie for #StarWarsnewbies ("virgin," we decided, was too much of a hot-button word), held at the *Change.org* headquarters in San Francisco.

The first thing we discovered was how hard it is to find anyone in the Bay Area in the twenty-first century who had never seen any *Star Wars* movies. This was, after all, ground zero for the first culture bomb; it only took until the end of 1977 before the number of people who'd bought a ticket to see *Star Wars* in the city exceeded its 750,000 population. Even with the combined recruitment efforts of StarWars.com, Change.org, and *Mashable*, we managed to unearth just thirty newbies, alongside a much larger number of friends and relatives who simply wanted to watch them watch it for the first time.

Before the screening, the newbies were interviewed to determine just how much they knew. Again, they surprised us. "I know it's out of order," said Jamie Yamaguchi, thirty-two, a mother from Oakley, California, of the set of six films. "I thought that was kind of strange." (Her parents' strict religious code meant she'd seen few movies to begin with.) The characters she knew: Princess Leia, Obi-Wan Kenobi, Artoo, Luke, "the gold guy, and that annoying guy who speaks funny. Oh, and Darth Vader."

Many answers were along the lines of this (also real) response: "Oh, I don't really know any of the characters' names—except for Luke Skywalker, Han Solo, Princess Leia, Darth Vader, Obi-Wan Kenobi, and Yoda. That's all I got."

"I know the big reveal," said Tami Fisher, a teacher at UC Hastings College of the Law and a former clerk to a California Supreme Court justice. "The father-son relationship between whatever their names are."

"My kids asked me if Luke and Leia knew they were brother and sister," said Yamaguchi. "I was like, 'They are?'"

It's increasingly hard to avoid *Star Wars* spoilers. They bombard us from birth whether we seek them out or not. A number of parents have come up to me during the process of writing this book and asked how come their younger kids know all the names of all the characters and planets in *Star Wars* and can recite the most obscure historical details behind almost every aspect of the franchise, despite the fact that those kids are too young to have seen any of the six movies yet. I've responded by asking either "Where did Luke Skywalker come from?" or "What are those teddy bear creatures in *Return of the Jedi* called?" When the parents answer "Tatooine" or "Ewoks," I say, "There you go. That planet was never named in the original *Star Wars*; those creatures are never actually named in a *Star Wars* movie. You picked their names up someplace else." (I found out what Tatooine was called at the age of four in 1978, years before I saw *Star Wars*, when I read it on the back of a cereal box; the revelation of the Ewoks came in a 1983 book of collectible stickers, months before *Return of the Jedi*.)

How far has this benign cultural infection spread? Is there anyone on the planet not carrying a little piece of *Star Wars* code in their heads? "We do not know how many individual people have seen a *Star Wars* movie in a theater," a Lucasfilm spokesperson told me, "but we do know that there have been approximately 1.3 billion admissions over the six films worldwide." That seems a conservative estimate, and it would be equally conservative to add another billion home video viewers on top of that, judging by the $6 billion the franchise has earned in VHS and DVD sales over the years. This does not even begin to count video store rentals or the vast market of pirated copies. How many billions more have watched it on TV, or seen an ad, or picked up one tiny piece of the $32 billion worth of *Star Wars*–licensed merchandise that's cluttering up the planet? Or, to look at the question the other way around, how many billions, or millions, of people have managed to avoid every last one of these trappings of the *Star Wars* franchise? And just who *are* these people?

I was naïve enough to think I could just come to somewhere like Window Rock and catch wide-eyed innocents watching *Star Wars* for the first time. But that hope was dashed the moment the Albuquerque and Salt Lake City Garrisons of the 501st Legion, a charitably minded bad-guy *Star Wars* costuming organization, rolled into Window Rock after epic long drives, donned their uniforms, and marched into the rodeo grounds at sunset. They were met with rapturous applause from the packed bleachers—a welcome greater than any I'd seen the 501st get at a Comic-Con or *Star Wars* Celebration convention. They marched in alongside the lines of viewers that had been forming for hours in 107-degree heat—a Stormtrooper, a snowtrooper, a biker scout, an Imperial guard, a bounty hunter, and of course, one Dark Lord of the Sith himself. Darth Vader was mobbed, with babies pressed into his arms while excitable mothers took pictures on iPads.

I also noticed a bunch of enterprising kids selling lightsabers. They were wearing Stormtrooper T-shirts with the legend "These aren't the Diné you're looking for." I asked Wheeler if the T-shirts were his doing, but he shrugged. He only made the sparkly "Navajo *Star Wars*" tops for the crew. He wandered off to have his picture taken with Boba Fett.

Help me, Elders, I thought. *You're my only hope.*

And then, as the mesas turned from sunset crimson to twilight indigo and a lightning storm started to crackle in the distance, I met George James Sr., Iwo Jima veteran and *Star Wars* virgin. It was as if I'd just been introduced to a unicorn leaping over a double rainbow. It had to be too good to be true. I ran through a list of names: Skywalker. Solo. Lucas. Wookiee.

James shook his head at all of them, uncomprehending.

I pointed out the tall guy in the black helmet, who was now dealing with a line of guys pointing and tapping their throats: they wanted to take a picture for a popular Internet meme called Vadering, where you leap in the air and pretend to be force-choked by the Dark Lord. James was perplexed. He genuinely had no idea why the kids from his tribe were doing battle with glowing sticks. When Wheeler got up to introduce the local Navajo voice talent, I had to tell James that no, this is not the Mr. Lucas I had just been talking about.

Then, just before the floodlights dimmed and the Twentieth Century Fox logo appeared on the screen, something occurred to James. He had seen something on someone's TV one time, he remembers, a clip from a movie set in space. "I saw wild birds," he says.

Wild birds in space? What could that be? I think for a second. I hold my arms up and then down at 45 degrees. "Like this?"

James nods; his eyes light up in recognition.

"Wild birds."

X-wing fighters.

Even eighty-eight-year old George James Sr., who lives in the mountains and sleeps under sheepskin in a home so remote that it is blockaded by snow for months at a time, was carrying inside his head a piece of *Star Wars* code—just like you and I and pretty much everyone else on the planet.

The Twentieth Century Fox fanfare ended, the screen went black, and an electric cheer went up from the crowd. Familiar blue letters appeared on the screen—but this time, for the first time in history, the phrase "A long time ago in a galaxy far, far away" was rendered in words so alien they had once been banned by the US government, so unfamiliar to the rest of the planet that they were used in World War II cryptography:

> Aik'idaa' yadahodiiz'aadaa,
> Ya' ahonikaandi . . .

That's all it took. The crowd roared so loud that I could barely hear the blast of the theme's opening chord. And *Star Wars* casually conquered one more Earthling culture.

This book is a biography of the franchise that turned Planet Earth into Planet *Star Wars*.

Its goals are twofold. First, to provide the first complete history of the franchise from its fantastical origins through Disney's $4.05 billion purchase in 2012 of Lucasfilm, the studio that created the movies. Second, and perhaps more interestingly, the book aims to explore the other side of the relationship: how *Star Wars* has affected, and been affected by, its planet of fans.

The story of the *Star Wars* franchise itself shows creativity at its most powerful. It is the tale of how something titled The Journal of the Whills, a couple of pages of impenetrable *Flash Gordon* fan fiction scribbled in pencil and then abandoned by its creator, transmogrified into a vast universe that has sold $32 billion (and counting) worth of merchandise around the globe. (Taking into account ticket sales, licensing, and other revenue streams, it's likely that *Star Wars* generated more than $40 billion between 1977 and 2013.) Much of that success had to do with the hard work of a small posse of dedicated believers whose names were not George Lucas. But *Star Wars* has millions of extremely devoted acolytes far beyond this initial cabal: collectors and costuming collectives, droid builders and lightsaber lovers, spoofers and satirists—and most of these groups have, in unexpected ways, become part of the franchise itself.

Even Lucas himself, at his most messianic, recognized that he was responsible for, at most, a third of what we talk about when we talk about *Star Wars.* "I am the father of our *Star Wars* movie world—the filmed entertainment, the features and the television series," he said in 2008. "I set them up and I train the people and I go through them all. I'm the father; that's my work. Then we have the licensing group, which does the games, toys and all that other stuff. I call that the son—and the son does pretty much what he wants. Then we have the third group, the holy ghost, which is the bloggers and fans. They have created their own world. I worry about the father's world. The son and holy ghost can go their own way."

Since Lucas spoke those words, the father has gone his own way, too. Lucas entered retirement after the Lucasfilm sale, and while new *Star Wars* features are barreling toward the cineplexes of Earth, they're doing so under the watchful eye of the franchise's stepmother, veteran film producer Kathleen Kennedy. When the next *Star Wars* film hits the big screen, it will be the first in history to emerge without the helicopter parenting of the Creator* himself.

With *Star Wars* poised to enter a new phase in its long history, it's an appropriate moment to pause and take stock of this creation. In particular, it's worth pointing out that behind the scenes, the world of *Star Wars* has never been as unified as Lucas's holy trinity metaphor suggests. The more you fall in love with the franchise, it seems, the more you recognize how rickety its space-fantasy foundations are. The greatest fans of the Expanded Universe (the collective name for the hundreds of *Star Wars* novels, thousands of *Star Wars* comics, and countless video games and other media that have developed characters and storylines outside of the *Star Wars* films themselves) are the first ones to tell you how much of it is self-contradictory and just plain sucks. And many lovers of *Star Wars* are intensely partisan about—and protective of—the films themselves. Fans of the original trilogy (*Episodes IV* to *VI*, released 1977 to 1983) have stewed obsessively over every change in Lucas's upgraded versions (tweaked for rerelease in 1997, 2004, 2006, and 2011) and remain bitterly divided over the prequel trilogy (*Episodes I* to *III*, released 1999 to 2005.) These twin passions, love and hate, are as constant companions to *Star Wars* fans as Jedi and Sith, or as the twin suns of Tatooine.

---

* This is a nickname Lucas applied to himself in 2007, after President George W. Bush famously referred to himself as "the Decider." Responding to a question from Conan O'Brien about fans challenging him, Lucas pointed out that he is another George W. He told the host: "I'm more than the Decider. I am the Creator!"

In 2005, a twenty-year-old in Vancouver called Andrey Summers witnessed the deep schisms within *Star Wars* fandom firsthand when he attended a midnight screening of *Episode III*. The screening was preceded by a costume contest, and Summers was shocked when, in the course of it, older fans actually started booing the homemade costumes of younger fans. "That's when I realized," Summers told me, "these fuckers aren't into joy. They're into canonical accuracy." He went home and penned a column for an online magazine called *Jive*, titling it "The Complex and Terrifying Reality of *Star Wars* Fandom." Like most of *Star Wars* itself, it was intended half-humorously but written in earnest.

The conceit was that Summers was having a hard time explaining fandom to his girlfriend, because true fans hate *everything* about *Star Wars*, from the whiny delivery of Mark Hamill as Luke Skywalker in the original trilogy to the CGI pratfalls of Jar Jar Binks in the prequels. "If you run into somebody who tells you they thought the franchise was quite enjoyable, and they very much liked the originals as well as the prequels, and even own everything on DVD, and a few of the books, these imposters *are not* Star Wars *fans*," he wrote.

Jive magazine is now defunct, but Summers's column went viral; translated into multiple languages, it bounced around the Internet on forum after forum. He was bombarded by emails from amused fans who got the point and angry ones who didn't. Summers was clearly onto something when he pointed out that love and hate are twin virtues of every true *Star Wars* fan—and though he didn't know it, his column was an echo of something that was said in the halls of Lucasfilm itself.

"To make *Star Wars*, you've got to hate *Star Wars*"—this is a maxim I've heard from more than one veteran of Lucasfilm's design department. What they mean is that if you're too reverential about what came before, you're doomed. You've got to be rebellious and questing. The franchise must constantly renew itself by pulling incongruous items out of a grab bag of outside influences, as Lucas himself did from the start. Likewise, fandom must constantly renew itself with new generations of viewers brought in by the prequels, by more recent additions to the canon like *The Clone Wars* and *Rebels* animated TV shows—and, soon enough, by the sequels to the first two trilogies.

Just as new fans are essential to keeping *Star Wars* alive and healthy, jaded old fans must renew themselves by going back to the thing that gave them joy in the first place. "To be a *Star Wars* fan," said Summers in his column, "one must possess the ability to see a million different failures and downfalls, and then somehow assemble them into a greater picture of perfection. Every true *Star Wars* fan is a Luke Skywalker, looking at his twisted evil father, and somehow seeing good."

"We hate everything about *Star Wars*," Summers concluded, before offering a line every fan in the world could agree with: "But the *idea* of *Star Wars* . . . the idea we love."

In Window Rock, lightning forked in the distant hills, but few in the audience seemed to notice or care. The people were cheering like crazy for the roll-up at the start of the movie, every word of it in Diné. Once the dialogue started, there was laughter for the first fifteen minutes straight—not laughter at the film or the performances, but the joyful laugh of a people seeing a movie in their own language for the first time.

To a viewer like me who had grown up watching *Star Wars* in its original English, a surprising amount of the movie sounded the same. Lucas loved cool sounds and sweeping music and the babble of dialogue more than he cared for dialogue itself. Much of the movie is either free of speech or filled with foreign chatter from aliens and droids. Think of Artoo, of the Jawas: intentionally unintelligible, and we love them for it. Think of how much time is filled with back and forth blaster fire or the roar of TIE fighters (actually a slowed-down elephant call) or the hum of lightsabers (a broken TV, an old projector). When I first learned that Wheeler's team of translators had been able to translate the movie from English to Navajo in just thirty-six hours, it had seemed a superhuman feat. In fact, there just isn't as much English in *Star Wars* as you might remember.

Some words are untranslatable and remain in English. "Princess Leia" has the exact same title, since Diné contains no concept of royalty. Likewise "Imperial Senate" and "Rebel Alliance." (The Navajo are so inherently egalitarian that the US government had to force them to set up a governing body it could deal with.) And while the translated dialogue is something of a mélange—the translators speak three different dialects of Diné—this turns out not to matter at all. After all, it doesn't sound weird to English speakers that half of the actors in the film are British and half American. (Carrie Fisher seems to be playing both accents, but we've grown to embrace that too.)

Humor translates differently, of course. The audience seemed to laugh at every word Threepio says. This may be partly because the droid is a drag act: voice actress Geri Hongeva-Camarillo matches his prissy tones perfectly. (Some months later I told Anthony Daniels, the original Threepio, about this gender switch. "The Navajo must be a very confused race," he said in his best clueless

Threepio voice, before winking and reminding me that concept artist Ralph McQuarrie—one of the largely unsung heroes of *Star Wars*—had originally envisioned Daniels's character as a waif-thin female robot.)

The biggest laugh of the evening, however, goes to Leia's line aboard the Death Star: "Governor Tarkin, I should have expected to find you holding Vader's leash. I recognized your foul stench when I came on board." There's a kind of earthiness to the phrase, it seems, that sounds especially hilarious in Navajo, even though Fisher found it one of the hardest lines of the movie to sell: Peter Cushing, who plays Tarkin, "actually smelled of linen and lavender," she said.

How strange it was to watch *Star Wars* in a foreign language and still get sucked in. I marveled once again at how flawlessly the story flows. Then came the CGI monsters of Mos Eisley, the shot from Greedo, the incongruous appearance of computerized Jabba, and I winced. I was reminded that, in approving this adaptation, Lucasfilm had required Wheeler to use the latest, highest-quality Special Edition version.

The movie starts to drag a little around the trash compactor scene. The kids in particular seemed distracted, preferring to play with their lightsabers in the aisles; they were caught up in the idea of *Star Wars* more than *Star Wars* itself. Families got up and left before the Death Star trench run, eleven pm being way past kids' bedtime. But for the hundreds who remained when the lights came up, the movie created its own little cult of celebrity, just as it has in every other culture it has ever invaded. There was a cast signing afterwards with the main seven voice actors, and the line to meet them coiled around the stadium. The actors are all amateurs (Darth Vader, for example, was played by local sports coach Marvin Yellowhair) and had been chosen from out of 117 people who had auditioned for the roles; they had been selected for their passion in performing, not for their knowledge of Diné. It worked: their exuberance, plus their familiarity with the subject material, carried the day.

I went looking for reactions from the few elders I saw in the line. This was the closest I was ever going to get to a complete adult newbie experience of *Star Wars*. Every one of the elders to whom I spoke shared George James's confusion over the title: Why are the stars at war? The elders also echoed one of the main complaints that had been leveled against *Star Wars* in 1977: it went too fast. (Modern audiences, of course, see it as too slow; the ethos of *Star Wars* helped beget the ethos of MTV.) Some were confused about exactly what each side was fighting for. You can translate "stolen data tapes" into Navajo, but you can't make it make sense.

Then I learned something spiritual from this group of elders: Manny was right about the Joseph Campbell connection bringing *Star Wars* full circle. "May the

Force be with you," it turns out, is a nearly literal translation of a Navajo prayer. "The Force," in their usage, can best be described as a kind of positive, life-filled, extra-sensory force field surrounding them. "We call for strength, for protection from negativity," Thomas Deel, eighty-two, told me via a translator.

Some of the elders glimpsed their belief system in George Lucas's creation. "Good was trying to conquer evil, and asking for protection in doing so," summarized Annette Bilgody, an eighty-nine-year-old in the traditional dress of a Diné grandmother. She also offered the highest praise of the evening: "I enjoyed it as much as my granddaughter did."

She wasn't alone. In the months to come, Wheeler would take his translated version of the movie on the road, screening it for Native American communities at film festivals around the United States. A DVD of *Star Wars* in Navajo sold out multiple times at Walmarts around the Southwest. Twentieth Century Fox and Lucasfilm got all the money, but that didn't matter to Manny. What mattered, he said, was that "the concept is blossoming." He was hearing one question constantly asked around the Nation: What films should we make in Navajo next? There was even interest in building another movie theater in Window Rock.

As for George James Sr.? He excused himself ten minutes into the movie and never returned. Perhaps, as a veteran of Iwo Jima, he hadn't wanted to see people blasting each other with weapons modeled on World War II military sidearms. Perhaps, as a Code Talker, he hadn't relished a story that revolves around an innocent hunted for the crime of carrying a message. But I like to think that, in leaving early, James managed to preserve some of the mystery he had brought to that evening and that he's still out there at his home in the mountains, wondering about wild birds and the stars at war.

1.

MARS WARS

Clearly, *Star Wars* is a grand, galaxy-spanning mythological epic. Except no, wait, it's a family-sized fairy tale in the land of far, far away. Unless it's a Samurai story, or possibly a World War II-style action adventure.

Since the first film in 1977, fans and critics have contorted themselves in all sorts of directions explaining the appeal of *Star Wars* by reference to a dozen different genres. No one is more adept at this than George Lucas, who variously compared it to a Spaghetti Western, Sword and Sorcery, *2001*, *Lawrence of Arabia*, *Captain Blood*, and the entire James Bond franchise—and that was all before the original movie was even filmed. Navigate past this asteroid field of influences, and what you find at the center of Star Wars is a simple, whimsical subgenre: space fantasy.

Space fantasy is to its parent genre, science fiction, as Luke Skywalker is to Darth Vader. George Lucas came closer to science fiction with his first movie *THX 1138*, and then abandoned it as too real, too dismal, too unpopular at the box office. Science fiction projects an image of the future through the lens of the present. The focus is on technology and its implications. There is some effort to adhere to the physical laws of the universe. It is fiction about science, whereas space fantasy is, well, fantasy set in space.* Science fiction echoes our

---

* Arguably, every movie Lucas ever made or had a strong hand in producing was some kind of fantasy or fantasia. *American Graffiti* was the latter; the genre he once offered for *THX* was "documentary fantasy."

world; space fantasy transcends our world. It is nostalgic and romantic, and more freely adventurous, and it takes technology as a mere starting point. It casts aside the laws of physics in favor of fun. "I was afraid science fiction buffs would say things like 'you know there's no sound in space,'" Lucas said in 1977. "I just wanted to forget science." In space, everyone can hear you go *pew pew*.

This great divide in speculative fiction, the possible versus the merely enjoyable, goes back to the fin de siècle rivalry between French science fiction pioneer Jules Verne and his upstart English contemporary, H. G. Wells. Verne was avowedly no scientist, but he wanted to be scientifically plausible. In *From the Earth to the Moon* (1865), Verne sends his lunar explorers off in a capsule shot out of a giant cannon; he includes pages of precise calculations in a brave attempt to prove that such a thing were possible.* Wells, like Lucas, was always much more interested in the workings of society and the individual than in the mechanics of science. When he got around to writing his own protagonist lunar novel, *The First Men in the Moon* (1901), Wells had his scientist declare that he'd never heard of Verne's book. He proceeds to discover an antigravity substance called "Cavorite" that simply floats his capsule, with him and a visiting businessman in it, moonwards. Verne sweated the details so much that his adventures didn't get to the moon until a sequel novel; Wells wanted to ship his heroes there as fast as possible so they could explore a fanciful lunar civilization he had invented. (This irked Verne to the point that he made a mocking and rather point-missing demand of Wells: I can show you gunpowder; show me the Cavorite!) When Lucas decided to make his version of outer space noisy with laser fire and screeching jets, he was establishing himself in the Wellsian tradition.†

They were at odds over means, but what united Verne and Wells was a crying need to expand the landscape of the human imagination. Myths, as Lucas once observed, are invariably set in "that place just over the hill"—the next frontier, real enough to excite interest but unexplored enough to be mysterious: distant Greek islands in the classical age, the dark forest in medieval fairy tales,

---

* Brave, but ultimately mistaken. It is not possible to shoot yourself to the moon via cannon. Do not try this at home.

† This Verne-Wells split can be seen in the earliest short, silent science fiction movies, too. This time the divide was the Atlantic rather than the Channel. Georges Melies made *A Trip to the Moon* in 1902, shooting his explorers in a cannon. Thomas Edison made *A Trip to Mars* in 1910, in which a scientist covers himself in antigravity dust and floats to the Red Planet.

the Americas in the wake of Columbus. By the twentieth century, with most of the planet explored, space became the last remaining place just over the hill. And one corner of space in particular fascinated authors and readers, and solidified the lineage that led to *Star Wars*: Mars.

The Mars craze spread steadily after an Italian astronomer, Giovanni Schiaparelli, famously spotted channels (*canali*) on the Red Planet in 1877. British and American newspapers, not understanding or caring much about the difference between *canali* and canals, loved to print large, illustrated, speculative features on Martian civilization, especially after amateur astronomer Percival Lowell wrote a trilogy of "nonfiction" books detailing what that civilization might look like. Writers with no scientific background started to pen novels of Martian exploration. Their methods of reaching the Red Planet varied wildly. In *Across the Zodiac* (1880), English journalist Percy Greg sends his explorers off in an antigravity rocket called the *Astronaut* (he coined the term). Gustavus Pope, a Washington, DC, doctor whose previous book had tackled Shakespeare, wrote *Journey to Mars* in 1894. In it, an American naval lieutenant encounters Martians on a small island near the South Pole; eventually they take him back to their planet in an antigravity "ethervolt car." (Wells, meanwhile, confounded genres by having his Martian invaders in the 1897 classic *War of the Worlds* arrive via capsules shot from Martian cannons—Verne in reverse.)

But where Mars first met space fantasy was in a book that is the unlikely great-granddaddy of *Star Wars*. An English writer and son of a newspaper baron, Edwin Lester Arnold, decided to cast aside spacecraft altogether; in *Lieutenant Gullivar Jones: His Vacation* (1905), he takes another fictional US Navy lieutenant and packs him off to Mars on a magical Persian carpet. Arnold's Mars is surprisingly medieval. The people of Hither, indolent and soaked in a strong wine, are beset by the barbarous hordes of Thither. The Hitherites have a slave class, a king, and a beautiful princess. When the princess is taken in tribute to Thither, Jones sets off on a planet-wide journey to free her. He is an oddly unappealing protagonist, prone to long speeches: too smug to be a hero, too upright to be an antihero. He carves "USA" into the side of a mountain during his journey. Arnold seemed torn between adventure story and anti-American satire, and the novel was a flop. Dismayed, he quit writing. (It would not be published in the United States until 1964.)

Arnold's idea of a fantasy Mars was rescued five years after he wrote it by an unlikely savior: a thirty-five-year-old manager of pencil sharpener salesmen in Chicago. The pencil guy had a lot of time on his hands, a lot of stationery in the office, and a desire for greatness that wouldn't quit. He read pulp fiction magazines, and noting that most of their stories were "rot," he tried his hand at one. Like Arnold's tale, it is narrated by an American officer who is magically transported to Mars—this time in the blink of an eye, by sheer willpower. No Cavorite, no carpets, just a man "drawn with the suddenness of thought through the trackless immensity of space." Like Jones, the pencil guy's protagonist meets outlandish humanlike characters and apemen, and fights heroically for the hand of a princess. The pencil guy thought his story childish and ridiculous. He asked for it to be published under a pen name intended to telegraph his sanity: Normal Bean. His real name he thought unsuitable for an author. It was Edgar Rice Burroughs.

The serial that became *A Princess of Mars* was first published in February 1912 in a monthly pulp magazine called the *All-Story*. It was a runaway success. Captain John Carter, Burroughs's larger-than-life hero (and fictional uncle), found a following that Gullivar Jones could only dream of. No confused satire, this; in Burroughs's book, lines of good and evil are clearly drawn. Carter is less wordy—there's not a line of dialogue in the first third of the book—and more consistently placed in peril than Jones. From chapter one, when he is attacked by (of all people) Native Americans in Arizona, Carter is beset by spears, swords, rifles, and claws. The lesser gravity of Mars (which Burroughs dubs "Barsoom") gives Carter just enough of an advantage in strength to help him overcome these considerable odds. He can leap buildings in a single bound. As well as kicking the space fantasy genre into high gear, Carter has a good claim on being the first superhero: he's the progenitor of both Superman and Luke Skywalker.

Burroughs bought a ranch called Tarzana in present-day LA, quit the pencil job, and churned out three more serialized sequels—plus the story he named for his new home, *Tarzan of the Apes*—before *Princess of Mars* even made it to publication in book form. Over the rest of a productive, affluent lifetime, Burroughs would return to Barsoom in eleven more books. Barsoom is a fascinating planet, and unprecedented in its mixing of past and future concepts. It is a dying and largely barbaric world, but an atmosphere factory keeps it breathing. It has military flying machines, radium pistols, telepathy, domed cities, and medicine that makes lifespans a thousand years long, but it also offers plenty of sword play, courtly codes of honor, a medieval bestiary of creatures, and a succession of chieftains carrying lances on their steeds. The exotic desert setting is straight out of *One Thousand and One Nights*.

Barsoom stories follow a trusty formula. Escapes, rescues, duels, and wars are the main attraction, but in between them Burroughs reveals aspects of this curious world with the confidence of a good travel writer. Territories are clearly delineated. Green Tharks are largely barbaric nomads; the red inhabitants of Helium are rational aristocrats. In his second book, *Gods of Mars*, we find blond-haired, white-skinned Barsoomians who are evil, decadent murderers, preying on the planet's inhabitants with the false promise of heaven.

Burroughs was modest and careful to say he was only writing for the money. But that's an understatement. Read him today, and you can easily get infected by the same powerful, pure, childlike enjoyment that enveloped the author as he wrote. Barsoom offers morally clear heroics with as much mythological depth as you care to invest in its mysteries. The thrill of exploration and the wonderment of a world that is able to cause us to suspend our disbelief are rendered with the same spirit Lucas would later describe in his movies as "effervescent giddiness." You can find this spirit in the work of artists as diverse as J. R. R. Tolkien and Stan Lee: ideal for the adolescent mindset, yes, but accessible to all and capable of greatness. Arthur Conan Doyle's epigraph to *The Lost World* (1912) would explain this principle so well that it would also later grace the press materials for the original *Star Wars*:

I have wrought my simple plan
If I give one hour of joy
To the boy who's half a man
Or the man who's half a boy.

That statement was wrong in one respect: it turned out early on that women and girls liked this stuff too. Dejah Thoris, John Carter's Barsoomian wife, who has his eggs (how that's possible, we don't know, except to reiterate: it's space fantasy) is hardly an empowered heroine by twenty-first-century standards (Carter has to rescue her from implied rape dozens of times in eleven books). But the eponymous princess of the first book is a scientist, an explorer, a negotiator; her famously bosom-filled portraits by fantasy artist Frank Frazetta in the 1960s turned her into a sexual icon, but they barely did her justice. By the standards of her day, Dejah Thoris was a suffragette. Princess Leia has a long line of antecedents, and they go back to Dejah.

Burroughs published his last Barsoom stories in 1943, and the last in a similar Venus series in 1942, eight years before he died. By then, the genre was variously known as space fantasy, space opera, planetary romance, and sword-and-planet, and had been taken over by Burroughs's many successors. Most memorable was his fellow Angelino Leigh Brackett, later known as the queen of space opera. She burst out of nowhere in 1940, at age twenty-five, selling an astonishing streak of twenty-six stories to pulp magazines in four years. All were set in what became known as the Brackett solar system. Her conception of each planet was fairly derivative—her Mars and Venus looked a lot like Burroughs's—but where Brackett excelled was in describing the interplanetary conflict between them. The scope had expanded, from Mars wars to solar wars. Brackett's scope was expanding too, and she started working on Hollywood screenplays such as *The Big Sleep*. She was unable to bring her two careers together until 1978, when she was named the writer of the first draft of *The Empire Strikes Back*.

Brackett's husband, Edmond Hamilton, would also contribute to *Star Wars*, albeit in a more nebulous fashion. His 1933 story in the pulp magazine *Weird Tales*, "Kaldar, Planet of Antares," contains this groundbreaking description of a weapon wielded by its hero—a saber made of light:

> The sword seemed at first glance a simple long rapier of metal. But he found that when his grip tightened on the hilt it pressed a catch which released a terrific force stored in the hilt into the blade, making it shine with light. When anything was touched by this shining blade, he found, the force of the blade annihilated it instantly.
>
> He learned that the weapon was called a lightsword.

Hamilton's story was reprinted in paperback in 1965, eight years before a young filmmaker named George Lucas would begin to devour every pulp science fiction story he could get his hands on.

Alongside Burroughs, the pulp magazines that published Hamilton, Brackett, and their ilk were, in many ways, the other grandparents of *Star Wars*. Two of the most important stories in the prehistory of the franchise both appeared in the August 1928 issue of *Amazing Stories*. The cover showed a man with a jetpack. He was the star of "Skylark of Space," a story written by E. E. "Doc" Smith, a food chemist who wrote fiction as a hobby when he wasn't trying to engineer the perfect doughnut. Smith had Burroughs's fizzing enthusiasm plus the desire to go farther in space. His heroes pilot a spaceship powered by "element X"—Cavorite on steroids—which shoots them out of the solar system and into the stars for the first time in fictional history. They bounce from planet to planet as if out for a day trip in a jalopy; a planet-wide war causes them less trouble than the double wedding and medal ceremony that follows. All the speed, romance and humor of *Star Wars* are in "Skylark." Smith would go on to write the Lensman stories—tales of mystical interstellar knights that would influence Lucas's concept of the Jedi. Smith expanded the scope of conflict to our entire galaxy.

That issue of *Amazing Stories* was even more important for another story, "Armageddon 2419 AD." The name of its hero, who is accidentally gassed to sleep in the twentieth century and wakes up in the twenty-fifth, was Anthony Rogers. He wasn't given his now-legendary nickname until his creator, the newspaper columnist Philip Nowlan, approached a national comic strip syndicate about doing a regular strip based on the character. Well, said the syndicate, "Anthony Rogers" sounded too stiff for the funny pages. How about something a bit more cowboy-like—say, Buck?

Buck Rogers is, essentially, John Carter in the future: a plucky, heroic fish out of water. But simply being five centuries old grants him no superpowers. And that provides an opening for his version of Dejah Thoris, Wilma Deering. Wilma is a soldier, like all American women of the twenty-fifth century, in which North America has been invaded by Mongol hordes. She is more intelligent and adept than Buck. In one early strip, she is shown fashioning a radio from a pile of electronic parts, to Buck's amazement. Captured and forced to wear a dress by the Mongol emperor, she exclaims, "What is this, a musical comedy?" What a difference suffrage had made.

Buck endures and evolves. After a few years, the Mongols are replaced as enemies by the traitor Killer Kane. Buck and Wilma are given a rocket ship and head for space—the first time this frontier had been portrayed in the comics. The strip took on new scope with Martian pirates, Saturnian royals, and interstellar monsters. In 1932, *Buck Rogers* became a CBS radio series, broadcast four times a week. This time, the Mongol plot was erased altogether, and Buck is simply resuscitated from five centuries of sleep by the Space Corps.

Other comic syndicates couldn't help but notice *Buck Rogers*'s lucrative cross-media success. At King Features, owned by the world's leading newspaper baron William Randolph Hearst, artists were told the company was looking for a *Buck Rogers* rival. A young artist named Alex Raymond answered the call. His contribution to the space fantasy genre would lead directly, in time, to

Star Wars. Like Lucas in later years, Raymond had to rework his idea several times, but when he got it right, its popularity exploded overnight. Once again, a derivative retread of the space fantasy idea would go further and faster than the original.

Buck Rogers was about to meet his match in Flash Gordon.

F lash Gordon was so vital to *Star Wars*, and such a sensation among Lucas's generation, that it's surprising to find there is little scholarship about the character. The comic strip and the movie serials it spawned formed a vital bridge between literary and visual space fantasy, but if Flash is known at all to most modern *Star Wars* fans, it is in his campy 1980 movie incarnation. Flash is unfashionable, for many good reasons, yet he deserves greater recognition. He was, after all, the first man to conquer the universe.

Flash debuted on January 7, 1934, five years to the day after Buck Rogers, and determined to go his rival one better in every area. Buck was a black-and-white daily; Flash was a color Sunday strip. *Buck Rogers* built slowly; Raymond raised the stakes right from his first panel. Astronomers find a strange planet rushing toward Earth (just like the one in the popular 1933 novel *When Worlds Collide*—this was a genre that liked to recycle plots). We meet Flash on a transcontinental plane hit by meteors from the strange planet; he saves another passenger, Dale Arden, from certain doom by bailing out with her in his arms. They land near Dr. Hans Zarkov's observatory. At gunpoint, Zarkov forces them aboard a rocket ship he intends to crash-land on the approaching planet. There our trio is captured by Ming the Merciless, Emperor of the Universe, who apparently never intended to crash into Earth at all (or at least Raymond seems to forget about that part of the plot; his early strips have a fuzzy, dream-like logic to them in the style of *Little Nemo*). Thus begin decades of adventure on the planet Mongo, with only the briefest of pit stops back on Earth during World War II.

Eight decades have now passed since his debut, and Flash has not aged well. Casual forms of racism and sexism filled the strip from the start. The second panel of the first strip shows African jungles where "tom-toms roll" and "howling blacks await their doom." Flash is introduced as a "Yale graduate and world-renowned polo player"—1930s code, observed Roy Kinnard, co-author of *The Flash Gordon Serials*, for the fact that Flash is "a WASP in good standing." Ming the Merciless is a barely disguised Mongol warlord with a Fu Manchu mustache and yellow skin. (Ming made the strip attractive to Hearst, purveyor of stories about the "Yellow Peril.") Dale Arden, meanwhile, is no Dejah Thoris—and certainly no Wilma Deering. We never learn Dale's occupation. Her sole motivation is to stay by Flash's side. "Men must adventure," writes Raymond in an early strip, paraphrasing a nineteenth-century poem, "and women must weep."

Despite its retrograde aspects, *Flash Gordon* set the gold standard for visual space fantasy. If you can make it past the early years of the strip, during which Flash spends a lot of time in his underwear wrestling various creatures Ming has set upon him, Raymond's increasingly confident representation of Mongo and its inhabitants is your reward. He starts drawing his characters in close-up, their overwrought faces reminiscent of Norman Rockwell paintings. He becomes devoted to drafting a world, its technology and scenery: rocket ships like submarines and cityscapes that anticipate the 1939 World's Fair, jumbled up with Arthurian towers and castles. On Mongo, as on Barsoom, science and chivalry, past and future, fairy tale and science fiction blend seamlessly.

The plots again followed a trusty formula, designed to produce a cliffhanger every week. Flash, Dale, and Zarkov are forever crashing their ships. Flash and Dale constantly declare their love without ever consummating it. They rush to rescue each other from peril. Flash sustains more concussions than an NFL player (which, as polo began to sound too snobbish, is what he would retroactively become). He tells Dale to stay behind because it's too risky; Dale tells him her place is by his side. Queens and princesses fall for Flash everywhere he goes. Dale is always walking in on compromising scenes and "naturally misunderstanding" them. Traitors are in the midst of each court; Flash is forever being suckered by their treachery, overcoming it, and forgiving their crimes, only to have the traitor escape again. It's space fantasy as soap opera.*

Flash is even more of a heroic cardboard cutout than John Carter or Buck Rogers. We never see him give into temptation or fail to forgive. (Only once, when Queen Fria of the frozen north of Mongo convinces him that Dale despises him, does Flash offer a willing extracurricular kiss.) One might call him Superman-like; the superhero arrived on the scene two years later, and Superman's early artists were clearly influenced by Raymond. But at least Superman spends half his life in his bumbling reporter guise, Clark Kent. The only time we see Flash's vulnerability is when he is unconscious. Still, that same

---

* The term "space opera" entered the language in 1941, used as a pejorative by snooty science fiction writers. Later, Brian Aldiss would reclaim the term in his seminal 1974 anthology *Space Opera*—just as George Lucas was constructing a space opera of his own.

relentless heroism that tends to make Flash boring to a modern adult audience still endears him to children—and it certainly endeared him to the adults of the late 1930s, a time when both relentless heroism and escapism became urgently necessary.

Flash Gordon quickly eclipsed Buck Rogers in the speed at which he crossed over into other media. A *Flash Gordon* radio series debuted a year after the strip, running for thirty-six episodes and staying faithful to Raymond's story throughout. A pulp magazine—*Flash Gordon Strange Adventure*—arrived the following year. Universal Pictures hastily acquired the movie serial rights for $10,000, and production began in 1936 on the first *Flash Gordon* serial: thirteen twenty-minute episodes with a budget of $350,000. (That would be $6 million in today's dollars). This was a record for a serial and more than the budget for a major feature film at the time. It wrapped in two months, shooting an incredible eighty-five scenes a day.

The star of the *Flash Gordon* film serial, Larry "Buster" Crabbe, a former Olympic swimmer, was himself a huge fan of the comic strip before taking the role. "When I went home in the evening I'd pick up the paper and find out what old Flash had gotten himself into with Ming," Crabbe recalled years later. Hearing about a casting call for the serial at Universal, where he had friends at the casting office, he went along out of curiosity: Who could possibly portray this hero? Crabbe himself, it turned out, once the casting office talked him into dying his hair blond. No expense was spared on the costumes, made to match the colors of the Raymond strip—even though the serial was shot in black and white. (Just digest that for a second. It was a different age.)

When *Flash Gordon* debuted, the film serial—like the comic strip—was an immediate sensation. First-run movie houses, which normally didn't screen serials at all, showed Flash as their main evening feature. The serial boasted state-of-the-art effects: two-foot miniature wooden rocket ships with copper fins, matte paintings, and split-screen shots that allowed Flash to fight a giant lizard. The city of the Hawkmen floated in billowing clouds of white smoke. The serial also offered some of the more revealing costumes yet seen on screen, particularly the Dejah Thoris–like outfit of Ming's lustful daughter and Flash's eventual ally, Princess Aura. The Hays Office, which enforced a set of moral standards agreed on by the studios in the hopes of heading off government censorship of the motion picture business, made its displeasure known. In future serials, Aura and Dale would look positively demure, while Flash would stop stripping to his shorts.

A second serial, *Flash Gordon's Trip to Mars*, followed in 1938, based on another Raymond storyline. Film historians have often assumed the setting was changed from Mongo to Mars to cash in on Orson Welles's sensational radio broadcast of *War of the Worlds* that year. But the timing doesn't add up: the serial was released in March, while Welles's fear-inducing play was a Halloween performance. Mars continued to excite the popular imagination no matter the month. Besides, Buck Rogers had been there, and anything Buck could do, Flash could do better.

That said, *Trip to Mars* is probably the weakest of the *Flash Gordon* serials. It adds comic relief in the hapless form of Happy Hapgood, a photojournalist who tags along for the rocket ship ride. The serial is most notable for the Martian enemies of Ming, the Clay People, who are eerie shapeshifters able to fade into cavern walls.

In 1939 came a *Buck Rogers* serial that cemented the relative position of the two franchises: it had a smaller budget and used *Flash Gordon's* hand-me-downs. Also made by Universal, also starring Crabbe (with his natural hair this time), it reused *Flash's* Martian sets and costumes. These days, serial fans consider it pretty much a fourth *Flash Gordon*. Somewhere in the home for retired space fantasy characters, Buck and Wilma must be livid.

Finally in 1940 came *Flash Gordon Conquers the Universe*. The slowest-moving and most cheaply made of all the *Flash Gordon* serials, it was also the most mature. Of course, mature is a relative term in a story that opens with Ming's rocket ships seeding "Purple Death dust" in Earth's atmosphere. But Ming, now dressed in the regalia of a European royal, was no longer the Fu Manchu stereotype; he was a stand-in for the real-life tyrant conquering Europe while the cameras rolled. Mongo's dissidents, we discover, have been locked up in concentration camps. Drunk on his own mad ambition, Ming has gone beyond declaring himself Emperor of the Universe; he now claims to *be* the universe. Thus, from the last line of the serial came its title, as Zarkov radios the outcome of their titanic struggle to Earth: "Flash Gordon conquers the Universe."

Plans were laid for a fourth *Flash Gordon*, but World War II intruded. Production stopped on all serials, and the format fell out of vogue when peacetime resumed. Alex Raymond had quit the comic strip to join the Marines; when he returned he focused on other cartoonish heroes, such as Jungle Jim and Rip Kirby. Flash Gordon, continued under the stewardship of artists Austin Briggs and Mac Raboy, was to outlast them all—including his creator.

Raymond's life ended prematurely and tragically, thanks to his love of fast cars. Unhappy in his marriage, with his wife refusing to grant him a divorce so he could marry his mistress, Raymond reportedly managed to get involved in four automobile accidents in one month in 1956. The last one killed him. Raymond was forty-seven.

As he met his end, Raymond had no idea that his most famous creation was reverberating around the head of a twelve-year-old boy in the unassuming town of Modesto, California. The boy also had a passion for fast cars and was just six years away from his own fateful appointment with an automobile accident. The flaming torch of space fantasy was about to be handed down to another generation—and this time, it would set the world alight.

2.

THE LAND OF ZOOM

Modesto is known the world over as the birthplace of George Lucas, but until 2013, most of the town's residents had never seen him. Even in 1997, when the town unveiled a statue dedicated to the wildly popular coming-of-age movie that made Lucas his first fortune, the movie based on his teenage years there, *American Graffiti*, Lucas declined to attend. It wasn't a snub; it was just George being George. He had more movies to produce, three kids to raise, and a world to fly around. Plus, for all his fame, Lucas has never been all that comfortable in front of an audience. "He's a behind the scenes guy; he's not out front," George's little sister Wendy, who still lives in Modesto, told the town in 2012. "People mistake that as being aloof."

Finally, for the fortieth anniversary of *Graffiti*, Wendy persuaded her big brother to be the grand marshal of Modesto's fifteenth annual classic car parade. On June 7, 2013, crowds braved the 103-degree heat that marks the height of a Modesto summer, lining the parade route three hours ahead of time. Here and there Modesto-ites chattered about the visiting VIP, trying to get his story straight. One might have expected a tall tale or two from his contemporaries, now in their late sixties, but classmates from Downey High had little to offer. "A nerd, but he was very nice," recalled one. Another remembered Lucas reading comic books between classes. A third, MaryAnn Templeton, barely knew the slight kid who hid behind his camera at high school games. "We all called him a little dork," she said. "Little did we know."

13

Inside the air-conditioned Gallo Center for the Arts stood Lucas himself, in trademark flannel shirt, jeans, and cowboy boots. Normally, when this most private man goes into public at a press-attended gathering, he wears the face best described by *Variety* editor in chief Peter Bart, who compared Lucas to a small-town banker: "impeccably polite and implacably distanced, as though fearing you might ask an inappropriate question or request a loan." But on this day, reunited with his sisters, he seemed almost giddy. The mood lasted for roughly one question from a reporter, and you can see it deteriorate in the follow-ups. What brought him back? His sister, "the small one," twisting his arm. Did he have a favorite memory of cruising? "It's like fishing," he said. "Mostly sitting around talking, having a good time." Did people here mostly talk to him about *Graffiti* or his other films? "I don't really talk to people on the street."

Finally, the *Modesto Bee* reporter pressed the question most residents were eager to ask: Did Modesto somehow influence *Star Wars*?

Lucas offered a smile that was one part pained grimace to two parts practiced politesse. "No, not really. Most of these things come out of your imagination."

Thus dogged once again by his most famous creation, Lucas stepped out into the street. A great roar went up, and a crowd of teenagers who had previously been dissecting the latest rumor of a Boba Fett spin-off movie pressed up to police barriers to get his autograph. Lucas signed their posters and fan club cards, his features once again arranged in the small-town banker configuration.

Certainly, the *Star Wars* films weren't conceived in Lucas's hometown; that happened a hundred miles to the west, in San Anselmo, where Lucas wrote the scripts for the films in the mansion that his *Graffiti* fortune had afforded him. Modesto did inspire the movie that allowed Lucas to purchase the home where *Star Wars* would be born. (The original *Star Wars*, as we shall see, was the indulgence of a multimillionaire director who would never really need to write a word, or direct a picture, again.)

Modesto gave Lucas his stepping-stone movie and much more besides; it was also the physical location for early *Star Wars* inspiration. But all that visionary stuff technically took place inside one boy's head. So if you want to glimpse the earliest glimmerings of the *Star Wars* universe, you'd be better off reading about World War II, or grabbing a pile of comic books from the mid-1950s, or (best of all) hopping on a rocket ship to Mongo than cruising around Modesto.

One place Modesto is not: Tatooine. The analogy to Luke Skywalker's desert-covered, double-sunlit home world has been drawn many times over the years by journalists who clearly don't live in Northern California. Their comparison seem reasonable enough, given that Luke is a character based on the naive side of Lucas's personality. But if the Tatooine experience on Earth is what you want, you'd find a much better candidate in the desert town of Mojave, hundreds of miles to the south: literally a spaceport, it also offers a roughneck equivalent of the Mos Eisley cantina, with curious-looking locals and sand that gets everywhere.

No, Modesto is verdant. The climate is positively Mediterranean. The town stands atop of California's central valley, the fruit, nut, and wine basket of the world. There's a lot of farming here, but you wouldn't call it moisture farming—unless you like your moisture infused with fermented grapes. The Gallo winery was founded here in 1933 by a couple of brothers who were so by-the-book that they waited until the moment Prohibition officially ended before digging up old winemaking pamphlets in the town library. By the twenty-first century, Gallo held 25 percent of the US wine market. It is still family-owned. A little education, a lot of hard work, and you can build a global empire: the example was not lost on Lucas, who just happens to grow pinot noir grapes at his own winemaking operation, Skywalker Vineyards.

Another misapprehension about Modesto: that it is extremely remote. "If there's a bright center of the universe, you're on the planet it's farthest from," said Luke of Tatooine. But the Bay Area is less than ninety miles due west of Modesto. If I-580 traffic is light and you have a lead foot, you can be in San Francisco in an hour and change. Sacramento is less than an hour to the north, Yosemite the same distance to the east. You can get to Hollywood faster from Modesto than from the Bay.

This doesn't mean it is easy to leave Modesto. The town exerts a strong cultural gravitational pull. It's just that, to see what else the world has to offer, you must be determined, and you must like fast cars—two qualities that the young George Lucas had in spades.

When George Walton Lucas Jr. was born, in the early morning of May 14, 1944, droves of German bombers were attacking Bristol. General Rommel was preparing a plot to assassinate Hitler. Britain's cryptographers were uncovering a plan by Göring to trick the RAF into bombing unused airfields. Japanese fighters harried American bombers over the Truk Atoll on their way to Wake Island. The British XIII Corps consolidated a bridgehead over the Rapido River, helping to open the road to Rome. In a school hall in London, workers prepared a giant map of Normandy as General Montgomery prepared to explain to Churchill and the king exactly how he and Eisenhower intended to liberate Europe.

The planet was on fire, but Modesto was about as far away from the conflagration as you could get. Lucas's father, George Walton Lucas Sr., had volunteered but was turned down—he was too slender, and he was married. The Lucases were even more insulated from the horrors of the war than they might have been. Still, the war left no one untouched, and its after effects—the warm glow of victory, the posttraumatic stress—went on for decades. Lucas later remembered growing up in a world where the war was "on all the coffee tables"— in *Time*, in *Life*, in the *Saturday Evening Post*, in living Technicolor.

The 1950s and 1960s were filled with war movies, each one a repolish of legendary heroics on the ground and—increasingly—in the air. *The Dam Busters* (1955), *633 Squadron* (1964), *Tora Tora Tora!* (1970)—These were the movies Lucas would record and splice to create the ultimate dogfight, a 25-hour reference reel that would form the basis for all the special effects of *Star Wars* (which would be shot by the same cinematographer who filmed *Dam Busters*).

If you look closely enough, you can see that wartime influence throughout the franchise. It's in the one-man fighters, the rebel's helmets and boots, the Stormtrooper's modified UK Sterling submachine guns, Han Solo's German Mauser C96 semiautomatic, the tall fascist in the black gas mask. "I like to say *Star Wars* is my favorite World War II movie," says Cole Horton, who runs the website From World War to *Star Wars*, which has documented hundreds of callbacks. "The story comes from myth. The physical, tangible things come from history."

The war's aftermath wasn't all coffee-table entertainment for young Lucas. Another conflict, this one on the Korean peninsula, broke out a month after he turned five. His sister Ann's fiancé was shipped out and killed in action there when George was nine. Even before that tragedy, Lucas had been subjected for years to the specter of an even more frightening war. His year of schoolchildren was the first to be shown the civil defense training film *Duck and Cover* (1951). Imagine seeing this at age five: not just a cartoon about a clever turtle who hides in his shell when the atom bomb drops, about also two schoolchildren who, "no matter where they go or what they do, are *always* trying to remember what to do if the atom bomb explodes right then."

Future war took terrifying shapes under the wooden desks of John Muir Elementary School. "We did duck and cover drills all the time," Lucas recalled later in life. "We were always hearing about building fallout shelters, about the end of the world, how many bombs were being built." No wonder, then, that he once called growing up "frightening" and said he was "always on the lookout for the evil monster that lurked around the corner." It couldn't have helped that he was a scrawny kid, an occasional target for older and larger boys at John Muir who liked to throw his shoes at the lawn sprinklers. More than once, Wendy had to step in and rescue him.*

War fears and bullies aside, Lucas was hardly suffering. He was the son of an increasingly successful and wealthy small businessman, George Walton Lucas Sr., who knew and supplied stationery to everyone in town. He was in the store at seven A.M., six days a week. Evenings were for golf, for the Rotary club; on Sundays, he and Dorothy, his wife and high school sweetheart, would do the accounts.

George Sr. had once dreamed of being a lawyer, and the career may well have suited him. Thin and ramrod straight, fond of dispensing Shakespeare quotes at the dinner table, he could have been a courtroom Lincoln. But he had been glad to have a job in a stationery store in 1933 when unemployment hit 20 percent. He talked himself into a 10 percent stake in the company, L. M. Morris, which the store's eponymous owner had founded in 1904. George worked his way up to a 50 percent stake and then took over and renamed the company when Morris retired. By 1950, the Lucas Company grossed a very respectable $30,000 a year (about $300,000 today). George Sr. made all that from stationery and—crucially for *Star Wars*, as it turned out—toys.†

George Lucas Sr. was no Darth Vader, despite the suggestion from Lucas biographer Dale Pollock that his relationship with his son inspired the paternal revelation in *Empire Strikes Back*. In fact, the young Lucas—Georgie, as he was affectionately called—seems to have been doted on. Lucas owned the best train set in Modesto, a three-engine Lionel Santa Fe, and all the Lincoln logs to go with it. Georgie got a great allowance for the time: 4 cents a week at the age of four, rising to $4 a week (that's $94 in 2013 dollars) by the age of eleven. In July 1955, George was packed off on his first plane ride—to Anaheim for the

---

* One older and larger boy in Modesto at the time was named Gary Rex Vader. No connection has yet been drawn to the Vader of his later years, but Lucas once said that he came up with the name "Darth" first and then tried "lots of last names, Vaders and Wilsons and Smiths." There are plenty of Wilsons and Smiths in Modesto, but only a handful of Vaders.

† In time, George Sr. became the 3M corporation's district agent and would focus on his corporate accounts, renaming his company Lucas Business Systems. Later sold to Xerox, it survives in Modesto to this day, with five branches across Northern California. Its website claims it has operated under the Lucas name since 1904.

grand opening of Disneyland. He just missed Walt Disney opening the park in person but arrived in time for day 2. "I was in heaven," Lucas said of the trip. In the shining realm of Tomorrowland, the nameless monster that haunted him back in Modesto was banished. The Lucas family would return to Disneyland every other year.

Certainly, George Sr. exerted a powerful influence over his children when he was around. "His dad was stern," says Patti McCarthy, a professor at the University of the Pacific in nearby Stockton, California, who thoroughly researched Lucas's life for Modesto's *American Graffiti* Walk, a series of video kiosks around the town. "But parents were stern then. Wendy Lucas always says, 'He was a stern man and a good father.'" Georgie and his sisters were expected to do chores; the boy detested having to mow the lawn with the family's battered old mower. His way of dealing with that was to save up his allowance, borrow $25 from his mother, and buy a new mower. Dale Pollock painted that incident as defiance. Hardly: it was the stuff of budding business genius—a sensibility that Lucas surely soaked up from his entrepreneurial dad. "My first mentor was my father," Lucas would tell Bill Moyers years later. (He named Francis Ford Coppola his second and Joseph Campbell his third.)

If anything, Lucas's mother was a more mysterious presence than his father. Dorothy, the daughter of a Modesto real estate magnate, was bedridden with inexplicable stomach pains throughout much of Lucas's childhood. At the age of ten, Lucas came to her with his first existential question: "How come there's only one God, but so many religions?" No satisfying answer was forthcoming, and Lucas would spend a good chunk of the next twenty years developing a new name for God that was embraced by religious and nonreligious alike.

Before Lucas Sr. became wealthy enough to move the family to an isolated walnut ranch outside town, Lucas enjoyed their modest tract home at 530 Ramona Avenue. Its most important feature was the alley out back, which Lucas shared with his tight knot of childhood friends: John Plummer, George Frankenstein, and Mel Cellini. The friends later called it "alleyway culture." They'd run in and out of each other's houses, always involved in some creative endeavor, constructing toy rail tracks and backyard carnivals. At eight, they made a roller coaster ride out of a telephone wire spool. "I liked to build things," Lucas recalled in 2013: "woodshop, treehouses, chess boards." He constructed forts and 3-D landscapes with papier-mâché mountains. He filled his room with drawings: landscapes, mostly, with people added as an afterthought. If asked what he wanted to be, he would suggest "architect." There was one exception to Lucas's impersonal artistic creations: in art class at school he drew—earning a rebuke from his teacher—pictures of "space soldiers." Such disapproval would not stop him for a second.

Lucas' writing and directing abilities were skills he had to acquire later in life with great effort and pain. His early years yield few portentous examples of either pursuit. But one of his surviving stories, from the third grade, foreshadows his love of speed, his lifelong sense of urgency, and his stick-to-itiveness: the qualities that would compel Lucas to complete every creative project he ever started. The story is called "Slow Poke," but the setting is the "land of Zoom"—in retrospect, a perfect name for the chrome-plated 1950s.

> Once upon a time in the land of Zoom, there was a little boy who was always slow. All the other people in the land of Zoom were fast.
> Once this little boy was walking down a trail when he met a horse. He wanted to talk to the horse, so he started to sit down on a stone where a bee was sitting.
> No sooner had he sat on the stone than he was up with a yell, and running down the trail.
> From then on, he was never slow again.

Brevity aside, this was quintessentially Lucas: a dreamer of a boy, slow at school, motivated by sudden moments of fear to be fast, an inveterate tinkerer restlessly searching for something cool in the Land of Zoom. "He was bored with school; he needed a bee sting," says Professor McCarthy. "The bee sting was the accident. It's almost a foreshadowing."

As for films, the focus of his later life? He went to the movies once every other week, if that, and while he enjoyed Disney movies—*20,000 Leagues Under the Sea* was a particular favorite—he said that in his teenage years he only went to Modesto's two picture houses to chase girls. Filmmaking was just one of many happy pastimes he tried out with Mel Cellini during the alley years. The pair had tried writing and editing a newspaper on Lucas's return from Disneyland, printed in George Sr.'s store; it lasted for ten issues. Cellini's dad had an 8mm movie camera, which could be used to make stop-motion animation. The boys played a lot of war games with toy soldiers, so they recorded their tiny green army moving across the alley a frame at a time. For special effects, Lucas would light tiny fires. "It was very critical to him that everything would look right," Cellini would remember. "It had to look real."

Even as a young auteur Lucas was learning to link art and profit. One fall he and Cellini built a haunted house in Cellini's garage. It was a sophisticated affair, with ghouls dropping out of the roof and strobe lights. Neighborhood kids were charged a nickel to see it. "We've got to change it around so it's different," Lucas said when the crowds started to drop off; then he relaunched the enterprise as a new and improved haunted house. "He did this a couple or three times; I marveled at it," said Cellini. "As soon as sales fell off, George would go back and redo it and retweak it, and the kids would come back again." It was a trick he would repeat many times with *Star Wars*.

Lucas turned ten in 1954—a transformative year, and one he has hearkened back to on many occasions. It was the year George Sr. bought a television. (He was not the first parent in town to do so, and George had been getting his *Flash Gordon* fix at John Plummer's house for years.) It was the year Lucas first declared his intent to become a race car driver. And it was the year he realized something he revealed publicly years later, in his first promotional short movie.

In 1970, when he was twenty-six, Lucas would make the ten-minute film *Bald* to promote his avant-garde dystopian movie *THX 1138*. The film opens with Lucas and his second mentor, Francis Ford Coppola, gravely introduced as "two of the new generation of filmmen," discussing what influenced the movie. Lucas could have mentioned many dark influences that would have resonated with his generation, such as *Brave New World* and the speeches of Richard Nixon. Instead, he proudly planted his flag in nerd territory. THX "actually came from reading comic books when I was about ten years old," Lucas said. "I was always struck by the fact that we were living in the future. If you wanted to make a film about the future, the way to do it would be to use real things, because we're living in the future."

By the age of ten, Lucas was already a voracious reader of comics. His and his sister Wendy's hoards grew so large that Lucas Sr. devoted an entire room to their comics in the family shed—more than five hundred comic books in total. Even that wasn't enough. On Sundays, while his parents did the accounts, he would go over to Plummer's house and read a stack of comics Plummer's dad got for free from the Modesto newsstand Nickel's News. The covers had all been torn off so they couldn't be resold. Lucas, however, wasn't about to judge a comic book by its lack of a cover.

The year 1954 was the tail end of the postwar zenith known to comics historians as the Golden Age. Superman and Batman were in the prime of their second decades. Subjects were diversifying—cowboy comics, romance comics, horror comics, humor comics, science fiction comics. This was the soup that Lucas swam in: supremely visual, wild, horrific, hilarious, boundary-stretching, authority-defying, and out of this world.

The comic book hero Lucas would recall in his earlier interviews is a largely forgotten character: Tommy Tomorrow of the Planeteers. For decades, Tomorrow clung tenaciously to the pages of *Action Comics*, the title that had given birth to (and in Lucas's childhood was still dominated by) Superman. In comic book terms, this was like opening for the Beatles.

Tommy Tomorrow sprang to life in 1947 as a cadet in what the comic called the "West Point of space." He then became a colonel in a solar system–wide police force called the Planeteers. At first young and naive, Tomorrow soon gained assistance from a sassy female character, Joan Gordy, and an older sword-wielding mentor, Captain Brent Wood. The most shocking twist in the strip: Wood learns that a notorious space pirate, Mart Black, is in fact his father.

Think that was shocking? If you really wanted to be shocked, there was EC Comics. Brash iconoclast William Gaines inherited the company from his father in 1949, and immediately instituted a long line of titles that delved into the smart and the spooky, from horror (*Tales of the Crypt*) to *Weird Science and Weird Fantasy*, which delivered four science fiction short stories per issue, each with a twist in the tale. "EC Comics had it all," Lucas later wrote in a foreword to a *Weird Science* collection. "Rocket ships, robots, monsters, laser beams. . . . It's no coincidence that all of those are also in the *Star Wars* movies." EC's storytelling style was inspirational, too: "mini-movies that managed to keep you enthralled and wanting more until the final page. . . . You read them with your eyes open wide, your mouth agape and your brain racing to take it all in."

But EC didn't have long to live. From April to June 1954, as Lucas sat on a blanket in the back yard reading comics, a Senate subcommittee grilled Gaines over an EC Comics title—one that would have been on newsstands on Lucas's tenth birthday—featuring a grisly image of a woman's severed head. Gaines spoke passionately in his comics' defense, but behind the scenes he was fatally eager to compromise. He helped found the Comics Magazine Association of America, which created the Comics Code Authority, which specifically targeted EC's distribution. Gaines's distributor went bankrupt the following year.

One of Gaines's publications survived unscathed, however, and would prove to be far more damaging to the established order of things than EC Comics. *Mad Magazine*, so quaint today, predated the great satirists of the 1960s. "*Mad* took on all the big targets," wrote Lucas in 2007:

Parents, school, sex, politics, religion, big business, advertising and popular culture, using humor to show the emperor had no clothes. This helped me recognize that just because something is presented to you as the way it is, doesn't mean that's the way it really is. I realized that if I wanted to see a change in the status quo, I couldn't rely on the world to do it for me. The impact this had on my worldview was enormous. I have spent much of my career telling stories about characters who fight to change the dominant paradigm. . . . For that, Alfred E. Neuman bears at least a little of the blame.

Carl Barks, a veteran Disney artist who created Scrooge McDuck and gave him his own comic book in 1952, was also partially responsible for sharpening the young Lucas's contrarian sensibility. The first piece of art Lucas ever bought, in the late 1960s, was a page of Barks's *Scrooge*. Barks comics were passed around at the very first *Star Wars* shoot in the Tunisian desert.

One of the earliest and most sophisticated *Scrooge* strips, a 1954 parody of the utopian novel and film that introduced Shangri-La, *Lost Horizon*, would find echoes in Lucas's later years. The strip opens with the billionaire duck being harassed by phone calls, letters, charity requests, speaking engagements, and the taxman. Seeking a respite, he and his nephews take off in search of the mythical Himalayan land of Tralla La. Scrooge is overjoyed to have found a society where friendship is the only currency. It all goes hilariously wrong when a local finds a bottle cap from Scrooge's now-discarded nerve medicine. A tidal wave of avarice rips through Tralla La, the bottle cap becomes the land's default currency, and the ducks are forced to escape again when the market is flooded.

The ten-year-old Lucas could not have guessed how much this strip foreshadowed his later life. He too would learn the peculiar isolating harassment that comes with being a famous billionaire. He too would use wealth to escape wealth, building his own whimsical Tralla La in Skywalker Ranch. Yet the need to sustain this utopia, and the people he hired to work it, would lead to a life that was far from carefree—and eventually he would sell his main enterprise to the same company that owns Uncle Scrooge.

Scrooge McDuck, Tommy Tomorrow, EC, and Alfred E. Neuman were all key influences on Lucas's growing mind, but they paled in comparison to Flash Gordon. Edward Summer can testify to this. Summer is a New York filmmaker, author, and former owner of the New York City comic book store Supersnipe; he became Lucas's friend and business partner in the early 1970s, when they were introduced by mutual friends and bonded over *Flash Gordon*.

Lucas was looking for original Alex Raymond artwork, and Summer had the connection. In 1974, Summer managed to sneak Lucas in via the back door at King Features, where two friends of Summer's were tasked with scanning Raymond's original strips to microfilm. They were then supposed to destroy it, but luckily for posterity Summer and his pals created an underground railroad that found the strips safe new homes.

Seeing those strips again—as well as borrowing reels of the serials for his own private screening room—allowed Lucas to realize how "awful" his favorite series was; he loved them still, but he came to the conclusion that he had been under a kind of spell as a child. He began to understand how rickety were the foundations of space fantasy. For modern viewers, the appeal of those cheesy, grainy old serials remains something of a mystery. But they connected strongly in children's minds at least until the end of the 1970s (which is when I first saw them). "It has to hit you when you're a kid," says Edward Summer. "When it hits you at the right age, it's indelible."

Flash's popularity with the first TV generation had a lot to do with the serial format itself. In the 1950s, newborn TV stations across America were desperate for content. There were a lot of live shows, and a surprising plethora of live TV science fiction (all of it sadly lost to posterity): *Captain Video and His Video Rangers* (1949–1955), *Tom Corbett, Space Cadet* (1950–1955), *Space Patrol* (1950–1955), *Tales of Tomorrow* (1951–1953). The people behind these shows were no dummies: *Captain Video*'s guest writer list reads like a who's who of 1950s science fiction (Arthur C. Clarke, Isaac Asimov, Walter Miller, Robert Sheckley). But while the talent may have been top-notch, the shows had too much time to fill—thirty minutes a day, five days a week—with almost no budget. "They had really cool spacesuits and really dumb sets," says Summer. "The production values were very poor. So when they started to rebroadcast the *Flash Gordon* serials, it was like being hit by lightning."

Serials had been enormously popular on the radio for years. This was the era of weekly hours with mysterious crime-fighters such as *The Falcon* and *The Shadow*. So it was hardly surprising that their cinematic counterparts turned out to be exactly what TV stations were looking for. Each chapter ran for about twenty minutes. That left time in a half-hour segment for a cartoon, or a local host recapping the story so far, or, most importantly, the sponsor's commercials. (Coca-Cola was a frequent *Flash Gordon* sponsor.) Between the original, 1936 *Flash* serial and the follow-ups from 1938 and 1940, there were forty episodes of *Flash Gordon*. You could run them end to end for two months every weekday with no repeats and then go back to the beginning—which was exactly what many stations did.

Flash Gordon isn't the most well-made or well-received production from the golden age of movie serials, the late 1930s and early 1940s; *The Adventures of Captain Marvel* (1941), a twelve-episode superhero serial from Republic Pictures, usually wears that crown. But *Flash* had twenty-eight more episodes, it was way more action packed, and the kids went crazy for it. Every true believer on the set of *Star Wars* remembered it fondly. Producer Gary Kurtz, four years' Lucas's senior, caught the tail end of *Flash*'s run in Saturday movie matinees before it even came to TV. "*Flash Gordon* definitely made the biggest impression of all the serials," said Charley Lippincott, *Star Wars*' marketing chief, who watched *Flash Gordon* projected onto the side of a library in Chicago. Howard Kazanjian, Lucas's friend and the producer of *Return of the Jedi*, said that visiting Mongo in a rocket ship was his childhood dream, to the point that he and his brother once tried to build their own rocket cockpit out of toothpaste tops. Don Glut, a film school friend of Lucas's and author of *The Great Movie Serials*, says Flash just seemed more alive than the protagonists of other serials: "Buster Crabbe was light years beyond any other actors in serials. He was handsome, he had the physique, he had charisma. Most serials had no connection between hero and heroine. Flash had personality, characterization, and an incredible sexual dynamic. When Dale says to Princess Aura 'I'd do anything for Flash,' it's pretty clear what she's talking about."

The world of special effects had barely advanced since 1936; there just wasn't that much call for it. "Nowadays you can see the spaceships are on wires, and it looks a little klutzy, but this was state of the art stuff," says Summer. "And on TV, the resolution was so poor you couldn't see the wires anyway." For years, Summer would dream of making a movie version of *Flash Gordon*. He wasn't alone; as we'll discover, Lucas only proceeded to pitch *Star Wars* after he couldn't get the movie rights to *Flash Gordon*. One early draft of *Star Wars* used a Raymond panel, Flash and Ming engaged in a fencing duel, for its cover.

Lucas has never been shy about refering to *Flash Gordon* as the most direct and prominent inspiration for *Star Wars*. "The original Universal serial was on TV at 6:15 [P.M.] every day, and I was just crazy about it," Lucas said after shooting *Star Wars* in 1976. "I've always had a fascination for space adventure, romantic adventures." The serial was the "real stand-out event" in his young life, he said on the set of *The Empire Strikes Back* in 1979. "Loving them that much when they were so awful," he said, "I began to wonder what would happen if they were done really well? Surely, kids would love them even more." Lucas paid direct homage with his roll-up—the words that scroll at the beginning of every *Star Wars* movie, just as they do in *Flash Gordon Conquers the Universe*.* His elaborate screen-wipes are recognizably inspired by the serial, too. Indeed, the thread between *Flash Gordon* and *Star Wars* is so obvious to the *Flash Gordon* generation that it sometimes even sees connections that aren't quite historically accurate. For example, Lucas friend Howard Kazanjian believes Luke Skywalker is Flash, Princess Leia is Dale Arden, Obi-Wan is Dr. Zarkov, and Darth Vader is Ming the Merciless.

The origins of those characters are actually more complicated, as we shall see. But there is one kind of masked *Star Wars* character whose origins may indeed go all the way back to *Flash Gordon*. In 1954, another *Flash Gordon* series had been produced directly for television. Made in West Germany by an international production company, it diverged significantly from the original; Flash, Dale, and Zarkov work for the Galactic Bureau of Investigation in the thirty-third century. There is no Ming, only a succession of villains in silver suits. Although this version of *Flash* only lasted for a single season, it had licensed the TV rights to the name "Flash Gordon," which had reverted from Universal back to King Features. This meant that Universal's *Flash Gordon* serial from the late 1930s, the one authorized by Alex Raymond, could not call itself *Flash Gordon* in the 1950s. Thus, when the original *Flash Gordon* serial was aired on TV, it bore a replacement title card that called the show *Space Soldiers*.† Those space soldiers that Lucas drew in art class, then, may have been his first *Flash Gordon* tributes. And in a way they are also a key—the first of many—to understanding why George Lucas made *Star Wars*. A young child's mind is set on fire by a serial story; he is drawn in by the dastardly villain, the love interest, the knowing sage, and most especially the clearly drawn hero. He is hooked on adventures with rocket ships in wildly different settings, with monsters everywhere and peril never more than minutes away, with a cliffhanger every reel. But he surely wonders, as most literal-minded children would, why the title card always says "Space Soldiers," "Space Soldiers on Mars," or "Space Soldiers Conquer the Universe." Who are these space soldiers? They don't seem to be anywhere in the show. There are Ming's guards, who walk around in Roman Centurion helmets with strange faceplates. But there never seem to be more than one or two of them hanging around at any one time. Tommy Tomorrow?

---

* *Star Wars* replicated the exact angle of the *Flash Gordon* roll-up and ended with the same unusual four ellipses.

† Ironically, "Space Soldiers" would have made a much better title for the West German series, which involved far more interplanetary travel than the original serial.

He's more of a space policeman. There are soldiers in all the magazines and books lying on coffee tables—heroic, charismatic soldiers, a soldier who became president—but they're not in space yet.

Then came the day Lucas picked up a 1955 copy of *Classics Illustrated*, issue 124: "War of the Worlds" by H. G. Wells. At the bottom of page 41 is a panel showing the future that the human survivors of the Martian invasion are afraid of: being hunted down by a futuristic army that has been brainwashed, trained, and outfitted by the Martian fighting machines. The soldiers wear sleek round helmets and carry ray guns. Years later, Lucas would leaf through original artwork from that comic at Edward Summer's house, turn to the page, and say that's it—that panel is where a lot of *Star Wars* came from.

Space soldiers also cropped up in *Forbidden Planet*, the movie Lucas saw for his twelfth birthday, in 1956, at Modesto's State Theater. Leslie Nielsen was the dashing captain of a whole flying saucer full of space soldiers visiting the mysterious planet of Altaria IV, with its hilarious deadpan robot, Robby, and its cavernous Death Star–like interior.

"He was really taken with it," remembered Mel Cellini of that birthday screening, to which Lucas brought a small gang of friends. "We were just enjoying the moment. He was learning it."

Lucas kept drawing space soldiers in art class, apparently even after the teacher implored him to "get serious." Years later at the University of Southern California, according to his roommate, Lucas would prefer to "stay in his room and draw star troopers" rather than go out to parties. His first wife, Marcia, would remember him talking about space soldiers on the silver screen from the day she met him. Little did any of them know what impact those space troop sketches would have, not just on the films themselves, but also on the foot soldiers who would prove instrumental in spreading Lucas's vision around the world.

After all, what do space soldiers fight in, if not star wars?

3.

PLASTIC SPACEMEN

S _tar Wars_ was the last thing on Albin Johnson's mind the grey, wet summer day in 1994 when he skidded into the back of a van in Columbia, South Carolina. The other guy didn't seem to have any damage, but Johnson got out to check anyway. His hood had popped up, and his grille had broken. Let's call it even, said the van driver. Johnson, relieved, stepped between the cars to put his hood down. That's when a third vehicle suddenly appeared, hydroplaned into the back of Johnson's car, and all but sliced him in two.

His surgeon told Johnson he had lost nearly all of the tendons in his left leg and was facing amputation; his exact words, according to Johnson, were "we're going to throw your leg in a meat bucket." Johnson fired him. He underwent twenty operations on the leg and then spent a year in a wheelchair while getting muscles removed, skin grafted on, and bones from elsewhere in his body chipped up and injected into the injury. At one point he nearly bled to death on the operating table.

A year later, left with what he called a "Frankenstein foot," Johnson finally elected for amputation and prosthesis. Dark days followed, and even his then-wife Beverly giving birth to their first daughter couldn't quite pull him out of the funk. "I kind of hid in my house and felt like a freak," Johnson says.

Johnson kept his workaday job at Circuit City—"putting my psychology degree to good use," he says—and it was there in late 1996 that a coworker, Tom Crews (yes, his real name), made a mission of cheering Johnson up. They talked about common interests: karate, rock and roll. Then they talked about *Star Wars*. Hey, did Johnson know the movies were coming back to theaters, in so-called Special Editions? Johnson brightened. "All we talked about that day was that opening scene where the Stormtroopers come tearing through the door of the *Tantive IV*. We couldn't let go of that concept."

Memories came flooding back. *Star Wars* memories.

Johnson had been born in poverty in the Ozarks in 1969. In the 1970s, his parents were called to a Pentecostal ministry in the Carolinas. His Sunday school teacher told him George Lucas had signed a deal with the devil and made his actors sign papers saying they were going to worship the Force. But Johnson went to see the first film twenty times anyway. Every time he came out of the theater he would run along its brick wall, imagining the gaps between the bricks to be the Death Star trench, and himself the pilot in the X-wing. He would run it so fast, and so close into the trench, he would occasionally skid his head painfully against the bricks. No matter—it was worth it to be Luke Skywalker.

Johnson laments that he didn't grow up to look anything like Luke, and then laughs: "Hey, at least we're both amputees." But then there are the space soldiers, the Stormtroopers pouring through the door in all that bright molded plastic. As he and Crews reminisced about *Star Wars'* most numerous icons, they realized that so long as the detailing on the suit was right, anybody could embody them. When you're a Stormtrooper, nobody knows you're an amputee. You're supposed to blend in, to be expendable—perfect for a shy, self-conscious guy.

Johnson became obsessed with the costume as "a passport to the *Star Wars* universe." He started sketching out ideas for how he could build his own, while Crews searched the nascent web, betting that he could find an authentic Storm-trooper costume—that is, one that matched the on-screen version in every detail, whether Lucasfilm-licensed or not—in time for the Special Editions. This was the pre-Google age, but somehow he stumbled on a Usenet posting in which a guy claimed to be selling an original movie prop costume in an "estate sale" for $2,000. The vendor was actually trying to avoid getting sued by Lucasfilm for selling a reproduction suit without its say-so, without Lucas getting a cut. This was risky, and reproductions in those days were rare. "It was like uncovering a 747 jet in caveman times," Johnson recalls.

Johnson cajoled Beverly, the real breadwinner of the family, into buying the suit in exchange for the next ten years' worth of Christmas presents. Soon, awkward plastic molding parts arrived in the mail. He nervously constructed them with Dremel and glue gun. It was horrible: the helmet hung loosely; the suit was constricting. He felt ridiculous: a plastic spaceman with a metal leg.

He had no line of sight in that helmet. No wonder Stormtroopers were such poor marksmen.

Still, Johnson wore it to his local one-screen theater for showings of *The Empire Strikes Back* Special Edition. Theatergoers poked him and laughed. "I had one guy after another saying, 'You loser, don't you wish you could get laid?,'" Johnson recalls.

But then Crews found his own costume online—another pricey, hard-to-construct model—and joined Johnson a few weeks later for the *Return of the Jedi* screening. This time, patrons looked awestruck and a little afraid as the pair confidently patrolled the lobby. "That's when the switch really flipped," Johnson says. "The more Stormtroopers, the better it looks. I resolved that somehow, in my lifetime, I would get as many as ten Stormtroopers together in one place. That's how big I was thinking."

The pair built a website and posted pictures of their exploits—at comic shops, State Fairs, and preschool graduation, whatever gigs they could get. Johnson wrote captions about a couple of Troopers who were always falling afoul of Darth Vader. He gave his trooper the name TK-210,* a denizen of detention block 2551 on the Death Star. Within weeks, four more Stormtroopers emailed him with pictures of their own. This was before Facebook, before flash mobs, before the golden age of geekdom dawned in the twenty-first century. The Internet had barely become a gathering place for *Star Wars* fans, let alone Stormtrooper costume owners. Yet somehow, here they were.

Johnson now pictured a whole Stormtrooper legion. He recalled several times back in grade school where he'd tried to organize some kind of juvenile army out of his friends; after *Star Wars* came out, he dubbed one attempt the Order of the Space Knights. Clearly, that name wouldn't work for Stormtroopers. He tried to think of names that recalled his dad's World War II fighter pilot squadron—"something zippy, something cool"—added some alliteration, and came up with the Fightin' 501st. He wrote a backstory that solved a question he'd formed watching the movies: How come Darth Vader always seems to have a detachment of Stormtroopers at his elbow whenever he needs them? The 501st, he decided, was a shadow legion, off the books, always ready: Vader's Fist.

---

* The only time a Stormtrooper is named in *Star Wars* is on the Death Star, where a commanding officer asks TK-421 why he isn't at his post. Johnson adopted this naming convention, using his birthday for the numbers. The 501st has since used up all its possible three- and four-digit TK numbers.

It was, friends agreed, a pretty neat idea. They helped him hand out leaf-lets at conventions: "Are you loyal? Hardworking? Fully expendable? Join the Imperial 501st!" In 2002, Johnson mustered roughly 150 Stormtrooper cos-tumers in Indianapolis at Celebration II, the second official *Star Wars* con-vention, and offered their services to a skeptical Lucasfilm to let the 501st help out as crowd-control when the event's security proved woefully inadequate for the thirty thousand attendees. Lucasfilm was won over by the tireless, hyper-organized troopers, and started to use the 501st as volunteers for all its events. Lucasfilm licensees followed suit. If you've ever been to one of the *Star Wars* Days held at dozens of baseball stadiums across the United States, if you've seen multiple Stormtroopers, or Darth Vader or Boba Fett at a store, a movie theater, or a mall, you've almost certainly been staring at the forces of the 501st.

Johnson's idea didn't stop at America's shores, either. The 501st Legion is now recognized as one of the largest costuming organizations in the world.* It has active members in forty-seven countries on five continents, divided into sixty-seven local garrisons and twenty-nine outposts (those units that comprise fewer than twenty-five members). More than 20 percent of the troops are fe-male. The 501st absorbed a once-independent UK garrison and established a garrison near Paris, though some French Stormtroopers have gone their own way with the 59*eme* legion. The Germans, meanwhile, have a garrison consist-ing of five squads that are all large enough to be garrisons on their own—but are loath to undergo any kind of de-unification.

The 501st elects local and legion-wide commanding officers every year. To Johnson's dismay, COs are imposing ever-more stringent membership requirements—your Stormtrooper belt must contain six pouches, not four—meaning that even the "authentic" (but not technically screen-accurate) Lucas-film-licensed suits sold online won't get you in the club. Most members make their own, hammering away at styrene sheets on vacuforming tables, sinking thousands of dollars and hundreds of hours into a single costume.

Such stringency notwithstanding, the 501st Legion is starting to stretch the limits of its name. Roman legions, world history's largest, rarely had more than 5,000 members; Julius Caesar crossed the Rubicon with 3,500. The 501st, at the time of this writing, numbers 6,583 screen-accurate active members. That, if you're keeping score, is 6,573 more troops than Johnson first anticipated.

---

* The Society for Creative Anachronism, an organization dedicated to celebrating the medieval and renaissance periods through activities like reproducing historic armor and clothing, has more than thirty thousand paid-up members—and a thirty-one-year head start on the 501st.

More importantly, Johnson and Crews's creation has reached that galaxy far, far away. In 2004 came the first official *Star Wars* novel to feature the 501st, written by famed franchise author Timothy Zahn—who happened to have first encountered Johnson and his crew at a convention, kicking back with a cooler full of beers after a long day. Johnson held onto sobriety long enough to explain the concept of the 501st. Zahn nodded thoughtfully, went away, and promptly wrote the novel *Survivor's Quest*, in which a squad from the 501st costarred with Luke Skywalker.

Even greater honors were to follow. The next year, George Lucas officially included the legion in his final *Star Wars* movie, *Episode III: Revenge of the Sith*. A detachment of Clone Troopers, the predecessors of Stormtroopers, follow the newly minted Darth Vader into the Jedi Temple as he prepares to massacre its inhabitants. In the script, they are designated the 501st Legion. But Johnson had no inkling of this until a member of his Tokyo Garrison mailed him a *Star Wars* action figure. Amid the Japanese script on the box was a number: 501. Hasbro has since churned out an impressive five million of these plastic 501st members. Ill-informed fans started to claim that Johnson was copying Lucas's name, rather than the other way around.*

The matter was settled in 2007, when George Lucas was made grand marshall of the Tournament of Roses Parade (associated with the Rose Bowl) in Pasadena. Lucas asked for the 501st by name and paid to fly hundreds of its troops from around the world to march five and a half miles with his float. Here they were, finally assembled, the space soldiers, going through actual army drills with actual drill sergeants. Lucas addressed them the night before the parade: "The big invasion is in a few days," he said, deadpan. "I don't expect all of you to make it back. But that's okay, because Stormtroopers are expendable." The legion roared its approval.

After a breather following the punishing march, the troopers put their buckets—as they call their helmets—back on and posed for photos with Lucas. Lucasfilm's Steve Sansweet insisted on introducing Lucas and Johnson, two shy men who prefer to run things from behind the scenes. "Good work on all of this," said Lucas.

"This is all you!" was all Johnson managed to sputter before the Creator.

---

* As great a compliment as that is, Johnson is uneasy about the fact that the 501st were heading into the temple to help kill Jedi children—including one played by Lucas's son Jett. This made for an awkward encounter years later, when Jett asked Johnson if he could become an honorary member of the 501st.

"No," said Lucas. "I made *Star Wars*." He gestured at the rows of white-armored troopers, standing stiffly at attention and carrying the flags of their garrisons. "You made this. I'm very proud of it."

It was enough to make a guy's head so big it would never again fit in a bucket. But even after that unparalleled moment of validation, Johnson retains a sense of perspective. "Y'all, if we're not having fun, this is just a drag," he tells his COs. "We're plastic spacemen. If anybody in the club is getting too serious, we'll throw out that tagline. 'Yep, we're plastic spacemen.'"

Every army needs someone to march behind, and the 501st is no exception. If the outfit is called Vader's Fist, then naturally every garrison needs more than screen-accurate Stormtroopers. It needs to walk in anonymous lockstep behind the most famous and frightening space soldier of them all.

Mark Fordham was a sniper on a SWAT team in Tennessee when he constructed a crude Darth Vader costume for his police department's 1994 Halloween party. The other officers raved about it, and that got Fordham thinking: How would people react to a screen-accurate Vader?

He called the main number at Lucasfilm and somehow found himself connected to a kindly soul who told him the pieces he needed: quilted leather jumpsuit with a blanket sewn in, wool crepe cape. "Vader is fairly comfortable," says Fordham. "He's just very hot."

Fordham paid local fashion students $200 to stitch the costume together. Now he had a new plan: visit the local schools dressed as Vader and offer a moral message: "Don't choose the quick and easy path like I did." But when he called Lucasfilm back to get their sign-off on his plan, the person he was randomly connected to this time around freaked out. Vader is our copyright, they said; we hire actors to portray him. You can't. "That kind of burst my bubble," said Fordham.

Still, the SWAT sniper figured there was nothing wrong in wearing the costume to the premieres of *Episode I* in 1999 and *Episode II* in 2002. He got the same result as Johnson: trooping alone is no fun. So he found some local 501st members and discovered to his surprise that the Stormtroopers enthusiastically welcomed a Vader. (Johnson would later drop "Stormtrooper" from the Legion's name to make this clearer.) Fordham practiced his James Earl Jones intonation listening to *Star Wars* tapes on his commute. He jury-rigged a mic and amp into his mask to approximate the mechanical sound of the helmeted archvillain. The amp used up two nine-volt batteries every thirty minutes—but for Fordham, there was nothing worse than being a voiceless Vader.

In short order, Fordham was elected garrison commanding officer and then CO for the entire global legion. He introduced awards and a rank system, promoting members who trooped more. When the 501st started to do more charity work, he felt it needed a common protocol, so he drafted a new charter to amend Johnson's "codex fundator"; the legion's goal, Fordham argued, needed to be more than "have fun." The 501st should be unified and identifiable, and the best way to achieve this would be through a franchise operation. "If you go to McDonald's in Chicago or Perth, you want to recognize you're in McDonald's," he says. "We wanted that common identity. When you invite us to something, you don't have to ask, 'Well, *which* 501st?'"

Fordham's philosophy about the 501st is, in many ways, the opposite of Johnson's. He likes the legion to be exact, standardized, and meritocratic. There are up to five Vaders in every garrison, and naturally no event should have more than one Vader. Currently, the legion offers them trooping opportunities in order of seniority. Fordham would prefer an annual audition in front of members to choose each year's Vader. "If that's me, great. If not, I would want the best Vader doing an event."

Fordham and his wife, Crickette, a Stormtrooper, had moved from Tennessee to Utah in the late 1990s. That was a full ten-hour drive away from Lucasfilm, but Fordham frequently drove to Skywalker Ranch and back on his own dime, "to show we take the brand seriously." It was on one of those visits that he was first told about Lucas and the Tournament of Roses Parade. While Albin Johnson marched in blissful Stormtrooper anonymity, Fordham was the Vader at the front of the pack, George Lucas's loyal enforcer.

During the coverage of the parade, one celebrity announcer joked that the troopers "needed to get jobs" and must be "marching home to their parents' basement." That kind of comment rankled: the troops were PhDs, doctors, technicians, aircraft mechanics, as well as many military and police personnel like Fordham. ("We're kind of drawn to the uniform element," he says.) The announcer was displaying exactly the perception of the legion that Fordham was fighting to change with his professional charter.

The conflict between Johnson's y'all-have-fun ethos and Fordham's style of strict screen accuracy and professionalism runs right through the legion. I've heard about intra-garrison conflicts over height restrictions (Mark says he would prefer to be a Stormtrooper but is too tall; Crickette would like to be Vader but is too short). One Asian member of the legion wanted to portray Anakin Skywalker before his transformation into Vader; that touched off a huge internal debate about whether he should have to wear makeup to look more Caucasian. There are even disputes over the proper level of interaction with the rival good guys' outfit, the Rebel Legion; I met a couple of 501st COs who also command their local Rebel outposts. The Rebels are about a third of the size of the Imperials and seem to prefer being outnumbered. "It kind of reflects the films," says Suzy Stelling, the CO of the hundred-strong UK Rebel Legion base. "The rebels are small, but we get through in the end."

The ultimate irony of the 501st is that for such a fascist-looking organization, it is actually profoundly democratic. There are local and global elections to the legion council every February, and they're not sham elections. There's a lot of healthy, rambunctious debate in the ranks. But ultimately they're all brothers and sisters under the Lycra; they've all literally bled for their uniforms at one time or another. The "armor bite," as the plastic panels' skin-pinching is known, is felt by everyone. (Everyone except the comfortably hot Vaders, that is.)

How do you get into the legion? By submitting multiple photos of your costume to a compliance officer, who will check the tiniest of details for screen accuracy; the six-pouch criterion is one of many. Would-be troopers have to work hard to get their costumes up to code—although some find it easier than others. "I've heard guys say they can finish their armor in a week or two, working nonstop with fast-acting glue," says Ed daSilva, CO of the Golden Gate Garrison in Northern California, who built his costume in two months. "If you can handle PVC, plumbing, irrigation work, it's similar."

Despite substantial economic pressure, the 501st has not succumbed to any kind of black market of armor making. Nor does it encourage the purchase of even Lucasfilm-licensed Stormtrooper replica suits. "Why would you want to spend $800 on eBay," daSilva says, "when you could spend $400 and be part of a club that sets standards for high quality?"

Some members sell pieces here and there, but "we stick to a simple rule of selling costumes at-cost, so there is no temptation to commercialize this," says Johnson. He describes the legion as "an eclectic and bohemian collective that trades tips and works to make good armor." There's money at stake, but it's not for them. Simply by appearing at charity events, the 501st helped raise $262,329 for all kinds of good causes in 2013, roughly double the amount raised the previous year.

A charity-loving, democratic bohemian collective of craft-minded Stormtroopers? Hard as it is to believe, it works: the 501st is getting stronger all the time. They get a lot of love from Lucasfilm—which invites the local Golden Gate Garrison to early screenings of new *Star Wars* animated fare at the Presidio headquarters—and they reciprocate with loyalty. This rambunctious democratic group will close ranks when it comes to the Creator's company. They'll not only work any Lucasfilm event for free but appear in any Lucasfilm-endorsed commercial (such as a recent Nissan ad in Japan, which featured a red Stormtrooper standing out from a pack of white ones).

It's often hard to figure out who's getting the better end of the deal, Lucasfilm or the legion. For example, at Lucasfilm's Celebration Europe II, held in Essen, Germany, in 2013, you could wander the vast show floor and find that the attractions pulling the largest crowds were provided by various branches of the 501st. The Belgian garrison provided a life-size TIE fighter they'd constructed, and it was Celebration's most popular photo spot—closely followed by a twenty-foot-tall, wooden AT-AT, also constructed in Belgium and signed by Lucas ("May the Force NOT be with you, Imperial dogs!" he wrote). On the one hand, Lucasfilm has at its disposal a passionate, disciplined, and creative militia—the kind of fans any company would kill for—for free. On the other, the legion gets more genuine value and cachet out of making this stuff in the first place than any company could accrue. Lucasfilm would never dare offend it, and it gets to sit on the front line of fandom, exactly where it wants to be.

The legion has made itself indispensable. It has inducted a select hundred or so authors, actors, and Lucasfilm employees as honorary members; you could spot them across the Celebration halls in their metallic badges with multicolored squares in the style of Imperial officers. The legion hosted an extremely exclusive dinner, with most of the stars of the original trilogy in attendance; the media couldn't get anywhere near it. The space soldiers have become the hottest ticket in the hottest franchise on Earth.

It's strange, then, that one man who had an enviable role in bringing the soldiers into being in the first place all those years ago has become something of a pariah in the *Star Wars* community.

If you want to see where the iconic plastic armor for Lucas's army of space soldiers first sprang into three-dimensional life, you have to go to Twickenham, a leafy old suburb in the far southwest of London just down the road from Elstree, where the original *Star Wars* was shot. Here, across from a bucolic cricket green, in a building that was formerly a Dickensian candy shop, you will find the polar opposite of the 501st: a one-man operation producing Stormtrooper armor for commercial gain, more interested in asserting his rights than he is in the subject of *Star Wars*, and most definitely not licensed by Lucasfilm. You will find a man who beat Lucas in court, sort of, but is losing his appeal in the court of fandom. You will begin to unravel the curious case of Andrew Ainsworth.

Ainsworth is a wiry, friendly fellow with a neatly trimmed black and white beard and a twinkle in his eye. He's an industrial designer, skilled in vacuum forming, and he gets especially animated discussing the quality of reflected light that makes these uniforms look like much more than plastic. At such moments, Ainsworth looks quite a bit younger than his sixty-four years.

When I met Ainsworth at his shop, we sat for hours drinking cups of tea amid Stormtrooper replicas. Ainsworth brought out to me what he claimed was one of the first Stormtrooper helmets ever made. He told the story behind the helmet—how his friend, artist Nick Pemberton, got him involved in the production of *Star Wars* in January 1976. Pemberton told Ainsworth to buy him a pint if anything came of it. "I had no idea what it was," he says. "I thought it was a puppet show; Nick used to work on those for television."

Pemberton brought Ainsworth a maquette of the Stormtrooper helmet that was based on Lucasfilm concept sketches and paintings. Ainsworth had an oversized vacuum-forming machine he used to make plastic canoes and fish ponds; Pemberton asked Ainsworth if he could make the helmet prototype. He made one in two days. "He took that in to Lucas, and Lucas said, 'That's great—I'll have fifty more,'" says Ainsworth. The production was rushing to get sets and costumes to Tunisia at the time. Ainsworth remembers a line of white limos idling outside the shop, each one waiting for the next helmet. "The studio was so keen to get them, as soon as we finished one they'd drive away with it," he chuckles.

As he told the story, Ainsworth fiddled with the rim of the supposedly historic helmet, causing a little tear in the side. He didn't even blink. The *Star Wars* fan, the historian, the preservationist in me all want to scream at him: *No, stop, put that thing under glass!* This was my first inkling that Ainsworth, despite his boasting of a place in the franchise's history—and it is, alas, a rather expandable thing, this boasting of his—failed to get the *idea* of *Star Wars*.

Ainsworth and his partner, Bernadette, have been together since the 1960s, when he used to make cars in shipping crates outside her south London flat. Then they bought this former candy shop and founded Shepperton Design Studios. No one disputes that SDS produced Stormtrooper helmets and armor, TIE fighter pilot helmets, Rebel pilot helmets, and Rebel troop helmets—all from outside the UK studio system, which was rigidly controlled by unions at the time. Ainsworth's uncredited role made him £30,000—more than most of the names that showed up on screen at the end of *Star Wars*.

And that was the last of his involvement with the franchise. Ainsworth showed remarkably little interest in the *Star Wars* phenomenon as it exploded around the world, and only caught the original movie once on TV years later. In the late 1990s, looking to pay school fees for his kids, he dug up the old forming tools, made another batch of helmets, and tried selling them at a local market. He found few buyers, and they ended up on the top of the bedroom wardrobe. In 2002, Bernadette declared she was going to sell them online. Ainsworth says he didn't think they'd get a penny; as it turned out, when they were listed on Christie's as "original" helmets, they got $4,000 each. Shepperton Design Studios launched its website and went into the Stormtrooper helmet business in 2003. After selling nineteen helmets to customers in the United States for £35 apiece, Ainsworth got a call from Howard Roffman, head of Lucas Licensing. Ainsworth recounts the call:

"Who are you?" Roffman demanded.

"I'm the guy who made these Stormtrooper helmets."

"No, you're not. We did."

Lucasfilm legal does not mess around. The company promptly sued and won a $20 million punitive judgment against Ainsworth in a US court. A UK bailiff brought Ainsworth the demand some weeks later. Ever affable, Ainsworth made the bailiff a cup of tea.

After four years of fighting Lucasfilm in the UK High Court of Justice, Court of Appeal, and finally Supreme Court, Ainsworth won something of a split decision. The Supreme Court ruled that the US judgment was enforceable in the United Kingdom. Ainsworth was still on the hook for $4 million, all for selling nineteen Stormtrooper helmets in the United States.*

But the court also ruled that Stormtrooper costumes were props—not sculpture, as Lucasfilm had insisted. It was an important distinction: the copyright on sculpture lasts for seventy-five years in the United Kingdom; the copyright on props runs out after fifteen. So while Ainsworth had an enormous legal bill, he was also free to keep selling Stormtrooper helmets and armor. And sell them he does, for hundreds of pounds apiece, along with "original Dark Lord" costumes and "original R2 Droids"—so original, apparently, he dare not fully name the characters.

One of Ainsworth's legal tactics was to countersue Lucas, on the grounds that he had designed the Stormtrooper costume himself and Lucas was breaching

---

* After Disney bought Lucasfilm, the company settled with Ainsworth for a mere £90,000. Ainsworth was still stuck with legal fees around a million pounds.

his copyright. This patently ridiculous claim was thrown out of court, but that hasn't stopped Ainsworth repeating it ever since. In 2013, Ainsworth participated in a London art show at the Saatchi Gallery in which various artists were given Stormtrooper helmets as canvases; he was described on the gallery literature as "the creator of the Stormtrooper." I wasn't surprised to read that the High Court judge had described him as "viewing events through his own Ainsworth-tinted spectacles."

Ainsworth made something of a splash in *Star Wars* forums around the time of his court case, but fans soon suspected they were dealing with someone who didn't seem to know very much about the franchise and was willing to make up his own details. For example, his explanation in one interview for why he didn't work on *The Empire Strikes Back* or *Return of the Jedi* is that Lucas didn't return to the United Kingdom after his experience with the unions (which is untrue). He claims that his armor was reused on the subsequent movies and that it "looked pretty ratty by the end"; in fact, the armor was recast for *Return of the Jedi*. It's not surprising that he didn't know that, because he told me he had only watched *Star Wars* once on television, and neither of the other movies of the classic trilogy.

It's a shame, because Ainsworth did play a small but vital role in the making of the original film, and somewhere under his miasma of self-justification and faulty memory is a small business success story. The judge gives him credit for the design of the X-wing pilot's helmet, for instance, because the Marine helmet he was supposed to be basing the design on never arrived from the United States. At nearly forty years distance, however, it is doubtful whether this particular tale will ever be objectively told.

Adding to the confusion is the testimony of Brian Muir, a sculptor who worked at Elstree and sculpted the maquette, or scale model, for Vader's helmet, which was made in-house out of heavier fiberglass. In court, Muir claimed that the Stormtrooper helmet was sculpted not by Ainsworth's friend Nick Pemberton but by another sculptor, Liz Moore, who also sculpted the prototype Threepio costume. (Moore died tragically young some years later.)

In court, Muir's claim was quickly thrown into question. Moore's boyfriend at the time testified that she sculpted in a different kind of clay than the one seen in the only photo of the Stormtrooper sculpture that exists. The judge found that Pemberton, not Moore, sculpted the Stormtrooper helmet, which makes sense: How else would Ainsworth have become involved in the first place, except through his friend Pemberton? But that didn't stop Muir from taking to the Internet—including 501st forums—with vehement attacks on Ainsworth and a spirited defense of Liz Moore's memory.

Digging deeper into Muir's story, however, it becomes clear that he isn't actually claiming to have firsthand knowledge of Moore's sculpture—just that other unnamed people in the crew told him she had produced it. Muir told me in a testy email explaining why he didn't want to be interviewed that it "actually doesn't matter" who sculpted the helmet—"so long as it wasn't Ainsworth."*

The contrast between these tangled tales and the more laudable efforts of Albin Johnson and Mark Fordham is dramatic, but also instructive. When *Star Wars* fans work for free, fired up by a love of the franchise, you get the 501st. But when there's business at stake, a chance to make some money from the phenomenon, you get unseemly feuds like Ainsworth's and Muir's. It's the kind of unintended consequence that the Creator, sketching space soldiers in art class, could never have foreseen.

---

* In 2011, after the Supreme Court gave Ainsworth the go-ahead to continue selling Stormtrooper helmets and armor, another UK company called RS Prop Masters happened to start selling its own screen-accurate Stormtrooper suits, recast from a set of armor from the original movie that had been found in an attic. Muir added his endorsement. His daughter started a Facebook page devoted to ridiculing the quality of Ainsworth's Stormtrooper reproductions. The feud between Muir and Ainsworth, it seems, has moved into the marketplace.

4.

HYPERSPACE DRIVE

Space soldiers, in their Tommy Tomorrow and Flash Gordon guises, were far from the only obsession in the young Lucas's life. Soon enough, they weren't even the central one. In his teens, Lucas's attention shifted from drawing and comics to cameras and cars. An auto accident, the most important turning point in Lucas's entire creative history, led him to rethink his approach to school; he discovered the study of humanity and became fascinated by photography. Only then, belatedly, did he fall into film, take the key classes and meet the key people who would set him off down the path to the stars.

None of these other obsessions ever left Lucas entirely, however. They all informed his most well-known work. So as tempting as it is to detour around Lucas's turns as boy racer, greasy mechanic, reformed anthropology student, and artsy film school prodigy, this scenic route actually has much to tell us about the *Star Wars* story. Quite simply, that story would not have developed in the way it did without these twelve key stops along the road.

1. CAR CULTURE

Every Lucas movie features a fast-paced chase or race in some kind of hot rod or pod. The *Star Wars* films felt faster at the time of their release than anything else on screen, and their speed didn't just come from Lucas's years of obsessive TV watching. Rather, it came from that sense of flow and motion, excitement and danger one can only get from behind the wheel of a speeding vehicle. In *Star*

Wars, Lucas would say that he wanted "space ships that people got into and drove around like cars." This was his version of a magic carpet to Mars.

When Lucas was sixteen, his ever-benevolent father bought him his first car, a tiny Italian supermini called a Bianchina. George Sr. probably figured the kid couldn't do much damage with this 479cc Fiat-made motor and top speed of 60 miles per hour. Lucas called it a "dumb little car" with a "sewing machine engine."

But Lucas had a knack for making a little go a long way. He spent his spare hours and his allowance at the Foreign Car Service, a garage for hot-rodders with a go-kart track out back. He made some special modifications himself, adding a straight pipe and a roll bar, and a seatbelt from an Air Force jet, and learned how to hug the curves at top speed. It didn't look like much, but it had it where it counts. The first time he flipped the car, he tore the roof out rather than repair it. You can almost feel the horror creeping up the spine of George Sr., who still entertained hopes that his son might take over the Lucas Company business someday.

Lucas Jr. acquired a fake ID that said he was over twenty-one; this let him enter autocross contests in parking lots and fairgrounds, winning more than his share of trophies. He became good friends with Modesto's autocross champion, Allen Grant, who would assume briefly the role of an elder brother figure for the young racer. Grant described a kid who was quiet until he got to know you, and then wouldn't stop babbling. Who knows what space soldier–filled ramblings got cut short when Grant told Lucas, as he frequently did, to shut up. "He was always jabbering about a story, and what about this and doing this and you know," says Grant. "We didn't take him too serious."

When George Jr. was a teenager, the upwardly mobile Lucas family moved to a walnut ranch on the edge of town. Until he got his car, he was a quiet loner who kept to his bedroom outside of meal times and TV time, ate Hershey bars, drank Cokes, read comics, played rock and roll and jazz 45s, and shot the occasional BB pellet out of the window. But cruising culture put him in the swing of Modesto's social scene. Tenth and Eleventh Streets on Friday nights were a fascinating parade of chrome. There were ritual courtesies: kids left their cars unlocked so friends could sit in them; if you had a favorite parking spot, other kids would hold it for you.

Lucas slid into a phase of minor juvenile delinquency, filling a glove compartment with speeding tickets and appearing in court after he'd racked up too many. He didn't join the real-life gang depicted in *American Graffiti*, the Faros, but he did become their enabler. His job, the story goes, was to lure local toughs into fights by sitting his scrawny self next to them in the local burger joint. When the inevitable challenge came, he would run away, leading his quarry to the Faros. It's a telling image: George Lucas, young, beardless, with a bowl haircut, five foot six inches in flannel shirt and blue jeans blackened by engine grease, waltzing straight into danger, facing it like a Zen master, secure in the knowledge that he had backup. He never had to put up his fists.

2. THE CRASH

The cracks in the facade of young Lucas's grease-soaked life appeared at school. For years, his grades had hovered around Cs and Ds. He was only saved from Fs by his younger sister Wendy's homework help. He knew he was going to be a race car driver or a mechanic, so who cared about grades? Answer: George Sr. and Dorothy Lucas, who had been model students—class president and vice president in their day. They tried encouraging his visual sensibilities, buying him a Nikon camera and constructing a darkroom. Lucas took the camera to the race track.

But Lucas's alleyway friend John Plummer was going to the University of Southern California for business school, and George Jr. wondered whether college was right for him too. Never above nudging his son with elaborate gifts, George Sr. agreed to send the kid on a backpacking trip to Europe with Plummer if Lucas graduated high school.

That became the goal of the summer of 1962. Lucas hit the books in the local library. It was a grind. His heart wasn't in it. Bored, he returned early one hot afternoon, making an illegal left turn on the road to the Lucas family ranch. At the same moment a Chevy driven by a Downey High classmate—one Lucas probably couldn't see in the rearview for his own dust—had run a red light and was trying to overtake him on the left.

The force of the impact flung Lucas through the roof he had made. He only survived because his jury-rigged Air Force seatbelt snapped. A proper belt would have locked him in the car as it wrapped around a walnut tree.

Lucas's lungs hemorrhaged, but he was extraordinarily lucky. He was out of Modesto's Kindred Hospital within two weeks, albeit with months of physical therapy ahead of him. The crash had destroyed the Bianchina, wrecked his chances of backpacking around Europe, and garnered one more traffic ticket from the cops for that illegal left turn. But it also gave him a pass: Downey High graduated him without looking at his grades. Still, a profound lesson had been learned. "He became quieter and more intense," remembered Mel Cellini. The Foreign Car Service tried to cheer him up by bringing him a racing helmet with a roller skate taped on top. Lucas's head was somewhere else.

The crash changed everything; that is about the only constant when Lucas has told the story of his life over the years. It made him more mindful and more fearless. "It gave me this perspective on life that said I'm operating on extra credit," Lucas told Oprah Winfrey in 2012. "I'm never afraid of dying. What I'm getting is bonus material."

If Lucas had died in the crash, what kind of *It's A Wonderful Life* alternate universe would we be in? Not just one without *Star Wars* and its imitators, but also without much of a special effects industry. If we had summer blockbusters at all, they would be more disaster movies in the style of *Jaws* and less science fiction or fantasy spectaculars. There would probably be no *Star Trek* on the big screen, and certainly no *Battlestar Galactica* on the small one. It's distinctly possible that Twentieth Century Fox would have gone bankrupt after 1977; certainly the pattern of investor takeover would have been different, and Rupert Murdoch might not control it today. We'd have fewer cineplexes and fewer screens for movies overall; we also wouldn't have *The Godfather* in its Coppola-directed incarnation, nor *Apocalypse Now*.

What's most interesting to consider, however, is whether this *Star Wars*–less universe would still have come to pass if George Lucas hadn't made that illegal left turn in the first place, failed to graduate, and gone off in search of glory on the Grand Prix circuit like he'd wanted his whole teenage life. Some stories, it seems, require a blood sacrifice.

3. *21–87*

Several months after the accident, Lucas enrolled in Modesto Junior College for the next two years, earning an A in anthropology and a B in sociology. For the first time he was getting an education he craved, one that engaged him, one he was even able to apply to the rituals of the cruising scene around him. He went through that twentieth-century rite of passage for smart adolescents: reading *Brave New World* and *1984*. Both renditions of dystopian futures left their usual indelible mark, especially at a time when the world seemed inches from the brink of suicide—as it did during the Cuban Missile Crisis that October 1962. But where were the uplifting, positive stories to counterbalance and help make sense of frightening times? There was, Lucas says he realized at this point, "no longer a lot of mythology in our society."

More important than his graduation certificate to Lucas—and the *Star Wars* saga—was a growing interest in art house or "personal" films, kindled on weekend jaunts to Berkeley and San Francisco with Plummer. It was his first taste of the North Beach coffee house scene, where independent artists in black turtlenecks would hang bedsheets from ceilings and project their latest dream. By far the most influential short Lucas ever saw was *21–87*. The film's vital statistics make it sound light years away from *Star Wars*, and yet there's a key connection. Lasting less than ten minutes, *21–87* was made in 1963 by a troubled young filmmaker in Montreal, Arthur Lipsett, who used random audio and discarded footage from the National Film Board of Canada.

What Lipsett came up with, however, was the definition of transcendent. The images in *21–87* are mostly of people, up close and personal, looking at the camera, caught in candid moments. Men feed pigeons and stare up at their city, pensive in an everyday sort of way. "There are no secrets, just the plain facts of life," says one man offscreen. "Why can't we bring these things out into the open?" Over the faces of old people, a lady declares, "I don't believe in mortality. . . . I believe in immortality." The film itself opens with the title over a picture of a skull. It's a *memento mori* as well as a *memento machina*: the title comes from a discussion about the mechanization of society and how it fulfills our need to fit in. "Somebody walks up and says, 'Your number's 21–87,'" says the voiceover, twice. "Boy, does that person really smile."

This notion would find its reflection in *Star Wars*—think of how many beings in it, from droids to Stormtroopers, are identified by their number. But it was not *21–87*'s greatest contribution to the future movie. About three minutes in, as birds fly over a cityscape and old men watch and feed them, we hear this: "Many people feel that in the contemplation of nature and in communication with other living things, they become aware of some kind of force, or something, behind this apparent mask which we see in front of us, and they call it God."

Some kind of force, or something. In later years Lucas would point out that religious writers had been using the phrase "life force" for thousands of years. But he also acknowledged a debt to *21–87* and stated that the Force in *Star Wars* was an "echo" of Lipsett's film. At film school, he would load *21–87* onto the projector more than twenty times.

4. HASKELL WEXLER

In 1963, while Lucas was still a student at Modesto Junior College, his parents bought him his first 8mm film camera, just like the one he played with back in the alleyway. He took it to speedways around the state, as he had with the Nikon they had given him in high school.

While filming at these racetracks, Lucas worked as a mechanic in the pit with a racing group known as the AWOL Sports Car Competition Club.* If

---

* Lucas also edited the AWOL newsletter, known as BS. (Seriously.)

he wasn't meant to race cars, he could at least tinker with them. That was how, one weekend afternoon at Laguna Seca, Lucas got chatting with a customer who noticed his camera: Haskell Wexler, famed cinematographer. Immediately Wexler could tell the kid had a certain eye, a certain hunger for the visual.

Lucas's friendship with Wexler would pull his life powerfully in a new direction. Wexler showed the student around his commercial film house; it was the first time Lucas saw the movie industry in the wild and became aware that movie careers existed. Wexler said he would have gotten Lucas a production assistant job—possibly on a documentary Wexler was working on, *The Bus*—but that it was nixed by film unions. Lucas said that was the point he "turned his back on Hollywood." In fact, Wexler would keep trying to get Lucas a job within the Hollywood system for the rest of the youngster's time in school, with little success.

Around the time he met Wexler, Lucas was figuring out his next move beyond junior college. The first to accept him was San Francisco State, where he would have pursued a degree in anthropology. He also applied to do illustration and photography at the Art Center College of Design in Pasadena; his father torpedoed that dream by telling his son he'd have to pay for it himself. Lucas says he was too lazy to even consider that. Meanwhile John Plummer was thoroughly enjoying his time at USC and thought Lucas might get a kick out of the film school's photography program. "It's supposed to be easier than P.E.," Plummer told Lucas. That was all the kid needed to hear. Wexler called up a USC instructor called Mel Sloan; legend has it his words were "For God's sake, watch this kid." This may have tipped the scales, or Lucas's newfound aptitude may have shone through on the test. It mattered not. USC accepted Lucas, and the young man continued to be pulled inexorably toward film.

His father came up with a generous solution: he would pay George Jr.'s way through school as an employee of his company. Lucas would get $200 a month. Lucas Sr. may have reasoned that film school would confer a valuable lesson. After all, nobody graduated from film school and immediately found work at a studio. They were first taken on as apprentices. If you made it to the dizzying heights of assistant editor after four years of apprenticeship, you would have to wait another four years until you could edit film.

Hollywood was a closed fortress of nepotism, yet there was always a place where nepotism would work in Lucas's favor: Modesto. "You'll be back in a few years," George Sr. told his son.

"No I won't, I'm going to be a millionaire before I'm 30," Lucas shot back. Or at least, so he remembered as a millionaire in his thirties.

5. USC

When did *Star Wars* first emerge as a cinematic concept? Where did the love of *Flash Gordon* transmogrify into the idea of putting some version of it on celluloid? Lucas's answer is frustratingly imprecise: sometime during film school. "You end up with a little stack of ideas for great movies you'd love to make," he told *Starlog* magazine in 1981. "I had this idea for doing a space adventure. . . . It was such an obvious thing that I was amazed no one had ever done it before."

No student was less likely to have emerged as the star of the class. Lucas began at USC as a junior, and he was a photography major, not a cinema major; he began with only two classes at the film school. Film was not the cool subject it is today, and the department was banished to a spartan building called the Stables on the edge of campus. In his opening address, the dean of the school told students there was still time to get their tuition back. "Conditions were crowded, equipment limited, and scheduling editorial and mixing equipment was challenging," remembers Lucas's classmate, Howard Kazanjian. "We learned to work together. We created the feeling of family. The facility was old and funky, but I would have had it no other way."

Lucas was increasingly drawn to the "geeks and the nerds" of his film classes, despite their pariah status. "No one wanted to be around us," he remembered in 2013. "We were bearded and strange." He compared his compatriots to modern-day Googlers and Facebookers. Something exciting and new was going on within the Stables, and the kids sensed it.

Lucas shunned the screenwriting class, run by the infamous Irwin Blacker, from which students had been known to emerge in tears. He didn't care for plot or dialogue. Sound and vision were all he wanted to learn about. He took a history of film class with Arthur Knight, whose enthusiasm was infectious. Knight screened *Metropolis*, the 1927 masterpiece by Fritz Lang. It imagined a future city where an imperious "master" is challenged by rebel workers. The master's son ventures into the underworld in pursuit of the female leader of the rebellion, and the master orders a machine made in her image in order to discredit her. Lucas would file that iconic golden robot away in his mind, where it would stay for years, becoming fluent in over six million forms of communication.

6. CLEAN CUT CINEMA

Don Glut arrived at USC the same year as Lucas; he, like George, started as a junior. The two met when Lucas and his dorm roommate, Chris Lewis, along with

Glut's roommate, Randall Kleiser, founded the Clean Cut Cinema Club, where members took turns screening movies. Glut joined too, though he didn't quite fit in with the club's deliberately uncool ethos. "I was the only one in the club with long hair," says Glut. "After the Beatles came out, everyone grew their hair long. That's what girls wanted, so that's what we did. But Lucas and Kleiser and Lewis were groomed perfectly." (Lucas wouldn't gain a beard until he returned to USC as a graduate student.) Indeed, the CCCC had a reactionary bent aimed at the "beatnik guys dominating the cinema department," the ones exhorting them to follow Jean-Luc Godard into independent filmmaking and telling them they couldn't get a job in the industry. Lucas and his cohorts had a different concept of what that industry could be.

The CCCC tended to shy away from screening the then-fashionable works of new-wave French cinema. That's what the professors were into, so the CCCC wanted to be into something else. Glut was a brash blue-collar Chicagoan who loved comic books and superheroes. A friend at Republic Pictures got him reels of old serial episodes, which is what he screened for the club: *Captain Marvel, Rocketman, Spy Smashers, Zorro.* Despite his love for *Flash Gordon* serials, Lucas was seeing most of these other serials for the first time, Glut recalls.*

In his second year, Lucas rented an $80-a-month place up in Benedict Canyon, the name of which may well have inspired Tatooine's Beggar's Canyon. Kleiser moved in, and the pair threw a party at which Glut screened an episode of *The Adventures of Captain Marvel.* Glut loved this stuff, but he also recognized the dumber scenes when he saw them. In one, Captain Marvel is following a car whose driver has been knocked unconscious. The car careens down a winding road, somehow managing to avoid going off the edge. "That's impossible," laughed Glut.

Lucas looked at him very seriously. "No," he insisted. "The car would follow the contours of the road."

The two shared a love of cheesy serials, but Glut's passion for them got him into trouble. Each classroom had a 16mm projector; you could screen anything if there wasn't a class in session. Glut was screening his serials for an audience one night when he was ejected by Herb Kosower, the animation teacher. In 1965, Glut had to take his camera class over again after turning in a movie

---

* It should be noted that Glut has an ax to grind against Lucas, who failed to help Glut out of his dire financial straits with further work after he wrote *The Empire Strikes Back* novelization. He let me interview him with the understanding that he would not be made to appear to say anything positive about Lucasfilm.

called *Superman vs. The Gorilla Gang* for his final assignment. It fulfilled the requirements, but the teacher failed him. Why? "Because it's a Superman movie."

Lucas, by contrast, kept his own love for such things out of school bounds, although it ate up his extracurricular life. Kleiser remembered trying to urge him out of his room and go to parties, but Lucas "just wanted to stay in and draw star troopers," Kleiser said. All those years after art class, he was still picturing space soldiers.

7. LOOK AT LIFE

As a junior, Lucas took Kosower's animation class. While Glut hated Kosower, Lucas sat in the front row, intent on learning how everything worked, ready to overachieve. Almost immediately, he discovered he had a talent for animation—and how.

In 1965, George Lucas made his first short movie, born of an early homework assignment that couldn't have been more basic. The students had been instructed to take a minute of 16 mm film, run it through the Oxberry camera, and make something move. What Lucas did with that minute was extraordinary and still holds up today as if it were a great YouTube short (which it now effectively is). It's called *Look at Life*. The title referred to the two popular weekly photo magazines *Look* and *Life*. Lucas cut out his favorite pictures and strung them together in a collage, in the style of Lipsett's *21–87*.

As in all subsequent Lucas films, the music was in the driving seat: in this case, the first track from the soundtrack to the Brazilian film *Black Orpheus*, which happens to be a minute long. It opens with a lilting guitar, over which Lucas zooms out from an eye, a face behind wire mesh. Then an urgent samba bursts in, appearing as rudely as would years later the first chord of John Williams's *Star Wars* theme. We see snarling dogs in Alabama, Dr. Martin Luther King Jr., Klansmen, Khrushchev, soldiers in Vietnam, all in rapid succession. Five frames per image: extremely fast for 1964, even a little shocking today. It ends with the title cards "anyone for survival?" and "End?"

That last card may have been a portentous step too far, but there it was: America at the tipping point of the 1960s, anxiety over war and racism, the emotion behind that year's big protest anthem "Eve of Destruction," all within a single minute of film. The result was a hit with faculty and went on to win a total of eighteen awards at student festivals around the world. Lucas's confidence exploded in an instant. "When I did that film, I realized I was able to run circles around everyone else," he said. "That's when I realized these crazy ideas I had might work."

8. THE MOVIOLA

After *Look at Life*, Lucas went to town on class projects. For lighting class, he and classmate Paul Golding produced a simple meditation on the hood of a car. Set to Miles Davis's "Basin Street Blues," it was called *Herbie*, for the mistaken belief that Herbie Hancock played piano on the track. Hypnotic shots of neon diffusing over chrome were cut to the music. At the snap of a drum you saw, for a second, something that looked like a galaxy being born.

Lucas had the chance to meet and take a class from the mighty French director Jean-Luc Godard; after that, he seems to have had the zeal of a convert about new-wave cinema and the auteur theory. By the time of his third short, *Freiheit*—the story of a young man, played by Kleiser, escaping across the border between East and West Germany, played by Southern California scrubland—Lucas had veered so far into the avant-garde that he was experimenting with dropping his first name. "A film by LUCAS," says the title card.

The primary film-editing machine at the time, the upright Moviola, seemed custom-built for a car-loving youth. It had gears and sprockets, it needed to be greased, and it growled. Foot pedals controlled speed and motion. Lucas had to break into the editing room, known as the Bullpen, so he could drive the film all night, cutting a scene just a hair's breadth before he got bored with it, the whole session fueled by Hershey bars, Cokes, and coffee. He gave himself the supremely geeky nickname "Supereditor."

For his graduation project, *1:42:08—A Man and His Car*, Lucas brought his two main loves together: fast cars and fast films. It was technically excellent but cold: you didn't see much of the man. Its soundtrack was the roar of the engine. He'd been inspired by another National Film Board of Canada film called *12 Bicycles*, which used the same kind of long lenses Lucas would employ in *1:42:08*.

Lucas used color film, which students were theoretically barred from using, and took more than a semester to complete the project, another breach of the rules. He was dressed down for breaking into the Bullpen and editing at night. The faculty may have grumbled, but Lucas was basically untouchable at this stage. The award-winning wunderkind had attracted a coterie of student friends, which became known—in retrospect, at least—as the Dirty Dozen. At one end of the spectrum was John Milius: girl-chasing, outlandish, conservative, militaristic, a man who would have joined the Marines but for his asthma. At the other end was Walter Murch, a refined East Coast intellectual. Murch first met Lucas when the young savant told Murch he was developing film all wrong. That kind of approach didn't seem to stunt relationships in a school that was all about meritocracy: "If you saw an exciting film," said Murch, "you became friends with the guy who made it."

Both Milius and Murch would come to have an indirect effect on *Star Wars*, but Milius's impact was the most immediate: he insisted on taking Lucas to see the samurai films of the Japanese director Akira Kurosawa that played at the Toho cinema on La Brea in Los Angeles. Kurosawa had turned Milius's life around when he'd been declared 4-F; a weeklong festival of Kurosawa's movies had convinced him to apply to film school. Lucas only had to see *Seven Samurai* once to know he was hooked. Kurosawa shared his love of long lenses and wide shots; he told irresistible stories that built slowly to a grand conclusion; he loved to build the audience's anticipation for something that was about to happen, something just off the edge of the screen.

And there was something more in those samurai films, something that would have been obvious to any child of the 1950s: Kurosawa loved Westerns. Asked once where he received his inspiration, the Japanese director responded: "I study John Ford." Ford, the multiple-Oscar-winning director of movies such as *The Searchers* and *The Man Who Shot Liberty Valance*, is considered the past master of the Western. Although born to an Irish family in Maine, Ford was able to find and frame the spirit of the American West. His characters struggled against vast, rugged terrain, reached for far horizons, and spoke only when necessary. Kurosawa translated Ford's Westerns to medieval Japan. *Star Wars* would owe significant debts to both directors. Lucas may have taken a circuitous foreign route to the Western influences that would show up on Tatooine, but was hardly impoverished for doing so. It was like learning about American rock and roll by listening to the Beatles.

9. GOVERNMENT WORK

On graduating in August 1966, Lucas got the draft letter he'd been expecting. The Vietnam War was sucking an entire generation into the major maelstrom of the Cold War. He considered following the exodus to Canada; friends who had been drafted had weighed that option, but thought better of it when they heard back from homesick classmates. The best Lucas could hope for was Officer Candidate School, perhaps leading to assignment with a military filmmaking unit.

When he reported for medical inspection, however, Lucas got a nasty shock: he was diabetic. Not only did that rate him 4-F, but he also had to quit his constant companions: Hershey bars and Cokes. John Plummer said Lucas compared the diagnosis, once it was confirmed by his doctor back in Modesto, to a second car crash. But it was to give him a heroic dose of self-discipline and a leg up on his contemporaries. Desperate to outrun the need for insulin injections, he would remain substance-free for the rest of his career: no smoking, no drugs, no sugar, barely any drinking. Such choices would set him apart from many other filmmakers of his generation, and not in a bad way. In 1977, the year the first *Star Wars* film was released, Martin Scorsese admitted he was too coked up to face the challenge of making much-needed changes to the disastrous *New York New York*; Francis Coppola sat amid a haze of pot smoke on the horrifically over-budget, long-delayed *Apocalypse Now* while friends feared for his sanity. Meanwhile, Lucas—boring old Mr. Clean—churned out the year's top movie on a tight budget, then turned around and started its sequel.

Since he was spared from military service, Lucas's next obvious step was USC graduate school, but he was too late to apply for the fall. While he waited for the next year's admissions process to begin, he cut movie reels for the US Information Agency, working in the living room of editor Verna Fields.

This first taste of professional moviemaking forced Lucas to rethink his aspirations. After being told that he'd made a story about a crackdown on an anti-government riot in South Korea look "too fascist," he had an epiphany: he didn't want to be an editor. He wanted to be the one telling the editors what to do.

His year off from school afforded Lucas another revelation. Fields hired a second editor to work alongside him. Her name was Marcia Griffin. She was as shy and willful as Lucas, and they had both been born in Modesto. (Griffin was a military brat from a nearby base.) "Neither one of us would take any shit from the other," Lucas said. They began to date. And it didn't take long for George to start telling Marcia about an idea he had for a space fantasy. "That damn movie was whirring through the editing machine in George's head on the day we met," she would say two decades later, from the other end of a bitter divorce. "He never doubted it would get made. . . . He spent a lot of his time thinking of ways to get those spaceships and creatures on the screen."

Those spaceships and creatures were to change her life forever, too—and not necessarily for the better.

10. *THX 1138 4EB*

The dream of spaceships and space soldiers seems to have been entangled with the dream of an easier-to-make movie—more science fiction than space fantasy—whirring through the editing machine in Lucas's head. Walter Murch and another classmate, Matthew Robbins, had come up with a treatment for what was originally called *Breakout*: a man escaping from an underground lair in a dystopian future. Lucas loved the concept. How to make it, though? He wasn't in film school at the time. He didn't have access to equipment, and he certainly couldn't afford to buy any on his own.

But these obstacles were surmountable with a little bit of lateral thinking. Lucas realized that if he took a second job as a teaching assistant in a USC class for navy cadets (USC trained military filmmakers) in return for the lease, he would have access to their color film. He organized the navy guys into two teams, framing the class as a competition to see who could shoot a film with the best natural lighting. He took charge of one team. His guys had access to military installations. Hey presto: instant film crew, instant locations. It wouldn't have failed to remind Lucas of Jean-Luc Godard's own strange dystopian film *Alphaville: A Strange Adventure of Lemmy Caution* (1965), filmed in the strangest, most fascist-looking locations he could find around Paris.

THX 1138 4EB was the name Lucas gave to the uncut feature he loaded up on the Moviola at Verna Fields's house some weeks later. It would take him twelve weeks of late-night editing to finish it. THX was pronounced "Thex" and appears to have been a joking reference to "sex," though Lucas had trouble persuading anyone other than his closest friends to say it that way. The "EB" stood for "Earth Born." A year later, when the film was wowing audiences at student film festivals, he amended the title—another signature Lucas move—adding *Electric Labyrinth*.

The result was light years beyond the average student film. Lucas and Murch had warped the sound, making much of the dialogue deliberately unintelligible. All the audience needed to understand was that THX 1138 is a man on the run from some sort of Orwellian government security apparatus. Not much acting was required. THX is seen in close-up only for a second. The surveillance guys hunting him are supposed to be dispassionate, which the navy guys found easy. One wears a numbered helmet that covers his eyes while he pulls levers—the first embryonic Stormtrooper Lucas committed to film.

The major innovation in the movie is what Lucas did in the optical lab: adding numbers and captions to the film, almost at random. He points his camera at TV screens. An organ drones deep discordant notes in the background. Viewers feel like voyeurs, ghosts in the government machine. Today it feels like it's full of student film cliché, but Lucas practically invented those clichés. Not only did the short win armfuls of awards, but it also won him his first appearance in *Time* magazine in February 1968. Lucas babbled to the interviewer that THX's pursuers have a whole backstory, that they are two separate races of "erosbods and clinicbods."

Suddenly Lucas the odd-bod was making all sorts of interesting friends with this award-winning film as his calling card. "*THX* was not of this earth," said a Long Beach film student who was introduced to Lucas at a student screening that included Lucas's completed short, Steven Spielberg. It was to be another decade before they became collaborators, but they were already well on the way to becoming each other's biggest fans. "*THX* created a world that did not exist before George designed it," Spielberg enthused.

That may be overselling the fifteen-minute version of *THX* somewhat. "It's a chase film," says Charley Lippincott flatly. "It's about paranoia." But however you define it, the fact remains that Lucas managed to put a nightmarish future on film years before Hollywood started doing the same thing. The film industry would produce a slate of sour science fiction futures in the 1970s, such as *Omega Man* in 1971, *Soylent Green* in 1973, *Logan's Run* in 1976. Lucas was to effectively launch that slate with the feature version of *THX*, and he would effectively bring it to an end with *Star Wars*.

11. THE EMPEROR

Lucas reentered USC as a graduate student in triumph, a fifteen-minute color film in the can. No other student had ever done such a thing. For an encore, he would crank out his first graduate film on an even tighter schedule, learning just how fast he could push himself. *Anyone Lived in a Pretty [How] Town* was a five-minute confection named for an E. E. Cummings poem. The plot: a photographer makes his subjects disappear. That's it. Like most of Lucas's student shorts, it featured no dialogue and felt a little inhuman—and you weren't sure how deliberate all of that was.

The final film Lucas shot as a student, *The Emperor*, was different. For the first time, Lucas focused his lens on a human subject: Burbank radio DJ Bob Hudson, the self-styled "emperor of radio." It was an interesting choice, and not because the name would be echoed in the prime mover of evil in the *Star Wars* movies.

Hudson was a self-confessed fantasist. He opened the short by talking about Emperor Norton, an eccentric character in nineteenth-century San Francisco who declared himself emperor and began to be treated as such. Hudson took the example to heart with his grandiose title. Lucas evidently warmed to this notion: someone becoming exactly what he wanted to be, no matter how outrageous it sounded. Like Norton, Hudson declared it and then lived it. This was to become Lucas's philosophy too: dream yourself an empire. "As corny as it sounds," Lucas declared years later, "the power of positive thinking goes a long way."

Perhaps because of such eccentric grandiosity, Hudson got himself ejected from a steady stream of stations. "I'm disagreeable," he tells the camera, though we only see his whimsicality. These days, Hudson would be an AM radio shock jock; he had the look and the loose mouth of a Rush Limbaugh. But in the 1960s, radio voices were more benign: they played records, told stories and jokes, kept you company.

Lucas had fun with the format, and viewers of his films got a strong sense of his oddball humor in *The Emperor* for the first time. He put the credits in the exact middle of the movie, right before the punch line of one of Hudson's jokes. "It's fantasy," Hudson says at the end of the movie, echoing the title card at the beginning. "Radio is fantasy." He fades out, leaving an empty chair.

Film was fantasy too—that's what Lucas learned at USC. Film was fantasy; your fantasies could appear on film. And he had the potential to spin that fantasy, to drive that Moviola, like no other filmmaker. Well, *almost* no other.

12. FRANCIS FORD COPPOLA

After Lucas graduated, he retreated into the desert. Classmate Charley Lippincott had turned down a $200-a-week scholarship offered by Columbia Pictures to work on a Western called *McKenna's Gold* that was being shot in Arizona, and Lucas took the gig instead. But he became angry at the scholarship, which he later called "a ruse to get a bunch of cheap, behind the scenes documentaries." Lucas pocketed the cash, withdrew from the shoot, and made a silent film about the desert itself. Still in love with numbers, he called it *6.18.67*, for the day he finished shooting.*

The next opportunity was another scholarship—one that Lucas won (on the strength of THX) and Murch lost, but not before they'd made a pact that the winner would help out the loser. This one gave Lucas six months at Warner Brothers at $80 a week. Later, Lucas would spin the fantasy that his first day on the lot was Jack Warner's last. In fact, Warner would stick around, on and off, for years. But the studio was in a bad way, sold to a business consortium, many of its departments shuttered. One that was in the process of closing was the animation department, home of *Looney Tunes*, which is where Lucas had wanted to spend his scholarship time. Prior to the scholarship, Lucas had tried

---

* Exactly one decade later, Lucas would be reaping the first rewards of a far more difficult desert shoot.

and failed to get a job at Hanna-Barbera; he had briefly assisted animator Saul Bass on the Oscar-winning short *Why Man Creates*. It would take Lucas until 1985 to succeed in becoming a producer of animated fare—having taken the long way 'round.

Instead, Lucas picked up the phone in the moribund animation department and made a fateful call to his classmate Howard Kazanjian, who happened to be on the lot as assistant director on the only movie then in production: a musical called *Finian's Rainbow*. Kazanjian told Lucas to come on down so he could introduce him to Francis Ford Coppola, a self-confident wunderkind from UCLA, the only student filmmaker in the country whose star had eclipsed Lucas's. After a spell working for B-movie maestro Roger Corman, Coppola had landed a Hollywood directing gig. That alone seemed impossible. But the fact that he just happened to be on the Warner's lot at the same time Lucas was despairing of something to do? That had to be destiny.

Coppola found room in the budget for Lucas to work as an assistant, and their ever-lively relationship was off to the races. Coppola challenged Lucas to come up with a brilliant idea for the film every day. Lucas delivered, but Coppola, four years his senior, still teased his charge mercilessly, calling him a "stinky kid." Lucas's second lifelong mentor after his father was also, he said, his tormentor. They were polar opposites: loud and quiet, impetuous and cautious, womanizing and distantly devoted. Lucas once said his career was a reaction to Coppola's as much as anything else. Still, the two had something crucial in common. "George broke the rules at USC," Kazanjian would later observe; after all, he literally broke into the editing bullpen. "Francis likes breaking rules."

On late nights back at the office with Kazanjian, Lucas and Coppola kept talking about how much they hated the Hollywood scene and wanted to tear down its stodgy structure of unions and old-guard studio bosses. So it was another extraordinary stroke of luck when Coppola got the go-ahead from the studio to film his screenplay *The Rain People*. He put together a twenty-person road shoot: a caravan across America on a shoestring budget, all handheld cameras and motels. The movie's heroine was doing a Kerouac, going on the road to find herself. The young filmmakers were doing the same. Lucas came along as a jack of all trades: he would record sound, carry equipment, manage props. He filmed a documentary that captured Coppola's tempestuousness, as well as the fun and chaos of the road trip, with fireworks being shot from car to car, their drivers wearing Prussian military helmets.

Around this time, Lucas was captured on documentary film cameras himself for the first time, for a segment of a short on new filmmakers that was ostensibly focused on Coppola. Introduced as the director's assistant—no, no, insists Coppola, his *associate*—Lucas smiles shyly and looks down at his camera. Then the film cuts to Lucas in thick-framed glasses, the beginnings of a goatee, and a Mao-style military jacket, in full revolutionary flow. "Student films are the only real hope," he lectures. "I think they [the studios] are starting to realize that students know what they're doing. You know, they're not just a bunch of silly kids playing around."

The Creator-to-be, the self-determined Emperor of film, was about to become much more than a silly kid playing in an alleyway.

But first, he would have to learn to write.

5.

HOW TO BE A JEDI

The God of the state was a lie. Our hero was determined to find the truth behind all religions.

"There must be something independent," said THX 1138. "A Force."

Lucas wrote those lines in 1968, as he was adapting *THX 1138 4EB* into what would be his first-ever feature film. The echo from Arthur Lipsett's *21–87* could still be heard. Sometime in the following year, he decided to cut the Force scene from his *THX* script. But the Force would continue to flow through him, demanding to be born as a concept. In 1977, it would explode into the minds of millions; thereafter, Francis Ford Coppola suggested to Lucas that the two of them actually start a religion using the Force as its scripture. Lucas feared for his friend's sanity. But it wasn't out of character for Coppola, a man who once joked that he was modeling his career on Hitler's rise to power—and who, Lucas often said, had a habit of finding a parade and jumping out in front to lead it.

Even if Coppola had his tongue in his cheek, it wasn't an unprecedented idea. Science fiction writer L. Ron Hubbard had by then spent three decades building his religion, the Church of Scientology. Lucas has more adherents than Hubbard could ever have dreamed of. If he had let the charismatic Coppola build a church of Force-ology, there seems little doubt we'd be living in a different world.

But Lucas's intent in the movies had been to distill religious beliefs that were already in existence, not to add a new one. "Knowing that the film was made for

57

a young audience, I was trying to say, in a simple way, that there is a God and that there is both a good side and a bad side," Lucas told his biographer Dale Pollock. "You have a choice between them, but the world works better if you're on the good side."

The Force is so basic a concept as to be universally appealing: a religion for the secular age that is so well suited to our times precisely because it is so bereft of detail. Everyone gets to add their own layers of meaning. Lucas, through a long process of trial and error, seems to have deliberately encouraged viewers' unique interpretations. "The more detail I went into, the more it detracted from the concept I was trying to put forward," Lucas recalled in 1997. "So the real essence was to deal with the Force but not be too specific about it." In *Star Wars*, Obi-Wan Kenobi explains the Force to Luke Skywalker in just twenty-eight well-chosen words: "The Force is what gives a Jedi his power. It's an energy field created by all living things. It surrounds us, penetrates us. It binds the galaxy together."

Other than that, the Force is largely a mystery. We learn that it has a strong influence on the weak-minded; that there is a Dark Side of the Force that seduced Darth Vader. We know that Vader believes the Force to be far superior to the technological power of the Death Star and that he can use it to choke people he disagrees with from across a room. Luke is taught to "let go your conscious mind" and "reach out with your feelings." He is told the Force "will be with you, always." Han Solo believes the Force to be a "hokey religion," no substitute for a good blaster, but later grudgingly wishes for the Force to be with Luke. Obi-Wan disappears when Vader's lightsaber strikes him; audiences presumed this had something to do with the Force, but it was left unexplained for five more movies. Luke was able to destroy the Death Star because he puts his targeting computer aside and relies on the Force—you might just as well call it intuition.

And that's all he wrote—Lucas, at least. The explanation provided by Jedi master Yoda in the next movie, much of it written by Lawrence Kasdan rather than Lucas, may have been more poetic, more spiritual ("luminous beings are we, not this crude matter") and more demonstrative (Yoda lifts an X-wing fighter out of a swamp after explaining that the Force is connected to all things). But we learn little more from this than we did from Kenobi's twenty-eight words.

Indeed, later attempts to examine the Force in more detail seemed out of keeping with the movie's space fantasy origins. The moment Lucas decided to add a kind of rational, scientific component to Jedi knowledge of the Force, in *Episode I*—the infamous "midi-chlorians," microscopic organisms that are supposed to help the Force bind to living beings—long-time fans revolted. It didn't matter that, as Lucasfilm protested, the midi-chlorians are not supposed to be what the Force is actually made of—just a biological indication of its presence. If you dig deep enough into the Lucasfilm archives, you'll find Lucas talking about midi-chlorians as early as August 1977. "It is said that certain creatures are born with a higher awareness of the Force than others," he said during a role-playing exercise designed to help him flesh out *Star Wars* concepts after the original movie. "Their brains are different; they have more midi-chlorians in their cells." This didn't matter either. What fans actually want, it seems, is as little detail as possible. They want twenty-eight words, and nothing more.

Lucas, by that stage, may have been trying to use his powers for the good of science education; as much is suggested by the midi-chlorians' homonymity with mitochondria, the energy source for most of our cells. That's commendable, but if we want to see the Force of the movies manifest in real life, you have to look to religion and art, not biology. The Force is a Navajo prayer, an echo of a comment in an art-house film, and many more things besides. "The grandest form of active force / from Tao come, their only source," says the Tao te Ching. The Tao, like the Force, is the basis for a form of martial arts. So are the concepts of chi, or energy, prevalent in traditional Chinese Buddhist culture, and *prana* in India, Sanskrit for "life force."

The Force is all of these things; it is none of them. The Force has been embraced by Jews and Hindus and Wiccans. Everyone sees what they want to see in it, especially if—like those kids watching *Flash Gordon*—they first encountered the Force at the right age.

Just how widely the Force has been embraced by people from different walks of life became clear in 2004, when Dr. Jennifer Porter, a religious studies professor from the Memorial University of Newfoundland, conducted a survey at a Disney World *Star Wars* Weekend. "When I was 12, something about that universal connection to the Force really grabbed something within me," said one Jewish respondent. "That and the concept of the Jedi respecting and protecting all life and developing mind, body and soul reflected my own path in life. From that point I made it my personal journey to become a Jedi. I wasn't counting on being able to move objects with my mind and the thought of creating a true functioning lightsaber didn't even cross my mind, but I did seek to control my emotions, to be more aware of the consequences of my actions, to honor and respect all life in both people and creatures, and to find peace and serenity and beauty in everything around me."

That was a surprisingly representative sentiment. "The theme that emerges most strongly in the comments," says Porter, "is that of the Force as a metaphor for godhood that resonates and inspires within them a deeper commitment to the godhood identified within their traditional faith." In other words, the Force is like an Instagram filter through which to view any established religion. It isn't oppositional enough to even appear to attempt to supplant any traditional religion, the way John Lennon had his brief flirtation with the notion that the Beatles had more active supporters than Christianity. The Force is friendly and enhancing to all. Therefore, the Force conquers all.

Christianity could easily have set itself up in opposition to a theology that appeared to embrace Eastern culture. Instead, for the most part—except for isolated locations like Albin Johnson's Sunday School—Christians embraced the Force. It was ethereal enough to be construed as the Holy Spirit. "May the Force be with you" sounded an awful lot like the *dominus vobiscum* of traditional liturgy: "the Lord be with you."* Indeed, the earliest attempt to layer a contemporary earthly religion over the Force—one of the earliest books written on *Star Wars*, period—was a Christian one. In 1977, Frank Allnutt, a former Disney publicist (he worked on *Mary Poppins*) turned evangelist, rushed out a book called *The Force of Star Wars*. Rather than being an escape from reality, Allnutt wrote, *Star Wars* was a signpost to something more real. "It says to the viewer, 'Listen! There's something better in life than wallowing in the mud of pornography, dope, materialism and vain philosophies. You have a higher calling—a calling to be somebody, to do something. You have a date with destiny. You have potential in you that you haven't begun to develop. There is a Force in the universe that you need to be plugged into.'" Lucas was pointing toward Jesus, Allnutt wrote, "perhaps unknowingly." He said that when Kenobi talked about the Force, "his eyes sparkled like he was talking about a dear old friend, not an impersonal Force." He compared Kenobi's sacrificial moment of death to the crucifixion. (In later years Allnutt would refine his philosophy, pointing out that "Jedi" could be a contraction of "JEsus DIsciple.")

Allnutt's book became an instant bestseller and resonated with both fans and the broader Christian community. When I mentioned Allnutt's book to Albin Johnson, he laughed nostalgically. "I devoured that book," he said. "It was plain English enough that I followed along; I must have read it three times." It allowed young Albin to reconcile *Star Wars* with his parents' Christian faith and made him resolve to "stick it out and harbor a secret love for *Star Wars*."

Lucas himself was never much of a Christian, as much as he had been raised Methodist. He certainly carried around a concept of God—"I'm simply struggling through life, trying to do God's bidding," he told Dale Pollock in

---

* *Star Wars* producer Gary Kurtz remembers that comparison was exactly the intention.

1982—but his use of the G-word diminished in later years as his views evolved. In 1999, Lucas was told by the dean of the Graduate School of Journalism at UC Berkeley, "You sound awfully Buddhist to me." Lucas responded: "My daughter was asked at school, 'What are you?' And she said we're Buddhist Methodists. I said, well, I guess that's one way to describe it." A few years later, he elaborated to *Time* magazine: "I was raised Methodist. Now let's say I'm spiritual. It's Marin County. We're all Buddhists up here." *

Much of what we learn of the Jedi in the prequel trilogy follows this part-Christian, part-Buddhist theme. We see an order similar to the Knights Templar or celibate warrior monks. We hear a lot about nonattachment, a key Buddhist tenet; we learn that "anger leads to hate, hate leads to suffering"— suffering being the result of all attachment, according to the Buddha. Anakin Skywalker becomes a fallen angel, the Satanic Vader. But this biblical downfall happens because he is too attached to the idea of defeating death and saving his wife.

The prequels complicate our notion not just of the Force but of the Jedi knights themselves. We see the Jedi in repose, in what looks like prayer or meditation, depending on your point of view. But we also see an order that is too rigid, an order destroyed, like the Templar, because it was dragged into war by its attachment to being "guardians of peace." Everything in the original trilogy tells us the way of the Jedi is the last hope of the galaxy. But everything in the prequels tells us the Jedi themselves had flaws that were all too human. It's as if Lucas built a religion by accident and then decided to tear it down at its foundations.

A t the same time as Lucas was making the prequels, a grassroots effort to create a kind of Jedi church was under way—but in a far less serious sense than you might think.

In February 2001, New Zealand was one week away from its usual once-a-decade census. Someone in the country, anonymous to this day, took a look at question 18, which dealt with religious affiliation, and saw a chance to have some fun. "We are trying to encourage people to tick the 'other' box and then fill their religion in as Jedi," said an anonymous email. "All *Star Wars* fans will

---

* Indeed, Lucas's long-time assistant, Jane Bay, is a dedicated follower of the Dalai Llama and has written books about her experiences of traveling to Tibet, adopting a daughter there, and then dealing with the grief of losing her.

understand." The writer claimed, falsely, that the country would be forced to recognize Jediism as an official religion. His or her second objective: "it's a bit of an experiment in the power of email."

It's safe to say the experiment succeeded. With one week's notice, some 53,715 New Zealanders ticked the "Other" box and wrote in "Jedi." The government refused to recognize it as an affiliation—but unofficially, "Jedi" became the country's second largest religion.

For the census in Australia that August, the same email was overhauled. This time it was claimed ten thousand was the official barrier to a new religion. There was a new incentive: "Remember, if you are a member of the Jedi religion then you are by default a Jedi Knight." In some versions, there was a coda: "If this has been your dream since you were 4 years old . . . do it because you love *Star Wars*. If not, do it out of badness."

The Australian government struck back, warning that anyone who went to the Dark Side by putting a false answer on a census form was liable for a penalty of $1,000. Though the idea of the government issuing a fine to any or all of the self-declared Jedi beggars belief, census officials were in earnest. "For a group to be included in the Australian Bureau of Statistics' classification of religion, it would have to show that there was an underlying belief system or philosophy," said Hugh McGaw of the Census Processing and User Services. Some seventy thousand Australians risked the fine and wrote in Jedi anyway, perhaps in the hope that someone would come along and reveal that underlying belief system. (Nobody was ever fined.)

New Zealand and Australia were just the beginning. Jediism spread to Canada courtesy of a couple of DJs in Vancouver; twenty-one thousand Canadians wrote it in their census. Subsequent counts in Croatia, the Czech Republic, and Montenegro all found thousands of Jedi living in their country. Ireland has refused to divulge how many Jedi live on the Emerald Isle. But the all-time prize for the Jedi chain-mailers was the United Kingdom, which reported more than four hundred thousand Jedi within its borders, after the government made it clear that nobody would be fined for writing it in, and indeed embraced it as a method to increase census response rates among teens and twentysomethings. Those four hundred thousand respondents represented 0.7 percent of the population, making Jedi the United Kingdom's fourth largest stated religion after Christianity, Islam, and Hinduism.

So far, so amusing. But how much of this was a real reflection of the spread of Jediism, rather than just done to annoy officialdom or to make a point about having to put your religion on your census form? Turns out, not so much.

Consider that in the 2001 census, 14.7 percent of the United Kingdom put down "no religion." For *Star Wars*–loving atheists and agnostics, "Jedi" may be simply a more interesting personal statement than "no religion." Consider also that the largest percentages of Jedi in the United Kingdom seemed to live in major college towns: Brighton, Oxford, and Cambridge all had roughly 2 percent Jedi. Much of the response was essentially a student prank.

Still, there followed an onslaught of Jedi headlines. Politicians found they could get attention by latching on to the notion of a Jedi religion. In 2006, Labor's Jamie Reed used his maiden speech in Parliament to declare himself the first Jedi MP. His office confirmed that this was a joke; he was trying to prove that religion, in the context of a parliamentary bill on hate crimes, was a hard thing to define. But the headlines didn't hurt. Nor did they for a Conservative MP who brought up a possible Jedi exclusion to a religion bill in 2009.

Ordinary UK residents also made the news by claiming affiliation with the Jedi. A couple of Londoners calling themselves Jedi delivered a petition to the United Nations Association calling for the forthcoming UN International Day of Tolerance to be renamed the UN Interstellar Day of Tolerance; the *Daily Mail* couldn't resist doing a photo feature. Then, in 2009 in Bangor, North Wales, a man named Daniel Jones was asked to remove his hoodie in a Tesco supermarket; he claimed he was the founder of "the International Church of Jediism" with "500,000 followers worldwide." Newspapers reported this without comment; in fact, Jones's church has little more than 500 followers on Twitter. "It states in our Jedi doctrination [*sic*] that I can wear headwear," Jones said, after he had presented the Tesco manager with a church business card and was ejected. A Tesco spokesman put his best spin on the incident: "If Jedi walk around our stores with their hoods on, they'll miss lots of special offers."

The closest thing one can find to a Church of Jediism is the website Jedichurch .org; this international umbrella group currently claims 6,300 members on Facebook. That may be the same size as the 501st Legion, but the group has none of the 501st's coherence. The content is largely the same as any Facebook group: jokes, news items, inspirational images, the occasional political cause. A member writes that they're getting the Jedi Code as a tattoo. Someone posts a quote from the Dalai Llama; another posts a video of lightsaber twirling; yet another updates us on a unicycling Darth Vader in Portland, Oregon, who plays flaming bagpipes.

More power to them all. But having a fun Facebook group does not a religious order make. The Wikipedia page on Jediism says it all: "Jediism has no founder or central structure." Imagine a religion with no religion. As Lucas's third mentor, Joseph Campbell, put it: "All religions are true. None are literal."

The number of Jedi in censuses since 2001 has also risen and (mostly) fallen. In her research, Jennifer Porter draws a distinction between "Jedi realists," who call themselves Jedi but reject the religion label and prefer to think of Jediism as a philosophy of life, and Jediists, who claim to follow an entirely new creed. Some Jediists claim to follow something called the Twenty-One Maxims (Prowess, Justice, Loyalty, Defense, Courage, and I'll spare you the rest) gleaned from the now inactive website jediism.org. Porter estimates that there are at least five times more Jedi realists than Jediists. "There was an ideological power struggle," she says, "and the Jediists got stomped."

That sounds about right. The Jedi I've encountered are very postmodern about the whole thing. Things are just as one Presbyterian respondent to Porter's survey wrote: "I suspect that all or most of these Jedi are not really practicing the faith they profess to believe in anyway. They just want cool lightsabers."

I can't seem to spin my lightsaber forward. This is a problem. Spinning your lightsaber forward is the first thing you learn in lightsaber class. If I can't master this basic move, my training will be limited indeed.

Alain Bloch, our instructor, is doing his best to show us. Looking the part in robes, long leather Jedi boots, and feathered hair à la Anakin Skywalker, he points out what he's doing in the studio mirrors. "Forward spin, thumb and forefinger. Forward, open up your palm, palms open out." My wrist doesn't want to turn like that. I can't even see how his is turning. It's a blur. "Just let the momentum of the blade carry you through the spin. Now you can go a bit faster."

Regardless of my poor ability, the class moves on. Soon we're practicing spinning our sabers backward, slashing them in figure eights with each hand, and whipping them out from behind our backs. Bloch has *Star Wars* soundtracks playing in the background, accompanied by the occasional echoing clunk as another lightsaber falls to the floor.

We're at the regular Sunday afternoon meeting of the Golden Gate Knights, a three-hour Jedi training school held in a dance studio steps from the start-ups of San Francisco's South of Market neighborhood. Bloch's two-year-old class was featured on the websites of the BBC and *Los Angeles Times*. Then the BBC turned to him for comment when a Scottish clergyman expressed fears that the disestablishment of marriage in the UK would lead to people "being married by a Jedi." Bloch declined to contribute: he's a Jedi realist. "All of it is rather crap," he says of Jediist tracts. "I tell people, just go to the source: Buddhism,

Taoism, Hinduism, whatever. Because all of the pseudo-religious philosophy in *Star Wars* is just that."

I found a surprisingly diverse crowd in Bloch's class—about as many women as men, young as old, Caucasian as not. There was a healthy stream of couples on dates, gay and straight. Every week, we had visitors from foreign climes. One guy came all the way from Madrid; it turned out he had started leading a similar class there. If you want a snapshot of the *Star Wars* audience, it's right here. It looks like everyone.

Lightsabers, in short, are a global obsession. There's an annual worldwide contest for the best lightsaber video on YouTube called Sabercomp. (The results are spectacular and well worth looking up.) In Germany, I met the Saber Project, a large and earnest group of fluorescent lightsaber makers that performed a mass battle demonstration before a thirtieth anniversary screening of *Return of the Jedi*. In 2013, Harvard and MIT scientists were able to bind together tiny molecules made out of photons. "Scientists Create Lightsaber Technology," the headlines screamed. In Shanghai, one company has gone so far as to sell an extremely powerful handheld laser as a "lightsaber"—it might not be able to slice off someone's arm and cauterize the wound, but it will certainly take your eye out.

But who wouldn't want the chance, at least once, to swing something you can convince yourself is a real lightsaber? The sabers the Golden Gate Knights use are a vast improvement over the $10 telescoping kind found in Toys "R" Us. Bloch offers blades in abundance, all custom built by groups similar to the Saber Project as well as assorted online individuals. Each handle has a different style, a different grip, a well-honed metal sheen. They emit just the right hum; some are modified with accelerometers and impact sensors and make the famed clashing sound when they meet. A tough translucent tube houses a beam from a powerful florescent LED; it's enough to feel there's a laser blade in front of you when the lights are on and to make everyone in the class go "ooooh" when the studio lights are dimmed and the mirrors reflect our blades into infinity.

The easiest way to describe lightsaber class is that it's one part fencing, one part yoga. The goal is to learn a numbered system of fight choreography worked out by Bloch and his cofounder Matthew Carauddo, who runs the same class in a studio in Silicon Valley. You and I could meet for the first time with our lightsabers at a Comic-Con, say, and I could utter a string of numbers and you would know that I was going to slice around your body in a star formation and parry appropriately. We could even throw in flourishes such as the figure eight, or something more elaborate Bloch calls the "Obi-Annie" (but which is actually a move called "plum blossom" from the martial art Wushu). We would for one moment shed our nerd shells; we would look cool.

It's a far cry from the rolled-up newspaper and "zhoom, zhoom" noises my friends and I would employ as kids. I was delighted to learn that everyone— even Ewan MacGregor and Liam Neeson, when they began training with sticks for their lightsaber battles in *Episode I*—makes the noises when they start out. As kids in the 80s, Bloch and his friends would battle with flashlights in darkened rooms. "We had our rules about it," he says. "Usually we would have to stop and decide if someone had blocked the blade in time. I suspect we spent more time refereeing the fights than actually fighting."

Bloch came to learn the way of the lightsaber after an unusual experience at the annual Burning Man festival in Nevada in 2006. One attendee, in an act of the kind of bizarre generosity that permeates the event, handed out ten thousand lightsabers, with the instructions to "meet at sunset for an epic battle royale." Two sides, each hundreds strong, charged at each other in the middle of the desert, in the nerd version of a giant pillow fight.

The experience changed Bloch. He felt inspired to start walking the streets of San Francisco dressed as a Jedi. One day in Dolores Park, the palm tree mecca of the Mission District, a man came up to him and said, "I see you have two lightsabers."

Bloch, who indeed was carrying two lightsabers for the first time—red and blue, Sith and Jedi—said, "Yes I do."

"Well," said the man thoughtfully, "we should do battle, then."

And battle they did. Bloch came armed with rules: if you touched the other guy's torso three times with the lightsaber, you won. Later Bloch met another man at a party who challenged him to a duel and asked if he remembered the epic battle royale at Burning Man. This was Hib Engler, the guy who handed out the ten thousand lightsabers in the first place. They fought twice. Both men won a duel. The circle was complete.

Bloch tried to brush up his skills through fencing class, stage combat class, and martial arts. But nothing on offer was quite like being trained to use a lightsaber. Finally, Bloch found Carauddo through a YouTube video demonstrating his technique and his custom sabers. Carauddo gave Bloch one lesson, and Bloch said, "You know, people would pay to do this." He found the studio and started to prove himself right. The guy from Dolores Park was one of the first; two years on, Bloch estimates he's had nearly a thousand students. The suggested donation (ahem, Lucasfilm) is $10.

A few more lightsaber-spinning exercises—doing a reverse figure eight behind your back, letting the lightsaber leap from hand to hand—and then we move into the fight choreography. "First, chamber your attack," Bloch says, meaning pull the blade into your side, held with two hands (always hold your lightsaber with two hands unless you're doing a spin or flourish), pointed up and ready. Then swing at your opponent, pivoting the handle with your higher, leading hand at its fulcrum, using the back of the blade as a lever with your lower hand. If you get it right, it should snap to a halt just before it hits them.

When you watch experts like Bloch and Carauddo do this, it's a marvelous, energetic whirlwind, very much in the style of the movies; Carauddo, short and stocky, moves like a Jedi Tasmanian devil. But when I look at myself in the mirror, trying to remember whether attack 3 or attack 4 is on the left or the right, I don't see a Jedi. I see Ghyslain Raza.

G hyslain Raza is probably the best-known figure in the world whose name almost nobody knows. In November 2002, he was a heavyset fourteen-year-old attending St. Joseph's Seminary, a private school in Trois-Rivières, Quebec. There was a school play coming up, and Raza was directing a *Star Wars* skit. He needed to work on some moves for the actors.

Raza was also in the school AV club. So one day he grabbed a golf ball retriever, took a VHS tape with an old basketball game on it, and decided to record his lightsaber moves. The retriever was too long to act as anything other than a double-headed lightsaber, of the kind that martial arts expert Ray Park wields as Darth Maul in *Episode I*—very advanced moves, in other words. Raza didn't care. He would swing the retriever around for about twenty seconds, huffing and grunting with serious purpose, then stop, pause the video, and try again. In his final pass, he got so animated he almost fell over. In total, Raza recorded one minute and forty-eight seconds.

"I was just goofing around," Raza told Canada's *Maclean's* magazine in his one and only interview on the subject, eleven years later. "Most 14-year-old boys would do something similar in that situation. Maybe more gracefully."

Raza put the video back on the shelf and thought nothing more of it until the following April, when he found a friend in the AV club had taken a still from the practice footage and was using it as his desktop background image. "There's a video doing the rounds," the friend explained. "Didn't you know?" One classmate had found the VHS tape; another transferred it to digital format; a third posted it on the web. Right away, Raza got a sinking feeling—but he had no idea how bad it was going to get.

It's hard to estimate how many people have seen the video, now universally known as "*Star Wars* Kid." Visit it on YouTube today, and you'll see it has racked up almost twenty-nine million views, adding a million views every six months or so. But "*Star Wars* Kid" went viral in May 2003, two years before YouTube was even founded. The video did the rounds on the now-defunct file-sharing service Kazaa, where it was downloaded a million times in its first month. It hit the nascent blogosphere, which was hungry for just this sort of quirky content. A popular website called waxy.org posted it, alongside a version with Raza swinging the saber at superspeed, and from then on it was shared by email. The *New York Times* did a story. Parodies aired on *Family Guy* and *Arrested Development*.

Today, the remixes are almost as popular as the original. In "Drunken Jedi" (thirteen million views), a special effects company called Kalvascorp turned Raza's golf ball retriever into a real lightsaber and showed it fending off blaster fire. There are versions showing Raza battling Yoda (four million views) and Agent Smith from *The Matrix* (two million views).

In November 2006, a marketing company called the Viral Factory estimated that "*Star Wars* Kid" had been seen nine hundred million times in its first three years. That would make it the second most popular Internet video of all time, behind only Psy's monster 2013 hit "Gangnam Style." By 2014, it seems fair to say that "*Star Wars* Kid" in its many forms has been seen at least a billion times—in other words, as many times as all tickets sold for all *Star Wars* movies.

Raza went through some very dark times. So many reporters called after the *New York Times* story that the family had to unplug the phone. At school, students clambered onto tabletops to imitate him. The crueler side of the Internet was out in force; a commenter called him a "pox on humanity"; more than one suggested he commit suicide. He never considered it but "couldn't help but feel worthless." He did his exams in a high school affiliated with a local hospital, sparking rumors that he'd been sent to a psychiatric ward. His family hired a lawyer that sued the three kids responsible for uploading the video. They sought damages of $160,000, but the settlement they got didn't even cover the lawyer's costs.

Raza got his school life on track with the help of a private tutor and was able to return to St. Joseph's Seminary for his senior year. He studied law at McGill University and became the president of a local conservation society.

He decided to speak out against cyberbullying after another Canadian teen committed suicide when pictures of her rape were posted on the Internet by her accused rapists—a truly horrific case that rather put Raza's experience in perspective. His message for kids who fall victim to cyberbullying: "You'll survive. You're not alone. You are surrounded by people who love you. You have to overcome your shame and get help."

It was entirely understandable that Raza was as mortified as he was. What he never quite appreciated, or cared about, was that he had a posse. As soon as the video went viral, before the *New York Times* had even written about it, far more readers were apologizing for the behavior of the minority. Waxy.org got remorseful and helped organize donations to Raza as a way to apologize. The blog asked for enough to buy him an iPod; 135 readers immediately contributed a total of $1,000.

Alain Bloch, for one, appreciates Raza and his moves. "We weren't laughing so much at him as much as we were laughing at ourselves," Bloch says. "We've all picked up a broomstick and waved it around like a lightsaber. That's why his video became so popular: it was funny and awkward, but ultimately we connected to him. He made us feel more comfortable with our own awkwardness. Our own dreams of being a Jedi."

A t the end of the Golden Gate Knights class, Bloch gathers everyone into a circle. We sit meditation-style, lightsabers balanced on their ends in front of us, painting our faces in the dark. Luminous beings are we.

"Take some deep breaths," says Bloch. "Close your eyes. If you can't keep them closed, just look at your blade. We have a little Jedi oath, a mantra. So if you want to be a part of it, repeat after me."

This is what we repeat:

There is no emotion.
There is only stillness.
There is no thought.
There is only silence.
There is no ignorance.
There is only attention.
There is no division.
There is only perception.
There is no self.
There is only the Force.

This mantra turns out to be the Jedi Code—or rather, Bloch's version of it. There seems to be some disagreement, on planet Star Wars, about exactly what the Jedi Code is. At the Jedi Academy in Disney World, Orlando, instructors tell young padawans to repeat the following "Jedi Code" before they are given their "trainee lightsabers":

> A Jedi uses the Force,
> For knowledge and defense,
> Never for attack.
> If I disobey these rules,
> Into the crowd I will go back.

(The kids usually get very quiet on the last line.)

In *Star Wars* lore, the Jedi Code is supposed to go back to an ancient order that embraced both the Dark and the Light Side of the Force, called the Je'daii—which means "mystic center," according to *Wookieepedia*, a crowd-sourced online encyclopedia—and the code has since changed over time. Here's its best-known iteration, as used in a hip-hop track called "Jedi Code," by Rapsody:

> There is no emotion, there is peace.
> There is no ignorance, there is knowledge.
> There is no passion, there is serenity.
> There is no chaos, there is harmony.
> There is no death, there is the Force.

Bloch says he changed his version of the code for two reasons. First, the original is licensed Lucasfilm material, and you do not want to mess with Lucasfilm on matters of copyright. Second, it didn't make a whole lot of sense. Couldn't you call peace a kind of emotion? The lack of passion is kind of a downer; why rob yourself of that? Plus that "there is no death" line might make the casual visitor think they'd stumbled into a religious cult. And if there's one thing we've learned about the Force, it's that it keeps resolutely refusing to turn into a religious cult.

Several months after my first class with the Golden Gate Knights, I was asked to participate in Course of the Force. A charity relay race organized by the website Nerdist, it would charge runners with taking a single lightsaber from Lucas's Skywalker Ranch in Marin, in the north of the San Francisco Bay Area, all the way down to San Diego Comic-Con, the biggest event on the geek calendar. All proceeds were to go to the Make-a-Wish Foundation. Participants would run behind a replica of Jabba's sail barge one at a time, each taking a leg of the marathon distance, swinging a lightsaber for multiple video cameras.

I'm self-conscious at the best of times, and I shuddered to think of myself caught on video with a lightsaber. The mirrors at Bloch's studios were bad enough; this would be a broadcast on one of YouTube's most popular channels. I'd have to *run* and spin a lightsaber at the same time. Was I setting myself up to be the next Ghyslain Raza? I would have used that old mainstay "I have a bad feeling about this," the ominous phrase that features in all six *Star Wars* movies, but that would hardly be in the spirit of Lucas's positive thinking. The key to that phrase is that it only ever makes the expected disaster more likely to happen, according to *Empire Strikes Back* and *Return of the Jedi* cowriter Lawrence Kasdan. "It's certainly been true in my own life," he says.

Kasdan, it turns out, is kind of the Saint Paul of Force-ology. He may have kept his in-screenplay descriptions of the Force to a mysterious minimum, but he has plenty of his own thoughts on the matter. He believes the Force really exists in terms of being "the combined vibration of all living things," something we humans contribute to. His personal religion, so far as it goes, is to believe that there is "so much more going on than we can see or perceive, that we're not alone in this space, that everything that has happened in this space is still there." It was Lucas and Kasdan together who came up with the immortal line "Try not; do or do not, there is no 'try'"—the fact that these words came from the mouth of a green puppet does not diminish the fact that they form a profoundly useful dictum that marries purpose and mindfulness, and sticks in the brain for life.

A lot of pronouncements in Lucas's philosophy have this kind of straighten-up-and-fly-right feeling to them. He's warned us about the selfishness and self-destructiveness of the Sith, the Jedi's mortal enemies. He's beaten the drum for years on the importance of empathy and our responsibility to one another. Frank Allnutt's Christian tract was right in one respect: Lucas eschews wallowing in mere pleasure for a higher calling—the joy of doing good for others. But he does so in very humanist language. Take this secular sermon Lucas delivered to the Academy of Achievement in Washington, DC, in 2012:

> Here's something I learned along the way. Happiness is pleasure, and happiness is joy. It could be either one. Pleasure is short lived. It lasts

an hour, a minute a month, and it peaks very high. It's like drugs, like anything—whether you're shopping, engaged in any pleasure, it all has the same quality to it. Joy doesn't go as high as pleasure, but it stays with you. It's something you can recall. Pleasure you can't. So the joy will last a lot longer. People who get the pleasure say, "Oh, if I can just get richer, I can get more cars. . . ." You will never relive the moment you got your first car. That's the highest peak. . . .

Pleasure's fun, but just accept the fact that it's here and gone. Joy lasts forever. Pleasure's purely self-centered. It's all about your pleasure. It's about you. A selfish, self-centered emotion created by a selfish moment for you.

Joy is compassion. Joy is giving yourself to something else, or somebody else. It is much more powerful than pleasure. If you get hung up on pleasure, you're doomed. If you pursue joy you'll find everlasting happiness.

This, as most of us know, is a hard rule to follow; there are far too many temptations to pleasure. But he's right: the moments we want to remember are the joyful ones, the things we do with and for others. Take, for example, the time I ran behind Jabba's sail barge in full Jedi robes, holding a lightsaber high for charity, numerous cameras on the barge capturing every second for Nerdist. And all I could think was I needed to do a forward spin of the lightsaber without messing it up, while running. I felt as alone as Ghyslain Raza. Then I realized I wasn't alone, because I was running with the hardcore of the Golden Gate Knights, who'd offered to drop everything on a weekday morning and have a jog in the cold San Francisco fog, accompanying me in violation of the rules.

I thought about the joy of doing dumb things for a good cause; I thought about the kid who lost his dignity, and the billion people who had laughed with or at him. I hoped that he too, someday, would experience a moment of joy from having been *Star Wars* Kid. Then, after flailing around with the thing, I suddenly executed a perfect forward spin of the lightsaber, and I thought, *That's for you, Ghyslain.*

6.

BUCK ROGERS IN THE TWENTIETH CENTURY

The fact that George Lucas wrote out, typed up, and then deleted a "there must be a Force" scene from *THX 1138* was just one sign of the turmoil his one true science fiction movie was going through in his mind. He slashed away at anything that sounded like space fantasy: this was to be a dark debut, in a setting at once futuristic and familiar. But translating all that, from the fluid images in his head into static words, would be one of the most painful operations of his life—alongside the writing part of just about every *Star Wars* movie.

"I bleed on the page. It's just awful." That's how the filmmaker has described his writing style, from his first script onwards. The bleeding began in 1968, when Coppola persuaded Warner Brothers to take an option on a feature-length version of Lucas's award-winning *THX* short. The $150 weekly checks would also serve as Lucas's salary on the *Rain People*. That would buy him time to bleed.

Lucas was eager to get his ideas on the screen but desperate to outsource the scripting part. Coppola, however, insisted: a director had to learn how to write. Lucas showed him a draft. "You're right," Coppola said, horrified. "You can't write." They tried writing a draft together. They tried hiring an experienced screenwriter, Oliver Hailey. Neither result adequately translated the images in Lucas's head onto the page. And so Lucas struggled forward on his own, as he would so many times in the course of his career. Lucas's talent, time and again, would boil down to this absolute devotion to his wordless ideas, this obstinate opposition to anything that didn't look like them. *THX* would not get made until the script was as much as 70 percent the way he'd imagined it, according to his own estimate. It was to be the second highest such number he'd achieve in his scriptwriting career, after the 90 percent figure he offered for *The Phantom Menace*.

Lucas scribbled away in motel rooms every morning and evening during the *Rain People* shoot. Mona Skager, Coppola's script supervisor, was the designated typist for Lucas's early drafts. One evening, she said, he was watching television and began to babble about "holograms, space ships, and the wave of the future." Was this *THX* trying to work itself out, or something else?

One gets the sense of a coin spinning in Lucas's head. On one side was science fiction dystopia: a heavy, meaningful film about who we are and what we've done to our world. On the other side: that seemingly lost space fantasy utopia of rocket ships and swashbucklers. "I really loved adventures in outer space," Lucas would say years later, in response to Skager's recollection. "I wanted to do something in that genre, which is where *THX* partially came from. [But] *THX* really is Buck Rogers in the 20th century, rather than Buck Rogers in the future."

Lucas was quite literal about that Buck Rogers connection. He would open the movie with a trailer for *Buck Rogers*, the 1939 serial. The announcer's intonation of "Buck Rogers in the twenty-fifth century" was familiar to its audience, having been made famous by the earlier radio serial. (Director Chuck Jones had parodied it in a 1953 Daffy Duck cartoon, a favorite of Lucas's and Spielberg's, which screened before all 70mm prints of *Star Wars* in 1977: "Duck Dodgers in the twenty-fourth-and-a-half century!")

But in the opening seconds of *THX*, a redubbed announcer can clearly be heard saying, "Buck Rogers in the twentieth century!" Most viewers paid no heed to the date. They simply assumed the trailer was ironic juxtaposition with the dystopian nightmare that followed. Not for the last time, the meaning of a Lucas movie would be buried in plain sight.

Lucas finally finished the *THX* script with the help of Walter Murch. He didn't hire Murch just to honor their pact that the winner of the Warner scholarship would help out the loser; Murch was on his weirdness wavelength, he said. They brainstormed scenes and shuffled them like cards. The result was resolutely anti-story, full of disjointed moments and snatches of dialogue. It refused to explain anything to the audience. "The problem that George and I found with science-fiction films was that they felt they had to explain these strange rituals," Murch said. "A Japanese film would just have the ritual and you'd have to figure it out for yourself."

Here's what we figure out: THX 1138 is a citizen in a nameless underground society that has been drugged into sexless happiness by the state. This version of dystopia is far more *Brave New World* than *1984*. No one says the population is unhappy, Lucas later pointed out; it's just that they're in a cage. Robot-faced policemen are everywhere—the masked space soldier slowly taking form—as are confessional booths with the face of Jesus from a Hans Memling painting; this is the state deity, OMM. THX spends his evenings in front of the holograms, drugged out, masturbating to erotic dancers, enjoying police beatings. His female roommate, LUH, cuts down her own and THX's drug supply, which awakens them. They start a tender sexual relationship.

A coworker, SEN, wants THX as his roommate and fixes things so LUH is transferred. THX and SEN turn each other in for crimes against the state. Tried and tortured, they find themselves with other outcasts in a prison of pure whiteness. SEN tries to organize the group with rhetoric: "One idea could get us out of here!" THX simply walks out. SEN tags along. The pair meet a man claiming to be a hologram and emerge from the white limbo into rush-hour human traffic. SEN can't go on. While waiting to be taken away, he talks poignantly to children, marveling at how small their drug-based learning tubes are these days. THX and the hologram learn that LUH is dead, her name now repurposed for an embryo in a jar.

Cars, of course, provide the escape route. THX is pursued by police robots on bikes. Both crash. THX makes it out into the city's shell, fends off attacks by strange dwarf creatures, and then starts climbing up a long hatch toward the light. A robot policeman pursues him but is shut down when the chase exceeds its strict budget. In the final shot, THX emerges into we-know-not-what world, a silhouette against a sunset.

As depressing as it is to watch, THX now seems prescient, a glum presaging of America's medicated, couch-potato consumerism. Nobody says *we're* not happy, either—just that we're spending much of our lives indoors, with a variety of interactive screens rather than holograms. The social commentary was pretty heavy-handed, as you might expect from a small-town twenty-four-year-old living in LA in 1968. Here was a man angry at our drug cultures (prescription and otherwise), at a world that had gone plastic and sterile, at authority figures obsessed with restricting sex, money, and power.* Call it *Brave New World* meets *The Graduate*.

---

* Some of SEN's rhetoric—"We need dissent, but creative dissent!"—was lifted verbatim from Richard Nixon's 1968 campaign speeches.

A month after Nixon's inauguration in January 1969, as Lucas and Murch were still tweaking the script for *THX*, Marcia Griffin and George Lucas got married at a Methodist church just south of Monterey (he'd proposed just prior to the *Rain People* trip). The Lucas family drove down from Modesto to attend. Coppola came, as did Lucas's closest friends from USC: Walter Murch, Matthew Robbins, Hal Barwood. For their honeymoon, the bride and groom drove down the California coast to Big Sur before doubling back to San Francisco and across the Golden Gate. Lucas wanted his wife to see the charms of Marin County. He had good reason: Marin was where Lucas had recently glimpsed his future. Toward the end of production for *The Rain People* in June 1968, Coppola had wriggled out of a commitment to speak on a panel in San Francisco about film and the written word, sending Lucas in his place. There Lucas had fallen under the spell of another filmmaker on the panel, John Korty. Over the previous four years, Korty had made three prize-winning independent films out of a $100-a-month barn in Stinson Beach. His total outlay was $250,000, and he was making a profit.

Once they saw the barn, Lucas and Coppola were converts. They wouldn't continue to be cogs in the studio system; they would go independent. Coppola was further convinced when he visited a commune of filmmakers on a trip to Europe. He nearly bankrupted himself buying and shipping state-of-the-art editing equipment back to the United States. The instructions were in German. To fix it, an engineer would have to fly in from Hamburg. Still, now they had everything they needed.

It is hard not to be enamored with Marin, even in February when the Lucases arrived. The San Francisco vistas from the Marin headlands, the world-class hikes, the benign gaze of Mount Tamalpais over the whole place—this was so attractive that a developer backed by Gulf Oil was planning to build an entire city in the headlands, called Marincello. "It is probably the most beautiful location in the United States for a new community," said the developer. The locals hated the idea. By the time the Lucases arrived, Marincello was mired in lawsuits and red tape. It would never be built.

In stark contrast to LA, Marin was perfect for a small-town kid. It was all about bucolic small towns, such as Sausalito, where the hippies lived on houseboats (Murch and his wife would move into one). There was Mill Valley, enshrined in a song by Rita Abrams (Coppola would direct the idyllic music video). In San Rafael, Frank Lloyd Wright's Marin Civic Center had just been completed. (The futuristic building with its soaring spire would feature in *THX* and later in the 1990s science fiction film *Gattaca*; it also houses Lucas's divorce papers.)

South of Mill Valley was a tiny neighborhood called Tamalpais–Homestead Valley, full of windy roads, overgrown hedges, and picket fences. Here the Lucases rented a one-bedroom Victorian with a large attic for $120 a month. They moved in that spring. An Alaskan malamute called Indiana, which Marcia would strap into the passenger seat, completed the domestic scene. Marcia wanted kids, but Lucas demurred: they weren't financially secure yet.

One birth, at least, took place in the Lucas's new home in the hills. While editing his *Rain People* documentary, *Filmmaker*, on a Moviola in the attic, Lucas declared their home the headquarters of a fictitious company, Transamerica Sprocket Works. But on screen, for copyright purposes, he used a more prosaic name: Lucasfilm. This, too, was still technically fictitious. Lucas would not file corporate papers until 1971.

The next month, Coppola and his crew arrived to start scouting locations for their film company, which was slouching toward San Francisco to be born. Lucas led them around Marin like an eager tour guide. Coppola made offers on two separate Marin mansions but couldn't scrape together the down payment fast enough. Time was tight; the editing equipment was about to arrive. Korty, of all people, the Stinson Beach idealist, found a former recording studio in SOMA, the most urban, warehouse-filled neighborhood of San Francisco. Lucas argued against it—the whole idea was to have a retreat *outside* of a big city—but Coppola was holding all the cards. Sorry, George, and by the way, the company name is going to be American Zoetrope, not Transamerica Sprocket Works.

American Zoetrope was the epitome of 1969 cool. The offices of *Rolling Stone* were just around the corner. Jerry Garcia was a frequent visitor. Woody Allen dropped by, as did the mythical Akira Kurosawa himself. Even Stanley Kubrick, the reclusive director fresh from *2001*, called from self-imposed exile in the United Kingdom, wanting to learn more about these crazy kids and their high-tech editing machine. The market was obviously on their side; *Easy Rider*, a film by a motley gang of Lucas and Coppola's contemporaries, was on its way to making $55 million at the box office, on a budget of $400,000. Every studio suddenly wanted a piece of the young filmmaker revolution. Zoetrope was it. Nobody thought they were just stupid kids playing around anymore. Coppola was getting $2,500 a week in seed money from Warner Brothers to set up the new company, part of a proposed $3.5 million deal. Warner would distribute Zoetrope's first movie, with an option on several more, sight unseen. Zoetrope would be able to produce the movie without Warner interference, at least until it was done. It was a great deal for the time, made in one brief shining moment when the big studios felt lost and desperate for young moviemakers to show them the way. But the problem with the contract was baked in from the start. The money was actually a loan; Coppola would have to pay it back if Warner didn't like his output. Still, it included a budget for *THX*, the company's first picture. Coppola's lucky number was 7, so he whimsically decided to fix the budget at $777,777.77—a lowball figure for a feature, even then.

That summer, as men walked on the moon, Lucas assembled his cast. Robert Duvall from *Rain People* would play THX; San Francisco actress Maggie McOmie would play LUH. Not for the last time, Lucas used a renowned older British actor—in this case, Donald Pleasance as SEN. Lucas's crew scoured the Tenderloin for addicts in treatment programs, forced to shave their heads as a sign of commitment. They'd be useful as extras.

Shooting began on September 22, 1969, and wrapped two months later. Lucas and the crew ran through a hectic schedule of shoots in and around the city. He would have loved to film in Japan, to give THX even more of the sense of alienness (for American audiences) he and Murch craved. But the budget wouldn't even stretch to a scouting trip. Instead, it was a guerilla movie, much of it shot without permission in the still-empty tunnels of San Francisco's Bay Area Rapid Transit. The pace was intense, the work stressful. Lucas talked about his "needle going into the red" on day 1 and staying there. He noticed his crew loading film the wrong way into a camera and had an epiphany: professional crews can be just as clueless as student filmmakers. He built his own special effects with model cars and $10 fireworks. As for the actors, he let them perform the way they wanted, as if he were shooting a documentary. On one night in a closed set, Duvall and McOmie went for it in a sex scene that was risqué even in 1971.*

Lucas wanted his underground world to look a little scuffed and dirty and lived-in. The actors wore no makeup. The whiteness of their uniforms tended to obscure this, but Lucas hoped to achieve the look in later films. He was already thinking about a sequel to *THX*—after all, he'd spent all this time creating this world, it seemed a shame to limit it to one picture. There was one vague scene he had in mind for the sequel: his hero would be trapped in some kind of giant garbage masher.

As overwhelming as it all was, and as many difficulties as he had with the crew, Lucas was breaking new ground, and the experience invigorated him. "It

---

* So much so that it earned a review in *Playboy*.

was the only movie I really enjoyed doing," he said a decade later. The photo on his *THX* set pass showed something very unusual in the history of Lucas portraiture: a big, cheesy grin on his face.

American Zoetrope was officially incorporated in November 1969. Lucas was named vice president, but the position was unpaid. To make ends meet, he and Marcia took a variety of freelance assignments. Inspiration and occasional gigs came from Haskell Wexler, who had recently arrived at Zoetrope, fresh from the August release of his movie *Medium Cool*, a drama-documentary filmed at the 1968 Democratic National Convention in Chicago. Lucas and John Milius planned to do something similar, documentary-style, in Vietnam. Milius, mocking a hippie button that said "NIRVANA NOW," suggested calling it *Apocalypse Now*; he wanted to base it on Joseph Conrad's *Heart of Darkness*, having been incensed by a teacher's claim back at USC that the book was unfilmable. It would go through ten drafts. Lucas was to direct it, even though, as Milius later put it, George didn't know Conrad from *Mary Poppins*; he just wanted to do a documentary-style Vietnam picture. Before long, Coppola optioned it to Warner without asking either Lucas or Milius. He'd found another parade to jump in front of.

Wexler's next assignment was to shoot a documentary about a free concert at a racetrack over in the East Bay. Organized by the Grateful Dead, it was to feature Jefferson Airplane, Crosby, Stills, Nash & Young, and the Rolling Stones. Wexler had been trying to film the Stones for years. Would Lucas like to help capture crowd footage? Rock and roll on a racetrack with a camera, and he'd get paid? It must have sounded like a dream come true.

The racetrack was Altamont. The concert was badly planned and horrifically overcrowded. Hells Angels were running security. During the Stones' set, a Berkeley student named Meredith Hunter started waving a gun on stage. The Angels tackled and stabbed him. The drug-fueled crowd freaked out. To this day, Lucas says he can't remember what he shot. But Albert Maysles, director of the *Gimme Shelter* documentary that used the footage a year later, says Lucas was responsible for the moody moments of concertgoers in silhouette, panicked, trying to find their way out. Said Maysles, with an odd kind of pride: "It's like a sci-fi scene."

Lucas spent much of 1970 in his attic in Marin, retreating into his own cautionary tale of sex, drugs, and escape. "It's a kind of therapy" was how he described editing. Just as well—he despised the regular kind. He had even been irked when Coppola tried to get him to sit down with the crew and discuss difficulties during the *THX* shoot.

Coppola came to visit and introduced Lucas to Gary Kurtz, an older USC grad just returned from three years as a filmmaker with the Marines in Vietnam, whom Coppola had worked with in his Roger Corman days. Kurtz, a quiet Quaker with an Amish-style beard, was now associate producer on a road movie called *Two-Lane Blacktop*. Lucas had shot with an unusual film stock, Techniscope, on *THX*; for a lot of technical reasons, Techniscope makes it easy to make a reel of film last twenty minutes rather than the usual ten. "For low budget pictures, that was perfect," Kurtz says. "Especially pictures with car stuff." Coppola had an ulterior motive for getting the two together; Kurtz was the only filmmaker he knew who'd seen action in Vietnam, which would make him a perfect producer for *Apocalypse Now*.* Given the subject was film and cars and the war, Kurtz and Lucas bonded instantly. Lucas offered to make Kurtz producer on his next picture, whatever that might be—but with the strong presumption it was going to be *Apocalypse*.

For the moment, Lucas had all the backup he needed. Marcia helped edit *THX*, although she found it emotionally cold even after she was done with it. At night, Walter Murch cut an audacious avant-garde soundscape: less music than distorted noises, feedback, free-floating electronica. For the prison scenes, while Duvall was tortured on screen, Murch got improv actors to record ad-libbed lines as if they were bored and casually sadistic air traffic controllers. One of the voices belonged to Terry McGovern, a local DJ and actor who, during his session, would unwittingly create the name for one of the *Star Wars* universe's most famous creatures. McGovern was in the army reserves at the time and was running late from his once-a-month training weekend. So he drove to the studio with his best friend and fellow reservist, Private Bill Wookey.

McGovern and Wookey looked pretty ridiculous that day. It was 1970, and like everyone else in their twenties, the two pals had long hair, but for the sake of the army they squeezed it into short-hair wigs. "We had these huge heads," Wookey remembers. "We must have looked like aliens." Wookey was a pretty hairy guy in general (he still is, and started growing a long beard to match his hair the moment he got out of the reserves in 1972). He had fuzzy, red-brown locks and stood six foot three inches tall. Believe it or not, that's all sheer coincidence. Wookey has never met George Lucas. All that happened was that during

---

* Kurtz too had an ulterior motive: he wanted to borrow Coppola's fancy French Éclair cameras.

his ad-libbing, McGovern threw out a line for the benefit of his friend: "I think I just ran over a Wookey back there." Memories are fuzzy at this four-decade distance, and nobody knows if Wookey was actually in the studio at the time. There's a good chance the pair were high: "We smoked an awful lot of dope at the time," remembers Wookey. McGovern says he "probably just dropped his name to be silly."

The wonderfully silly line didn't even make it into *THX 1138*. But Murch was amused by it, as was Lucas when he heard it. The filmmaker filed the name away in his notebook, where it gained an extra couple of vowels and became "wookiee." McGovern kept on working as occasional voice talent for Lucas. One day in early 1977, he would be paid all of $200 to record another bunch of lines that didn't make a lot of sense at the time: "These aren't the droids we're looking for," he was told to say in a slightly dazed voice. "You can go about your business." It was only when he saw *Star Wars* several months later that he was blown away by the result: "I was paralyzed with joy," says McGovern. "I'm in a scene with fucking Alec Guinness!"

Similarly, Bill Wookey was blissfully unaware of what had happened until he saw *Star Wars* with everyone else in 1977. By that time he had a steady job as a clothing salesman in San Rafael and took his two young boys to see the movie their Uncle Terry had been working on. Then he heard the family name on the screen for the first time: "Droids don't rip people's arms out of their sockets when they lose; wookiees have been known to do that," says Harrison Ford of his large hairy friend, who suddenly looked strangely familiar. "I definitely thought right away it was cool," Wookey said. "It wasn't until the next few weeks and months that I started getting a little uncomfortable with people making references and assuming I was the role model for Chewbacca." But the embarrassment soon turned into pride—especially for his sons, who began a *Star Wars* action figure collection that now fills the family basement. "When my boys went off to school, they just thought it was the coolest thing in the world," the hirsute clothing salesman, now age seventy, remembers. "They were Wookiees."

By the time THX was ready, Lucas feared his first feature film would also be his last. He knew the movie was off the wall. In November, Coppola came by to collect the final product. After Murch screened a reel for him, Coppola shrugged: "It's either masturbation or a masterpiece." But if George was happy, Francis was happy. He packaged it up for the journey to Warner, together with boxes of Zoetrope screenplays ready for production, including *The Conversation* and *Apocalypse Now*. The quirky little *THX* was supposed to be the appetizer. Even if they didn't like it, the suits at Warner wouldn't refuse the main course. Would they?

As it turned out, they would and did. The day Coppola took *THX* south—November 19, 1970—was so disastrous that Zoetrope employees took to calling it Black Thursday. The suits detested *THX 1138* so much they didn't even glance at the other screenplays. They owned this film whether they liked it or not, but they didn't intend to support another. On the spot, they cancelled the whole deal and called in Coppola's loan. Suddenly he owed Warner $400,000.

Lucas's baby was a hostage to Hollywood. This was the metaphor he offered repeatedly about this formative moment: you raise a child for two or three years, and then someone comes along and cuts one of her fingers off. It's okay, they say, she's fine—she'll live. "But I mean, it hurts."

Warner forced Lucas to cut four minutes from *THX 1138*. Lucas ignored the studio's entreaties to edit more. The studio pushed the movie out in March with little fanfare. Big theaters didn't book it. It got good but tiny notices in *Time* and *Newsweek*. "Some talent, but too much 'art,'" sniffed the *New Yorker*, calling the white-suited dystopia "gloomy and blinding."

The film had left Lucas in a bad way financially, and Zoetrope in an even worse spot. The studio started to turn a small profit by renting its editing machines to makers of commercials, but it wasn't enough to dig Coppola out of debt. Then he got a call from Paramount, offering $150,000; he was their third-choice director on the adaptation of a Mario Puzo potboiler from 1969 called *The Godfather*. Coppola refused the first couple of times Paramount asked. That was *old* Hollywood stuff. But Lucas talked Coppola into it: "We need the money," he said. "What have you got to lose?"

Off Coppola went for his date with destiny. He threw Lucas a bone by letting him shoot close-ups of the newspaper where Michael Corleone learns his father has been shot. Lucas returned the favor by editing another key *Godfather* scene, in the hospital, to add more tension.

Lucas badly needed a new project. Columbia Pictures was going to bankroll *Apocalypse Now* but got cold feet at the last minute. He and Marcia were down to $2,000 in savings. At one point Lucas and Kurtz discussed adapting a Kurosawa movie, just as *The Magnificent Seven* had recently remade *Seven Samurai*. *Hidden Fortress*, perhaps. Why that particular Kurosawa flick, the favorite of neither filmmaker? "Because it's a fairly straightforward action adventure through hostile territory," says Kurtz. "It's a handful of characters and it's elegantly told"—perfect for a low-budget picture. Not that Lucas and Kurtz didn't dream about bigger-budget fare. One night the new friends were at a diner and looked in the paper to see what was playing at the local theaters. There was nothing they wanted to see. They enthused about how great it would be to see *Flash Gordon* on the big screen, in color.

Nobody can remember at a forty-year remove what was said in that conversation or who started it (Lucas and Kurtz were both *Flash Gordon* fans). Kurtz says they were talking in more general terms about how science fiction pictures hadn't really been enjoyable since *Forbidden Planet* in 1955. "They all seemed to go downhill towards either genre horror, *Creature from the Black Lagoon*–type movies, or alien invasions, or just dystopian stories about postapocalyptic societies," Kurtz says. "And none of that was fun. It was just the idea of capturing the energy of *Flash Gordon, Buck Rogers*–style space opera, really, which hadn't been done for so long."

Whatever was said in the diner seems to have lit a fire under Lucas. On a visit to New York in early 1971, "on a whim," he says, Lucas went to visit King Features to inquire about the film rights to *Flash Gordon*. The King executives agreed to meet with him because they were thinking about the film rights too; they mentioned Frederico Fellini as a possible director. The Italian maestro was also known to be a *Flash Gordon* fan.* There was no way Lucas could compete with Fellini at this point in his career.

This seems to have been Lucas's lightbulb moment. The vague space movie idea he'd been running through the projector in his head for years—there was no reason that couldn't be *better* than *Flash Gordon*. After his meeting at King Features, he and Coppola dined at the Palm Restaurant in Manhattan, and Coppola could sense his friend's disappointment—but also his new outlook. "He was very depressed," Coppola would recall in 1999, over lunch with Lucas and producer Saul Zaentz. "And he says, 'Well, I'll just invent my own.'"

Coppola paused to consider. "What a limitation, if they had sold him *Flash Gordon*."

"I'm glad they didn't,"† concluded Lucas. Years later, he reflected on why that was. "*Flash Gordon* is like anything you do that is established. You start out

---

* Indeed, Fellini was said to have drawn a *Flash Gordon* substitute for an Italian paper during World War II, when Mussolini banned *Flash*. No comic strips have ever been brought forward to substantiate this rumor. Comic book and *Flash Gordon* expert Edward Summer is skeptical.

† Not least because at that very moment in 1971, unbeknownst to Lucas or King Features, a production company in LA was shooting a campy pornographic parody called *Flesh Gordon*, which would eventually see release in 1974. The company's name, in another odd coincidence: Graffiti Productions.

being faithful to the original material, but eventually it gets in the way of the creativity. . . . I would have had to have had Ming the Merciless in it, and I didn't want to have Ming. I wanted to take ancient mythological motifs and update them—I wanted to have something totally free and fun, the way I remembered space fantasy."

In the meantime, though, Lucas needed a more bankable movie. If Fellini was to take *Flash Gordon*, maybe Lucas could take something from Fellini—for instance, the idea behind the movie *I Vitelloni*, about four teenagers in a provincial town who talk about leaving for Rome but never do. What if you followed a bunch of guys, on the cusp of leaving a small town, and follow them through one night of cruising—a ritual that had died out in the last decade?

Lucas would set his version in the summer of 1962, the moment everything changed for him, and end it with a car crash. He came up with a semi-Italian title: *American Graffiti*. It sounded odd to contemporary ears. The Italian word had not yet gained common currency. New York subway trains were about a year away from being covered in spray-painted signatures. Lucas hadn't intended that debased usage of the word in any case; he meant the word invented at Pompeii in 1851 that means nostalgic etchings. He wanted to record the legacy of a lost decade: an American Pompeii, frozen in time forever.

The title aside, *Graffiti* was intended as a very mainstream, commercial project. Lucas was determined to combat the perception that he was an emotionless science fiction nerd. It had become the butt of jokes around Zoetrope. "Everyone thinks you're a real cold fish," Coppola told him. "Why don't you do something warm?" Muttered Lucas as he wrote: "I'll give you warm." He worked up a fifteen-page treatment with another pair of USC friends, Willard Hyuck and his wife, Gloria Katz. Lucas put the word "MUSICAL" in capital letters on the title page; it was a confusing way of emphasizing the rock and roll soundtrack he imagined for the film.

Meanwhile, the world was starting to call him. That spring, Lucas appeared in both *Newsweek* and a PBS documentary in which he railed against the Hollywood system while walking below the Hollywood sign. Lucas's first major newspaper profile, published in the *San Francisco Chronicle* around the same time, nailed him in its very first line: "Those who know George Lucas say that he has the temperament of an artist who works alone in his attic, plus a keen business sense aimed at the preservation of his work." Those two essential facets of his personality were now locked in place and would not change for the rest of his career.

Then, in May 1971, Lucas learned *THX* had been officially selected for the Cannes Film Festival. Lucas was the beneficiary of circumstance: a revolt by young European filmmakers, demanding that more films by under-thirties be screened at the festival. George and Marcia cashed in their savings—no one was paying for him to attend the event—and took off for Europe. They stopped off in New York for a week, staying with Coppola (who was at his lowest ebb while shooting *The Godfather*) and his long-suffering wife, Eleanor, who was nine months pregnant. The Lucases slept in the Coppolas' living room and just so happened to leave for JFK the same early morning Sofia Coppola was born.

Even before he arrived at Cannes, Lucas could see his luck changing. While in New York he met David Picker, president of United Artists, to pitch *American Graffiti*. Arriving in London on his twenty-seventh birthday, Lucas called Picker from a pay phone around the corner from a dingy flat costing less than $5 a night. Picker made a $25,000 deal for *Graffiti* on the spot.

Elated, the Lucases took a ferry to France and the train to Cannes on their Eurail passes. They had to sneak into one of the two *THX* screenings, which were sold out. They didn't show up at a hastily arranged press conference; nobody even knew they were there. It didn't matter; only one meeting at Cannes, with Picker, was to have any consequence. They met at Picker's suite in the Carlton—Lucas's "first big-time movie experience," a nice change from the offices of underlings. Picker confirmed the *Graffiti* deal and asked Lucas if he had anything else for UA.

Lucas sensed his opening, and he took it. "I've been toying with this idea of a space-opera fantasy film in the vein of *Flash Gordon*," he said. Picker agreed to take an option on that too.

It was the first time Lucas had pitched his dream movie, and he was shocked to find it pivot so fast from fantasy to reality. "That was really the birth of *Star Wars*," Lucas remembered later. "It was only a notion up to then; at that point it became an obligation."

Picker, sadly, can't remember anything about the encounter now. For him, it was one of many deal-or-no-deal meetings he had in that hotel. "You can imagine how many meetings I had on that terrace," Picker says. "More deals were made, more hearts were broken than any level of the business anywhere." What he does remember is that Lucas has never let him live down his eventual divestment from the project. The filmmaker has needled Picker thusly on every subsequent meeting: "Hey, David, you could have had *Star Wars*."

On August 3, 1971, United Artists officially registered the name "The Star Wars" as a trademark with the Motion Picture Association of America. The definite article, as strange as it sounds to our ears, would remain oddly attached to those two more famous words for the next five years.

The origin of this historic name—whether it harkened back to the space soldiers or was inspired by a more recent phenomenon, *Star Trek*—is frustratingly unclear. All we know for sure is that Lucas had the name long before he had the slightest inkling of a story. "The discussion about [the title] was that it was *Flash Gordon*–like, space-opera-type adventure about wars in outer space," says Kurtz, "and then that kind of gestated into *The Star Wars*." Patrick Read Johnson, a filmmaker who became the first kid in the world to see the movie when he covered it as a fifteen-year-old cub reporter for *American Cinematographer* in 1977—Gary Kurtz calls him "fan 1"—is convinced that there's no way you could write about that title and not think about the elder science fiction franchise. "The name, before it came out, always got a laugh from my friends," Johnson told me. "It sounded goofy. Like someone had tried to make *Star Trek* but just added the word 'Wars' at the last minute."* Kurtz says that was a "fairly common reaction" at the time.

Lucas was certainly a fan of *Star Trek*. He took afternoon breaks, during the long years of writing *Star Wars*, to watch *Trek* reruns. "I liked the idea that you could gallivant around the galaxy," he told *Star Trek* creator Gene Roddenberry's son in 2004. He was attracted to the show because it "got rid of the mundane boring action of real space, and said let's just get out and go where no one else dared to go." (Roddenberry Jr. was, ironically, a far greater fan of *Star Wars* than *Star Trek* as a child.)

The original *Star Trek* series debuted on television in 1966. It was canceled in 1969 after a seventy-nine-episode run, short of the hundred episodes normally needed for syndication—but, by 1972, Paramount had syndicated it to 125 local TV stations around the United States. Network executives called it "the show that won't die." In January 1972, some three thousand eager fans crowded the first annual *Trek* convention in New York, snapping up Vulcan dictionaries, books of Vulcan songs, and more than one hundred fanzines. By 1975, fans were holding two conventions a year in the city, attracting fourteen thousand visitors between them; by 1976, there were four *Star Trek* cons a year around the country, with the cast gratefully plucked from obscurity into superstardom.

---

* In the early 2000s, Johnson would turn his experience of seeing *Star Wars* before anyone else into an independent movie called 5–25–77 (*Star Wars*'s release date) for which Gary Kurtz acted as producer. It has still not been released.

Legendary science fiction writer Isaac Asimov reported from these cons as one might report on Beatlemania, describing "teenage girls screaming for Spock."

Lucas went to some of these early *Trek* conventions, at a crucial time when he was struggling to turn *Star Wars* into reality. "He did talk about *Star Trek* quite a bit," remembers Gary Kurtz. The show was "inspiring in a way. It freed up the mind to think about what it would be like to travel to distant galaxies and encounter other species."

Before fans of either franchise get too apoplectic, let me clarify: it would of course be an exaggeration to say that *Star Wars* is just *Star Trek* with a facelift. The concepts behind the two franchises are pretty much diametrically opposed. *Star Trek*, as we know from its opening sequence, is about a starship on a five-year mission of exploration. Many of the plots are fantastical, but it is science fiction, not space fantasy. It is our own galaxy, in our own future, using the tools of science to further the progress of a rational Federation. "*Star Trek* was more intellectual," Lucas said. "It wasn't action-oriented."

Still, there's more than a passing resemblance between Flash Gordon and Captain Kirk—and between Lucas and Roddenberry. Both creators used speculative fiction to make political points. "If I went to a strange planet I could talk about war and race and all the things you couldn't talk about on television," Roddenberry told the AP in 1972. "Kids today are growing up at a time when people are saying there is no tomorrow, that it may all be over in 20 years. *Star Trek* said there is a tomorrow and that it can be just as challenging and exciting as the past. It said that we shouldn't interfere in the lives of other people. Maybe the kids saw something about Vietnam in that."

In 1971 Vietnam was hard to avoid, even for a young couple like the Lucases, bumming around Europe on a Eurail pass post-Cannes, mostly visiting Grand Prix racetracks. That summer's biggest album, Joni Mitchell's *Blue*, has a song called *California*—about bumming around Europe, longing for the US West Coast, but being horrified by the news from home: "more about the war and the bloody changes." Later, Lucas would wax lyrical about how the war might have been avoided: the vast numbers of decent Americans who could have spoken out against it but chose not to. "To not make a decision is to make a decision" is how he was putting it by 1976. "By not accepting the responsibility, people eventually have to confront the issue in a more painful way." He was extremely sensitive to the fact that the war had knocked the country off balance. Lucas referred to that balance as "the poetic state."

Lucas was determined now to make movies about the war in three modes: past, present, and future; absence, reality, and allegory. *American Graffiti* would take people back to a time before Vietnam ripped America apart. *Apocalypse Now*, which Lucas hoped to direct before or after *The Star Wars*, would show it in the present tense. If *THX* was the movie he expected to get him banned from Hollywood for life, *Apocalypse Now* was the movie he felt would lead to the government running him out of the country.

The third mode that Lucas intended to use to depict Vietnam—the allegorical, futuristic lens—was only just taking shape, but already it was being influenced by Lucas's thinking about the present tense.* Lucas was fascinated by the notion of how a tiny nation could overcome the largest military power on Earth, and this was baked into *The Star Wars* right from its earliest notes in 1973: "A large technological empire going after a small group of freedom fighters."

B ack in California following his Cannes trip, Lucas officially incorporated his own brand of freedom fighters: Lucasfilm Ltd., the name he'd copyrighted back in 1969. It was just a shell corporation for the moment, and friends were confused by the British-style name; why "Ltd." and not "Inc."? The alliteration just sounded better, says Kurtz—and it looked better too, because the pair were sketching out logos on paper and had the notion that they'd make a big, brassy, Cinemascope-style graphic in which the letters went from large to small to large again. They never got around to it.

Whatever it was called, Lucasfilm was barely a zygote at this stage, let alone an embryo. Lucas and Kurtz hired their first two secretaries, named Lucy Wilson (who also did accounts) and Bunny Alsup respectively, and that was it for employees. Lucasfilm's first legal headache concerned the *Graffiti* draft Lucas had assigned to a USC classmate of his, Richard Walter, who had grown up in New York and didn't understand car culture. Kurtz had already paid Walter most of what Lucas had received up front; Walter fought for weeks to get paid for his desultory second draft. Lucas resigned himself to writing the third draft from scratch—time to bleed on the page again.

There was a way out. Lucas's agent, Jeff Berg, had been trying to sell him as a contract director for months, and now there was an offer: a crime picture called *Lady Ice*. It would pay $100,000. He could take the money, pay off all the money he'd borrowed over the years from his dad, make a name for himself, and achieve financial security. But he would have to postpone the dream of those three movies. The dreams were just too big. He decided to plow on in penury.

---

* Though *Star Wars* was ultimately set "a long time ago," Lucas's earliest plan was to set it in the thirty-third century.

In December 1971, the UA development deal was sealed into a memo. It described *The Star Wars* only as "a second picture" after *Graffiti*, despite the fact that the company had just registered "The Star Wars" as a trademark. Lucas's space fantasy project, it seems, was still at such a protean stage that even the placeholder name wasn't certain.

Lucasfilm's first movie deal was incredibly short-lived. Shortly after the UA deal memo was issued, Lucas sent Picker his third draft of *Graffiti*. He asked for more money for a fourth draft, and promised he would cowrite with Hyuck and Katz. Picker says he loved it, but his boss at UA didn't get it. The *Graffiti* deal was dead, but Picker still had the option to produce *The Star Wars* whenever Lucas got around to writing a treatment.

There followed four months of rewriting and shopping *Graffiti*. Finally, Ned Tanen, head of the "youth division" set up to fund low-budget independent pictures in the wake of *Easy Rider*, agreed to take it on. He was a former cruiser himself; he got that part of it. He didn't get the title. Gary Kurtz still has a letter from Tanen complaining that *American Graffiti* made him think of "an Italian movie about feet." Universal had a half-dozen suggested titles. Lucas was writing about his hometown; why not call it "Another Quiet Night in Modesto"? Lucas and Kurtz thought that ridiculous. "The way we solved that was by saying, 'You come up with a better title, because we don't love this one but it's better than anything we've heard,'" remembers Kurtz. It was good practice, as it turns out; a year later, he would use the exact same line with another set of studio bosses over the title *Star Wars*.

Tanen conceded the title fight but had one other stipulation: the film had to have a star actor or a star producer. What about that guy who just directed that amazing movie, *The Godfather*? Coppola readily agreed.

Lucas's space fantasy project was shopped a second time. When Universal agreed to take on *Graffiti*, Lucas sold his other ideas as part of the deal: the contract gave Universal options on *Apocalypse Now* and *The Star Wars*, although it would only have a chance to pick up the latter project if UA declined its option.

The Star Wars was now named in a legal contract, not just a trademark document. Lucas was to get $50,000 for cowriting and directing *Graffiti*—a pay cut compared to *THX*. The budget was $650,000, also lower than that of *THX*. For enduring that ignominy, however, Lucas would get 40 percent of any profits.

The *American Graffiti* shoot, in July 1972, was a frenzied month of vampire hours, dusk till dawn. That one night the movie is set in would, for the cast and crew, happen sixty times: a nocturnal *Groundhog Day*. Lucas was not a night person. Nor was he keen on dragging his crew back to Modesto; instead he chose San Rafael and then, when it became clear the city was too noisy to stand in for the quiet town of his youth, the small farming town of Petaluma further up in Marin. At first Lucas tried to be the cameraman as well—he really thought he could do it all. But the results looked terrible. So Haskell Wexler flew up from LA to help out, gratis.

The story was simple: Two friends, Curt and Steve, are class stars trying to decide if they are going off to college in the morning. Their other two pals are polar opposites: a hot-rodder, Milner, who gets lumped with someone's kid sister for the night and is being pursued by an out-of-town hotshot driver, and a hapless scooter rider, Terry the Toad, who borrows Steve's car for a night and picks up a cute but demanding date. Lucas later suggested three of the friends represented aspects of his Modesto life. Terry was Lucas the dorky comic-reading kid. Milner was Lucas the Bianchina boy racer. Curt was the junior college version, the Lucas who had knuckled down and was moving on to bigger and better things.

Graffiti's story threads were united by Wolfman Jack—an actual contemporary DJ whose location no one knew (just as they didn't back in Modesto—it turned out Wolfman was broadcasting from a powerful tower down in Tijuana). The four stories intercut, an unusual idea at the time, as if viewers were bouncing between cars on radio waves. Wolfman himself appears at the end to help Curt contact a mystery blonde he had glimpsed through a car window. It is the DJ as benign force, the voice that answers prayers: like Lucas's student film *The Emperor*, but from the point of view of the radio audience.

Coppola was wrapped up in *Godfather* publicity at the time, and barely took part in the film he was nominally producing with Kurtz. But thanks to Fred Roos, a friend of Coppola's who also did casting for *The Godfather*, Lucas was gifted what may be the best cast of unknowns any second-time director has ever had. Ron Howard and Richard Dreyfuss stole the show. Then there was the guy playing Bob Falfa, the mystery driver who challenges Milner. He was a former bit player for Columbia who'd gotten out of the business and taught himself carpentry, which paid better. His name was Harrison Ford, and Kurtz had a set-to with him about how much he had been drinking at the crew's Petaluma motel before shooting the crucial drag race scene at dawn. "Don't show up like this again," Kurtz remembers chiding Ford, who stayed sober on the set from then on.

Lucas wasn't about to stop the party, or give his cast much of anything in the way of direction. "The set was very wild, very loose," remembers Terry McGovern, who played a teacher. "George is not an actor's guy." McGovern had his hair cut hours before playing his scene opposite Dreyfuss when someone pointed out that teachers didn't have long hair in 1962. Another member of the cast, Charlie Martin Smith, remembers Lucas getting much more animated in describing his next movie than discussing the one at hand. "It sounded great to me," recalled Smith. "A big science fiction adventure with these short furry creatures called Wookiees. Richard Dreyfuss and I kept begging George to let us play them. . . . Then he turned around and made the Wookiees seven feet tall, which knocked [us] out of the running for that part."

But for the most part, Lucas faded into the background like Wolfman Jack. He hid from the actors in most every scene—jammed under a diner's counter-top, prostrate atop a car—and let the cameras capture what they would. He frequently fell asleep during a take. "I'm really going to direct this in the editing room," he told Ron Howard. And so he did, but not in his attic this time. He talked Coppola into buying a house in Mill Valley and turning its granny flat into an editing studio. Verna Fields was the main editor, but Marcia played a major role after Lucas pleaded: "I made it for you." It was a tough needle to thread. The crosscutting between stories had to work perfectly, never losing the delicate mood of teenage fantasia. Getting the sound right was just as challenging. Lucas and Murch spent hours moving speakers to and fro in the garden of Coppola's Mill Valley house, trying to perfect the sound of a song heard from a passing car. (The film's soundtrack would be drawn from the songs Lucas had listened to in 1962—all except those by Elvis, who wouldn't give up the rights.) They worked through cans marked with reel (R) and dialogue (D) numbers. One night Murch called out: "I need R2, D2." Lucas was amused; he was still a fan of curious letter-number combinations. "R2D2," the friends repeated, laughing. Lucas wrote it down in a notebook he'd started carrying around.

By January 1973, *Graffiti* was ready for its preview. The Universal executives were invited to the screening, which was held in front of a packed house at the Northpoint Theatre in San Francisco's Fisherman's Wharf. Most of the audience loved the film, laughing throughout, but Universal's Ned Tanen hated it. A self-confessed manic depressive, he genuinely didn't see the warmth or the comedy. He wanted cuts. He threatened to release it as a TV movie. Coppola stepped in to defend his friend, offering to buy the movie from Tanen on the spot, at cost, reaching into his pocket for a nonexistent checkbook.

As gallant a gesture as that was, it didn't work. Tanen refused to make a decision about releasing the movie; he seemed determined to keep *Graffiti* in limbo. Lucas was inconsolable. Once again, his child had been kidnapped by

Hollywood. Again he was deep in debt to his parents, to Copolla, to everyone. He went home and refused to return Universal's calls. Kurtz, meanwhile, had gone on scouting trips to the Philippines and South America to find the country most suitable as a stand-in for Vietnam on *Apocalypse Now*, as well as a country that could supply the maximum number of helicopters. While he was waiting, Lucas said, he might as well start "whipping up this treatment for my little space thing."

It was time to bleed on the page like never before.

7.

HOME FREE

When Lucas prepared to sketch out his space fantasy film for the first time, he wasn't alone. Across America, across the world, film makers were dreaming of similar projects. Just as *THX 1138* was barely the first of numerous American dystopian movies in production in the early 1970s, *Star Wars* was one of a crop of ideas for speculative, fable-like space films, many of which were germinating as the decade progressed.

The starting gun had been fired by Stanley Kubrick in 1968 with the $10 million epic *2001: A Space Odyssey*. Audiences didn't get it back then, but filmmakers certainly did. Nascent talents like Martin Scorsese, John Carpenter, and Steven Spielberg were all sniffing around the science fiction realm, searching for a breakout mainstream hit—something that would follow the lead of Douglas Trumball, the twenty-five-year-old special effects technician Kubrick had hired for *2001*, but in the service of a more accessible story.

Lucas's success in this race was by no means assured. One of his closest friends had already conceived of a science fiction film that may well have been the successor to *2001*. It almost snagged Steven Spielberg as a director. The project fizzled, but not before it propelled Lucas's film into hyperspace, providing the young director with the most important introduction of his career.

Once upon a time, a USC film school graduate was kicking around a treatment for a science fiction movie without a name. He was also dabbling in a computer language called BASIC. To help figure out what his movie should be called, he decided to write his computer program in BASIC. He would input hundreds of words he and his friend were using in the script, and the computer would spit them out in random two- and three-word combinations.

When the printout came, most of it was garbage. But as he ran his finger down the list of names, one random combination stood out. The first word was "Star." The second was "Dancing."

Star Dancing. Coming soon to a theater near you. "That's kind of cool," thought Hal Barwood. He took it to his cowriter, Matthew Robbins, and they tried the name out for a few months. Eventually, however, they decided they preferred one of the titles they'd come up with on their own: *Home Free.* That was the name under which their agent sold the treatment to Universal. So much for two-word titles starting with "Star." Humans 1, Computerized Name Generator 0.

Yet Barwood's computer program would eventually be vindicated, because every time this lost film has cropped up in the telling of the *Star Wars* story, it has been rendered as *Star Dancing.* Barwood spoke to me with the express wish that I set the record straight about the movie's name.

Barwood and Robbins were key witnesses to every stage of the Lucas saga, the Rosencrantz and Guildenstern to Lucas's Hamlet. They were friends with him at USC; introduced Lucas to their agent, Jeff Berg; rented rooms from him on the grounds of his million-dollar mansion in the mid-1970s; and were among the first few readers of early *Star Wars* drafts. Barwood later cropped up at Skywalker Ranch in his second career, making games for LucasArts, although he would not retire on the best of terms with his old friend or his company.

Barwood, a New Englander who married his high school sweetheart, had been a science fiction fan from a young age. At USC he made the award-winning short *A Child's Guide to the Cosmos* (1964). When he graduated in 1965, he, like many USC film school alumni, went into industrial films. But he was haunted by an idea for an animated film he wanted to make called *The Great Walled City of Xan.* Barwood managed to wangle his way back into USC as a teaching assistant in 1967, just as Lucas was doing the same thing with the navy class that filmed the first *THX.* In the following years, Barwood cemented his friendships with Lucas, Robbins, and Walter Murch.

After graduation, Lucas would visit Barwood and his family in LA. The two of them geeked out over film, animation, and science fiction. They played a 1970 game called Kriegspiel—a more complex and warlike version of chess, played on hexagons rather than squares. "I beat him pretty regularly," Barwood remembers.

The script latterly known as *Home Free* was written at the instigation of a producer named Larry Tucker, who'd just had a big hit with the 1969 swinger film *Bob & Carol & Ted & Alice*. Tucker didn't exactly know what he wanted next, but he knew he wanted it to be science fiction, and he wanted it to be odd. "He said, 'Maybe there's an alien who jumps up in the air and comes flying down and sticks his nose into the ground like an arrow,'" Barwood recalls. "We thought, 'What the hell is he talking about?'"

What, indeed? Science fiction in its literary form had gone in some wonderfully weird directions in the 1960s; at times it seemed to be leading the way for youth culture. The decade kicked off with *Stranger in a Strange Land* (1961), Robert Heinlein's seminal novel about Valentine Michael Smith, an Earthman raised by Martians. Returned to Earth, Smith finds he is a fish out of water, yet his psychic powers and sexually liberal attitude win many converts to his way of understanding, or "grokking." He founds a church and tells his followers they are about to evolve into a new species, Homo Superior. The free speech movement, the civil rights movement, the hippies: they all grokked it.

Four years later came another breakout science fiction novel, Frank Herbert's *Dune*. If *Stranger in a Strange Land* was a cult, *Dune* was a global religion. It is still believed to be the best-selling science fiction book of all time. Herbert built a universe in the space of a novel: specifically, a Galactic Empire 210 centuries in the future, where computers are outlawed and great aristocratic houses are at war over access to a mystical, addictive spice that grants a user longer life and enhanced awareness.

Dune centers on Arrakis, the desert planet where the spice is found, and it started a fad for desert planets. Hardscrabble warriors called Fremen are forced to harvest moisture from the atmosphere. A young aristocrat named Paul Atreides flees the massacre of his family, enters the desert, undergoes ordeals, takes the spice, and becomes a terrifying kind of messiah—as in Heinlein's novel, the figurehead of a new religion. (There was a lot of that going on in the '60s.) The sequel, *Dune Messiah* (1969), showed a dark side to Atreides just in time for the Charles Manson murders.

It took a while for Hollywood to catch up to the imaginative brand of science fiction in literature like *Stranger* or *Dune*. "Science fiction movies ran roughly 20 to 25 years behind written science fiction," says Lucas's friend and filmmaker Edward Summer. There were sound financial reasons for this. As great a critical impact as *Forbidden Planet* had made in 1956—"If you've an ounce of taste for crazy humor, you'll have a barrel of fun," said the *New York Times*—the film took years to recoup its $5 million budget. The audience, it was thought, just wasn't there. Preteen boys like Lucas and his pals had rushed to see it, but the rest of the family hadn't. What chance did any other science fiction have? "You'd exhaust the audience on the first weekend, and then you were in trouble," remembers Barwood of the conventional wisdom at the time.

The received opinion in science fiction filmmaking was that you would make your money back only if you made a movie cheaply enough. James Bond could give you return on investment. *Doctor Zhivago* and *The Sound of Music* could give you a return on investment. But guys in astronaut suits just couldn't. So the '60s continued the trend of the '50s, with low-budget schlock in the style of Roger Corman. While readers devoured *Dune* in 1965, theaters were still offering *Santa Claus Conquers the Martians* (cost: $200,000). That was a big budget epic by the standards of 1967's *Mars Needs Women* (cost: $20,000). And so long as they were chronically undersupported by studios, there seemed little chance that science fiction or fantasy films would ever overturn the perception that the category was moribund by commercial and artistic standards.

That state of affairs started to shift on April 3, 1968, when by a startling coincidence the two most important science fiction films of the decade were released on the same day. One was *Planet of the Apes*. The other was *2001: A Space Odyssey*. Trying to imagine a world before either film existed is almost as hard as trying to imagine a world before *Star Wars*. Was there really a time our pop culture memory did not contain the line "Take your stinking paws off me, you damned dirty ape?" Were we once able to hear the opening notes of "Also Sprach Zarathustra" without thinking of black monoliths, or "The Blue Danube" without seeing spinning space stations and zero-gravity stewardesses?

2001 was ultimately a more significant movie than *Planet of the Apes*. The obsessive, reclusive Kubrick—an idol of Lucas's on a par with Kurosawa—had devoted three years of effort to this film, as had coscriptwriter Arthur C. Clarke. It was visual science fiction with as much music and as few words as possible. Its timing was exquisite. The special effects, which still hold up today, took audiences to the moon and beyond months before NASA had made its first lunar orbit. Then there was the final act: astronaut Frank Bowman's dialogue-free trip into the monolith on Jupiter, through death and rebirth, a mere year after the acid-soaked Summer of Love.

The movie divided critics and audiences. In the United Kingdom, a young mime artist named Anthony Daniels, seeing his first science fiction movie, would walk out before the end. But the visual style of *2001* made a strong impression on one American filmmaker who preferred to tell stories with as few words as possible. "To see somebody actually do it, to make a visual film, was hugely inspirational to me," Lucas said. "If he did it, I can do it."

At the time, however, Kubrick's masterpiece lost out to its release-date rival. *2001* didn't make its $10.5 million budget back until it returned to theaters in 1975 (it has since earned more than $100 million). *Planet of the Apes* was shot for half the cost and made $32.5 million at the box office that same year: score another victory for small science fiction budgets. Critics went ape for *Apes* too, and Twentieth Century Fox released a sequel every year from 1970 to 1973, followed by a TV series in 1974. Each one was weaker and cheesier and brought in fewer dollars than the last.

But the original was pitch-perfect and had much in common with *2001*. Both films feature actors in monkey costumes, hunted astronauts, and profound paradigm-changing twists in their closing minutes. Both carry an implicit threat: our technology—whether self-aware computers or atomic weapons—will be the doom of us all. But both films also hold out hope that we can evolve, either into smarter apes or into star-bound embryos.

Between them, the two movies expanded the possibilities for the genre as never before. As did current events: when Neil Armstrong and Buzz Aldrin walked on the moon eighteen months later, the sense of wonder was infectious. All bets seemed to be off. Maybe there really *were* aliens who jumped into the air and stuck their noses in the ground like an arrow. Or maybe the break-through movie would have something to do with spaceships, holograms, the wave of the future.

In 1973, another young, bearded USC graduate called John Carpenter filmed a semiserious spoof of *2001* that focused on the claustrophobic confines of a long-haul starship. Its stir-crazy crew has adopted a bizarre beach ball–like alien; it jumps in the air, at least. The movie was *Dark Star*, and it featured film history's first depiction of a ship going into hyperspace, created by Carpenter's friend Dan O'Bannon. Not bad for a $60,000 budget.

Dark Star caught the attention of a frenetic independent filmmaker who'd made a couple of hallucinogenic movies of his own, the Chilean director Alejandro Jodorowsky, known as Jodo. Having bought the film rights to *Dune* for next to nothing, Jodo had come to Hollywood to try to persuade Douglas Trumball to do the visual effects. Jodo wanted to open the movie with the greatest panning shot he could possibly imagine—across the entire galaxy without a single cut—and figured the only one who could do it was the effects wizard behind *2001*'s spaceships. But Trumball was arrogant in their meeting, interrupting Jodo several times to take long phone calls. The director walked out and went to see *Dark Star* instead. He was so impressed he promptly arranged a meeting with O'Bannon, and after Jodo got him stoned on some particularly strong marijuana, O'Bannon agreed to pack up all his belongings, say au revoir to his wife, and move to Paris with him to work on the script.*

Jodo, appropriately enough for *Dune*, was something of a cult leader himself. He persuaded the great Orson Welles to act as the villain of the piece in exchange for hiring his favorite Parisian chef, and even managed to hector Salvador Dali into agreeing to a cameo as the Emperor of the Universe (for $100,000 a minute, Dali insisted). He got the Swiss artist H. R. Giger, possibly the only person in Europe weirder than Jodo and Dali, to do a bunch of nightmarish concept paintings, and recruited French comic book artist Moebius to storyboard the entire film at lightning speed. Taking the results back to Hollywood in 1975, he met with implacable opposition from the studios—not to the storyboards, or to the idea of a *Dune* movie, which had obvious potential, but to Jodo himself. His thundering insistence that it might be a three-hour movie, or even a twelve-hour movie if he felt like it, probably didn't help. He'd already raised $10 million, but for want of an extra $5 million, Jodorowsky's *Dune* was retired, never to be made.† Nevertheless, as with a lot of these failed 1970s space movies, its very existence would have some interesting unintended consequences.

Meanwhile on the East Coast, yet another young bearded filmmaker, Edward Summer, had graduated from NYU's film school with dreams of making a science fiction film. He'd made a short film called *Item 72-D*. Because everyone kept mistaking it for *THX 1138*, he added the subtitle *The Adventures of Spa and Fon*. While he waited to get funding for his other science fiction scripts, he opened a comic book store in Manhattan. Called Supersnipe, it soon became a mecca for comic book and film nerds including Brian de Palma, Robert Zemeckis, Martin Scorsese, and their friend George Lucas.

Years later, in 1999, the critic Peter Biskind wrote a book called *Easy Riders, Raging Bulls*. His thesis was that the "rock and roll generation" of directors split

---

* At that moment in the suburbs of Paris, a fifteen-year-old named Luc Besson was sketching out ideas for a space movie of his own. He would work on the script diligently for decades, and it would finally reach the screen in 1997 as *The Fifth Element*. Besson added one overt *Star Wars* reference: a female military officer with a Princess Leia hairstyle.

† It would find new life in a 2014 documentary about the unfinished project, *Jodorowsky's Dune*, from which most of these details are drawn. The documentary's only sour note: it suggests that some scenes in *Star Wars* were inspired by Moebius's storyboards. Gary Kurtz insists he and Lucas never saw them, although he did later employ Moebius to draw posters for *Star Wars'* European release.

in two in the 1970s: that Spielberg and Lucas went one way, into space fantasy and other popcorn fare, which changed the course of cinema and pushed out the edgier work of directors such as de Palma and Scorsese. But Biskind completely missed the fact that those edgy directors spent a good portion of the decade just as Lucas did: in comic book stores, reading science fiction, trying to get space movies off the ground.

"The 1970s was a perfect storm for something like *Star Wars* to happen," Summer says. He remembers Scorsese optioning stories by the great paranoid science fiction writer Philip K. Dick, while de Palma wanted to make a movie out of *The Demolished Man*, a science fiction classic by Alfred Bester. "Everybody, *everybody* wanted to make a movie of *The Stars My Destination*," Bester's other hit novel, Summer remembers. "I was involved with three separate productions of it, and nobody could get it right. The special effects were so difficult."

Universal, more than most studios, had caught science fiction fever. The buzz around *Home Free* built when Larry Tucker introduced Barwood and Robbins to a bright TV director named Steven Spielberg who loved science fiction as much as they did, and was a protege of the head of Universal. But unfortunately, as Barwood, Robbins, and Spielberg were chatting excitedly about *Home Free*, Universal handed Douglas Trumball a million-dollar budget to shoot a movie of his own. Called *Silent Running*, it would use some visual effects shots that hadn't been completed in time for Kubrick's movie.

Trumball's plot seemed like it should appeal to space geeks, acid freaks, and members of the growing environmental coalition that had recently celebrated its first Earth Day. In the distant year of 2008, all plant life on the planet has been eradicated, save for a bunch of geodesic-domed greenhouses in orbit. Their gardener is given the order to destroy his cargo and return to Earth; instead, he kills the crew and goes rogue with a pair of robots. Joan Baez sang two full songs on the soundtrack. It was something else.

Home Free was to be something else, too. It had a little *Forbidden Planet* in its DNA, a little *2001*, and a little something for the stardust generation. It was the story of a space expedition checking out a couple of planets in a distant star system. Two guys are investigating the less interesting planet, the atmosphere of which is barely breathable. They scour its grassy plains in something like a giant RV. All of a sudden, the RV's computers start printing out the protocols for a first contact: it has detected alien life nearby. The protocols have been in the works for centuries and are inviolable. Accordingly, the senior guy departs for the other planet, leaving his underling behind as a guinea pig.

The junior guy has a series of archeological adventures on the planet—shades of Indiana Jones—while uncovering evidence of an ancient alien civilization. He can't find anything alive except a bunch of mysterious clean-up robots, which he brings back to the RV. They start disassembling the vehicle faster than he can put it back together. His oxygen starts running out.

That's when the real aliens arrive, like the cavalry to the rescue. "They're these angelic creatures," says Barwood. "They communicate with each other via light-emitting patches on their bodies. And they're sort of on vacation." The creatures recognize the astronaut is in danger, form a ring around his ship, start a dance, and "by powers beyond human understanding," lift the RV into orbit, where the young astronaut can be rescued by his compatriots.

When *Silent Running* bombed at the box office in 1972—it was way too preachy, its protagonist insufferable—Universal lost all interest in science fiction. *Home Free* went to the graveyard of lost Hollywood projects. Barwood laments that the film would have cost too much to make anyway and would probably have done better thirty years later, as "a nice little CGI movie."

Barwood went on to success with Steven Spielberg, for whom he and Matthew Robbins wrote his first main feature, *Sugarland Express*. After that, as we'll see, Lucas asked Barwood to cowrite *Star Wars*, but Barwood turned him down. He did a lot of uncredited script polishing on Spielberg's own movie about a first contact, *Close Encounters of the Third Kind*, fleshing out the beginning and the end. Uncredited too was Barwood's impact on *Star Wars*, which may never have turned out the way it did were it not for a vital connection that Barwood provided to Lucas after his own space dream died.

Back in his industrial film days, Barwood had worked on a series of movies for Boeing. The idea had been to promote a rival to the Concorde jet—itself another project that never came to fruition—called the SST, for Supersonic Transport. At the aviation company, Barwood met an artist who'd done some amazing gouache paintings of the SST. The artist's name: Ralph McQuarrie.

In 1971, while Barwood was still working on *Home Free*, he discovered that McQuarrie had moved to Los Angeles. They met to discuss the movie, and Barwood and Nobbins hired McQuarrie to create four concept paintings for it. Once McQuarrie had finished the first, he invited Barwood and Robbins to his studio one afternoon to make sure he was on the right path.

The pair came over and brought their pal George Lucas, with whom they'd just been having lunch. The meeting that followed would quite literally change cinematic history.

McQuarrie's painting—an astronaut next to an RV in a field of grass—stunned everyone. Yes, they said, he was on the right path. "George looked at Ralph," recalls Barwood, "and said, 'You know, I'm going to make a science fiction movie. I'll remember you.'"

Before he could afford to enlist McQuarrie's help in visualizing his space story, however, Lucas would have to sit at the kitchen table in his Mill Valley one-bedroom and struggle mightily to come up with the right words.

8.

MY LITTLE SPACE THING

How do you build a universe from scratch? It was a question George Lucas grappled with in 1973 as he sat down to hash out what, exactly, *The Stars Wars* was all about. He had done something approximate in *THX* and still carried notions of a sequel. But to do a *THX* movie was not really to tell stories. Lucas was now trying his hand at space fantasy, at storytelling on a galactic stage. And for that, he would have to relearn the art of writing.

Lucas began by scribbling a list of names, just to see what they would look like written down. Emperor Ford Xerxes the Third. Xenos. Thorpe. Roland. Monroe. Lars. Kane. Hayden. Crispin. Leila. A baby name book in one hand, history books in the other, he added descriptions that wore their real-world inspirations too clearly on their sleeve: Alexander Xerxes XII, Emperor of Decarte. (Presumably a warrior-philosopher king.) Han Solo, leader of the Hubble people. ("Solo" came from the paper cup brand, Hubble from the astronomer.) Oh, and here's a good one, a name kind of based on his own: Luke Skywalker, "Prince of Bebers."

This is the point at which you want to yell, Wait, George, go back to those two names! Lose their ridiculous titles, dig up those R2-D2 and Wookiee names from your notebooks, and you'll be well on your way.

But the course of creativity rarely runs smooth. Lucas focused first on another character: Mace Windy, a noble space samurai in the Kurosawa mode. Windy is a "Jedi-Bendu," a title which hailed in part from the name for samurai films, *jidai geki* (which actually just means "period drama"). The guy who will

102

tell Mace's story, his apprentice or "padawaan," is either C. J. Thorpe or C. 2. Thorpe (nothing more futuristic-sounding than a name with a number in it). Either way, his nickname will be "Chuie," pronounced "Chewy."

Lucas had roughly one scene in his head at this point, although he wouldn't actually write it out for three years. He wanted to see a dogfight in outer space. Rather than stay static, or move very simply in one direction the way models did in *Star Trek*, the ships would hurtle and tumble around after each other like World War II fighters, like wild birds. For now, Lucas focused on the big picture questions. How to frame the movie that had been spinning in his head since USC? A movie that he now had to will into being, just the way he willed *THX* and *American Graffiti* into existence.

Whills. That was it. Lucas saw an ancient order of galactic guardians called Whills. We wouldn't get to see them; they would be chroniclers in the background. The whole movie would be drawn from a book we never see, a book he could keep fleshing out for years if this little space thing worked. "Journal of the Whills," he wrote. "Part 1. This is the story of Mace Windy, a revered Jedi-bendu of Ophuchi, related to us by C. J. Thorpe, padawaan learner to the famed Jedi."

Like many an amateur science fiction or fantasy writer, Lucas got bogged down in names, in planets and spaceships and interplanetary organizations, without first finding reasons that his audience should care about them. Thorpe hailed from Kissel. His father was chief pilot on the intergalactic cruiser *Tarnack*. Windy was "Warlord to the Chairman of the Alliance of Independent Systems." Thorpe becomes his apprentice at the "exalted Intersystems Academy."

Mired in detail after just a few paragraphs, Lucas decide to cut to Part II: four years later. Now Windy and Thorpe were "guardians on a shipment of fusion portables to Yavin" when they were "summoned to the desolate second planet of Yoshiro by a mysterious courier from the Chairman of the Alliance." This was to be their greatest adventure . . .

And then the narrative ended. The Creator had two pages of a rough outline of the first in a series of films set in this new universe, but went no further. The man who finished every project he ever started was balking at the threshold of his hero's journey. Which is, of course, exactly what a hero is supposed to do.

While Lucas was staunching this latest bleeding, Universal still declined to distribute *American Graffiti*. William Hornbeck, one of the most respected editors in the business, called it "totally unreleasable." Tanen had two scenes cut. Both scenes mocked authority figures: one in which Ron Howard's character Steve confronts his old teacher at the sock hop and tells him to "go kiss a duck," and another in which Terry the Toad is accosted by a used-car dealer. Lucas was apoplectic—his child was having her fingers cut off again—and sullenly refused to participate in the mutilation. Kurtz got Verna Fields to do the editing.

In early 1973, while *Graffiti* was stuck in limbo, *THX 1138* was shown on network TV. *Newsday* critic Joseph Gelmis loved it. The author of *The Film Director as Superstar*, Gelmis naturally wanted to know more about Lucas. Could he be a superstar? He arranged a preview screening of *Graffiti* and was baffled that the studio couldn't see its worth. He took the Lucases out to dinner in Sausalito and got the sense they were glad to have a free meal. What was Lucas working on next? Gelmis asked. Perhaps fearing the big-time movie critic would laugh at a *Flash Gordon* reference, Lucas called his new project "a $4 million space opera in the tradition of Edgar Rice Burroughs." It was an attempt to push himself into the realms of plot, he said, the way *Graffiti* pushed him into dealing with characters.

In fact, when Lucas produced a second draft in April 1973, it was a kind of overcompensation for not liking plot all those years; a ten-page treatment stuffed, suffused, and sprinkled with plot. It bore no relation to the "Journal of the Whills" two-pager. Instead, it found its structure in a number of Kurosawa movies, most notably *Hidden Fortress*.

Here we reach a favorite assertion of film nerds: Did you know *Star Wars* was based on *Hidden Fortress*? Except no, it really wasn't. Lucas has acknowledged the influence of Kurosawa's long lenses and wide shots and was happy to be interviewed for the DVD release of the Japanese movie, in which he offers the faint praise that *Hidden Fortress* is his fourth favorite Kurosawa movie. But both he and Kurtz, who rarely agree on anything about *Star Wars* history, say the comparison between that film and *Star Wars* has been overblown. While Lucas had seen *Hidden Fortress* within a year of writing the treatment, this was 1973: he couldn't exactly rent the video and do a scene-by-scene analysis. All he did was copy the summary in Donald Richie's 1965 book *The Films of Akira Kurosawa*, which became one paragraph in the treatment's introduction.*

---

* Richie's summary reads: "It is the sixteenth century, a period of civil wars. A princess, with her family, her retainers, and the clan treasure is being pursued. If they can cross enemy territory and reach a friendly province they will be saved. The enemy knows this and posts a reward for the capture of the princess." Lucas's paragraph reads: "It is the thirty-third century, a period of civil wars in the galaxy. A rebel princess, with her family, her retainers, and the clan treasure, is being pursued. If they can cross territory controlled by the Empire and reach a friendly planet, they will be saved. The Sovereign knows this, and posts a reward for the capture of the princess."

Hidden Fortress focuses on two peasants in sixteenth-century Japan, torn by civil wars. They were supposed to fight for a winning clan but showed up late, were taken for defeated soldiers and captured, and then escaped. They bicker over which way to go next, split up, and are both captured again. Again, they escape. After finding gold in a piece of driftwood by a riverside, they encounter its source: the defeated clan's general and a supposedly mute girl hiding in a fortress in the mountains and hoping to move the gold out of enemy territory. The peasants tag along, hoping to earn or steal a share of the gold. The girl is revealed to be the defeated clan's princess, for whom the enemy has posted a bounty. She and the general use the gold to restore the clan's territory. The peasants end the movie with a single coin as a reward.

Lucas's second treatment opened with a scene from a different story altogether:

> Deep Space.
> The eerie blue-green planet of Aquilae slowly drifts into view. A small speck, orbiting the planet, glints in the light of a near-by star.
> Suddenly a sleek fighter-type spacecraft settles ominously into the foreground moving swiftly toward the orbiting speck. Two more fighters silently maneuver into battle formation behind the first and then three more craft glide into view. The orbiting speck is actually a gargantuan space fortress which dwarfs the approaching fighters.

Only after this foreshadowing do we cut to the paragraph cribbed from Richie's summary. An outlaw princess, a gruff general, and their treasure ("priceless aura spice," Lucas wrote, his first reference to *Dune**) are traveling in "land speeders" across enemy territory.

Two bickering Imperial bureaucrats eject themselves from the Space Fortress, crash-land on the planet below, and are captured by the general. The general's name, a favorite from Lucas's list: Luke Skywalker. It sounded like an old man, a Gandalf or a veteran Samurai, ambling in the clouds with a walking stick. Lucas would never begin a single draft thinking of it as a name for a young hero.

In a nod to Lucas's greatest influence, the treatment sent the small band toward a spaceport called Gordon. There they hope to find a spacecraft to take

---

* His first, but by no means his last. Science fiction geeks have noted the comparisons for years: *Dune* features Princess Alia, pronounced "A-Leia"; both featured vehicles called Sandcrawlers; the hardscrabble inhabitants of both Arrakis and Tatooine farm for moisture. "Jedi Bendu" may have been partly inspired by the self-control combat technique found in *Dune*, "Prana Bindu."

them to a friendly planet. Seeking shelter in a storm, Skywalker finds ten lost boys in an abandoned temple. He overhears them plotting to attack the empire in defense of the princess. Here the treatment veers off entirely from *Hidden Fortress*: Skywalker trains these lost boys into manhood. "The boys are angered at his cold and relentless directions, although they grow to respect him when they begin to see the results of his training," Lucas wrote, in what may have been his most accurate description of his relationship with his father.

The band of rebels reach Gordon. Here we get the one scene that was to survive unaltered through all drafts and into the movie: the group enters a cantina, hoping to find a contact that will yield passage off the planet. "The murky little den is filled with a startling array of weird and exotic aliens laughing and drinking at the bar," Lucas wrote. A group of aliens lays into one of the boys, and Skywalker is forced to take his "lazer sword" from its sheath. In a matter of seconds, an arm lies on the ground.

So far so exciting. But the pace continues exhaustingly, with no slow beats. The rebels are led into a trap by a trader, steal a space fighter, battle Imperial ships across half a galaxy, hide in an asteroid, are attacked again, and crash-land on the "forbidden planet of Yavin." And that's just one paragraph.

Yavin brings us aliens riding on giant birds who capture the princess and sell her to the empire. Skywalker and the boys fashion "jet-sticks" from their rescue packs. A mob of aliens throw Skywalker into a boiling lake. He clings to a vine, finds the lost boys with the help of an alien farmer, attacks an Imperial outpost, learns the princess has been taken to the Empire's home planet, and trains the boys again, this time to fly one-man fighters. They fly into the prison complex, blast their way to the princess, and take her to the friendly planet they were aiming for in the first place. There's a parade. The bureaucrats see the princess "revealed as her true goddess-like self" and then go and get drunk. "The End?" Lucas wrote, leaving the door open to sequels and echoing *Look at Life*.

We're as far from *Hidden Fortress* here as we are from the finished *Star Wars*. Lucas offered many nods to other Kurosawa movies: General Skywalker encountering the boys in the temple echoes a scene in *Yojimbo*; the cantina scene is inspired by the sequel, *Sanjuro*. It's pretty dense stuff, even for a seasoned *Star Wars* fan reading it in hindsight. For someone not attuned to science fiction, it's pretty much impenetrable. Lucas's agent Jeff Berg found it incomprehensible. Still, he had no choice but to show the treatment to United Artists and Universal.

If Lucas was trying to produce a treatment that would get him out of his obligation with both studios, he couldn't have done better. Clearly, this picture was going to cost more than $4 million. David Picker at UA, which still had the first option on the film, rejected it out of hand. (It would take a few more months for the studio to release its trademark on the name *The Star Wars*.) In June, Berg sent the treatment to Universal, which held the second option, accompanied by a terse note: if the company wanted it, it had ten days to say yes. Universal never actually turned *Star Wars* down; it just didn't respond.*

With UA and Universal both having passed on *The Star Wars*, Lucas was free to shop his treatment around other studios. He took it to Disney, but that studio was a walled castle producing few great movies at the time—1973's *Robin Hood* was the exception—and beginning what would become a decade of decline. "Disney would have accepted this movie if Walt were still alive," Lucas insisted. Ironically, Disney would never get its hands on the film, not even after it bought Lucasfilm some four decades later; the original movie is the only *Star Wars* film to be distributed by another studio in perpetuity.

The lucky studio, of course, would be Twentieth Century Fox. In 1973 it was the home of the last successful big-budget science fiction adventure, *Planet of the Apes*. More importantly, it had a keen hunter of talent in the form of its new vice president of creative affairs, Alan "Laddie" Ladd Jr. Laddie was the son of a Hollywood star, a former agent, and a former producer. He was shaking things up at Fox with his contractual ability to give movies the initial go-ahead to start production using the studio's money—or "greenlighting," as Hollywood calls it. The first movie Laddie greenlit was *Young Frankenstein*. The second was *The Omen*. Both would become monster hits. To interest Laddie in Lucas, Berg managed to get him a print of *Graffiti*. Laddie loved the film so much he asked Berg if there was any way Fox could buy it from Universal. Berg communicated this to Tanen, which in turn spurred Tanen to finally schedule the long-suffering movie for a summer release.

A fair number of falsehoods have clustered around Laddie's role in *Star Wars* over the years. One myth is that he was president of the studio at the time; in fact, he wasn't even on the board of directors. Another is that Laddie couldn't understand what Lucas was talking about when the young director tried to explain *Star Wars*, and merely decided to bankroll him based on his passion for the project. Not true, he says. "I understood completely," remembers Laddie, now seventy-six. "He explained it to me in terms of other films." *Flash Gordon* was not one of them. Evidently Lucas had already solidified his lifelong habit

---

* Universal would make nice with Lucas soon enough, taking an option on another treatment he wanted to develop, called *Radioland Murders*.

of discussing *Star Wars* differently depending on who he was talking to. For Laddie, his influences were old Errol Flynn capers such as *The Sea Hawk*, *Robin Hood*, and *Captain Blood*.

Star Wars would borrow their sense of adventure, their bloodless deaths, their clearly delineated conflict between good and evil. Even now, Laddie keeps spotting echoes of the movie in old Hollywood—such as the Gene Kelly version of *The Three Musketeers* (1948), which ends with a medal-giving ceremony very similar to the medal-giving on Yavin IV.* "Like everyone else, he stole from what he loved," Laddie says. But there were ways in which Lucas was clearly exceptional: "He was a very intelligent human being. I was very impressed with his brain. I believed in him completely."

On July 13, 1973, Laddie snapped up *The Star Wars* in a deal memo that gave Lucas $150,000 to write and direct. The memo also gave Lucasfilm a budget of $3.5 million and 40 percent of the movie's profits. It stipulated that sequel rights, soundtrack, and merchandising would be negotiated before production got under way. *Star Wars* legend has it that these were inconsequential things, known to Hollywood lawyers as "the garbage." Few films got sequels; even fewer sequels made money. Soundtracks didn't sell unless they were musicals. Merchandising for movies? Impossible. That said, the fact that the lawyers would keep fighting over the precise details for the next two years shows that Fox was not as asleep at the switch as we've been led to believe.

Even turning the deal memo into an actual deal took a few months. Meanwhile in August, *Graffiti* was released, and Lucas's life would never be the same again. It was a hit—and not just one of those slow-to-build indie hits, but the kind for which *Variety* reserved its finest neologisms, "socko" and "boffo." It opened strong in New York and LA, and lost no momentum as it spread across the country. This was summertime, there were still drive-in theaters, and this was the perfect drive-in movie for hot summer nights. You saw it and felt seventeen again.

Graffiti would make $55 million that year. When it was reissued in 1978, after *Star Wars*, it made another $63 million. By the twenty-first century, its take would exceed $250 million. Given that its budget was $600,000, the film gave Universal and Lucas one of the greatest returns on investment in movie history. Lucas's agent knew he could get another half million up front for *The*

---

* Others have looked at this ceremony and seen a similarity to Leni Riefenstahl's 1938 Nazi documentary *Triumph of the Will*, which Lucas has said he saw in the late 1960s, but he dismissed any connection.

Star Wars, at the very least, if he renegotiated his fee with Fox. Instead, his client wanted to press the case on his rights to the garbage.

By the end of 1973, to his great surprise, George Lucas was a millionaire small business owner. After taxes, *American Graffiti* earned $4 million for Lucasfilm that year. In 2014 dollars, that's $16.5 million. It was an astonishing turn of events for a couple in a one-bedroom in Mill Valley, who were getting by on less than $20,000 a year with both of them working.

But the Lucases weren't about to copy Coppola, who had moved into a massive Pacific Heights mansion and started leasing a jet after the runaway success of *The Godfather*. For one thing, they had to pay debts back to just about everyone they knew, including Coppola and George Lucas Sr. Then the couple spent cautiously. They moved further into Marin and paid $150,000 for a one-level Victorian mansion on Medway Road in San Anselmo. Working from old photographs of the house, Lucas reconstructed a second-floor tower with a fireplace, wraparound windows, and view of Mount Tam. Inside, he made a desk out of three doors. Drafts of all six *Star Wars* movies would be written on its surface.

In October 1973 Lucas began loaning his wealth to a shell company, the Star Wars Corporation. Marcia was away in LA and Tucson, editing *Alice Doesn't Live Here Anymore* for Martin Scorsese. He visited Tucson a few times, feeling a little protective—Scorsese had a rowdy reputation. Lucas brought hefty tomes with him: *Isaac Asimov's Guide to the Bible* and a giant study of mythology called *The Golden Bough* by the nineteenth-century anthropologist Sir James George Frazer. *The Golden Bough* was enjoying something of a revival in the 1970s. It aimed to boil down all religious beliefs and rituals to their common elements, but Frazer's prose requires something of an effort to slog through. Scorsese asked Lucas: Why all the heavy reading? I'm tapping into the collective unconscious of fairy tales, Lucas explained.

Back home, he retreated to the writing tower at eight every morning. His goal was five pages every day; when he finished, his reward was music on the Wurlitzer jukebox. Usually he got one page done by four P.M. and reached the rest of his target out of sheer panic in the next hour, in time for the CBS *Evening News* with Walter Cronkite.

The news offered little respite. The world seemed to be falling apart. The ceasefire in Vietnam broke down. US troops were heading for the exits. Watergate engulfed the Nixon White House. The Arab nations attacked Israel again. OPEC was withholding its oil; suddenly even millionaires like Lucas had a hard time filling their cars.

Lucas channeled the news into his notes. With *Apocalypse Now* on hold until Coppola, then just its producer, could persuade a studio to fund it, *The Star Wars* became the only place he could comment on present-day politics. Thus the planet of Aquilae becomes "a small independent country like North Vietnam," he wrote in late 1973. "The Empire is like America ten years from now, after gangsters assassinated the Emperor and were elevated to power in a rigged election. . . . We are at a turning point: fascism or revolution."

Politics blended with escapism. Lucas bought armfuls of comic books again. Jack Kirby, the best-loved comic artist in the United States, had just finished a series called *The New Gods*. The hero uses a mysterious power called the Source. The villain is called Darkseid, a black armor–plated character; he happens to be the hero Orion's father. Away those influences went into the filing cabinet of Lucas's brain.

Lucas had never been a particularly avid reader of science fiction novels. But he made a serious effort now. There was one 1960s author for whom he had always made an exception: Harry Harrison, a former illustrator and former *Flash Gordon* comic strip writer. Harrison offered stories that could be read on two levels: rollicking space adventures and satires of the science fiction genre. *Bill the Galactic Hero* (1965) spoofed Robert Heinlein's masculine tales of space soldiers. *The Stainless Steel Rat* was a series of novels whose protagonist, Jim diGriz, is a charming rogue and interstellar con man, in it for the fun of it: a proto–Han Solo.

By the time *Star Wars* came out, Harrison was in Ireland, trying to eke out a tax-free living from his novels. The film rights to his 1967 classic *Make Room! Make Room!* had been sold to MGM for one dollar by an unscrupulous lawyer; MGM turned it into *Soylent Green*. In the early 1980s, Harrison read in an article that Lucas loved his work and became apoplectic: "I thought, 'well, why the hell didn't you write to me and have me do a god damned script for you, you know, if that's what you feel, old son. I'd be very happy to come over and make some money from this rotten field.' Oh, there's no justice."

When he was writing *Star Wars*, however, Lucas wasn't really thinking about making money from the rotten field. He was just absorbing its pulpier classics. Though he long understood Burroughs to be a primary influence on *Flash Gordon*, Lucas only read *A Princess of Mars* cover to cover in 1974. He picked up the Lensman books by E. E. Doc Smith, featuring a race of interstellar superhuman policemen. The Lensmen travel the galaxy finding particularly smart individuals to join them via the Lens, a mysterious crystal that tunes into the "life force" and turns its wearers into mind-reading telepaths.

Lucas seems to have turned influences over in his brain as if he were tossing a salad. "*The Star Wars* is a mixture of *Lawrence of Arabia*, the James Bond films and *2001*," he told the Swedish film magazine *Chaplin* in the fall of 1973, which oddly enough appears to be his first published interview about the movie in any language. "The space aliens are the heroes, and Homo Sapiens naturally the villains. Nobody has done anything like this since *Flash Gordon Conquers the Universe*." The homo sapiens line wasn't strictly true of any draft he finished, but it did show the breadth of possibilities he was playing with. He also managed to come up with one more dramatic metaphor for the moviemaking process: "It's like mountaineering," he told the Swedish reporter. "It's freezing cold, you lose your toes, but then you reach the top and it's worth it."

In May 1974, Lucas turned thirty, the age by which he had promised his father he'd be a millionaire; he had achieved that goal many times over. He had also summited first-draft mountain, and it was quite a height he'd scaled. This first complete draft of *The Star Wars* stood 191 scenes and thirty-three thousand words tall. In movies of the early 1970s, the average scene lasted two minutes; even if Lucas was planning on making his scenes a minute each on average—a tall order, given the weight of dialogue—*The Star Wars* would last three hours and ten minutes. Nevertheless, Lucas made four copies and sent them to Coppola, Robbins, Barwood, and Willard Huyck—who, along with his wife, Gloria Katz, had provided that essential humorous rewrite in *American Graffiti*'s fourth draft.

None of these early readers would give the *Star Wars* script rave reviews. Like the *Hidden Fortress*–inspired ten-page treatment, the first draft was overflowing with plot, albeit an entirely different plot. It had moved in the right direction in some respects—no longer was this taking place in the thirty-third century, but in some nameless time. And the eternal conflict of Jedi against Sith, the fall of the Jedi, and the rise of the Empire, which underpinned the whole story of six *Star Wars* movies, was mentioned at the very beginning. In a *Flash Gordon*–style "roll-up"—the opening crawl—we learn that the Jedi Bendu were the Emperor's personal bodyguards and "chief architects of the Imperial Space Force." Then a rival warrior sect, the Knights of Sith, hunted down and killed them for the "New Empire." We cut to a moon, where an eighteen-year-old called Annikin [*sic*] Starkiller sees a spacecraft zoom overhead and then rushes into a rocket ship to alert his father, Kane, and ten-year-old brother, Deak, who has been tasked with a philosophy problem.

That's right: the first script of *The Star Wars* opens not with explosions and droids and Darth Vader, but with homework.

ANNIKIN: *Dad! Dad! . . . They've found us!*

Deak looks up from a small cube he has been studying. His father whacks him across the shoulder with a braided wire connector.

KANE: *Continue with the problem. Your concentration is worse than your brother's. (to Annikin) How many?*

ANNIKIN: *Only one this time. A Banta Four.*

KANE: *Good. We may not have to repair this old bucket after all. Prepare yourself.*

DEAK: *Me too!*

KANE: *Do you have the answer?*

DEAK: *I think it's the Corbet dictum: "What is, is without."*

Kane smiles. This is the correct answer.

Deak is promptly killed by a seven-foot Sith knight and his character forgotten. If the sprawling script has a protagonist, it is probably Annikin Starkiller. Kane takes him back to their home planet of Aquilae, now threatened with Imperial invasion. He asks his old friend, General Luke Skywalker, to train Annikin as a Jedi, while Kane visits another old friend—a green-skinned alien called Han Solo. Aquilae's leader, the improbably named King Kayos, squabbles with his senators about whether the empire actually plans to invade. Kayos sends them off with a blessing: "May the Force of Others be with you all." To General Skywalker, a few scenes later, he says: "I feel the Force also." The Force goes unmentioned and unexplained for the rest of the script. The concept Lucas first explored in the writing of THX was almost as hesitant to break out into his writing now as it was in his first screenplay four years earlier.

Annikin has a tryst in a closet with a female aide. General Skywalker is so angered by this that he and Annikin lock lazerswords.* But there's no time for dueling: a giant space fortress is on the way. Annikin jumps in a land speeder to save the king's daughter, Princess Leia, just before the planet is struck by two atomic explosions. Pilots attack the space fortress in retaliation. "There's too much action, Chewie!" one pilot tells another. The readers tended to agree.

Halfway through the script, we cut to the space fortress and a couple of construction robots, "ArTwo Deeto," a "claw-armed tripod," and "SeeThreePio," who boasts a "totally metallic surface of an Art Deco design"—in other words,

---

* The spelling of this weapon would keep changing between drafts, from "lazer sword" to "lazersword" to "laser sword." It would only become "lightsaber" in the fourth draft.

the *Metropolis* robot. Notable about their dialogue: it is *dialogue*. ArTwo talks:

ARTWO: *You're a mindless, useless philosopher. . . . Come on! Let's go back to work; the system is all right.*
THREEPIO: *You overweight glob of grease. Quit following me. Get away. Get away.*

Another explosion, and the robots cling to each other in terror. They find an escape pod and head for the planet below, where Annikin and Princess Leia encounter them. ArTwo is shocked into speechlessness. Darth Vader, a human Imperial general, lands on Aquilae, preparing the way for Valorum, a knight of the Sith. Luke and Annikin go to the spaceport of Gordon, where they have that lazersword brawl in a cantina. They meet Han Solo, who takes them to Kane. Kane powers Han's ship by ripping a powerpack out of his own cyborg chest, killing himself. Pursued by the Empire, the ship hides in an asteroid belt and makes an emergency landing on the forest world of Yavin. Here they encounter giant "Wookees" [*sic*] led by Chewbacca—no, not the same Chewie as the pilot in the earlier scene. The princess is captured and taken to the space fortress. Annikin sneaks aboard but is captured and tortured by Darth Vader. Watching this, Valorum decides to switch sides and save Annikin and Leia. The trio tumble into a garbage chute, where they are almost crushed, but they manage to escape just before the Wookees—trained by General Skywalker—destroy the Fortress in one-man fighters. Leia returns to Aquilae, is crowned queen, and names Annikin lord protector. Confused? Lost? Overwhelmed? You're not the only one. "It was a universe nobody could understand from the scripts," said Huyck. "Not until George acted it out." But when he did, his enthusiasm for the scene helped him communicate it. Lucas can easily paint pictures with words, by all accounts, but only when he's speaking them.

Lucas leaned heavily on Huyck and Katz during the early stages of the drafting process. Every time he went down to LA, he paid a visit to the couple, showed them the draft in progress, and left with notes on what to fix. For the version he sent to Laddie at Twentieth Century Fox a few months later, he changed a bunch of names—again, from our perspective, moving in the wrong direction. Annikin Starkiller became Justin Valor. The Jedi, shockingly, became the Dia Noga.

The horror of writing a second draft seemed almost too much to bear. Lucas had been getting stomach pains from the tension of writing. "You beat your head against the wall and say, 'Why can't I make this work?,'" he recalled a decade later. "'Why aren't I smarter? Why can't I do what everybody else can do?'" In March 1974, he had told *Filmmakers Newsletter* that he would "hire somebody to do a rewrite."

Hal Barwood remembers Lucas, on one of his trips to LA post-*Graffiti*, trying to persuade him to write a draft. "George approached me in an oblique way to see if I might be a collaborator on writing *Star Wars*," he says. Barwood is bashful about it now. "I would've been the wrong guy to write a movie like this," he says. "I am interested in science fiction rather than space opera, so it would have been a big problem for me. I didn't realize how much of a taste I had for adventurous movie making. I was very interested in much more arty stuff. And I was a huge fan of *Star Trek*."

So Lucas dragged himself back to the door desks for another round. Kurtz's secretary, Bunny Alsup, remembered Lucas getting so miserable over the script that he would tear his hair out—cutting one unruly curl at a time, filling a wastebasket with them. "You go crazy writing," Lucas said decades later. "You get psychotic. You get yourself so psyched up and go in such strange directions in your mind that it's a wonder all writers aren't put away someplace. You can just get so convoluted in what you're thinking about that you get depressed, unbearably depressed. Because there's no guideline, you don't know if what you're doing is good or bad or indifferent. It always seems bad when you're doing it. It seems terrible. It's the hardest thing to get through."

In January 1975, the second draft was ready. Now titled *Adventures of the Starkiller, Episode One: The Star Wars*, it was about five thousand words lighter than its predecessor. Lucas wrapped it in a gold-embossed folder, as if to emphasize how seriously he was taking it.

The first thing any reader who was paying attention would have noticed about the second draft: the Journal of the Whills is back. The movie opens with a Bible-like prophecy, supposedly taken from its pages: "And in the time of greatest despair there shall come a savior, and he shall be known as: THE SON OF THE SUNS." *The Golden Bough* seems to have sunk in, because religious statements—and the religion of the Force—are front and center this time. In the roll-up, we read that the Jedi Bendu "learned the ways of the mysterious Force of Others," until they were eradicated when the Empire took over. But there's one Jedi out there still fighting the good fight, known only as the Starkiller.

The roll-up may be more ponderous than its predecessor, but the opening scene is far more action-driven: a small rebel spacefighter is being chased by not one but four giant Imperial Star Destroyers. The rebel ship returns fire and destroys one of them. We cut to the droids, now rendered as "Artoo" and "Threepio," aboard the smaller ship; they are now on the side of the rebels. Artoo "makes a series of electronic sounds that only a robot could understand."

The placement of these droids lends credence to an otherwise dubious story that Lucas tells about the creation of the *Star Wars* trilogies. Ever since 1979, two years after the first movie's release, Lucas has attempted to convince us that his writing process was some variation on the following: taking the first draft of *Star Wars*, cutting it in half, choosing the second half, then chopping the resulting story into three parts, which became the original trilogy. But it's a dubious claim once you read the first three drafts, which are three completely different stories containing some similar scenes in roughly the same position. "That's not true," Kurtz says bluntly of Lucas's assertion. "There were lots of little bits and pieces that were reasonably good ideas and ended up in the final draft." After which, "there wasn't enough material to do other movies." He admits that both he and Lucas gave post–*Star Wars* interviews in which they talked about the movie being "a section out of the middle" of a larger story—but that this was in the fictional Journal-of-the-Whills sense of a larger story. "It's very easy in hindsight to make things a lot simpler than they actually were," Kurtz adds.

If there is any evidence for Lucas's halves-and-thirds anecdote, it is this: the droids who showed up halfway through the first draft are now at the beginning of the second. Artoo and Threepio's ship is boarded by Stormtroopers—the first real appearance of the space soldiers in any draft thus far. Their still very human leader is General Darth Vader, still just Sith Knight Valorum's right-hand man. Deak—one of the sons of the Starkiller—makes short work of the Stormtroopers. Deak, a Jedi, uses a blaster, while the Stormtroopers wield laser swords. Vader defeats Deak because he is "strong with the Bogan"—Lucas's initial name for the Dark Side of the Force.

The droids escape to the desert planet below, where Artoo is instructed to make contact with one Owen Lars. Threepio tags along only because his "prime directive is survival." When Lucas imagined Threepio talking, he heard a public relations guy or a sleazy used-car dealer, perhaps like the one Universal cut from *American Graffiti*. The droids are captured by hooded, robot-nabbing dwarves, "sometimes called Jawas." (Coincidentally, Lucas's friend Steven Spielberg was about to make a movie based on the novel *Jaws*; Lucas had spent some time down in LA to see the faulty mechanical shark close up and gotten briefly stuck in its giant grey maw.) There's a robot revolt inside the Jawas' wagon. The robots escape, much like the *Hidden Fortress* peasants. Arriving at a "small moisture ranch," they find Lars, his nephews Biggs and Windy, his niece Leia, and our hero, eighteen-year-old Luke Starkiller.

Lucas had lost interest in writing about a gruff old general. He preferred Luke as a young hero: son of the Starkiller, brother of the recently defeated Deak, himself a Jedi trained by his Uncle Owen. We find him in the desert at laser sword practice, fending off blasts from a floating chrome baseball. Luke is now a sensitive artist type, a historian who would much rather "catalog the ancients" than fight in a galactic war. "I'm not a warrior," he says. (So why was he practicing?) Artoo plays a hologram of Deak, informing Luke "the enemy has constructed a powerful weapon" to use against their father—we know not what—and Luke must take the "Kiber Crystal" to him on Organa Major.

After a dinner of "thanta sauce" and "bum-bum extract," Luke embarks on a long-winded, jargon-filled explanation to his younger brothers about the Force of Others. Originally discovered by a holy man called the Skywalker, the Force is divided into the good half, "Ashla," and the "paraforce," called the Bogan. To prevent people with "less strength" from discovering the Bogan, the Skywalker only taught it to his children, who passed it on to theirs. And there you have it: as conceived for the first time, the Force was an exclusive, aristocratic cult.

Luke isn't done. Like a boring uncle at a family dinner, he drones on and on about politics: how the Senate grew too large, fell under the control of the Power and Transport guilds, and then "secretly instigated race wars and aided anti-government terrorists" with the aid of a Bogan-influenced Jedi called Darklighter, who turned a bunch of pirates into Sith knights.

The next morning Luke and the droids head off to Mos Eisley and its cantina. There, he meets Han Solo, now a "burly-bearded but ruggedly handsome boy dressed in a gaudy array of flamboyant apparel"—Coppola, basically. Han hangs out with an eight-foot "gray bush-baby monkey with baboon-like fangs"—Chewbacca, here wearing cloth shorts—and a science officer called Montross.

The bar brawl plays out. Luke and his laser sword win handily. Han leads him to his ship, via a stop for a steaming bowl of "Boma-mush" (there's a lot of food in this draft), and demands "an even million" for passage to Organa Major. Luke sells his speeder as a down payment; his father the Starkiller will pay the rest. (The moment where a Jawa fawns over the speeder, to Threepio's horror—"nice zoom-zoom"—offers the funniest line in this difficult draft.)

Solo turns out to be a cabin boy who's talking a big game. His unnamed ship is owned by a bunch of pirates, one called Jabba the Hutt. The pirates are addled by spice, which here appears to be simply an addictive recreational drug in the style of *THX*'s pills, rather than the mysterious life-extending chemical found in *Dune*. This allows Solo to create a diversion, steal the ship, and take his passengers to Organa Major. The planet has been destroyed; they don't know what by. So they head to the planet of Alderaan, to a city in the clouds—much like the Hawkmen city in *Flash Gordon*—where Deak is held prisoner. They free him by dressing up as Stormtroopers, using Chewbacca as their prisoner.

As they start blasting their way out, Han is overcome by a mysterious attack of depression:

HAN: *It's no use. We're lost.*
LUKE: *No, no, there's a debris chute. It's the Bogan force making you feel that way. Don't give up hope. Fight it!*
HAN: *It's no use, it's no use.*
LUKE: *Well, we're going anyway. Think of good things. Drive the Bogan from your mind.*

It's astonishing how much the word "Bogan" crops up in this draft: thirty-one times in total, versus ten mentions for the light-side Ashla Force. It's not hard to picture the depressed writer whiling away the long hours at his door desks, trying to drive the Bogan from his mind.

Down the garbage chute go our heroes, into the belly of the beast, to do battle with a creature called a Dia Noga in a trash compactor that the droids are able to shut down before it crushes them. The gang escapes Alderaan in classic adventure serial style, taking a bunch of bad guys hostage. On the ship, it turns out Deak is badly injured. Threepio can't do anything for him: "These are spiritual wounds," he explains. "The Bogan arts often run contrary to the ways of science and logic."

Also defying logic is Luke's sudden certainty that his father is on the fourth moon of Yavin (Yavin IV), out on the edge of the galaxy. On their way, they pass an enormous mysterious something—"as big as a small moon," says Montross—heading in the same direction. On Yavin's fourth moon, Luke and Han find the Starkiller's allies, including the Grand Mouff Tarkin—"a thin, bird-like commander." The mysterious approaching something is finally identified as the Death Star. More of a spiritual than a technological terror, it contains "all the force of Bogan." But the Starkiller has seen a weakness, a small thermal exhaust port at the Death Star's North Pole. Finally, we meet the Starkiller: a wizened old man with a long silver beard and shining grey-blue eyes, whose "aura of power . . . almost knocks Tarkin over."

Tarkin fears the Bogan is too strong and the Starkiller too old—that is, until Luke hands his dad the Kiber Crystal, which seems to restore his vital essence. All the Starkiller says to his long-lost son: there'll be time for full Jedi training later. Luke suits up and joins the attack on the Death Star. Han gets his reward: eight million in "neatly minted chrome bars." (Of course, a car nut would create a galaxy where the currency is chrome.)

Strangely, there hasn't been a villain in the script for two hours. Not until Darth Vader, feeling the presence of the Ashla Force, leads a team of TIE fighters from the Death Star. He destroys all the rebel ships but Luke's, before being destroyed himself by a returning Han. Vader crashes into Han's ship. Han and Chewie eject in a life pod. And who gets to fire the fatal shot that destroys the Death Star? Not Luke, but Threepio, riding shotgun. Back on Yavin IV the Starkiller offers his thanks—no medals here—and announces that "the revolution has begun."

Before the closing credits, we get a second roll-up. It promises a sequel: *The Adventures of the Starkiller Episode II: The Princess of Ondos*, in which the Lars family will get kidnapped, the Sith will return, and the Starkiller's sons will be put through further trials.

So much for chopping the first draft into halves and thirds; even at this point in the drafting process, Lucas planned to enter uncharted territory with the sequel.

Note the name of that supposed sequel—and how readily Lucas seemed to abandon the *Star Wars* name for the franchise as a whole. He may have honestly preferred *Adventures of the Starkiller*, which does sound rather *Flash Gordon–* esque. But there may have been a different calculation at work here.

Budget talks with Fox were deadlocked. Nobody had any idea how much a movie like this was supposed to cost. Lucas kept insisting this was "the first multi-million dollar *Flash Gordon* kind of movie." Kurtz tried pricing it out but admitted his figures were arbitrary. One of his budgets came to $6 million, another to $15 million. At one point Fox's moribund visual effects department estimated that the effects shots alone would cost $7 million. "That was definitely a finger-in-the-wind time."

However, there was progress in the "garbage" portion of the contract that would turn out to be crucial. Lucas got sequel rights, so long as he started producing one within two years of the movie's release.

Then there was merchandising. Contrary to legend, the contract didn't give Lucasfilm exclusive rights to all movie-related products; Fox could sell those too. It was more of a marriage than a giveaway. But it did give Lucas's shell company complete control over the name: "The Star Wars Corporation shall have sole and exclusive right to use . . . the name The Star Wars in connection with wholesale or retail outlets for the sale of merchandising items."

Given that the main title of this and subsequent movies in the second draft was now *Adventures of the Starkiller*, Lucas's control of the name *The Star Wars* might not have seemed a big deal to lawyers at the time. And, for all we know, that may well have been the point. If Lucas changed the name of the movie series for the purpose of contract negotiations, that would have been one of the most shrewd script switches in history.

Lucas showed the second draft to his trusted coterie. He held Friday night BBQs during which he brought Barwood, Robbins, and a rotating cast of friends back to his office to read chunks of the script and tape-record their reactions. The second draft met with little more enthusiasm than the first. "Anyone who read those drafts said 'what are you doing here? This is absolute gobbledygook,'" recalled Kurtz.

Coppola, ever the cheerleader, couldn't understand why Lucas had "chucked the [first] script and started again." But Barwood points out that Coppola always thought he was writing alone like Lucas, even though he invariably had assistance: "With all due respect to Francis, he's never been able to figure out how to properly tell a story without a little help. Mario Puzo saved his butt." Still, even Barwood the science fiction fan had a hard time understanding Lucas's story. If he didn't get it, Fox would have no clue. Lucas needed visuals, fast. Luckily, he had decided to call that artist guy Barwood introduced him to.

Lucas had commissioned Ralph McQuarrie in November 1974, before completing the second draft. McQuarrie finished his first *Star Wars* painting on January 2, 1975, the day after Lucas officially completed the draft script. Even though McQuarrie hadn't had a full script to work from, his earliest concept paintings would indelibly shape not just the first film, but the entire *Star Wars* saga.

McQuarrie's painting showed the two characters people had the hardest time imagining: the droids, lost in the desert of Utapau (an arid planet that would eventually be supplanted in the script by Tatooine; the name would have to wait thirty years to find its place in the saga). Threepio's humanoid eyes looked directly, pleadingly at the viewer. (I asked Anthony Daniels whether he would have played Threepio without McQuarrie's painting to explain the character for him. "Absolutely 100 percent not," he said.)

As guidance for Artoo, Lucas had mentioned the squat, slinky-legged, wheeled robots from *Silent Running*: Huey, Duey, and Louie. Since they were square, McQuarrie decided to make Artoo round. In one of many sketches, as a tripod, so McQuarrie imagined him as a tripod who throws his center leg forward by propping himself on his side legs, as if on crutches.

For the second painting, completed the following month, McQuarrie tackled the laser sword duel between Deak Starkiller and Darth Vader. Lucas supplied McQuarrie with a book on Japanese medieval military culture, suggesting that Vader might wear a flared samurai-style helmet. He also provided pulp illustrations in which the villain wore a cape. But Lucas still imagined Vader as fully human, his face "partially obscured" by cloth, Bedouin-style.

McQuarrie spent just one day on the Vader painting. He considered that Vader had just entered from the vacuum of space, and so he gave him a full-face, military-style gas mask. It was McQuarrie who created the instant emotional bond with Threepio that Daniels cannot shake to this day.

Gas mask and black Samurai helmet together: the effect was immediately stunning. Vader towers over young Deak, the perspective giving the impression he's supposed to be a Frankenstein-like giant. But this is, in fact, the most fortuitous misunderstanding in *Star Wars* history. McQuarrie in fact saw Vader as a short villain, a "ratty little guy" in the words of Paul Bateman, an artist McQuarrie later collaborated with. His perspective decision in that one painting would later inspire Lucas to cast six-foot-five bodybuilder Dave Prowse in the role, making Vader one of the tallest villains in cinematic history.

Within a couple of months, McQuarrie completed three more paintings. Now Lucas had visual aids to explain the Death Star, the Cloud City on Alderaan, and the cantina sequence. In the last, a Stormtrooper was seen in his "fascist white uniform" for the first time. Luke Starkiller had not yet been visualized. But it was enough. "They were done as a substitute for handwaving" in budget talks, McQuarrie said modestly of his paintings. Little could he know how effective a stand-in they would be.

The concept paintings helped clear up some of the confusion over Lucas's vision, but there was one more complicating factor: Lucas's second draft was embarrassingly crowded with men. He'd already gotten a lot of heat over the fact that *Graffiti* ended with on-screen text catching us up with the next ten years in the lives of the male characters, and nothing about the women. With the feminist movement growing more powerful with each passing month, *Star Wars* seemed on track for similar criticism. In March 1975, Lucas decided to fix that at a stroke: Luke Starkiller became an eighteen-year-old woman. After all, he'd been reading an awful lot of fairy tales as research into the mechanics of storytelling, and it's rather hard to ignore the convention that the protagonist of fairy tales is almost always female. (Think Cinderella, Rapunzel, Snow White, Red Riding Hood, and Goldilocks—as much as they have to be saved by princes or woodcutters, we at least see the story through their eyes.)

This gender reversal lasted for a couple of months, long enough for the female Luke to show up in a McQuarrie painting of the main characters. By May 1975, when Lucas wrote a crucial six-page synopsis for Fox executives—a synopsis not of the second draft, but of an entirely new story—Luke was back to being a boy. But Princess Leia had returned from the purgatory of the first draft, and in a much more prominent role. Now she was a leader of the rebellion from the outset, replacing Deak Starkiller in the opening scene and in the prison on Alderaan. (That latter part meant that she would be rather visibly tortured by Vader; it would take Lucas one more draft to develop a distaste for putting a bruised and battered woman in his movie.)

The Starkiller himself was absent in the synopsis. Now, it turned out, he had been killed in battle many years ago. Instead, Luke is mentored by an old general named Ben Kenobi who has become a hermit on Luke's home planet.

Armed with these new characters, Lucas threw himself into a third draft. His writing process began to accelerate. A year had elapsed between the treatment and the first draft. The second had taken him nine months. Lucas wrote the third draft in seven months. It was slightly shorter than the second, at roughly twenty-seven thousand words. If you go through it and delete any scene or dialogue that was not ultimately filmed, what's left is about seventeen thousand words. That meant Lucas had the majority of *Star Wars* in his hands by August 1975.

The third draft still opened with that Journal of the Whills quote about the son of suns; it was too clever a line for Lucas to let go. The roll-up was still way too long. But a key change had happened in the dialogue: there was less of it. Lucas the editor had taken the reins. Where previously he had burbled on for paragraphs, Threepio now opens the movie with four short sentences, the first of numerous lines from this draft that would make it into the final film: "Did you hear that? They've shut down the main reactor. We'll be destroyed for sure. This is madness!"

The number of special effects called for in the script had been edited down, too. Lucas was mindful of the budget and more realistic about costs. At some point during the scriptwriting process, Fox shuttered its entire special effects department—indeed, of the major studios, only Universal had a special effects department left. So Lucas and Kurtz hired their own special effects guy, the brilliant and difficult John Dykstra. Dykstra was a protégé of 2001 and *Silent Running* spaceship guru Doug Trumball, who was Lucas's first choice and suggested Dykstra. In an industrial park in the seedy Van Nuys district of Los Angeles, Dykstra began assembling a young team eager to work long hours for little pay ($20,000 a year on average) in return for the chance to get some incredibly real-looking spaceships up on the screen. Lucas gave the group an appropriately awesome name: Industrial Light and Magic. As cheap as they were, however, in total they were already costing the director $25,000 a week out of his own pocket. No wonder he reasoned that one terrifyingly large Imperial Star Destroyer could be just as effective in the opening chase sequence as four.

The third draft cuts from the space battle to the surface of the planet below, where Luke Starkiller is trying to persuade his friends he saw two ships, through his "electrobinoculars," exchanging laser fire. Of course, the battle is over before they get to see it. One of his friends, Biggs Darklighter, has just returned from the Imperial Academy and confides to Luke in hushed tones that he's going to jump ship and join the rebellion.

The Ashlan Force is gone in the new draft, but Lucas clung to the name of the evil Bogan force, eager to have us understand it. "Like Bogan weather or Bogan times," Luke says when he learns about it from Ben Kenobi. "I thought that was just a saying." The Bogan only crops up eight times in this draft, however.

There is still a scene in which a grizzled veteran slams his arm down in sorrow to reveal he is part cyborg. This role had now passed from Kane to Montross to Kenobi. The old Jedi general, whom Luke has studied—he knows his "diary of the Clone Wars" by heart—is much more of a reluctant warrior than he would ultimately become. Luke has to drag him out to adventure into the galaxy, rather than the other way around. Ben Kenobi really is getting too old for this sort of thing.

Still, Kenobi brings with him a new element to the script: comedy. Luke is attacked by Tusken raiders just before he meets Ben; they leave him handcuffed to a giant spinning wheel. Kenobi approaches with a "good morning!"

"What do you mean, 'good morning'?" Luke responds. "Do you mean that it is a good morning for you, or do you wish me a good morning, although it is obvious I'm not having one, or do you find that mornings in general are good?"

"All of them at once," replies Kenobi.

It's a great laugh line. It is also lifted, word for word, from *The Hobbit*. J. R. R. Tolkien's work was so widely read by the 1970s that Lucas could never have gotten away with the theft; it vanishes in the fourth draft. Still, it does reveal Obi-Wan Kenobi's origins, as well as Yoda's, rather plainly. This version of Kenobi is the acknowledged father of both of them, and he's a giggling galactic Gandalf.

Tolkien had died in 1973, just as Lucas was getting started on the first draft, and Middle Earth books had never been more popular. There was a surprising amount of overlap between the third draft of *Star Wars* and Tolkien's trilogy *The Lord of the Rings*. Both are full of strange creatures burbling meticulously made-up languages. Artoo and Threepio are Frodo and Sam, the innocents abroad, whether they're carrying the stolen data tapes or the One Ring. Both pairs of innocents are guided and guarded by ensemble casts. The Death Star, the hellish war machine, is Mordor. Stormtroopers are Orcs. Grand Moff Tarkin, now on the side of evil, is a dead ringer for Sauruman. Darth Vader, the Dark Lord of the Sith, is Sauron, Dark Lord of Mordor. Gandalf—Kenobi—carries a magic sword and eventually sacrifices himself only to return in slightly altered and more magical form.

There was another book that loomed large in Lucas's mind at the time and that he would often bring up in later interviews: Carlos Castaneda's *Tales of Power*, part of Castaneda's supposedly autobiographical series about the revealing philosophical trials he went through to gain sorcerer-like powers. The relationship between Luke and Ben would come to echo that of Castaneda and the Yaqui mystic Don Juan.

We're a long, long way from *Flash Gordon* now. We've mixed space fantasy with classic or "high" fantasy, added a layer of mysticism, and sprinkled on a few jokes and comic characters. Then there was just the right pinch of something else: backstory.

Luke's allusion to Ben Kenobi's "diary of the Clone Wars" in the third draft is the first mention of a conflict that would become a major part of *Star Wars* lore. It was around this time that Lucas began writing notes on the backstory of his universe—not much more than seven or eight pages of notes, by Lucas's reckoning, by the time the next draft (the fourth) came around. But it was enough to give him the confidence to throw in two references to the Clone Wars—one from Luke, the other in Princess Leia's hologram message. We learn that Kenobi served Leia's father during them. We get the picture. The Clone Wars were a World War II to this current Vietnam-like guerrilla action against the Empire (which, in the third draft, Luke calls the "Counter Wars"). Lucas would guard the Clone Wars' details more jealously than any other plot point; in years to come, they would be off-limits even to Lucasfilm's licensed writers. We would not find out who the clones were, or on whose side they had fought, for nearly three decades—during which time a million imaginary versions of the conflict would play out in a million minds.

Chewbacca comes to the fore in the third draft as well. Ralph McQuarrie's sketches of the creature, based on an image Lucas had provided him from a science fiction story magazine (McQuarrie added the bandolier), seemed to bring him into sharper relief in Lucas's mind. There was another influence in front of Lucas's face every day, of course. Wookiees may have gotten their species name from Bill Wookey, and Lucas may have been thinking about Wookiees ever since he chatted about them on the *Graffiti* set. But Chewbacca in particular—and the notion of him as Solo's copilot—came from the enormous Lucas dog, Indiana, strapped into the front seat of Marcia's car. Lucas was so enamored with Wookiees by the filming stage that, according to Mark Hamill, he once flirted with the idea of adding a Journal of the Whills–like framing device to the movie—one in which the whole narrative is a story being told by a mother Wookiee to her baby.

Then there is Han Solo, who in the third draft has become a full-fledged pirate rather than a cabin boy. He is ever more like Coppola, a suave huckster who can talk his way into anything, a foil to Lucas's Luke.

As Lucas tore through the third draft in mid-1975, Coppola was much on Lucas's mind. Coppola was at that point pressing his protégé to put his space fantasy hobby movie on the back burner and direct the hard-hitting Vietnam film he'd long talked about: *Apocalypse Now*. After *The Godfather: Part II*, Coppola could afford to write his own ticket. He wanted to be the producer and to whisk Lucas off to the Philippines pronto.

To Lucas's friends, this seemed like the smart move. Lucas was, after all, an independent movie guy. It was his turn to make a big statement, something dark and gritty: his *Chinatown*, his *Taxi Driver*. Kurtz had spent more time scouting for *Apocalypse* than he had for *Star Wars*. Lucas had been planning for the Vietnam movie for four years and writing *Star Wars* for just two. The last

American helicopters had left the rooftops of Saigon on April 30, 1975, just as Lucas was between his second and third *Star Wars* drafts. If he made *Apocalypse Now*, Lucas could help write the first draft of the conflict's history.

It would have been so easy to postpone the pain of *Star Wars*. One word to Coppola would have done it. There was still no agreement with Fox on the budget. In fact, Fox put the project on a moratorium in October, pending a December meeting of the whole board. Laddie was still a strong supporter, but even he was nervous about spending more than $7 million on the project. The chance of *Stars Wars* being made had never seemed more remote.

So what stopped Lucas from walking away? Why did he beg Coppola to wait and then finally, in frustration, tell him to go make *Apocalypse Now* himself?

To hear Lucas tell it, it was all about the kids. He'd been getting letters from teen fans about *American Graffiti*. They had been into drugs. Then they saw his movie, jumped in their cars, chased girls—it was pretty much all guys who wrote to Lucas—and "it really straightened some of them out," Lucas reported. That led him to wonder what a good old-fashioned adventure movie could do for younger kids who at that point had nothing to watch but *Kojak* and *The Six Million Dollar Man* and what Lucas called "movies of insecurity." Kids like Coppola's sons, ten-year-old Roman and twelve-year-old Gian-Carlo. Lucas talked to them about *The Star Wars*. They got it when the grown-ups didn't. (Roman would later become the first official member of the *Star Wars* fan club.)

But Lucas was also in too deep to quit now. He hadn't been sweating blood over the *Apocalypse* script like this; *Apocalypse* was John Milius's writing obsession. Lucas's interest in *Flash Gordon* preceded his interest in Vietnam. True, his vision of what *Apocalypse Now* should be was completely different from Coppola's. The George Lucas version would be "more man against machine than anything else," he said in 1977; "technology against humanity, and then how humanity won. It was to have been quite a positive vision." But it did not escape his attention that he was dealing with every one of those themes already in *Star Wars*, albeit in more shrouded allegorical form.

Besides, Lucas had just come across a fascinating book about telling stories through allegory, one written in 1949. He had digested hundreds of fairy tales by 1975, as he attempted to boil down some basic story elements for the *Star Wars* script, and this book jibed with a lot of things he'd been doing in picking apart story and myth and religious ritual. It was *The Golden Bough* as a user's manual. The author claimed that all tales could be boiled down to a single story with a defined arc. Borrowing a term from James Joyce, he called it the "monomyth."

The book was *The Hero with a Thousand Faces*. The author was Joseph Campbell.

The influence of Campbell's book on the original *Star Wars* has been overstated; it was far more influential in the drafting of the next two films. Kurtz eschews the influence of the book, and "the whole idea of *Star Wars* as a mythological thing," because "all coming-of-age stories fit that model, and Hollywood has done those kinds of stories since the beginning." He points out that the Campbell connection wasn't mentioned in interviews until after Lucas met the author in 1983. But Campbell's book did help Lucas tighten up his plot and may have encouraged him to make the first film's fairy tale connection more plain. As 1975 drew to a close, Lucas decided he wasn't writing an interstellar Bible story any more. He cut the "son of suns" line from the opening. In its place, he added:

> A long time ago, in a galaxy far, far away, an amazing adventure took place.

In the end, Lucas was simply guided by everything he liked. "*Star Wars* is a sort of compilation," he would tell an interviewer, "but it's never been put in one story before, never been put down on film. There is a lot taken from Westerns, mythology and samurai movies. It's all the things that are great put together. It's not like one kind of ice cream, but rather a very big sundae."

On January 1, 1976, Lucas finished the fourth draft. Barring one more minor revision, a good chunk of witty dialogue rewrites from Willard Huyck and Gloria Katz, and some cut scenes, this version is pretty much what audiences saw the following year. On December 13th, the Fox board had finally, officially agreed to a budget of $8.3 million. Another vital piece of good luck: *2001* was rereleased in 1975, and the movie finally broke even the same month the Fox board met. "We wouldn't have made *Star Wars* without the success of *2001*," says Charley Lippincott, the movie's marketing guru.

Another odd fact: *Star Wars* might never have been funded without the consent, or at least the consenting silence, of Grace Kelly. The Monaco princess had been named to the Fox board in July 1975, ostensibly to get away from her oppressive husband and back to Hollywood as often as possible. "She was fairly quiet about the whole thing," Laddie said when I asked him if he remembered the late princess's take on this tale of a galactic princess. "I didn't feel she was really that fond of it, but don't remember her saying anything negative." On a board that was bitterly divided over the movie Laddie had greenlit, her silence may have been enough to tilt the scales in favor of funding it. In any case, she got her reward in January 1978, when a rigged lottery gave Princess Grace and her children the very first preproduction set of *Star Wars* action figures.

Thus far Lucas had spent $473,000 of his own money on *The Star Wars*. He knew this dessert would take far more ingredients than could be bought for $8.3 million. That was a fairly low figure; the average studio comedy at the time, with no special effects, cost around $20 million. How on Earth could Lucas realize his vision on that budget? He cut the Alderaan prison scene from the script, placing that whole sequence aboard the Death Star, purely to save money. Instead he had the Death Star destroy Alderaan from a distance as a demonstration of its power. To us, in hindsight, it may seem like a natural fix; back then, it seemed more like having to take the banana out of the sundae.

Still, it was almost time to serve it up.

9.

SPOOF WARS

We tend to go overboard with hindsight when examining the history of something successful. We build creation myths out of the creation of a myth. The creator himself, seeking a simple solution to the questions he must answer over and over, is often more than happy to help in this deception.

But *Star Wars* was not made in a heavenly moment with the muses; it did not arrive on stone tablets. It was far more of a light, wispy thing. As tempting as it is to think of the entire franchise as some preordained feat of genius, it's far more revealing to view it as *Flash Gordon* fan fiction meets fairy tale, made by a film nerd who, suddenly finding himself with a lot of time and money on his hands, was experimenting more than anything else. "He acts now like he knew it was going to be a big hit," says Charley Lippincott. "He didn't. He was just farting around."

When did Lucas hit on the right formula? When he added a sense of humor to the stodgy old space-fantasy mixture. The jokes started to creep into the third draft, with its giggling Ben Kenobi, and really piled on in the fourth (with a little help from his friends). If you listen to the way Lucas talks about *Star Wars*, beyond responding to our loaded questions about myth and legend, there's a distinct sense of levity to his answers. Back in early post–*Star Wars* interviews he would talk about this strong sense of "effervescent giddiness" he'd detected in rewatching *American Graffiti* and *Star Wars* back to back; he felt the movies were of a piece. Later on he would half-joke that he wrote *Star Wars* to give *Mad Magazine* material. I've heard more than one fan express this notion: "George Lucas is trolling us all."

In 2010, on stage with his preferred interviewer, Jon Stewart, we saw the goofy way Lucas likes to play with the franchise even now. Stewart asked a question that had bugged him for years: On what planet was Obi-Wan Kenobi born? "This is one of the first things I wrote in the very first script," Lucas said. Really, responded Stewart. You're not just making this up? "No, I wouldn't do that. He comes from the planet Stewjon."

Lucas was joking and serious at once. The serious part came when Lucasfilm confirmed that yes, the planet of Stewjon, homeworld of Obi-Wan Kenobi, had now been added to the official *Star Wars* galactic atlas. Previously printed works that claimed Kenobi had been born on the planet of Coruscant, the galactic Imperial capital, were no longer accurate. The Creator had spoken.*

Should *Star Wars*, then, be classified as a comedy? Certainly one of the film's three lead actors thought so. "I laughed all through *Star Wars*," said Mark Hamill. "I thought they were comedies. It was absurd having a big giant dog flying your spaceship, and this kid from the farm is wacko for this princess he's never met, that he's seen in a hologram, the robots are arguing over whose fault it is. . . . They hook up with a magic wizard and they borrow a ship from a pirate. . . . It was goofier than hell!" No wonder Hamill would play Luke Skywalker just as fervently during his guest appearance on *The Muppet Show* as in the movies—for him, it was practically one and the same.

Of course, Hamill and his compadres played this humor deadpan, just the way Lucas does with his jokes. The movie was performed in earnest; there was to be no winking to the audience. Viewers might laugh, but they'd also be immersed in the galaxy Lucas had created. Come for the comedy; stay for the world building.

In a sense, Lucas and company have been performing an elaborate, Galactic-sized improv for decades, with participation from a massive troupe of improv artists. That explains why *Star Wars* has attracted more than its share of spoofs, skits, and whimsical fan-made ephemera over the years—and why those spoofs have almost all taken a surprisingly reverential approach to the source material. It seems everyone wanted in on the exact same joke Lucas was telling in the first place, laughing along with him rather than at him. Take Stormtroopers,

---

* And this wasn't even the first time the Creator had jokingly changed *Star Wars* canon on the fly to flatter a late-night talk show host. Chatting with Conan O'Brien in 2007, Lucas claimed that the full name of Death Star admiral Motti, the first Imperial to be force-choked by Darth Vader, was Conan Antonio Motti. The writer of the Lucasfilm novel *Death Star*, who had decided to give Motti the first name "Zi" in the book, had to scramble to change it.

who manage to look simultaneously badass and ridiculous. As seriously as the 501st takes its costume accuracy, it can't resist spoofing the Stormtroopers by holding, for example, Hawaiian shirt contests. "That's a powerful aspect of comedy: debasing authority figures," says Albin Johnson. "They're modern-day tin soldiers."

One of the most recent case studies of this planet-wide improv act is the Death Star White House petition. Here's how that got started. In January 2012, a student at the University of Leicester in England was watching *Return of the Jedi* when a question popped into his head about Star Destroyers. These sleek triangular battleships of the Galactic Empire are seen on screen at the beginning of every movie in the original *Star Wars* trilogy. Most of us look at them and think, *Wow*. Sean Goodwin looked at them and thought, *How much steel would it take to build those? Is there enough iron in the Earth to construct one?*

The question wasn't entirely idle. Sean had an old boarding school friend in the United States, Anjan Gupta, an Indian-born economics student at Lehigh University who was making a name for himself writing an economics blog for his class called *Centives*. In its first year, *Centives'* greatest scoop was proving that it was cheaper to pay for the buffet in the dining hall than to go on the meal plan, which irked the administration and won the blog a few hundred admirers. Then Anjan, on a whim after reading the Harry Potter books, had decided to calculate the cost of everything you'd need to go to Hogwarts' school for wizards. The resulting blog post went viral, getting picked up on CNN and *The Daily Show* and garnering more than ten million page views. It had been hard to go back to college-level blogging after that, so Anjan had enlisted Sean to help write more quirky pop culture economics entries.

Sean's first post, a calculation of how many zombies it would take to overthrow history's greatest armies, had seen little interest. Maybe Star Destroyers would do better? Or better yet, how about the largest piece of battle technology in the *Star Wars* universe: the planet-killing Death Star itself. "Because if you're going to ask for the impossible, let's find the most ridiculously impossible thing," laughs Sean.

Goodwin decided to focus on the original Death Star, also known as DS-1, whose dimension was easier to calculate than that of the filigree, half-finished-but-fully-operational version in *Return of the Jedi*. A quick Google search later, *Wookieepedia* gave him the diameter of DS-1: 160 kilometers, or roughly one-tenth the size of Earth's moon. Instead of spending weeks trying to estimate how many floors, hangars, elevators, ventilation shafts, and garbage mashers were in the DS-1—as a hardcore fan might—Sean simply assumed the steel distribution would be roughly similar to that of an aircraft carrier, because "they're both essentially floating weapons platforms."

So all Sean had to do was get a number for the amount of steel in an average-sized aircraft carrier and calculate the number of aircraft carriers that could fit inside the Death Star. Barely an hour later, he had his number: the Death Star contains one quadrillion tonnes (metric tons) of steel.

There was, Sean discovered, more than enough iron in the Earth's core to construct two million Death Stars. Assuming you could find a way to siphon it out, however, turning it into steel would take 833,315 years at the current rate of production. That, Sean reasoned, wouldn't make for a particularly interesting article: "The Death Star can be built, sort of." Almost as an afterthought, he wondered: How much would it cost? The answer, for the steel alone, was 852 quadrillion dollars, or 13,000 percent of global GDP. He wrote that at the bottom and emailed the entry to Anjan. Anjan loved the dollar amount so much he made it the headline. "We sat back and said, 'Well, that's a really big number. We don't need anything else,'" says Sean. "'Let's just put that on the Internet and see what happens.'"

At first, nothing happened. On its first day, the article got a few hundred readers and one comment: "Awesome!" On day 2 came the question "When do we get started?" Day 3 saw queries about the cost of copper for all the electronics, an offer of a wheelbarrow as seed capital, and an estimate of staffing requirements based on the same scale: thirty-four trillion crew members. But the article wasn't taking off in the same way the Harry Potter one had, and Anjan felt bad for telling Sean the Death Star post was going to go viral. Sean's response was legendary: "I cannot conceive of a world where people would not want to know this."

Then a popular economics blog, *Marginal Revolution*, picked the story up and got its readers chattering. An Australian newspaper reprinted it. Tech blogs started to take notice. *Forbes* added its own analysis, pointing out that you had to take into account the entire galactic GDP, not just that of one measly planet. *Mother Jones* quibbled over the cost of steel, putting it closer to 1.3 million times global GDP. By June, Paul Krugman was talking to *Wired* about just how much financial sense it made to build a $852 quadrillion Death Star.

Traffic to *Centives* exploded. The server crashed. Lehigh agreed to host the blog post on the university site. Anjan started taking his laptop to class, not hearing a word the professor said as he watched the page views stack up in real time.

But the real craziness began in November, when a man in Longmont, Colorado, identifying himself only as John D., started a petition on the White

House website, We the People. John D. demanded that the US government "secure funding and resources and begin construction on a Death Star by 2016" as a "job creation" measure. Nobody knows for sure if John D. was inspired by *Centives'* post, but every news story on the petition made mention of Sean's estimate. *Centives* actively promoted the petition, and in just two weeks it had secured the 25,000 signatures then required for a White House response.

In January, the White House responded. It wasn't required to do so in a timely fashion under the rules of We the People. Washington was deadlocked over the budget and debt negotiations known as the "fiscal cliff." This clearly frivolous petition could have been filed away in the virtual equivalent of a desk drawer for years. But President Obama, who had played with toy lightsabers on the White House lawn with the US Olympic fencing team and who had once been described as a Jedi Knight by George Lucas himself, couldn't resist. Paul Shawcross at the Office of Management and Budget was directed to draft a response. NASA was consulted. The result would shoehorn in just about every *Star Wars* reference known to a mainstream audience.

Titled "This isn't the petition response you're looking for," the response asked: "Why would we spend countless taxpayer dollars on a Death Star with a fundamental flaw that can be exploited by a one-man starship?" Shawcross pointed out that a human-made fortress called the ISS already orbited Earth—"that's no moon, it's a space station!"—and a laser-wielding robot was currently roaming Mars. He compared science and technology education to the Force, just so he could quote Darth Vader: "Remember, the Death Star's power to destroy a planet, or even a whole star system, is insignificant next to the power of the Force."

But for Sean and Anjan, the most important part of the letter came right at the beginning: "The construction of the Death Star has been estimated to cost more than $850,000,000,000,000,000," Shawcross wrote, with a link back to the Lehigh page. "We're working hard to reduce the deficit, not expand it." Later, Lucasfilm sent a tongue-in-cheek response from Galactic Empire Public Relations: "'The costs of construction they cited were ridiculously overestimated, though I suppose we must keep in mind that this miniscule planet does not have our massive means of production,' said Admiral Motti of the Imperial Starfleet."

The two bloggers were, so to speak, over the moon. "We wanted to see what the president had to say," says Anjan, "but we never expected to be referenced." It was a historic moment, to be sure: one student's idle thought while watching a *Star Wars* movie had gone all the way to the White House in the space of a year. And all it took was a Death Star reference, a little math, and a finely tuned sense of buffoonery.

An alien observer watching the hubbub surrounding the Death Star petition might well have surmised that our planet had lost its mind. Millions of us, including the leader of the free world, were caught up in what appeared to be an earnest discussion over building a "ridiculously impossible thing " a giant planet-destroying orbital laser a tenth the size of our Moon. The alien observer would probably be justified in vaporizing us for such talk.

It would be easy to miss the humor beneath the deadpan tone of the whole affair. It wasn't satirical; there was no target. *Star Wars* itself was not being mocked. The goal for the people who participated was to stay in character, as if they really were endeavoring to bring the "ultimate weapon" of *Star Wars* into our galaxy, here and now. The humor of the whole episode was predicated on people knowing and caring intently about details—some of them extremely minute—from the films and their attendant media.

The comments section on the *Marginal Revolution* blog post about the Death Star calculation is a case in point. Here, even now, sober economists hash out questions about the variables: Whether to factor in the slave labor of Wookiees (which was partly responsible for its construction, according to the novel *Death Star*). Or whether you could fund the whole thing from taxes on the population of Coruscant (which is said to have a trillion inhabitants, thus funding the Death Star at a cost of roughly $8,000 per person). Or whether a quality assurance engineer should have nixed a thermal exhaust port two meters wide that led directly to the main reactor shaft, and what effect this oversight might have had on the Empire's chances of getting an insurance policy on its second Death Star.

What's particularly odd is that these sorts of conversations have been going on for years and show no signs of slowing down. Perhaps the best known Death Star riff is captured in *Clerks*, the 1994 no-budget movie that made director Kevin Smith famous. One of the titular store clerks and his friend discuss the independent contractors who must have been aboard the second, under-construction Death Star when the Rebel Alliance blew it up. Wouldn't they have been innocent victims? A roofing contractor who happens to be listening in assures the clerks that no, in his experience, contractors have to make political decisions—for instance, whether to work for Jersey mobsters. Those people on the Death Star knew what they were getting into.

The *Clerks* contractors conversation prompted an equally goofy response, some years later, from George Lucas. In *Episode II*, Lucas included a scene in which we see the Geonosians, an insect race, handing over a hologram of what would become DS-1. "They would be the ones that were probably contracted to build the Death Star," Lucas said on the movie's DVD commentary track, casually contradicting the story of slave Wookiees. The *Clerks* characters, Lucas acknowledged, "were worried that they got killed on the Death Star, but they are after all just a bunch of large termites."

There's something about *Star Wars* that makes this kind of geeky rumination acceptable to a mainstream audience. (You can't imagine a roofing contractor saying the same thing about a Borg Cube from *Star Trek*.) Even when the aim is to be utterly silly, an earnestness emerges. This pattern was in evidence right from the start, in the very first *Star Wars* parody: *Hardware Wars*.

The writer-director of *Hardware Wars*, Ernie Fosselius, saw *Star Wars* the week it came out in 1977 and says he was already plotting the parody while he was in the theater. *Hardware Wars* was shot in four days by a bunch of broke twentysomethings—the Seans and Anjans of their day—in less than glamorous locations around San Francisco: the backs of bars, garages, and an abandoned French laundry. The costume designer provided the $8,000 budget. Fosselius and filmmaker Michael Wiese came up with the tagline: "you'll laugh, you'll cry, you'll kiss three bucks goodbye."

Hardware Wars was a twelve-minute version of *Star Wars* in the form of a trailer. On the surface, you might think it a zany low-budget parody and nothing more. The characters have names like Fluke Starbucker, Darph Nader, Augie Ben Doggie of the Red Eye Knights, Princess Anne-Droid with her cinnamon buns strapped on, Ham Salad, and Chewchilla the Wookiee Monster, a brown furry Cookie Monster puppet.

But there's a distinct sense of affection about *Hardware Wars*. The filmmakers are really trying, gosh darn it, to make a steam iron stand in for a Star Destroyer as it chases after a Rebel toaster, or to replicate the destruction of Alderaan with an exploding basketball. Fossellius and Weise hired veteran voice actor Paul Frees to narrate the whole trailer (and when they said "hired," it turned out they meant "agreed to do maintenance work for"). "His voice is so rich you actually think you are seeing 'incredible space battles,'" Wiese says, "when in fact it's only a Fourth of July sparkler."

Most of all, there was the assumption that everyone watching would be inherently familiar with the subject matter. It was a safe bet: this was San Francisco, after all, the first all–*Star Wars* city, the Creator's town, his first step in the conquest of the universe.

The bet paid off. *Hardware Wars* grossed $500,000 in a year. That was a 6,250 percent return on investment, making it one of the most successful short films of all time.

Lucas wasn't about to launch a lawsuit. He called *Hardware Wars* "a cute little film" and later declared it to be his favorite fan tribute. Wiese, flush with success, won a meeting with Alan Ladd Jr. and "three lawyers with expensive suits" at Fox. They watched the short, Wiese said, without so much as a giggle.

"Well, kid," said Laddie, "what do you want us to do?"

Wiese had no hesitation. "I want you to show this with *Star Wars*. You know, make fun of your own movie!"

"I'll get back to you," Laddie said.

"And I'm sure he will," Wiese said, decades later.

The closest Lucasfilm ever got to getting litigious over a parody came in 1980. *Mad Magazine* had mined *Star Wars* for material, exactly as Lucas had predicted. Now artist Mort Drucker and writer Dick De Bartolo had produced their send-up of the sequel, *The Empire Strikes Out*. Perhaps because there had been such a culture of secrecy around certain revelations in the plot of the original film, Lucasfilm's legal department sent a cease and desist letter, demanding that *Mad* turn over all profits made from the issue. *Mad* just smiled and sent back a copy of a letter from *Mad*'s number 1 fan: some guy named George W. Lucas.

"Special Oscars should be awarded to Drucker and DeBartolo, the George Bernard Shaw and Leonardo da Vinci of comic satire," Lucas had written. "Their sequel to my sequel was sheer galactic madness." He couldn't resist pointing out a gaping inconsistency in the parody—Han Solo appears in the *Millennium Falcon* several panels after he has been frozen in carbonite. "Does this mean I can skip *Episode VI*?" Lucas wrote, which was probably more of a cry for help than the magazine realized. "Keep up the good Farce!"

Lucasfilm's legal department never wrote *Mad* again. One of its members, Howard Roffman, told the magazine many years later the incident happened because no one in the legal office, then based in LA, had talked to anyone in San Anselmo about it. Charley Lippincott, meanwhile, had been actively sending *Mad* some *Star Wars* gags of his own. "I wrote them and said I didn't think they went far enough," Lippincott said. He chuckled at the legal department's temerity. "You can't sue *Mad Magazine*."

Like *Star Wars* itself, the parodies seemed to pretty much die out after the original trilogy ended in 1983. The one notable exception—Mel Brooks's feature-length *Spaceballs* in 1987—seemed outdated on arrival. "It should have been made several years ago, before our appetite for *Star Wars* satires had been completely exhausted," wrote Roger Ebert. "This movie already has been made over the last 10 years by countless other satirists." (A handful of the jokes, such as the princess's hair buns turning out to be ear warmers, arrived direct from *Hardware Wars*.)

But again, like *Star Wars*, the spoofs came roaring back in 1997, bigger and better than ever. That was the year a character designer at the Fox Kids Network named Kevin Rubio unveiled a film at San Diego Comic-Con called *Troops*. It was *Star Wars* meets *Cops*, the ride-along reality show known for its theme tune "Bad Boys," which Rubio also used.

Cops, not *Star Wars*, was the parody target of *Troops*: witness the Stormtrooper with the Minnesota accent who likes the "small town feel" of Tatooine and resolves domestic disputes with the world-weary diplomacy of local lawmen everywhere. Instead of being a send-up of *Star Wars*, *Troops* affectionately imitates the films as closely as possible. We get Stormtroopers on speeder bikes and brief shots of Imperial ships landing that wouldn't look out of place in the original trilogy. The CGI era had dawned, and far more was possible on a tight budget than in the *Hardware Wars* days.

If anything, *Troops* gets more immersive as it moves along. The ten-minute short turns out to be an elaborate alternate explanation for what happened to Luke Skywalker's Uncle Owen and Aunt Beru. Without the *Cops* layer, it would be an earnest fan film—which in some senses it still is. "I couldn't do a serious piece," lamented Rubio—for want of budget, he meant, not for want of trying. "The only person who can do a serious piece is George."

Troops was an instant sensation and inspired hundreds of other filmmakers. In 2010, it topped a *Time* list of the top 10 *Star Wars* fan films. Lucasfilm decided to embrace the genre and established the Official *Star Wars* Fan Film Awards; *Troops* won the "Pioneer Award." Other categories included best comedy, best mockumentary, and best parody of a commercial. Even the winners of the ultimate trophy, the George Lucas Selects Award, tended to be on the spoof side.

As Lucas embraced the parodies, the parodies embraced back. *George Lucas in Love* was a 1999 short by Joe Nussbaum, a recent USC graduate, and his fellow grads. Once again, the comedic target was something other than *Star Wars*: the recent Oscar winner *Shakespeare in Love* and the way it imagined the playwright's inspirations to be constantly in front of his face. Set at USC in 1967, and filmed on the campus, it showed Lucas struggling to write an agricultural fantasy called *Space Oats*, while a stream of influences surround him unheeded: a dorm-room rival breathing like Darth Vader with an asthma inhaler; a large, hairy, car-fixing friend; a Yoda-like professor. Finally there's his muse, Marion, who leads the "student rebellion," wears her hair in buns, and in a twist ending turns out to be Lucas's sister.

The short launched Nussbaum's directorial career after Steven Spielberg got hold of a copy and sent it to Lucas, who sent Nussbaum an approving letter commending him for doing his research (he'd spotted a line from *American Graffiti*.)

There's a kind of mutual love affair between Lucas and spoofs that feature him as a character. He is never the target; he is the sage one does not cross. A 2007 short called *Pitching Lucas* stars a Lucas look-alike who is offered three *Star Wars* live-action TV show ideas by sleazy Hollywood executives (variations on *Six Million Dollar Man*, *CHiPs*, and *Charlie's Angels*); Lucas dispatches each executive to a variety of grisly endings. "And that," he concludes, "is why I always write my own scripts." *Pitching Lucas* won the George Lucas Selects stamp of approval from the Creator himself, as did the 2004 short *Escape from Tatooine*, which ends with Boba Fett crash-landing on an alternate Earth where Lucas has been enshrined in a giant statue at the Lincoln Memorial.

It was surprisingly late in the day, the mid-2000s, before parodists started to explore the possibilities of putting Darth Vader in mundane situations. Perhaps they were taking the lead of Lucas, who had by then fleshed out all of Vader's backstory; perhaps they were simply waiting for the rise of YouTube. In 2007, users of the nascent online video service were treated to *Chad Vader, Day Shift Manager*, in which a Vader-like character (said to be the Dark Lord's brother) has to manage recalcitrant employees at a very Earth-bound supermarket. The pilot episode was seen twelve million times; the show went on for thirty-eight episodes split into four seasons. British comedian Eddie Izzard imagined Darth Vader attempting to navigate the Death Star canteen; a stop-motion version of the Izzard skit starring Lego *Star Wars* figures now has twenty-one million views on YouTube.*

---

* YouTube also offers some wonderfully surreal Dadaist cutups of the source material itself. *The Vader Sessions* (which has more than five million views) took every one of Vader's scenes in the original *Star Wars*—which amounted to a mere ten minutes—and dubbed in James Earl Jones quotes from other movies, modulated Vader-style. "I know you have been inconvenienced, and I am prepared to compensate you," Vader now says to the dead rebel troops in the corridor of the Tantive IV, in a line from *Coming to America*. "Shall we say one million American dollars? Very well then, two million!"

There was, it soon became clear, comedy gold in treating Vader—a Jedi-killing, child-murdering, daughter-torturing, son-amputating man-machine—as a fragile, everyday kind of fellow. "He's like the most evil guy in the galaxy, but there's a part of you that wants to know what that feels like," says Jack Sullivan, the thirty-two-year-old, Boston-based asset manager who runs @DepressedDarth, one of Twitter's most popular *Star Wars* parody accounts. Sullivan started the account in 2010 to promote a YouTube short he was planning to make of Vader walking around Boston begging for spare change. The short never got made, but the account gained more than five hundred thousand followers thanks to a steady diet of sad Vader jokes and *Star Wars* puns. Sullivan is already making a respectable $5,000 a month from selling ads on his Depressed Darth website and is considering retiring from the financial industry to go into full-time tweeting.

Perhaps the most telling Vader spoof, for an aging generation of parents who'd grown up on *Star Wars*, is Jeffrey Brown's *New York Times* best-selling volumes, *Darth Vader and Son* (2012) and *Vader's Little Princess* (2013). This was Vader at his most mundane, facing the challenges of single parenthood with Luke and Leia respectively in a series of heartwarming cartoons. Every modern mom or dad who'd identified with Luke or Leia in the 1970s, only to grow up and find themselves the Vaders of their households, could relate.

When everyone wants in on the joke, and the source material is this widely recognized, what you get is endless iterations of everything the franchise could possibly be. The first *Star Wars* spoof to win a Primetime Emmy—the epic *Star Wars Uncut*—could not have been more collaborative. The brainchild of twenty-six-year-old web developer Casey Pugh, *Star Wars Uncut* chopped the original movie into 473 segments lasting fifteen seconds each and then let fans sign up online to reshoot each segment in their own way—each with the no-budget earnestness of *Hardware Wars*, and each given roughly the same amount of time to shoot it (thirty days). It was so heavily oversubscribed that Pugh added an extra step, letting fans vote on the best versions of each segment. Stitch them together, and you get two hours of nonstop gut-busting hilarity—humor born of the shock of recognition (it's basically the same movie) as well as the gleefully earnest recreations by delightful amateurs.*

So there are certain common elements in this litany of *Star Wars* spoofs. They either add to the myth in some subtle, subversive way, or they lovingly

---

* I was particularly amused to discover a couple of my friends had made it into the movie. The husband played Han Solo. The wife, eight months pregnant, played Jabba the Hutt.

replicate it; they add a layer of something else in pop culture or put *Star Wars* concepts in incongruous, mundane situations. But the idea of *Star Wars* is always respected. The franchise's reality is unsullied; if anything, it is boosted by the flattery. *Star Wars*, it turns out, is a broad church, able to absorb all laughter.

Is any comedian truly capable of getting under the skin of *Star Wars*, skewering it more than wallowing in a version of it? There have been a few attempts. In 2007, a couple of friends with animated TV shows—Seth McFarlane, creator of *Family Guy*, and Seth Green, cocreator of Cartoon Network's *Robot Chicken*—began to use their respective platforms to produce some epic *Star Wars* meta-next-level spoofs. It's fair to say Green had the idea first (as his character, Chris, complains on the *Family Guy* spoof, "Blue Harvest"*). It's also fair to say, as McFarlane's character shoots back, that *Family Guy* has the larger viewership.

"Blue Harvest," which got the greatest audience share of any *Family Guy* episode to date, goes the route of layering its Griffin family humor over a *Star Wars* animated homage. It does have a few moments of true satire—such as the opening crawl, which marvelously manages to both spoil and belittle the entire classic trilogy:

> It is a time of civil war, and renegade paragraphs floating through space.
> There's cool space battles, and the bad guy is the good guy's dad, but you don't find that out 'til the next episode.
> And the hot chick is really the sister of the good guy, but they don't know it, and they kiss. Which is kind of messed up. I mean, what if they had done it instead of just kissed?

After that, there is the occasional joke aimed squarely at the holes in *Star Wars* logic, such as the laser operators on the Star Destroyer who let R2-D2 and 3-CPO's escape pod go because there were no life forms on board: "Hold your fire? What, are we paying by the laser now?" But McFarlane seems to lose interest in attacking the franchise at that point, falling back on his usual winning blend of toilet humor and pop culture callbacks. His *Star Wars* references for most of the feature-length episode consist of lovingly recreated, animated homages to iconic special effects scenes from the movie, such as the *Millennium Falcon* taking off from Mos Eisley. One of the most irreverent popular satirists

---

* Named for the undercover title for *Return of the Jedi*.

of our age, it turned out, could little more attack the franchise than throw a chair through a stained-glass window. For the "Blue Harvest" DVD release, McFarlane traveled to Skywalker Ranch and conducted an unusually fawning interview with Lucas.

Green's stop-motion puppet show *Robot Chicken* kept its satirical knives out for the franchise itself far longer than McFarlane did, even though its spoof was supposed to be a one-off sketch. In "The Emperor's Phone Call" (three million YouTube views), Emperor Palpatine is informed of the destruction of the Death Star (there it is again, the most humorous object in the universe) via collect call from Vader. The conversation that follows skewers both *Star Wars* and *Return of the Jedi*. "I'm sorry, I thought my Dark Lord of the Sith could protect a small thermal exhaust port that was only two meters wide. That thing wasn't even fully paid off yet!" yells the Emperor, voiced by McFarlane. "Oh, just rebuild it? That'd be real fucking original!" It was as if *Mad* had finally gone far enough for Charley Lippincott.

To Lucasfilm's great surprise, Lucas—encouraged by his son Jett to watch the show—adored the *Robot Chicken* parody. The Creator brought Green and his cowriter Matthew Senreich to Skywalker Ranch. The pair got Lucas to not only agree to two full-length Robot Chicken *Star Wars* episodes, but to participate as voice talent—his first professional acting role. "I don't know what I was thinking," said Lucas, as his doll reclined on a couch in a therapist's office, on his decision to let *Robot Chicken* do a special. But Lucas's participation didn't preclude the sketches from pointing out more previously unseen flaws in the movies. Take the moment Luke sits down in the *Millennium Falcon* after escaping the Death Star, and Leia puts a blanket over his shoulders as he mourns Obi-Wan Kenobi. "I can't believe he's gone," says Luke. Instead of sympathy, the *Robot Chicken* version of Leia offers this: "Oh, did the eighty-year-old man you met yesterday just die? Sorry if I didn't notice. I was just busy thinking about my entire family and the other two billion people from Alderaan who were just vaporized into dust about three hours ago." Leia's voice was provided by Carrie Fisher, who read it like she'd wanted to say that for a long time.

No matter how edgy the pair got, it didn't seem to matter. Green and Senreich soon found themselves the court jesters of Lucasfilm Animation. They collaborated on a new project, which they and Lucas announced to fans at Lucasfilm's Celebration convention in 2011, called *Star Wars Detours*, aimed at more of a family audience. Six trailers were released online. Fans didn't take to it. "It seems the show is really just *Robot Chicken* neutered," sighed *Badass*

Digest, one of the few news sites to cover it. After Disney bought Lucasfilm, *Detours* was put aside. Those six trailers were taken down from YouTube. Nearly forty episodes had been completed, but at time of writing, remained unseen. Said Green: "We didn't think it made any sense, in anticipation of these new movies coming out, to spend the next 3 years with an animated sitcom as kids' first introduction to the *Star Wars* universe." Especially not if the humor of that sitcom was to fall flat with the *Star Wars*–loving adults who would invariably watch it.

That's the danger with Star Wars spoofing—you're always just one step away from widespread derision if you say something jarring, or if you don't quite catch the elusive effervescent giddiness of the movies. Obama may be the *Star Wars* president, but even he messed up a month after the Death Star petition response, mangling his franchises in a later speech, joking that he wasn't going to "somehow do a Jedi mind-meld" on Congress. Millions of *Star Wars* geeks and Trekkers suddenly cried out in anguish: the president had conflated "Jedi mind trick" with "Vulcan mind meld."

Which brings us to the coda to the whole *Centives* affair. In December 2012 Sean Goodwin tried another whimsical Death Star post suggested by a commenter: How long would it take to mop all the floors on the Death Star? Sean did the math on the floor space—359.2 million square kilometers, roughly the area of the Earth—and figured it would take 11.4 million years' worth of hours to mop it all. To get the job done in a year would take forty-eight million workers; if they all took minimum wage, the mopping would cost $723 billion a year.

The article went nowhere. No one cared about mopping the Death Star. Why had it failed while its predecessor succeeded? "Suspension of disbelief," suggested Anjan. "People could just about imagine building a Death Star, but not keeping it clean. They assumed robots would do it."

Their brush with intergalactic greatness was over. Sean and Anjan handed the keys to the *Centives* blog over to a new generation. Anjan became a management consultant in New York, and Sean taught English in Bangkok. They fondly remember the days when their ridiculously impossible idea went all the way to the White House, but they don't really claim too much credit. "We were inspired by the Death Star because it's the Death Star," Anjan said. "What really sparked it all was the fact that *Star Wars* made a difficult concept seem real."

10.

STAR WARS HAS A POSSE

By December 1975, the month the Fox board met to decide the fate of *Star Wars*, George Lucas had all his difficult concepts in place. He was wrapping up the fourth draft and knew how most of the pieces would fit together. He had explained the Force in twenty-eight words. The Stormtroopers now carried blasters, not lightsabers (though the lightsaber-carrying tubes on the back of their costumes would last into the movie, like a vestigial tail). The Death Star came into focus, no longer eclipsed by long scenes on Alderaan.

The flow of blood onto the page was ebbing, and Lucas was even starting to enjoy himself. "I've loosened up a little bit," he confessed to Charley Lippincott. "It's more fun to have other people make suggestions, so you don't have to do all the work."

Loosened up, of course, is a relative term; 1976 would see Lucas drive himself harder than ever—into sickness, into the hospital. He would have trouble del- egating simple tasks such as which lights to turn on or off during a given shot, leading to friction with his more experienced British crew. But at the same time, Lucas had overcome his instinct to go it alone. He would solicit more advice than ever before—more than with *THX*, cowritten with Walter Murch, or *American Graffiti*, cowritten with Huyck and Katz. This was a big universe, and he was still building it—some of it from spare parts. There was a lot of room for other craftspeople, so long as Lucas trusted their competence.

Star Wars, then, was no longer just a script written in agonizing isolation on a door desk. As 1976 dawned, Lucas found himself the ringleader in a circus of genius, the head of one of those once-in-a-generation teams of fiery young turks eager to prove themselves. As seems appropriate, given the influence it drew from Westerns, *Star Wars* had a posse—and it was more vital in producing the look, feel, and content of the film than history, seeking a single creator, has given it credit for. Lucas himself understood the power of teamwork and appreciated the contributions of any collaborators already in his inner circle. The Creator, said Ralph McQuarrie, "was very happy if you came up with ideas that were very different."

McQuarrie, who died in 2012, remains the most beloved and most crucial member of the *Star Wars* posse. His production paintings pushed the wavering Fox board into Lucas's camp in December 1975: "McQuarrie sold it, needless to say," said Lippincott, who put together that crucial presentation. Without McQuarrie, Lucas might never have gotten the budget he needed to make his "little space thing." But the artist had many more contributions to the franchise.

We've already seen how McQuarrie helped create the mechanized version of Vader and the heartbreakingly human droids. He also casually offered a floating block orb from an animated film he'd been working on; this became the robot that tortures princess Leia. McQuarrie's sketches and paintings would inform the look of every character and every set, from the Jawa droid market to the Death Star to the fourth moon of Yavin, where Lucas wanted the rebel ships to be outside in the jungle. But they're in hiding, McQuarrie pointed out. They should have their ships squirreled away somewhere. How about inside a temple?

Like Lucas, McQuarrie started to think up backstory that would never make it onto the screen. He was fond of dozing off on a comfortable couch, allowing ideas to rise unbidden "like bubbles in champagne," he said. In one such liminal moment he saw the rebel ships on Yavin IV taking refuge in ancient temples with a special kind of stone that counteracted gravity, allowing the fighters to move in and out of the hangar more easily.

McQuarrie, self-effacing to the end, would argue that any decent artist could have gotten *Star Wars* past the Fox board. Other artists disagree. "If I had a hundred people working for me, none would come up with what Ralph imagined," says Paul Bateman, a concept artist who collaborated with McQuarrie in his later years. Bateman helps take care of McQuarrie's extensive archive. "Artistically, *Star Wars* is Ralph's vision, even when he felt he was just interpreting the words."

Star Wars wasn't only Lucas and McQuarrie's baby, of course—not by a long shot. There was producer Gary Kurtz, the posse's longest-serving member. Kurtz fell out with Lucasfilm after he allowed *Empire Strikes Back* to go massively over-budget, as we'll see, which may explain why the company's official history tends to underplay his contribution. But it seems fair to say that Kurtz was the kind of sounding board Lucas needed at this stage in his career, the kind that talked back. For example, Kurtz studied comparative religion in college, with a particular interest in Buddhism, Hinduism, and Native American religions. He was earnestly unhappy about the way the Force was treated in those early drafts, the way it seemed to get all its energy from the Kaiburr Crystal. He also wasn't a fan of the Bogan and Ashla concepts that lingered on, even into the third draft. He showed Lucas a lot of his college textbooks. There was plenty of time, as the years dragged on, for director and producer to chew this sort of thing over. "We did have long discussions about various religious philosophies and how people related to them and how we could simplify it," Kurtz remembers. Whether Lucas was on that path already with his *Golden Bough* studies, or whether Kurtz nudged him in the right direction in some late night talk about karma, *prana*, and the universal energy of the Navajo, is a question that will likely never be resolved.

What is black and white: if *Star Wars* had won the Best Picture Academy Award it was nominated for, it would have been Kurtz alone bounding onto the stage to accept it, and with good reason. He took charge of the constant, penny-pinching budget revisions required by Fox. He scouted for the best combination of experienced workers and low-cost soundstages and chose Elstree Film Studios, hidden in the drab wasteland of a suburb called Borehamwood, just outside of London. He made some unusual but brilliant hires, including John Mollo, an expert in military uniforms and historical dramas who would win an Academy Award for his costume design in *Star Wars*.

Kurtz also hired Ben Burtt as sound designer, on the recommendation of Walter Murch. Burtt would go on to become one of the most significant and long-lasting members of the *Star Wars* posse; he's still in it today. Again, it was the McQuarrie paintings that sold it to him; "Immediately, I could see this was the kind of movie I'd tried to make as a kid," said Burtt, an amateur camera enthusiast. Back then Burtt was the epitome of the young and hungry Lucas employee, fresh out of school, whip-smart, but not too proud to be a gofer. He ran Carrie Fisher to hairstyle test appointments; he went to the zoo and asked for a bear to be starved for a day, then have a bowl of milk and bread wafted under its nose so he could gain enough anguished hunger to make the roar that became, with the judicious application of a sea lion, the sound of a Wookiee. "Bears in zoos are too content," explains Burtt.

Still, Burtt set his expectations really low, as did much of the posse. It wasn't humility so much as a sign of the times, of how ridiculous it was to think that any kind of space movie could go mainstream. He though it might do well for a couple of weeks. "The best thing I could imagine," said Burtt, "was that we would get to have a table at next year's *Star Trek* convention."

As crucial as the behind-the-scenes posse was, the movie would have gone nowhere without the right on-screen posse. That meant getting the casting just right, which was especially difficult considering Lucas was mostly looking for unknown actors to populate his galaxy. *Star Wars* boasted a trio of talented casting directors—Vic Ramos, Irene Lamb, and Diane Crittenden—but the most influential voice in casting the lead actors turned out to belong to a guy who wasn't on the books at all. Fred Roos had assembled the unparalleled ensembles of *The Godfather* for Coppola and *American Graffiti* for Lucas. He had since gone on to producing Coppola's movies *The Godfather: Part II* and *The Conversation*. For *Star Wars*, "George just asked me to come along and consult," Roos recalls. "I was never hired, so to speak. I was just family."

Roos's first contribution was to push for a friend of his, the teenage daughter of Hollywood icon Debbie Reynolds and her long-ago ex-husband Eddie Fisher, for the role of Princess Leia. Roos had hung out with Carrie Fisher on a number of occasions and found her to be charming and sexy with a quick wit and a nascent writing talent. Fisher did herself no favors by missing the first casting call; she was enrolled in the Central School of Speech and Drama in London at the time and didn't think it worth skipping class for. But Roos kept bringing her name up with Lucas, who was leaning toward choosing actress Terri Nunn for the role.

Lucas finally met Fisher when she was back in LA over the Christmas break—on December 30, 1975. He asked her to read the speech that Leia gives in hologram form to R2-D2. At that point, the speech was extremely wordy. Many actresses had been defeated by it. But Fisher had just been schooled in elocution. She had gained a mild British accent and a propensity for tongue twisters. Her favorite was, and remains, "I want a proper cup of coffee from a proper copper coffee pot. If I can't have a proper cup of coffee from a proper copper coffee pot, I'll have a cup of tea." She nailed the speech.

Roos's second contribution to *Star Wars*—albeit a more unintentional one—was to bring in Harrison Ford, whom he had hired for that bit role back on *American Graffiti*. Lucas was adamant that no one who had appeared in *American Graffiti* would also appear in *Star Wars*; he had a stubborn notion that it would distract the audience. But after Roos brought Ford in to do some carpentry around the American Zoetrope office in LA, where casting meetings were held, Lucas decided to have Ford read the role of Han Solo opposite a string of potential Princess Leias and Luke Starkillers.

All other versions of this story have credited Roos with a clever piece of manipulation in throwing Ford into Lucas's path like that. It's a nice story, Roos says, before reluctantly admitting that wasn't his intention—the Zoetrope office just happened to need a new door, and he knew a carpenter. "Harrison had done a lot of carpentry for me; he needed money, he had kids, he wasn't a big movie star yet," Roos says. "The day he was doing it, George happened to be there. It was serendipitous." Credit that missing door, then, for one of the great scoundrels of cinematic history.

As for Luke Starkiller, Lucas liked a TV actor called Will Seltzer. He had earlier dismissed a young soap opera actor known for his role in *General Hospital*, Mark Hamill. But the casting directors insisted that Lucas see Hamill again, and brought him in on December 30, the same day Carrie Fisher finally showed up. Like Fisher, Hamill had memorized one of the most wordy pieces of dialogue his character had in the third draft; like Fisher, he nailed it.

Still, the casting wasn't a sure thing. Lucas ended up with two slates of actors for the three main roles: Ford, Hamill, and Fisher on one hand; Christopher Walken, Will Seltzer, and Terri Nunn on the other. The first slate was chosen simply because they were available and willing to shoot in London (and in Hamill's case, Tunisia) that March. All accepted the fee Lucas offered them: $1,000 a week. Ford demanded a change in his contract: he wasn't interested in the sequels George kept talking about and didn't want to be obligated to appear in them. It would be reasonable to assume they were just going to be carbon copies of the original.

Fox was pushing for at least one big name in the cast. Lucas reportedly made overtures to Toshiro Mifune, one of the most famous actors in Japan and a star of Kurosawa movies. He had played the fearsome Samurai general in *Hidden Fortress* and a tempestuous wannabe knight in *Seven Samurai*. Lucas offered Mifune the role of Obi-Wan Kenobi, according to Mifune's daughter Mika; later she claimed her father was also offered Darth Vader. In any case, it came to naught.

Alec Guinness just happened to be in LA playing a butler in a satirical movie, *Murder by Death*, at the end of 1975. The venerable British actor was a legend of Ealing comedies as well as weightier roles, such as his Oscar-winning obsessive Lt. Colonel Nicholson in *Bridge Over the River Kwai*, a movie Lucas had seen and loved as a kid. Lucas and Kurtz made overtures, sending a screenplay to Guinness's hotel. Guinness's first reaction wasn't encouraging: "Good God, it's science fiction! Why are they offering me this?" The dialogue was "pretty ropey," he wrote. But he did agree to meet Lucas for dinner before he left town, encouraged by the fact that his director on *Murder by Death* respected Lucas's works so far: "There's a real filmmaker."

In his diary, Guinness remembered a "small neat-faced young man" with "poorish teeth, glasses and not much sense of humor." There wasn't much of a connection: "the conversation was divided culturally by eight thousand miles and thirty years." Still, Guinness liked Lucas's description of Kenobi as Gandalf-like, which gave him something to work with. And he could get on with Lucas, Guinness thought, "if I can get past his intensity."

In January, Lucas and Kurtz offered Guinness an intense sum to appear in the film: $150,000, as much as Lucas was getting paid to write and direct it. Guinness would also get 2 percent of Kurtz's profit points. The script was a little silly, and the points probably wouldn't mean anything, Guinness reasoned, but the salary would at least allow him to live in the style to which he was accustomed if his latest West End play was a flop.

As 1976 dawned, Lucas rushed up and down the California coast trying to take care of a laundry list of items before heading to London to begin filming. Dykstra's special effects operation in Van Nuys was running far behind schedule, and Lucas got to know the nine a.m. Monday Pacific Southwest Air (PSA) jet from SFO to LAX very well, with its large painted smile underneath the nose. He spent more than $8,200 on plane tickets and rental cars (which Fox still hadn't agreed to cover). On a typical day in LA, he would get up at three a.m. to do twenty-five storyboards, finish them in time for a nine a.m. casting meeting, and then go to ILM until nine p.m. That brutal schedule didn't factor in Lucas's obsessive revisions to the fourth draft of the script. "A writer-director ends up working 20 hours a day," he complained to Lippincott; it was only a slight exaggeration.

Some of those working hours were enough to make Lucas miss the agony of writing. At ILM, Lucas and Dykstra were already butting heads over how long it was taking to build the revolutionary camera system, the Dykstraflex. Despite its name, the Dykstraflex was a group effort between all the artist-engineers at ILM. It was a Frankenstein's monster of old VistaVision cameras hooked up to the spaghetti wires of integrated computer circuits. In theory, and there were an awful lot of theories involved in the Dykstraflex, you could program it to move through seven axes of motion. In other words, it should be able to swoop up, around, over and under one spaceship model, giving the model the illusion of perfect movement. And because you could simply repeat the same program for the next ship, when you spliced them together, you could make it look like one was following the other.

Assembly of the Dykstraflex had put the nascent ILM far behind schedule, but Dykstra was proving hard to motivate. Lucas's friends heard complaints that ILM under Dykstra and his young charges had become a "hippy commune," although the special effects wunderkind preferred the term "Country Club." Weed was smoked freely; these young geniuses, most in their early twenties, were often stoned out of their gourds. A tiny "cold tub" was set up outside to escape the heat of the warehouse. At night they would blast old spaceship prototypes into the sky and watch the occasional porno. Still, there was reason to tolerate all this: if the Dykstraflex worked, it could cut the cost of special effects in half.

ILM's artists were proud of their spaceship models, but there was already a major problem with one of them. Local stations across the United States had started screening *Space: 1999*, a science fiction TV show imported from the UK, in late 1975. It was set on the moon, which is knocked out of orbit and into interstellar space by a nuclear explosion. *Space: 1999* had been aimed at the US market, with American actors and a hefty $3 million special effects budget for the first season. It was bad enough that the characters mentioned a "mysterious force" that was supposedly guiding the moon's journey or talked about the problems of "going to the dark side" (of the moon). Worse that the moonbase's major ship, the *Eagle*, looked a lot like Han Solo's long, sleek pirate vessel, which ILM model makers had just completed, and which Lucas had just named in the fourth draft: the *Millennium Falcon*. *Eagle*, *Falcon*: Lucas was going to look like a plagiarist.

So ILM had to come up with a bold and costly new design,* and the answer to the question of who gets the credit for it is as fuzzy as the *Falcon's*

---

* The original *Falcon* had cost $25,000—a third of the whole model budget. It was reused as the rebel ship at the beginning of the movie, the *Tantive IV*.

copilot. The official Lucasfilm account has Lucas coming up with the concept on a plane, basing it on a hamburger. But Joe Johnston, who'd painted the first *Falcon* and was to become one of the franchise's most important visionaries, remembers Lucas's only instruction as "think of a flying saucer"; Johnston thought that too cheesy and 1950s, and added the other essential elements of sticking the old ship's cockpit to one side and adding those large pincers at the front. Still a third story I heard from a Lucasfilm veteran is that Lucas had a eureka moment in the ILM cafeteria: peeling the bun from his burger—Lucas ate a lot of burgers in those days—he stuck an olive on one side and made the tines of a fork represent the front. That sounds like a classic Lucas moment: lightly, unself-consciously building something unusual out of whatever was to hand; sketching the big picture and leaving it to others to work out the details. "Look around you," Lucas once told Howard Kazanjian, his old USC friend whom he tried to bring into the *Star Wars* posse but who had too many other movie commitments at the time. "Look around you. Ideas are everywhere."

Ideas, props, and happy accidents were everywhere in London, too. While Lucas was readying his California crew, their counterparts in England were laying vital groundwork for the deliberately grimy, scuffed-up props and sets that were soon to take shape at Elstree.

Production designer John Barry had his team scouring junkyards and flea markets for washers, pipes, parts of cameras, parts of guns. It was all in the best British tradition, as science fiction shows in the United Kingdom did not normally have *Space: 1999* budgets. Prop masters had to get creative; *Doctor Who* had literally begun in a London junkyard thirteen years earlier. That was fine with Lucas, who was looking for a kitbashing aesthetic himself. "I'm trying to make props that don't stand out," he told Lippincott. "I'm working very hard to keep everything nonsymmetrical. I want it to look like one thing came from one part of the galaxy and another from another."

The used universe: it was the same concept Lucas had for *THX*. This time it came with nonsymmetrical clothing, not blinding white uniforms. John Mollo made do on a budget of $90,000—less than the cost of a single set. In his sketchbook, amidst phone numbers and to-do lists, and notes on how much he'd spent parking, you can see Mollo's naive early images slowly transform into the characters we know today. Darth Vader's costume, perhaps the most infamous villain's outfit in all of cinema, cost Mollo a mere $1,100 to put together, mostly out of motorcycle leathers. Luke's costume cost twice that;

Mollo assembled it out of a pair of white jeans, boots, and a Japanese-style robe.

The first shoot of the film took place in the Tunisian desert, with the critical—and at times unexpected—gear provided by Barry and Mollo's teams. When Kurtz had to charter a Lockheed Hercules to fly some forgotten equipment from London to Tunisia—spending $22,000 to move $5,000 worth of essential gear—it just so happened that there was space on the plane for a skeleton the British crew had uncovered; a diplodocus from the Disney movie *One of Our Dinosaurs Is Missing*, shot at Elstree a couple of years earlier. Up went the cry: just throw it on the plane. That became the skeleton we see when Threepio and Artoo crash land on the desert planet. In later years it was named the Krayt dragon and, like many other things in the *Star Wars* universe, given a weighty backstory by someone other than George Lucas.

The adversity of that Tunisia shoot would become legendary. A truck carrying robots caught fire. A freak thunderstorm, the first in that location in fifty years, devastated the set. The remote control R2-D2 wouldn't move the way it was designed to. Kenny Baker, the diminutive actor inside one version of the trashcan droid, kept falling over. Anthony Daniels, encased in C-3PO for the first time, managed to rip the fiberglass costume at the leg, soaking the shards in decidedly un-droid-like blood.

Lucas was "compromising left and right" to get the shoot done. Still, even as they shot, he kept tinkering with the fourth draft, on a French typewriter where the keys were all wrong. Here he had his last major revelation about the script, which had to do with the Death Star. Here's the problem as it stood: The "dirty half dozen," as Lucas called them—Luke, Han, Obi-Wan, two droids, and a Wookiee—arrive in the *Millennium Falcon*. The dirty half dozen, plus one Princess, leave in the *Falcon*. If they all slipped in and out unchallenged, what threat was this mighty battle station? There needed to be some sacrifice—something to make clear that the Death Star was a danger to be reckoned with.

Marcia Lucas, a reluctant part of the *Star Wars* posse from the very beginning, had two suggestions. The first was to kill Threepio, which Lucas simply couldn't bring himself to do. Then she suggested sacrificing another character, one who had nothing to do after the Death Star but utters a few sage statements during the final dogfight. In retrospect, it's obvious: Obi-Wan Kenobi must die during his lightsaber battle with Darth Vader.

The venerable Sir Alec and Lady Merula Guinness had only just arrived in Tunisia. A party was arranged for his birthday. He was getting into the used universe spirit: before his first scene, the great actor rolled around in his costume on the desert floor. Having coaxed the famous man this far, Lucas was loath to cut him out so quickly; he would wait till they got back to London to make the final decision.

In the meantime, Lucas added a couple more changes in the revised script. First, he wanted to find a new name for the planet Tunisia was supposed to represent. For one thing, *Star Trek* fans might point out that the name, Utapau, sounded a little too much like T'Pau, a famous female Vulcan character. For another, Lucas had developed a useful habit of saying the names he was writing aloud; if he ever faltered on the pronunciation, he went looking for alternatives. Luckily there was a nearby city in Tunisia Lucas liked the sound of. The Tunisians transliterate it from the Arabic most commonly as Tataouine. Lucas decided to spell it Tatooine.

Second, Lucas needed to find a new name for the character played by Mark Hamill, the only leading American actor who had come to Tunisia for the shoot. Lucas was sick of people asking him if "Luke Starkiller" had anything to do with cult murderer Charles Manson, sometimes known as the Star Killer. This conflation of the two meanings for "star" would continue to dog Lucas; Fox's marketing department complained that people would assume *The Star Wars* was a movie about conflict between Hollywood luminaries. The studio's market research, which consisted of posing twenty questions to passersby in a mall, also concluded that people would confuse the title with *Star Trek*. And most urgently, the majority of respondents, fatigued by Vietnam, simply didn't care to see any more films with "war" in the title. Lucas and Kurtz postponed conflict over the name by removing the definite article and asking Fox executives to come up with alternate names for the film. They failed to do so because "there weren't a lot of people there who were that interested" one way or the other, says Kurtz. As far as Lucas was concerned, pre-Tunisia, the full title of the movie was *The Adventures of Luke Starkiller as taken from the "Journal of the Whills," Saga I, Star Wars.*

For the name of Luke's character, at least, Lucas was prepared to compromise. He dragged up his second-choice name from the first draft: thus Luke Skywalker reentered the *Star Wars* universe, this time as a young hero, and the Starkiller name was put on ice (until 2008, that is, when "Starkiller" became the name of Darth Vader's apprentice in the video game *Force Unleashed*). Luckily, no dialogue would have to be reshot. Luke's full name isn't mentioned in the script until he announces it to Leia on the Death Star, a scene that would be shot back in London.

Luke's inspiration, meanwhile, had driven himself into the ground. Lucas described himself as "depressed" and "desperately unhappy." He shunned the Tunisia wrap party in favor of sleep. Worse days awaited him in London.

I n April 2013, speaking at Windsor Castle before the queen and an audience of British film luminaries, Lucas would put a nostalgic gloss on his early trips to London: "I've been coming here since 1975," he says, "so for me this is like a second home." To drive home the point, he added a curious use of the royal we: "The White House, the government there, doesn't support the film industry the way we do in Britain."

But in 1976, during one of the hottest summers on record, Lucas's experience of Britain—and especially its film industry—was ghastly. The crew was openly hostile to the "crazy American" and his children's film. "80 percent of the crew of the original movie thought it was a load of rubbish and said so at the time," said Pat Carr, production coordinator. "Some very high-up people who should have known better were overheard on the set saying that Kurtz and Lucas didn't know what they were doing." The greatest offender was Gil Taylor, director of photography and veteran of the *Dambusters*, but even Anthony Daniels, a true believer in Threepio as a character, thought the film itself was "rubbish." Taylor gave Lucas bright, blazing studio lights instead of the more natural documentary lighting he asked for. The cleaning department kept wiping down the unclean "used universe" surfaces.

It was all too much for Lucas. There were a thousand people on the payroll, compared to the fifteen crew members he had for *American Graffiti*. He barely talked to the British crew. Kurtz, also not the world's most talkative person, was left to play intermediary. Elstree was a strict union shop; there were mandatory twice-daily tea breaks (taken on the go, with tea ladies wheeling carts and assistants delivering mugs to their superiors) and an hour-long lunch. Work would end at five thirty sharp—unless they were in the middle of a scene, in which case the crew would vote on whether to continue for another fifteen minutes. Lucas always pushed for a vote; it always went against him.

Alec Guinness was frustrated with the "hot, boring and indecisive" shoot. Lucas's bad news—or at least the young director's handling of it—didn't seem to have helped. In the Lucasfilm version of events, Guinness was mollified after Lucas took him out to lunch to explain the importance of Obi-Wan's sacrifice. But on April 12, a week after the crew had returned to England and the other American stars had joined them there, Guinness wrote in his diary that

Lucas still hadn't made up his mind to kill him off or not. "A bit late for such decisions," he fumed. "Harrison Ford referring to me as the Mother Superior doesn't help." Four days later: "I regret having embarked on the film . . . it's not an acting job. The dialogue, which is lamentable, keeps being changed and only slightly improved."

The dialogue changes came courtesy of Willard Huyck and Gloria Katz. Lucas had invited the couple to England to give the fourth draft a final polish, for a one-off payment of $15,000. Modestly, he estimated they tweaked about 30 percent of the script. That may be overstating the case. Still, pick a sharp and witty line in *Star Wars*, particularly one of Han Solo's, and chances are it came from Huyck and Katz's typewriter. For example:

> In the holographic chess scene where Threepio suggests a new strategy to Artoo: "Let the Wookiee win."
> Inside the Death Star, where Luke persuades Han that Leia has more wealth than he can imagine, and Han responds: "I don't know—I can imagine quite a bit."
> Further into the rescue attempt, where Han has a nervous conversation over the intercom with a Death Star commander: "We're all fine here, thank you. How are you?"
> When Leia, frustrated with Han and Chewbacca, asks: "Will someone get this walking carpet out of my way?"

Ford, then thirty-four, and Fisher, then nineteen, brought more levity to the proceedings, but they were hardly enamored with the dialogue either. Famously, Ford told Lucas: "You can type this shit, but you can't say it." The young trio were shot documentary style, as on *American Graffiti*; that is, Lucas would let them play the scene as if they were having a normal conversation, with no instructions. Fisher called the cast "trick talking-meat." She and Ford smoked pot during the shoot, until it became clear that Ford's weed was too strong for Fisher. They had a clandestine affair after Ford surprised her by hiding in her closet naked but for a tie.

The director seemed barely present. Ford, almost as famously, said Lucas offered only one of two instructions after a scene: "Do it again, only better" or "Faster and more intense." The biggest smile Fisher got out of Lucas was when she presented him with a *Buck Rogers* helium pistol at the wrap party.

The London shoot wrapped in July 1976. Even then, the crowd scenes in the cantina weren't complete; Stuart Freeborn, the British designer and *2001* veteran making the alien costumes, had fallen sick. There was no working shot of R2-D2 rolling down a long desert canyon. The rough cuts Lucas assembled for Laddie were a complete mess, and Lucas acknowledged as much: "It's not what I want it to be."

Whether Lucas knew it or not, this was a particularly good moment to be honest. Laddie was being hounded at Fox for his championing of *The Blue Bird*, a romantic fantasy film starring Elizabeth Taylor and Jane Fonda, a joint production with a Soviet studio. It tanked at the box office, and Fox, already cash-strapped, was down another $8.5 million. That was exactly *Star Wars'* budget. If Lucas had not shown a measure of honesty and responsibility by recognizing that *Star Wars* was in a state of confusion, Laddie might have withdrawn his support. As it was, Fox pushed the *Star Wars* release window from Christmas 1976 to spring 1977.

The only bright light for Lucas, perversely, was how badly the British economy was doing. Inflation was soaring, and sterling was sinking. In March 1976, the UK government had to go cap in hand to the International Monetary Fund. Investors panicked. By the time Lucas had to pay his contractors, the pound had dropped below $2 for the first time in history. Kurtz got to shave nearly $500,000 off the film's costs. They were now over-budget by a mere $600,000. Kurtz and Lucas sat down at one point and made a darkly humorous calculation: based on their salaries, the pair was earning $1.10 an hour.

On the way back to the United States following the London wrap, Lucas took a two-day layover in Alabama to see Spielberg. *Close Encounters of the Third Kind* had begun shooting, with twice Lucas's budget, on an enormous set near Mobile, and everyone (Lucas included) assumed it would beat *Star Wars*. Few people seemed to be screaming for a modern *Flash Gordon*—but Spielberg's subject, UFOs? They were a national craze. "George came back from *Star Wars* a nervous wreck," Spielberg remembered years later. "He didn't feel *Star Wars* lived up to the vision he'd originally had. He felt he'd just made this little kid's movie." Spielberg's crew would remember Lucas as thin, pale, tired, and hoarse: a man on the edge of a breakdown.

The breakdown came after Lucas stopped in LA next to check in on ILM. Dykstra had spent fully half his budget building the Dykstraflex. He had to nail an unprecedented 360 special effects shots by spring. Lucas took a look at the seven shots they had in the can and deemed one to be useable. Tempers flared. Dykstra was fired. On the plane back to SFO, Lucas started feeling chest pains. Driving to San Anselmo, he decided to check himself into Marin General Hospital. Next morning the doctors told him it wasn't a heart attack, just exhaustion: a warning shot from his body. "My life was collapsing around me," Lucas said.

Still, he kept plugging away, maintaining his punishing schedule. He brought Dykstra back but hired a production supervisor to keep ILM in line: no more hippy commune. His first editor had produced a disastrous rough cut; Lucas fired him too and started cutting while he figured out a replacement. The goal was to get a rough cut ready by Thanksgiving. In need of placeholders for the special effects shots and soundtrack, he dug up the World War II dogfight scenes he'd been videotaping and spliced together tracks from his favorite classical LPs.

But the production seemed cursed—especially when the trouble-prone Mark Hamill flipped his car trying to make the freeway exit on the way to a recording session. He needed facial reconstruction surgery and fell into a deep depression. Meanwhile, pick-up scenes of Luke in his land speeder on Tatooine had to be shot without Hamill, so were filmed at a distance.

No one who visited ILM in run-down industrial Van Nuys in among the chop shops and porn distribution warehouses could imagine anything great springing from it. "*This* is where you're shooting the movie?" the then-struggling young actor Rob Lowe, visiting his aunt and uncle at ILM, exclaimed. Lowe wrote that it looked more like a hideout for the Symbionese Liberation Army. There was a terrible smell from the Bantha costume that had been placed atop an elephant for pick-up scenes. The Death Star trench was a small number of foam core parts covered in egg cartons and toy pieces; the ILM crew had to keep swapping them around to create the illusion that it was more than a few hundred feet long. Occasionally, exhausted, the technicians took naps in the trench.

Many elements were missing right until the last minute. Phil Tippett, a stop-motion animator with friends at ILM, was recruited into the posse in the waning days of *Star Wars* because Lucas desperately needed anyone who could design and act inside newer, scarier creature costumes for the Cantina. "The originals were a little too Beatrix Potter for George," Tippett remembers. Then when Lucas found out Tippett did stop-motion, he asked him to create a chess game with moving monsters for the *Millennium Falcon*'s rec room; Lucas had originally intended to shoot actors in masks as the chess pieces. This was so late in the day, Tippett would end up animating the monster game at night, while ILM had its wrap party.

Even after ILM wrapped up its work, there was still the long nightmare of sound mixing. Lucas and Kurtz had wanted the movie to employ Sensurround, a bass-heavy sound system used in the 1974 disaster movie *Earthquake* and little else since. But Sensurround was owned by Universal, which wanted a whopping $3 million up front and 10 percent of all *Star Wars* revenue. A brash young Dolby sound engineer called Stephen Katz met with Lucas and Kurtz and persuaded them that you could get the same effect much more cheaply using the then-novel technology of Dolby six-track Stereo. But only some theaters could afford to install the necessary Dolby system, so Lucasfilm's workload was tripled—it had to come up with a six-track mix, a stereo mix, and a mono mix all by the May 25 deadline. Kurtz booked a mixing theater at Warner Brothers, but his booking was rescinded when the world's hottest action star, Clint Eastwood, needed the theater for his upcoming movie *The Gauntlet*. Kurtz scrambled and found a mixing theater at Goldwyn Studios, but only the graveyard shift—eight P.M. to eight A.M.—was available. It was the worst possible outcome for Lucas and Kurtz, the vampire hours of *American Graffiti* all over again. Neither could sleep well during the day this time, either.

One day during the sound mix Kurtz got a call out of nowhere from Dennis Stanfill, chair of the board at Fox. "The board would like to see the picture," he said. In they trooped—Princess Grace and company—at eight P.M. that evening to screen a rough cut of *Star Wars* for the first time. Out they trooped at ten P.M. without saying a word. "No applause, not even a smile," says Kurtz. "We were really depressed." The last to leave was Stanfill, who lingered to reassure Kurtz on his way out: "Don't worry about them. They don't know anything about movies."

It was a sadder, wiser Lucas who sat down with Charley Lippincott for a postgame interview, intended for a "making of *Star Wars*" book. Neither man expected a huge readership. "It wasn't particularly the movie I set out to make," Lucas said. "Given another five years and $8 million, we could get something spectacular." He foresaw a backlash against his "comic book movie," and remembered Gene Roddenberry saying it had taken ten or fifteen episodes of *Star Trek* before the show found its footing: "You have to walk around the world you've created a bit." Lucas dreamed of doing another *Star Wars* film someday, one closer to the original movie he saw in his mind. The closest he got to that illusion was when he saw the trailer; cut together really fast, it gave the illusion that this was a movie absolutely jam-packed with spaceships and aliens. There was consolation in the fact that Fox had signed the final contract in August, giving the Star Wars Corporation complete control over any sequels until 1979, in the event that he could scrape together the money to make one.

Could this film still work? Possibly, Lucas conceded glumly. Maybe the kids will dig it. Maybe it will make as much as the average Disney picture—that is,

$16 million. That meant Fox would lose a little money when all the marketing and overhead were calculated, but he and Fox might both make some money on the toys. $16 million was a better outcome than anyone around Lucas could imagine, save for Spielberg. Even Marcia believed that the most recent Scorsese movie she helped edit, *New York New York*, would do better at the box office. "Nobody's going to take yours seriously," she warned her husband.

Marcia had done meticulous editing work on *Star Wars*, as well, but she was displeased with the results. She burst into tears after one screening: "It's the *At Long Last Love* of science fiction!" (*At Long Last Love* was another famous flop from Fox. Luckily, Laddie, who was sitting nearby, did not overhear.)

Lucas was seeing discouraging signs everywhere, even among his closest friends and strongest supporters. In fall 1976, he and Edward Summer set up the Supersnipe Art Gallery on Manhattan's Upper East Side, a few blocks from the Supersnipe Comic Euphorium, with the idea that the offshoot might morph into a boutique selling *Star Wars* art. Lucas had a vision of three such boutiques, the others in San Francisco and Beverly Hills, but there seemed to be little interest even in New York. His temper was frayed; crossing Eighty-Sixth Street with Lucas and Kurtz one day, Summer mentioned that he'd just seen *Logan's Run*, the big science fiction movie of 1976, set in a silver-jumpsuit-wearing future society of hedonistic youths who are not permitted to live past thirty. "It's kind of a bubble gum movie," said Summer. Lucas scowled. "Well, I don't think you're going to like *Star Wars* much," he said. "It's kind of bubble gum." Summer protested: He'd read the script. He was in the posse.

Movie theater owners certainly weren't in the posse. Fox had been hoping that theater owners' advance guarantees for *Star Wars* would reach $10 million. They got to $1.5 million. There were a bunch of great pictures supposedly coming out in May 1977: William Friedkin, who had made *The Exorcist* and *The French Connection*, had one of those paranoid 1970s thrillers that seemed to do so well, *Sorcerer*. There was a World War II picture, *A Bridge Too Far*; a post-apocalyptic science fiction thriller, *Damnation Alley*; a buddy movie, *Smokey and the Bandit*; and Fox's main film of the summer, for which *Star Wars* was to be a mere curtain raiser, *The Other Side of Midnight*. Based on a best-seller by Sidney Sheldon, it was a very edgy 1970s kind of romance, its soap opera plot suffused with the hot-button topics of abortion and murder.

Fox was so afraid of potential losses from *Star Wars* that it tried to force theaters to take the movie if they wanted *Other Side of Midnight*. And if that didn't work, which it didn't, the company's lawyers were looking into selling the movie as part of a package deal to a company in West Germany, then Hollywood's new favorite tax haven. The price tag Fox lawyers had slapped on *Star Wars* was less than what it would end up costing the studio: $12 million. Appropriately enough, Fox also made arrangements to dump a movie in West Germany called *Fire Sale*.

And that's the way things might have turned out, but for the fact that Charley Lippincott had a posse of his own.

These days, even Lucasfilm doesn't know how to reach Charley Lippincott. He's in his happy retirement in a farm house in New Hampshire, the state where he grew up, having had his fill of marketing big-budget Hollywood science fiction movies. "Thirty years in Los Angeles was enough," he says.

Lippincott was a science fiction, comic book, and film geek, cut from the same cloth as Lucas. After Lippincott's family moved to Chicago, he watched the *Flash Gordon* serials projected on the wall of a local library. He was hooked, and followed Flash's exploits in the *Chicago Examiner*, which his parents wouldn't take for political reasons; he had to sneak the comics page from a girl down the street. A rising star at USC, he was film professor Arthur Knight's assistant and a friend to the younger Lucas. He was the one who brought the French auteur Jean-Luc Godard to campus and made sure Lucas got to sit in on Godard's seminars.

After graduating from USC, Lippincott made a name for himself promoting movies at MGM. The guy who hired him, Mike Kaplan, had done the publicity campaign for *2001*. Lippincott was eager to learn what had gone wrong in the selling of that movie. He wondered why it hadn't done better. Had Kaplan tried connecting to the fan base at, say, the World Science Fiction conference? Kaplan sighed: that was just what he'd wanted to do, but the movie wasn't ready in time. So Lippincott knew what he was going to do if he ever got the chance to promote another movie that nerdy: "I was going to build an underground cabal. I would be the one who broke all the barriers."

Lippincott had stayed in touch with Lucas since graduation, cutting a promotional reel for *THX* for the princely sum of $100. By 1975, their paths had dovetailed again. That year, Lippincott had his big break at Universal, devising a tow to promote Steven Spielberg's *Jaws*, the first movie in history to make more than $100 million at the box office. Lippincott's stock was high, to say the least. Kurtz and Lucas kept their offices at Universal after *American Graffiti*; they tracked Lippincott down, and Lucas had a three-hour discussion with him in the lobby of the MCA Black Tower, the intimidating building where Universal's executive offices are located. That weekend, Lippincott read the third draft of *The Star Wars* end to end. He was sold. Here, finally, was a movie for which he could put the Kaplan plan into effect.

When he started work on *The Star Wars* as the film's marketing director in November 1975, Lippincott took an immediate interest in the novelization of the script. Lucas wanted a novel, and his lawyer, Tom Pollock, was about to auction off the rights to New York publishing houses. But Lippincott knew the perfect home for it: Ballantine Books, the most successful publisher of science fiction in the United States. Lippincott took *Star Wars* to Judy-Lynn Del Rey, editor and wife of the legendary science fiction editor Lester Del Rey. Lippincott walked out of that meeting having sold not one but five *Star Wars* titles: two novelizations, two "making of" books, and a calendar.

Lucas's first idea for the author of the novelization was to tap Don Glut, a member of his old USC cohort. Glut had called Lucas and said, "I heard you're making a movie called *Space Wars*. Is there anything I can do?" Lucas offered Glut the novel but said there were a couple of catches: it only paid $5,000, there were no royalties, and Fox was insisting that Lucas's name be on the cover. It was a ghostwriting job. Thanks, Glut said, but no thanks.

As a Plan B, Del Rey recruited a pulp science fiction writer named Alan Dean Foster; she'd enjoyed Foster's novel *Icerigger* and knew that Foster had also written the novelization of *Dark Star*—not to mention a whopping ten *Star Trek* novelizations based on that franchise's animated series. Foster agreed to the terms and had a brief meeting with Lucas at ILM. Making conversation, Foster asked Lucas what he was going to do when all this was over. "I'm going to retire and make small experimental films," Lucas said.

Foster was a natural addition to the posse. He too had grown up reading comic books, and that influenced how he wrote: fast. "I'm watching a movie in my head, really," Foster says. "I write fast because I just describe what I'm seeing." *Star Wars* was just another job, and he wrote the novelization of the script in less than two months using the unreconstructed fourth draft as a basis. He made a few tweaks along the way, starting with that "a long time ago in a galaxy far, far away" thing. He felt "another galaxy, another time" worked better. He wrote that Mos Eisley was a "wretched collection of villainy and disreputable types." Foster has since been credited with coming up with the name of the Emperor of the *Star Wars* galaxy, Palpatine, in his prologue. But Foster says he can't remember doing that; the name may well have come from Lucas's notes.

The book isn't bad, per se, but it is a relic from a time when *Star Wars* was still a title to be giggled at. With no one standing over his shoulder reminding him that this was supposed to be utterly divorced from terrestrial reality,

Foster threw in a few lines that now sound strange to *Star Wars* fans, such as "he wouldn't know a Bantha from a panda" and "Luke's mind was as muddy as a pond laced with petroleum." He mentioned one animal specifically so he could throw in one of his favorite comedy lines: "What's a duck?" Luke asks Obi-Wan, a reference to the Marx Brothers movie *Coconuts*, in which Groucho says "viaduct" and Chico mishears it as "Why a duck?"

After selling the novelization rights to Ballantine, Lippincott made his portfolios for the crucial December 1975 Fox board meeting that got the film's budget approved. Then it was off to give the same presentation at a Fox sales convention in Los Angeles: "Twenty-Six in '76." (This was when *Star Wars* was still intended to be one of the twenty-six movies Fox was going to release in the bicentennial year.) The audience of theater owners didn't care for *Star Wars*. "I bored the shit out of the old cusses with their big cigars," Lippincott remembers, "but the young people who came with them loved it." He bought the kids dinner and kept in touch. His underground cabal was just getting started.

Another way to hook the kids in advance of the film's release was through comic books. Again, Lippincott made it happen. He did his damnedest to get a meeting at Marvel Comics. Publisher Stan Lee wouldn't take his calls, but Edward Summer got the ball rolling, setting Lippincott up with editor in chief Roy Thomas, who had just written a comic book adaptation of Edwin Arnold's 1905 space fantasy *Lieutenant Gullivar Jones: His Vacation*. Thomas insisted he would also write the *Star Wars* adaptation, and called a meeting with Stan.

The deal Lippincott cut with Marvel was extremely unusual at the time. Normally a movie would be adapted into one or two issues of a comic book. Lippincott insisted on a minimum of five issues, with two to be released before the movie. Fine, said Lee, but Lucasfilm wouldn't see a dime of royalties on a given issue until they'd sold 100,000 copies. *Spider Man*, Marvel's best-selling title, sold 280,000 copies per issue. "That didn't faze me one iota," Lippincott says. "Because either the comic book was going to work, or screw it." Back at Fox, "they thought I was the biggest fool in the world," he says. Not because of the 100,000 copies clause, but because nobody cared about comics. What did they have to do with bringing in a movie audience? When the first comic book hit newsstands and didn't sell out its 100,000-copy run, the doubters seemed vindicated.

Still, Lippincott doubled down on his strategy. He'd been teaching film part-time at UC San Diego, and one kid in his class had helped found a convention for comics, rather unimaginatively named Comic-Con, a few years earlier. So

Lippincott went to San Diego Comic-Con 1976 and prepared to do something the small convention had never seen before: present a panel about an upcoming movie.

Today, Comic-Con is packed with Hollywood studios and TV companies touting their wares. It is widely accepted that the convention's early adopter audience can make or break a franchise that has even the slightest relationship to science fiction, superheroes, fantasy, or horror. The studios will closely monitor attendance at the big panels, and woe betide the publicist who can't get a good turnout. When I told Lippincott I was about to visit Comic-Con for the first time, he apologized for what I was about to experience. "What I did led to something I'm appalled at," he said.

Lippincott's Comic-Con presentation, however, wasn't anything like what you'd see today. He showed slides; he talked about the story and the characters. There was no teaser, no trailer. The special effects weren't even close to finished. The stars didn't show. There were a couple hundred people in the audience. He sold posters for $1.75 apiece; they didn't exactly fly off the tables at his booth.

Still, Lippincott persisted. He went to a Science Fiction and Fantasy Society conference in the San Fernando Valley, where he was heckled by one successful author for daring to promote a movie. "The students were all for it," Lippincott recalls. "The older writers thought I was a two-bit salesman." He flew to Kansas in September for the thirty-fourth World Science Fiction Convention, in the same hotel where the Republican Party had just that week renominated President Gerald Ford after a bruising primary battle with Governor Ronald Reagan. Lippincott took Mark Hamill and Gary Kurtz and a whole bunch of costumes from the movie along for the ride, although even here he ran into suspicion and misunderstandings. Having never seen a movie promoted like this before, the convention organizers had to be persuaded to let Lippincott show the costumes.

Lippincott read up on the history of space fantasy. He talked to fanzines. He studied *Star Trek* in order to understand what about it had won such devoted fans (he wasn't one himself). His marketing plan, however, called for him to steer deferentially clear of Trekkie circles for fear that they would create a backlash against this upstart movie with a too-similar name. Even without targeting that market segment, however, Lippincott watched as the buzz in the science fiction community started to build.

Foster's novelization, titled *Star Wars: From the Adventures of Luke Skywalker*, was published in December 1976, six months before the movie was to be released. That was partly a result of the fact that the release date had shifted from Christmas to May. But holding to the novel's original release date was Lippincott's idea: it would get the story out to science fiction fans early, as many as 250,000 of them (the size of the initial print run), and get them all telling their friends. The novelization (with a stunning McQuarrie cover) was launched in paperback, hit the best-seller list, and sold out by February. Strangely, Del Rey didn't want to take a chance on a second print run just yet, but Lippincott managed to get it serialized in the *Los Angeles Times*. The book's success was a tremendous morale booster at ILM, where the special effects team was still scrambling to realize the scenes Foster had so casually described.

Lippincott's underground cabal, like the book's mass-market audience, was growing as the film's release date of May 25 loomed. The Friday before the Wednesday release, he held a special screening at Fox for the critic from *Variety* and invited twenty college-age kids to watch it too. The critic accused Lippincott of trying to sway his reaction with a bunch of cheering kids, but he had it all wrong. They were there because they were about to start a phone network, frantically calling other kids around the country and telling them all about this amazing thing they had just seen.

Star Wars was only going to open in a mere thirty-two theaters across America, but thanks to Lippincott's cabal at least one of these venues was a prime one: the 1,350-seat Coronet in San Francisco, renowned for having the best projection and sound quality in the city. Gary Meyer was the booking agent for both the Coronet and United Artists' secondary theater in the city, the Alexandria. Meyer was so enthused by Lippincott's campaign that over dinner one night, he told Fox's head of distribution all about this hot new movie, *Star Wars*.

The executive was incredulous. The last rumor he'd heard about *Star Wars* was that the Fox board had fallen asleep watching it and the movie was going to be shelved. He pressed Meyer: he was going to put *The Other Side of Midnight* in the Coronet and *Star Wars* in his second best theater, right? Oh yes, said Meyer, and promptly booked *Star Wars* in the Coronet.

11.

THE FIRST REEL

May 25, 1977, was another grey day in San Francisco, the brief candle of spring snuffed out by the same Pacific fog that made Mark Twain shiver a century earlier. "The coldest winter I ever spent was a summer in San Francisco": Nobody knows if Twain actually said that, but every Bay resident knows the truth of it.

In the twenty-cent *Chronicle*, the news was just as dismal as the weather. A cargo plane at Oakland Airport had exploded the previous night, leaving two maintenance workers dead and eight injured. Terrorists in the Netherlands were still holding 160 children hostage. The Dow had closed below 1,000, its lowest level in sixteen months. Ex-president Nixon was still on TV after four nights and counting of blather with that British interviewer, David Frost.

Readers would just as soon forget all about Watergate. They'd also like to forget Vietnam, but the fingerprints of the war were everywhere, even in 1977. The *Chronicle* reported that the Pentagon was moving a load of Agent Orange across country by train so it could be burned in the Pacific (harmlessly, officials said). A short blurb noted that the government had just tested the safety of a nuclear fuel shipping cask by running a train into it at eighty-two miles an hour. Something that wouldn't be known for years: a new round of underground atomic blasts were under way in Nevada on that day.

None of these stories got the coveted feature slot on the front page. That was reserved for an article on weddings in Las Vegas—the hot new thing, apparently. A shocking fifty thousand couples would get married in Vegas in 1977 alone, it said. They didn't even need a blood test. "Most of them will get free pizza," the story said, as well as "a roll of nickels, a discount on *Reader's Digest*, and packets of eucalyptus-scented douche."

Nukes. Nixon. Terrorists. Explosions. Chemicals. Casino weddings. Who would want to read more about any of that?

Readers who made it all the way to page 51 found the day's one piece of cheery news. In a review with the economical four-word headline "*Star Wars*: Magic Ride," writer John Wasserman—a veteran local character known for reviewing live sex shows—reported on a new work from a local filmmaker that was about to make its debut in the city that morning—a movie judged so unimportant by its studio, it hadn't even received a proper premiere.

Wasserman's review was breathless. "With the opening today at the Coronet of 'Star Wars,' writer-director George Lucas makes a spectacular return to the screen," he wrote. *Star Wars* was "the most exciting picture to be released this year—exciting as theater and exciting as cinema. It is the most visually awesome such work to appear since '2001—A Space Odyssey,' yet is intriguingly human in its scope and boundaries."

If this wasn't selling it enough, Wasserman described a film "as embraceable by children or teenagers as by us older folks . . . a contemporary 'Star Trek,' a stylish 'Space: 1999' that will whisk us on the magic carpet of our imagination." The film even offered a feel-good message:

> The only audible preaching by Lucas—in a whisper, to be sure—suggests that man is man and creatures are creatures, and it doesn't really matter how far forward or back you go to check it out. God is here The Force, feelings defeat the calculation, good conquers evil—but not without sacrifice—and love will keep us together. "Star Wars" is that rarest of creatures: The work of art with universal (excuse the pun) appeal. There is in all of us the child who dreams of magical beings and fantastical adventures. . . . If "Star Wars" doesn't garner at least half a dozen Academy Award nominations, I will eat my Wookiee.

Flipping past Wasserman's review—and puzzling over that bizarre word he just promised to eat—a reader of the *Chronicle* would have stumbled on a full-page ad for this strange-sounding film. In cheesy Frank Frazetta–style, it showed a youth with his shirt open and some kind of sword made of light, a young woman with a gun, and behind them a spectral apparition with a face that looked like a cross between a samurai, a wolf, and a gas mask.

So this was it, the "most exciting picture to be released this year." It was playing exclusively at the finest theater in the city: a fine way to escape the fog. The Coronet's first showing was at 10:45 A.M. What did you have to lose, except $3? Who wouldn't at least give it a try?

Back when Warner Brothers wrested *THX 1138* from Lucas's control, Fred Weintraub—the studio's "youth expert"—gave the young director this advice. "If you hook the audience in the first ten minutes," he said, "they'll forgive anything." Those ten minutes, roughly the length of a film's first reel, could make or break a movie—especially one that required viewers to make a leap of faith, as both *THX* and *Star Wars* did.

Lucas resented Weintraub, as he resented all studio interference, but he would proceed to follow Weintraub's dictum for the rest of his career. The entire set up of the plot of *American Graffiti* was conveyed in its first ten minutes. And more ground was covered in the first ten minutes of *Star Wars* than in—well, just about any other movie up until that point. Within this short timeframe the film won over skeptical audiences around the world, and earned itself and its Creator a place in cinematic history.

The first reel of *Star Wars* was vital—and yet a surprising amount of the credit for it belongs to people whose names are not George Lucas. It's an object lesson in how filmmaking is a fundamentally collaborative endeavor, and the collaboration often extends across decades. Take the first thing the audience at the Coronet would have seen in that first public screening on the morning of May 25, after the *Duck Dodgers* cartoon: the Fox fanfare. Five seconds of thumping drums and bright brass in B-flat major, the fanfare was composed way back in 1933 by prolific movie composer Alfred Newman, a friend of Irving Berlin and George Gershwin, and expanded in the 1950s for the launch of CinemaScope, the studio's wide-screen movie format. The fanfare had fallen into disuse by 1977, but George Lucas loved Newman's work and asked that it be revived for *Star Wars*. If you're counting, that's one point for Newman and one for Lucas.

For generations of kids, that fanfare would not mean Twentieth Century Fox so much as it would mean *Star Wars*. The part of the fanfare that was extended in the '50s is the bit that plays over the Lucasfilm logo; many viewers wrongly assume it to be some kind of separate Lucasfilm fanfare. Indeed, while not technically part of the film, the fanfare has become so widely associated with the following two hours of entertainment that it was rerecorded by John Williams in 1980 and placed at the beginning of every *Star Wars* soundtrack album.*

After the fanfare dies away, the screen falls silent and black. Up pop ten simple words, lowercase, in a cool blue:

A long time ago, in a galaxy far, far away . . .

These are Lucas's words, as edited by Lucas: the corny addendum "an amazing adventure took place" from the fourth draft is gone. No title card in the history of cinema has been more quoted; no ten words are more important. Watching the movie in a theater in Colorado, the beat poet Allen Ginsberg read those ten words and said aloud to his companion: "Thank goodness. I don't have to worry about it."

It was a revolutionary statement—but why? Leave aside the fairy tale cadence, which lulls us into story time. Consider instead that this is exactly what every fantasy epic needs to give you right off the bat: a setting in space and time that says, relax. Don't bother trying to figure out the relationship between what you're about to see and your own Earthbound reality, because there isn't one. This isn't *Planet of the Apes*; the Statue of Liberty isn't going to turn up in a last-reel twist. No other movie had ever announced its divorce from our world so explicitly before; with the exception of *Star Wars* sequels, none would ever be able to do so again without seeming derivative.

The perfect simplicity of those ten words appears to have been hard for a lot of people to understand in the run-up to the movie's release. The words that open Alan Dean Foster's novelization ("another galaxy, another time") aren't quite the same—that might place us in the future, rather than in a story that is safely in some history book. Fox didn't get it at all: its trailer for *Star Wars* opened with the words "somewhere in space, this may all be happening right now."

The ten words remain on the screen for exactly five seconds, long enough for the casual viewer to think, *Isn't this supposed to be a science fiction movie? Aren't they all set in the future? What kind of thing is—*

---

* Years later, when Lucasfilm was sold to Disney, fans realized the Fox fanfare would likely be replaced by "When You Wish Upon a Star" for *Star Wars Episode VII*. The Internet was inconsolable.

Boom. The largest logo you've ever seen fills the screen, its yellow outlines nudged right up to the top and bottom of the frame, the color a deliberate contrast with the blue of the preceding ten words. It is accompanied by a violent orchestral blast in the same key as the fanfare, B-flat major. Both were placed there by Lucas; neither were his work. Let's take a closer look.

The on-screen logo was initially supposed to be the work of a veteran logo designer, Dan Perri. His is the foreshortened, star-filled "*Star Wars*" seen on theater marquees and in most print advertising. But the logo that made it into the first reel actually came into being in a far more roundabout way. In late 1976, Fox needed a brochure that was going to be sent to theater owners. To design it, the company turned to an LA ad agency called Seiniger Advertising, known for its movie posters. Seiniger gave the job to its newest art director, a twenty-two-year-old named Suzy Rice who had just arrived at the company from a gig at *Rolling Stone*.

Rice found herself at ILM in Van Nuys, getting a tour of spaceship models. She met with Lucas in his office. First, he impressed on Rice how fast this needed to be turned around. Second, he knew he wanted a logo that would intimidate the viewer. Something that would "rival AT&T." His final direction was that he wanted it to look "very fascist," a choice of words that caused Rice no end of headaches when she retells the story. She happened to have been reading a book on German font design. She thought of the concept of uniformity. She chose a modified Helvetica Black and set about flattening each letter in a white-on-black outline.

At a second meeting with the young art director, Lucas said the result looked like "Tar War." So Rice connected the *S* and the *T*, the *R* and the *S*. After a third meeting, her logo got the OK from Lucas. At a fourth meeting—squeezed in while Lucas was shooting inserts for the cantina scene, when the door was opened for her by the green alien Greedo smoking a cigarette through a straw— the brochure got approved.

A couple of days later, Kurtz called Rice to let her know they were going to use her logo in the main titles as well, albeit with a flatter *W* (hers had pointy tips). They'd tried Peri's design in the opening credits. Then they tried her design instead and, in Kurtz's words, "Wow."

Wow indeed. The result looks like the world's hottest rock band logo, as if *Star Wars* might be the next Led Zeppelin rather than a space-fantasy film. Instead of putting the logo at the top of the crawl, going in the same direction as the text to come—the layout that was planned for Peri's logo—Rice's design pulls back fast into the stars, as if daring you to give chase.

Rice, like a lot of people with tangential involvement with the *Star Wars* legend, would spend the rest of her career trying to live up to it. "Many people have expected me to work a miracle for their project," she says. She has seen her design everywhere, for decades, on T-shirts and caps and lunch boxes and every other single piece of *Star Wars* merchandise, out of the corner of her eye, everywhere she goes. Rice still loves the franchise and has seen every movie; she is sanguine about the fact that she doesn't own it and, as an outside contractor, didn't even get a movie credit. It's what the logo represents, rather than the work itself, that she says she enjoys.

The musical contribution, unlike the logo, has been widely credited: composer John Williams's *Star Wars* march (not to be confused with the Imperial March, which would debut in 1980) is frequently voted the greatest tune in movie history. Williams had been introduced to Lucas by Spielberg in 1975, prior to the release of *Jaws*; that movie's ominous theme sealed the deal. Lucas knew that, for his space epic, he wanted something bombastic and brassy in the style of old Hollywood—such as the *Flash Gordon* serials, which used very romantic, 1930s-style scores. The images were going to be wild; the music would have to anchor you in familiar emotions. The temporary track Lucas had assembled contained snatches of English composer Gustav Holst's ominous *Mars, Bringer of War* over the start of the film. Lucas's only direction for the main theme was that it contain "war drums echoing through the heavens" during the opening crawl. Williams obliged, and did so much more.

Williams wrote the entire score over the course of two months, January and February 1977. The soundtrack was recorded with the London Symphony Orchestra over the course of a few days in March. It was, Lucas later said, the only part of the movie that exceeded his expectations. Jubilant, he played half an hour of it over the phone to Spielberg, who was crushed—Williams still had to score *Close Encounters of the Third Kind*, and it sounded like Lucas had squeezed the composer's best work out of him. In a sense, he was right. Williams's music is often venerated by fans as the "oxygen" of *Star Wars*, in McQuarrie collaborator Paul Bateman's phrase.

How had Williams been able to create this iconic music so fast? The answer seems to be one part genius, one part pastiche. Williams has often said he owes a debt to the movie composers of the 1930s and 1940s; specifically, the *Star Wars* main theme shares its opening notes with the theme from *King's Row*, the 1942 drama that launched Ronald Reagan's acting career.

Few of us hear these influences today, of course. It is impossible to separate the *Star Wars* theme—or the rest of the soundtrack, for that matter—from the visuals of *Star Wars*; cut a thirty-second TV segment on anything to do with the franchise anywhere in the world, and you're going to get a grab-bag of images (lightsabers, spaceships, creatures, droids, troopers) under the main melody from Williams's march. A supremely self-assured, soaring tune, it can confer a sense of optimism and adventure on any images it overlays as surely as the *Benny Hill* "yakkety sax" theme can make any video funny. The decision to replace Holst's minor key menace with this major key exuberance is pure Williams. (Hands up any readers not hearing it in their head right now.)

Next up for the viewers at the Coronet: the opening crawl. In 1977, this scrolling text immediately followed the *Star Wars* logo, without an interposed title. It would not be preceded by "Episode IV: A New Hope" until the movie was *re*-rereleased in 1981.

The disconnect between the *Star Wars* films' titles and their release order often confuses casual viewers—and fans debate to this day whether the numbering system that began in 1980 with *Episode V* reflected the Creator's true intent in 1977. George Lucas has claimed in recent years that he really wanted to open the movie with the title *Episode IV*, but that he either "chickened out" or "Fox wouldn't let me." The written evidence points in the other direction: The shooting script calls the movie *Episode One of the Adventures of Luke Skywalker*. The first drafts of the *Empire Strikes Back*, written after Lucas had the upper hand over Fox, call that movie *Star Wars II*.

Gary Kurtz lends credence to Lucas's claim but insists that the notion was far less precise than the Creator remembers. "We were toying with the idea of calling it *Episode III*, or *IV*, or *V*—something in the middle," he recalls. "We were a bit clouded by the fact that we wanted it to be as much like *Flash Gordon* as possible"—that is, he and Lucas wanted to "capture the flavor" of encountering a serial halfway through its run, but never got so far as choosing an episode number. "Fox hated that idea," Kurtz confirms, "and actually, they were right. We thought it would be really clever, but it wasn't that clever at the time. If you go see what's been touted as a new film, and it says *Episode III* up there, you'd say, 'What the hell?'"

Numbering aside, Lucas had hit on something important during all that redrafting. *Star Wars* remains one of the best examples of the storytelling dictum that it is best to begin in the middle of things. (Quite literally so, as it would turn out: Lucas's six-episode saga was the first in world history to open at its precise midpoint.) And he did insist that the roll-up remain, in the face of Fox executives who complained that children wouldn't read any kind of scrolling text at the start of a film. About the time they started, Lucas said.

Credit for the words that roll up the screen following the *Star Wars* logo is only one part Lucas; the other credit goes to the unlikely duo of director Brian De Palma and then *Time* movie critic, later filmmaker, Jay Cocks. Lucas had screened an unfinished cut for them in spring 1977, along with a house full of other friends. Over dinner afterwards, while Spielberg declared the film was going to be a huge hit, the naturally acerbic De Palma—who had sat in on most of the *Star Wars* casting sessions, looking for actors for *Carrie* at the same time—openly mocked Lucas: "What's all this Force shit? Where's the blood when they shoot people?" Perhaps urged on by Marcia, who knew George deeply respected De Palma, Brian later made a peace offering: he offered to rewrite the roll-up.

Lucas was crushed but agreed: the opening crawl had been too wordy in each of its four drafts, and he was down to the wire. His pastiche of lengthy, *Flash Gordon*-style introductions clearly wasn't coming across to viewers. De Palma sat down the next day, with Cocks at the typewriter. The result: an object lesson in the power of editing. Here's how a line editor like myself might respond to Lucas's version of the crawl:

It is a period of civil wars in the galaxy. [Redundancy: we've already been told we're in a galaxy far, far away. Also: civil wars, plural? The rest of the crawl only mentions one.] A brave alliance of underground freedom fighters has challenged the tyranny and oppression of the awesome GALACTIC EMPIRE. [Too much cheerleading and editorializing. What is this, a propaganda film? Let us decide which side to take. And the word "awesome" is starting to acquire a different, more positive meaning—might be best to avoid in this context.]

Striking from a fortress hidden among the billion stars of the galaxy, [redundancy again; we already know how huge galaxies are. Also, does it matter that it's a fortress, and might that be too clever a reference to *Hidden Fortress*?] rebel spaceships have won their first victory in a battle with the powerful Imperial starfleet. [Isn't it understood the Empire would be more powerful than rebels, by definition?] The EMPIRE fears that another defeat could bring a thousand more solar systems into the rebellion, and Imperial control over the galaxy would be lost forever. [Why is this all-powerful Empire suddenly on the defensive? Why would a thousand star systems make a difference if the galaxy has a billion of them? And why are you making me do math at the movies?]

To crush the rebellion once and for all [redundancy: things that are crushed tend to stay crushed], the EMPIRE is constructing a sinister new battle station. [Name it here, perhaps?] Powerful enough to destroy an entire planet, its completion spells certain doom for the champions of freedom. [We haven't been introduced to these champions yet; perhaps name one of them? How about Princess Leia, whom Threepio will mention in the first few minutes of the film? Also, the movie opens with a ship that has stolen plans to that battle station, on which the whole plot hangs. Explaining that here might help raise the stakes.]

The De Palma and Cocks edit is the crawl that survives to this day. It is a spare and simple four sentences, revealing exactly what you need to know, with not a word going to waste:

> It is a period of civil war. Rebel spaceships, striking from a hidden base, have won their first victory against the evil Galactic Empire.
>
> During the battle, Rebel spies managed to steal secret plans to the Empire's ultimate weapon, the Death Star, an armored space station with enough power to destroy an entire planet.
>
> Pursued by the Empire's sinister agents, Princess Leia races home aboard her starship, custodian of the stolen plans that can save her people and restore freedom to the galaxy. . . .

This new ending primes the audience to expect a starship on the screen—but even with that tantalizing prospect, viewers might well be getting antsy by the time they're done reading. Even this pithy version of the crawl takes a precious one minute and twenty seconds to climb up the screen and vanish into space. Just eight minutes left to knock our socks off.

To make up for lost time, Lucas has done something very unusual: he has given the film no opening credits. It was an astonishingly self-effacing decision for the time, and one that would later get Lucas into trouble with the Directors Guild and Writers Guild. You would have no idea who directed this movie unless you were to intuit it from "Lucasfilm Ltd." Yet Lucas was determined that nothing would break the fourth wall of his fairy tale set-up.

Until 1977, the number of movies without opening credits could be counted on one hand. They were all visionary films of one sort or another. Disney's *Fantasia* (1940) was the first, followed by *Citizen Kane* (1941) and *West Side Story* (1961). More common in the 1970s was the practice of overlaying credits over the opening scene. In his slow-moving classic *Once Upon a Time in the*

West (1969), Sergio Leone added captioned credits for a record-breaking fifteen minutes. Score another point for Lucas for arresting this trend.

So the crawl has done its job, at least for the readers in the audience. (For the rest, too dazzled by the music, it might as well just be saying, "AWESOME AWESOME AWESOME.") We're expecting the arrival of a starship carrying Princess Leia and the stolen plans. But first, Lucas pans down over one moon, two moons, to the beautiful luminescent curvature of a desert planet (a point for Ralph McQuarrie's matte painting). And here our eyes rest for a full twenty seconds—a very, very long break, compared with what is to follow. Meanwhile, during the panning shot, the London Symphony orchestra has taken a much shorter break, a brief moment of pianissimo to acknowledge the beauty of the heavens. Then, as viewers' eyes rest on the desert planet, the orchestra takes a dark turn, spending most of those twenty seconds giving musical warning of some ominous doom just offscreen.

Finally, there it is, the first special effects shot of the movie and perhaps the most groundbreaking moment in special effects history: the tiny ship *Tantive IV* being chased by and trading laser fire with a massive Imperial Star Destroyer. We come in low under the hull of the Destroyer, which, according to everyone who saw it, seemed to keep going and going and going until we reached its engines.

In fact, the Star Destroyer shot lasts just thirteen seconds—less than half the length of a TV ad. But by the end of those thirteen seconds, the film has effectively established just how powerful and evil the Empire is, and just how overmatched the rebels are. (The best sight gag of the *Family Guy Star Wars* spoof "Blue Harvest" imagined the Star Destroyer as the SUV of space, placing a giant "BUSH/CHENEY" sticker on its rear.)

ILM recognized that this was by far the most important shot of the film and the greatest possible test of its computer-controlled, jury-rigged Dykstraflex camera. If it went wrong, if the Star Destroyer was seen to wobble even slightly, the illusion would be broken, and the audience's suspension of disbelief ruined, possibly for the duration of the film. Like much of *Star Wars*, this special effects shot teetered on the brink between genius and laughingstock. "We had seven or eight hypotheses that had to prove right in order for all that stuff to work," Dykstra said of the Dykstraflex. Which is one of the reasons why only one shot was in the can when Lucas visited ILM after the shoot and had his near heart attack: the fledgling company had been spending all its time and money on research and development, learning how to program motors by pushing the right sequence of buttons.

The *Tantive IV* was the last model to be completed by ILM, meaning the first ship on screen in the movie is also its most professional looking. In real life, the model was six feet—twice the size of the supposedly giant Star Destroyer following it. Lucas wanted to build a much larger destroyer to match. ILM convinced him that there wasn't time and he didn't need to—optics and the Dykstraflex would take care of it. Still, they spent a couple of weeks adding detailing to the Destroyer to please the Creator.

ILM first cameraman Richard Edlund admitted losing sleep over the thought of someone in the audience standing up and shouting "model!"—but instead, the audience at the Coronet cheered. It was a scene repeated around the world, absolutely unprecedented: people driven to cheering for a thirteen-second special effects shot. In Champaign, Illinois, a physics PhD student named Timothy Zahn would become a lifelong fan—and later, the world's most celebrated *Star Wars* author—because of this moment. In Los Angeles, a twenty-two-year-old truck driver who had been dreaming of exactly this kind of spaceship model would be so angered by the movie, so consumed by the question of how Lucas did it, that he would quit his job and enter the film industry full time. His name was James Cameron, and he would go on to direct two special effects–rich movies that beat *Star Wars* at the box office: *Titanic* and *Avatar*.

A quick reverse shot of the Star Destroyer from the front, a quick shot of a laser blast exploding on the *Tantive IV*, and we cut to Threepio and Artoo walking down the corridor. Credit Ralph McQuarrie for their design, with inspiration from *Metropolis* and *Silent Running*. But for Threepio's voice, score a point for Anthony Daniels. His prissy English butler take on the golden robot was never what Lucas intended. The director went through a couple dozen voice actors back in the States, listening for the sleazy used-car salesman he had in mind when writing the script. But none matched Daniels's jerky, fussy movements as well as Daniels himself, who was eventually invited to loop his own lines. Artoo's bleeping and blooping came courtesy of sound designer Ben Burtt, who ran his own voice through a synthesizer to get the trashcan robot's baby-like babble.

Intercut with the droids are quick cuts of the *Tantive IV* being sucked into the belly of the Star Destroyer, while rebel soldiers prepare to be boarded via one particular door at the end of a corridor. None say a word, but we get close-ups of their anxious faces, looking up and reacting to the sound effects. An oft-overlooked point: none of the extras seen in close-up are young. These are veteran space soldiers, evidently, and even they are afraid of what's coming. Without a word from them, we're already invited to fill in the movie's backstory in our minds.

This goes on for about a minute with no dialogue, effectively ramping up the tension. This was one of the scenes Lucas shot in his last frenzied days in London when the crew was divided into three, and it had yielded a few minutes of footage shot from three different camera angles, just so there'd be more to play around with in the editing stage.

Already, what we see on the screen represents the full resources of the Creator stretched gossamer-thin, just barely holding the illusion together—as would be the case for the next two hours.* The fact that the shots come together so seamlessly is nothing short of a miracle—and for this we must give points to Lucas's editing team.

Film editors Richard Chew, Paul Hirsch, and of course Marcia Lucas had to use every editing trick in the book to make *Star Wars* work. Once you see some of the fixes they came up with, you can't unsee them. When Luke is attacked by a Tusken raider on Tatooine, for instance, the actor in the Tusken suit raised his weapon above his head just once before Lucas said, "Cut." In the editing stage, Chew jogged the film back and forth until it looked like the Tusken was shaking his Gaffi stick menacingly, while Burtt helped mask the edit with the signature Tusken war cry: the sound of the crew's Tunisian donkey braying.

Marcia was the only Lucas who ever won an Academy Award for a *Star Wars* movie; George would never win an Oscar specifically for any of the films, but Marcia and her coeditors walked away with the Best Film Editing Award at the 1978 Oscars. Marcia was also responsible for making George keep in a couple of audience favorites he was intent on cutting—Leia kissing Luke "for luck" before they swing across the Death Star's canyon and the tiny Death Star "mouse" robot that ran in terror from a growling Chewbacca. For all that Lucasfilm publications would minimize her role postdivorce, it is undoubted that she did the most important work of the movie's three editors—including the vital Death Star dogfight, which took her eight weeks to cut together.

Meanwhile, back on the *Tantive IV*: the door at the end of the corridor fizzes and explodes. Enter the fascist-looking Stormtroopers, for whose white plastic suits the credit is disputable—but let's say one point for McQuarrie's design, and a half point to Nick Pemberton and Andrew Ainsworth for three-dimensional amendments. Battle begins, laser bolts streaking across the screen, rebel soldier stuntmen throwing themselves backwards in bloodless death. Three minutes in, and we have now seen war both between vast starships and

---

* Kurtz had to beg Laddie for an extra $50,000 just to shoot this scene.

on a human level. We know how battles are fought in this faraway galaxy: with bright florescent gee-whiz laser fire (the sound effect is Burtt scraping the guy wire of a radio tower in Palmdale with his wedding ring), lots of cool explosions, ships immobilized but not really damaged, and soldiers dying dramatically the way they did in old movies—the way kids do on the playground. The deaths play out in a way not seen since before Sam Peckinpah and Francis Coppola. There will be no blood.

Next comes a key moment: the droids escape the battle by crossing a corridor full of laser fire without getting a scratch. This improbable outcome teaches us that the droids are our Kurosawa peasants, our Shakespearean fools: they will apparently understand little of what is going on around them, and ultimately escape unharmed. If you accept this scene, or laugh benignly at it, you've already taken the leap of faith that *Star Wars* requires.

From the ridiculous to the sublime: the battle is won, the Stormtroopers stand to attention, and through the fog of war emerges a tall figure clad in all black, a cape swirling behind him and a gleaming helmet masking his face. He inspects the dead soldiers. Williams's score stops for the first time in the entire movie thus far, so that we can hear this grotesque new character breathe.

The sound of Darth Vader sipping in air through his respirator is horrific, claustrophobic, like he's in an iron lung. In fact, it's Ben Burtt again, breathing through a scuba mask. He recorded himself breathing at three different speeds, which was all the movies would ever use, depending on how animated Vader got. More than any character, Vader is a composite, for whom credit must go multiple ways: Lucas, McQuarrie, Mollo, Burtt, and sculptor Brian Muir, as well as actors Dave Prowse and James Earl Jones. Then there was Fred Roos, casting guru, who fought hard for James Earl Jones as the voice of Vader. Lucas objected to putting one black man in the film only to have him voice the villain. But Roos insisted that this went beyond racial politics: Jones simply had the best baritone of any actor alive.

The importance of Darth Vader's entrance so early in the film cannot be overstated. For the few theatergoers not on board with the story so far, it is a moment of clarity. At this first appearance, Vader says nothing, just walks out of the frame—enough to leave viewers guessing about who this character is, what's under his mask, and how much we'll see of him in the movie to come.

Vader, perhaps more than anything else, accomplishes the task of hooking the audience in the first reel—especially the kids. Take this anecdote from New Zealand–based web designer Philip Fierlinger, who was a seven-year-old in Philadelphia in the long hot summer of 1977 when his father took him to the movies. Fierlinger desperately wanted to see *Herbie the Love Bug* but was forced by his dad to see *Star Wars* because it had air conditioning. He was bored and irritated by the long scroll of words, and confused by the space battle. "Who's the good team, and who's the bad team?" he whined to his father, who couldn't tear his eyes from the screen to respond. "Then Darth Vader emerged," Fierlinger recalled, three and a half decades and dozens of viewings of *Star Wars* later. "I simultaneously shat my pants and got a boner."

That may be a slight exaggeration, but it is indicative of the general reaction to Vader: he hits you in the primeval parts. You want to either kill him, run from him, or march in lockstep (like the 501st) behind his glorious badness. Todd Evans, a young audience member at the first showing at the Piedmont in Oakland, remembered: "When Vader came out of the darkness, the entire audience starts going, 'Sssssssssss'! Some lizard part of their brain instinctively knew to hiss the bad guy." It was a scene repeated around the country, a sound that had not been heard at the movies for—well, we don't quite know when hissing at the villain fell out of favor, but you may have to go all the way back to the melodramas of the silent movie era, which Lucas adored. The fact that the music cut out at this point made that reaction easy, Kurtz suggests: "it was an invitation to hiss."

Back we go to our trusty droids, who have become briefly separated off-screen. (There was supposed to be a shot at this point of Threepio stuck under an exploded mass of wires, but that was cut by the editors and placed later in the movie, after the *Millennium Falcon* defeats its pursuing TIE fighters, to great comic effect.) We see Artoo being fed a disc of some kind by a mysterious white-robed figure—the princess mentioned, though apparently not seen, by Threepio. As the droids amble off, she removes her hood, revealing a double-bun hairdo that Lucas modeled on the hairstyles of revolutionary Mexico at the turn of the twentieth century. He was, he says, deliberately looking for a style that was unfashionable at the time.

We're five minutes in.

The battle won, the rebel prisoners are marched down a corridor along with captive droids. Vader gets his first line, interrogating the ship's captain about the location of the Death Star plans, and we hear the terrific deep basso rumble of James Earl Jones run through a synthesizer.

Vader's voice is another minor revelation for viewers and an unwelcome revelation for one of the actors. David Prowse, the British bodybuilder inside the Vader suit, was expecting his dialogue to be used in the final film, much as Anthony Daniels was for Threepio. Prowse claims Lucas had promised he would rerecord (or "loop") the lines with him later. But Prowse's Devonshire accent, which is stronger than he seems to realize, just didn't fit the role. The crew took to calling Prowse "Darth Farmer." Instead, Jones was brought in for a single day's voice work, receiving a flat fee of $7,500. Prowse, with more than a touch of bitterness, later claimed Jones was chosen when Lucas realized he didn't have a single black actor in the film (In fact, as we know from Roos, Lucas disliked that kind of tokenism). Lucas, for his part, told *Rolling Stone* in 1977 that Prowse "sort of knew" his voice wasn't going to be used in the final film.

Vader's strangulation of Captain Antilles, the rebel commander of the *Tantive IV*, is another one of those moments that plays as horror or as comedy, depending on the perspective of the viewer. Many grown-ups laughed at the brief shot of the captain's boots dangling off the floor, a shot that emphasizes Vader's height and strength. But for many of the film's younger viewers, the scene is at least mildly traumatic. At the moment when Captain Antilles expires and is hurled against a wall, one child at the May 1 test screening in San Francisco's Northpoint Theatre burst into tears. Kurtz knew this because he had been pointing microphones at the audience throughout the screening; he was able to use that recording to convince the RIAA ratings board to give the movie a teen-friendly PG rather than a Disney-esque G. Score a point for Kurtz and that San Francisco child, whoever he or she is.

We cut back to the princess attempting to evade Stormtroopers. "There's one," they say. "Set for stun." Fisher fires first, wielding her gun with an ease that had eluded the other actresses trying out for the role. This scene had nevertheless caused much hilarity for Lucas pals Hal Barwood and Matthew Robbins when they had first viewed it one day at Lucas's ever-expanding compound in San Anselmo in the fall of 1976. The pair had stopped by Lucas's editing suite to grab him for lunch at a Chinese restaurant on the main drag. Yeah, sure, said Lucas, but take a look at this scene first.

"We see Carrie Fisher in this funny gown with apple fritters on the side of her head," recalls Barwood. "Matthew and I couldn't concentrate over lunch because we were appalled by what we'd seen." The pair ran around for most of the afternoon yelling, "Set for stun," over and over. "Oh Jesus God, George," Barwood said. "What are you doing?" It wasn't until he saw a rough cut at Christmas that his attitude changed. "I was rather stunned by how much better it kept getting," he said. Still, he and Robbins have the honor of being the first people in the world to reenact a *Star Wars* scene ironically.

Back in the *Tantive IV*, Artoo, a MacGuffin on a mission, makes for the escape pod. Threepio argues with him but gets in anyway. This scene lasts twenty-three seconds. Then comes the special effects shot (the first that ILM had filmed and Lucas had approved) of the pod ejecting like an Apollo capsule, the Star Destroyer gunners declining to blast because there are no life forms aboard, the droids inside the pod thinking the distant Star Destroyer is their undamaged ship: this all takes twenty-two seconds. Princess Leia and Darth Vader have their first meeting, which lasts another thirty seconds. Vader and his underling have a conversation about the merits of imprisoning her with dark hints of torture—"leave that to me"—and a debrief on the stolen data tapes. All of which takes—you've guessed it—about half a minute.

There's already a rhythm to the film's taut editing, which—while not particularly fast by today's standards—gives us just as much as we need in each moment and no more. "When it was first released, people felt it moved very fast," said Lucas of *Star Wars* in 2004. And that speed was to the movie's advantage: cinemagoers would want to go back to the theaters to watch it again not just because it was a fun, action-packed story, but because there was so much stuff packed into each scene that you could watch it four times and still not catch every odd robot or strange creature in the background. Maybe you caught that silver replica of Threepio right behind our droid heroes in the very first scene? No? Sorry, things were moving too fast. You'll have to come back.

"The whole thrust of the film was movement," said Laddie. "That's what he was going for—to not give anybody a chance to say, 'My God, what a wonderful set.'" But Lucas's haste was also borne of a sense of embarrassment. He just didn't believe ILM's special effects were up to snuff—specifically, not up to the standard Kubrick had set in 2001. So he made sure each shot cut quickly, in the hope we wouldn't notice the film's imperfections. (Even long after it became obvious that we didn't notice or care, he still felt that way: "*Star Wars* was a joke, technically," he said of the original visual effects in 2002.)

Lucas also understood that he needed to slow down occasionally. One of those moments fills the next few minutes: Artoo and Threepio have walked out of their pod and begin to wander the desert planet, disagreeing over which way to go. And that's where we are at the movie's ten-minute mark: with the two going their separate ways on the dunes of Tatooine. Threepio delivers an ineffectual kick to Artoo's wheel unit before the odd couple splits, and as the first reel's dramatic space fantasy introduction ends, we enter the portion of the movie that simultaneously pays homage to Kurosawa and John Ford.

Are you hooked yet? Presuming the special effects haven't wowed you, and Darth Vader hasn't terrified you, then the answer depends largely on how much the two droids have transfigured into real, humanlike characters with whom you can sympathize. Artoo especially, a roller-skating trashcan with a single HAL-like camera for an eye, would seem to stretch the limits of anthropomorphism. But Ben Burtt's electronic bleeps manage to convey an improbably wide range of emotions, while Anthony Daniels's excruciatingly mannered portrayal of Threepio evokes its own strange kind of sympathy.*

These droids have personalities enough to capture the affections of many viewers who might have thought themselves above such things. "Full marks for the creation of two adorable mechanical objects which become a science-fiction apotheosis of Don Quixote and Sancho Panza," wrote Alec Guinness's friend, the successful English actor and director Peter Glenville, in a 1977 letter to Guinness after Glenville had seen the film in New York. "They make you laugh and care desperately." From Glenville, who had recently aborted his attempt at a movie version of *Man of La Mancha*, this was high praise indeed.

Yet perhaps most remarkable about the first ten minutes is who isn't in them: no Luke, no Han Solo, no Obi-Wan. The only sympathetic human character is Princess Leia, and she only has two lines. Early viewers could be forgiven for thinking the droids are actually the movie's heroes. It proves to be an ensemble film, of course, with every apparent hero leading the audience on to another apparent hero: Leia to the droids, the droids to Luke, Luke to Obi-Wan, Obi-Wan to Han, Han and Luke back to Leia.

On paper, this overpopulated plot seemed far too confusing for anyone to handle. Who is our hero, really, and where are they? "You've left the audience out," Brian De Palma told Lucas in his rant after that 1976 screening, referring to the first act. "You've vaporized the audience. They don't know what's going on." Don Glut would have a similar reaction when he saw *Star Wars* for the first time: it's *Flash Gordon*, he thought, but put through too much of an *American Graffiti*–style ensemble filter. "Who's the hero?" Glut asks, even now.

That kind of reaction was why Lucas inserted those scenes in the third draft of the script, which survived into the fourth, where the space battle was intercut with Luke Skywalker watching it from the ground. Luke then tells a bunch of fellow teens about what he had seen, while his old friend and mentor Biggs

---

* Daniels's portrayal was so droid-like, in fact, that Charley Lippincott told a reporter from science fiction magazine *Starlog* at the movie's release that Threepio was played by an actual robot—and the reporter believed him.

Darklighter returns from the Academy to tell Luke he's going to jump ship and join the rebellion.

Although he distrusted this scene and felt it a little too *American Graffiti*-esque, Lucas went so far as to shoot it because Barwood and Robbins insisted it would help clarify the movie and make it more human.* But looking at it today, it's clear it would have stopped the movie in its tracks. It was nearly five minutes of dusty dialog about the Empire nationalizing commerce in the central systems—backstory that took up half the first reel. Biggs wears a strange miniature black cape and towers over Luke. Had it made it into the final cut the scene might not have killed *Star Wars*, exactly, but it would certainly have bored and confused a good chunk of the audience far more than the ensemble effect.

Biggs's absence does leave a few confusing lines in the script: "Biggs is right, I'm never going to get out of here!" Luke complains to Threepio. But there's so much in medias res anyway, it still works. Biggs? Sure, Biggs, a friend, whatever. When Biggs actually shows up on the rebel moon of Yavin IV, suiting up and preparing to join the mission to destroy the Death Star, it's a nice reward for the repeat viewers.

The fact that Luke doesn't show up until the seventeenth minute works to the movie's advantage in another way: it's useful for latecomers. A lot of people missed the first reel while the movie was playing in theaters, especially as the word about *Star Wars* spread and lines outside the theater began to grow. As much as has been packed into the first reel, and as fast as those cuts are, the movie is still pretty easy for newcomers to pick up at the second reel: these funny robots are wandering this desert planet, easy pickings for a race of hooded dwarves with glowing yellow eyes. Got it. They've been captured and imprisoned in some kind of massive angular robot U-Haul. Looks like they're going to be sold into slavery. Who's going to buy them?

The opening reel is proof that the greatest strength of *Star Wars* is what it doesn't tell you. After all that world building he did while drafting the script, Lucas left almost all of the story's context offscreen. We never learn, for example, if this galaxy far, far away has any sort of date and time system; fans would have to invent their own chronology on the basis of the first film, with the destruction of the original Death Star marking year zero. We don't know

---

* Opening the movie with the droids, Barwood and Robbins suggested, made it look like Lucas "was making *THX 1138* all over again."

what currency Solo and Obi-Wan are using to make their deal at the cantina. We hear Solo claiming that his ship can do the Kessel Run in less than 12 parsecs, and we may wonder why he's talking about a unit of distance equivalent to 19 trillion miles (or roughly 228 trillion for the whole Kessel Run) as if it's a unit of time. Was Solo boasting about how short a distance he had to go via hyperspace? Was he just supposed to be a bullshit artist, as suggested in the shooting script? ("Ben reacts to Solo's stupid attempt to impress them with obvious information.") Or did the word "parsec" have a different meaning in the galaxy far, far away?

Some of these questions are answered in Foster's novelization (Foster changed "parsecs" to "standard time units" because he "just couldn't let that one go"), and it is the poorer for it. Mysteriousness is what fires our imaginations. We acquire just enough knowledge to incubate the idea of *Star Wars*, and a backstory of our own invention starts spilling out of us. Lucas, despite his negative experience with the uninformative nature of *THX 1138*, trusted the audience to dream up the missing details, and the audience paid him back in spades. The next four decades would be spent filling in every conceivable gap—the name of every droid on every ship, the species of every alien in the background of the Mos Eisley cantina, every detail of the Clone Wars.

But that wasn't where moviegoers' heads were at in 1977. In the warm afterglow of that rebel medal ceremony, they had more pressing questions than the origin of the hammerhead creature in the cantina, or how Luke's proton torpedoes managed to make a 90-degree turn to go down the ventilation shaft, or why Chewbacca didn't get his own medal. The movie, after all, had left lots more urgent loose ends: What had happened to Obi-Wan? Who will wind up with the princess, Han or Luke? Who was Luke's father? What evil lurked beneath Vader's mask, and is he still alive after being spun off into space during the Death Star battle? Did the rebels just win the war against the Empire? Probably not; there was some talk of the Emperor, and he wasn't anywhere to be seen. It says *Star Wars*, plural. There have to be more, right?

12.

RELEASE

The cards seemed stacked against *Star Wars* from the beginning, but never more so than at its opening in theaters. It was released on the Wednesday before Memorial Day. Those ten- to fourteen-year-old kids Lucas had intended as the target audience were still in school. (In theory, that is; there were at least four kids playing hooky at that first 10:45 A.M. showing at the Coronet.) The movie had opened in just thirty-two theaters, with eleven more scheduled to join in over the next few days. (By comparison, *A Bridge Too Far* and *New York, New York* were opening in four hundred theaters around the same time.) And how well had *Star Wars* been advertised by that most traditional of means, the trailer? Just that one trailer for the film had come out the previous Christmas, disappeared, and returned at Easter.

Yet on that first day, the movie took in $255,000, or about $8,000 per location. In 1977, that was what most theaters took in during an entire week. It was a record for most of the thirty-two houses that showed the movie. The take wasn't distributed evenly, of course. Mann's Chinese Theatre in Hollywood saw its largest ever one-day box office for a single movie: $19,358. At $4 a ticket, that meant about 4,800 Angelinos squeezed into five showings in a single day. (A dozen or more of those tickets were bought by Hugh Heffner and his Play-boy Mansion posse, who parked a fleet of limos in front of the lines at Mann's, determined to see what all the fuss was about; Heffner ended up watching it twice.)

Charley Lippincott's cabal got to work alerting the media, but the media were slow to act. *Variety* and other newspapers would report the first day's record-breaking ticket grosses, but on-the-scene reports from the lines outside theaters would not appear in newspapers until the weekend. Still, it didn't take long for a new breed of fan to emerge: the repeat viewer. Kurtz was doing an east coast media tour on May 26, flying from TV appearances in Boston and New York, when he was caught off-guard during a show in Washington, DC, by a caller who phoned in to say he'd already seen *Star Wars* four or five times already—exactly as many times as the movie had shown in his town at that point.

In May 1977, repeat viewers didn't necessarily add to the ticket gross: they could simply stay in the theater, wait an hour or so, and watch the movie again. This was not something viewers had tended to want to do before. Indeed, it was because of *Star Wars* that most cinemas instituted a policy of clearing the audience out of the theater between shows. But as soon as they left the theater and came back, the repeat viewers were responsible for an incalculable amount of box office takings. For many—and this is something you see time and again in television and newspaper reports from 1977—the number of times they'd seen *Star Wars* took on the tone of a competitive sport: "I've seen Star Wars twenty times!" But for many more who weren't quoted by the news media, it was simply a thrill to invest themselves in a story with such eminent repeatability. You could see it twenty, thirty, forty times and not get bored.

One such fan was Christian Gossett. The son of an actor and an *LA Times* reporter, Gossett was nine years old when he saw *Star Wars* at Mann's Chinese Theatre on opening day. "My father had this wonderful habit—when there was a movie he wanted to see, he'd let us out of school that day and we'd go in the afternoon," Gossett remembers. "*Star Wars* was the first film that was so good, we unanimously agreed that as soon as Mom got off work, we were going to drag her to see it again. There was this wonderful warm glow, the feeling that you could just jump in the car and go to the theater and be in that world again. It was like the analog 1977 version of Video On Demand." Gossett would grow up to become the artist who invented the double-bladed lightsaber used in *Episode I*.

On Friday, two days after the movie's debut, *Star Wars* opened in another nine theaters. There was still far too much demand and far too little supply. Other theater owners, the "cusses with their big cigars" Lippincott had bored to death, would have loved to join in on the *Star Wars* sensation immediately but had to honor preexisting bookings first. Fox had also inadvertently helped to create this publicity-boosting shortage by grossly underestimating demand. The executives, Laddie excepted, simply hadn't thought *Star Wars* was worth the celluloid it was printed on; Fox began with less than a hundred prints and had to start cranking out extras as fast as it could once it became clear *Star Wars* was the event of the season. As early as May 25, the company cannily turned the *Other Side of Midnight* strategy on its head: now, they told owners, if you want to book *Star Wars*, you have to book *Other Side of Midnight* as well.

The lines at theaters stretched around the block from that very first 10:45 A.M. showing at the Coronet, and they did not quit. The Avco Theater in Westwood had to hire sixty new staffers just to control the crowds and take their tickets. Its manager boasted, somewhat ruefully, that he had to turn away five thousand people on Memorial Day weekend. The manager of the Coronet, a cranky old soul named Al Levine, had never seen anything like it. He offered a now-famous description of the crowds: "Old people, young people, children, Hare Krishna groups. They bring cards to play in line. We have checker players, we have chess players; people with paint and sequins on their faces. Fruit eaters like I've never seen before, people loaded on grass and LSD."

Levine was onto something. The release of *Star Wars* coincided with record levels of marijuana usage among high school students; according to government statistics, the trend would peak in 1978 and has been falling ever since. Almost every review described the movie as a "joyful fun ride" or a "visual triumph"—a surefire lure for heads wanting to kill a few hours in mindless, psychedelic bliss. And as for the title—well, Fox's marketing department could not have been more wrong in its assessment that audiences would see "star" and think of Hollywood celebrities. The Woodstock and post-Woodstock generation saw "star" and thought not of Hollywood celebrities, but Ziggy Stardust, the Starland Vocal Band, Ringo Starr, the Atlanta rock band Starbuck, "we are stardust, we are golden," "Good morning starshine," "There's a Star Man waiting in the sky." Lucas's creation arrived at the tail end of the glam rock and the height of the disco years. The Sex Pistols were to release "God Save the Queen" on May 27, 1977, igniting the punk era—but for now, stars were still cool. *Star Wars* may not have needed the assistance of the drug culture; it was groundbreaking for the straights, too. But 1970s America's fondness for toking up before heading to the theater certainly didn't hurt those first-week grosses.

Nor did the growing popularity of *Star Trek*. The show that wouldn't die was stronger than ever in early 1977, with plans for a second TV show in the offing. But in the absence of a big-screen *Star Trek* movie, something Gene Roddenberry had been trying to get off the ground for years, *Star Wars* certainly seemed like the next best thing. Charley Lippincott had deliberately avoided making overtures to the Trekkers out of respect; most came anyway. "I was a *Star Trek* fan first," says Dan Madsen, then a fourteen-year-old in Denver. "But I've got to be honest, when *Star Wars* came out, I took down all *Star Trek* posters in my bedroom and plastered my wall with *Star Wars*. It took over our territory." Madsen would grow up to befriend both Gene Roddenberry and George Lucas, and he would end up running both *Star Wars* and *Star Trek* official fan clubs. But in 1977, there was no question where his loyalties lay.

You can see this shift most readily in the pages of *Starlog*, the most widely read science fiction monthly of the era. *Starlog* had launched in 1976, packed to the gills with *Star Trek* episode guides and breathless reports on the conventions. In the June 1977 issue, on newsstands when *Star Wars* debuted, there was a single one-page article about the movie that Lippincott had urged the magazine to run. The unsigned, unheadlined article was barely more than a caption to a couple of old McQuarrie paintings, yet it still managed to botch the details of *Star Wars* in spectacular fashion: the movie apparently featured a "laser sabre," white-clad "robot guards," and "an ancient mysterious technique for working one's will, known simply as 'The Power.'" But from that point on, *Starlog* might as well have called itself *Star Wars* magazine. The movie reigned as the cover story of the July issue; for the August number, now stuffed with ads for *Star Wars* merchandise, editor Kerry O'Quinn composed an unusually gushing editorial. He recounted leaving the theater after his first *Star Wars* viewing and encountering "two people arguing about the scientific accuracy of some of the film's dialogue," to which someone overhearing in the next aisle boomed, "So what!" The pendulum of attention swung from science fiction to space fantasy, from Verne to Wells, from Roddenberry to Lucas, almost overnight.

Star Trek fans started talking about having "graduated" from *Trek*. A cartoon published in a *Trek* zine reflected the growing anxiety about *Star Wars* within *Trek* fandom. "That's mutiny!" declared Captain Kirk, glowering at a line of Starfleet officers waiting to see *Star Wars*. "Yes," responded one carefree officer in the cartoon, "I guess it is." *Trek* fanzine *Spectrum* reported that "two extremes have already formed: one saying that '*Trek* is Dead,' citing *Star Wars* as its killer; and the other faction maintains a grin-and-bear it attitude, assuming that the enthusiasm will eventually wane, leaving ST fandom intact, and that *Star Wars* 'is just another rerun movie.'"

Neither faction's prediction would turn out to be correct. *Star Wars* was a rising tide that lifted the *Star Trek* boat soon enough. But in the short term,

Trek fans started turning out *Star Wars* fiction fanzines almost immediately after the release of the movie. They had names like *Moonbeam* and *Skywalker*, *Hyper Space* and *Alderaan*. Their writers received dire warnings from *Trek* fans that Lucasfilm was likely to have a harsher attitude toward fan-written fiction than did Paramount, the studio that owned the *Star Trek* franchise. But that wasn't quite the case. Sure, when it came to clamping down on the *sale* of anything with a *Star Wars* name, Lucasfilm would prove to be a testy and controlling rights holder, harsher than even those knowing Trekkers could have predicted.

But the intent at Lucasfilm was to give a lot of leeway to the fans. "We're working out a policy about fanzines," wrote Craig Miller, Lucasfilm's first head of fan relations, in a thank-you note to the editor of *Hyper Space* in 1977 (the editor had sent Lucas an early copy of the zine; Kurtz had read and enjoyed it, and directed Miller to respond). "A problem with copyright has to be resolved." Later, zine editors were told the nature of that problem: the Fox lawyers were suspicious of zines, and Lucasfilm was trying to convince them of the positive effects of fandom. Most zine writers felt safer publishing stories that were obvious satires (satire having more legal protection under copyright law). The spoof-friendly nature of *Star Wars* struck again.

The only line that could not be crossed, as far as Lucas was concerned, was the erotic one. Hetero- and homoerotic "slash fiction"—the name comes from the slash in "Spock/Kirk"—had been a staple of *Star Trek* zines for years. But Lucas made it clear early on that he only wanted to see PG-rated fan stories. Lucasfilm's legal department later sent stern warnings to writers of two X-rated fan stories: one Swedish fan story that featured Darth Vader sexually torturing Han Solo, and one American tale in which Solo and Leia hooked up. "The word has come down from George Lucas himself," wrote Maureen Garrett, director of the official *Star Wars* fan club, "that *Star Wars* pornography is unquestionably unacceptable." Garrett cited the "damage done to the wholesomeness associated with the *Star Wars* saga." Lippincott learned that Lucas was in earnest about this when he returned from a press tour of Japan with Mark Hamill and brought some *Star Wars* pornographic manga back for the boss as a joke. Lucas hit the roof, demanding the makers be sued. There were no grounds: the copyright for *Star Wars* had not yet been registered in Japan because it hadn't been released there yet. But Lippincott never heard the end of it. "I really learned to watch it with George," he said. It was a lesson many others would learn in time.

B y day 6, at the end of the Memorial Day weekend, *Star Wars* had brought in $2.5 million in ticket sales. That did not technically make it the highest grossing movie in America; *Smokey and the Bandit*, which opened that weekend, beat it with a take of $2.7 million. But Smokey was showing on 386 screens, and *Star Wars*, by that point, was only on 43.

Besides, nobody was making buttons out of quotes from *Smokey and the Bandit*. The kids were doing that with *Star Wars* faster than Kurtz and Lippincott could keep up. And it wasn't just buttons. The 70s was the age of the everyday T-shirt and button entrepreneurs, too. So before you could say "cult favorite," youngsters everywhere were making "May the Force Be With You" buttons and donning "I'm Hot for Han Solo" T-shirts. Many fans remember buttons being handed out, and T-shirts being sold, outside theaters even on day 1.

Every news publication did its requisite *Star Wars* story. *Time* magazine, at the height of its powers and readership in 1977, had flagged its Jay Cocks story in a corner at the top of the cover. It simply read "Year's Best Movie." *Star Wars* would have had the whole cover, but for the election of Menachem Begin in Israel; last-minute switches like that happened all the time at Time. It didn't matter; the corner was poking out of every newsstand, creating buzz even if you didn't buy the magazine. Every TV news program had done a segment on the crowds waiting to see this amazing movie—up to and including the voice of America, CBS news anchor Walter Cronkite. His coverage marked a major milestone. In 1968, President Lyndon Johnson famously declared after Cronkite's negative report on the war in Vietnam that "if I've lost Cronkite, I've lost Middle America." The converse was true in 1977: if *Star Wars* had won Cronkite, it had won Middle America. This wasn't just a movie for kids, science fiction fans, stoners, and assorted weirdos. In the space of a week, space fantasy had gone mainstream.

The Cronkite segment, which George and Marcia Lucas watched from the comfort and safety of Hawaii, was the first they saw of the media hype. They had arranged months previously to fly to Hawaii two days after the movie opened, partly to escape what Lucas was certain was going to be a disaster. The couple had not had a proper vacation since Europe in 1971, six years earlier. It was time to get away, and the Lucases had their sights set on the Mauna Kea hotel on the Big Island with Willard Huyck and Gloria Katz.

Greater need had no man for a tropical escape than Lucas had at that moment. The final push at the sound-mixing theater had taken the last drop of his energy. Of course, Lucas had to micromanage the process, along with the final edits. He pulled thirty-six-hour days. Carrie Fisher found him collapsed on a couch at his little editing facility, the office long ago leased on the Universal lot, muttering that he never wanted to do this again. Lucas ran the deadline of May 25 hard: the legend that cans of film were being rushed over to theaters as the first reels were already playing may not be true, but it's not that far from reality.

And still he wasn't satisfied. Special Edition haters take note: George Lucas started reworking *Star Wars* not in 1997, but on May 25, 1977. As the opening day dawned, Lucas was still unhappy with the Dolby 5.1 stereo sound mix; there were a few lines of Mark Hamill's that didn't sound quite right. All day Lucas beavered on the mix while lines were forming at thirty-two theaters around the country. By nightfall, he still hadn't finished. When Marcia clocked in for her shift night-editing *New York, New York*, they were both zombies.

George and Marcia's dinner break that night would become one of the most famous and oft quoted meals in entertainment history. The Lucases sat in Hamburger Hamlet, directly opposite Mann's, one of the world's most famous theaters, watching the crowds and the Playboy limos outside without realizing that *Star Wars* was playing there. It wasn't just that they were exhausted; it's that William Friedkin's *Sorcerer* was supposed to have been playing Mann's. But it had been delayed, and nobody had told Lucas *Star Wars* had been booked instead. Score another one for Lippincott's persuasive posse.

And what did Lucas do after finding out that it was his movie, not Friedkin's, that was causing a ruckus at Mann's? He headed back to the studio to call Mark Hamill. He at least had the decency to be gleeful first: "Hi, kid, are you famous yet?" Then he asked Hamill to come in—not to celebrate, but to rerecord some of his dialogue. Hamill declined. Marcia, at least, had the sense to buy two bottles of champagne.

That night, Lucas refused to believe his luck. It was too early to celebrate. He was running on fumes; it was time to head for the beach. In Hawaii with Marcia and Huyck and Katz, he wanted to forget the movie even existed. Then a few days in, Laddie telephoned the hotel. "I said 'Laddie, I'm on vacation, I don't care what happens to the movie, it doesn't make any different to me,'" Lucas recalled. "He said 'turn on Channel 5, turn on Walter Cronkite, wait till you see what's going on." It took Cronkite, Lucas's preferred news anchor, to drive the message home. "Well," said Lucas, "I guess maybe this is a huge hit."

In June 1977, the monster crowds at the four theaters in New York showing the film each required police on horseback for crowd control. All walks of life rubbed shoulders in those lines. Johnny Cash, Muhammad Ali, and Senator Ted Kennedy waited at their theaters like everyone else. Elvis Presley tried a different tack; the King was in the process of securing a *Star Wars* print to screen for himself and Lisa Marie at Graceland the day before he died.

Even the stoic Gary Kurtz was starting to believe *Star Wars* was a huge hit. "We were dismissing the lines on the basis that for the first three or four weeks it would probably have nothing but science fiction fans," he says. "It's only after a month, and they were still there, that we realized it was becoming a self-perpetuating phenomenon."

The posse's instincts had been proved correct beyond their wildest imaginings. There had been enough word of mouth in the science fiction community to draw first-week crowds. Glowing reviews brought in the week 2 and 3 crowds. News stories about the size of the crowds brought in the post–Memorial Day crowd. The lines metastasized, producing yet more stories about neighbors being frustrated, trash piling up at the end of the day, and local merchants making a fast buck from the whole scene.

Those who saw the film, those who were in the know, were familiar with funny-sounding names and catchphrases. They had joined an exclusive club that knew about "the Force," even if everyone had a different theory on what it actually was. Suddenly *Star Wars* was a lot more than the sum of its box office. It was famous for being famous.

There was one more factor driving audiences back time and again: the stunning, immersive, rarely heard-before Dolby stereo setup. This was an era when most theaters still offered a single paltry mono speaker behind the screen, and most theater owners figured their patrons cared little for sound quality. Fox was having a hard time persuading the owners to spend the $6,000 or so necessary to upgrade to Dolby stereo, so it started paying for the installations itself. The deal was that if the movie turned out to be a success for the theater, the owners would pay Fox back for the system. This was a pretty safe bet on Fox's part.

The studio recognized its good fortune faster than Lucas and Kurtz did. Laddie was instantly and widely feted as having believed in a difficult project, stuck to his guns, and saved an ailing company. "There could be a 21st Century Fox after all," marveled *People* in July. Fox stock was worth $13 a share just before *Star Wars* was released. A month later it hit $23. A stock rising 76 percent in a month would be front-page news in any era, but in the depressed market of the late 1970s, that was a leap worthy of the *Six Million Dollar Man*. Laddie's salary took a massive jump too, from $182,000 to $563,000. He was elected to the board of directors in July. The accountants began parking the company's newfound wealth by investing in an Aspen ski resort and Pebble Beach golf course. Fox's fiscal 1977 profits, $79 million, were double the previous record annual profit. "*Star Wars* was like they struck gold," Laddie says. "They went crazy with the money they made."

A couple of things were quickly and quietly forgotten on the Fox lot. One is how close the company came to selling *Star Wars'* profits to its West Germans partners. Laddie says he never knew about the complicated tax shelter scheme (which would not be uncovered by reporters until 1980; also kept quiet until then was the unsuccessful $25 million lawsuit that ricocheted back from the West Germans). Fox had withdrawn from its verbal agreement with the tax shelter after the company's executives saw the positive feedback cards from the preview screening in San Francisco at the Northpoint Theatre on May 1.*

Laddie was about as jubilant as Laddie gets. His daughter Amanda, then four, remembers him driving her past the lines at the Avco theater in West Hollywood. By July 1977, he had seen *Star Wars* thirty times. Officially, the Fox boss's repeat trips were to check and triple check that the audience approval really was universal. But you don't go to sit through something thirty times without loving it. Laddie, it seems, was entranced just like everyone else.

For Fox, however, the triumph was bittersweet. The company's deal with Lucas had been the essence of penny wise and pound foolish. Because the film had gone over-budget—thanks in large part to ILM spending twice its $1.5 million allotment—Fox was able to dock $15,000 from Lucas's relatively meager $150,000 salary. At the same time, however, it had to hand him 40 cents of every dollar the studio made out of renting the film to theaters, and 50 cents out of every dollar made from merchandising. That last concession now stood to lose the company millions even as it made the company millions.

But because Fox still had a contractual ability to put out its own *Star Wars* product, there were already $39.95 "metallic-looking vinyl" C-3PO, Storm-trooper, and Darth Vader whole-head masks on the market; the Chewbacca mask was rubber "with hand-applied hair." That summer you could pick up an R2-D2 thermos for $3.95. A company called Factors Inc. got the license to make T-shirt transfers, printed them up on the cheapest, Mexico-made, white

---

* Not all the cards were positive. Kurtz still has one framed in his office, penned by an anon-ymous twenty-two-year-old man. "This is the worst film I've ever seen since Godzilla versus the Smog Monster," is all it says.

T-shirts it could find, and flooded the market with them. Few fans seemed to know or care that in its haste, Factors had misspelled Darth Vader's name. Fox let Weingeroff, the jewelry company, rush out a line of cheap Threepio, Artoo, Vader, and X-Wing earrings. Topps was hard at work on its first line of *Star Wars* bubble gum cards, designed by a young underground comics artist working a day job there, named Art Spiegelman.

And then there was the wall art. In May 1977, the most popular poster in America was an image of Farrah Fawcett, chief Charlie's Angel, in a bathing suit, with a noticeably aroused nipple. By July, *Star Wars* posters were outselling Fawcett five to one.

Fox's greatest problem, however, wasn't that it would have to hand Lucas half of everything they'd already made on those deals. It was that Lucas had complete control over the now-inevitable sequels. The best Fox could hope for was that Lucas would stay in Hawaii until 1979 and ignore the clause in the contract that would revert sequel rights to Fox if he didn't start filming the follow-on movie within two years. Somehow, that seemed unlikely. The best they could do was go looking for the next *Star Wars*—and never make the same mistake again.

Meanwhile in Hawaii, Huyck and Katz had bid farewell to the Lucases, and George, in a moment that feels like a distinct changing of the guard, invited Steven Spielberg, the only other director in the world to have had this much success, to come and take a break from *Close Encounters*. Coppola, stuck in the Philippines and slowly going crazy on the washed-out *Apocalypse Now* shoot, where costs and egos were spiraling out of control, sent Lucas a congratulatory telex. It contained a terse request, one of those asks when a friend in need tries to sound as if he's joking: "send money."*

Lucas and Spielberg built sandcastles and vaguely discussed their future. They knew they were in the ascendancy, the two most financially successful directors in the business. With *Jaws* and *Star Wars*, it was clear, Lucas and Spielberg had created a new genre: the summer blockbuster. A team-up seemed inevitable. Lucas and Spielberg were cut from the same cloth: both ruthless perfectionists who managed to stubbornly retain a childlike sense of wonder. Naturally, there was some competition between the two friends, but they were

---

* At the same time, Coppola's entourage was bitterly deriding *Star Wars* as "twerp cinema."

both invested in each other's success—quite literally. Back in Alabama on the set of *Close Encounters*, Lucas, convinced that Spielberg's would be the bigger movie, had granted his friend 2.5 percent of the profits of *Star Wars*, and Spielberg reciprocated—a kind of blood-brothers ritual known in the industry as swapping points. Today we know that Spielberg got the better end of that deal; that 2.5 percent has made him $40 million and counting. But in the summer of 1977, Lucas could still win the bet: with Douglas Trumball special effects and a John Williams soundtrack, *Close Encounters* could conceivably leapfrog *Star Wars* the way *Star Wars* was set to leapfrog *Jaws*.

And after that? Spielberg vented his frustration to Lucas on that vacation, complaining that he really wanted to do a James Bond movie, but that Bond producer Cubby Broccoli had turned him down three times already. Lucas said that he had something better than Bond. He told Spielberg about an idea he'd had for an homage to other action-adventure movies of the 1930s—the Errol Flynn epics, *King Solomon's Mines*, that sort of thing. The hero would be a dashing archeologist called Indiana Smith. Unlike *Star Wars*, he conceived it as a franchise even before it was written: "a series of films he hoped would reinstate high adventure," Spielberg recalled a few years later. He was excited—this was "James Bond without the hardware"—but, he said, the name Indiana Smith was too dull. Okay, said Lucas. How about Indiana Jones?

That was about as far as the conversation got before Lucas was interrupted by more phone calls from Fox about *Star Wars* grosses.

Lucas had one more specific daydream in Hawaii. With giant amounts of wealth coming his way, he realized, he would finally be able to make his Marin County–based filmmaker's utopia—a fantasy deferred since the early days of American Zoetrope—a reality. It was time to return to the mainland and to the universe that *Star Wars* had reshaped in his absence.

B y the time George and Marcia flew home, *Star Wars* had an even greater stranglehold on the popular imagination. Laddie was increasingly certain that *Star Wars* would overtake the highest grossing movie of all time, *Jaws*, at some point that year—just as soon as *Star Wars* could get in enough theaters. *Jaws* had only had half of *Star Wars'* viewers per screen.

If he was going to have any chance of surfing this rising tide of interest, Lucas would have to expand his business, fast. The Star Wars Corporation was still only comprised of a dozen people operating out of trailers on the Universal lot. How rough they must have looked compared to his Marin County dream.

While in Los Angeles, Lucas hired a personal assistant, Jane Bay, a Universal staffer who happened to be thinking about moving to Northern California herself. Bay would become his staunchest protector, sticking with Lucas until they both retired in 2012.

From this point on, Lucas would need a buffer: the world's press, and assembled fans and crazies, were beating paths to his doors. He'd been told of one instance of a knife-wielding man walking into the LA offices, claiming he wrote the movie and demanding his cut. For Lucas, who couldn't even stand to be stopped in the street by strangers, it was too much. "I'm an introvert. I don't want to be famous," Lucas pleaded to *People* in July. "I get nervous when people recognize me and say, 'I loved your movie.'" The magazine helped his cause by leading the article with a large photograph of Laddie instead.

As Lucas went to New York for the premiere of—what else?—*New York, New York*, he clung to anonymity as tightly as he could. At a party at the Sherry-Netherland Hotel, he learned of hundreds of autograph hunters waiting in the lobby. Lucas tried to convince Edward Summer to take his place. Both men had beards and glasses. "They don't know exactly what I look like," Lucas said. "Just go out and sign some stuff; they'll never know the difference." Around that time, Lucas decided he and Summer should hide out by going to a near-empty theater showing William Friedkin's *Sorcerer*. Lucas enjoyed the thriller; as they emerged into daylight, Summer remembers him shaking his head in amazement at the long lines for *Star Wars* across the street. He still couldn't quite believe it had come to this.

If he didn't want adulation, what did Lucas want to do next? That high adventure movie with Spielberg, for sure, but "more than anything else," he told Lippincott, "I would like to see high adventure in space. . . . Science fiction still has a tendency to make itself so pious and serious, which is what I tried to knock out in making *Star Wars*." The old Wells-Verne rivalry between space fantasy and science fiction was to be settled once and for all.

One of the most interesting and pivotal interviews of Lucas's career came on this New York visit, as he talked to *Rolling Stone*'s managing editor Paul Scanlon in his hotel suite. By now, it seems, Lucas's luck had sunk in, and he knew he was about to become the most financially successful filmmaker in history. The interview captures him in an expansive, forward-thinking mood. Despite declaring that *Star Wars* was just 25 percent of what he wanted it to be because he "cut corners" and engaged in some "fast filmmaking," Lucas was finally able to take a measure of pride in some of its scenes. Scanlon told Lucas that the moment when the *Millennium Falcon* hits hyperspace got a cheer every time he'd seen it. Lucas was quick to point out how easy the shot was to do, and indeed it was when you looked closely—a green-screen light field in the cockpit, and then the camera pulls back from the *Falcon* very fast while the stars rotate. But finally he conceded the point and offered the kind of homily you can imagine Lucas saying in his boy racer days: "There's nothing like popping the old ship into hyperspace to give you a real thrill."

He had grandiose dreams for the *Star Wars* series and more modest visions of what Lucasfilm's corporate side could become. In time, the two would flip. This was the first time Lucas publicly discussed the possibility of more *Star Wars* movies—plural. "This film is a success, and I think the sequels will be a success," he said. "The sequels will be much, much better." His vision was that *Star Wars* would be another kind of James Bond franchise, with room for a variety of directors and interpretations. He would be executive producer. He was done directing them—for now:

> What I want to do is direct the last sequel. I could do the first one and the last one and let everyone else do the ones in between. . . . The people are there, the environment is there, the Empire is there . . . everything is there. And now people will start building on it. I've put up the concrete slab of the walls and now everybody can have fun drawing the pictures and putting on the little gargoyles and doing all the really fun stuff. And it's a competition. I'm hoping if I get friends of mine they will want to do a much better film, like, "I'll show George that I can do a film twice that good," and I think they can, but then I want to do the last one, so I can do one twice as good as everybody else.

At this moment of triumph, Lucas shunned his second mentor in favor of his first. "I have never been like Francis and some of my other friends," he said, "constantly in debt and having to keep working to keep up their empires." Lucas's empire would be more modest—apparently, after that Hollywood adventure of the past decade, he wanted to become a shopkeeper like his father. "I want to be able to have a store where I can sell all the great things that I want," is how he put it. That would include comic art, which the Supersnipe store he'd opened with Summer was already selling, as well as old rock and roll records and antique toys. Revealing for the first time his diabetes, Lucas said his magical store would also sell "good hamburgers and sugarless ice cream, because all the people who can't eat sugar deserve it."

It all sounded so easy—use his *Star Wars* income as seed money for a cool entrepreneurial venture and, as a hobby, go back to making those experimental films he'd told Foster about. He would be the wizard in the wings, the man behind the curtain, the low-sugar Willy Wonka. The continuing *Star Wars* story? That would run itself.

13.

THE ACCIDENTAL EMPIRE

At the end of 1954, the golden year when the Lucas family first acquired a television, Disney aired four one-hour films about the life of a Tennessee congressman who lost his life in the Alamo. The company was caught off guard by the show's popularity, which led to an incredible $300 million merchandising bonanza in the space of a year. Kids went wild for the show's hero, pestering parents to buy his toy guns, sheets, watches, lunch boxes, underwear, mugs, towels, rugs, and pajamas. Most especially, they bought his headgear, a coonskin cap, which reportedly sold at a rate of five thousand caps per day in 1955 alone. The price of raccoon fur jumped from 25 cents to $8 a pound.

Most of the windfall went to independent sellers; at the time, licensing as we know it today simply didn't exist. But the young Lucas saw the results all around him, stored the example away in his memory, and would draw on it some twenty-one years later as he labored over his third film.

In 1976, talking to Lippincott after shooting *Star Wars*, Lucas cast his mind back to this 1950s craze. He was trying to explain how his movie might just be the first feature film to have an impact in merchandising, and this Disney TV miniseries was the biggest merchandising hit in his memory.

"*Star Wars*," Lucas mused, "could be a type of Davy Crockett phenomenon."

That, of course, turned out to be the understatement of the century.

To understand the degree to which Lucas's creation outstripped Davy Crockett, to see the true scope of four decades of *Star Wars'* physical presence— both its merchandise and fan-created gear—you need to visit a chicken ranch in Petaluma, Northern California.

Appointments are required to enter through the ranch's wrought-iron gate, which is adorned with a portrait of Alec Guinness. You park by flagpoles flying the banners of the rebellion and the Empire, and walk past the private home that says "Casa Kenobi." There used to be twenty thousand chickens on this property; now there are fewer than six in a single coop, near the corner of Yoda Trail and Jedi Way. The others have been replaced, in a long former chicken barn, by what the Guinness Book of Records recognized in 2013 as the world's largest *Star Wars* collection. Welcome to Rancho Obi-Wan.

Up a narrow stairway Steve Sansweet greets you near an alcove with a talking head of Obi-Wan. The bust looks like Guinness, Obi-Wan number 1, but it has the prerecorded voice of James Arnold Taylor, Obi-Wan number three, from the *Clone Wars* cartoon. "Your visit may provoke feelings of intense jealousy," the voice warns. "But do not give into hate. That leads to the Dark Side. If you're lucky, you won't also give in to a spending spree. So get ready for a galactic, physical and spiritual reawakening . . . from a certain point of view."

Sansweet is snarky and avuncular, bursting with knowledge—he cowrote the official *Star Wars Encyclopedia*, the *Ultimate Guide to Star Wars Action Figures*, and many more besides. He's somewhere between a vaudeville comedian and a gossip, always ready with a quip and another collector's item to show you. With bushy black eyebrows framed by a silver beard, he looks like a mischievous Santa Claus. You might think him a retired TV host, which in fact he is: he helped QVC sell *Star Wars* gear during sixty hours of shows during the 1990s. "And I always bought one of whatever I was selling," he says. He's not kidding.

Sansweet was raised in Philadelphia, went to journalism school, and reported on the JFK assassination for the college paper. As a *Wall Street Journal* reporter in Los Angeles in 1976, he started collecting toy robots after writing a front-page story about a collector; the robots reignited a long-held passion for science fiction. Then one day at the office, he noticed another reporter toss an invitation in the trash. It was to the media preview of a new movie called *Star Wars*. Sansweet fished it out, and a few days later his life changed forever. That invite, and the movie program, are the first items in his collection. "I was already in my 30s," he wrote, "but realized this was what I had been waiting my whole life for."

Sansweet had to wait another twenty years until he could parlay his love of *Star Wars* into a job at Lucasfilm, as head of fan relations. By then his house in LA had gained an extra two floors and five storage lockers, all to hold his collection. And that was before the prequel movies, which saw by far the largest explosion in *Star Wars* merchandise in the franchise's history. Sansweet is a collecting machine: a scavenger of sets, a friend to every licensee and fan artist. He swoops on eBay offerings and divorce sales. He has a black belt in price negotiation. There's a poster in his office, signed by George Lucas, which confers on Sansweet the title of "ultimate fan."

At first, Sansweet was determined to keep his collection private. His Petaluma chicken farm, the only place his real estate agent could find near Skywalker Ranch that was large enough to hold his stuff, was too remote to seriously consider turning it into a museum. But after leaving Lucasfilm in 2011 (he's still a part-time adviser), Sansweet was convinced by friends that there was enough interest to convert the place into a nonprofit. It would offer regular tours for anyone who takes out a membership. With just two employees, Rancho Obi-Wan already has one thousand members, paying $40 a year each.

Sansweet provides a quick tour of the library—which contains books from thirty-seven countries in thirty-four languages—and the art and poster room, where all the unopened boxes live. His assistant, Anne Neumann, is usually to be found here, still struggling to catalog everything in the collection; her official estimate, after seven years and ninety-five thousand items catalogued, is that there are at least another three hundred thousand items and counting. To put that in perspective, the British Museum has fifty thousand items on display at any one time.

We travel down a cramped corridor of movie posters, and you can't help but wonder where the real goods are. Then Sansweet knocks at a door. "Mr. Williams," he says, "are you ready for us?" Then in a stage whisper, he adds: "Very temperamental."

As the door swings open and John Williams's *Star Wars* theme begins, you gaze down the stairs at what a twenty-first-century type of Davy Crockett phenomenon looks like.

It's the large items you notice first: the life-size Darth Vader with red lightsaber drawn (codpiece and helmet from the original costume), the original mold of Han Solo in carbonite, the larger-than-life Boba Fett, the head of Jar Jar Binks, the stuffed Wampa, an animatronic version of the Modal Nodes band from the Mos Eisley cantina, the iconic bicycle from Skywalker Ranch with lightsabers for handlebars and a Vader-shaped bell (known as the Empire Strikes Bike).

Seconds later, as your eyes adjust, you take in the rows upon rows of stuff. It's packed tightly into shelves as if it were a department store where space is at a premium—except the space seems to go on forever, with at least two sets of shelves on every wall, vanishing into the distance, where stands a life-size Lego Boba Fett and a *Star Wars* marquee from 1977. There are rooms beyond that, just out of sight: a corridor constructed to look like one on the *Tantive IV* leads to the artwork, the arcade games, the pinball machines.

This is the point at which grown men and women have been known to weep. It is also the point at which one of two things tends to dawn on their partners: "I get it now," and "Okay, maybe that collection at home isn't so bad after all."

Star Wars has generated more collectable paraphernalia than any other franchise on the planet—but it had surprisingly little help from its creator. At some point in 1975, working on the interminable second draft and sipping coffee, George Lucas thought of dog breed mugs. They were all the rage in the 1970s. Wouldn't it be fun to have a mug that looked like a Wookiee? That, and the fact that R2-D2 looked like a cookie jar, were the only specific pieces of merchandise that Lucas has admitted envisioning while writing the film.

But Lucas knew the movie was ripe with possibilities for spin-off products. Having grown up the son of a stationery and toy store owner, having constructed his own toys, he remained fascinated by their potential and wasn't the least bit ashamed of his interest. When the director George Cukor told Lucas at a film conference in the early 1970s that he hated the term "filmmaker" because it sounded like "toymaker," Lucas shot back that he would rather be a toymaker than a director, which sounded too businesslike. Movie sets were play sets; actors were action figures. "Basically I like to make things move," he said in 1977. "Just give me the tools and I'll make the toys." Toys "followed from the general idea" of *Star Wars*, he told a French reporter later that year.

Before *Star Wars*, no one had ever made a dime out of toy merchandising associated with a movie. The previous attempt had accompanied *Doctor Dolittle* in 1967, when Mattel produced three hundred *Dolittle*-related items, including a line of talking dolls in the likeness of Rex Harrison and his menagerie. The producers licensed multiple soundtrack albums, cereals, detergents, and a line of pet food. They placed toys inside puddings and waited for the revenue to roll in.

Even though *Doctor Dolittle* was a hit, an estimated $200 million of its merchandise went unsold. And this problem with movie merchandise was not limited to the pre–*Star Wars* era. The Doolittle tale was to repeat itself with *ET* in 1982. *ET* was wildly successful—it overtook *Star Wars* in the all-time box office stakes (at least until the Special Editions were released at the end of the next decade)—but *ET* computer games and toys in the shape of the movie's alien protagonist had been overproduced and gathered dust on store shelves. Atari produced so many unsold *ET* game cartridges that it decided to bury them in a giant pit in the New Mexico desert. The movie was a charming story; it was not, as industry parlance had it, a particularly "toyetic" story. The protagonist did not look especially cute in the cold light of Toys "R" Us.

In retrospect, of course, it seems obvious that *Star Wars* was the very definition of toyetic. The characters and vehicles were profoundly unusual, the uniforms (plastic spacemen!) bright and arresting, the blasters and lightsabers mesmerizing. Had it been a TV show, merchandising deals would have been no problem. Just look at the *Star Trek* toys, the dolls, the Starfleet napkins, the Dr. Pepper tumblers featuring Kirk and Spock that you could pick up at any Burger King in 1976. But *Star Wars* was a movie, not a TV show, and every toy executive in the mid-1970s knew that movies were here today and gone tomorrow. By the time manufacturers got their toys made in Taiwan, *Star Wars* would most likely be out of theaters and forgotten.

Still, as the release date approached, Lippincott persisted. He tried to sell toy companies on the then-bizarre idea of *Star Wars* action figures. His top target was the Mego Corporation, which produced Action Jackson and a line of World's Greatest Superheroes. But the movie wasn't finished until the last minute, and with only still photographs from the film available for pitching potential merchandising partners, Lippincott struck out. Mego was importing a line of action figures from Japan called Micronauts. They were the best-selling toys in America. Who needed *Star Wars*? At the February 1977 toy fair in New York, Lippincott was asked to leave the Mego Booth.

Finally, Lippincott got a bite from a Cincinnati-based company called Kenner, which had invented the Easy Bake oven in 1963 and had just found success again with twelve-inch *Six Million Dollar Man* dolls. Kenner was owned by cereal company General Mills. The toy company's CEO, Bernie Loomis, had been persuaded by the *Star Wars* deal simply because Fox dangled the possibility that *Star Wars* might be made into a TV show. Loomis and Lippincott signed a contract that committed Kenner to producing four action figures and a "family game."

The terms of that deal, signed a mere month before the release of the movie, have never been revealed. Mark Boudreaux, a designer who started working at Kenner in January 1977 and was thrust straight into making vehicles for the *Star Wars* line, remembers the deal being described around the office as "$50 and a handshake." Certainly, Lucas—who had been too busy finishing the film to micromanage Lippincott—was furious when he found out what he'd been locked into once the movie came out. "He thought he should have had more of the money," Lippincott says. "But we made it at a time when nobody wanted a toy deal. The Monday morning quarterbacks say we should have waited. I don't think anybody could have."

In the lead-up to the film's release, Lippincott gave Kenner the trailer for the movie. The toy designers went wild for it, and set about making three-and-three-quarter-inch action figures. One story has it that the figures were that size because Loomis asked his vice president of design to measure the distance between his thumb and his forefinger. In fact, the figures were simply the same size as Micronauts. *Star Wars* dolls couldn't be the standard eight or twelve inches tall; they had to fit in vehicles. If Han Solo was twelve inches tall, the *Millennium Falcon* would have to be five feet wide. Toys "R" Us would have had to take over the entire mall. Instead, *Star Wars* toys would have to be content with taking over entire walls of stores.

For that first holiday season, Kenner couldn't swing into action fast enough. Scrambling in early June when it was clear the movie was a monster hit, the company would have needed to start shipping the action figures in August to make it in time for Christmas, an impossible deadline at the time. A very junior designer at the company, Ed Schifman, came up with an infamous solution: a $10 piece of cardboard that promised you the first four action figures as soon as they were ready. It was called the "Early Bird Special." Some fans mock it, some remember it fondly, but there's no denying it did the trick. "Okay, we sold a piece of cardboard," says Boudreaux. "We still kept *Star Wars* toys top of mind at Christmas 1977." (Like just about every action figure in *Star Wars* history, the Early Bird Special was too famous to produce just once: in 2005, Walmart sold a replica version.)

Once it was clear *Star Wars* was a hit, Lucas sat down with Kenner and made sure there would be other toys beyond the action figures. Top of his mind: blasters. Loomis had banned guns from the Kenner line after Vietnam; the generation that protested the Vietnam war were now parents and were horrified by the prospect of their kids playing with weaponry. Loomis tried to tell Lucas this. Loomis was planning on making inflatable lightsabers, so at least the kids could do battle with *something*. Lucas took this all in, then repeated his question: "Where are the guns?" Loomis relented; Kenner started selling blasters.

In 1978, the company sold more than forty-two million *Star Wars* items; the majority, twenty-six million, were action figures. By 1985, there were more *Star Wars* figures on the planet than US citizens. Then came a lull of a decade, before a new licensee, Hasbro, came along with the "Power of the Force" line; though the figures were derided (by Sansweet, among others) as being ridiculously muscular, they still sold like hot cakes. Hasbro hasn't left off since.

After 1977, Lucas started to develop some hard-and-fast rules about the *Star Wars* brand. The hardest and fastest was that the *Star Wars* name was not be slapped on any old piece of crap. The movies were made with incredible care and precision; the merch should be too. Sansweet can show you a prime example made by Kenner's Canadian division in 1977, which hadn't got the memo: a Batman-style utility belt and a dart gun, with Darth Vader's image on the box. Lucas was enraged when he saw it. His licensing division, then called Black Falcon, was supposed to ensure that sort of thing never went on sale again. It nixed the Weingeroff jewelry deal. *Star Wars* was also never to be associated with drugs or alcohol. (There were exceptions to all these rules in the chaotic beginning; Sansweet gleefully shows off a piece of sheet music from 1977, the cantina band theme, that shows Chewbacca with a martini glass.) Until Lucas relented in 1991, there would not be *Star Wars*–themed vitamins for fear that children might get a taste for pill popping (the maker of *THX 1138* still resented drugs).

Lucas professed to take a hands-off approach to merchandising, but in practice he retained a tremendous amount of control over it. "If you do something I don't like, I'll let you know," he told Maggie Young, Lucasfilm's vice president of merchandise and licensing from 1978 to 1986. As a management technique, that did the trick: Young was too terrified to make anything but the most conservative choices. There do seem to be a few strange blind spots in the history of licensing: Lucas, a diabetic, held out against sugary breakfast cereals for years (until Kellogg pitched low-sugar 3POs in 1984), even though some of *Star Wars*' most long-term partners included sugar water makers Coca-Cola and Pepsi.

Inconsistency aside, it worked. More than $20 billion of merchandising has been sold over the lifetime of the franchise. That's half the lifetime sales of the Barbie franchise—quite a feat, considering that the anatomically unrealistic blonde doll had a twenty-year head start. And Barbie is struggling to remain relevant in the modern world; the doll's sales declined by 40 percent in 2012. *Star Wars*, meanwhile, is only getting stronger; now that Disney, a publicly traded company, has bought the formerly private Lucasfilm, we know that it generated about $215 million in licensing revenue in 2012 alone.*

Sansweet is quick to correct anyone who might have worried that the sale of Lucasfilm to Disney would lead to a sudden slew of *Star Wars* Disney products. "People got all upset online and complained they were going to make Darth Goofy," he says. "Well, guess what—they made it seven years ago, and it was great." He points to his shelves of Jedi Mickeys, Stormtrooper Donald Ducks, and yes, Darth Goofy—fruits of a twenty-five-year partnership between Lucasfilm and Disney.

Sansweet's tour seems unending, and he likes to keep it unpredictable. You never know when he's going to pick up a plush puppet of Princess Leia in her slave bikini, say, and start talking in a falsetto voice, or threaten you with a felted wool blaster. Often he affects bafflement about the items in his collection, as if he just woke up to find all this stuff here. He will mock unusual objects no matter where they came from, and he's delighted to show off some of the worst official products ever to emerge from Lucasfilm licensing: a C-3PO tape dispenser where the tape emerges suggestively from between the golden droid's legs; a Williams Sonoma oven mitt in the shape of the space slug from *Empire Strikes Back*; Jar Jar Binks candy where you have to open the Gungan's mouth and suck on his cherry-flavored tongue. Sansweet shakes his head sadly, suppresses a smile. What were they thinking?

But the officially licensed *Star Wars* products are incomparable—both in terms of numbers and strangeness—to the paraphernalia that fans and bootleggers have produced. Sansweet can show you some of the earliest bootlegged figures, replicas of which—replicas of bootlegs!—now go for hundreds of dollars. A good chunk of Rancho is given over to fan-made ephemera from around the world. We're talking a beautiful Bantha piñata and Leia and Han as Day of the Dead skeletons from Mexico; tins of Cream of Jawa soup and potted

---

* Barbie can't even count on strict gender divisions in toys any more—certainly not since Wear *Star Wars*, Share *Star Wars* Day was started by blogger Carrie Goldman in 2010. Goldman was incensed when her daughter was bullied for bringing a *Star Wars* water bottle to school, and she struck back with an annual event promoted far and wide online, designed to draw attention to the fact that girls love *Star Wars* too.

Ewok; a Stormtrooper painted on a ten-thousand-year-old mastodon bone. There are dozens of tricked-out Stormtrooper and Vader helmets, each one painted by a different artist for the Make-a-Wish foundation. Australian fans studiously ignored Lucasfilm's alcohol ban and sent Sansweet a bottle of Mos Eisley Space port.

"The fan-made stuff turns me on more than anything," says Sansweet. "It shows their passion, their skills, and what sets *Star Wars* apart from any other major fandom of the last fifty years. I love Harry Potter, but you don't see people building miniature Hogwarts castles. You don't see a lot of kit Quidditch teams. People love those movies. They don't have the same passion for them."

Being around Steve Sansweet—here at the Ranch, at a book signing, laughing and backslapping with fans at Celebration—is like living in a *Star Wars*–themed version of *The Orchid Thief*. Except that Sansweet's obsession is more stable, more legal, and more constantly fed than John Laroche's pursuit of rare flowers. It's hard not to be jealous of Rancho Obi-Wan—not necessarily of the collection itself, though I have met many people who would kill to own it, but rather of the kind of certainty and focus it reflects. To be immersed in an unrivaled global network of fandom, with merchandising as your MacGuffin. To be the ultimate fan—yet to still retain a finely tuned sense of the ridiculous. To shake your head at the folly and still love every second of it. This is a big part of the idea of *Star Wars*.

I have never been a collector of anything—I generally align myself with the view expressed by Dr. Jennifer Porter, the Jedi academic and religion expert, who described the kind of gear she saw at Disney's *Star Wars* weekend as akin to "tacky pilgrim mementos from Lourdes" that people have a disturbing tendency to "cherish as contact with the sacred." Still, *Star Wars* is about the closest I ever got. I started buying the action figures and receiving them as gifts in 1980, just in time for *The Empire Strikes Back*. In those days before video rentals, before *Star Wars* had even been shown on network TV, the figures were a way of taking little pieces of the movie home—even when the figure in the plastic blister pack looked significantly more generic than the actor on the cardboard back of the packaging.

Just as importantly, the figures were a way of feeding my imagination in the absence of new *Star Wars* movies. The three-year wait between the *Empire Strikes Back* and *Return of the Jedi* seemed interminable. There were innumerable ways the cliff-hanger ending of *Empire* could have worked out. My figures, and millions of others around the world, played out the possibilities. Countless *Millennium Falcons* chased after *Slave-1*, the ship owned by Boba

Fett, which came with a free Han Solo frozen in carbonite. Who knows how many times Luke Skywalker—the Cloud City version—repeated his show-down with Darth Vader's figure, demanding to know if what he said about being his father was true?

One thing that would never have crossed my mind as a kid was keeping the figures pristine in unopened blister packs. That was what I feared seeing at Rancho Obi-Wan: an unhealthy obsession with mint-condition collecting and trading, the joyless commodification of playthings. So I was glad to learn from Hasbro, which bought Kenner in 1991, that the majority of *Star Wars* consumers don't take that approach. "About 75 percent of our fans do liberate their figures," says Derryl DePriest, Hasbro's vice president of global brand management and chief evangelist for the *Star Wars* line, who conducts surveys on these sorts of things.

DePriest has been liberating his *Star Wars* figures since the age of twelve. When I first met him at San Diego Comic-Con, he pulled out his smartphone and showed me how he stores his collection at home. They were arranged on dozens of shelves, each shelf representing a major ensemble scene from a *Star Wars* movie. You could reenact the original trilogy in three and three-quarter inches, right there. (It was the first time I'd seen something Rancho Obi-Wan actually didn't have.)

As DePriest thumbed through his photos, I pointed out a shelf full of Stormtroopers surrounding the *Millennium Falcon*, and recalled that one of the most puzzling things I had done with my collection as a child was to trade a Snowtrooper from the Hoth base in *The Empire Strikes Back* for a friend's regular Stormtrooper figure, one that was more beaten up than the regular Stormtrooper figure *I already had*. It's hard for an adult to remember what kind of logic was at work there: Aren't collectors supposed to crave the dissimilarity of collector's items? But DePriest was able to absolve me and reminded me why I did it: everyone needs a whole bunch of Stormtroopers. "Part of the fun is having the good guys outnumbered by the bad guys," he said. "The rebels always have to be fighting against an overwhelming force. So we make sure we have those figures in abundance." Call it the spirit of the 501st in miniature. No trooper should troop alone.

Despite this inherent advantage, the Stormtrooper is only the second-best selling action figure in Hasbro's line. Consistently on top, year after year, is Darth Vader. We're drawn to the iconic villain, it seems; no wonder Lucas evolved him from a second-tier role in the original *Star Wars*, with little more than ten minutes of screen time, to the centerpiece of the first six movies.

As the technology of model making improves, Hasbro is able to sell more and more varieties of *Star Wars* action figures—and Vader is the primary ben-eficiary of this shift. This is quite a shock for a casual fan from the 1970s and 1980s, when there was only one model of Vader sold (because why would you make more when the guy never changes his costume?). From 1995 through 2012, there were fifty-seven new versions of Vader, and that's not even counting the dozens of Anakin Skywalkers produced during that time. Those on the light side of the Force will be glad to know that Luke has his dad beat in sheer num-bers, with a grand total of eighty-nine figures in every conceivable costume and pose. Sadly, Princess Leia has a mere forty-four figures in her name. In total, there are now more than two thousand kinds of *Star Wars* figures—a far cry from the three hundred sold by Kenner.

I put the latest Hasbro figures next to my old Kenner models; it was like looking at a Rembrandt next to a medieval fresco. The old figures, so vibrant in my youth, now seemed like blobs of plastic with eyes and a mouth drawn on. Their twenty-first-century counterparts were exquisitely crafted miniature humans. DePriest explained that Kenner's factories in China used to crank out millions of figures from the same plastic mold. As the molds degraded, the figures looked less and less screen-accurate. The factories were rushing to feed a phenomenon that could have collapsed at any moment. These days, with *Star Wars* on a stable footing, the molds are precision-made and can be changed every few hundred figures.

Star Wars has proved to be a strong prop for Hasbro. In 2013, the company scored a hit by collaborating with videogame company Rovio on *Star Wars* Angry Birds. In one month, the company sold a million *Star Wars* 'telepods'—physical toys that interact with the app. Not only does the company have a range of figures in the works for *Episode VII*, it still has figures left over from the first six movies that have never been made. You may think every single character in every single scene has been made into an action figure by this point, but DePriest says there are still plenty of aliens from the cantina and Jabba the Hutt's Palace that have never seen the inside of a plastic mold.

Still, the real money is in the more popular characters and in making ever more precise, screen-accurate versions of them you can sell to collectors. There are whole teams at Hasbro dedicated to doing just that. At Comic-Con, De-Priest showed off a forthcoming figure, a $20 version of Princess Leia in her eye-opening slave bikini from *Return of the Jedi*. The blueprints were covered in notes to the design team: "Eyes should be more sultry. More petite overall. Smaller breasts. Outer parts of nostrils not so tall. Please sculpt some under-pants!" I couldn't help but think of Carrie Fisher's acerbic attack on a Leia model she once received that seemed a little too revealing. "I told George, 'You have the rights to my face,'" she said. "You do not have the rights to my lagoon of mystery!'"

But the audience of collectors, men and women, were thrilled. Then De-Priest asked how many of them actually take their figures out of the packaging when they buy them. Only a smattering of hands went up.

"Play with your toys, people," DePriest sternly told the crowd. "Play with your toys."

14.

HERE COME THE CLONES!

As Kenner scrambled to sell those Early Bird Special certificates for Christmas 1977, its toy executives could at least console themselves that the phenomenon they were eager to cash in on wasn't going away any time soon. Its market research that summer found that, out of one thousand children surveyed, a third had already seen the movie, and 15 percent had seen it more than once. Kids who hadn't seen it were desperate to. The peer pressure of the playground was just too much, even without the toys. "We used to play cops and robbers," says James Arnold Taylor, who would grow up to be the voice of Obi-Wan Kenobi but who at this point in our narrative was a seven-year-old in San Jose. "After the summer of 1977, we played *Star Wars*."

It wasn't just kids, of course. The American public in general hadn't been this crazy about a single cultural focal point since the Beatles. It was completely in vogue (and in *Vogue*). And it was about to attract that sincerest form of flattery: imitation.

By Labor Day 1977, *Star Wars* boasted $133 million in total ticket sales from just under a thousand theaters. It had long since surpassed *Jaws* to become the best-selling movie of all time, unless you adjusted *Gone with the Wind*'s ticket sales for inflation.* The attendant media was headed for the stratosphere, too.

---

* And unlike *Gone with the Wind*, here was a story that post-1960s America could be proud of itself for telling. The cantina bartender's refusal to admit droids—"We don't serve their kind here"—was widely interpreted as a civil rights parable.

The soundtrack album had sold 1.3 million copies. A disco version of the main theme, rushed out by a producer called Meco, had sold 130,000 copies in its first few weeks. Meco's album, *Star Wars and Other Galactic Funk*, hit the top of the *Billboard* charts in October. Alan Dean Foster's paperback, bearing Lucas's name, was the fourth biggest best seller in America. Foster was obliged to lie to friends about whether he wrote it. He claims he didn't mind, and he's easygoing enough that you believe him. But it had to sting a little.

In the LA area, *Star Wars* made a triumphant return to Mann's Chinese Theatre after *Sorcerer* completed its contractual six-week run. To celebrate, Darth Vader, Threepio, and Artoo had their names and footprints set in the concrete, next to Betty Grable's, while three thousand people watched. Even the reporters were wearing *Star Wars* T-shirts. Kurtz told them not to expect another movie for two years. "It will be a separate story—we want to do a different adventure each time, not 'sequels' as such—but with the same characters," he said. But then he wasn't so sure: "We could go in 14 different directions with this."

Behind the scenes, preliminary steps for *Star Wars II*—very much a sequel, despite what Kurtz said—were already under way. Lucas was scribbling notes for a treatment. Ralph McQuarrie's services were secured. Kurtz started scouting for locations; he booked Elstree for the stage shooting eighteen months ahead of time.

Brian Johnson, the model maker from *Space: 1999*, was brought on in place of John Dykstra to head up the special effects. Dykstra, never a diplomat, had butted heads with Lucas one too many times; neither wanted to work with the other again. Lucas was sometimes generous with his points, dishing out roughly 25 percent of his stake in *Star Wars* to actors, crew, and friends. Hamill would get around $600,000 a year from his point. Dykstra, the Academy Award winner whose hypotheses about cameras and computers changed the face of special effects forever, got nothing.

Not knowing how long *Star Wars* would stay hot, Lucas's lawyers pressed their advantage with Fox and presented a sequel contract in September. The negotiations did not last long. Lucas had Laddie over a barrel, and both of them knew it. He could take his sequel rights to any other studio. At the next board meeting in Monte Carlo, where Princess Grace won her first-edition *Star Wars* figures, Laddie remembers calmly telling his fellow board members: "Either we make this deal, or we don't make the movie." He also remembers that they were angry enough to start a campaign that would eventually edge him out of the company: "They wanted to give George a 10% increase, and George didn't have that in mind, and he was right."

Lucas would get quite a bit more than an extra 10 percent. His company was to grab the lion's share of *Star Wars II* profits: 52 percent of the first $20 million, 70 percent of the next $40 million, and 77 percent of everything after that. A couple of Lucasfilm subsidiaries were created to manage the windfall that the company expected. The Chapter II Company would handle the new film. Black Falcon Ltd. would handle all new merchandising deals, getting 90 percent of licensing fees from 1981 onwards (an extra impetus for Fox to make even more licensing deals immediately).

If the next movie was anything like as big a hit as *Star Wars*—a huge if, to be sure—Lucasfilm would make out like a bandit. Fox didn't even get to be the money; Bank of America would offer loans to Lucasfilm based on Lucas's $20 million collateral. That would be his entire stack of chips from *Star Wars*, barring merchandising. It was a measure of the power of the phenomenon that the deal was signed almost immediately, on September 21, 1977, before a single word of the *Star Wars II* treatment (as it was then known) was written.

The announcement of *Star Wars II*, when it came, went little noticed by the press. It was a foregone conclusion. Why should it matter? Sequels never, ever did as well as the original; everyone knew that. There was a *Rocky II* in the works; there was a *Jaws II*. For that matter, there was a *More American Graffiti* under way at Lucasfilm. So what? With the sole exception of *The Godfather Part II*, sequels were all rote. They were almost never done by the same director. Didn't Lucas just say he was stepping back from directing? What schmo was going to stand in the shadow of *Star Wars*?

Star Wars was almost certain to be a flash in the pan: this was conventional wisdom until 1980. And Lucas stood to lose big if that proved to be the case. Finance a movie with a studio, and the studio would at least cover your losses; finance it with the bank, and your house could be on the line, as Coppola's was with *Apocalypse Now*.

This didn't slow the Creator down one bit. George Lucas just took the fat stack of chips he'd won on a single turn of the roulette wheel and put it all right back on the same square. Trouble was, the entire TV and movie industry seemed to be putting their chips there too. The Creator didn't seem to care. "I want *Star Wars* to be a success so everyone will copy it," Lucas told *Starlog* in the summer of '77. "Then I can go see the copies, sit back and enjoy them."

Well, at least he got the first part of his wish.

They came from all corners of the entertainment universe, converging on the-aters like Star Destroyers in battle formation. The signal had been received: science fiction was in, no matter the content (and no matter that Lucas called his thing "space fantasy"). If you could slap something on screens fast enough, perhaps you could catch a few million dollars from the *Star Wars* juggernaut before it careened off a cliff.

As often happens in space travel, there were strange time dilation effects. The first movie to arrive seemed to have been in transit for more than a decade. An Italian film from 1966 called *2+5: Missione Hydra* was repackaged, dubbed, and pushed into US theaters in October 1977 under the name *Star Pilot*. No matter that the plot—aliens crash-landing on Sardinia and taking a scientist hostage—had more to do with monster movies of the 1950s and there were no special effects to speak of. It was a movie available to theaters at the same time as *Star Wars*, and it had "Star" in the title.

If that wasn't low enough for you to sink as a theater booker, another option presented itself in the September 26, 1977, issue of the trade magazine *Boxoffice*. A West German porn flick from 1974 alternately called *Ach jodel mir noch einen!* (*Oh, yodel for me again!*) or *Stosstrupp Venus bläst zum Angriff* (*the Venus patrol blows its attack*) was repackaged as *2069: A Sex Odyssey*. The ad, from a shameless distributor called Burbank International Pictures, called this "erotic science fiction fantasy" the "sensuous sequel to *Star Wars*." If that didn't drive the point home, the first *s* in "sensuous" was a dollar sign.

Star Wars had put dollar signs in filmmakers' eyes around the world. Lucas's sensibilities "showed there was twice as much money out there," Lucas's old friend and *Apocalypse Now* screenwriter John Milius said. "Studios couldn't resist that. No one had any idea you could get as rich as this, like ancient Rome." Some directors and screenwriters would adjust wholeheartedly to the new reality (like Milius himself, who went on to direct *Conan the Barbarian*, which made $130 million at the box office). Others would not. William Friedkin watched his grim trailer for *Sorcerer*—which he considered his finest work—playing before *Star Wars*. "We're fucking being blown off the screen," his editor, Bud Smith, had told him, which was what brought him into the theater to see Lucas's movie. "I dunno, sweet little robots and stuff—maybe we're on the wrong horse," Friedkin glumly admitted to the manager of Mann's Chinese Theatre. The manager simply warned him that if *Sorcerer* was indeed the wrong horse, *Star Wars* would be right back in the saddle, which of course it was. *Sorcerer* went on to worldwide failure, unable to make its $22 million budget back. Friedkin would never direct another big-budget picture again.

With hindsight, it's obvious what horses the studios should have been betting on. We have demonstrated so much propensity as a society for rollicking summer movie action adventures, for PG-13 tales of good against evil—pictures that kids and grown-ups can enjoy together that are at once old-fashioned in their morality and up-to-the-minute in special effects. Since those days of *Sorcerer* versus *Star Wars*, we've sat through so many *Harry Potters*, cheered for so many hobbits, sailed with so many pirates on the Caribbean. We've been agog at costumed superheroes and comic book flicks for so long that these oeuvres seem normal, as American as apple pie. *Star Wars* and its inheritors are as ubiquitous as large soda and popcorn.

But in 1977, the impulse was not to take the quintessence of *Star Wars* and bottle it in a new container, but rather to make the cheapest science fiction possible and hope for the best. Old prejudices died hard. Wasn't this stuff for kids, anyway? Would they really be able to tell the difference? Budgets were somewhat bigger than before, largely to accommodate special effects that wouldn't be laughed off the screen in a post–*Star Wars* universe. Still, a lot of movies made in the following years looked more like *Star Pilot* than *Star Wars*.

Much of this schlock was international. Canada offered *Starship Invasions* (1977) and *HG Wells' Things to Come* (1979); Wells's book was full of serious warnings about World Wars II and III, but the movie wanted nothing to do with that. Its trailer promised "a universe of robots, men with the will to destroy worlds, interstellar blackmail and intergalactic heroism." Italy was the source of a couple of movies even more shameless in their plundering. *Starcrash* (1978), opened with a poor man's copy of the Star Destroyer shot, featured smugglers and robots doing battle against an imperial villain and his planet-destroying space station; it also features Christopher Plummer as the emperor and a young David Hasselhoff, wielding a light saber. The main villain in *The Humanoid* (1979) wears a black, samurai-style helmet and black cape, looking identical to Darth Vader from the rear. Both failed the box office test.

From the United Kingdom came *Saturn 3* (1980), which seemed to have all the right elements. *Star Wars* production designer John Barry came up with the story, a thriller about murder on an isolated space station; the script was written by young literary turk Martin Amis. Kirk Douglas, Harvey Keitel, and Farrah Fawcett were the stars, the latter wearing a variety of skimpy outfits. It cost $10 million and made $9 million. What went wrong? Too much script doctoring, a sixty-four-year-old Douglas trying to prove his virility at every step (the shoot would inspire Amis's novel *Money*), and various disputes that saw Barry walk out—straight on to *The Empire Strikes Back*, where, tragically, he died a week later from a sudden attack of meningitis.

Japan offered came *Message from Space* (1978), made for $6 million—not much by American standards, but a record in Japanese moviemaking. As a nod to the US market, it starred crusty old action actor Vic Morrow. Again, the plot seemed to have all the right elements: an evil empire, sword battles mixed with laser fire, a seedy alien bar. United Artists, the studio that had first refusal on *Star Wars*, snapped up the US rights for $1 million. It didn't make its money back. "The only thing it cleaned up was the red inkwell," UA vice president Steven Bach lamented.

To make a movie look like *Star Wars*, it soon became clear, you had to spend *more* than *Star Wars*. Lucas liked to say he'd made a $20 million movie on a $10 million budget. By outspending him, a handful of other directors managed to attain comparable success. Spielberg had spent $20 million on *Close Encounters*, which would eventually gross $288 million around the world. Warner Brothers spent $55 million on *Superman*, a risky bet given that the superhero genre had been as moribund as science fiction before *Star Wars* came along to rescue it; with the help of another stirring John Williams march, it became the studio's biggest hit in its history, bringing in box office receipts of $296 million worldwide.

So studios started to knuckle down and spend on science fiction and fantasy. Disney nodded in *Star Wars*' direction in 1978 with two low-budget comedies— *The Cat from Outer Space* and *Unidentified Flying Oddball*, also known as *The Spaceman and King Arthur*, an update of Mark Twain's *A Connecticut Yankee in King Arthur's Court*. By 1979, Disney had developed a script called *Space Station One*, later renamed *The Black Hole*. It boasted a $20 million budget and 550 special effects shots, and it was to be a moody, action-filled melodrama set on the edge of known space with toyetic robots.

The Black Hole marked the first time Disney came calling to Lucasfilm—in this case, because the Mouse House wanted to rent the Dykstraflex camera. Lucasfilm's terms were too steep, so Disney created computer-controlled cameras of its own. The director, Gary Nelson, made sure that the robots—V.I.N. CENT and B.O.B—looked dirty and scuffed up; the used universe concept was gaining traction. It had stars—Ernest Borgnine and Maximilian Schell, with Roddy McDowell and Slim Pickens voicing the robots. It was one of Disney's first PG movies, the first to throw in a little cursing to attract teenagers. What could go wrong?

Lots, apparently—because Disney had forgotten to care about the script. In the United States, *Black Hole* barely made its budget back. Roger Ebert called it "a talky melodrama whipped up out of mad scientists and haunted houses." The evil black robots that battled V.I.N.CENT and B.O.B were "ripped off from Darth Vader." The Maximilian Schell character trying to drive the space station *Cygnus* into a black hole was a carbon copy of Doctor Morbius from *Forbidden Planet*. It wasn't space fantasy; it was yet another tale about the hubris of science. Did we really need more of those?

The most successful science fiction movies commissioned in the wake of *Star Wars* came from the geeks who had been marinating in this stuff long before Lucas was a household name. In this sense, they were much like Lucas himself (and some of them had worked for him on *Star Wars*). Studios would have been better off cloning him rather than attempting to clone his work.* They needed writers and directors who were that passionate about their material, not carpet-baggers. Caring about the details was reflected on the screen—and at the box office.

The prime example was Dan O'Bannon, coauthor of *Dark Star*, the 1974 John Carpenter hyperspace comedy with the beach-ball alien. After *Dark Star*, O'Bannon got the idea of doing a similar movie, this time as horror; he wanted to call it *They Bite*. But he got caught up working for Alejandro Jodorowsky in Paris on the abandoned version of *Dune*. It turned out to be worth it, because H. R. Giger was also working for Jodorowsky, and his gothic alien paintings influenced O'Bannon no end. O'Bannon went back to LA in 1975 and wrote a script, then called *Star Beast*. It soon became *Alien*.

Like Lucas, O'Bannon was quite above board about his grab bag of science fiction influences, such as *The Thing from Another World* (1951). "I didn't steal *Alien* from anybody," he said. "I stole it from everybody." His cowriter Ronald Shusett contributed the idea of an alien bursting from a spaceman's chest.

In late 1976, casting around for a studio to produce the movie, O'Bannon and Shusett aimed low. They turned to B-movie maestro Roger Corman and were about to sign a deal with him when a friend suggested a new production company that had a relationship with Fox.

---

* Warner and Universal tried the next best thing to cloning Lucas: they rereleased *THX 1138* and *American Graffiti* respectively, both with the few minutes of footage they'd cut, to Lucas's extreme chagrin, now restored. *Graffiti* was once again a hit; *THX* was once again a dud.

Laddie liked the basic idea but didn't feel *Alien* was strong enough to fund immediately. He may well have been hedging his bets, given how much of a turkey *Star Wars* was expected to be in nearly all quarters of the company. Who would want to risk green-lighting another science fiction script in that environment? "Hollywood is like a bunch of lemmings," Laddie complains. "They get one hit, and everyone chases it." After *The Sound of Music*, he remembered everyone chased musicals for a few years. For big budget fantasy or science fiction movies to progress, that one big chase-worthy hit was essential.

In the meantime, O'Bannon made ends meet by working for his fellow USC alum George Lucas, who needed some animation that looked like a targeting computer showing a strange X-shaped space ship; Lucas remembered O'Bannon had done something similar for *Dark Star*. O'Bannon didn't make a lot of money out of his work in *Star Wars*—just enough to get him off his cowriter's sofa and into an apartment of his own.

But *Star Wars*, once it became a chase-worthy hit, helped Fox birth *Alien*. "They wanted to follow through on *Star Wars*, and they wanted to follow through fast, and the only spaceship script they had sitting on their desk was *Alien*," said O'Bannon. He was granted the exact same budget as *Star Wars*: $11 million. The British director, Ridley Scott, had decided to switch from historical epics to science fiction after seeing *Star Wars* at the Chinese Theater. He hired Charley Lippincott, now something of a good luck charm in Hollywood. *Alien* was released on May 25, 1979, two years to the day after *Star Wars*. It made $104 million at the box office. "*Alien* is to *Star Wars* what the Rolling Stones were to the Beatles," its producer David Giler said. "It's a nasty *Star Wars*."

Helping to shepherd *Alien* to the screen was one of the last tasks Laddie had at Fox. His spat with the board over whether he should have made the *Star Wars II* deal on Lucas's terms blew up in fall 1979, when the former producer declared his intention to go round up a posse and form a production company. Fox shortened his contract, the nicest possible way of showing Laddie the door. In October, the Ladd Company was founded. Laddie rounded up Ridley Scott, who was hired to direct a script penned by a rather high-strung actor called Hampton Fancher, based on a novella by a strung-out science fiction writer. Fancher and Scott clashed, and Fancher left the movie. Thus was *Do Androids Dream of Electric Sheep* by Philip K. Dick transmogrified into something equally brilliant but rather different, *Blade Runner*, by a team that had been utterly inspired by *Star Wars*. No wonder Harrison Ford was the perfect choice to play the replicant-hunting protagonist, Deckard.

Not that what they created was anything like *Star Wars*—or was it? On the surface, *Blade Runner* seemed more like a big-budget, storytelling-positive version of *THX 1138*. It had that same slow-moving feeling, the lingering scene-setting of a future dystopia, a robotic humanity. Lucas had abandoned that whole bummer of a notion and laid claim to our dreams instead. Ridley Scott successfully inhabited our nightmares. Yet the two directors had much in common at this stage: a desire to tell an economical story that preserved as much mystery as possible; a story that was told through the eyes of nonhuman constructs, whether droids or replicants, who bear witness. "I've seen things you people wouldn't believe," said Deckard's last replicant victim, Roy Batty, in a famous dying speech penned by actor Rutger Hauer (yes, he wrote it himself, on the same night it was shot). "Attack ships on fire off the shoulder of Orion. I watched c-beams glitter in the dark near the Tanhauser Gate." In this, its most memorable moment, *Blade Runner* briefly shed its science fiction skin and became a space fantasy about war in the stars.

Even low-budget filmmakers who were old hands at science fiction were driven to spending unusually large amounts on their next space flicks. Roger Corman had taken his entire Venice Beach staff to see *Star Wars* at the Chinese Theater on day one. It was the kind of thing he'd always dreamed of making. Left in the lurch when Fox grabbed *Alien*, in 1979 he filmed *Battle Beyond the Stars*, an homage to *Star Wars* that also liberally plundered the plot of *Seven Samurai*. At $2 million, it was Corman's most expensive movie ever, largely because of the salaries of its stars, George Peppard and Robert Vaughn. It was also one of Corman's most successful movies, earning $11 million at the box office. It is perhaps best remembered today as the movie James Cameron got his start on. The former truck driver who quit his job after watching *Star Wars* had made an experimental science fiction special effects movie called *Xenogenesis* and taken it to Corman, who was always on the lookout for passionate kids like Cameron. Corman put him in charge of the spaceship model shop on *Battle Beyond the Stars*.

Cameron became a one-man ILM. He worked one eighty-five-hour shift on nothing but coffee. He slept on a gurney in the studio and suggested special effects ideas that Corman hadn't thought of. When Corman fired his art director, he found Cameron on his gurney, shook him awake, and offered him the job. Thus began the meteoric career of the only man to beat *Star Wars* at the US box office twice.

Everywhere you looked, would-be filmmakers with fantastic dreams were coming out of the woodwork. Perhaps the biggest unrealized dream belonged to Barry Geller, a serial entrepreneur obsessed with the fringes of science and comparative religion. In 1978, Geller optioned the movie rights for the Roger Zelazny novel from 1967, *Lord of Light*, which fit his temperament perfectly. The plot: a group of space colonists have used future technology to make themselves immortal and have assumed the names of Hindu gods. They are challenged by a young iconoclastic Buddha figure, Sam; it is hinted in the novel that time is a wheel and the story's events will repeat themselves over and over.

Some producers believed the novel's circular plot and religious digressions made it unfilmable. Not Geller. He turned out a script, raised $500,000, and got comic book legend Jack Kirby to do production sketches. The aim of the film, he wrote, "was to bring attention to our extraorinary [*sic*] mental powers, just as Star Wars brought recognition of life in the Galaxy." He envisioned a massive theme park based on the movie in Aurora, Colorado, called Science Fiction Land; Kirby drew that too. It would include a mile-wide Buckminster Fuller dome and a mile-high spire called Heaven.

Geller's dream foundered in December 1979, when he and his business partner, Jerry Schafer, were arrested by the FBI on suspicion of fraud. Geller was cleared, but his partner was indicted for theft, conspiracy, and three counts of security fraud. Prosecutors alleged Science Fiction Land would have given Schafer his own zip code for various nefarious schemes. The whole project, tainted by association, died.

But the script had a now-famous afterlife. The same month the project perished, the script found its way into the hands of the CIA. The spooks were looking for a *Star Wars*–like project to help get a fake film crew into revolutionary Iran to rescue six American diplomats from their hiding places in the Canadian embassy. The *Lord of Light* script and Kirby drawings were repackaged under the name *Argo*, the diplomats were saved, and Geller knew nothing about it until the operation was declassified in 2000. When the Oscar-winning Ben Affleck movie retelling of 2012 failed to mention Geller or *Lord of Light*, Geller was livid.

One visionary who got a happier ending was animator Steve Lisberger. In 1976 Lisberger became fascinated by Atari's first video game, *Pong*, and imagined a feature-length movie, part live-action actors, part computer animation. In 1977, Lisberger's studio created a thirty-second sample of a backlit neon figure throwing two spinning discs. The character was electronic; they nicknamed him Tron. The Boston firm moved to California en masse and pitched the idea to major studios. Eventually Disney came calling. Its old guard wasn't sure about the idea, but the younger, video-game-playing executives were into it. *Tron* was guided in to land at Disney by Harrison Ellenshaw, a matte painter on *Star Wars* and *Black Hole*. Ellenshaw was "the ambassador and the young prince of the Disney lot," Lisberger says; it was his belief that sold it. Score another point for *Star Wars* alumni.

Even the most established of franchises were not immune to the *Star Wars* effect. James Bond, moviegoers were informed at the end of *The Spy Who Loved Me* in July 1977, was to return in a sequel called *For Your Eyes Only*. But by the time those credits rolled on screens around the world, the producers were having second thoughts. Why not go for something flashier, a little more *Star Wars*? Ian Fleming had written a novel called *Moonraker* back in 1954. Its plot, featuring Bond playing bridge with a wealthy industrialist called Sir Hugo Drax who later tries to destroy London with an atomic weapon, was promptly tossed out. Instead, Bond was to investigate the theft of a space shuttle and discover his archenemy, Drax, has built a city in orbit. "Other films may promise you the moon," boasted the trailer, "but we deliver!" *Moonraker*, released in 1979, was criticized for taking Bond into new realms of silliness; the film still holds the record for most actors on wires in a single (zero gravity) scene. But it also took 007 to new heights at the box office. Its gross was larger than any previous Bond film. Adjusted for inflation, only *Thunderball*, *Goldfinger*, and *You Only Live Twice* beat it.

So it seemed *Star Wars* was bad for imitators, good for true believer filmmakers, and even better for established franchises, so long as they were set in space. Which brings us to *Star Trek: The Motion Picture* (1980). Gene Roddenberry had been trying to spin his TV show's newfound popularity into a movie for the better part of a decade. Paramount had just scrapped the project, and Roddenberry was working on a brand new *Star Trek* TV series called *Phase II* when *Star Wars* came out. *Phase II* was itself scrapped, and the pilot episode—written by none other than Alan Dean Foster—was turned into the basis of the movie. It didn't work so well at that length, however. The movie's costs spiraled out of control, reaching $46 million. (Lucas saved it, after a fashion, when ILM took over the special effects contract.) Still, it made $139 million at the box office worldwide, a respectable amount and enough to guarantee a lower-budget sequel. Leonard Nimoy would later credit *Star Wars* with kick-starting the *Star Trek* movie franchise—though the latter would never outperform the young upstart.

The franchise Lucas had imitated all along would return to the screen because of *Star Wars* but would pale in comparison to it. That much became clear in 1980, when, at long last, *Flash Gordon* got a full-length movie. Producer Dino De Laurentiis had bought the rights from King Features years before *Star Wars* came out, but he failed to persuade Frederico Fellini to direct it. So *Flash* lay fallow until his progeny, *Star Wars*, exploded onto screens. Then De Laurentiis moved fast.

Reviving *Flash* after a near forty-year absence wasn't so easy. There were fundamental differences of opinion about which direction the movie should take. Scriptwriter Lorenzo Semple figured the caricatures of Flash, Dale, Zarkov, and Ming, not to mention the Birdmen, were impossible to play with a straight face in the 1980s. He wrote a campy version in the style of the 1960s *Batman* TV series, which he had written much of. But his sense of humor didn't translate for De Laurentiis, who assumed everything would be played straight and ordered up no-expense-spared sets and costumes. "I told Dino I didn't like it," said Lippincott, who ended up working as the movie's marketing director. (Charley Lippincott: the Zelig of 1970s and '80s space movies.) "It was making fun of the whole thing. You had to do it as a fantasy that would work in the eyes of the audience." The budget soared to $35 million. The star Sam Jones, a former Playgirl pet, fell out with director Mike Hodges, which led to all Jones's lines being dubbed by a still-unknown voice actor.

The result divided audiences. In the United States, *Flash Gordon* tanked with $27 million in box office. In the United Kingdom, it was a rousing success, aided by the film's Queen soundtrack and an over-the-top performance by Brian Blessed. But none of this gave De Laurentiis the *Star Wars*–style franchise he craved. *Flash Gordon* would live on as a comic, a cartoon, and eventually a Syfy Channel series, which lasted for one season. Flash's one consolation, in the home for retired space fantasy screen heroes, is that he escaped the fate of the $250 million film version of John Carter, the Edgar Rice Burroughs character on which he was based, in 2012. *Carter* barely made its money back, and was even slammed as a *Star Wars* copy. A century-long experiment was complete: *Star Wars* had finally, definitively outlasted its space fantasy forefathers, as surely as Luke Skywalker would become stronger and wiser than his dad.

Many movies pillaged *Star Wars* after its release, but not a single one of them became the target of a copycat lawsuit from Lucasfilm. However, there was one TV show that managed to earn the legal wrath of Lucasfilm and Twentieth Century Fox—even though the show was first conceived long before *Star Wars*.

In 1968, the same year George Lucas was struggling to organize his thoughts around "spaceships, holograms, the wave of the future," TV producer Glen A. Larson wrote a script called *Adam's Ark*, in which a ragtag fleet of spacecraft flees the destruction of Earth and searches for humans on other planets. After *Star Trek* folded, however, no network seemed keen on science fiction shows. Larson turned his attention to a string of hit shows, such as *The Fugitive, Alias Smith and Jones*, and *The Six Million Dollar Man*.

After May 1977, coincidentally or otherwise, Larson returned to the *Adam's Ark* concept. He flipped the script so that the ragtag fleet is fleeing the destruction of its own set of planets and searching for the mysterious, legendary Earth. Adam is renamed Adama and given an admiralty. He is the one holdout against a peace treaty that the humans of twelve worlds are planning to sign with a race of robots, the Cylons; Adama's resistance proves prescient, as the Cylons launch a sneak attack in the middle of the treaty celebrations. (The Soviet ambassador would later complain about the show, seeing a Cold War metaphor in this tale of treachery and mistrust.)

Executives at Universal had put out a call for some kind of TV version of *Star Wars*. The five-hundred-page script that Larson turned in, dated August 30, 1977, was duly named *Galactica: Saga of a Star World*. Larson was given $7 million to make a pilot, the largest budget ever for an episode of a TV show and not far from the official budget for *Star Wars*. The armor-covered Cylons looked a little like Stormtroopers, albeit in blindingly bright silver—no "used universe" here.

The story of *Battlestar Galactica* was at least a few light years removed from that of *Star Wars*. Lucas's rebellion had never been conned into seeking a peace treaty with the Empire; no one in that long-ago galaxy far, far away had ever heard tell of a planet called Earth. *Galactica's* brand of mysticism brought it much closer to the *Chariot of the Gods* concept of humanity being planted on Earth by superior ancient races—an idea as prevalent in the 1970s as a belief in UFOs.

Still, Universal was cautious enough to send Lucas the Larson script. Lucas didn't damn it outright. Instead he asked Universal not to use the phrase "Star World." So Larson came up with a new class of spaceship, a "Battlestar." Lucas felt that the name for Adama's son, Skyler, was too close to Skywalker; Larson changed it to Apollo at the last minute. Lucas also felt that the name Starbuck was too reminiscent of *Star Wars*; that, for Larson, was a step too far.

What really irked Lucas, however, was that Larson contracted John Dykstra to do the special effects for the *Battlestar Galactica* pilot and Ralph McQuarrie to do the concept art. Dykstra brought much of ILM with him, reforming the Country Club as a new company, Apogee. He still had much of ILM's equipment, but it wasn't clear whether he had to return it to Lucas: legally speaking, ILM had temporarily ceased to exist. The paychecks stopped coming as of May 25, 1977. The special effects industry was still moribund at that point; members of the Apogee crew were glad of any work they could get.

Fox was upset too: the studio had pitched the concept of a *Star Wars* TV show to Kenner CEO Bernie Loomis and other potential licensees. Now it seemed Universal was going to beat them to the punch, making it that much harder for any *Star Wars* show to make it to the TV screen. Furthermore, the *Battlestar* premiere episode was shown in theaters in Europe as a movie, meaning it had started to compete on *Star Wars'* home turf. Fox sent Universal a cease and desist in December 1977. When work continued on *Galactica* regardless, Fox filed a lawsuit the following June, alleging thirty-four ways in which *Galactica* had ripped off *Star Wars*. Universal countersued, alleging that *Star Wars* had ripped off the 1939 *Buck Rogers* serial, to which Universal still owned the rights. Slightly less preposterously, the suit also alleged theft from *Silent Running*, the 1972 bomb that sunk Barwood and Robbins's film *Home Free*. But of course, McQuarrie had consciously based the design of R2-D2 on the reverse of *Silent Running*'s robots, making Artoo round where his predecessors were square. They waddled; he mostly glided.

When the *Galactica* pilot finally aired on television—in September 1978, the same month most theaters finally stopped showing *Star Wars*—the science fiction community rallied around Lucas. "*Star Wars* was fun and I enjoyed it, but *Battlestar Galactica* was *Star Wars* all over again," opined Isaac Asimov in a newspaper column. "I couldn't enjoy it without amnesia." Writer Harlan Ellison dubbed *Galactica*'s creator "Glen Larceny." Prior to the premiere on ABC, *Time* magazine called it "the most blatant rip-off ever to appear on the small screen."

But not everyone agreed that they were watching a rip-off. Dykstraflex spacecraft shots and laser fire from fighter craft in space do not a copycat make. The more the show developed, the more it staked out its own territory—just as Gene Roddenberry noted that *Star Trek* had to go fifteen episodes to find its footing. "The characters are given more psychological dimension than the comic-strip cutouts engaged in *Star Wars*," wrote *Newsweek*'s critic on viewing the pilot.

Galactica lasted a single season on ABC. Ratings started out high, but an irregular time slot torpedoed the show. Outraged fans protested outside the network's headquarters; one young fan in Minnesota committed suicide. Larson would reuse many of the sets and equipment for another, more successful TV show: a remake of *Buck Rogers*. *Galactica* returned for one more series in 1980 without much of the main cast. Some twenty-three years on, the Sci-Fi Channel (later Syfy Channel) would remake the entire series in a darker fashion, altering one essential detail: the Cylons could now look like humans. It ran for four successful seasons, and would come to influence Lucas in the late 2000s, when he finally got around to planning a *Star Wars* live-action TV show.

Fox's suit against Universal was thrown out of court in October 1980; Universal's case against *Star Wars* was likewise dispatched the following May. Fox's case was restored on appeal two years later, with the court declaring that it "raised genuine issues of material fact as to whether only the *Star Wars* idea or the expression of that idea was copied." In 1984, Universal paid Fox $225,000 to make the whole thing go away.

The claim and counterclaim left one odd piece of legal trivia in its wake. In a decade-long deluge of science fiction movies with borrowed concepts, after black samurai helmets and planet-sized weapons, only one US feature film was slapped with a lawsuit accusing it of outright copying: *Star Wars*.

Early in 1978, Twentieth Century Fox contracted TV producer Dwight Hemion to executive produce an hour-long *Star Wars Holiday Special* for CBS. Fox believed three years was going to be too long to wait between *Star Wars* movies. Lucas agreed. The Emmy-nominated Hemion had spent a decade producing specials for the likes of Frank Sinatra and Barbara Streisand. In 1977, he had produced the last TV special to star Elvis Presley, one of Lucas's idols. Hemion had also directed a well-received version of *Peter Pan* starring Mia Farrow and Danny Kaye, suggesting he could handle children's fantasy. If his holiday special worked, it could be the pilot for a *Star Wars* TV series.

Lucas suggested a story that focused on Chewbacca's relatives and a galactic holiday called Life Day on his home, Kashyyyk. The Wookiee planet had been recently rejected for *The Empire Strikes Back*. Now, because Lucas liked to recycle just about every concept ever considered for *Star Wars*, and because he still had a soft spot for Wookiees, it was revived. Ralph McQuarrie produced paintings of the planet. Lucas provided the names of Chewie's family: his wife, Malla; his father, Itchy; and his son, Lumpy. Lucasfilm produced a "Wookiee bible" with everything the writers would need to know about the apelike species, including how they reproduce: "Wookiees have litters." Lucas would also tell one of the writers of the show that Han Solo was married to a Wookiee, "but we can't say that."

The *Holiday Special* is legendarily awful—not in that so-bad-it's-good kind of way that heralds a cult classic like *Starcrash*, but in the sense of monumentally boring. (Look it up on YouTube and see how many minutes you can suffer through.) Before it aired, Lucas and Gary Kurtz took their names off the project. "We were kind of appalled," Kurtz told me. "It was a bad mistake." A quote falsely attributed to Lucas by practically the entire Internet has him expressing a desire to destroy every copy of the special in existence "with a hammer." But he told *Starlog* magazine in 1987 it would be released on videotape "soon." Here's what he said in 2002: "That's one of those things that happened, and I just have to live with it." (Lucas was less restrained in his appearance on Seth Green's *Robot Chicken* spoof, where within the safety of satire he offered his only real public critique of *Holiday Special*: "I hate it, I hate it, I hate it!" his character screamed from the therapist's couch. Green says Lucas requiered little coaching.)

Did it have to be that bad? When McQuarrie died in 2012, something turned up in his papers: a treatment for the special, dated March 1978. The author remains unknown, but it reads a lot like Lucas. The treatment begins with Chewbacca arriving at his home and reuniting with his family. Han Solo appears on a video screen, congratulating the Wookiees on the fact that their planet has been chosen to host the galactic festival called Life Day. Solo gives us the stakes: Life Day isn't illegal, yet, but the Empire fears it could unify the galaxy and is scheming to shut it down in any way it can. Chewie, the most famous Wookiee, will be the focus of the festival. The Starship *Musica* is on its way to kick off the ceremonies.

Meantime, a trader arrives at the Wookiee residence. Chewie buys a "Video Book" for his son as a Life Day present, though the trader makes it clear that Life Day isn't a commercial festival. Chewie relaxes with a "Mind Evaporator" that plays rock and roll, which Wookiees apparently enjoy. (As weird as that sounds, it wouldn't be out of character for George Lucas, rock and roll fan and the man who gave us an equally incongruous Benny Goodman–style swing band in the Mos Eisley cantina.) Chewie then discovers to his horror that

Lumpy has gone missing: he's stowed away aboard the trader's ship, destination Tatooine. The trader is eventually reached at that familiar cantina, and he agrees to return Lumpy to Kashyyyk via the *Musica*. Meanwhile, an Imperial commander dispatches a guest star—the treatment suggests Raquel Welch—to make sure the *Musica* never makes it to Kashyyyk. She seduces its commander, dances (literally) into its control room while explaining to Lumpy how starships work, and "screws everything up." The droids follow her and notify Leia and Luke, who alert Chewbacca, who takes a shuttle to the starship and flies it to safety. Life Day and Lumpy have been saved. And Chewbacca would finally get the medal he was denied during the final ceremony of *Star Wars*.

Would that have made for the greatest holiday special ever? Probably not, but it might have provided the foundation for a campy cult classic. The treatment appears to have been transformed, however, by Hemion's producers, Ken and Mitzie Welch. Chewbacca was removed from most of the show; instead we see his family wondering if he's ever going to show up at all, and watching various entertainments to distract themselves. Life Day remains utterly unexplained throughout the final version; at the end, it appears to be a festival composed entirely of Wookiees in red robes.

The show's writers realized with a dawning sense of horror that they were now writing a script dominated by characters that didn't speak a word of English. "The only sound they make is like fat people having an orgasm," writer Bruce Vilanch noted. Heavyset himself, he told Lucas he would create the show's dialogue by leaving a tape recorder in his bedroom. Lucas was not amused. Nor was he particularly interested in keeping tabs on the show. He appointed David Acomba, a frat brother of Charley Lippincott's, as director. But Acomba was not accustomed to TV directing; the crew found him high strung. He quit the production after shooting a few scenes. "These people don't know what they're doing," he told Lippincott.

The writers did the best with the treatment they were given by the Welches, creating what they hoped were charming scenes of family life on Kashyyyk. Itchy the young rascal steals cookies, annoys his grandfather with a toy spaceship, and amuses himself with a hologram of circus tumblers. Malla watches a cooking show. She checks in on Chewie's progress via video screen with Luke and Leia, and distracts Imperial troops who search her home for the unauthorized video screen.

The first ten minutes after the opening credits is nothing but Wookiees roaring at each other. If the writers had left it at that, the *Holiday Special* might at least have gone down in history as a kind of avant-garde insurgency, a mime's delight that baffled the mainstream. But this was a variety show. Songs were written. Jefferson Starship was to perform its single "Light the Sky on Fire." A cartoon, featuring the debut of bounty hunter Boba Fett, was in production. Bea Arthur, of Maude fame, was to sing a song in the Mos Eisley cantina to the tune of the cantina band's swing music, called "Goodnight but Not Goodbye." It all had to be shoehorned into the show somehow. (Mark Hamill, at least, resisted plans for Luke to sing a number.)

In the most horrific example of how the *Holiday Special* went completely off the rails, Chewie's father, Itchy, relaxes with the Mind Evaporator provided by the trader. But what he witnesses isn't rock and roll. It's singer Diahann Carroll, cast by the Welches with two explicit intentions: one, make sure the cast was multiracial, and two, perform an erotic song that was PG enough for the censors. "I'm your fantasy," she coos to the old Wookiee. "I am your pleasure." The Wookiee growls with orgasmic delight. "Ooh," giggles Carroll, "we are excited, aren't we?"

But even Carroll's song is easier to stomach than the special's ending. Carrie Fisher was going through what Vilanch described as "her Joni Mitchell period." Showcasing her singing talents, such as they were, was the quid pro quo for her participation. The Welches duly wrote a ballad for Princess Leia—celebrating Life Day to the tune of the *Star Wars* theme itself. Fisher, who loved to sing but hated the song, appears glassy-eyed and struggles to hit the high notes.

By the time Lucas and Gary Kurtz saw what was going on, it was too late to do anything but remove their names. "In the long run, it wasn't necessary," Kurtz remembers. "Fox was worried that three years was too long to wait for the second film and something needed to be out there in the meantime. It really didn't." But the studios and networks had spoken. CBS was overjoyed to have what would surely be the holiday season's biggest ticket. So many advertisers had climbed on board, the one-hour show was stretched into two. Del Rey published a Wookiee storybook. Kenner, the lead advertiser, prepared to release a line of Wookiee action figures. Never again would they be caught flat-footed by demand!

The show was teased for months beforehand. Kids were thrilled that *Star Wars*, which had only just left theaters, was now showing up on TV. Folks who didn't go to the movies, and had only *Battlestar Galactica* to go on, would finally get to see what was all the fuss was about. That applied not just in the United States but around the world; the *Holiday Special* was sold and screened in at least six other countries, including Canada and Australia.

At first, it seemed to have paid off. An estimated thirteen million people in the United States alone tuned in for the start. But ratings dropped precipitously after the Boba Fett cartoon at the end of the first hour. By the time Fisher performed her song, most viewers had switched over to ABC or NBC, or switched off altogether.

The special, strangely, clung to the edges of *Star Wars* canon for years. Since it marks the first appearance of Boba Fett and the first time the Wookiee home world is mentioned, Lucasfilm couldn't ignore it altogether. (That was until 2014, when Lucas took a scorched earth approach to all *Star Wars* media in which Lucas's name was not in the credits; only then did the worst *Star Wars* clone of all vanish from the *Star Wars* galaxy.) It was never released on home video, despite what Lucas said he hoped in 1987, and was only kept alive by fans on bootleg tapes until the YouTube era arrived.

At the time, the *Holiday Special* seemed the startling self-immolation of a promising franchise—proof, if any were needed, that the sequel was likely to bomb. For George Lucas, it was an object lesson: never again would he cede so much control over how his universe was represented. When it came to his sequel, if he was to avoid losing every penny of his *Star Wars* wealth, he would have to watch the process like a falcon.

Manuelito Wheeler, Director of the Navajo Nation Museum, with a scale model of the truck-mounted screen he used to show the first movie in the Navajo language: a little something called *Star Wars*, to which his office is a shrine. CHRIS TAYLOR

Fascination with the space frontier mixes with nostalgia for an age of chivalry in this publicity still for *Flash Gordon Conquers the Universe*. In the cockpit of their rocket ship, dressed for the region of Arboria, from left: Dr. Zarkov (Frank Shannon), Flash Gordon (Buster Crabbe), Dale Arden (Carol Hughes), and Prince Barin (Roland Drew). UNIVERSAL PICTURES

In 2013, George Lucas made his one and only public homecoming to Modesto for the fortieth anniversary of *American Graffiti*, down the streets he used to cruise—and here, past his father's old stationery and toy store. Asked if Modesto was the home of *Star Wars*, he responded: "not really. Most of these things come from your imagination." CHRIS TAYLOR

Albin Johnson, founder of the 501st Legion, is a shy, retiring, behind-the-scenes kind of guy—not that you'd know it from this rare shot of Albin with a couple of what he calls "Trooper Groupies." ALBIN JOHNSON

Mark Fordham, then-CO of the 501st and its premiere Darth Vader, shows the power of the Legion at the Tournament of Roses Parade in 2007, with Grand Marshall George Lucas. Both men had ambitions to turn their organizations into franchises. MARK FORDHAM

The day that changed everything and eventually birthed *Star Wars*: June 12, 1962. The crash quelled George Lucas's driving desires, committed him to education, and led to a love of anthropology, sociology, and the visual arts. THE MODESTO BEE

THE MODESTO BEE

McClatchy Newspapers Service

MODESTO, CALIFORNIA, WEDNESDAY, JUNE 13, 1962   PAGE D

Youth Survives Crash

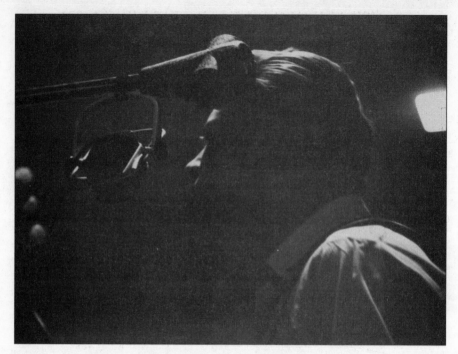

A rare portrait by photography student Lucas, never before published, shows his love of dramatic lighting. The rock guitarist subject is Don Glut, fellow member of the Clean Cut Cinema Club at USC and future author of the *Empire Strikes Back* novelization. COLLECTION OF DON GLUT

Alain Bloch, co-founder of the Golden Gate Knights, teaches a weekly three-hour lightsaber class—a cross between fencing and yoga, with a few moments to meditate on the Jedi Code. Jedi organizations tend to be action-oriented more than spiritual. CRISTINA MOLCILLO AND ROS'IKA VENN

A fan-made model of Barack Obama as a Jedi, seen at Rancho Obi-Wan. Obama is the first president to have been a teenager when *Star Wars* hit theaters. He crossed lightsabers with the US Olympic fencing team, responded to a petition requesting a Death Star, and was dubbed a Jedi Knight by George Lucas—then confused a Jedi mind trick with a Vulcan mind meld. CHRIS TAYLOR

Gary Kurtz, here with Lucas on the throne room set from *Star Wars*, was four years Lucas's senior and had the Vietnam experience he was looking for in a producer for *Apocalypse Now*. But he was also a *Flash Gordon* fan, and ended up producing a remarkable string of hits for Lucas instead: *American Graffiti*, *Star Wars* and *The Empire Strikes Back*. His level of influence over the early franchise, before his sudden departure from it, is still debated. KURTZ/JOINER ARCHIVE

Phil Tippett and Jon Berg were recruited to help reshoot the aliens in the Cantina. When George Lucas found out they were also stop-motion artists, he asked them at the very last minute to animate the chess set on the Millennium Falcon. Previously, Lucas had planned to use actors in leotards for the chess pieces. TIPPETT STUDIOS

The Millennium Falcon, the Dykstraflex, Richard Edlund, and Gary Kurtz at ILM in 1976. The homemade computer-controlled camera was the hidden hero of *Star Wars*, creating the illusion of multidirectional spaceship motion for the first time—and turning the moribund special effects industry on its head. KURTZ/JOINER ARCHIVE

The bright, compelling cast that, according to Carrie Fisher, used to jokingly call itself "trick-talking meat": Harrison Ford (Han Solo), Peter Mayhew (Chewbacca), Mark Hamill (Luke Skywalker), and Fisher (Princess Leia). KURTZ/JOINER ARCHIVE

The wait outside the 1,350-seater Coronet in San Francisco on the weekend after opening, May 28, 1977. It took three days after the movie opened for newspapers to start photographing the lines outside theaters across America. CORBIS / SAN FRANCISCO CHRONICLE

The first *Star Wars* merchandise ad ever to grace the
pages of the science fiction magazine *Starlog*, in the
issue that hit stands July 14, 1977. These vinyl masks
(and Chewbacca's "hand applied hair") were some
of the first products licensed by Twentieth Century
Fox, which at this stage had just as much right to
sell *Star Wars* tchotchkes as Lucasfilm did. STARLOG/
INTERNET ARCHIVE

Mann's Chinese Theater in Hollywood, where Threepio, Artoo, and Darth Vader placed their
feet in wet concrete in August 1977. The ceremony celebrated the return of *Star Wars* after
a mercifully brief engagement with what was supposed to be the hit of the summer, William
Friedkin's *Sorcerer*. A few hundred attendees were expected; five thousand showed up. KURTZ/
JOINER ARCHIVE

Lucasfilm veteran and ultimate fan Steve Sansweet now holds the Guinness World Record for the largest *Star Wars* collection ever. His nonprofit museum Rancho Obi-Wan boasts 300,000 items, such as this 8mm one-scene viewfinder, the closest audiences in the 1970s could get to taking the movie home with them. CHRIS TAYLOR

The author dressed in a Boba Fett costume, hand-crafted by the 501st Legion, wandering the halls of the Salt Lake Comic Con in 2013. CHRIS TAYLOR

ATAQUES ESTELAR DEL TERCER TiPO

con MARJOE GORTNER · CAROLINE MUNRO · DAVID HASSELHOFF · JOE SPINELL · ROBERT TESSIER · NADIA CASSINI · CHRISTOPHER PLUMMER | dir. LEWIS COATES
TECHNICOLOR

Of all the *Star Wars* rip-offs, by far the most blatant was Italian cult classic *Star Crash*, seen here in a Spanish-language version. The movie featured a lightsaber battle and a planet destroying super weapon; the poster boasted what appeared to be a Star Destroyer and the Millennium Falcon. The title translated to "Star Clashes of the Third Kind." NEW WORLD PICTURES

Cinematographer Peter Suschintzky, artist Ralph McQuarrie, Gary Kurtz, and production designer Norman Reynolds discuss an early scene in *The Empire Strikes Back* over a maquette of the Rebel Base hangar on Hoth. KURTZ/JOINER ARCHIVE

The Dagobah set at Elstree hosted a few special visitors from their Borehamwood neighbors, the Muppets—and you can see just how little love was lost between *The Empire Strikes Back* director and his little green star. From left: Miss Piggy, Irvin Kershner, Frank Oz, Yoda, Kermit the Frog, Kathy Mullen, Jim Henson, and Gary Kurtz. George Lucas consciously based Yoda on Kermit; this was their first meeting. Both characters are now owned by Disney. KURTZ/JOINER ARCHIVE

Jeremy Bulloch, aka the original Boba Fett, poses with two astromech droids at Celebration Europe II. CHRIS TAYLOR

The main room at Rancho Obi-Wan in Petaluma, California. CHRIS TAYLOR

Cast members from *Return of the Jedi* reunite on stage, months before it is announced that four of them would be returning for *Star Wars: Episode VII* in 2015. At this point prior to his operation, one of the returning cast, Peter Mayhew (Chewbacca), is unable to walk without the use of a lightsaber cane. CHRIS TAYLOR

The only photograph taken of the historic one-time meeting between Gene Roddenberry, creator of *Star Trek*, and George Lucas, creator of *Star Wars*. At "Starlog Salutes Star Wars," the tenth anniversary celebration at the Stouffer Concourse Hotel in Los Angeles, May 1987. DAN MADSEN

The fans who became buddies for life after they camped outside the Coronet theater in San Francisco for what was then a record thirty-three days before the release of *Episode I: The Phantom Menace*. Most would not look this excited after seeing the film. CHRIS GIUNTA

Artoo builder Chris James and an army of astromechs. The entirely fan-built droids range from the original-style R2 Unit to the black-domed R4-K5—a dark side droid said to work with Darth Vader in one *Star Wars* novel. CHRIS JAMES

Star Wars: the Clone Wars director Dave Filoni shows a picture he drew while an animator on *Avatar: The Last Airbender*, of that show's characters in *Star Wars* garb. A hardcore fan of the franchise from age 3, Filoni almost didn't get the *Star Wars* directing job—because when Lucasfilm called, he thought it was a prank committed by friends at *Spongebob Squarepants*. CHRIS TAYLOR

Eight years after narrowly escaping arrest for wearing a Darth Vader costume when the character was completely unknown, Turkish 501st Legion founder Ates Cetin finds himself leading a protest towards Taksim Square in 2013 while protesters hum the Imperial March. GIZEM AYSU OZKAL

The museum that never was: the original rejected plan for the Lucas Cultural Arts Museum or LCAM, permanent home for much *Star Wars* artwork, on the waterfront of San Francisco's Presidio. LUCAS CULTURAL ARTS MUSEUM

15.

HOW TO EXCEED
IN SEQUELS

In July 1978, actor Dave Prowse toured the United States as Darth Vader for the first time. The former British bodybuilding champion was irked by Lucas's insistence that no publicity photographs were to be taken of him on the set of *Star Wars* in Vader costume with the helmet off, and further irritated that no information about him had appeared in the movie's press materials. When Vader had placed his footprints in the wet concrete outside Mann's Chinese Theatre in Hollywood, Prowse had been stewing in London.

"I created Darth Vader," Prowse insisted to a reporter in November 1977. "His movements, his mannerisms are what I and no one else put in the character. . . . So where does Fox get off pretending to the public that the real Darth Vader is inside my black suit when I'm 6,000 miles away? It's disgraceful and dishonest." It was around this time that Prowse started signing photographs, to Lucasfilm's chagrin, "David Prowse IS Darth Vader."

The 1978 trip was an attempt to assert his rightful place, as Prowse saw it. His publicist arranged a West Coast tour. He gave a talk at Marin Civic Center, a few miles from Lucas's home, and fielded questions outside a Berkeley comic store surrounded by roughly a thousand *Star Wars* fans, many in costume. Asked about his first meeting with Lucas, Prowse recalled: "I was confronted with what looked like a young boy." Asked about the sequel, he said it would start filming the following February. Then he offered what a *San Francisco Examiner* reporter described as "a glimpse of a possible plot": Darth Vader and Luke Skywalker are in a do-or-die lightsaber duel when Luke learns that Vader is his father. "Father can't kill son, son can't kill father," Prowse said—so the two characters would live to star in the next sequel. His audience cheered wildly.

Now, according to Lucasfilm lore—and Prowse's autobiography—he had no foreknowledge of the plot twist coming in *The Empire Strikes Back*. It was kept under wraps to the point where Prowse was given fake dialogue for the famous scene ("Obi-Wan is your father"). Mark Hamill was only clued into what was really going on minutes before the scene was shot. The voice of Vader, James Earl Jones, was the only other actor to receive the correct line. The story goes that Prowse learned that Vader was Luke's father during the London premiere in 1980. (In fact, he'd already seen a number of press preview screenings by that point.)

So how come Prowse was casually discussing it as a "possible plot point" a year before filming even began? The plot twist itself was only a few months old; Lucas wrote the key second draft of the script, in which Vader announces his parentage for the first time, in April 1978. He was obsessively secretive about the revelation and wouldn't even allow his secretary to type up that page. Perhaps Prowse had a mole inside Lucasfilm? Nope. He'd said the same thing at a convention around October 1977, according to an interview with a London fanzine called *Little Shoppe of Horrors*: "Vader didn't kill Luke's father, Vader IS his father."

This was decades before the advent of Internet-driven fan culture. The word "spoilers" was not in common currency. Prowse's words vanished in the vacuum of forgotten fanzines and a single paragraph at the end of a local newspaper article. Still, they throw a spanner into the works of *Star Wars* history. After all, this was the twist that transformed everything. The moment Darth Vader officially became Anakin Skywalker, everything in the *Star Wars* universe changed. The path of the next four *Star Wars* films became clear: the third movie would be about his redemption; the prequels would cover his fall. The entire arc of *Star Wars* would become nothing less than the tragedy of Darth Vader.

Lucasfilm would like to be able to say that the plot twist was planned way ahead of time, and that its secrecy campaign to prevent anyone finding out about it worked. The official history is questioned by blogger and Toronto-based cameraman Michael Kaminski, who expended a great deal of energy in *The Secret History of Star Wars* (2008) attempting to show that Lucas had no overarching plan for the series and came up with the Vader twist in 1978 on a whim. But what if neither of these explanations was true? What if Lucas happened to mention this "possible plot point" to Prowse on the set of *Star Wars* in 1976, for a future movie that then didn't seem very likely, and Prowse decided to reveal it out of spite at a company he felt was spurning him?*

The more I studied this strange twist, the more obsessed I became with finding out the truth. Prowse's agent did not respond to repeated requests for an interview, so I tracked down Prowse at the inaugural Salt Lake Comic-Con and asked Bryan Young, who was moderating an on-stage interview with Prowse, to ask him about the 1978 article. "Never heard of it," Prowse said, rather quickly. The following day, I waited in Prowse's autograph line and presented him with a copy of the article. "I'd be interested to read it," he said. "Can I keep it? I'll be here tomorrow."

I came back the next day. Prowse had no memory of the article. He is eighty now and uses a wheelchair. I felt bad for harassing a senior. But he is also an important part of *Star Wars* history, and I knew this might well be the last chance anyone would get to uncover the mystery. So I explained my question again. In a low voice, Prowse reeled off a litany of complaints about his treatment at the hands of Lucasfilm over the years. (He is banned from the official *Star Wars* convention, having "burned too many bridges"—Prowse's words—with Lucasfilm.) "Sometimes," he confessed, "you get in trouble just for speculating on what's going to happen."

"Thanks for stopping by!" the controller of the autograph table said to me with cheery menace.

Was that it? Was Prowse just speculating when he predicted the big reveal? Gary Kurtz says he "vaguely" remembers "something like that". In *Making of "Return of the Jedi"* (2013), Lucasfilm said Prowse was persona non grata on the set because he "had *inadvertently* leaked story points early on while making *Empire*" (emphasis mine). And here's one thing I didn't mention about that *Examiner* article: Prowse actually 'revealed' that the paternal twist would come in a *third* movie.

That throws a different kind of wrench into *Star Wars* history. Fans and Creator alike had been hewing to the notion that this twist was not just unforeseen

---

* Complicating matters still further is a story mentioned in *Starlog* in 1987, which supposedly came from a source close to Lucas. Apparently the Creator had walked into a small San Francisco science fiction convention shortly after *Star Wars* was released and casually told a group of fans in an impromptu Q&A that Darth Vader is Luke's father. "This was an experiment on Lucas's part to see how far and how fast information would be spread in the SF fan community," *Starlog*'s Bill Warren wrote.

but unforeseeable. Yet nasty paternal surprises have been a staple of world literature since Sophocles had the idea for *Oedipus Rex*. We've seen examples from
comic books: Mart Black in *Tommy Tomorrow*, Orion Darkseid in the *New
Gods*. We've also seen how Lucas began to be influenced by Joseph Campbell's
notion of the hero's journey in 1975—too late for the book to matter much
to *Star Wars*, but right on time for its sequel, whereupon Luke the hero had
reached the stage in his journey of "atonement with the father."

Perhaps you didn't need to be George Lucas to know where the next film
was headed. Evidently, even the guy inside the sight-obscuring helmet could
see it coming.

In late 1977, months before Prowse's trip to the States, Lucas had begun making lists of planets again, just as he had in early 1973. There was Chewbacca's
home planet, Kasshook—or is it Kazzook? Or Ganaararlaac? There was a gas
planet called Hoth, as well as an ice planet, as yet unnamed. A garden planet
called Besspin. A swamp planet called Dagobah.

Lucas began to see disconnected images: A metal castle in the snow. Vader's
office, with torrents of lava. Some sort of snow battle. Artoo after a crash landing, his snorkel sticking out of a swamp. Two guys riding on giant two-legged
snow lizards (straight out of the Queen Fria storyline in *Flash Gordon*). One
of them gets attacked by a large snow monster. All of these descriptions went
straight to Ralph McQuarrie for immediate visualization.

Lucas wasn't intending to write the script, just to help come up with its outline. Armies of screenwriters would have killed for the chance to write the first
draft, but Lucas wanted someone with old-time pulp science fiction experience.
A friend introduced him to the space fantasy novels of Leigh Brackett. It wasn't
until Lucas called her in and asked if she'd ever written for the movies that he
discovered she was also the Leigh Brackett who wrote the screenplays for *El
Dorado* and *The Long Goodbye*, and cowrote the adaptation of *The Big Sleep*
with William Faulkner.

Lucas knew he wanted the second movie to be more character-driven, more
mature, more romantic: *Gone with the Wind* in outer space. (*Gone with the
Wind*'s box office take, adjusted for inflation, was the final mountain for *Star
Wars* to scale.) Brackett seemed to be exactly the writer he was looking for.

There was no time to lose. Even in his moment of triumph, Lucas was still in
the Land of Zoom, and would never be slow again. The fame could be illusory;
the fortune could evaporate. Time to strike while the iron of creativity was hot.

In November 1977, Lucas sat down with Brackett for a three-day story conference that formed the basis of a script treatment he wrote shortly after. Sadly, only Lucas's side of the conversation was recorded. But the 51-page transcript showed Lucas had learned the lessons of his last two movies. He wanted to give each of the main characters their own plot line, *American Graffiti*-style. And in the wake of those years of struggle with sprawling *Star Wars* scripts, he wanted to keep this one to 105 pages at most: "short and tight."

Many of the plot points followed naturally from the first film. For Luke to continue his Jedi training without Obi-Wan, he would need a new teacher. Someone more like Ben Kenobi from the third draft of *Star Wars*: a crotchety, crazy creature who is "constantly making fun of Luke" and reveals "the simplest truths almost like a child." Lucas decided to make him small and puppet-like, and wondered aloud if Muppet maestro Jim Henson—whom Lucas had met while Henson was shooting *The Muppet Show* across the street from Elstree— was available. "It should be like Kermit the Frog," he said of the character, "but an alien."

Brackett had to make clear that the Empire was still a force to be reckoned with after the destruction of the Death Star. The Emperor must be mentioned again, and for the sake of future movies, his power would have to grow. The rebellion could be under attack from the very start, perhaps on the ice planet, which would also allow for some *Doctor Zhivago*–style romance amid the snow. And Darth Vader? There's a "personal agenda between him and Luke," Lucas told Brackett. "He might use Leia and Han to find Luke." There will be a titanic battle between Luke and Vader, ending with Luke escaping "down a vacuum tube." Lucas already knew how the third movie will end: "When we kill [Vader] off in the next one, we'll reveal what he really is. He wants to be human. He's still fighting in his own way with the dark side of the Force."

As for Han Solo, Lucas knew he wanted to develop him further but was still struggling with how. Harrison Ford hadn't signed up for a third film yet, so he had to be removed from the action with a degree of uncertainty about his return. Perhaps he could be sent off on a dangerous mission to secure the support of his stepfather, a ruthless merchant or the head of a galactic transportation union. Perhaps we learn more about how he hooked up with Chewie, which is how we get to see the Wookiee planet. Lucas also wanted to introduce one of Han's old friends, a suave gambler type, who may be a member of a clone family that was apparently responsible for the Clone Wars. The movie would end, he said, "with Luke and Leia looking up at the stars wondering if they'll ever see Han again."

Leia, by contrast, was barely developed in the original treatment—except in as much as she is caught in a romantic triangle between Han and Luke: "She rejects Han, though she is excited by him." Eventually, he gets to land "an Errol Flynn kiss that knocks her off her feet." Meanwhile, and very clearly separately, Lucas offers the notion that Luke has a twin sister on the other side of the universe—placed there for safety, she too is being trained as a Jedi.

Notice a pattern here? Like any wise businessman, Lucas was buying insurance for his main moneymaking assets. These developments all allowed the business to continue for as long as possible. The introduction of the Emperor allowed Vader to be killed off; the introduction of the gambler meant we can afford to lose Han. The puppet creature was a hedge against Alec Guinness, who was at that point refusing to participate as the ghost of Obi-Wan. Mention of a sister, another Jedi child planted somewhere safe, would allow us to lose Luke in future episodes.* The creator was moving as fast as he could to build a decades-long franchise—and to extend the *Star Wars* universe past the point where it was dependent on any single actor.

Inspired by the conference with Brackett, Lucas whipped up a quick story treatment. The vague imaginings from his notes got names. The puppet creature: Minch Yoda. The ice planet: Hoth. The snow lizard: a Taun Taun [*sic*]. And for the first time, the sequel itself got a name, which was announced to little fanfare. *The Empire Strikes Back*: it sounded hokey to some, reminiscent of old-time adventure serials. But it would achieve Lucas's main goal: announcing on every theater marquee that the destruction of the Death Star was just the beginning.

I n the outside world, the *Star Wars* craze continued unabated—and manifested itself in ways that Lucasfilm would never authorize today. The November issue of *Vogue* included a feature headlined "The Force of Furs"; inside, Threepio cuddled up to a couple of models in pelts, while Vader looked sternly at a couple more, and Stormtroopers tried to strong-arm fur-wearing women. Cantina aliens and skating Stormtroopers appeared on *Donny & Marie*, the Osmond siblings' show. Bill Murray sang the "*Star Wars* song" on SNL.

---

* Of course, Lucas had almost lost Mark Hamill, thanks to his car accident in January 1977, during *Star Wars* postproduction. To explain away Hamill's facial scar, Lucas knew he would need to have Luke attacked by a monster at the very beginning of the script.

It was too late to put together any kind of *Star Wars Holiday Special* for 1977, but Mark Hamill showed up in Skywalker garb on the *Bob Hope All Star Christmas Special* and arrested Hope—dressed as "Bar Vader"—for "malicious mutilation of a marvelous movie." By late 1978, that was no laughing matter: the company had got its legal and licensing act together to the point where it sued the singer Neil Young for dressing small actors as Jawas during his stage show.

There was a sense of urgency at Lucasfilm: the company needed to get organized. Lucas brought his old USC friend Howard Kazanjian on board as vice president of development, ostensibly to produce the *American Graffiti* sequel required by Lucas's contract with Universal. In fact, Lucas was already thinking of severing ties with his *Star Wars* and *Empire Strikes Back* producer, Gary Kurtz. Why isn't exactly clear; Kurtz says he wasn't aware of any problems until *Empire* started to go way over budget, but it seems Lucas may have been unhappy with the simple fact that *Star Wars* had gone over budget too. Says Kazanjian: "During pre-production on *Empire*, long before a script, George said I should attend as many meetings on *Empire* as possible, as I would be producing the third film." Notably, Kazanjian was always able to keep his Lucasfilm movies on budget.

The company hired its first CEO, Charlie Weber. A veteran of real estate, Weber was picked largely because he'd never heard of George Lucas. He led the acquisition of what became known as the Egg Company, a former egg wholesaler's million-dollar piece of property across the street from the Universal lot where Lucas kept his LA office. This would be the center of all Hollywood-based operations; everything that couldn't be done from Marin. In their best moments, said Kazanjian, "we were trying to build Camelot." Even if worst came to worst in the movie business, Lucas knew, the Egg Company building's value would go up regardless.

Lucas had personally earned $12 million from *Star Wars* alone by the end of 1977. Yet Randall Kleiser (once Lucas's roommate, now the successful director of *Grease*) remembered visiting George and Marcia around this time to find they were still eating from a stack of TV dinners in a large icebox. Kleiser pointed out that they could now hire a cook, and watched the lightbulbs go off above their heads. As generous as he was with friends, giving away 25 percent of his *Star Wars* profits, Lucas was drawn to relatively simple living. He bought a Ferrari but mostly drove his 1967 Camaro. His plan was to keep $50,000 a year for living expenses and plunge the rest into building the company. He took more breaks and gave his growing staff presents at Thanksgiving and Christmas.

Otherwise, 1977 ended the way it began: with Lucas and everyone around him hard at work on a *Star Wars* movie.

One of the most challenging tasks, of course, was finding the right director. Lucas and Kurtz came up with a hundred possibilities, before whittling it down to twenty, and finally one: an old hand at movies, a mentor from USC. Irvin Kershner, age fifty-four, had judged the National Student Film competition that *THX 1138 4EB* won ten years earlier. Now that prize student was asking him to take the reins of the sequel to the world's biggest film. Kurtz took Kersh, as he was known, out for a drink to float the idea; the two had worked together before. When Lucas called Kersh days later, he used a couple of winning tactics: reverse psychology ("you'd have to be crazy to take this on") and outright praise ("I want somebody who under tremendous pressure will not cave in, somebody who has vast experience in films and likes to deal with people and characters").

"I felt very flattered," Kersh said. "He knew how to get to me, the rat."

Kersh's solicitousness in the face of Lucas's flattery may have obscured one important point about the mentor figure. "I think George had it in mind that he could direct the film remotely by telling Kersh what to do," says Kurtz. "And Kersh was not that kind of director."

Kersh did get the *idea* of *Star Wars*, though. He had watched the original movie with his ten-year-old son, and saw through his young eyes the movie's appeal and core strengths. He was a Buddhist, and understood the force implicitly. He described *Star Wars* as a morality play, but one that had to move speedily to keep a modern audience's interest. The Lucas-Kershner relationship moved fast too, and a deal memo was signed by Valentine's Day.

January ended with another story conference, this one with Steven Spielberg and an advertising-executive-turned-writer Spielberg had plucked out of obscurity, Lawrence Kasdan. The trio gathered for the first time to discuss the Indiana Jones movie. Lucas was on fire, spitting out at a rapid clip. There are pages and pages of the transcript in which no one says a word but Lucas. "What we're doing here, really, is designing a ride at Disneyland," Spielberg said. He occasionally offered ideas; Lucas gently shut him down. The relationship reflected their standing: *Close Encounters* opened strong—very strong—but nowhere near the box office records set by *Star Wars*. The championship of the movie world remained in Lucas's hands for now.

Brackett, who had been typing away since her own story conference with Lucas, turned in her draft in late February. It contained some intriguing might-have-beens: Minch Yoda, known here simply as Minch, is able to call Obi-Wan's ghost "by the power of the Force" and then proceeds to duel with him, winning a highly formal bout. Luke's father, known simply as Skywalker, also appears in ghostly form and leads his son through the oath of the Jedi Knights. There is a lot of saluting with lightsabers. Luke salutes the *Millennium Falcon* when Han leaves to find his stepfather at the end of the script.

But Brackett's draft seemed oddly static, especially after all those roller-coaster cliff-hangers in the *Raiders* conference. Luke moons after Leia in the ice base and gets hypnotized by a crystal that pops out of his lightsaber. Han and Leia spend half the movie flirting and canoodling in the broken-down *Falcon*, just drifting in empty space. Threepio and Chewie repeatedly bicker about the brewing romance. When Vader captures our heroes in Cloud City, he sits them down to an awkward dinner and then lets them roam about the place while under arrest. Cloud City owner Lando Kaldar, not yet Lando Calrissian, talks wistfully of missing his clone family.

Brackett made odd choices of tone and mistakes in continuity. She winked at the audience a lot, seeming not to get that *Star Wars* drew its humor from being deadpan earnest. Han tries a line on Leia—"We're just two people alone in the immensity of space"—then collapses in a fit of giggles: "I'm sorry, that's too much, even for me." Han also says the ice base is safe in obscurity because "I doubt even God remembers where he hung this star," casually introducing a deity to the Force-filled galaxy. Vader, whose name Brackett occasionally misspells, pursues Luke out of revenge for blasting his ship at the end of the battle for the Death Star—despite the fact that it was Han who did that. (To be fair, this was an error Brackett may have picked up from the Alan Dean Foster novel *Splinter of the Mind's Eye*—on which, more later.)

Lucas must have experienced a familiar sinking feeling when he read Brackett's draft. It happened on *THX*, it happened on *American Graffiti*, and it was happening again: he outsourced the troublesome task of script writing to a professional, and what came back failed to match the content of the movie in his head. Reading the draft in his first meeting with Lucas after he'd signed on as director, Kershner was equally concerned.

A call was duly placed to Brackett—which was when Lucas learned she was in the hospital. Leigh Brackett died less than a month later. She'd been in the final stages of cancer throughout the script-writing process and hadn't wanted to say anything. *The Empire Strikes Back* was to be her last hurrah. Lucas determined to keep her name on the movie. "I liked her a lot," he said. "She really tried her best." Her script had, at least, shown him the way he didn't want *Star Wars* to be.

Lucas set about writing a new draft by hand. He produced much of it while on vacation with Marcia and friends in Mexico—a second vacation in less than a year, unprecedented for the Lucases. Also unheard of was the speed at which Lucas wrote the second draft: he started writing in April and was done by June. No longer was he slumped at the door desks, battling the Bogan Force. This is the draft on which Lucas admits he had the most fun: "I found it much easier than I expected," he said. "Almost enjoyable."

In typical Lucas fashion, the dialogue of the sequel's second draft—his first—was wonderfully stilted. At the end of the draft, after Lando and Chewie leave in the *Falcon*, Luke tells Leia: "I will be leaving also. I have left unfinished things." Leia responds: "You know it's Han I love, don't you?" Luke: "Yes, but I have been swept into another sphere. Han is better for you." *Gone with the Wind* this ain't.

Still, much of what we now know as *The Empire Strikes Back* settled into place in the second draft, with only minor differences in structure. The Imperial invasion of Hoth now featured "huge walking machines," which had already been sketched out by designer Joe Johnston.

This is as good a point as any to address a falsehood that has persisted for years in the Bay Area—namely that the AT-ATs, as those Imperial walkers became known, were inspired by the giant four-legged cranes at the Port of Oakland. Lucas denies this. The truth is wilder: Joe Johnston was inspired by a four-legged tank, a concept vehicle designed by General Electric in 1968 called the Cybernetic Anthropomorphous Machine. The CAM had been commissioned by the army for possible use in Vietnam; GE only abandoned it when the design turned out to be too exhausting to operate. Intentionally or otherwise, Lucas and Johnston were continuing the analogy between the Empire's fight against the rebellion and America's fight in Vietnam.

Han hides the *Falcon* in an asteroid field, a scene ripped from the first draft of *The Star Wars*. Luke leaves Yoda and Ben precipitously on Dagobah, leading Yoda to declare that they "must find another." When he appears in Cloud City to welcome our heroes, Lando is no longer a clone. When Vader captures Han and Leia, he tortures both of them. Han is frozen in carbonite and handed over to bounty hunter Boba Fett—a plot point that deals with the recalcitrant Ford, who was consistently asking that Han be killed off.

And then, in the first handwritten version of his post-Brackett draft, Lucas arrived at his twist in the tale. During the climactic lightsaber battle with Darth Vader, the Sith lord is trying to get the young Skywalker to come over to the Dark Side. He encourages Luke's hatred: "I destroyed your family. I destroyed Kenobi." Then he makes an incongruous offer: "We will rule the galaxy as father and son."

"What?" says Luke, and we're right there with him. *Wait. Back up.* Why would Vader give the game away in what amounts to a Freudian slip? The dramatic reveal comes a few lines later: "I am your father." Search your feelings, he insists. You know it to be true.

Lucas would later claim that he had Vader in mind as Luke's father all along. But he has also copped to a whole lot of spontaneity in his writing. "When you're creating something like that, the characters take over," he said in 1993, "and they begin to tell the story apart from what you're doing. . . . Then you have to figure out how to put the puzzle back together so it makes sense."

Here's how it may have played out, the moment when the "maybe" of Luke's parentage collapsed into a certainty. Lucas wrote the lightsaber battle on vacation in Mexico, working feverishly fast, caught by the muse. He understood the audience would know Luke isn't going to die; they needed a reason to fear for him in this moment. The jeopardy, as Lucas had noted in his story conference with Brackett, is that Luke might get turned to the Dark Side of the Force. So he peppered Vader's dialogue with reasons for Luke to give into his hatred. What reasons might they be? Well, we know from the first movie Vader killed Luke's father, so let's have him say something like that, maybe make it even bigger: "I destroyed your family."

Your family. Your father. Anakin Skywalker, the loose thread that refuses to be tied up. Darth Vader, the mystery man inside the iron lung suit. We know so little about them; the movie thus far had stubbornly refused to advance either character. It was especially irritating given that the Joseph Campbell formula calls for some intense father action at this point in the story. In *The Hero with a Thousand Faces*, Campbell explains that the hero reconciling with the father is an essential, almost religious component of all myth: "The problem of the hero going to meet the father is to open his soul beyond terror to such a degree that he will be ripe to understand how the sickening and insane tragedies of this vast and ruthless cosmos are completely validated in the majesty of Being."

But wait a second: "We will rule the galaxy as father and son," the character makes him write. Finally, definitively, whether he'd thought of it before or not, new worlds opened up for Lucas to conquer. Vader was already supposed to be a Jedi Knight who turned to the Dark Side and betrayed the Jedi. But if Vader were simply a new name for Skywalker, well, that would bring the betrayal up to decidedly operatic levels. It would explain at a stroke why everyone from Uncle Owen to Obi-Wan to Yoda has been so concerned about Luke's development, and whether he would grow up to be like his father.

The unification of Anakin Skywalker and Darth Vader removed a lot of redundancy from the storyline. You can see the problem plain as day in Brackett's first draft, where Yoda summons Obi-Wan, who in turn summons Skywalker père. "Suddenly Dagobah is full of old, noble Jedi ghosts who are basically the same character," says author Michael Kaminski.

For the rest of the production, Vader's secret was kept under wraps as much as possible. Lucas was careful even about telling Kershner. He really wanted the twist to reach as many audiences as possible in an unspoiled state. Only one thing would ultimately give the game away, and with Lucasfilm's blessing: the novelization of *The Empire Strikes Back*, written by Lucas's USC pal Don Glut, which would come out one week in advance of the movie and sell three million copies. Once again, the plot of the entire movie would be hidden in plain sight, perfectly accessible to the literate and interested; once again, *Star Wars* would prove to be more than just a movie franchise.

Glut had turned down the novelization of *Star Wars* but still had his "finger in the *Star Wars* pie," as he puts it. He had originally been contracted to write a Wookiee-based novel. After the disaster of the *Holiday Special*, Glut got a call from Carol Titleman, Charley Lippincott's former girlfriend, who was now in charge of Lucasfilm's nascent publishing division as well as the upcoming National Public Radio adaptation of *Star Wars*. Titleman took Glut out to lunch and said: "Forget the Wookiee novel. We want you to write *The Empire Strikes Back*." This time, he would be allowed to put his own name on the cover. Glut was offered a "relatively small" advance on royalties, rather than the flat fee Foster was granted for the *Star Wars* novelization. It wasn't the best deal in the history of publishing, but Glut was told: "If you turn it down, there are people who will pay us to write it."

Glut found Lucasfilm a hive of self-imposed secrecy. "They were so paranoid," he says. "Some people could look at the scripts but not see the artwork; some people could see the artwork but not the scripts. They literally locked me inside a trailer with all the McQuarrie paintings." He made sketches in a notebook and remembered showing an employee one sketch when he came out. "Is this Yoda?" Glut asked. The employee threw his hands over his eyes. "Don't tell me! I don't want to know."

While the talent at Lucasfilm raced to prepare for the making of a second film, Lucas seemed less interested in the movie than he did in the utopian future film community of Bulltail Ranch, soon to be renamed Skywalker. Here, finally, was the Marin County dream Lucas had nurtured since John Korty had first invited him up there in 1968. It was hidden away on Lucas Valley Road, the name of which was a happy coincidence—John Lucas was a nineteenth-century Marin-ite who inherited the land from his uncle. The 1,700-acre valley was wild and grassy, green in the spring and yellow in the summer and fall. It was utterly enclosed, a world unto itself, with deer bounding through the valley and mountain lions patrolling the tree-lined hills.

Skywalker Ranch was to remain as secret as the script throughout the making of *Empire*. Initially, the land deed was in the name of Lucas's accountant. Which was just as well, since the combination on the padlocked fence at the ranch entrance was ridiculously easy to guess: 1138.

Just as he gave his scripts to trusted friends, Lucas brought Hal Barwood and others to the ranch in June 1978. He explained the dream: it would remain, for the most part, a ranch. They would plant walnut trees, just like the ones on the ranch home he spent his teenage years in. They would build a vineyard and raise cattle, maybe horses. The buildings would be few and far between, so sparsely arranged that you wouldn't be able to see one building from another. That plan was partly due to the fact that Marin had not zoned the land for development. But it also reflected Lucas's vision of an agrarian utopia for filmmakers and writers. Creative types, Lucas believed, couldn't work traditional eight-hour days. They weren't at their best in cities. They needed to refresh the well with long midday breaks, games of Frisbee, or walks in the hills, perhaps with the extra adrenaline boost of running into a mountain lion.

For the time being, Skywalker Ranch was just a vision that Lucas kept sketching out on his notepads. The land was a place for picnics, an off-roader's paradise where Gary Kurtz enjoyed driving around at top speed. But the fact that the ranch was just an idea didn't diminish its power—not when it came from the guy who had been doodling space troopers in those notepads not so long ago. Lucas brought Kershner to his office to show him his plans for the ranch and impressed on him that only Kershner could make them real. All he had to do was direct the most successful sequel of all time. No pressure.

Throughout 1978, Lucas lured a half dozen ILM staffers out of Van Nuys north to Marin, but he had to put them in another industrial building in nearby San Rafael. To shield it from curious fans, there was no ILM branding; instead, the building bore the logo of a fictional entity, the Kerner Company Optical Research Lab. Some twenty-seven new ILMers were hired by the new year. This was the state of a filmmaker at the height of his powers: life at top speed with an empire to build; a focus on big picture ideas, and an increasingly large cast of people who were worrying about the details, eager to please. Something Coppola once told him was starting to come true: fame and fortune were a kind of death, in the sense that you were reborn as a new person.

Casual fans could be forgiven for thinking Lucas had little to do with *Empire Strikes Back*. His name was only the fourth on screen in its closing credits: "based on a story by." Leigh Brackett and Lawrence Kasdan are credited as the screenwriters, with no suggestion of the crucial second or third drafts Lucas wrote in between their work. Still, of the two screenwriters who are credited instead of Lucas, Lawrence Kasdan had by far the greater impact. Kasdan had been brought into Lucas's discussions with Spielberg about *Raiders* because Spielberg loved an earlier script of Kasdan's, *Continental Divide*. As soon as Kasdan turned in his *Raiders* script, Lucas tapped him to do his third ever script, a draft of *Empire*, without so much as reading his work on *Raiders*. Post-Brackett, it was a vulnerable moment. "I was desperate," Lucas later admitted.

Kasdan was to be to *Empire* what Huyck and Katz were to *Star Wars*—only instead of heavily rewriting 30 percent of the dialogue, he would lightly rewrite pretty much all of it. Yoda owed his backwards grammar to Lucas, who thought this was how a guru might sound. But he owes the brevity and memorability of his lines to Kasdan. You can also credit Kasdan with lengthening Leia and Han's romantic scenes, and introducing the word "scoundrel" into their dialogue. The back of Vader's head is seen in his private cubicle by an underling as a machine slips on the Dark Lord's helmet; this tantalizing glimpse was also a Kasdan invention.

Kasdan and Kershner "challenged everything in the script," Lucas said later—and that was what he wanted. "If they had a great idea or they had a point, it immediately went in." Lucas wanted the script to move fast; Kasdan wanted emotional depth. It turned into a gentle tug of war—Lennon and McCartney if one of the Beatles had been a thousand times richer than the other.

But the scriptwriting was just one of many elements that made *Empire* so memorable. Yoda's body, rather than his dialogue, was the major fear of the preproduction phase. If the puppet didn't work, Lucas knew, the whole illusion of the movie would be sunk. Joe Johnston came up with the look of the wizened alien guru, but turning it into reality was harder than expected—and trying to pull it off with a Henson-style Muppet was no sure thing. At first, the 2001 veteran Stuart Freeborn experimented with dressing up a baby monkey in a Yoda suit. Only when that clearly did not work did Kurtz make a pilgrimage to

Jim Henson's house, taking Edward Summer along for the ride and swearing him to secrecy.

Henson paused long enough to make a pun—the mass market version of this thing, he quipped, should be called a toy-yoda—before passing on the project. He was far too busy with *The Muppet Movie*. Days later, however, he showed the Yoda sketch to his collaborator Frank Oz, who wasn't too busy. What Oz did with Freeborn's designs and Kasdan's words not only made Henson proud but created a guru for the ages. In 1980, Yoda was to spark serious debate over whether a puppet could be nominated for an acting Oscar. By 2013, he was to receive the most votes from Starwars.com visitors in Lucasfilm's first official online character tournament—beating the might of Darth Vader himself in the final round.

With Oz at the helm of the puppet, locating his voice somewhere between Miss Piggy and Fozzie Bear, Yoda started to take shape. But it would take all of Lucasfilm's ingenuity—and all of Kershner's patience—to create and film multiple realistic puppet versions of the creature, offering the illusion that he could move independently of Oz. Kershner would curse the little green guy's name for the rest of the picture. Meanwhile, what his boss was going through—and insulating Kershner from—was ten times worse than the proper positioning of a recalcitrant puppet.

Financing *Empire* was a serious and constant headache for Lucas. The budget had inflated to $18 million. Payroll alone in 1979 was more than $1 million a week, with another $2 million a week being spent on the shoot after March 1979. The movie was behind schedule almost immediately. In an echo of the problems on *Star Wars*, there was a natural disaster on the first week of location shooting in the northernmost climes of Finse, Norway. This time it was a freak avalanche rather than a freak desert storm. Instead of cutting days and scenes out of the shoot as Lucas had been forced to, Kershner and Kurtz let it fall behind schedule. Kurtz announced to Lucas that the budget was now $22 million.

Toy sales came to the rescue. Despite the movie no longer being in theaters, despite the disastrous *Holiday Special*, and against all expectations, Kenner announced that it had its strongest holiday season yet. Sales of *Star Wars* action figures, spaceships, and play sets had crossed the $200 million mark, funneling more than $20 million into Lucasfilm subsidiary Black Falcon. Without that cash injection, there's little question *Empire* would have been sunk. There's something poetic about it: millions of children joyfully acting out the further adventures of Luke Skywalker literally funded the further adventures of Luke Skywalker. Call it a karmic Kickstarter.

Even with the Black Falcon revenues, Lucas found himself constantly having to put out fires. In July 1979, the Bank of America loan was automatically halted when Lucasfilm's payroll hit $1 million. This was red tape at its reddest, the rigid policy of a new loan manager who looked only at the numbers and was unfamiliar with his client. Lucasfilm was days away from defaulting on paychecks. Oddly enough, some of the blame lay with Coppola. B of A had a nightmarish experience funding *Apocalypse Now*; Coppola asked for an extra $16 million over his initial budget. The bank still wasn't sure it would get the money back. Once bitten, twice shy, B of A cut Lucas off. Ironically, Lucas had been devoting a few spare days here and there to helping Coppola edit the mounds of film he had brought back with him from the Philippines. Lucas was trying to make sure that the movie he washed his hands of back in 1975 made Coppola proud—and made B of A's money back. He was doing a good deed for his friend, and it was not going unpunished by his friend's bank.

Lucas had to turn to his real-estate business CEO to end the financial crisis. Weber worked the phones, and Bank of America handed over the loan to the First National Bank of Boston. Lucas had some breathing room: the budget could now extend to $27.7 million. But the shoot kept getting further and further behind schedule; by late July, when the Dagobah set was under construction, Kersh was lagging by more than a month. To compound the problem, Kurtz had currency trouble—the exact opposite situation from what they had during *Star Wars*. The pound was rising against the dollar. The markets had given a vote of confidence to Margaret Thatcher, who was elected prime minister as Kersh was filming in her country. Suddenly Lucas's set bills ballooned by $3 million, bringing the total to $31 million. Francis Coppola, Bank of America, and Margaret Thatcher nearly torpedoed *The Empire Strikes Back*? Sounds crazy, but it's true.

Lucas vowed to the Boston bank that he would pay the loan off for the rest of his life if the movie didn't break even. It wasn't enough. First Boston required Fox to act as a guarantor. That was the last thing in the world Lucas wanted, but it was either that or he would be forced to shut down the shoot. Fox agreed, in exchange for a better cut of the distribution money. They didn't have to put any cash down to get it. When Lando Calrissian talked about his deal with the Empire "getting worse all the time," it would have been hard for Lucas not to think of his own situation with Fox. The more *Star Wars* money Fox had, the less went to the ranch. This dream was getting worse all the time.

Lucas decamped to London several times during 1979. He had hoped to stay away. He was trying to tell Kurtz that it was his job to stop Kersh overrunning the schedule, at a cost of $100,000 of Lucas's money each day. Kurtz would say that he'd done what he could, even directing a second unit himself to film the scenes with Luke in the Wampa's ice cave to try and reduce the overrun. "I tried to rein Kersh in a bit," Kurtz pleads. "He was very good with the actors, and he was a bit slow." The visual effects team took to rolling their eyes at the director when, for example, filming the scene where the bounty hunter Boba Fett shoots at Luke Skywalker in the corridors of Cloud City. They'd ask Kersh a simple question: Where do you want the squibs, the little explosive devices that simulated Fett's laser blasts hitting the wall behind Luke? Kersh would point to an area, frowning, uncertain. "Are you sure now?" the team would ask. They would drill holes, put the squibs in, cover them up, do a rehearsal—and then Kersh would change his mind about the location of the squibs.

But ultimately, Kersh was hard to speed up because Kurtz was enamored with every scene the older director was coming up with—the lighting, the framing, everything. "Kersh did an outstanding job" on *Empire*, Kurtz says. "The difference between *Star Wars* and *Empire* is striking. It's not only better written, but its performances are much less comic book-y, darker and more realistic." And ultimately, Lucas can't blame Kurtz—because Lucas was enamored with Kersh's transcendent cinematic output at the time as well.

We know this, and a lot more besides, thanks to the diary of Alan Arnold, *Star Wars*' most refined chronicler. Arnold was an English publicist and journalist of the old school, whose résumé read like he'd stepped out of a Graham Greene novel. He was a former press officer for Her Majesty's government who served in Cairo and Washington, DC, and a former foreign correspondent who had visited thirty countries. He had worked with Marilyn Monroe and Marlene Dietrich; he counted Eleanor Roosevelt and Edward Murrow as acquaintances. His books included *How to Visit America*. Now he was serving Lucas as the unit publicist for *Empire Strikes Back* at Elstree, and as part of his role he got to visit crew in Marin and LA.

Arnold was the Lippincott of *Empire Strikes Back*: he made hours of interview tapes with all the principals. (Unlike Lippincott, he published his work in a stream-of-consciousness diary format, the now sadly out-of-print *Once Upon a Galaxy*.) Kershner was Arnold's most frequent interviewee, but he also captured wonderful sketches of Fisher, Ford, Hamill, and newcomer Billy Dee Williams, who had been picked to play Lando because Lucas loved him in the Billie Holliday biopic *Lady Sings the Blues*.

But it was Lucas who proved to be Arnold's most intriguing interviewee. The Creator was now floating the notion that he had written six discrete treatments

in the form of two trilogies before finishing *Star Wars*, and that "after the success of *Star Wars* I added another trilogy," for a grand total of nine movies—or,
as he claimed in another interview around this time, twelve.* How much Lucas
actually wrote, we don't know, but in 2005 he said he never wrote anything at
all for *Episodes VII* onwards. He was already changing his tune as early as 1987:
"I'll guarantee that the first three are pretty much organized in my head, but
the other three are kind of out there somewhere," Lucas said. There's a pattern
here: the pattern of an artist enamored with positive thinking, trying to will his
work into being by talking about it as if it existed. Lucas told Steven Spielberg
he had written two more treatments for Indiana Jones movies after *Raiders of
the Lost Ark*: "It turned out George did not have the stories in mind," Spielberg
recalled later. "We had to make up all of the subsequent stories."

To Arnold, Lucas appeared to be quite Zen about the possibility of losing all
his money before he had a chance to finish the second of those twelve movies.
"I'm willing to take that risk because I started with nothing," he said. "Five years
ago I had nothing. . . . If this is just one of those mildly successful sequels, I'll
lose everything. I could end up being millions in debt. It would probably take
me the rest of my life to get out from under." But the risk was worth it for the
ranch: "Mostly it will be a place to think," he mused, and to "make films without
regard for commerciality."

As much as Lucas loved *Star Wars*, it was now a means to an end: the creation of a filmmaking paradise. How soon Lucas's dreams had outstripped his
money in the bank. "The money needed is so enormous that the money I have
doesn't amount to anything," he told Arnold. "The only way to do it is to create
a company that will generate profits." That would mean turning *Star Wars* into
a self-sustaining entity, a franchise that Lucas wouldn't have to get completely
involved in. Sending the universe, in other words, out of the nest on its own.

But in order to relinquish complete control over the growing *Star Wars* franchise, Lucas would have to ensure that the audience knew the quality wasn't
going to drop as it had during the *Holiday Special*. And that meant making *Empire Strikes Back* the best movie it could possibly be. He understood that Kersh
was doing that, and Lucas was clearly conflicted about it, and about whether
he'd do a better job. He said he hired Kersh "because his reputation is one of
being a fast director, and a very good one." Could he speed up the process?

---

* Lucas walked the twelve-movie claim back in an interview with *Prevue Magazine* in 1980, in
which he said movies ten to twelve were potential spin-offs he had abandoned—movies or droids,
movies or wookiees—rather than episodes in the saga.

Probably, said the boy from the Land of Zoom. Kurtz's assessment was different; Lucas had been laid so low by *Star Wars* that the pressures of directing this film would have "laid him out" completely, the producer told Arnold.

The real trouble with Lucas's plan to let go of *Star Wars* was that the idea of it wasn't ready to abandon its host. "The truth of it is I got captivated," he says. "It's in me now. I can't help but get upset or excited when something isn't the way it's supposed to be. I can see that world. I know the way the characters live and breathe. In a way, they have taken over."

Kersh, for his part, had his own ideas about why the shy Lucas might have had a hard time confronting his elder mentor director over the speed of his work: "I've caught him looking through a camera only twice so far, and he looked at me as guiltily as if he'd stolen a cookie." All Lucas would tell him about the rushes he was receiving was "I love them." Behind the scenes, according to Kurtz, Kersh's blunt response whenever he was confronted with how long he was taking was simply: "You guys hired me to do this job. Let me do this job."

Kersh was most at home with his young leads, taking his time to mentor them. In particular, Kersh recognized Harrison Ford was mature and strong enough to shape his own role. Arnold captured many moments where Ford riffed on his dialogue, with Kersh acting as a wise old sounding board. When Han and Leia land in Cloud City and Lando plants a flirtatious kiss on Leia's hand, Ford's line as written was "She's traveling with me, Lando. And I don't intend to gamble her away, so you might as well forget she exists." But that seemed a burst of jealousy too far, not to mention a little paternalistic. Ford came up with a line that had plenty more interpretation to it: "You old smoothie."

Arnold also captured a crucial moment in Ford's trailer, where the star and the director were discussing Han's final moments in Cloud City before he gets frozen in carbonite:

> FORD: *I think I should be manacled. It won't stop the love scene. I don't have to put my arms around Leia to kiss her. As I pass her by, I think Leia ought to say very simply, "I love you."*
> KERSHNER: *And you say "Just remember that, Leia, because I'll be back." You've got to say "I'll be back." You must. It's almost contractual!*
> FORD: *If she says "I love you," and I say "I know," that's beautiful and acceptable and funny.*
> KERSHNER: *Right, right. You know what? I may keep Vader out of this till the end.*

In case you missed that (because Kersh seems to have done), Harrison Ford came up with one of the most memorable lines of the film—of the entire series—in his trailer, over coffee and fruit. A Lucasfilm documentary, *Empire of Dreams*, would later suggest that Ford only spoke that line as the last of a dozen or more takes. That may had been true, but it left out the essential fact that it was premeditated by Ford and preapproved by Kersh. The script supervisor's final notes from the set had the "I know" line in there. Lucas screened two different versions of the movie for a test audience, one with the line in and one without it. Audiences laughed at the line. Lucas didn't understand why. Kersh and Ford had to explain: laughter was the only way you get an emotional release in what is clearly a very powerful and difficult scene.

If Kersh was content to let the actors rework their dialogue, he was not so easygoing about everything on set. This director was even more of a perfectionist about lighting than Lucas. He came up with the movie's most memorable visual palate on the carbonite freezing set: "We didn't want the comic strip look, but a look of diffused color," he said, describing an aesthetic that contrasted markedly with the first movie. "People's faces have green on one side and red on the other, or the scene is orange and blue." When the cast was taken of the Han Solo frozen in carbonite prop, it was Kershner who suggested the iconic, arresting pose: Han would have thrown his hands up to protect himself against the process.

Ford complemented Kershner's creative style perfectly. Fisher was, well, a different kettle of fish. Kershner had a much harder time dealing with the actress and her frequent illnesses. Some really were illnesses, and she did go to hospital for a stomach checkup. But more than a few of the incidents could be explained by the combination of her party-central flat in St. John's Wood, her friendships with the Rolling Stones, her newfound coke habit, and—at least on one occasion—a bottle of harsh Tunisian liquor brought over by Eric Idle of Monty Python. As he compiled his record of the filmmaking process, Arnold dismissed a bout of crew gossip that she'd been up all night (when in fact she had) and delicately drew a veil over Fisher's private life: she was "allergic to a lot of things" and "doesn't always look after herself as she should," he wrote.

It was harder to draw a veil over Fisher's on-set freak-outs. She was frustrated with Ford's freedom to change his dialogue on a whim and paranoid that much of the script was being changed behind her back. She yelled at Ford, she told Kersh at one point, and "it kind of screwed me up." Kersh encouraged Fisher to yell at him instead. They discussed whether Leia should slap Lando; Billy Dee Williams was concerned because Lando gets slapped around a lot, but he was game to try it. Fisher lashed out so hard you can hear it on the tape:

WILLIAMS: Don't hit me like that!
FISHER: Did it hurt?
WILLIAMS: Of course it hurt.
FISHER: I'm sorry. How do you hit someone?
WILLIAMS: If you want to hit me, fake it.

Fisher, alone among the lead actors, was utterly frustrated with her character. "I know Leia's favorite color is white," she said, but that was about it. "She is more of a caricature, somewhat one dimensional." Luke had to grapple with the lure of the Dark Side after a disturbing revelation; Han got his sacrificial freezing scene; Lando got to redeem his betrayal and bad deal with the Empire. Leia? She was still handy with a blaster, sure, but all she got to learn was how to tremble in Han's arms, how to "use a good kiss," how to tell a man you love him. It wasn't that playing opposite Ford in the romantic scenes didn't have its virtues: "special effects gave him a very good mouth," she said. It was that Fisher was starting to discover the curse of *Star Wars*: her career had stalled outside of this caricature. "I function exclusively in space, it seems," she said. Fisher was the first *Star Wars* actor to make this disturbing discovery, but she certainly would not be the last.

Meanwhile at ILM, Lucas was more willing to urge his underlings to do their best work as fast as possible. Phil Tippett, who had gone from animating the stop-motion chess set in the final days of *Star Wars* in that grimy warehouse in Van Nuys to heading up an entire stop-motion department* in San Rafael, remembers the moment he realized he had become more of a perfectionist than Lucas. When he wasn't happy with the movement of his Tauntauns, "I'd have to argue to do another take," Tippett says. "He'd say, 'It's fine'; then he'd say, 'Okay, one more take.'" Tippett knew that his thirty-three-year-old millionaire boss was caught between the demands of art and the demands of his bank, and it was clearly agonizing. Still, "he never micromanaged us," Tippett says. "He was very inclusive and respectful. We'd ask him, 'Does the Tauntaun do this or that?' and he'd say, 'That's what you guys do. Do what you want.' When you manage creative people that way, you get so much more work out of them."

---

* Or rather "go-motion," a technique that Tippett helped pioneer on *Empire*. It involved connecting models of Tauntauns and AT-ATs to tiny motors that moved them every time the camera shot its frame—so when you strung the frames together, the object's movement appears far more natural than in regular stop-motion. That's why AT-ATs don't move anything like classic Ray Harryhausen skeletons.

Lucas's frustration would only spill out once, when the shoot was over and Kurtz and Kersh were back in San Anselmo. Lucas decided to reedit the movie himself, insistent that Kersh had paced it too slowly—and this time, by all accounts, the result sucked. Supereditor was way too stressed out to do good work. Editor Paul Hirsch talked him down. "You guys are ruining my picture," Lucas fumed, but he relented.

Once the final footage was assembled the way Kersh intended, it was clear that what resulted from all this group effort was a hybrid.

On the one hand, the sequel was very much like the first *Star Wars*. Lucas had opted to make it clear that *Star Wars* was the name of a franchise, not a movie: he would open with the same "A long time ago" intro, the same Suzy Rice logo, the same fanfare. Only the crawl would reveal that we were in a different episode. (The "Episode V" thing confused a lot of audience members who wondered, not unnaturally, whether they had somehow missed episodes two through four.) The initial plan was to have the crawl fade in over the landscape of Hoth and open on the Tauntauns—you can still see it that way in the comic book version. But at the last minute Lucas decided that every *Star Wars* movie would open in space, with Star Destroyers—in this case, one launching probe droids.

On the other hand, the new film was a darker beast than its predecessor, a fairy tale of the grimmer, Grimm variety. The hellish sequence toward the end of the movie, in which Han is frozen in carbonite and Luke loses a lightsaber duel with Vader, loses his hand, learns about his father, and then tumbles down a wind shaft toward the gas planet—all within the space of twenty minutes—is one of the most terrifying and traumatizing moments in children's cinema. Waiting until the very last minute to tell Mark Hamill the line James Earl Jones was going to say certainly helped Hamill sell that crucial scene.

Vader's revelation was every bit as controversial as Lucas had hoped. Not everyone instantly believed that he was telling the truth. Even Luke muttering "Ben, why didn't you tell me?" as he hangs from a satellite below Cloud City, near death, wasn't necessarily enough to convince. (This line had been added in the very last draft.) If Vader was telling the truth, the saintly Obi-Wan had lied about Luke's father. James Earl Jones himself, reading Vader's line "I am your father," had this reaction the moment he said it: "He's lying."

Lucas says he talked to child psychologists who claimed that kids under a certain age—around eight or nine—would simply disbelieve Vader. (I count myself, age seven, among the disbelievers.) One thing is certain: debate about the veracity of Vader's claim raged in offices as much as on playgrounds around the world for the next three years. As a child, Lucas had been drawn to serial cliff-hangers and to the delicious anticipation of what happens next to our heroes. Now Lucas's second-draft switch had created the most hotly debated cliff-hanger in history, far outlasting the contemporary question of who shot J.R. on *Dallas*.

Something often forgotten today is that many members of the audience were less than okay with such open-ended endings. This kind of downer was a first for a family-friendly movie, and it was a major achievement for Lucas to be able to sell it. Not all the fans bought it, however. "It ends on a very bleak note that may leave certain younger members of the audience downright resentful," reported *Starburst*, the venerable UK-based monthly science fiction magazine, upon seeing the media preview of the movie.

> Now if the cliffhanging ending would be fine if we knew we were going to be able to see part 6 next week, next month or even six months from now. But I think expecting us to wait anything between 18 months and three years before we find out what happens next is a bit much on the part of Lucas and Company. For one thing, the cinema audience isn't a static entity. It keeps changing from year to year. Yet Lucas and Kurtz are behaving as if it's just one big *Star Wars* fan club that will patiently wait as the whole story is slowly unwound over a period of 10 to 15 years.

The cinema audience was indeed not a static entity; I was one of the ones who joined it for the first time for *The Empire Strikes Back*. What the *Starburst* writer could not see without retrospect is that my generation, my eight-to-thirteen age bracket, had just been handed the greatest gifts by this open-ended fairy tale: wonderment, the search for answers, and a desire to continue the saga ourselves. I made myself a little cardboard *Empire Strikes Back* logo—I hadn't quite gotten the message about Lucas's reuse of the Suzy Rice logo—so that I could open each "episode" of action figure playtime by pulling it away through my field of vision. I had Lando and Chewie and Luke and Leia perpetually save the Han in carbonite figure in a hundred different ways. No, my generation didn't *want* to wait between eighteen months and three years for the next episode, but *Star Wars* was kept top of mind while we did. We would gladly have waited that long between future movies—if only the saga *would* last as long as the ten to fifteen years suggested by *Starburst*. *Star Wars* was still a fragile thing.

Potential licences certainly didn't see *Star Wars* lasting that long. While Kenner was eager to replicate its success with action figures and play sets, few other companies had been interested in products related to *Empire Strikes Back*. Sid Ganis, who'd taken over from Lippincott, recalled going to a shoe department in a store in Cincinnati near Kenner where he failed to make a sale: "I would take out my portable slide projector, find a place to project it onto a wall, do my *Empire* presentation, and go home." Back then, nobody knew anything about a franchise as wildly lucrative as *Star Wars* was to become. "Trying to license *Empire* was like running into a brick wall," said Maggie Young, then the head of licensing. "People looked at the first film as a fluke."

The doubters, of course, couldn't have been more wrong. *The Empire Strikes Back* succeeded beyond any other sequel in history, making $500 million at the box office. Perhaps because we are overly familiar with the original *Star Wars*, the lingua franca of modern culture, *Empire* regularly beats its predecessor in polls of the top movies in history. In *Empire Magazine*'s rankings thereof (as voted on by prominent directors in 2013), *Empire Strikes Back* is number 3 while the original movie is number 22. The following year, *Empire*'s readers voted *Empire* the greatest movie of all time, greater even than *The Godfather*.

At the time, reviews tended toward the *Starburst* view of things; it seemed breathtakingly arrogant for a filmmaker to make their audience wait until a third movie for any kind of resolution. Still, once they'd seen it, there was a pervasive sense of certainty among reviewers that some enormous entertainment franchise the size of the Galactic Empire had just been born. "What matters at the moment is that there is no sense that this ebullient, youthful saga is running thin in imagination or that it has begun to depend excessively on its marvelous special effects—that it is in any danger, in short, of stiffening into mannerism or mere billion dollar style," wrote Roger Angell in the *New Yorker*.

Vincent Canby's review in the *New York Times* was the most famous negative one, written long before anyone knew the movie was a hit, and it ends this way (emphasis mine):

> *The Empire Strikes Back* is about as personal as a Christmas card from a bank. I assume that Lucas supervised the entire production and made the major decisions or, at least, approved of them. It looks like a movie that was directed at a distance. [But] at this point *the adventures of Luke, Leia and Han Solo appear to be a self-sustaining organism, beyond criticism except on a corporate level.*

The *Star Wars* phenomenon as we know it today was born at the moment it became clear that the second movie, for all its arrogance, was anything but a turkey. From this humble beginning the second film would grow in reputation, until the cinematic son overtook the cinematic father. Looking back on the movie, critics have called it important, weighty, life-altering for any kid of the time. Its denial of good feelings made young viewers grow up fast. "*The Empire Strikes Back* is the only blockbuster of the modern era to celebrate the abysmal failure of its protagonists," wrote cultural critic Chuck Klosterman. "It set the philosophical template for all the slackers who would come of age ten years later." We yearn to be Han Solo, but we end up in Skywalkerish situations, confronted by the Man, who turns out to have been our dad all along. Why, we wonder, didn't Ben Kenobi tell us the truth?

With the premiere of *Empire*, certain Lucas characteristics began to assert themselves: the perfectionist obsession with movie technology and the restless tweaking of his creations. He stubbornly insisted on opening the movie only in higher-tech (and harder to pirate) 70mm, which was much more expensive and kept the number of theaters *Empire* opened in to 100—little more than three times the number of theaters *Star Wars* opened in. This created another supply and demand problem, with long lines that looked great for the TV cameras (and this time, the cameras were ready on day one). The 35mm print arrived three weeks later, eventually reaching 1,400 theaters—far more than *Star Wars* ever played in simultaneously. In that three-week gap, Lucas decided to shoot an additional three special effects shots to make the ending clearer, causing a stir at ILM. "If you guys did this so fast," said Lucas when they were done, only half-joking, "why did it take so long to do all the other ones?"

As Lucas was busy cranking his effects-making empire back into high gear for those three shots, Darth Vader actor Dave Prowse wrote an angry entry in his diary. He had seen the twist ending at a press screening, he had heard the changed dialogue, and he had to record something that greatly concerned him. "They have done it again," Prowse said. "Would you believe it that Fox and Lucasfilm have just issued the press packs for *the Empire Strikes Back* without one jot of information about myself."

16.

BEING BOBA

When an actor takes on the role of a major character in the *Star Wars* saga, they're signing up for a lifelong relationship with that character whether they know it or not. Some thespians, like David Prowse, feel more ownership over their characters than Lucasfilm might like. Others, like Mark Hamill (who went on to a prolific career as a voice actor for animated TV shows), have kept their alter egos at a healthy distance. Some, like Anthony Daniels and Peter Mayhew, completely embrace their inner droid and wookiee, respectively. "It's not ownership, it's kinship," says Anthony Daniels. "I actually like See-Threepio enough to want to look after him, and that is where insanity starts to come in."

A handful of other actors, Harrison Ford prime among them, really, really don't like to talk about their characters. Some, like Carrie Fisher, go public with their profound ambivalence. In 2013, Fisher wrote a characteristically hilarious and cutting letter to Leia Organa whom she was about to play again: "Here we are enacting our very own Dorian Gray configuration. You: smooth, certain, and straight-backed, forever condemned to the vast, enviable prison of intergalactic adventure. Me: struggling more and more with post-galactic stress disorder, bearing your scars, graying your eternally dark, ridiculous hair."

The main actors who signed onto the franchise in time for *The Empire Strikes Back* seem to be no exception to this rule. Billy Dee Williams has a complicated relationship with Lando Calrissian, the role he played twice on screen. On the one hand, the seventy-six-year old actor laments that his other movie roles were overshadowed by the suave gambler and administrator of Cloud City. On the other hand, he is strongly proprietorial of the character. When I interviewed Williams, he reminded me that he has reprised his role in every medium going: the NPR adaptation of *Empire Strikes Back*, the two *Star Wars: Battlefront* games, *Robot Chicken*, *The Lego Movie*, a Funnyordie.com video. If Lando were to show up in *Episode VII*, Williams is ready, though he hadn't gotten the call from Lucasfilm. Still, says Williams, banging his cane, "No one's going to play Lando but me."

And then there's Jeremy Bulloch, a quiet, friendly, yet reserved English gentleman—quite like me, if I may say. He's also ruggedly handsome, athletic, tall, a former footballer—quite unlike me. Bulloch, whose character also debuted in *Empire*, has had the honor of embodying one of the most cultishly popular personalities in the entire *Star Wars* universe, and managed to do so without letting it go to his head.

When I met Bulloch, he was dressed in a dapper pinstripe jacket that gave him—along with his well-parted white hair, bony features, and upper class accent—the air of landed gentry. All he was lacking was a pair of slippers, a pipe, and a regal-looking English dog. A more yawning gulf between actor and character couldn't be imagined.

"It's a character that sticks with you," said Bulloch, almost apologetically. "I was saying to my grandson the other day," and here he slipped into a husky Clint Eastwood voice, "'Remember, I'm Boba Fett. I'm an icon.' Then I thought, 'Wait, what am I saying?' You do get silly moments."

That's right: Bulloch was the actor under the helmet of the jetpack-wearing bounty hunter Boba Fett in both *Empire* and *Return of the Jedi*. If there's a character that embodies more cool than the relatively smarmy Han Solo, more mystery than the backstory-less Yoda, it's Fett. The Boba Fett Fan Club, founded online in 1996, precedes even the founding of the 501st Legion. The legions of devotees this character commands is out of all proportion to his screen time—less than 150 seconds in the original trilogy. His fame has been gained despite—oh, who am I kidding, because of—the brevity of his dialogue in the classic trilogy. Here are all the lines Fett gets to say in *Empire*: "As you wish. He's no good to me dead. What if he doesn't survive? He's worth a lot to me. Put Captain Solo in the cargo hold." Here's all Fett gets to say in *Return of the Jedi*: "Arrggghhh."

Curiously enough, that's twenty-eight words in all—exactly the number Obi-Wan uses to describe the Force. Lesson learned: in *Star Wars* script world, less is more.

I asked Bulloch if he knew an interesting fact that had been floating around Twitter for a while: that all of his dialogue fits in a single tweet, with space for attribution. He laughed uproariously for a minute. What was even funnier, he said, was that he messed up one of those lines during filming: "Put Captain Cargo in the Solo hold," he said on set. But nobody could hear him in that helmet anyway, and his lines were dubbed over, just like Darth Vader's.

Bulloch was far more self-effacing than Prowse about his role. He'd blundered into it, a bit part that came along because his half brother was associate producer on both *Star Wars* and *Empire*. His entire contribution to *Empire* took him just two days on set. It might interfere with the play he was then appearing in, Bulloch thought at the time, but it also might be fun for his kids to see.

He had no idea of Boba's origins, inside or outside of the *Star Wars* universe. He didn't know that George Lucas and Joe Johnston had sweated the finer points of the costume, first creating an all-white prototype and having an ILM artist run around in it at Skywalker Ranch, then putting the full-color version in a parade in *Star Wars'* hometown, San Anselmo, in August 1978, alongside Darth Vader, without explanation. He didn't know that Fett had been introduced in that disastrous *Holiday Special* or that he, Bulloch, was playing the most hotly anticipated new toy in the forthcoming array of *Empire Strikes Back* figures. You could send away box tops from boxes of Cheerios and get the action figure early. Kenner later determined that the figure's ejectable jetpack was a choking hazard; it is now one of the most valuable and sought-after toy figures in the world. Which makes it quintessential Fett: dangerous and rarely seen.

No, Bulloch knew none of this. What he did know was that the Boba costume happened to fit "as if a Savile Row tailor had made it," he said, right down to the size 10 spiked boots. "It was meant to be."

Even now, Bulloch is blissfully unaware of much of the culture surrounding the character. He didn't like that Boba died so stupidly in *Return of the Jedi*, knocked by a near-blind Solo into the Great Pit of Carkoon—the nesting place of the Sarlacc, the beast that gobbles him up. But as far as he was concerned, that's what happened. He's never read any of the Expanded Universe novels in which Fett escaped the Great Pit and went on to further adventures, including one in which he fights side by side with Han Solo. He'd never heard the MC Chris rap "Boba Fett's Vette," or seen the *Robot Chicken* sketch that shows Boba flirting with the carbonite-covered Solo in the *Slave I* hold ("your hands . . . begging for a piece of Boba") or the parody ad, "The Most Interesting Bounty Hunter in the World" ("he has never 'had a bad feeling about this'"). He certainly hasn't read Fett's entry in *Wookieepedia*, which runs to thirty thousand words, or a fifth of the length of this book.

When Bulloch began hitting the convention circuit, he was rather bemused by the rapturous welcomes he received. He felt he didn't deserve them. What had he done but fluffed his lines in a padded helmet and walked around a set toting a prop gun, channeling Clint Eastwood, all for a little over two minutes? He used to try to tell fans that anyone could have been inside that helmet. But the last time Bulloch sat on a panel in a room full of geeks and said that, a young boy stood up with tears in his eyes: "No, only you could play him, Mr. Bulloch."

Bulloch doesn't deny his Boba-ness any more. He embraced fandom, and fandom embraced back, sending him gifts such as the life-sized statue of the bounty hunter that now stands at the top of his stairs. He wishes it a good night on occasion before retiring to bed. "It's there to remind me," Bulloch says. "Don't mess with Boba."

First comes the jumpsuit: grey, utilitarian, slightly shiny, like a cross between a dystopian citizen's uniform and a low-budget 1950s astronaut. It has Velcro on the shoulders, pockets on the ankles with tools sticking out the tops, deliberately scuffed orange anklets. Then the spike-tipped boots, which are a tight squeeze as the owner of this particular costume is, like Bulloch, a size 10 and I'm an 11. I'm already sweating under the convention hall lights and I'm nowhere near the helmet yet.

Next up is the armored codpiece, which I can't say is something I'd noticed Boba wearing. Like a lot of elements of *Star Wars*, it makes sense only in the context of the ensemble. Then there's the leather belt with a dozen brown pouches and canvas saddlebags on the side, and a cloth tunic with a three-part breastplate, with scuffs in dull silver and yellow dotted on a deep military green. No wonder there's a global organization devoted to this kind of armor, the Mandalorian Mercs; no wonder some fans have what they describe as a "Fett-ish." Me? I feel simultaneously gleeful with recognition and completely ridiculous.

According to *Wookieepedia*, the fictional owner of this costume stands six feet tall. I'm afraid I'm a little short for a bounty hunter. Luckily, Michael Carrasco, the real as opposed to fictional owner of this costume, is my height. Carrasco, a real estate agent also known as TK-0534, is a trooper in the Alpine Garrison of the 501st. In exchange for a donation to the 501st's most vital charity of the moment—helping to buy a new set of knees for Peter Mayhew, the seven-foot-three actor who played Chewbacca, that he might walk from his wheelchair and play Chewie again in *Episode VII*—Carrasco has agreed to loan me his Fett costume, something the 501st doesn't normally do for outsiders. It's a work of art, a Fett costume, with two or three dozen paint colors applied to get just the right battered look, and it represents six months of hard labor from the owner. He affixes the jetpack—"one thing about this costume," he tells me, "you can't dress yourself"—and hands me that iconic helmet, battered and scratched and bullet-marked in all the right places.

It is not nearly as sweaty inside the helmet or as restrictive of vision as I'd imagined. The Mandalorians, the race that Boba Fett belongs to, evidently had the good sense to have visors through which you can see your feet. Troopers walk by and nod approvingly. "Watch out," says one. "Boba gets mobbed."

Carrasco hands me my BlasTec EE3 carbine rifle, shows me how to hold it, and offers to accompany me onto the floor. We get a Stormtrooper escort. I pass through the curtains into the roar of the Comic-Con crowd. It's a little overwhelming, and I walk slowly, carefully, clutching my rifle, looking from side to side to make sure I'm not about to bump into anything. I worry a little about getting in character; then I remember—these movements *are* in character. I'm doing exactly what I need to do—walk slowly and menacingly. *Just be cool.* I can't remember what I'm supposed to say, until I remember that Fett is something of an introvert.

Carrasco advises me to hold one gloved hand up to the visor and pretend to be scanning the crowd on some infrared frequency, looking for bounties. Part of me wants to say, "Don't be so silly." Then I start doing it, and meaning it, and find that it starts drawing interest. Suddenly, I'm mobbed for pictures. Before I know it, I'm interacting with the crowd in the Boba voice. "I suppose so," I'm saying to smiling, wide-eyed children when they ask if Mom or Dad can take a smartphone picture. "They're not on my list."

Then one eight-year-old boy, brown tousled hair, furrowed brow, looking much like me at eight, comes up and asks just the kind of question I would have asked Boba Fett at that age.

"Hey," he says with an air of innocent suspicion, as if he's asking about the mysterious nonarrival of Santa Claus, "how did you escape the Sarlacc?"

The Sarlacc, of course, is supposed to digest its victims over the course of a thousand years. How *did* Boba escape it? I vaguely remember reading his explanation of the feat in a comic book series called *Dark Empire*. I could pull out my smartphone and look it up, somewhere in Boba Fett's thirty-thousand-word *Wookieepedia* entry, but there's a chance that might spoil the illusion. Besides,

I'm not entirely sure that's what the kid is asking. He may only have seen the movies, and therefore his question could mean: How come you are standing here at all, right now, in front of me? *Explain yourself, Mr. Supposed-to-Be-Digested Bounty Hunter.*

Boba's propensity for brevity is what saves me. I lean down to the boy, use my deepest, most hoarse Jeremy-Bulloch-doing-Clint-Eastwood voice, and say the magic words: "I have a jetpack."

The kid's face brightens like an exploding Death Star, and I get one of those fleeting moments of *Star Wars* magic that are too easily forgotten. I have been looking for a moment that explains why the 501st Legion does what it does, and I got more than I bargained for. I feel as if I just made, or saved, a *Star Wars* fan. Albin Carrasco grins and gives me the thumbs-up. And I catch myself thinking: I could do this all the time. "The experience will change you, seeing kids' eyes light up when you walk by," Johnson promised. He was right. An accurate masked bad guy costume really is your passport into the *Star Wars* universe. For a moment I was that guy, there in Cloud City, witnessing Solo's freezing, floating him back to *Slave I* through mythic white corridors, demanding Captain Cargo be put in the Solo hold.

I pose for pictures next to the Alpine Garrison's full-sized Solo in carbonite—every good garrison needs one of those—and part of my brain wonders about Lucas, who has expressed wistfulness at the fact that he is no longer "allowed" to wander the floor at this kind of nerd convention. If he'd been able to do this in 1980—wandered around as Boba Fett and experienced the reaction—maybe he wouldn't have killed off the character so precipitously. Maybe, just maybe, he wouldn't have hastily wrapped up every last thread of the saga in a third movie, then taken the franchise out, and buried its body amid the redwoods.

17.

END OF THE JEDI?

In the summer of 1981, an exhausted George Lucas gave the longest published Q&A of his career. He chose to give it to *Starlog*, the US science fiction fan magazine that had been born in the same year as *Star Wars* and grew up alongside it. "I don't want to upset your readers too much," the filmmaker told *Starlog's* founder, Kerry O'Quinn, "but *Star Wars* is just a movie." It was a surprising admission from someone who had spent the better part of the last decade dreaming up the world depicted in the films, but it also spoke to the deep ambivalence with which Lucas had come to view his most widely admired creation.

Lucas was getting ready to produce one more sequel before putting the franchise that had taken control of his life into deep storage and moving on to new filmic pastures. He was writing what was then called *Revenge of the Jedi*—the name bounced around between "Return" and "Revenge," depending on the draft—and was about to go look for a director in London. At the same time, he had just finished postproduction on *Raiders of the Lost Ark*, the first of the Indiana Jones films he had dreamt up with Steven Spielberg; Spielberg had directed, while Lucas had settled happily into the role of executive producer. He and Marcia had recently adopted a baby girl, Amanda Em, whose arrival changed Lucas's perspective on everything. Marcia was pestering him for more vacations. (Something was the matter with Marcia, he didn't tell O'Quinn—something that even Amanda wasn't fixing.) The script writing process "never gets easier." Why was he working twelve-hour days again?

The world's most famous filmmaker wasn't exactly pulling a Greta Garbo, but he was tired of fame. "It happened despite my best efforts," he told O'Quinn, "and it's something I don't really want." He admitted to doing a few interviews a year only so people wouldn't think he was a hermit. He was cynical about the reason for the attention: "It's all monetary," he said. "They [the press] don't care about the movies. They just care about 'Gee, this guy's really rich!'" As for film critics, they weren't worth a dime either: they "don't realize the effort and pain and struggling that went into something."

Effort, pain, and struggling were all around Lucas: nearly all of his friends had embarked on their own troubled special effects–filled movies. Hal Barwood and Matthew Robbins were mired in *Dragonslayer*, the movie that would make Barwood quit movies altogether and become a games designer; John Milius wrote letters to Lucas venting about wanting to quit from the director's chair of *Conan the Barbarian*. Once again, we see the lie in the notion that Lucas and Spielberg were the only filmmakers interested in big-budget science fiction, fantasy, or adventure films: rather, they were the only ones able to produce them without tearing too much of their own hair out.

Lucas airily dismissed O'Quinn's question about whether *Star Wars* was an "important film" or "had changed lives." He was "baffled" by the reaction to it. Overall, his message to the fans was: stop overanalyzing. For that matter, stop analyzing at all. "The people who are saying 'it's nothing, it's junk food for the mind' are reacting to the people saying 'this is the greatest thing since popcorn!'" Lucas said. "Both of them are wrong. It's just a movie. You watch it and you enjoy it . . . like a sunset. You don't have to worry about the significance. You just say 'hey, that was great.'"

The significance of *The Empire Strikes Back* to Lucasfilm was that it had earned the company a healthy $92 million of revenue, and indeed, that was great. But it had also cost Lucas far more of his money, time, and personal attention than he had anticipated. Relying on the banks, and then having to go back to Fox for a loan, had rankled. Lucas had no intention of going through that again, so he held Fox's feet to the fire. As early as 1979, Lucasfilm had suggested that Fox hand over $25 million for the rights to distribute the third *Star Wars* movie, a loan that would be payable out of the movie's receipts. Fox suggested $10 million, so Lucas walked away from the contract altogether. Negotiations would drag on for two years—but in the end, Lucasfilm would accept the $10 million figure. It was something, but not nearly the sum Lucas had been hoping for—and he would have to make up the difference out of his own pocket.

If there was one constant to Lucas's life between 1980 and 1983, it's that he was trying to rein in everything that had gotten out of his control. His work hours had gotten out of control. *Star Wars* had most definitely gotten out of control, which was why Lucas had resolved to wrap everything up in a third and (for now) final movie. Lucasfilm, split between the Egg Company in LA and its creative arm in Marin, had gotten out of control; CEO Charles Weber had a fundamentally different vision from Lucas's, wanting to grow the company and diversify its holdings into a range of industries, including energy. Weber wanted to project an image of success, so everyone at the Egg Company—down to the secretaries—drove expensive company cars. At Lucasfilm North, Joe Johnston couldn't even get the company to pay for a $13 electric pencil shapener, and sticklers everywhere reminded employees to turn the lights off when they left a room.

Lucas barely tolerated Weber's largesse, and the final straw came when Weber suggested that Skywalker Ranch—now under construction, Kershner having risen to Lucas's challenge that he finance the project with a successful *Star Wars* sequel—was an unnecessary expense. In January 1981, Lucas suddenly fired Weber, laid off half of Lucasfilm South, and told everyone else they had to move north. There were generous severances and six more months of salary while folks found other work, but there was no going back. Skywalker Ranch was to be the company's center of gravity, and it was to be sacrosanct.

Meanwhile, ILM had expanded its business—not just to keep Lucasfilm profitable in the years between *Star Wars* movies, but also to keep the special effects team from defecting. *Star Trek the Motion Picture* (1979) was to mark the beginning of ILM's total dominance of the special effects business, a position cemented by *Raiders of the Lost Ark*, filmed during the summer of 1980.

Compared to *The Empire Strikes Back*, *Raiders* was a walk in the park. Paramount was putting up the money. Spielberg was a natural director, and he had an extremely bright and capable new production assistant, the young Kathleen Kennedy. Lucas called it the best fun he'd ever had on set—and he barely even needed to be there. If *Star Wars* was like laboring in the salt mines, and *Empire Strikes Back* was paying other people to labor in the salt mines (taking the first few shifts in there yourself and then agonizing as your underlings barely mine fast enough to keep the bank from repossessing the salt mine), then *Raiders of the Lost Ark* was like having one of the world's greatest chefs cook up a great meal according to your recipe, and occasionally sprinkling in a little salt. Not only that, but *Raiders* made more money than *Empire*.

Which would you rather do again?

Gary Kurtz claims that Lucas was changed by his experience on *Raiders*—that from this point on, Lucas started talking cynically about popular movies being a roller-coaster ride, in which thrills and spills trumped the need for an adult plot. Kurtz insists that an early version of the third movie had no Ewoks and a much darker ending: one in which the Empire was ultimately defeated but Han died, Luke walked off alone, and Leia was left to govern a Rebellion in tatters. This was thrown out after *Raiders*, he says, partly because of "discussions with the marketing people and the toy company," which didn't want Lucas to kill off one of his main characters, and that's why he and Lucas agreed that Kurtz should quit the franchise. "I just didn't want to do another attack on the Death Star," Kurtz says.

But Kurtz is something of an unreliable witness when it comes to the development of *Return of the Jedi*. He retired from the *Star Wars* production company in December 1979, before *Empire* had even finished production and well before *Jedi* was written. Howard Kazanjian took his place on *Empire* to help Lucas appease the banks; Kurtz's departure was made public in a press release two months before the release of *Empire*. By then Kurtz was deeply involved in preproduction on Muppet maestro Jim Henson's fantasy movie *Dark Crystal*, filmed back in Elstree, across the street from *The Muppet Show*. It was a project Henson had asked Kurtz to work on for years. *Dark Crystal* was replete with enough mythology to scratch Kurtz's comparative religion itch. Kurtz changed his country of residence, and Lucas seemed happy to let him go.

Did the darker version of *Return of the Jedi* exist? Not according to Lucasfilm's recently released and apparently exhaustive accounting of its archives, *The Making of "Return of the Jedi"* (2013). Author J. W. Rinzler dredged up three of Lucas's early undated treatments for the third movie, the first one running to little more than a page. Even that one featured a new Death Star and small bearish creatures that were then called "Ewaks." (There are also "Yussem," which in 1980 concept sketches from Ralph McQuarrie and Joe Johnston are as gangly and tall as the "Ewaks" were short.) When I pointed this out to Kurtz, he backtracked and said he was referring to preliminary discussions about a third movie during the development of *Empire*. "I'm not sure that ever got to a complete story outline," he says. "It was dismissed very early on as being too melancholic."

A popular myth has it that Lucas initially wrote a script for *Jedi* where the role of the Ewoks would be played by Wookiees, and that he got the name for the teddy bear creatures by reversing the "wook" and "iee" syllables. But Ewok, whatever its spelling, was actually inspired by the Miwok Indians, native to Marin. As for using Wookiees, that's a reference to how the first draft of *The Star Wars* ended. "The whole story had really been about a primitive society overcoming the Empire at the end," Lucas said. But the Wookiees had long since become more sophisticated creatures; witness the fact that Chewbacca can fly and fix a starship. He couldn't retroactively make them primitive.

Lucas knew he was going to have the Ewoks help destroy a Death Star the way the Wookiees had in that long-ago draft, so he needed the Empire to build one or two more. He needed to introduce the Emperor, who had been seen in hologram form during *Empire* but who was still waiting in the wings for the final act. The rest of the script was essentially filler, he said, albeit filler that had the task of resolving the Solo situation—the carbonite fix that Lucas had come up with as a hedge against the possibility that Harrison Ford would refuse to sign on for a third movie. "I had to come up with another hundred pages of stuff to make it work," Lucas said, "because Han Solo had become such a popular character and I thought it would be fun to go back to Tatooine." Not that Lucas necessarily had an actor to play Han Solo at the outline stage; Harrison Ford had still not agreed to return for a third film; the fate of carbonite-frozen Han was as uncertain in real life as it seemed at the end of *Empire*. Kazanjian, more of a communicator than Lucas, took the lead and personally talked Ford and his agent into coming back. (Ford would come to regret doing so.) "Okay," Lucas declared on getting the news from Kazanjian, "we'll defrost him."

I n the third and fullest undated summary of *Return of the Jedi*, likely written in 1980, Lucas scribbled a little note next to Leia's name. It was right at the end of the treatment, during the Ewok celebration after the rebels destroy the Death Star and defeat the Empire. It was one word that was to have massive implications for the whole franchise: "Sister!" it said, the exclamation mark suggesting that Lucas had just decided the matter.

Lucas wrote the first full script for *Jedi* alone—there would be no Leigh Brackett–like draft from another writer this time—cloistered in his writing tower in January and February 1981. Luke learns that little bit of sibling knowledge from Yoda, and then it is forgotten until the very end of the script, where it is skipped over quickly and treated very lightly. We see Luke talking to her in the background, while in the foreground, Han shakes his head: "Her brother! I just can't believe it." Whodathunk?

In the history of *Star Wars*, few decisions—including the decision to make Jar Jar Binks a character in the prequels—have been as consistently controversial as the decision to make Leia Luke's sister. This was, after all, a romantic triangle that had lived in the memory of popular culture for six years. Fans had laughed at her kissing Luke "for luck" before their rope swing in *Star Wars* and whooped when she gave Luke a longer, more sensual kiss in the medical bay in *Empire*. Now it turned out that any fan rooting for Luke and Leia to get together had in fact been rooting for incest. The decision may have definitely settled the question of who Leia would end up with, Luke or Han, but it left a bad taste in its wake.

Even if you left that thorny issue aside, the revelation that Luke and Leia shared the same blood may have been one too many familial revelations for the series. Vader being Luke's father had elicited gasps; Leia being Luke's sister got furrowed brows. Even Mark Hamill, veteran of fifty episodes of *General Hospital*, thought it a soap opera step too far. "I said 'oh come on,'" Hamill remembers. "This just seemed a really lame attempt to top the Vader thing." He joked that Boba Fett should remove his helmet and give Luke one more surprise: "oh my God, it's mom!"

How long had Lucas been considering the sister revelation? In the Lucasfilm tome *The Making of "Star Wars"* (2008), Rinzler made a halfhearted stab at suggesting that its origins come from the moment Lucas decided to turn Luke Starkiller into a girl, and back again, before quickly digressing on to the topic of how often twins crop up in mythology. But that explanation ignores what Lucas told Alan Dean Foster in 1975, about the second book he wanted Foster to write: "In the next book, I want Luke to kiss the princess." Indeed he did, and snuggled with her, and the pair flirted outrageously. Foster is adamant that if Lucas had the slightest inkling of who Leia would turn out to be, he had plenty of chances before *Splinter of the Mind's Eye* was released. "It adds an odd frisson to the book," Foster says. "He would have caught that immediately if he was sure they were going to be brother and sister."

A more likely scenario is that Lucas was trying to tie up loose ends he had inadvertently created at the end of *The Empire Strikes Back*. When Luke leaves his Jedi training too early to help his friends in Cloud City, and the ghost of Obi-Wan laments that he was "our last hope," Yoda says ominously: "No, there is another." Lucas has said he meant this as a throwaway line that would enhance the audience's perception of Luke's jeopardy: the story doesn't need him! Separately, he had mentioned to Brackett the possibility of Luke's twin sister being hidden away somewhere on the "other side of the universe," being trained as a Jedi. Blogger Michael Kaminski suggested this meant the twin sister would have been the subject of the sequel trilogy, *Episodes VII, VIII,* and *IX*, as Lucas then conceived them—though Lucas has since insisted that he had never planned the story for those three movies.

Yoda's reference to the "other" aroused a lot of interest among fans in 1980, with many of them suggesting—to Mark Hamill and others—that the princess was the "other." After all, watch *Empire Strikes Back* multiple times, and the identity of the "other" is not the only mystery you're left with. Here's another:

How was Leia, aboard the *Millennium Falcon* as it fled Cloud City, able to hear Luke, who was clinging to an antenna far away, calling her for help? The catch-all answer was "the Force," of course, but in that case the scene suggested Leia was as Force-sensitive as Luke—and perhaps that they had more in common than viewers knew.

In other words, by making Leia the secret Jedi twin sister of Luke, Lucas was actually giving the fans what they most expected, resolving all remaining issues, and taking the fastest route to closure. Having the hero and heroine discover they were siblings all along was a soap opera twist, yes, but it was also the slightly twisted kind of resolution you might expect from a tale of the brothers Grimm. "People have perceived [*Star Wars*] sort of different from the way it is," Lucas told O'Quinn, "and in this one, it becomes obvious what it was all along—which, essentially, is a fairy tale."

With a script in hand, Lucas was ready to pick another director. Kershner had declined the opportunity to stay with the franchise for another two years. "I didn't want to be a Lucas employee," he said in 2004. "And I'd read the script of *Jedi*, and I didn't believe it." Lucas's first choice for Kershner's replacement, after the experience of *Raiders*, would have been Spielberg. Lucas had quit the Directors Guild of America over a spat about whether Kershner's director credit should have been placed at the beginning of the movie, and Spielberg remained a member, but the lawyers didn't deem this a problem. The problem was that Spielberg was deeply entrenched in his latest science fiction project, a movie about a friendly alien based on an imaginary childhood friend of Spielberg's.

Kazanjian drew up a shortlist of a hundred possible directors that was quickly whittled down to twenty, then twelve. At the top of the list was David Lynch, the young auteur behind *Eraserhead* and *Elephant Man*, and a particular favorite of Lucas's. Lynch was brought up to Marin and extensively wooed. But as soon as he was shown around the art department and saw the first pictures of the Ewoks, Lynch got a headache that developed into a full-blown migraine. This, evidently, he saw as a bad omen. Three days after Lucas made him the offer, Lynch declined. It later emerged that he had received what seemed like a much better offer: the chance to direct the big-screen, big-budget version of *Dune*, the rights to which had just been renegotiated by Dino De Laurentiis. Once again, De Laurentiis had beaten Lucas to something he wanted. And once again, it would not turn out as well as planned: Lynch would spend $40 million on a long and troubled shoot. *Dune* would earn only $30 million of it back, becoming the most infamous turkey in science fiction movie history—to the gleeful delight of would-be *Dune* director Alejandro Jodorowsky.

Shorn of proven top-tier directors, Lucas briefly considered coming out of directorial retirement. "I wanted to get it out of my system and finish the damn thing off," he explained to *People* magazine in 1983, "but I was stopped by the amount of work." Instead, he picked a relative unknown, the Cardiff-born director Richard Marquand, best known for a TV movie about the Beatles as well as a Ken Follett spy drama with Donald Sutherland, *Eye of the Needle*. Marquand came well equipped with metaphors: *Star Wars* was "the most exciting and grandiose film of all time," he said, "the myth of the 70's and the 80's, just as the Beatles were the myth of the 60's and early 70's." He was so impulsively eager to do it that, during the selection stage, he called up to request a second interview with Lucas, at which he proceeded to rhapsodize about how right he was for the film. He would, as Kazanjian said, prove "flexible." Lucas would be executive producer, but as he would later point out, this was more like the executive producer on a TV show—someone who came up with the scripts and the overall direction of the series, while the director handled the tricky business of dealing with actors.

Marquand readily agreed and would spend the next two years professing how overawed he was with the responsibility in front of him. He would variously compare directing *Jedi* to directing *King Lear* "with Shakespeare in the next room" and to conducting the Ninth Symphony with Beethoven listening in. That may have been a little hyperbolic, but Lucas would indeed spend nearly all of the shoot on the set. Nominally he was a second-unit director, but effectively he acted as codirector—very much the senior partner. You can see it in clips from the set: Marquand gives orders, but the crew is listening to Lucas. When the orders were in conflict, there was no question who was in charge. This time, there would be no sneaking looks through the camera like a kid stealing a cookie.

With a director selected, Lucas wrote a rushed second draft, and then came one of the most enjoyable parts of the production: sitting around a table at his growing Parkway mansion in San Anselmo with Kazanjian, Marquand, and Lawrence Kasdan, who had been reluctantly brought back into the *Star Wars* fold. Kasdan agreed to write a draft in exchange for the promise of Lucas's help on his first directorial feature, *Body Heat*. The four of them talked about the story of *Revenge of the Jedi*, as it was at that point, for five days, ten hours a day, getting lost in the details and the possibilities. There were no sacred cows in this discussion. Marquand may have been in awe of the creator, but Kasdan set out to provoke him into interesting responses and a darker alternative to what he called a "wimpy ending":

> *KASDAN: I think you should kill Luke and have Leia take over.*
> *LUCAS: You don't want to kill Luke.*
> *KASDAN: Okay, then kill Yoda.*
> *LUCAS: I don't want to kill Yoda. You don't have to kill people. You're a product of the 1980s. You don't go around killing people. It's not nice. . . . I think you alienate the audience.*
> *KASDAN: I'm saying that the movie has more emotional weight if someone you love is lost along the way; the journey has more impact.*
> *LUCAS: I don't like that and I don't believe that. . . . I have always hated that in movies, when you go along and one of the main characters gets killed. This is a fairy tale. You want everybody to live happily ever after and nothing bad happens to anybody. . . . The whole emotion I am trying to get at the end of the film is for you to be real uplifted, emotionally and spiritually, and feel absolutely good about life.*

Eventually, Lucas conceded the point: somebody would have to fall along the way. For a while, it was to be Lando Calrissian, nobly killed in the destruction of the second Death Star, and the quartet agonized over how they were going to tell Billy Dee Williams. Eventually, however, Lucas decided it made sense to show us Yoda dying of old age near the start, ending his life by confirming to Luke that Vader was his father and revealing that Leia was his sister, after which he would disappear like Kenobi.

Much of what we now know as *Return of the Jedi* was hashed out around that table in those fifty hours. In his second draft, Lucas had actually given us two Death Stars, both under construction over the city-planet that governed the galaxy, then called Had Abbadon. Kasdan declared that two Death Stars gave the rebels "too many targets." Marquand contributed the idea that the remaining Death Star should appear to be under construction, but should in fact be fully operational. Had Abbadon was reluctantly abandoned: it would be a prohibitively expensive thing to film. In Lucas's early scripts, Vader brings Luke to the Emperor in the Emperor's palace on the planet, a place of stone walkways over bubbling lava. By the time the conference was over, the Emperor had been transferred to the one remaining Death Star.

Then there was the problem of Darth Vader. In Lucas's early drafts Vader has an unusual story arc: not redemption, but irrelevance. The Grand Moff

Jerrjerrod, the Emperor's new favorite, makes his superiority to Vader clear and the Emperor's displeasure over Vader's failure to turn Skywalker to the Dark Side even clearer. Vader's loyalty wavers until the Emperor Force-chokes him, silencing that familiar iron lung breathing and seemingly pacifying his apprentice. There is a showdown involving Luke and the Force ghosts of Obi-Wan and Yoda on one side and Vader and the Emperor on the other, which is brought to a conclusion when Vader suddenly throws the ruler of the galaxy into the lava, possibly under the influence of Yoda.

In the second draft, Lucas—under the influence of his brains trust—gave Vader a death scene on the Death Star in which Luke removes his mask. In that moment, Vader is redeemed; we see a sad old man, relying on bionics to keep him alive. "The whole machine thing becomes a partial metaphor for the Dark Side of the Force," Lucas realized, "which is: machines have no feelings." For all his relative lack of influence, Marquand was able to interject with one more good idea—that Anakin Skywalker, now redeemed, should say a few words with the mask off before he dies.

The redemption of Darth Vader would rub some fans the wrong way: the ultimate screen villain of the twentieth century turns out to be a Wizard of Oz figure, and that somehow makes everything that came before it acceptable. Some *Star Wars* luminaries wondered what message that sent. "It's like Hitler's on his deathbed and he repents and everything's okay," said Alan Dean Foster. "'I've murdered eight million people, but I'm sorry.' I just couldn't go with that." Kazanjian, a devout Christian, would have that problem as well, until Lucas pointed out that his religion emphasized forgiveness. Thereafter, Kazanjian was a convert and came up with the suggestion that Anakin Skywalker's ghost should make an appearance at the end alongside Obi-Wan and Yoda.

The only character to fare poorly out of the redrafting process was Leia. In Lucas's early scripts, she got her first command on the as-yet-unnamed "Green Moon" where the Ewoks live. By the time Kasdan wrote his draft, she was just one member of Han's mission to the moon. Carrie Fisher had asked Lucas for some sort of edge to the character, perhaps a drinking problem; something, at least, to suggest the suffering the princess had been through, the genocide of her entire planet. She got a slave bikini.

The filming of *Return of the Jedi* proceeded in an atmosphere of even greater secrecy than *Empire Strikes Back*. Coproducer Jim Bloom came up with the brilliant idea to book his location shoots under a fake movie title and tagline,

Blue Harvest: Horror Beyond Imagination. The purpose was less to distract fans than to get reasonable feees out of vendors, who were by now overcharging for anything that said "Star Wars" on it in the same way that businesses increase their rates for anything to do with a wedding.

The main trio of actors would be given code names on set—Martin, Caroline, Harry—and kept in the dark about the movie's key twists. Harrison Ford repeatedly protested that Han should be killed off—at least until he found out that Luke and Leia were siblings, and that he would end up with Leia. Dave Prowse was almost completely sidelined, wrongly fingered as the source of a UK newspaper story that revealed Darth Vader was to die. His fencing coach and stunt double, Bob Anderson, appeared in many of the shots. Prowse was utterly unaware that Sebastian Shaw, an actor friend of Alec Guinness's, was being used as the face of Vader in his death scene, a fact that still upsets the former bodybuilder today.

The Elstree set wasn't entirely closed. Lucas had accepted one important interloper: a *Los Angeles Times* journalist named Dale Pollock. After he'd written up a few early stories on the movie, Pollock had been contacted by Crown Publishers: they wanted a biography of Lucas, tied to the release of *Return of the Jedi*, but they didn't want the book to be controlled by Lucasfilm. Pollock met the company halfway: a legal agreement was drafted that allowed Lucas to review the manuscript and make any changes he felt were factually inaccurate. In exchange for that concession, Pollock would have more access to the Creator than even *Starlog* got. It seemed too good to be true—and indeed, it was.

The bulk of Pollock's work for the book, interviews that lasted a total of eighty hours, would come once Lucas was back in the United States and the film was in postproduction. But in Elstree, Pollock could already see in Lucas the symptoms of a control freak. Marquand was clearly intimidated by Lucas; there was no question who was in charge on the set. Marquand was out of his depth and trying to assert himself when Lucas wasn't around. The film's nominal director didn't ask for help from his crew. He compounded his problems, by all accounts, by kowtowing to the big movie star, Harrison Ford, and being less friendly to the rest of the cast, a sin for which Ford did not forgive him.

Lucas was in charge and getting every shot he wanted, but he wasn't having fun. By day 72 of the shoot he was utterly exhausted. "I smile a lot, because if I don't everyone gets depressed," he complained to a *New York Times* reporter on set. "But I'd rather be home in bed watching television. No matter how much I think everyone knows *Star Wars* now, they don't. I've given Richard the answers to a million questions over the last year, filled everybody in on everything I can think of, and yet when we get here the crew comes up with a thousand questions a day—I'm not exaggerating—that only I can answer. 'Can these creatures do this or can't they? What was the culture behind this artifact?' I'm the only one who knows where we're going and where we've been." So much for the Bond-esque franchise of multiple directors. Lucas now claimed that his original plan had been to "be a real mercenary" and turn the entire franchise over to Fox, "take a big percentage of the gross," and watch the movies when they were done. That had always been Lucas's biggest regret: he was the only nerd in America who couldn't just go stand in line for the new *Star Wars* movie. He shrugged. "I started it, now I have to finish it. The next trilogy will be all someone else's vision."

The shoot wrapped in eighty-eight days, which was sixty-six days less than it took to shoot *Empire Strikes Back*. Marquand had indeed proved flexible—at least on the set. Afterwards, tasked with overseeing the first edit of his footage, the British director had something of a breakdown. He said he either was unable to sleep or would wake up screaming. He would often be found walking the streets of San Anselmo at three a.m., the latest victim of *Star Wars* mania. Months later, he presented his final cut at Lucas's home screening room and declared the movie would never get any better than that. Lucas sighed, thanked Marquand for his work, and took the movie off him. Marquand died four years later of a stroke at the age of forty-seven. If there ever were such a thing as the curse of *Star Wars*, he could well have been one of its earliest victims.

Something was clearly off during the final editing and special effects stage. It wasn't just the sense of finality, the end of a trilogy. ILM employees sensed that Marcia Lucas was more tense than usual, and they were having trouble getting feedback from George. Dale Pollock had done weeks' worth of interviews with George, but he was unable to get Marcia to commit to a sit-down interview, and he couldn't figure out why. When Howard Kazanjian asked George if Marcia would be involved in the editing process, he got a terse reply: "You'll have to ask her."

What not even their closest friends knew was that Marcia had asked George for a divorce after he returned from London. The marriage had broken up over "irreconcilable differences."

The most immediate irreconcilable difference was named Thomas Rodrigues, a stained-glass artist employed at Skywalker Glass Studio. Marcia had hired him back in 1980 to design and manage the production of the beautiful glass dome that still sits over the library in Skywalker Ranch. Rodrigues was nine years her junior; he was recently divorced himself and managing a team of six glassmakers. Marcia fell in love with him at some point over the next two years. She says she remained faithful to George; Lucas, however, refused any form of marital therapy. He settled glumly into the role of cuckolded martyr and would remain as such on the few occasions he ever spoke of it again.

The Lucases successfully kept their domestic problems a secret until after the movie was released. Even the journalist assigned to watch the Lucases' lives didn't realize what had happened. "As open as I thought he was being with me, he was clearly keeping one whole part of his life off limits," Pollock says.

George threw himself into the edit, once again dragging out those reels of World War II footage to substitute for the special effects shots of the Rebel attack on the Death Star. He cut the movie so that each scene was faster than in its two predecessors: this was the MTV generation he was dealing with now, after all, and he had to keep pace. As much as he wanted the movie to be done, as much as he was reeling from Marcia's revelation, his perfectionist side was stronger. The number of special effects shots he wanted in the movie had nearly doubled. "You can't be sick," he would say later of the responsibility that weighed on him during this final push. "You can't have normal emotions. . . . You've got a lot of people depending on you."

Lucas was terse, and he snapped one day when editor Duwayne Dunham pointed out that there wasn't a scene that dealt conclusively with what happened to Vader. He was last seen dying on the Death Star, but that left open the notion that he might come back. This was a problem, as Lucas wanted to finally, utterly, and conclusively kill off Darth Vader. So a pickup scene was shot one night at Skywalker Ranch, weighty with even more meaning than the participants knew about: Luke burns the body of Vader in a funeral pyre.

Still, Lucas wasn't satisfied. On November 22, 1982—soon known as "Black Friday" around ILM—the Creator tossed out more than a hundred special effects shots, effectively deleting 250 model spacecraft from the movie altogether. Before they got good and drunk, the ILM model makers screamed at Lucas. Years later, Lucas the father would compare the frustration of his artists to the crying of babies, and explain the importance of interpreting the emotion behind the noise: "You can actually tell why they're crying. . . . You can tell whether it's a real scream or just kind of whiny." He pushed hard for shots from his Computer Division, which was another brilliantly risky business bet, an expensive skunkworks project he'd set up after *Empire*. "It was a case of 'okay, that fire is out, I guess I'll start another one,'" Lucas later laughed. Computer graphics,

Lucas knew, was the future—but all the team could contribute for *Jedi* was one special effect, the Death Star as seen from the Rebel briefing room. It was, in other words, the exact same shot that had been rendered on a computer for *Star Wars* in 1976. This time, at least, the computerized Death Star appeared to be in 3D, hovering in thin air like a hologram, rather than appearing in blocky pixels on a large screen.

Lucas procrastinated until the very end on the title of the movie. Kazanjian still felt that "Return" was too weak a word—it made him think of *Return of the Pink Panther.* A marketing report based on 324 telephone interviews, in which participants were asked to choose between "Revenge of the Hero" and "Return of the Hero" confirmed that "Revenge" was felt to be more exciting, but that it didn't match the image of a hero, particularly among the under-thirties.

The film's title was changed, after much debate, on December 17, 1982—less than six months before the release date. This didn't just mean that posters had to be remade and the trailer had to be recut. Practically every license was affected. Kenner had already produced somewhere around $250,000 worth of action figure packaging bearing the title *Revenge of the Jedi;* all of it had to be destroyed. The company had already produced Ewok toys against its better judgment, purely on Lucas's insistence. He didn't really care if they succeeded or not—he just wanted his daughter Amanda, now firmly at the center of his domestic life, to have one.

On April 17, 1983, with the release of *Return of the Jedi* a month away, Lucas marked an important anniversary: it was ten years to the day since he had sat down to write his first *Star Wars* treatment, the one that had cribbed a few notes from *Hidden Fortress.* And here he was, still rehashing it, still tinkering—three new special effects shots were being worked on even as the movie got its first secret audience preview at the Northpoint Theatre in San Francisco. Here the world was more obsessed with the saga than ever, awash in *Return of the Jedi*–themed Pepperidge Farm cookies, AT&T Darth Vader phones, and Coca-Cola *Star Wars* collectible glasses. Kids donned their *Return of the Jedi* roller skates to visit the Jedi Adventure Center at their local mall.

Star Wars, it seemed, was everywhere. And in just a few years, it would be nowhere at all.

18.

BETWEEN THE WARS

The year 1983 should have been one of triumphal, Ewok-like celebration for George Lucas. At last, he thought, he was finally free of the story that had dogged him for ten years. He had just turned thirty-nine, and though his friend Steven Spielberg had taken back the crown of biggest blockbuster of all time with *ET: The Extra Terrestrial* the previous year, Lucas had made the best-selling movie *trilogy* of all time. *Return of the Jedi* was a smash hit. Opening in just over a thousand theaters, it made $6 million in its opening day—a new record—and $45 million in its opening week. There were even reports that some hard-core fans had camped out all night to be the first in line, which was then unheard of. By the end of the year, the movie had raked in more than $250 million.

Reviewers professed to like *Jedi* somewhat less than *Empire*, now recognized as a classic of the genre, but moviegoers were voting the other way. Meanwhile, the official *Star Wars* fan club hit its first peak in 1983 with 184,000 members. The novelization of the movie was the best-selling book in America. With the profits from all of this, Lucas could finally complete Skywalker Ranch, the design of which he had been restlessly tinkering with for years (most recently adding a giant water feature, Lake Ewok). It should have been heaven.

Instead, it was arguably the worst year of his life.

The first blow, even before news of Lucas's divorce became official, was the arrival of the manuscript of *Skywalking*, the biography written by Dale Pollock.

The experience apparently scarred the intensely private Lucas for life. Pollock remembers being summoned to Lucas's home in San Anselmo shortly after the filmmaker read the manuscript. Inside, spread out on a large workbench, "was just about every page of the manuscript with a red paperclip on it," Pollock says. "It was clear we were not going to agree on what was inaccurate. He would say things like 'It says here I'm frugal. I'm not, I'm very generous. I want that changed. It's inaccurate.'"

Of course, one can be frugal in business and generous with friends and charities at the same time. Indeed, this is the picture that emerges in the book; we learn of Lucas carefully accounting for every dollar spent at his company, while sharing his *Star Wars* points when he didn't need to, and keeping his charitable giving under wraps for fear of being labeled an easy mark, à la Scrooge McDuck.

Pollock pushed back as best he could. "I told him, 'I'm happy to put in something that says you disagree with this,'" he remembers. "'But I'm not taking out what I wrote. Matters of opinion are not subjects of accuracy.' What he said to me at the end of our unfruitful conversation was 'I'll never do this again; no one will ever do this to me again; I will control everything that's written about me.' He's stayed pretty true to that."

To this day, Lucasfilm contends that some of the eighty hours of interviews Lucas gave to Pollock were off the record; Pollock, now a film school professor, says he would have turned his tape recorder off if he'd heard Lucas utter the words "off the record." There were rumblings of lawsuits, from both Lucas and Coppola, whom Lucas had attacked in his interviews, alleging that Coppola had stolen *Apocalypse Now* and never really stood up for *American Graffiti*.

But Pollock had actually held back on some of the worst things Lucas had said about Coppola. (They remain unpublished; Pollock has refused entreaties from publishers to print the Lucas tapes in their entirety.) He sent both men copies of tapes that proved his point. The threats of lawsuits vanished. Lucas even signed a copy of *Skywalking* for the author, an inscription that may well go down in history as the most lukewarm dedication from a subject to his biographer. It reads:

> To Dale. You have captured an imprint of the first thirty nine years of my life. I am now able to close the book on the past (your book) and look forward to the future. It has been an interesting and sometimes unnerving experience. I'm glad we were able to do it together.
>
> May the force be with you.

It was only after the book was published, Pollock says, that Lucas's friends told him of the filmmaker's true intent in participating: to help him reconcile with Marcia. "He hoped my recreation of their meeting and their early time together would help make the case why they should stay together," Pollock says. Even unbidden, he did the best he could. When he finally got hold of Marcia, she complained to him that George "never wanted to go anywhere, hang out with anyone—he was very insular and it just drove her crazy." This is rendered in the book as "he and Marcia avoid parties, restaurants and travel." He writes that the "resiliency of their relationship is impressive," and quotes Lucas's long-time assistant, Jane Bay: "They just keep getting stronger as a couple." Marcia is quoted talking about the "tender and cuddly" side of her apparently cold husband, the side that liked to imitate commercials in silly voices and blushed at her off-color jokes. We see Marcia encouraging George to play tennis and go skiing. The fact that Marcia had to make her husband endless rounds of tuna sandwiches with the crusts cut off, the way his mother used to make, goes unmentioned.

When it came to editing *Star Wars*, writes Pollock, "Marcia is indispensable to Lucas because she compensates for his deficiencies. Where George is not unduly concerned with character and lacks faith in the audience's patience, Marcia figures out how a movie can be made warmer, how the characters can be given depth and resonance." Lucas's less laudatory way of putting this was to say that Marcia was great at the "dying and crying" scenes; she edited the Yoda death scene in *Return of the Jedi*, one of the slowest and most tender moments of the series. According to Marcia, the conclusion of *Return of the Jedi* marked the only time George paid her a compliment on her work—telling her she was a "pretty good editor." How that rankled.

Skywalking came too late to have any effect on the Lucases' marriage. George and Marcia Lucas officially separated on June 30, 1983. (It would be almost thirty years to the day before Lucas married again.) At the beginning of that month, they had held a tearful meeting to tell the staff at Lucasfilm; the press announcement was made about two weeks after that, on June 13. The Lucas marriage was officially dissolved on December 10, 1984.

The divorce papers in the public record are minimal, both parties having signed a settlement that remains sealed to this day. All we know is that they would share custody of Amanda and that Marcia had agreed to the deal George offered, waiving her rights to receive further spousal benefits under California law. A Marin County judge agreed to keep the settlement under wraps because of the harm that media attention could inflict on the Lucases' daughter.

We might agree with the judge and draw a veil over the whole sad scene. But as much as the company would prefer to forget it, the fact remains that Marcia's departure was one of the most costly financial disasters in Lucasfilm history. The company had, in effect, just lost its cofounder. "I think people sometimes forget that Marcia Lucas owns half of this company," Lucasfilm's second CEO, Bob Greber, pointedly told Pollock before the divorce. He added that her unofficial title was "Lucasfilm's cheerleader." Her departure cast a pall over everything. Greber himself would leave in 1985, after trying and failing to persuade Lucas to make more *Star Wars* films.

Losing his wife cost George Lucas more than the budget of another *Star Wars* film, with no return on investment. He was determined to be done with Marcia, and he was determined not to part with Skywalker Ranch. That made for an expensive settlement. Press reports at the time of the divorce pegged Marcia's payout at between $35 million and $50 million. Her prenuptial agreement with Rodrigues, signed five years later, states that she still has a forthcoming note from Lucasfilm worth around $25 million, which is to remain solely her property. By the time Marcia and Rodrigues separated in the summer of 1993, her ex estimated Marcia's net worth at $60 million. Her income—from real estate and from points in *Star Wars*—was $7 million a year.

None of that, of course, guaranteed Marcia happiness or made up for her lack of a career later on. Nor did the fact that she and Rodrigues had a child, Amy, in 1985, or their wedding on Maui in 1988. According to court documents, they had five cars, including three Mercedes and a Jaguar. On top of their $1.6 million home in Marin, they owned a million-dollar ski home in Utah and a million-dollar beach condo in Maui. They would fly first class with Amy and her nanny on the Concorde to Paris, and stay at a $2,500-a-night suite in the Ritz. But Marcia found herself shunned by many former friends of the Lucases and was unable or unwilling to return to a film-editing career.

Marcia and Tom were divorced in 1995 after two years of separation. She gave Rodrigues most of the cost of a substantial house in San Anselmo, and a generous amount to make sure Amy had equal access to anything she could get at Marcia's home. But Rodrigues complained that he'd had to put his career on hold while Marcia wanted him available to "play and travel." Thus began a long and contentious legal wrangle over the size of their settlement. Ultimately, the judge concurred with Marcia that Tom's cut was more than generous, and he retreated to a winery he'd bought north of Marin.

George and Marcia would stay in touch only as much as necessary for Amanda. Their subsequent activities would often make it seem as if they were in competition. Marcia funded a postproduction center at USC that bore her name; Lucas donated his $175 million building to their alma mater. Marcia bought a house in Pacific Heights; Lucas moved his company to the nearby Presidio. Marcia never quite understood what George was doing with his company. In 1999, she told author Peter Biskind that the Lucasfilm empire was "an inverted triangle sitting on a pea, which was the *Star Wars* trilogy. But he wasn't going to make more *Star Wars*, and the pea was going to dry up and crumble, and then he was going to be left with a huge facility and enormous overhead. Why did he want to do that if he wasn't going to make movies? I still don't get it."

Lucas could have recouped his losses from the divorce with one more *Star Wars* movie. But he was adamant: the trilogy was over. He was tired, worn out by the divorce and the unbearable stress of trying to bring his fantastical visions to life with limited budgets and inadequate technology. He would not make more big-budget explorations of his universe until the technology was ready to make it look exactly the way he saw it in his head, no rubber monsters required.

This didn't mean that *Star Wars* was a shriveled-up pea, as Marcia put it. Not quite. There were a handful of deals in the works after *Return of the Jedi*. There were to be two ABC TV movies starring the Ewoks. The first, *Caravan of Courage: The Ewok Adventure*, arrived in 1984. It was aimed at children, far more so than anything in the *Star Wars* universe thus far. But this was George Lucas: anything made for children had to be high quality, or as close as possible on a $2 million budget.

After the disaster of the *Star Wars Holiday Special*, Lucas had learned his lesson. He kept a close eye on the production of *Caravan of Courage* and came up with the story behind it: a family crash-lands on the moon of Endor, the parents and children are separated, and the Ewoks help reunite them. It was directed by the independent filmmaker who had lured Lucas to Marin in the first place, John Korty. Still, *Caravan of Courage* suffered from one major problem of the *Holiday Special*—a large portion was furry creatures burbling in a language all their own—so actor Burl Ives was recruited to do a folksy voice-over.

The sequel came in 1985, and it was a much darker affair, called *Battle for Endor*. The parents, who have been reunited with their children at the end of the previous movie, are murdered—along with a whole forest full of Ewoks—by off-world marauders and an evil sorceress. As with *Indiana Jones and the Temple of Doom*, a darker movie than *Raiders* and one that Lucas says he intended as a direct metaphor for how he was feeling at the time, *Battle for Endor* reflects the darkness of Lucas's postdivorce world—a darkness that seemed to be annihilating the innocence of the *Star Wars* universe.

"The divorce kind of destroyed me," Lucas admitted years later. He began a rebound relationship with singer Linda Ronstadt, another feisty brunette; they broke up when Ronstadt declared she had no interest in getting married or having children. He experimented with new looks, switched from glasses to contacts, and even tried shaving his beard off. It was, as he said, a classic divorce situation. He called up and reconciled with his old friend and mentor, Coppola. Perhaps most importantly, he was to meet his third and final mentor in the flesh—and not a moment too soon.

Lucas had put Joseph Campbell's *The Hero with a Thousand Faces* to good use between the third and fourth drafts of *Star Wars*. But it seemed at that point a rather utilitarian work and failed to light a spark in the young Lucas. It was not until some indeterminate point after the first movie, he said, that a friend gave him a series of Campbell lectures on tape. Lucas felt Campbell was much more powerful as a speaker than a writer; he described the experience of listening to the lecture as "immediately electric" and resolved to meet Campbell next time he was in town.

Lucas had to wait until May 1983 before finally meeting the famed mythologist, who was almost forty years his senior. Barbara McClintock, a Nobel Prize–winning scientist who was then in her eighties, was holding a symposium at the Palace of Fine Arts in San Francisco: The Inner Reaches of Outer Space. *Dune* author Frank Herbert was in attendance, as was *Apollo 9* astronaut Rusty Schweikart. But when Lucas called McClintock to ask for an introduction, it was not to any of these famed personalities. Rather, it was to Campbell, whose talk was the centerpiece of the symposium. Lucas the space fantasist and mythology nerd must have sat in the audience enraptured as Campbell described his concept of galactic space in soaring rhetoric: "a universe of unimaginable magnitude and inconceivable violence: billions of roaring thermonuclear furnaces scattering from each other, many of them actually blowing themselves to pieces." The stars are at war.

McClintock's introduction didn't go so well. Campbell and Lucas were seated next to each other, not speaking. Campbell had enjoyed silent movies back in the 1920s; he didn't really go for talkies and certainly didn't care for modern fare. He had a tendency to hold court, and Lucas was not the greatest at breaking the ice. So McClintock called over magician David Abrams, who did a trick that involved putting George's hand on Joe's. "That was it," McClintock recalled. Lucas and Campbell started talking about the impact of a *Hero with a Thousand Faces* on Lucas's movies, none of which Campbell had yet seen. They met next for dinner in Hawaii, where Campbell lived. A friendship began to bloom, Lucas later told Campbell's official biographers.

Campbell and his wife, Jean, came to stay with Lucas in his ever-widening San Anselmo estate for a week, and Lucas gently suggested showing him the *Star Wars* trilogy at Skywalker Ranch: "Would you be interested at all in seeing it? I can show you one, or all three of them." Campbell opted for all three. Lucas suggested stretching them out over three days; Campbell insisted on doing the trilogy in a day. It marked the first time Lucasfilm had screened all three as a movie marathon. They took breaks for meals between each screening. When the credits rolled a third time, the eighty-year-old Campbell sat in the dark and declared: "You know, I thought real art stopped with Picasso, Joyce and Mann. Now I know it hasn't." That, McClintock noted, made Lucas's day.

"I was really thrilled," Campbell said of the *Star Wars* series in a later interview. "The man understands the metaphor. I saw things that had been in my books but rendered in terms of the modern problem, which is man and machine. Is the machine going to be the servant of human life? Or is it going to be master and dictate? That's what I think George Lucas brought forward. I admire what he's done immensely. That young man opened a vista and knew how to follow it and it was totally fresh."

Lucas returned Campbell's compliment in February 1985 at the National Arts Club, where Campbell was being presented with the Medal of Literature. In a potted revisionist history of his writing of *Star Wars*, Lucas gave a speech in which he said that prior to reading Campbell, he had been reading "Freudians and Donald Duck and Uncle Scrooge, and all the other mythical heroes of our time." When he finally came across *The Hero with a Thousand Faces*, he said, it helped him carve a five-hundred-page script down to two hundred pages. "If I had not run across him," Lucas said, "I might still be writing *Star Wars* today." Of course, as we know, the script emerged more organically, with a far greater range of mythic influences, such as *The Golden Bough*. Campbell's book arrived very late in the day, and the majority of the first movie's script was in place by the time Lucas read *Hero*. But Lucas was not about to let that fact get in the way of his burgeoning relationship with Campbell, one that reflected well on the saga in retrospect. "He is a really wonderful man and he has become my Yoda," Lucas concluded.

The following year, PBS broadcaster Bill Moyers, another mutual friend of Lucas and Campbell, told Lucas he was interested in filming multiple interviews with Campbell. "Bring him out to the Ranch," Lucas insisted. He would cover out-of-pocket expenses for the show. "Just point the camera at him and turn it on. Let's not make a big deal of this, let's just get him talking." The result, some forty hours of interviews edited into a five-episode special called *The Power of Myth*, hit screens shortly after Campbell passed away at the age of eighty-three; it became one of the most-watched and best-loved shows in PBS history. The franchise that Campbell had inadvertently helped to shape, meanwhile, was not faring nearly as well.

By 1985, the year George Lucas lionized Joseph Campbell at the National Arts Club, *Star Wars* was far from its mythical heights. The franchise seemed to be petering out as a brand for anyone but the youngest children, and even they were losing interest. There was a *Droids* cartoon, starring Artoo and Threepio, which lasted for one season, and an *Ewoks* cartoon, which lasted for two. Initially these cartoons were shown as a *Star Wars* adventure hour on ABC Saturday mornings, and a new line of Kenner figures and a *Star Wars* comic book were created to go with them. Viewership figures were great—in a few European and Latin American countries, that is.

Not for the last time, Lucas turned to Disney to help revive the brand. The first Lucas-Disney collaboration was the Michael Jackson vehicle, *Captain EO*, executive produced by Lucas and directed by Coppola. That blossomed into a Star Tours theme park ride, which opened in Disneyland in January 1987. Disney CEO Michael Eisner helped Lucas open the proceedings with a lightsaber, a couple of droids, an Ewok or two, and a pair of large mice. Star Tours was situated at the same Tomorrowland that entranced a young Lucas back in 1955, and it had the singular honor of being the first Disney ride based on a non-Disney movie.

Ironically, the concept for Star Tours was based on an idea for a ride related to Disney's *Star Wars* clone from 1979, *The Black Hole*. The total cost of what was to be the first version of Star Tours, $32 million, was twice the original cost of Disneyland itself and exactly the budget of *Return of the Jedi*.

Outside of Disney Parks, however, the whole *Star Wars* machine was creaking to a halt. The power in the toy world now resided with Mattel, which was still smarting from its failure to pick up the *Star Wars* license in 1976. Starting in 1981, Mattel did a reverse George Lucas: the company came up with the toy line first and then built a story around it. The toy was called He-Man. To create a story around the character, Mattel turned to Lucas's former friend, Don Glut. Working from Polaroids of the toys, Glut created the whole concept of Castle Grayskull, a mysterious location called Eternia. The result was called *Masters of the Universe*, and inferior as it was, it would steal a good deal of the *Star Wars* universe's thunder.

Similarly, in 1982, the GI Joe franchise had been revived as a series of *Star Wars*–sized figures, together with a whole mythology, a Marvel comic, and a brand new enemy, the evil Cobra Force. Once again, it was the *Star Wars* playbook, but this time married to a muscular Reagan-era patriotism. GI Joe was Stallone's Rambo writ small. He-Man seemed more like Arnold Schwarzenegger writ small (with so much similarity that Mattel had to fight off a lawsuit brought by the owners of *Conan the Barbarian*).

Kenner, which was still using the tagline "*Star Wars* is Forever," saw the writing on the wall as early as 1984. Sales of action figures had dropped off precipitously after *Return of the Jedi*; the movie had so much finality to it that there was nowhere left for kids to go. Darth Vader and the Emperor were definitively dead—what stories could you act out without the bad guys? (An avid action figure director at the age of ten, I remember getting around this problem for a while by claiming the Emperor had been cloned—but got bored and packed my *Star Wars* figures away in the attic by the age of twelve.)

Desperate to keep *Star Wars* alive, Kenner designer Mark Boudreaux led a team effort to come up with a whole story that would follow on from *Return of the Jedi*, and they kitbashed some prototype action figures using spare parts. The concept was called "The Epic Continues." The idea was that the Emperor's death had allowed a "genetic terrorist" called Atha Prime to return from the galactic exile he'd been banished to after the Clone Wars, bringing with him a whole bunch of Clone Warriors. Simultaneously, Grand Moff Tarkin was to return, revealing that he had somehow survived the destruction of the Death Star and lead resurgent Imperial forces, and Luke and Han were to enlist the help of a bizarrely named new species from Tatooine called the Mongo Beefhead Tribesmen.

Boudreaux gave the presentation to Lucasfilm, fully aware that the future of Kenner could hang in the balance. Years later, he still vividly remembered Lucasfilm's response. "They said, 'Thank you very much, you guys have done an awesome job, but for now we'd like to do some other awesome things.'" He wasn't to know that Lucas was jealously guarding his vision for the Clone Wars—or that in the perfectionist universe of the Creator, there was no room for Mongo Beefhead Tribesmen. Kenner, Lucasfilm's longest-running licensee, shut down its *Star Wars* line in 1985, and General Mills spun the company off the same year.

Marvel had been running into similar problems in its attempt to keep the *Star Wars* comic book relevant. The writers found a way to place Luke and friends in the throes of conflict with an alien invasion of the galaxy following the events of *Return of the Jedi*, but they could only keep that going for three years. The art looked tired, despite its attempts to keep up with the times: Luke Skywalker sported a mullet, a headband, and six-pack abs. After nine years, the comic ceased publication with its 107th issue in May 1986. The newspaper comic strip had shut down two years earlier.

In the mid-1980s, you were more likely to read about *Star Wars* in a political context than anything else. The popular moniker for President Reagan's new missile defense system was first used by the Democrats and intended as an insult, but the name stuck, and Reagan didn't correct it until after his reelection. For Lucas, a lifelong liberal, it was the ultimate irony, given the fact that the prime evil of the *Star Wars* galaxy had been based on the previous two-term Republican president. Lucas, as you may remember, wrote the original movie in the shadow of Vietnam and with *Apocalypse Now* buzzing around his brain. The Empire is granted the superior technology of the United States and a Nixonian leader we barely see, and the first draft of the script sees its space fortress brought down by creatures inspired by the Viet Cong. By the time those creatures make it onto the screen in *Return of the Jedi*, they have been deliberately disguised as cute teddy bears. (The signs Lucas stuck up around ILM at the time—"dare to be cute"—suddenly take on new meaning.) The Nixon character, Emperor Palpatine, is cloaked in the garb of a Sith, but did you notice something about the room in which we meet him on the second Death Star? As Lucas pointed out to Ian McDiarmid on set, Palpatine's office is oval.

By the time the classic trilogy had wrapped up in 1983, Lucas's original intent had become so buried under layers of interpretation that *Washington Post* reviewer Gary Arnold praised his feel-good epic for helping to "close some of the psychological wounds left by the war in Vietnam." Other reviewers at the time, and cultural critics since, have made the same mistake: how clever of Lucas to put America in the underdog position, they said. Arnold was nearer the mark when he said that the franchise "tapped into inspirational depths that transcend political allegiance. It reflected politically uncomplicated yearnings—to be in the right, to fight on the side of justice against tyranny."

No one knew this better than Reagan, who had been elected in the same year *Empire* won the box office.* Reagan had described the Soviet Union as

---

* The question of whether a couple of uncomplicated, feel-good, California-made movies nudged voters toward this uncomplicated, feel-good, California-made movie actor candidate is one I'll leave to the psephologists, though the very idea would horrify the liberal Lucas.

an "evil empire" in a speech before the National Association of Evangelicals in March 1983, a month after the first US screening of *Star Wars* on HBO and two months before the release of *Return of the Jedi*. The full quote is "I urge you to beware the temptation of pride, the temptation of blithely declaring yourselves above it all and label both sides equally at fault, to ignore the facts of history and the aggressive impulses of an evil empire." Reagan's chief speechwriter Anthony Dolan says no *Star Wars* reference was intended; there have, after all, been one or two empires throughout history, evil or otherwise. What the world heard, however, was a reference to a fictional galactic empire.

There was a similar situation later that month, when Reagan unveiled the concept of defensive systems that could intercept intercontinental missiles during a half-hour live TV address on the defense budget. He left the details hazy, probably because the notion of space satellite X-rays powered by nuclear explosions may have made the technology seem as incredulous as it in fact was. (In terms of its feasibility, Reagan had been sold a bill of goods by Edward Teller, father of the H-bomb and the inspiration for Dr. Strangelove.)

The front page of the next day's *Washington Post* carried a rebuttal quote from the lion of the Left, Senator Ted Kennedy, blasting Reagan's proposals as "misleading Red scare tactics and reckless Star Wars schemes." Perhaps realizing that a "Star Wars scheme" sounded a little too exciting to pin on his opponent, Kennedy threw a few other, less appealing and more preposterous metaphors into a speech at Brown University in June: Reagan was proposing a "supersonic Edsel," a "Lone Ranger in the sky, firing silver laser bullets and shooting missiles out of the hands of Soviet outlaws." But it was too late. The "Star Wars" nickname stuck. Cartoonists showed Reagan introducing his latest advisers, Artoo and Threepio. *Time* magazine had a cover story about Reagan and defense in April; it was only the second occasion the words "Star Wars" had appeared on the cover of *Time*. (The first was its cover on *Empire*; that vital review in 1977 had only said, "Inside: Year's Best Movie.")

Reagan was suspiciously slow to defend his Strategic Defense Initiative against the *Star Wars* comparison: he waited two years. It evidently didn't hurt him in the 1984 election, which he won in one of history's greatest landslides. Finally, in March 1985, the president gave a speech before the National Space Club. "The Strategic Defense Initiative has been labeled 'Star Wars,' the president said, "but it isn't about war, it's about peace . . . and in that struggle, if you will pardon me stealing a film line, the Force is with us." It was a masterful piece of political jujitsu on the Great Communicator's part—but pedantically speaking, that wasn't the line Reagan was looking for. "The Force is with us" was not used in a *Star Wars* movie until *Attack of the Clones* in 2002, when it was spoken by a Sith.

Meanwhile, the Soviets were doing their best to pin the evil empire label back on the United States. The movies would not be shown in Russia until the 1990s, but the Washington bureau chief for TASS, the Soviet Union's centralized news agency, did his best to put a political spin on his *Return of the Jedi* review. "Darth Vader in America now," said the reviewer, "is not only a cosmic brigand in an iron suit." An unnamed "local journalist," he said, had "pinned the same tag on President Reagan." The magic mirror of *Star Wars* always reflected your enemies as the Imperial evildoers.

Lucasfilm took pressure groups on both sides of the political debate to court for using the words "Star Wars" in ads for and against the Strategic Defense Initiative. Its argument was that a real-life conflict damaged a franchise built entirely on imaginary warfare. The company ultimately lost the case, with the judge arguing that those two words were way too common in the English language for him to grant the plaintiff relief. "*Star Wars*, your honor, is a fantasy," complained Lucasfilm lawyer Laurence Hefter. "It's something that doesn't exist." By the time he said that, it was starting to feel like the franchise didn't exist either.

As the tenth anniversary of the original movie approached, there was little left of the franchise but nostalgia. The *Star Wars* fan club sent out its final issue of the *Bantha Tracks* newsletter in February 1987 and promptly shut down. Dan Madsen, the kid from Colorado who had replaced his *Star Trek* posters with *Star Wars* posters in 1977, was now running the *Star Trek* fan club. Lucasfilm contacted him in early 1987, brought him out to Skywalker Ranch, and asked him if he would also run the successor to the *Star Wars* fan club. It was to be called the Lucasfilm Fan Club, and it would focus on non–*Star Wars* movies on the Lucasfilm docket. "I definitely got the feeling he was trying to step away from *Star Wars*," Madsen says. "It was hard to be a *Star Wars* fan at that moment." Disappointed, he nevertheless accepted the offer: "I just had fun covering the other movies and bided my time."

Starlog magazine, at least, couldn't let the tenth anniversary of the first *Star Wars* release pass without commemoration. That May, it threw a convention at a hotel near LAX; ten thousand fans showed up. George Lucas was the guest of honor and gave a speech after being presented, by R2-D2 and C-3PO, with a giant birthday card, signed by thousands of fans. He was surprised by how much *Star Wars* had taken off, he said, and someday—no promises—he hoped to get back to it. That got a loud cheer.

Then there was a surprise Madsen had helped arrange: Gene Rodden-berry, the creator of *Star Trek*, bounded onto the stage. Lucas wasn't one for surprises—and looked shocked. Roddenberry, a big bear-hugger of a guy, enthusiastically grasped the arm of the quiet, reserved Lucas, who was about a foot smaller. It was the one and only time these giants of the geek world were to meet. Madsen was the only one who thought to snap a picture.

Also speaking at this first tentative *Star Wars* convention was Howard Roff-man, the new vice president of Lucas Licensing. Roffman, an ambitious and ac-complished young lawyer, had joined the company in 1980 at age twenty-seven, the week *Empire Strikes Back* came out. He was quickly promoted to general counsel. In 1987 he had been given the seemingly impossible task of fighting the power of He-Man and GI Joe. Could *Star Wars* toys be revived without any Kenner-like plan for new stories? "It was not a great time to get that job," Roffman remembered in 2010:

> But I thought, "I'll show them. I'll be the greatest salesman who ever lived." I went out to every retailer, every licensee, trying to convince them to restock *Star Wars*, and to a one they told me, "Kid"—I did look like a kid back then—"*Star Wars* is dead."
>
> I had to go back to George Lucas and deliver the news. That was a meeting I wasn't looking forward to. I thought it was going to be a sit-uation where he presses a button and your chair falls through the floor and into a tank of piranhas.
>
> I'll never forget it. . . . He looked at me and narrowed his eyes and said:
>
> "No it's not dead; it's just taking a rest. A lot of kids really love those movies. Someday they're going to grow up and have kids of their own. We can bring it back then."
>
> That was the moment I realized that George Lucas really is Yoda.

Meantime Roffman, and Lucasfilm, focused their attention on other brands. The company had a couple of notable failures in 1986 with *Howard the Duck* and *Labyrinth*, both produced by Lucas (and directed by Lucas friends Wil-lard Huyck and Jim Henson respectively), but Lucasfilm had high hopes for its movies in production: a fantasy called *Willow*, starring Warwick Davis, who had played the lead Ewok, Wicket, in *Return of the Jedi*; a Coppola biopic of automaker Preston Tucker; and the third Indiana Jones film. There was also Lucasfilm Games, a profitable new division that was later renamed LucasArts. It produced a string of hits such as Maniac Mansion, an adventure video game with a TV show tie-in, and had many more titles in the works. Ironically, the one thing the games division couldn't produce at the time was *Star Wars* games, for which Atari, and later JVC, held the license.

There was one form of *Star Wars* game that Roffman's team was able to license, however, and it was the geekiest version of them all. The *Star Wars* role-playing game, made by a tiny company in Pennsylvania called West End Games, launched in October 1987. For the next three years, it would be about the only thing going on in the *Star Wars* universe. Those Dungeons & Dragons players who switched to playing *Star Wars* would be like the Irish monks who saved civilization by copying ancient scrolls through the Dark Ages.

It's an apt metaphor, since the role-playing game wasn't just preserving the memory of *Star Wars*. It was cataloging and enhancing it. To create the source-book for all those dungeon masters out there, West End Games editor Bill Slavicsek had to invent names for all the alien races, all the ships, all the weapons and droids. He had to figure out the nuts and bolts of how Lucas's universe worked, and fill in all the gaps that the Creator hadn't bothered to think about.

At the time, it seemed about the nerdiest thing you could possibly do. But Slavicsek's work—and the contributions of writers who came after him—would prove incalculably important to the coming *Star Wars* revival.

19.

THE UNIVERSE EXPANDS

The Expanded Universe, it was called, and what a universe it was. Some 260 novels; dozens of short stories; 180 video games; more than 1,000 comic books. More than 120 book authors alone who got to contribute their own little piece to *Star Wars* legend. So much creativity—and according to the internal rules of *Star Wars* canon, any bit of it could be overwritten by Lucasfilm's on-screen work at any time. Indeed, *Episode VII* has already banished the Expanded Universe to the universe next door.

Like so much of *Star Wars*, the Expanded Universe was dominated by activity in the 1990s and 2000s. But it actually got its start in 1976—earlier than the original movie—courtesy of Alan Dean Foster. The world wouldn't see the result of his labors until February 1978, but the ghostwriter's *Star Wars* contract demanded a second book. So once he'd spent two months writing up the original *Star Wars* novelization and mailed it off to Lucas's lawyer, Tom Pollock, Foster turned right back to his IBM Selectric typewriter, loaded another piece of blank paper into it, and started work on the first ever *Star Wars* tale not created by George Lucas. No biggie.

Before the world even knew who Luke and Leia were, then, Foster packed them off to the fog-shrouded, cave-filled planet of Mimban. It was fog-shrouded and cave-filled because one of the few directions Lucas had given was to write something cheap. The novel was little more than an insurance policy. If *Star Wars* only broke even, or made just a tiny bit of profit, he could use Foster's book as the basis for a screenplay and make a quick sequel on a Roger Corman budget while the sets were still lying around. When Foster wrote a thrilling battle in space for Chapter 1, Lucas nixed it. No doubt the massive cost overrun at ILM was weighing heavy on his mind. In the potential future of the cheap *Star Wars* sequel, there'd be no more Dykstra-driven headaches.

"Make it work as a Sergio Leone Western," Lucas suggested to Foster in one of their two meetings to discuss the book. "It can go more into the middle of no-where where these really slimy creatures live. Essentially, space can be boring. . . . Now that we've established the space fantasy, we can move away from that."

The book Foster produced was called *Splinter of the Mind's Eye,* and it was shaped by more constraints than just Lucas's presumed budget. Only Luke and Leia were in the book, because Harrison Ford was not signed up for a sequel. Only Vader's face was on the Ralph McQuarrie cover, with Luke and Leia seen from behind, because Lucas did not at that point have the rights to use Mark Hamill and Carrie Fisher's faces. The plot was a movie Foster constructed in his head out of spare parts Lucas had left lying around. Luke and Leia meet Halla, a Force-sensitive old woman, and go off in search of the Force-enhancing Kaiburr crystal—something Lucas discarded after the third draft of *Star Wars* as he felt it turned the Jedi into hard-to-root-for superhumans. Darth Vader, alerted to their presence, meets them there. He and Luke have their first lightsaber showdown, but not before Leia has taken Vader on with a lightsaber herself. In an odd reversal of what would come to pass in *Empire,* Luke slices Vader's arm off. Vader falls down a deep cave shaft. At the end, though, Luke senses Vader is still alive.

Foster was simply having fun; few elements of *Star Wars* were sacrosanct at this point, least of all Vader and his tragic arc. Surprisingly, Lucas declared in those 1976 conversations with Foster that Vader was a weak villain, that, the killing of Obi-Wan Kenobi aside, "he never does anything to anybody. I mean, he chokes one guy." He would have to be built up as a villain in this second book, Lucas declared, and "Luke kills Vader in the end." Luckily, Lucas's word was hardly law at this stage. Foster effectively saved Vader's life.

As hokey as its plot was, *Splinter* was another best seller; by the time it was published in February 1978, nine months after the first film's release, the world was hungry for any new *Star Wars* story. Children would reread the paper-back until it fell apart in their hands. Foster was offered more *Star Wars* novel deals by Del Rey—"the story of Chewbacca's second cousin's uncle, that kind of thing," he recalls—but declined. It was time to move on.

Apart from *Splinter*, there were surprisingly few *Star Wars* novels during the original trilogy years. Those two scoundrels, Han Solo and Lando Calrissian, got pulp-ish paperback trilogies of their own. (Han got exciting Western-style adventures at the outpost called "Star's End"; Lando got odd, almost psychedelic adventures with "the Mindharp of Sharu.") Before she died, Leigh Brackett was signed up to write a Princess Leia novel; she was not replaced, and once again Leia would get short shrift. The Expanded Universe was left to Marvel comics, which produced characters that would sometimes irk Lucasfilm—the most infamous being one of the earliest, a wisecracking green cartoon rabbit called Jaxxon, modeled on Bugs Bunny. Jaxxon offered the first inkling of the disastrously off-base concepts and creations that could swirl out of the Expanded Universe—but for every Jaxxon, fortunately, there was a Mara Jade or a Grand Admiral Thrawn.

One afternoon in the fall of 1988, Lou Aronica came back from lunch in midtown Manhattan, shut his office door, and wrote an impassioned letter to George Lucas. His lunch buddy had told him he'd read someplace that Lucas had officially announced there were going to be no more *Star Wars* movies. "There's just so much wrong with that," thought Aronica. The Rebel victory at the end of *Return of the Jedi* had seemed tenuous at best. He was a Luke Skywalker guy: What happened next to the galaxy's only trained Jedi? "This body of work is too important to popular culture to end with these three movies," Aronica wrote.

Aronica wasn't just an aggrieved fan. He was the head of mass-market publishing at Bantam and had founded the company's popular science fiction imprint, Spectra. His pitch to Lucas: if you're not doing anything more with the franchise, let us produce quality books under your supervision. Aronica didn't want to churn out two so-so novels every month the way the *Star Trek* franchise did. He envisioned one well-written hardback a year, starting with a trilogy that advanced the whole *Star Wars* story, written by an award-winning author. "We can't do these casually," he recalls saying at the time. "They have to be as ambitious as the movies were."

Aronica heard nothing back for nearly a year. At some point, Lucas Licensing VP Howard Roffman went to sound Lucas out about the idea. "No one is going to buy this," said Lucas, but gave his assent anyway. Ground rules were laid down: the first novel would take place five years after *Return of the Jedi*. Events prior to the original movie, such as the Clone Wars, were untouchable; Lucas was mulling the possibilities of prequels and didn't want anything to interfere with his creative process. No major characters could be killed off. And no one who was already dead in the movies could be brought back.

Aronica agreed, gleefully. He cast around for writers but didn't have to look too far: Spectra had just signed up Timothy Zahn, a Hugo award–winning author who had written the Cobra trilogy, a tale of intergalactic war. Aronica called up Zahn's agent and learned that the author was an even bigger *Star Wars* fan than Aronica was. When Zahn turned in his manuscript, it was Aronica who came up with the title: *Heir to the Empire*.

Zahn's novel was released on May 1, 1991. Lucasfilm lore claims that it was as instant a hit as the first *Star Wars* movie. "I'll never forget the day that Lucy [Autrey Wilson, Lucasfilm finance director] came into my office in 1991 to deliver the news that Tim's *Heir to the Empire* had premiered at number one on the *New York Times* bestseller list," Roffman wrote in the introduction to the twentieth anniversary edition of the book.

In fact, *Heir* was on a slower boil than that. The book first appeared on the *Times* best-seller list on May 26, debuting at number 11. The next week it reached number 6, leapfrogging James Michener's *The Novel*. Another two weeks and it overtook John Grisham's debut *The Firm*, reaching the number 2 spot, held back by Dr. Seuss' *Oh the Places You'll Go*—the only cheaper hardback on the list than *Heir*, which was priced at a deliberately low $15.

On June 30, 1991, two months after it was released, *Heir to the Empire* became a coveted *New York Times* hardcover fiction list number 1 best seller. It remained at the top for exactly one week, though it stayed on the overall list for a total of nineteen weeks. Its initial print run of seventy thousand copies was gone within months. Four more print runs followed that year. Not bad at all, but you'd need a pretty selective memory to remember it debuting at number 1.

Aronica is aggrieved by another claim Roffman makes in his introduction: that it was Lucy Autrey Wilson who came up with the idea of pitching publishers rather than the other way around, and that Bantam just happened to be the only publisher that believed in the idea. "They didn't approach us; they responded to my letter," Aronica says. "I knew a lot of other people in the science fiction publishing world, and they were all furious that I'd been able to make this deal."

After having to convince his bosses that *Star Wars* could sustain one hardback a year, Aronica now found himself having to hold back a deluge of books. "There was a lot of money to be made," he says. "The program grew out a little faster than I would have liked." After Zahn completed his trilogy, there were six, then nine, then twelve books a year; 1997 saw a record twenty-two *Star Wars* novels for all reading ages. The quality, and sales, suffered accordingly.

There was no year between the 1991 release of *Heir* and 2013 in which we have seen fewer than ten *Star Wars* novels. They sometimes nudge the bottom of the best-seller list for a week or so, like *Star Trek* paperbacks. Zahn's most recent *Star Wars* novel, *Scoundrels*, sold a respectable seventeen thousand copies. but it's a far cry from Aronica's vision of one movie-like "event" book a year—or from the sales of *Heir*, which has been purchased more than a million times and which still moves about five thousand copies a month. "We could have made *Star Wars* a best-selling author, like a Grisham or a Clancy, and retained the audience," Aronica laments. "If every book was as good as *Heir*, maybe they'd be top 5 best sellers every time out."

So what was it that made *Heir* so good? It was a case of making new *Star Wars* by loving the idea and hating many of the preceding details. Timothy Zahn was a huge *Star Wars* fan and had been since 1977, when he was a physics student in grad school and took no fewer than eight separate dates to see the movie. "I was a physicist," he says. "They had to know what they were getting into." He had listened to *Star Wars* soundtracks while writing every prior science fiction novel. But as with any true *Star Wars* fan, there was something that bugged him. He didn't like the fact that the Jedi seemed to have no inherent limit on their ability to operate the Force other than their own belief in it. "If they can do anything," he says, "they're just superheroes."

So when Zahn was pacing around his house in November 1989, in those first few days after getting the call from his agent about Aronica's offer, excited about the chance to play in the *Star Wars* sandbox and nervous about the notion of failing spectacularly in front of the hard-core fans, this was his first vision: a cage constructed of creatures that could negate the effects of the Force. A cage fit for a Jedi.

Zahn is fond of modestly insisting he didn't revive *Star Wars* fandom; the fans were there, he says, ready for anything that said *Star Wars* on its cover. "I got to stick my fork in the pie crust and show how much steam there was underneath," he says. But he also made key choices about the directions the universe would expand in—choices that would lay down a template for what worked in *Star Wars* literature. (Zahn would also be reminded of what didn't work when he made the apparently innocent choice to have Luke drink a cup of "hot chocolate" in the early pages of *Heir to the Empire*; fans howled with protest at this Alan Dean Foster–like insertion of a very Earth-bound beverage.)

Anyone faced with the task of picking out the threads Lucas had tied up at the end of *Return of the Jedi* would have been presented with some major problems. Lucas had killed off the series' two main villains, the Emperor and Darth Vader. The Empire was on the run. It needed a seriously good bad guy at its helm to keep readers' interest. With the Rebellion ascendant, here was a chance to create a villain who was also an underdog—one who, unlike his predecessors, ruled by loyalty rather than fear.

So Zahn came up with the character of Grand Admiral Thrawn, a blue-skinned, red-eyed humanoid who had worked his way up imperial ranks, a brilliant tactician who studied the art of any species he was in conflict with in order to understand their culture and thus outsmart them. A guy like that could uncover those obscure, Force-negating, anti-Jedi creatures that Zahn decided to call "ysilamari." (Zahn did not always follow Lucas's habit of writing easily pronounceable names.)

With that, Zahn was off to the races. He had a notion for a Dark Jedi with whom Thrawn could make common cause. He would be an insane clone of Obi-Wan Kenobi, created in the Clone Wars. Who better to throw Luke for a loop? He wanted to investigate the Sith, since Vader was always being called the Dark Lord of the Sith, and nobody knew what the Sith were. Zahn imagined a race of diminutive assassin aliens with faces that looked like Vader's mask. He wanted a wily smuggler in the Han Solo vein, but one who was operating on a larger scale and could be even more wily. Along came Talon Karrde, supplier of ships that the Rebels were in desperately short supply of, and his ship the *Wild Karrde*.

And then there was Mara Jade, whom Zahn created specifically to fix something he hated about *Return of the Jedi*. His main problem with the film: the opening act in Jabba's Palace seemed disjointed from the rest of the movie. What did any of that have to do with the struggle against the Empire, the topic of the entire trilogy? So Zahn retroactively inserted an Imperial assassin into Jabba's Palace who tried, but failed, to ensure Skywalker's death offscreen. The assassin worked directly for the Emperor, whom, Zahn decided, no longer trusted Vader's plan to turn his son to the Dark Side. Mara Jade, the Emperor's Hand, would put Luke in jeopardy throughout his trilogy. She was to become, after Thrawn, the Expanded Universe's most popular character. She would marry Luke Skywalker in a later book, even though that's not what Zahn originally intended. She would inspire the first online mailing group (and later the first blog) to cover the Expanded Universe, Club Jade. With her vibrant red hair, green eyes, and full-figured leather jumpsuit, Mara is fast becoming one of the more popular *Star Wars* costume choices for women on the comic convention circuit; she offers all of the feisty, fiery personality that Leia should have developed, but ultimately lacked.

Zahn had all of these concepts and characters in place in a mere two weeks and turned in a rough outline before Lucasfilm and Bantam had even inked a contract. The first draft of *Heir to the Empire* was written in six months.

Then came the pushback. Lucasfilm wouldn't let him clone Obi-Wan Kenobi, that flouted the ban on avoiding the Clone Wars and resurrecting old characters. The race of assassins could not be called the Sith. Zahn had come up with his own laws of physics, his own background bible to the universe; Lucasfilm wanted him to use the sourcebook from West End Games' *Star Wars* role-playing game.

Zahn chafed against what seemed like arbitrary restrictions. This was 1990. The *Star Wars* universe was still ill-defined; there was no internal digital database of its components at Lucasfilm (yet) and certainly no fan-edited encyclopedia (yet). Zahn chafed further when he found out that Lucasfilm was simultaneously restarting the *Star Wars* comics line with a publisher called Dark Horse, and wanted Zahn to coordinate his efforts with them. The comic series, *Dark Empire*, was to show Luke confronting a clone of the Emperor. For Zahn, that was a clone too far: "It destroys Darth Vader's sacrifice in killing the Emperor at the end of *Return of the Jedi*," he says. "It unravels the whole original trilogy."

Compromises were reached. The insane clone of Kenobi, which Zahn fought the hardest for, became a Dark Jedi called Joruus C'boath (pronounced suh-boa-th). The Vader-worshipping assassins became the Noghri. Zahn's ideas for the book title, *Wild Card* and *Emperor's Hand*, were nixed by Aronica; *Heir to the Empire* it was. But Zahn wasn't done hating *Dark Empire*, even though the comics referenced Grand Admiral Thrawn in their introductions. In a later novel, *Visions of the Future*, Zahn had Mara Jade and Luke recall having dealt with a cloned Emperor. "Whatever," says Mara. "I'm not even convinced that was him." (To its credit, *Dark Empire* is the source for the notion of a repository of Jedi knowledge—a "Holocron"—which would play an important role in the Expanded Universe in years to come.)

These days, having seen the Clone Wars unfold, Zahn is grateful that Lucasfilm fought back. There are still things he chafes against, one of them being the fact that a later writer—spoiler alert—killed off Mara Jade in a duel, after infecting her with mysterious intergalactic spores. "It would have been nice to let me know and to let me argue why not," he said. "I know that Lucasfilm owns everything I put down on paper and give them. But it still feels like losing your daughter." The Expanded Universe fans at Club Jade were right there with him. "They shunt her to the side and give her a stupid disease," complains Tracy Duncan, a Detroit journalist known to the Internet as Dunc, proprietor of the *Club Jade* blog. "It was like 'Oh, we only have two or three female characters; let's kill off one of them.' Such a waste."

The Expanded Universe may have been two steps below the movie canon at all times, then erased from the canon altogether. But having authors and a story and characters messed with could hurt as much for fans as it had once hurt for Lucas.

S helly Shapiro likes to say she saved Han Solo's life. Del Rey, where Shapiro is an editor, took over the Lucasfilm publishing license from Spectra in 1998, part of a deal connected to the forthcoming release of the prequel movies. Lucasfilm had wanted the Expanded Universe to slowly build up a vast and complex mythology, but the plan had worked too well and too fast: the novels had already gotten too sprawling, the quality uneven. One trilogy follows Luke Skywalker as he sets up a Jedi Academy in the mysterious ruins of Yavin, the jungle planet seen at the end of *Star Wars*, which turns out to be haunted. Han and Leia get married, and a book devotes itself to the backstory of the wedding. Derided as one of the worst novels of the Expanded Universe, *The Courtship of Princess Leia* sees Han kidnap and control his future wife with the laughably titled "gun of command" after she receives a marriage offer from a well-connected prince.* The Solos then have three kids: Jaina, Jacen, and Anakin. Bring on the Young Jedi Knights series!

Lucasfilm called a summit at Skywalker Ranch, at which Shapiro was thrown straight into the deep end of the *Star Wars* universe. She, her first three authors, and a contingent from Dark Horse Comics were there to discuss what became known as the New Jedi Order, a series that would send the Expanded Universe off in a new direction over the course of twenty-nine novels (a number later whittled down to nineteen). There was to be an alien species invading the galaxy (the concept suggested by Kenner and used by Marvel comics was to be given a fresh coat of paint). But to inject a sense of jeopardy and gravitas into a universe where Luke and the Jedi had—despite Zahn's best efforts—become

---

* Tracy Duncan's suitably snarky commentary on the plot of *Courtship*: "He doesn't need a gun of command! He's Han Solo!"

way too much like superheroes once again, the licensees would also dust off the idea proposed by Lawrence Kasdan during that *Return of the Jedi* story conference: a main character must die.

Lucas had evidently moved on from the days when he felt that it wasn't "nice" to kill our favorite characters. "Early on we got the all-clear to kill anyone," says Mike Stackpole, an author at the table. "Literally anyone was fair game." Shapiro, a serious Harrison Ford fan, says she put her foot down: Han Solo would live.

Stackpole remembers it differently. He says there was a simple, methodical process of deciding which of the leads—Han, Luke, Leia, Lando, the droids, Chewbacca—it would hurt the least to lose. From whose viewpoint would it be hardest to describe the grief? "After two days," Stackpole says, "we had Chewie locked down."

When fan grief over the death of Chewbacca surpassed anything Shapiro or Stackpole expected, a rumor surfaced that Randy Stradley of Dark Horse Comics had told the meeting to "kill the family dog," and compared Chewie to Old Yeller. But Stackpole denies that, insisting they all stuck the knives in at the same time, like Roman conspirators. Shapiro, who would edit the book, was happy to wield a blade. "You've got to get people's attention. Otherwise it's just 'Oh, another adventure, another super weapon,'" Shapiro explains.

Vector Prime, the first novel of the New Jedi Order, would thus become the most controversial work in the history of the Expanded Universe, whose readers like to protest even more loudly than the average *Star Wars* fan. The author of *Vector Prime*, R. A. Salvatore, would receive death threats for his contribution to the oeuvre. He was, however, only obeying orders, and did at least give the Wookiee a heroic end. Chewie is killed helping to evacuate the population of a planet whose moon, thanks to the alien invaders, has fallen out of orbit. "Financially, it was successful, and it did work," Shapiro says. "Even people who complained about it couldn't put it down."

But for fans who mourned Chewie, there is one more figure to blame: a man largely unseen at the summit. As with all major decisions in the Expanded Universe, the ultimate go-ahead was likely granted via one of those lists of yes/no check boxes that Howard Roffman was constantly presenting to his boss—and you can't imagine this one would have just breezed past him. The decision to kill Chewbacca, the character based on the Lucases' dog Indiana, resides with George Lucas.*

---

* Years later, Stackpole apologized to Peter Mayhew, Chewbacca actor. Mayhew smiled and shrugged: "it doesn't matter. Chewie lives on in the movies." Years after that, when the Expanded Universe collapsed and *Episode VII* wiped over Vector Prime's continuity, it turned out Mayhew was right. Chewie lives on, thanks to new movies.

In 2002, Alan Dean Foster was ready to return to the universe he'd helped birth. He had been offered a contract for a book called *The Approaching Storm*. After he wrote his first draft at his usual speed, Foster was offered significantly more guidance from Lucasfilm than his previous "take out the first chapter—it's too expensive" experience. He spent days at Skywalker Ranch with an entire committee that went over the manuscript point by point and disagreed with his characters and their motivations. "It was guidance in the sense that you're in a Catholic school and nuns walk by with rulers," Foster remembered. "It was no fun."

Things had changed by the time Foster returned. The freewheeling levity of the late 1970s had vanished. The self-spoofing spirit of Jaxxon the bunny had been replaced, even in the comics, with gravely serious melodrama. Only one comic books title, the much-loved *Star Wars Tales*, managed to avoid the nuns with their rulers—and that was because it explicitly stated in each issue that its stories were not to be considered canon. Fans still fondly remembered its pastiches of *The Breakfast Club* with *Star Wars* characters, or its what-if tale in which Hans Solo travels to Earth through a freak wormhole; his skeleton is discovered years later by Indiana Jones. When *Star Wars Tales* switched to all-serious stories, readership fell off a cliff, and the title promptly shut down. The franchise had entered a whole new phase, and it would lead Lucasfilm to exert ever greater control as it struggled to accommodate a difficult new story from the Creator. The outrage from those cranky, critical Expanded Universe fans over the deaths of Chewbacca and Mara Jade was as nothing compared to the criticism that came in the wake of new additions to *Star Wars* canon: midi-chlorians, Gungans, and a very strange virgin birth.

20.

RETURN OF THE WRITER

According to Lucasfilm legend, the prequels began in the early morning of November 1, 1994. In plaid shirt, jeans, and white sneakers, George Lucas walked up the wooden stairs to his writing tower, to the door desks, to the franchise he had unceremoniously abandoned eleven years earlier. This time he'd brought a camera operator to record the moment. The results would be edited and shown on a brand new medium, the World Wide Web.

"My oldest daughter was sick all night," Lucas confided. "I got no sleep whatsoever." He walked past the fireplace, the couch, the side table with the Tiffany lamp: on mornings when the fog has already poured over Mount Tam, one could imagine Lucas lighting a fire and ruminating.

It was the first time Lucas had shown fans "the cave I hibernate in," as he called it. He walked over to his door desks, little changed from the days when he struggled over early drafts of *The Star Wars*. "I have beautiful pristine yellow tablets," he said, picking up his long-standing paper of choice. He opened a drawer: "A nice fresh box of pencils." The camera captured his tired face, the bags under his eyes. "All I need," he said, collapsing dramatically into his chair, "is an idea." It seemed part exhaustion, part playing to the camera.

This was how *Episode I* began: bathed in absolute self-awareness that history was being made. The previous year, a few months after the release of *Jurassic Park*, Lucas had summoned a writer from *Variety* to Skywalker Ranch to inform the world that he had made the decision: work was to begin on the prequel movies, *Episodes I–III*. At that stage, he planned to shoot them all together. Every luxury Lucas had been denied in the making of the original film— luxury of time, of budget, of technology—was his for the taking. How could the prequels not succeed?

The only person who doubted George Lucas, as he pulled out the fabled three-ring binders with his notes on the *Star Wars* universe, was George Lucas himself. He was to remain pessimistic throughout the production process. "For every person who loves Episode I, there will be two or three who hate it," he predicted at its end.

"You just never know with these things," Lucas remarked one day during filming to Yoda puppeteer Frank Oz. "I made *More American Graffiti*. It made ten cents."

"Really?" said Oz.

"It just failed miserably."

Oz and Lucas looked at each other for a beat.

"You can do it," continued Lucas. "You can destroy these things. It is possible."

So why not leave well enough alone? Why not simply allow *Star Wars* to chug along in Expanded Universe form, in games and books and comics? Lucas had allowed adventures to take place after *Return of the Jedi*, and he could just as easily explore the prequel world that way too. Why risk being the destroyer of *Star Wars*, as well as its Creator? And why start then, that day, November 1, 1994?

A confluence of forces had brought the Creator back to his creation in the early 1990s. The technology was finally where he wanted it to be. Using puppets, models, actors in rubber suits, and the less jerky stop-motion animation (even "go-motion," the version pioneered by Phil Tippett) had always been painful stopgap solutions for Lucas; they were constrictions on his imagination more than they were expressions of it. You might have enjoyed the rubber puppet fest of Jabba's Palace, but it made the Creator wince.

Computer animation, however: Lucas had known that was the future since he first tentatively used it in 1977, in the rebel pilot's briefing room. ILM was making the future happen right under his nose. Advances in computer-generated imagery, or CGI, were coming thick and fast. The company used a computer program to remove wires from a few scenes in *Howard the Duck* in 1985. Then a young digital animator Lucas hired, John Lasseter, produced a stunning 3-D rendering for the movie *Young Sherlock Holmes*, in which a knight in a stained-glass window comes to life and attacks a priest. (The scene still holds up today.)

Many of ILM's experiments were less flashy, almost Easter egg–like, such as a plane seen in the sky for a few seconds of Steven Spielberg's *Empire of the Sun* (1987), but the technology was evolving rapidly and enabling feats of special effects that filmmakers previously could only dream of. *Willow* (1988) saw the first use of digital morphing; a character under a spell turned into various animals. James Cameron's *The Abyss* (1989) marked the first time computer-generated aliens had mingled with human actors, albeit for a five-minute sequence. But there was no missing the groundbreaking ILM effects in Cameron's next blockbuster, *Terminator 2* (1991), in which the T-1000 assassin from the future repeatedly turns himself into a sinister silver ooze of liquid metal.

Meanwhile, Dennis Muren, one of the few veterans of the original *Star Wars* and lead effects producer at ILM, was hard at work on a project for Steven Spielberg. The director had optioned Michael Crichton's novel *Jurassic Park*. Spielberg assumed he would have to go with animatronic or go-motion dinosaurs. Muren's job was to prove him wrong, and he had a secret weapon—state of the art animation hardware from Silicon Graphics.*

In 1992, when Spielberg and Lucas gathered to watch the result of Muren's labor—wire-frame dinosaurs running realistically across a screen—"everyone had tears in their eyes," Lucas said two years later. His reaction: "We may have reached a level here where we actually artificially created reality, which is of course what movies were trying to do all along." His only concern was that the dinosaurs might look clumsy in twenty years time. (They don't.)

Lucas's friendly rivalry with Spielberg was tilting toward Spielberg again. *Jurassic Park* was obviously going to be a huge hit and a landmark in CGI. It would have been natural for Lucas to feel the need to one-up his friend once more.

Luckily, Lucas's spirit of filmmaking adventure was back, spurred on by the *Young Indiana Jones* TV series. In development from 1989, and filmed from 1991 to 1993, the show was a tremendously happy experience for Lucas despite its untimely cancellation. Not only did it fill in a lot of the backstory for one of his best-known creations—call it the Indy prequels—but it was also a great chance to provide viewers with some lighthearted education, which was catnip for the Creator. Each week, young Indy would meet another famous historical figure. The episodes were relatively cheap compared to movies, costing

---

* In 1993, ILM and Silicon Graphics (also called SGI) inked a deal called Joint Environment for Digital Imaging, or JEDI, which essentially gave Lucas SGI workstations at cost. It's fair to say the prequels would never have been made without JEDI.

$1.5 million each. Each one would be a proving ground for digital special effects shots, of which there were around a hundred per episode. Most effects just deleted parts of the set that weren't historically appropriate, but it left Lucas enamored with and experienced in CGI backgrounds.

Young Indy marked the first time Lucas had gathered a team that used Skywalker Ranch the way it was intended. It was one of the closest things in his career to the small-scale filmmaking he'd long talked about getting back to. Filming was fun when you had someone else to direct, and above all, it got Lucas out of his businessman funk. "I could see George was looking for something else," said producer Rick McCallum. "He wanted to be in a world where things weren't taken that seriously."

Another factor driving the renaissance of *Star Wars*: McCallum himself. Lucas had met the American producer in the spring of 1984 while in London, visiting the set of *Return to Oz*, a dark and poorly received sequel to *Wizard of Oz* from Walter Murch and Gary Kurtz. Lucas had helped to bail them out of budget troubles. While visiting, he had wandered next door to the set of *Dreamchild*, a biopic of Lewis Carroll by playwright Dennis Potter, which McCallum was producing, and looked wistfully at the small-scale production.

When Lucas tapped McCallum for *Young Indy*, he had found his next Gary Kurtz—or rather, the producer he'd always wanted Kurtz to be: someone who would move heaven and earth for the whims of George Lucas, communicate with the crew on his behalf, and, most importantly, keep a tight rein on time and budget. With a bruiser of a producer like McCallum, Lucas could return to directing.

"The great thing about Rick is that he never says no," Lucas told Marcus Hearn, author of *The Cinema of George Lucas*. "He will screw his face up into a painful look—that's when I know I've gone too far—and he will eventually come back to me having found a way it can be done. . . . If I don't want to shoot a particular scene tomorrow but want something else, he'll say OK, then he'll work all night and move it all around."

McCallum agreed that this was the job of a producer. "Your talent, if you have any, is to enable the director to achieve everything he can," he said. "You want him to win." The days when Lucas would have someone on set who would push back were long gone, and they weren't coming back. Actors wouldn't be a problem, either. With more and more digital resources at his disposal, he could not only direct the movie in the editing room, the way he always did, but even move the actors' positions around in postproduction.

Star Wars fandom, meanwhile, was also pushing Lucas back toward the franchise. Aided by the explosion of the Expanded Universe during the early

1990s, the fans were back with a vengeance, and they were in Lucas's face. It was something he'd brought on himself. He had numbered the original trilogy IV, V, and VI. Demand for I, II, and III became a steady drumbeat. The fans were getting older, they were watching the originals on VHS, and they were impatient. Pretty much everything Lucas had produced in the late '80s and early '90s, barring *Indiana Jones*, was a flop. But *Star Wars* was the nearest he had to a sure thing. It was, Lucas came to realize, his destiny.

"Part of the reason for doing it," Lucas said of the *Star Wars* prequels at a press conference for one of those flops, *Radioland Murders*, in October 1994, "is that it's the first question I get asked. Not 'this is who I am' or anything, but 'when are you going to do the next *Star Wars*?' So if I do the next ones, hopefully people will introduce themselves first."

Lucas thought he could do the prequels cheaply and speedily. He would "never go above $50 million" per movie, he said. He would shoot them back to back and then focus on the all-important CGI. The first one would arrive in 1997, he decided, the second in 1999, and the third in 2001. The story would then be told, the fans would be sated and civil, Lucasfilm would never again be weeks from not being able to make payroll—as it was several times during the 1980s—and he would finally be able to get back to those small, experimental films. "It would hopefully make me financially secure enough to where I wouldn't have to go to a studio and beg for money," he recalled to Charlie Rose in 2004—a year when he was still fully preoccupied with the prequel-finishing task that should have been dispatched by 2001.

Anyone sitting down to write a screenplay on November 1, 1994, as Lucas apparently did, would have been interrupted eight days into the writing process by one of the most seismic midterm elections in postwar American history. Republicans took the House and the Senate for the first time in forty years. A resurgent GOP under House Speaker Newt Gingrich started pushing its tax-cutting, regulation-slashing "Contract With America." Democrats, whose messaging had improved since Ted Kennedy's "Star Wars" flub, started calling it a "Contract On America."

It was perhaps no coincidence, then, that Lucas started writing about a "Trade Federation," aided and emboldened by corrupt politicians, embroiled in some sort of dispute over the taxing of trade to the outlying star systems. We never learn what the dispute was about—whether the Trade Federation was pro- or anti-tax. But what we know is that the name of the leader of the Trade

Federation—never actually spoken in the movie, but noted in the script from the start—was Nute Gunray. By 1997, when the GOP Senate leader was Trent Lott, Lucas had named the Trade Federation's representative in the Galactic Senate: Lott Dod. We're a long way from the subtlety of his Vietnam metaphor here.

The older Lucas got, the more overt his politics became. By 2012, he was openly siding with the Occupy Wall Street movement, describing himself as a "dyed-in-the-wool 99-percenter before there was such a thing." It was increasingly clear to Lucas that his government had been "bought" by the rich, a process he abhorred. "I'm a very ardent patriot," he told Charlie Rose, "but I'm also a very ardent believer in democracy, not capitalist democracy." Asked by Rose why he didn't just make a political movie, Lucas explained that he had. The prequels were designed to "subliminally" convey the message of "what happens to you if you've got a dysfunctional government that's corrupt and doesn't work."

Contemporary politics weren't Lucas's only inspiration. He had brought out the secret file he'd been writing in since *American Graffiti*. There were folders marked "Character, Plot, Outline, Jedi, Empire." The original notes for the prequels added up to fifteen pages. There was plenty of drama inherent in these episodes: Anakin Skywalker would betray the Jedi order, somehow. But how? Why? The outline didn't always offer a lot of guidance. Here, for example, is what Lucas wrote for the man who was to become Darth Vader:

> Anakin Skywalker (age 9–20) a boy who builds Droids and races powerpods. [9–20? That's a pretty big range as far as movies go; this could be a children's racing movie in the style of *Herbie the Love Bug*, or an adult racing movie in the style of *Days of Thunder*.]
>
> Earnest and hardworking
>
> Who dreams of becoming a starpilot and a Jedi
>
> Good at heart
>
> Blue eyes.
>
> When ever he gets near a machine he gets an intuition and he knows what makes it work
>
> Is he a mutation? Who was his father?
>
> His mother outcast

Lucas loved no part of the process more than research. His desk was replete with books: *Your Child's Self-Esteem* by Dorothy Briggs and *The Gnostic Gospels* by Elaine Pagels; Simon Schama's *Landscape and Memory*, a sublime and meditative work on humans' relationship to nature. The two-volume *Peasant Questions and Savage Myths*, full of very strange historical folktales. *The Hounds of Skaith*, a science fiction novel by the late lamented Leigh Brackett. *Inherit the Stars*: a science fiction novel published the same month as *Star Wars*, it was the first of a well-received trilogy.

Lucas had likely been sitting with his books and his notes for some time before he brought the cameraman in to witness the screenplay's supposed birth on November 1, 1994. Once he decided to spring himself from the research trap and begin the screenplay of *Episode I* on that day, however, the Creator wrote like the wind, five days a week. Decisions were made. The uncertainty collapsed. Anakin would spend *Episode I* at the age of nine and then move up to twenty in *Episode II*. Lucas briefly considered starting Anakin as an adolescent, but he decided that Anakin leaving his mother would have more impact if the kid was just nine.

In theory, that made *Episode I* the story of how Anakin joined the Jedi order. To fill it out, Lucas came up with what he has since variously described as "a jazz riff" and "padding." When he realized his digital technology could take him to a place where his imagination was unbound, one of the first things Lucas saw was the pod race—the drag racing of his adolescence, but a kind of "Wacky Races" version that children would enjoy. He saw an entirely digital environment, the most thrilling natural racetrack in the universe. The plot would accommodate this somehow.

As for the rest of it? Well, Lucas could have structured *Episode I* using his old friend and standby, the hero's journey, as elucidated by his third mentor. But who was the hero? Lucas seemed reluctant to decide. He'd often talked about doing the back story of Obi-Wan Kenobi. That was his plan for the prequels as early as 1977: Obi-Wan as a young Jedi knight, how he met Darth Vader, what happened when he fought in the Clone Wars. Over time, however, Lucas's intent shifted toward creating a six-movie story arc that told the tragedy of Darth Vader.

Was the hero Anakin, then? Possibly—but in no draft of the script was Anakin on screen for the first forty-five minutes. That's three times the length of time it took us to meet Luke. Shorn of any kind of writing partner for the first time ever, Lucas returned to the anti-story approach of *THX 1138* and applied it to a retelling of the original *Star Wars* trilogy. He was once again more interested in sound and vision than dialogue. And where he did use dialogue, it was as if he were writing a Dadaist, William Burroughs–style cut-up poem, made out of random words and phrases from the original trilogy: "wizard!"; "it's a trap"; "how rude!"

Indeed, at various times during the production of *Episode I*, Lucas referred to his scriptwriting as poetry, a symphony, jazz. "With *THX* I became fascinated with that idea of visual jazz—take the same idea and just riff on it visually," he said on the commentary track for the *Episode I* DVD. "There's a lot of that going on in these movies. I like the idea of cyclical motifs that go on over and over." Later he suggested: "The films are primarily designed to be like silent films. Dialogue and effects are part of the musical composition. I'm telling the story visually rather than using a lot of heavy dialogue. . . . The films are composed along lines of music. Many themes are going on through the films, and the themes repeat using different orchestration. You have the same dialogue used by other characters in different situations, so you have a recurring theme going on constantly."

The first example of a thematic note that Lucas offers is Obi-Wan's first line of dialogue: "I have a bad feeling about this." Which is how you might respond to the idea of building a two-hour action adventure movie on the notion of a jazz riff.

Throughout much of the writing process, *Episode I* would simply be called "the beginning." There's one draft marked January 13, 1995, which would be astonishingly fast Lucas started on November 1. But it wouldn't be inconceivable, given Lucas's documented habit in later prequels of writing repeated, very fast drafts. Other dates that have been reported for drafts: June 13, 1996, for a revised rough draft, the following March for a second draft, and May 1997 for a revised second draft. A third draft is dated May 13, 1997, and a revised third draft from June 6, 1997, twenty days before filming began.

The first draft was markedly different from the final product. In the original *Episode I* script, Obi-Wan Kenobi has been sent alone by the chancellor of the Galactic Republic to resolve the Trade Federation's blockade of the peaceful planet of Utapau (there's that name from the original *Star Wars* again). The Trade Federation, persuaded by the mysterious Darth Sidious, a cloaked figure who is able to force-choke Nute Gunray long distance via hologram, attempts to assassinate Kenobi. The lone Jedi Knight escapes to the planet below and rescues a Gungan named Jar Jar Binks (who speaks in regular English sentences). With the help of the Gungan people, *all* of whom speak in regular English sentences, Kenobi travels through the ocean and the planet's core to the city of Naboo on the far side of the planet. There he rescues Queen Amidala and escapes with her retinue in a silver spaceship. Amidala repeatedly resists the notion of traveling with a Gungan. She physically shuns Jar Jar for most of the movie.

With some interesting tension between Amidala and Obi-Wan, our heroes land for repairs on the backwater planet of Tatooine. Padmé, supposedly the queen's handmaiden but in actual fact the queen, is sent to join Obi-Wan and Jar Jar on a mission to look for parts. She deflects unwanted attention from local thugs with a little martial arts. A slave boy named Anakin saves Jar Jar's life and takes them back to his hovel, where he introduces his mother and a droid he's working on: Threepio, who is entirely mute.

Anakin in this draft is full of ominous foresight—he claims to have seen Obi-Wan before, in a dream—and Jesus-like forgiveness of his enemies, who tend to be "in pain." He is wise beyond his years, as when he tells Padmé, "We're helping each other. That's the natural way of things." When Padmé asks Anakin if slavery is natural, Anakin responds: "Of course not. But the stupidity of many creatures is."

He gives her a kiss on the cheek, and they watch the twin suns of Tatooine set.

Before they leave the planet, Obi-Wan is attacked by a Sith Lord called Darth Maul. They have an exciting but inconclusive battle of Jedi powers while "vibrating to the point of becoming almost invisible." A Sith spacecraft follows the queen and the Jedi to Coruscant, the galactic capital and a planet city (the name was taken straight from Timothy Zahn's trilogy). On Coruscant, Anakin is taken for brief Jedi testing by Jedi master Quigon [sic] Jinn. Queen Amidala is refused permission to talk about the invasion of her planet before the Senate, so she gathers her forces and attempts to retake Utapau herself—against Obi-Wan's advice. Padmé and Jar Jar begin to develop common cause. Anakin helps out by evading the planet's blockade—bringing their ship out of hyperspace right above the surface, a miraculous feat that the ship's computers could not have achieved. He is apparently some kind of spatial savant.

The Gungans come to the planet's aid after an impassioned speech by Jar Jar. Again, it's in proper English. "I have traveled far," muses Binks, as wise and solemn as Anakin. "I have seen many wonders. We must become a part of the universe. In isolation, we will die."

He wishes Anakin well before they part for battle: "You are a wonder," says Binks, "and most amusing."

The Gungans attack the droids en masse. Obi-Wan and Quigon, who tagged along from Coruscant, liberate a planetary shield generator from a bunch of Trade Federation battle droids—taking the time to invoke Republic law and declare an illegal occupation. When the droids are defeated, Darth Maul attacks and kills Quigon. Despite the shocking death of his elder Jedi, Kenobi seems perfectly happy to banter with Maul on the topic of education—Lucas's passion ever since he started his educational foundation in 1991—before casually slaughtering him:

> OBI-WAN: *Your style of fighting is old, but I understand it now.*
> MAUL: *You learn fast.*
> OBI-WAN: *You don't bother to learn.*
> MAUL: *I don't have to.*
> OBI-WAN *slices the Sith in half.*
> OBI-WAN: *Learn not, live not, my master always says.*

Anakin and Padmé together deliver the killer blow to the orbital craft, he acting as pilot and her as gunner. There's a funeral for Quigon, for which Yoda flies in, and the old Jedi announces that Obi-Wan can train Anakin. There's a victory parade, for which Utapau senator Palpatine shows up and happens to mention that he's supreme chancellor now, though how he got the role isn't clear.

You'd get a lot of agreement among *Star Wars* fans that what is described in that first draft sounds better than what ended up on the screen. There are only a few exceptions: the banter between Obi-Wan and Darth Maul, which seems inappropriate after the death of Obi-Wan's elder Jedi, and the lack of explanation for Palpatine's elevation. These hiccups were cleaned up in subsequent drafts.

Trouble is, so much else got cleaned up too. Lucas's biggest change was to have Qui-Gon Jinn (now with a hyphen in his name) join Obi-Wan from the start, pushing him out of some scenes and distracting from what might otherwise be Obi-Wan's hero's journey. Obi-Wan was made to stay on the ship during the whole Tatooine sequence, in favor of Qui-Gon, and no longer developed any kind of connection to Anakin. Padmé was delighted by Jar Jar, not repulsed. Anakin was transformed from an ominous young Buddha to an excitable drag racer—more like Lucas at that age, perhaps.

The Jedi Council now had to tell us that the boy seems eerie, because nothing in his actions suggests it any more. Lucas cut a scene in which Watto removes the slave transmitter from Anakin's neck, which would've made him more sympathetic. He cut Anakin's ability to make the ship appear out of hyperspace right next to the planet. Lucas seemed to be doing his damnedest to prevent *Episode I* from being either Anakin's or Obi Wan's hero's journey.

There were changes large and small that dumbed the script down. Lucas added a wise-cracking, two-headed announcer to the pod race, rather than have Jabba the Hutt himself introduce the racers. And then there was the change that would cause Lucas no end of trouble: turning Jar Jar Binks from a wise, exiled, English-speaking Gungan to a clumsy buffoon spouting pidgin English. Lucas says he modeled this new comic relief version of Binks on the great physical comedians of the silent era—Buster Keaton, Charlie Chaplin, Harold Lloyd—with a little Jimmy Stewart and Danny Kaye thrown in for good measure. But in his pratfalls, loping gait, and falsetto voice provided by a black actor, Ahmed Best, critics saw something far less benign: a CGI minstrel show, a "Rastafarian Stepin Fetchit," in the words of the *Wall Street Journal*'s Joe Morgenstern, the first writer to make the comparison in his *Episode I* review. Lucas and Best had to insist repeatedly that was not the intention. "How in the world could you take an orange amphibian and say that he's a Jamaican?" a frustrated Lucas thundered to the BBC shortly after *Episode I* came out. "If you were to say those lines in Jamaican they wouldn't be anything like the way Jar Jar Binks says them." His protests fell on largely deaf ears, however, partly because the problem of unintentionally racist caricatures cropped up twice more in the movie. The Neimodians of the Trade Federation (Nute Gunray and his ilk) actually spoke with a soft Transylvanian accent; critics saw their imperial Chinese–style garb and heard Charlie Chan. Watto was speaking in a manner reminiscent of a gruff Italian shopkeeper; critics noted his trunk-like nose and saw an anti-Semitic cartoon. Lucas was still pulling random items from his grab bag of influences, but this time the influences conspired to make Lucas appear racially tone-deaf.

Why change Binks from sage to comedian in the first place? It seems Lucas was overly concerned about the prequels being darker than the original trilogy. They had to deal with the fall of the Old Republic, the fall of the Jedi, the rise of Vader, his all-but-destruction at the hands of Kenobi, the death of Luke and Leia's mother. Lucas seemed to be compensating with comedic moments, however ham-handedly. It wasn't just that he was trying to be his own Willard Huyck or Lawrence Kasdan–style script polisher and joke teller. A man raising three children may get used to driving the nighttime terrors away with goofy jokes and silly voices.

By the time Lucas had gotten around to the second draft, the movie he swore he would not make for more than $50 million was projected to cost $60 million. By the time he reached the fourth draft, that became $100 million—pretty much Lucas's entire fortune. Once more, Lucas was gambling all his chips. Here was his chance to fund Lucasfilm for a generation, and to beat or come close to James Cameron's *Titanic*, the new king of the box office. (Expected to be a monster flop, Cameron's epic had made a record-breaking $600 million gross in the United States alone in 1997.) But perhaps most importantly, it was a chance to seal Lucas's place in history as a groundbreaking pioneer of digital cinema.

But ILM's digital chops had yet to be tested when it came to creating the wild and wonderful creatures of space fantasy. What if there were a *Star Wars* movie they could practice on? What if they were to give the original movies, say, a digital makeover?

21.

SPECIAL ADDITION

In April 1996, George Lucas attended a dinner at the home of filmmaker and USC friend Matthew Robbins in honor of Arthur Penn, famed director of dozens of films including the Dustin-Hoffman-as-Native-American picture *Little Big Man* (1970). Penn was then in his seventies. The atmosphere was convivial, but Lucas sat down for dinner in a slightly irked mood. Now nearly fifty-two, he had just spent $500,000 on a painting and worried that he had overpaid. He was wistful about the passing of time: "I used to be able to catch the arrows. Now I can't even see them going by," he said. "You wake up in the morning, then you go to bed. If you're lucky you fit in lunch in between."

To a Pulitzer Prize–winning journalist who was present at the dinner, Lucas complained about media criticism of filmmakers, especially the flack Oliver Stone had received in 1992 for embellishing historical details in *JFK*. How could the media judge? They were dealing less and less in reality. Lucas drew a box with his fingers on the table. "We do our work in here," he said, "and they're out there."

Penn talked about the vagaries of filmmaking and how much was up to the fates. *Little Big Man* had been filmed in the snow, but then a Chinook wind came and melted it all. The crew had to wait around a month for more snow, as the temperature plunged to 40 below. They tried a variety of fake snow; nothing worked.

"That's the difference between then and now," said Lucas, suddenly triumphant. If he were in that situation now, he could simply add snow in with CGI. "I'd just make it," he said.

Penn, a filmmaking purist, looked aghast. He didn't say a word, but no none believed he would ever consider upgrading his movie with CGI snow.

But for Lucas, CGI was a natural solution to all the challenges of filmmaking. He'd been an animator, after all—that was the first class he took at USC, and it was the first career path he took outside of USC. By 1996, he was convinced there was nothing digital animation couldn't or shouldn't do.

But an artist, even an animator, needs canvases to practice on. He was a year away from the start of shooting on the still-unnamed *Episode I*, which had been slated for release in 1997. By 1996, it was clear that date would have to be pushed back to 1999. (To compensate, Lucasfilm coordinated an Expanded Universe event in 1996 in which variations on the same story, set after *Empire Strikes Back*, were told in a book, a comic, and a video game of the same name: *Shadows of the Empire*, described as "a movie without a movie.") In the meantime, there was a test bed for what CGI could do for *Star Wars*. Depending on your point of view, Lucas was either about to fix certain things that had long nagged him with modern tools—his equivalent of adding CGI snow to *Little Big Man*—or about to sacrifice his original movie on the altar of his new god, CGI. The truth of it depends a lot on your point of view.

Lucasfilm lore suggests the Special Edition arose as a last-minute idea, and that part of the motivation was Lucas's desire to show his son Jett, who was four years old in 1997, the movies on the big screen. It has also been suggested that Lucas was spending his own money on the *Episode IV* Special Edition. In fact, Lucas and Dennis Muren at ILM had been brainstorming how they might alter the original movie as early as 1993, the year Jett was born. Some restoration work needed to be done anyway; the negative was poor. It had been released in multiple versions. The audio had never been as good as Lucas intended, on neither the stereo nor the mono mixes (which, in any case, had slightly different dialogue). It was time to standardize the editions.

And as for putting up the money, Fox—now owned by Rupert Murdoch—was paying for the *Episode IV* revamp. The studio was happy to do anything Lucas wanted because it would help in the ongoing negotiations for the rights to distribute the prequels. Lucas would eventually give Fox those rights, but not before making Murdoch sweat by entertaining a bid from Warner Brothers.

Lucas had long chafed at the fact that he hadn't been able to finish the original film the way he had wanted to. On one occasion, he called it a half-finished film; on another, he said it represented as little as 25 percent of his vision. "It's like a screen door that doesn't fit right," he explained to *Newsweek*. Initially, the list of shots Lucas and Muren discussed to fix the screen doors was relatively short—somewhere between 24 and 100. Then ILM started pointing out shots that could be cleaned up, or altered, or added, or replaced. By the time the Special Edition was released in January 1997, the number of shots that had been altered in some way climbed to 277. It was as if Lucas had started with the screen door, overshot his goal, and ended up replacing the whole front of the house.

Many of the fixes were extremely minor and only noticeable to film nerds. The wipes between scenes were cleaned up. Luke's landspeeder got a more realistic digital shadow, replacing a hand-drawn black line. The Dia Noga, the monster in the trash compactor, was made to blink in the one shot where you can see its periscope eye. Some twenty-three shots saw minor content alterations, such as the addition of a floating probe droid in Mos Eisley. Another thirty-seven shots received major alterations, the kind that fill most of the frame. And seventeen shots were entirely new to the film.

Most of these completely new shots came in a scene Lucas had shot, but never used, in 1976. It features Han Solo encountering Jabba the Hutt, played by portly actor Declan Mulholland in a shaggy fur vest, just before Han boards the *Millennium Falcon*. The scene adds nothing to the plot that we're not told during Han's fateful meeting with Greedo in the Cantina (which Lucas had specifically extended to cover key information *after* the Jabba scene was cut). Like the deleted scene with Luke and Biggs that would have killed the first reel, the Jabba scene adds a couple of minutes of padding to a taut and exciting action movie.

Did restoring the Jabba sequence approximate Lucas's original intent? The answer isn't a clear-cut one, and it betrays the problem in trying to return to the messy process of making a movie two decades later. Yes, it does seem that Lucas originally considered making Jabba a puppet or stop-motion monster matted into the frame, erasing Mulholland. He asked Fox for an extra $80,000 in 1976 to cover both the Jabba scene and reshoots for the disappointing creature shots in the cantina. When Fox gave him just $40,000, Lucas spent it all on the cantina. He was ambivalent at best about Jabba's appearance. "If I had the money, I might have shot [the Jabba special effect] anyway," he recalled in 1982. "If it still didn't work, I'd have probably cut it out."

The complexity of matting in a figure like Jabba, given that Han Solo has to walk all the way around him during the scene, made the model prohibitively expensive for a perfectionist like Lucas—even when he was rich. For the 1981 rerelease of *Star Wars*, the one in which the movie officially became *Episode IV*, the notion of inserting Jabba went as far as someone in the art department drawing up storyboards. But even then, with Lucasfilm flush from *The Empire Strikes Back*, a special effects version of Jabba was considered either too expensive or too unimportant to even attempt.

Curiously enough, given that she was the one who cut it out of the film, Marcia Lucas was much more gung-ho about the Jabba scene at the time than her husband. Her reasoning? Two words: Harrison Ford. "I thought it was a very virile moment," Marcia said in 1982. "It made him look like a real macho guy. Harrison's performance was very good. I lobbied to keep the scene." She genuinely enjoyed it from an aesthetic filmmaking perspective, too. Lucas uses a long lens to make Ford look sharp and large next to tiny Jabba in the distance. But every other actor in the scene looked like Greedo, she recalled, and "George thought they looked pretty phony, so he had two reasons for wanting to cut the scene, the men and the pacing. You have to pick up the pacing in an action movie like *Star Wars*."

But in 1997, pacing be damned. Lucas was too curious about what he could do with his new toolbox, and naturally those long-ago dreams of a monster Jabba interacting with Han Solo returned. Could his perfectionism be satisfied with CGI? "The thing was to create a real Jabba the Hutt," Lucas told *Wired* in 2005. "Not a big rubber thing, but a digital actual character. I figured if I could do that, then I could do everything else." CGI Jabba, effectively acting as ambassador for Jar Jar Binks, was duly wire-framed in. To our eyes, two decades and a world full of CGI later, the 1997 version of Jabba looks crude, and not in a good old slimy Jabba kind of way. He's oddly antiseptic, unthreatening, and far smaller than the bloated version of the creature seen in *Return of the Jedi*. (Lucas was happy enough with CGI Jabba in 1997 but not in 2004, when the creature got one more digital makeover for the DVD release.) Fan favorite Boba Fett was also inserted into the scene, glaring at the camera at its conclusion—something Lucas most definitely didn't intend in 1976, given that Joe Johnston didn't design Fett until 1978.

There's also one little bit of cleverness too far. In the scene as shot, Harrison Ford walks closely all the way around Mulholland. Lucas could have just had the Jabba character face in a different direction, or move at the right moment to get out of Han's way. Instead, he had Han lifted up so that he appears to be stepping on Jabba's tail. It doesn't quite work from a visual perspective, falling into what roboticists and filmmakers call "the uncanny valley"—the gap between what looks real to our eyes and what looks artificial. It doesn't work from a plot perspective, either. If Han's going to antagonize his business associate by stepping on his rear end, surely there needs to be some motivation for it. Instead, it's just played as slapstick that makes Jabba squeal and his eyes bug out.

There are quite a few new slapstick moments in the Special Edition. Vast beasts called Rontos are all over Mos Eisley, throwing their Jawa riders as if on cue. Dewbacks turn and growl at our heroes at just the right moment. "Those animals moving actually distract from the principal purpose of the scene," Gary Kurtz complained. "If it had been a Western and those were horses, chances are the horses would have just been sitting there, because horses do that a lot." Though he lauded ILM's skills, Kurtz felt that "it does not fit in with the mechanical style of the original film." Phil Tippett, who at this point had been appointed ILM Visual Effects Supervisor, despite not having much love for the new computer-based techniques he was supervising, praised old Mos Eisley for being sparse, Western, and Sergio Leone–like. He once offered a succinct criticism of the CGI additions: "They're shit."*

For many Special Edition viewers, though, none of these alterations mattered as much as one amendment just before the Jabba encounter, during Han and Greedo's confrontation in the Mos Eisley cantina. In the 1976 shooting script, when Greedo is threatening Han over some cargo for Jabba that apparently never got delivered, here's how the scene was written:

> GREEDO: *I've waited for this moment a long time.*
> HAN: *Yes, I'll bet you have.*
> *Suddenly the slimy alien disappears in a blinding flash of light. Han pulls*
> *his smoking gun from beneath the table as the other patrons look on in*
> *bemused amazement. Han gets up and starts out of the cantina, flipping*
> *the bartender some coins as he leaves.*

Most moviegoers in 1977 saw that as a classic Western scene—the saloon gunfighter pulls a fast one on the bad guy and then casually compensates the

---

* In 2014, when he was apparently in discussions about returning to work at Lucasfilm on *Episode VII*, Tippett told me he'd been "kind of playing to the crowd" when he made that choice summary. "I didn't particularly care for the Special Editions," he said, "but I didn't really care one way or the other." He's still not quite sold on the value of CGI, despite running a CGI shop at Tippett Studios: "It's amazing what limitations can do for one's imagination," he says. "The big fish doesn't work in *Jaws*; the alien doesn't work in *Alien*. What do you do? You have to work really hard to create suspense."

barkeep for the mess. But in the 1997 version, Greedo was made to shoot a beat before Han, just missing his head. Han's shot was thus more clearly self-defense (although given that Greedo was pointing a gun at him and had just said Han was a dead man, it seems unlikely any court would have convicted Solo for murder in this situation).

After controversy erupted among *Star Wars* fans over the shot, Lucas changed the scene again. In the 2011 Blu-Ray version of *Star Wars*, the definitive version as far as Lucasfilm is concerned, Greedo's shot is moved forward by eleven frames—so that he and Solo shoot practically at the same time. In a 2012 interview, Lucas claimed for the first time that in 1976 he had intended Greedo to shoot back—and evidently to miss at point-blank range.

The fan outrage over what became known as the "Han shot first" controversy (though that's a misnomer, since Greedo didn't shoot at all originally—it would be better to call it "Han shot solo") isn't all that interesting. What is interesting is how much Lucasfilm seems to have done to stoke the controversy over the following years. In 2005, Lucas was photographed on the set of *Revenge of the Sith* wearing a "Han Shot First" T-shirt; he wore it again for 2007's *Indiana Jones and the Kingdom of the Crystal Skull*. A number of ILM animators kept "Han Shot First" postcards above their cubicles while working on the prequel trilogy. Lucasfilm has approved *Star Wars* spin-offs across many forms of media that include winking references to the controversy as well. Multiple novels and videos—even the Lego *Star Wars* series—have made reference to Han shooting first and to Greedo's terrible aim (Lego Greedo is seen in the cantina performing poorly at darts). "It's Solo, and he's shooting first!" Stormtroopers exclaim in the 2005 video game *Battlefront II*. "That's not fair!"

Changes aside, Lucas worried that the rerelease of the original film would barely make its money back. The reason? "We hadn't sold very many VHS tapes," he said in 2005. Although the video-buying public was warned that this was their last chance to own the original *Star Wars* on VHS, the 1995 release, Lucas says, only sold about three hundred thousand copies—or rather, the company had a "perception" that that's how well they'd done. "Which is nothing compared to the 11 million that *ET* did," he added, still focused on the friendly rivalry with Spielberg. "So I said that this would be an experiment, and hopefully we'll get our money back." (Perhaps for the sake of a good story, Lucas was minimizing his success: a total of thirty-five million VHS copies of *Star Wars* movies were sold by 1997.)

Fox would end up spending $7 million to do the restoration and digital work for the Special Edition and another $3 million enhancing the sound. The outlay

on the *Star Wars* Special Edition would be just short of the budget of the original film. But the expenditure was worth it—for Lucasfilm and its backers,
at least. The Special Edition release on January 31, 1997, would bring in more
than triple Fox's investment in its opening weekend alone—$30 million more
than its closest competitor, *Jerry Maguire*. In total, this re-re-re-rerelease of
Episode IV alone grossed $138 million in the United States and another $118
million abroad.

We have reached what is in many ways the tipping point of the whole *Star
Wars* franchise. In 1996, *Star Wars* had not conquered our cultural universe. It
may have become a best-selling title at the bookstore and in video games, and
the original movies were certainly remembered fondly, with more movies on
the horizon. But nobody had taken the temperature of the entire culture to see
how much of a *Star Wars* fever it had. Once it was clear the series had power
and longevity, to the point where it could make $90 million of pure profit from
the restoration of one old movie—once it was proved a decades-old movie could
completely dominate the box office and embarrass a really good contemporary
movie like *Jerry Maguire*—everything changed. All of the forms of fandom
explored in this book—the 501st, the Jedi Realists, the R2 Builders Club, and
more besides—got their start around or just after 1997. Lucas, formerly a mere
multimillionaire still struggling to pay off a divorce settlement, was secure and
firmly on the road to billionairehood after 1997. And of course, this is the tipping point of CGI, which was to slowly swallow *Star Wars* special effects from
this point on.

The release of the Special Edition immediately touched off a debate in the
media; stories cropped up everywhere about Lucas, and other artists, retroactively changing their own work. We were invited to consider the French
painter Pierre Bonnard, arrested for retouching his oil paintings in Paris's Lux-
embourg Museum; Bruckner revising his symphonies; Frank Zappa rerecord-
ing bass and drum parts for *Mothers of Invention* CDs. The same month as the
Episode IV Special Edition was released, a controversial Super Bowl ad showed
Fred Astaire dancing on the ceiling with a Dirt Devil in his hand. The era of
the digital retread had apparently begun.

Rick McCallum was wheeled out to make the case for Lucas. "Does a filmmaker have the right to go back and get the film the original way he envisioned
it?" he asked the *Chicago Tribune*. "Ask any director if he wanted to go back and
fix a film, because of all the compromises he had to make, and he would."

Outraged fans countered arguments like these by digging up testimony
Lucas had given to Congress in March 1988, when he had gone along with

Spielberg to protest a then hot-button issue: Ted Turner's colorization of classic movies, including classics such as John Huston's *The Maltese Falcon*. Huston had protested to no effect; he no longer held the copyright. Lucas was incensed. "People who alter or destroy works of art and our cultural heritage for profit or as an exercise of power are barbarians," he fumed. "In the future it will become even easier for old negatives to become lost and be 'replaced' by new altered negatives. This would be a great loss to our society."

Lucas's testimony had another theme running through it, however—a theme that Lucas has been remarkably consistent on throughout his life: the power of the creator to be the ultimate arbiter of his work. Could Huston himself have colorized *The Maltese Falcon* two decades after releasing it, if he'd so wished? For Lucas, the answer would have to be yes.

The more troubling aspect of the whole affair—with shades of *1984*—was the fact that Lucas's original negative was to remain hidden away from the public at Skywalker Ranch, with instructions that it never be shown. "To me, it doesn't really exist any more," Lucas said in 2004. Luckily, the 1977 negative has also been preserved in the Library of Congress's National Film Registry, which has now made a high-definition 4K digital transfer of it. The Library of Congress has never screened it, because the rights holder—Lucasfilm—will not allow it. Researchers can make appointments to view it at the Moving Image Research Center in Washington, DC. But for the casual viewer, it may as well not exist. Pull a DVD or Blu-Ray off the shelf, and you're getting the Special Edition, albeit in a slightly different version depending on when you bought it.

Lucas's stubbornness on his right to keep digitally altering his films put him out of step with his friends. Spielberg digitally altered *ET* for its twentieth anniversary edition in 2002, turning the guns of FBI agents into walkie-talkies; he later declared that he was "disappointed in myself" for doing so, and reverted to the original version for the Blu-Ray release. But even the changed version of *ET* had been sold alongside the original as part of a two-disc DVD set. Dennis Muren, the ILM mastermind who got the ball rolling on the Special Edition, assumed the same would happen with *Star Wars*: "I felt that so long as the originals were around for people to see that redoing them was okay," he said in 2004.

But that was never Lucas's intention. Drawing a contrast with *Blade Runner*—which he derided as having been released "six ways from Sunday"—Lucas insisted that there was only one *Star Wars*. All the accumulated changes piled on over the years—the 1978 audio remixing, the 1981 "Episode IV" addition, the 1997 Special Edition, the 2004 DVD release, the 2006 DVD rerelease, the 2011

Blu-Ray release—all amounted to a single film slowly progressing toward reali-zation. The time gap didn't matter; approximating the Creator's original intent, as determined by the Creator, was all that counted. In 1997, Lucas pointed out that the VHS tapes would degrade in a few decades; the Special Edition would remain in digital form for future generations. His attitude never changed, and he would only grow more tetchy on the topic. Here's what Lucas had to say to fans in 2004:

> I'm sorry you saw a half completed film and fell in love with it. But I want it to be the way I want it to be. I'm the one who has to take respon-sibility for it. I'm the one who has to have everybody throw rocks at me all the time, so at least if they're going to throw rocks at me, they're going to throw rocks at me for something I love rather than something I think is not very good, or at least something I think is not finished.

After multiple online petitions for such a thing gained tens of thousands of signatures, a poor quality version of the 1977 print was placed on a bonus disc as part of the 2006 DVD rerelease. Lucas insisted that he would not spend the millions necessary to restore it. So fans did it for him—in an incalculable num-ber of digitally altered "despecialized editions" available in the darker corners of the Internet, each one slightly different from the next, according to the whims of the editor. Lucas's insistence on a single standardized version of *Star Wars* has, ironically, led to *Star Wars* being available six hundred ways from Sunday.

A month after the first Special Edition hit theaters in late January 1997, Lucasfilm released a Special Edition of *Empire Strikes Back*. The film quickly claimed the number 1 box office position from its predecessor. It con-tained few noticeable changes, other than dubbing in Ian McDiarmid's voice for the hologram of the Emperor (his face would not be added until the DVD version in 2004) and fleshing out the Wampa that attacks Luke on the ice planet of Hoth—another monster breathing a little bit more life. Otherwise, it merely cleaned up the special effects. Was Lucas still displaying reverence toward Kersh, or was this a recognition that *Empire* was the most perfect film in the series and didn't need any amendments?

Certainly, there was a little less reverence displayed toward *Return of the Jedi*. For that rerelease, Lucas replaced the music sequence in Jabba's Palace—a three-minute song called "Lapti Nek," which had been written by *Hardware*

Wars' Ernie Fosselius and performed by a puppet called Sy Snootles—with a CGI Snootles singing a song called "Jedi Rocks," written by jazz trumpeter Jerry Hey. Snootles's band gained nine new CGI members. (To be fair to Lucas, even "Lapti Nek" had been a replacement for a track written by John Williams and sung by his son; it was a song derided by Richard Marquand for being "a little bit too disco.") Most crucially for the plot, Lucas added scenes of celebration around the galaxy after the second Death Star was destroyed, conveying for the first time the notion that the Empire actually had been fully defeated. (The Expanded Universe, the existence of which largely depended on the Empire *not* being defeated at the end of the movie, fought back. The comic book *Mara Jade: By the Emperor's Hand* featured one Imperial officer telling another that they'd rounded up all subversives involved in "victory" celebrations.)

The special editions of *Empire* and *Jedi* cost roughly $5 million each, with Lucasfilm footing the bill for both. They grossed $67 million and $45 million in the United States, respectively, and $57 million and $44 million abroad. The *Episode IV* special edition was so popular that it would help the movie regain the title of highest grossing film of all time from Spielberg's *ET*.* That ongoing rivalry between the two friends' highest-grossing movies might help explain why Lucas was so insistent on having one definitive version of *Star Wars*. If the 1977 and 1997 versions were counted separately, Lucas would never have regained the top spot.

It would have been hard for the heads of Lucasfilm not to absorb the lesson that the more bold and controversial the CGI, the bigger the gross. "The success of that rerelease not only told me that I could create these creatures and build better sets and towns than I could before," said Lucas in 2005, "but that the *Star Wars* audience was still alive—it hadn't completely disappeared after 15 years. I decided that if I didn't do the backstory then, I never would. So I committed to it."

Lucas's chronology here may be a little confused. By 1997, he was as deeply committed to *Episode I* as he had been to the original movie. He was into his third calendar year of writing, and his third draft, when the Special Edition came out. He had, in fact, confirmed that he himself would be directing the still-untitled movie back in September 1996.

Character designs such as the villainous Sith, Darth Maul, had been fully fleshed out by that time; concept designer Ian McCaig had been asked to draw

---

* *Star Wars* would hold the title only fleetingly. James Cameron's *Titanic* set sail in December 1997. Destination: highest-grossing movie of all time, until the next one.

the scariest thing he could think of. Lucas deemed the result, a pasty white crea-ture with blood-red ribbons for his hair, too scary by far. Back at the drawing board, McCaig sketched out his second-scariest idea, a circus clown in black and red makeup, feathers tied to his head with elastic, a feature that McCaig said would make him irritable. When feathers became horns, one of the most iconic characters of the prequels sprung to life. For a weapon Maul was given a double-bladed lightsaber, originally designed by artist Christian Gossett for the Expanded Universe comic *Tales of the Jedi*. Gossett would have to expend some energy in later years proving that he came up with the concept for the comic and had it approved by Lucas in 1994 and that it had not, as another designer once claimed in an interview, sprung from Lucas's imagination.

Meanwhile, casting director Robin Gurland had been rounding up actors since 1995. This time, it seemed like less consideration was given to the chemis-try between the actors and more to getting the biggest names imaginable. There wasn't an actor on the planet uninterested in appearing in the next *Star Wars* movie. In December 1996, Samuel L. Jackson had announced his intention to be cast in the movie on the British TV chat show *TFI Friday*. Jackson won his campaign some six months later, along with the Academy Award–nominated star of *Schindler's List* (1994), Liam Neeson, and rising teen actor Natalie Port-man. Ian McDiarmid would return to play Senator Palpatine, this time without makeup—he was finally the right age. Jake Lloyd, an eight-year-old who had been cast as Arnold Schwarzenegger's son in the holiday movie *Jingle All the Way* (1996), would play Anakin. Ewan McGregor, who had just burst onto the international scene with *Trainspotting* (1996), rounded out the big-name princi-pals, this who's-who of 1990s cinema.

A major fan of the original trilogy, McGregor recalled playing all the parts in the playground as a child, including Princess Leia. He said he'd been "deeply in love" with Leia for many years. Part of what sold Lucas on McGregor was his family connection to the original trilogy: his uncle, Denis Lawson, had played Wedge Antilles, the only Rebel pilot to survive all three films. Lightsaber-fighting on the set one day, switching from the clipped tones of Alec Guinness to his thick Perthshire accent as soon as Lucas's assistant yelled, "Cut," McGregor recalled the moment he got the casting call: "'Do you want to do *Star Wars?*' they said. I said, 'Too fucking right.'"

He wouldn't be quite so enthusiastic when he saw the result.

22.

THE LINE

The filming of *Episode I*—directed, according to its mischievous clapper-boards, by "Yoda"—began on June 26, 1997. Though Lucasfilm had leased Leavesden Studios in London for two and a half years, nearly all of that time was set aside for the grab bag of occasional last-minute shots known as "pick-ups." Lucas and producer Rick McCallum prided themselves on efficiency, and principal photography was finished by the end of September. Nearly all of it was shot against a green screen, except for location shoots in Tunisia (once again standing in for Tatooine and once again struck by a freak storm during shooting), Italy (for Queen Amidala's palace), and a park in Watford, ten minutes' drive from the studios. That was it. Lucas was perplexed when McGregor asked whether they'd be shooting the underwater scenes under water. "This isn't real," the digital director reminded the actor.

With a fledgling Internet full of fans hunting for details on the movie, security was tight. Actors would only receive the pages of the scenes they were working on. All pages had to be returned at the end of the day. Everyone on set had to sign confidentiality agreements, for which Lucasfilm was fast becoming famous.

The tightly controlled script was entirely Lucas's work—although that's not necessarily how he had wanted it. *Young Indiana Jones* writer Frank Darabont had at one point been approached to do a polish on the script, and he had agreed readily but never got the call; he did at least get to read the script and view a rough cut of the movie in advance. His fellow *Young Indy* alumnus Jonathan Hale was also mentioned by McCallum as a possible writer, but he wasn't even approached—not for this movie, anyway. Meanwhile, apparently eager for his old protégé's help, Lucas approached Lawrence Kasdan in June, shortly before shooting began, and asked him to take a second pass at a script that was already on its fourth draft and about to be filmed. Kasdan gave a polite but firm no. It wasn't just that he was a director in his own right now—it was that as a director, he recognized that it was important for this whole trilogy of prequels to kick off exactly according to Lucas's vision. "I thought he should take responsibility and make exactly the movie he wanted to make," Kasdan told *Eon* magazine, "and that's exactly what he did." Lucas later rationalized it: sure, Kasdan could "write better dialogue" and "better transitions," he said, but Lucas realized Kasdan would have insisted on what a lot of Lucas's friends were already telling him: "don't start the prequels with the story of a nine-year-old boy."

In London, Lucas spent more time in closed-circuit video conference calls with ILM back in San Rafael than he did directing the actors. The ILM-Lucas nexus was intended to be a symbiotic relationship of the kind the film was constantly referencing: ILM would create the digital background, Lucas would approve it, and fresh from that meeting he would describe to the actors what they were going to be playing against. ILM was feeling the pressure of 1,900 special effects shots, many of them featuring a kind of effect never done before. Notes were taped to doors quoting McCallum: "The film is going to come out in May 1999 no matter what."

It wasn't exactly a recipe for success. The set could feel like a prison; the actors were chosen for their names and past performances rather than their chemistry with each other. They had not been allowed to read the entire script, had no real idea what the story was, and barely even knew what environment they were supposed to be standing in. The film's director hadn't directed in twenty-two years; he tended to retreat into documentary style—just letting the actors do it the way they were going to do it—and was far more concerned about the technology he was using and its impact on the world than he was about the human dimensions of the film itself. ("I definitely feel a part of the transformation of cinema," Lucas told a press conference in July.) He fixated on details like whether Jar Jar was going to be an entirely CGI character or whether some of actor Ahmed Best's on-set suit was going to have to be used for more than reference. That take Natalie Portman just did? "Great," Lucas surmised, walking away from the set with McCallum one day early in the shoot. "Just great."

Portman and her fellow actors, fully aware of history's gaze, were stiffening up and giving the most somber performances of their careers. If they hadn't been instructed to speak in monotone, they were doing a good impression of it. But that was okay, because the director—who admitted he writes wooden dialogue and whose script had been vetted by precisely no one—wasn't listening to the words. To him this was music, a tone poem, a silent movie.

Perhaps the actors should have challenged him the way Harrison Ford used to; perhaps they should have worked their lines a little like Alec Guinness. But any such innovation was tough, even for the veteran actors, given their separation from each other. (Terence Stamp, playing the outgoing chancellor of the Galactic Senate opposite Natalie Portman, never actually worked with Portman. He had to emote to a piece of paper that marked where she would be standing.) Besides, at this stage in the Creator's career, which of the actors would dare talk back? "Now he's so exalted," Mark Hamill lamented about Lucas in 2005, "that no one tells him anything." Better to make their physical performance really sing. Swing those lightsabers, boys. (One actor who thrived on set: martial arts expert Ray Park, who played the dual-lightsaber-wielding villain Darth Maul.)

It wasn't just that the actors were being asked to perform in what was surely the most sterile, stilted environment of their careers. The film's producer agreed with everything the director wanted, and he would move heaven and earth to make it happen. The film's key performance came from a nine-year-old boy. Jake Lloyd was carrying the weight of the film and needed to convince the audience his character is something special, the product of a literal virgin birth, a potential Darth Vader—yet there he was, suffering from exhaustion in 125-degree Tunisian heat. The first generation of *Star Wars* fans, meanwhile, had been ginned up by the Special Editions and had inducted a new generation of fans—their kids—in the process. The media—especially a nascent online media—was chomping at the bit for a single grainy photo from the set. It was a level of anticipation few movies in history could actually have met.

In retrospect, it's amazing *Episode I* turned out as well as it did.

I n early 1999, ILM hosted a screening of the rough cut of what had now been named *The Phantom Menace*, a name reminiscent of the radio serials Lucas listened to as a kid. Documentary cameras caught the pall that descended over the viewers, Lucas's brain trust, as the credits rolled and the lights went up. They caught anxious looks and hair pulling.

After a few moments, Lucas speaks: "It's bold in terms of jerking people around, but . . . I may have gone too far in a few places."

Sound designer Ben Burtt, one of the longest-serving and most trusted Lucasfilm employees in the room, offers this reaction: "In the space of ninety seconds you go from lamenting the death of a hero to escape to slightly comedic with Jar Jar, to Anakin returning. . . . It's a lot."

"It boggles the mind," Lucas admits. "I've thought about this quite a bit, and the tricky part is you can't take any of those pieces out."

They were talking about the final few reels of the movie, which intercut four scenes: the Jedi versus Darth Maul, Anakin versus the Trade Federation station, Team Amidala versus the Trade Federation, Gungans versus the battle droids. It's an incredibly ambitious sequence, and yet Lucas was locked into its structure—which had become part of a pattern. The first *Star Wars* movie had one action scene at the end: the attack on the Death Star, spliced with reaction shots on board the station and back at the rebel base. *Empire* intercut two action scenes at the end: Luke's lightsaber battle with Vader, and Leia, Chewie, and Lando escaping Cloud City. *Return of the Jedi* ended on three simultaneous action sequences: Han and Leia and the Ewoks on the moon of Endor; Luke, Vader, and the Emperor battling it out aboard the second Death Star; Lando leading the rebel fleet's assault on the fully operational battle station.

So how could *Phantom Menace* not attempt to intercut four action sequences?

And yet even Lucas, who had been driving his special effects company to do the impossible for the past two years, seemed to know this was a step too far. To McCallum, shortly after the screening, Lucas expanded his comments to the film as a whole. "It is a very hard movie to follow," he said. "I have done it more extremely than I did in the past. It's stylistically designed to be that way, and you can't undo that, but you can diminish the effects of it. We can slow it down a little bit."

For the first time in his career, then, the "faster and more intense" director set about making a movie slower and less intense. At the same time, scenes that could do with a little more speed and intensity—specifically, the sitting around and talking scenes on Coruscant and in the Galactic Senate—were kept pretty much as they were. With four weeks to go, ILM was still working on the final parade scene; sound editing continued until a week before release. Even with all the resources of Skywalker Ranch, with tech geniuses and animation gurus aplenty, another *Star Wars* movie went down to the wire in almost the same way as the first.

This time the fans came to the Coronet early, more than a month ahead of the first screening on May 19, 1999. They came from all over. Chris Giunta moved from Maryland to San Francisco with his girlfriend, Beth, specifically so he could see *Episode I* at the theater where George Lucas liked to hold screenings, the theater that had become famous among fans: the Coronet, ground zero for the *Star Wars* phenomenon. Giunta found a job at Bank of America fixing ATMs and told his boss when he started that he would have to take off most of April and May 1999. When his boss found out why, he laughed and then asked, "Can you get me a ticket?"

In early April, Giunta started driving past the Coronet every other day to see if the line had begun. When he saw a tent appear for the first time, he rushed home to get his own camping gear. He returned to the Coronet, but the tent had mysteriously vanished. The lady at the box office had no idea where it had gone, but she saw no problem with him pitching his own tent at what was, presumably, the front of the line. Giunta slept there overnight and had just eaten his packed breakfast when a sedan rolled up hard, jumping the curb in front of him. A couple of guys shot out and started grilling Giunta: Who are you? Why are you here? What group are you with?

This was Frank Parisi, a video game reviewer, and his friend Shanti Seigel, and they had spent the last six months planning their *Phantom Menace* line strategy, mostly with a group called the Fraternal Order of Bounty Hunters. The friends had met and bonded on this very spot outside the Coronet for the Special Editions, near the front of the line. Seigel had been going to the Coronet since he saw *Empire Strikes Back* there at the age of four, and loved one seat in the theater more than any other—third row, seat 6—so much that he'd carved his name into it years before. "Everybody had different motivations for why they were planning to camp out," Seigel says. "Some people wanted to be first; some people wanted to do it for the glory; some people just wanted to have fun. I didn't give a shit about any of that. I just needed to make sure I got to sit in my seat for the opening show."

Seigel kept upping the ante on how early he, Parisi, and another friend would start camping out. Figuring *everyone* would arrive with tents in tow a month beforehand—including the Bounty Hunters, whom they could get a jump on— Seigel finally settled on a start date of eleven pm on April 15, or six weeks ahead of the release date. He was right; they were first. The trio stayed there for all of two days before the police kicked them off the sidewalk. Giunta had showed up two days after that, when Parisi spotted him and called Seigel, and that's when they did their *Starsky and Hutch* act with the car on the sidewalk. "Once we found out he was just some screwball lone wolf," Seigel says, "we immediately dropped our guard and befriended him." They all camped out together that night, and then the police kicked them all off again in the morning.

That's when another faction appeared on the scene, comprised of followers of Counting Down, a now defunct website that began as little more than a big clock ticking down the hours until the first midnight showing of *The Phantom Menace*. It soon became a clearing house for rumors about the movie—a nascent online community for the mostly male twentysomethings camping out in New York, LA, and San Francisco. More importantly, the Counting Down guys were the only ones with the foresight to get a $700 urban camping permit from city hall before they pitched tents outside the Coronet.

Team Counting Down invited all the other early campers to a summit meeting at the Round Table pizza next door to the Coronet. The factions of this fractious line were invited to unite. They devised a shift system: everyone who took a twenty-five-hour shift over the coming month would get one ticket. Giunta needed twelve tickets, so he signed up for twelve shifts. Everyone called him crazy. "Well," he explained, "I was going to do more than that anyway." Seigel declared that any night anyone else was camping, he would be there too.

Parisi came to the Coronet most days and kept Giunta company, talking movies. Some local hippie mom dropped her kid off at the line during the day; the line judged him the spitting image of Anakin Skywalker. "The kid goes to the front of the line," declared Parisi. "L'il Anakin" became a mascot; he forced the rest of the waiting fans to maintain good behavior and to tone down the drinking a notch or two. The truce of the factions held.

The line endured chilly summer wind and relentless fog. "It was nightmarish at night," said Todd Evans, one of the Counting Down guys who became best friends with Parisi. "But it was like summer camp for movie fiends." They stood firm when drivers on Geary stopped and yelled, "Get a life!" They weathered drive-by water balloonings and, on one particularly sticky occasion, an attack with a balloon filled with maple syrup. They took it in their stride when a local radio station, Wild 107, paid *Star Wars* fan Khari "Krazy K" Crowder to camp outside the Coronet for a month—in a well-appointed luxury van. The final indignity of the line warriors' struggle was that there wasn't even anything good on at the Coronet during that long month: only a Hollywood horror comedy, with all the quality that implies—a critical and commercial flop called *Idle Hands*. It was so bad, in fact, that Evans tried to watch it and left, preferring to sleep outside in the blustery cold. "And I never walk out of movies," he says.

If any passerby was ignorant enough to ask what they were waiting for, they'd point to the marquee. "*Idle Hands*," they'd say, deadpan. "We're camping out for tickets to *Idle Hands*."

Word of the line soon spread. Asian tourists came by the busload to take pictures of the happy few line warriors; one of whom, Travis, began making himself up as a note-perfect Darth Maul, yellow contacts and all. "We started to be the backdrop for local news," remembers Giunta. Round Table offered the line goers free pizza; the owner of a local bagel shop gave them a place to shower above the store. REI donated tents; IBM gave the line three Thinkpad laptops to share. Counting Down installed a T-1 line in a nearby copy shop and ran cables out the front door so the line had high-speed Internet, still a rarity in 1999. And what did the guys in line do with all this equipment? They watched a pirated copy of the *Star Wars Holiday Special*.

The number of the pay phone next to the Coronet was posted on Counting Down. Fans would call from as far away as Ireland, and the group outside the theater would take turns answering it. A rather odd young guy just out of high school named AJ Napper ran up and down the line yelling, reenacting Han Solo's famous Death Star battle cry as he chased, and was then chased by, a contingent of Stormtroopers. AJ started doing it every hour on the hour to relieve the monotony. Eventually, someone felt compelled to trip him up. Most evenings they'd all go to a dive bar over on Clement Street called the Other Place. The bartender gave all line warriors a 50 percent discount, and they invented a signature cocktail, the Flaming Darth Maul: Aftershock, Jaegermeister and/ or black vodka, and 151 rum on the top so you could set it on fire. Parisi got twisted drunk and stood on the bar tearing his shirt off and toasting, "To all my friends!" Seigel downed enough drinks another night that he almost considered letting a friend drive him home. Luckily, Giunta reminded him that his place was in the line, and Seigel was able to stagger back to his tent before passing out. Had he left, "I would have regretted it to this day," Seigel says.

A week before the midnight show came the great temptation. The Coronet hosted a special cast and crew screening for ILM and assorted VIPs. George Lucas showed up with his kids and shook a few hands. Everyone in the line tried desperately to play it cool, but some remember AJ rushing up to and gushing over Lucas. Robin Williams had a cunning tactic for getting in unmolested: he had a guy approach the theater dressed as Robby the Robot from *Forbidden Planet*, while Williams attempted to run in under cover. But AJ tracked him down, too.

Then, when all the celebrities and employees were inside and the doors shut, a Lucasfilm rep whispered to the kid and the guys at the front: "Okay, there are a few seats left; go in if you want." Tickets to an exclusive afterparty at the Marin Civic Center were included in the deal.

The members of the line paused. "Everybody looked at each other and said, 'These people are brothers in arms, committed to standing there every single day rain or shine,'" Evans remembered. They made a pact: anyone who went in now would be out of the opening-night line. Still, a whole bunch of line warriors took the Faustian bargain—including the kid. L'il Anakin went to the Dark Side, they said.

Those who went into the cast-and-crew screening missed a key warning sign: Francis Coppola exiting the theater with a large cigar, with which he proceeded to take a half-hour break. Giunta tried sneakily taking a selfie with his favorite director in the world in the background, but Coppola came up and smacked him. "If you want a proper picture, come over here," he said. The line got its fill of photos and then asked: Why was he missing the movie? Coppola shrugged: "I've seen bits of it before." *Bits* of it? Why wouldn't he want to watch *all* of it? But this was a time of innocence, a time of the firm belief that anything with the name *Star Wars* had to be golden, and so the line shrugged and kept on waiting.

Those who remained in line throughout the screening would receive incredible gifts from Lucasfilm. They remember some kindly lady, a veteran of the *Star Wars* fan club, driving a pick up truck to the Coronet with a six-foot chunk of the original foam-core Death Star trench from 1977; she took a hacksaw and started dispensing pieces of it to the line, which received it as if it were the true cross. Lucas had a Chewbacca-shaped chocolate ice cream cake delivered to the line. Producer Rick McCallum came to hang out with the guys a few times. Giunta got a special FedEx delivery to the line from his mom and hid it from Beth when she came to visit. But the fans who resisted the urge to enter the theater also had to suffer spoilers—particularly the moment when L'il Anakin, whom they couldn't shoo away, pointed to Travis, dressed as Darth Maul, and screamed, "You die!" The line warriors drew a collective sharp intake of breath.

Finally, the big day arrived. Evans coordinated a costume contest judged by the cross-dressing Sisters of Perpetual Indulgence, a San Francisco institution. Naturally, Travis as Darth Maul won. A dot-com founder came by—this was the height of the dot-com era—and gave everyone multicolored lightsabers. Evans dressed for the evening in tuxedo, though it was hard to maintain a cool façade. "Frank started doing this nervous bouncing, like a fighter before his Vegas title fight, just twitching with anticipation, and I was feeding off him," said Evans. When they opened the doors, no one can quite remember who was first in. Some say it was Krazy K from the radio station, carrying L'il Anakin in his arms. Parisi beat Evans in the door, but Parisi stopped to kiss the carpet in the lobby, and Evans ran straight past him.

Once inside the theater, the crowd was manic with excitement. The line warriors had an hour of mock lightsaber battles. One guy who'd perversely dressed as Captain Picard from *Star Trek* was chased up and down the aisles. Finally they sat and chanted for the movie they wanted: *"Idle Hands! Idle Hands!"*

Chris Giunta, who had served those extra shifts so he could bring his girlfriend, Beth, and ten other friends to the screening, had a surprise in store for Beth and the rest of the fans. Rick McCallum showed up at the front of the theater. The producer took one look at the packed house, the first in San Francisco to see the movie he'd worked on for nearly five years, and spread his arms wide: "This is fucking awesome." The line warriors cheered. Then McCallum asked if there was a Beth in the house. "I hate you," Giunta's girlfriend whispered—smiling, crying. Giunta, wearing Jedi robes, brought her up to the front of the theater and proposed to her with the ring his grandmother wore, the ring his mother had FedExed to the line. Beth said yes. The line warriors exploded. They ran out of the preferred seats they'd been planning and arguing over for months and rushed the couple in a giant group hug.

You could not have asked for an audience in a better mood as the lights went down and the Fox fanfare began. "Electricity was tingling in everyone's fingers," remembers Evans. "It was like the big bang, all this kinetic energy exploding in one giant release of fanboys all over the audience. Just this giant psychic orgasm."

Like all good things, the elation didn't last. After the movie, everyone trooped out of the theater, somewhat stunned. Outside, a TV crew was interviewing the luminaries of the line. What did they think? Was it all worth it? Giunta, his new fiancée on his arm, said he'd have to see it again to form an opinion. Evans still had images of pod racing and lightsabers dancing in his head and no coherent opinion just yet. Only one guy provided a concise sound bite. At fifteen years distance, no one can quite remember who it was; Giunta thought it was Parisi, who thought it was Seigel, who thought it was Travis. But they all remember what he said, the moment this aggrieved fan pushed past his friends, looked straight in the camera, and offered a choice three-word review of *Episode I*.

"Shit. Fucking. Sandwich," he yelled, and sulked off into the night.

23.

THE PREQUELS CONQUER *STAR WARS*

On May 25, 1977, the day the first *Star Wars* film had been released, the *San Francisco Chronicle* didn't mention the film until page 51. On May 19, 1999, by contrast, the paper was shot through with it. The NATO bombing of Kosovo, President Clinton's $15 billion spending request, the passage of a post-Columbine bill on child safety handgun locks: none of this made the front page. Instead, a giant headline wondered where the reclusive Lucas had gone on his big day: Back to Hawaii? (In fact, he was preparing for a vacation to Europe with his kids.)

Inside the *Chronicle*, readers could find an editorial titled "May the Hype Be with You" and an editorial cartoon showing a world filled with *Star Wars* signage. The city's board of supervisors had just voted in a ban on the sale of laser pointers to children, because parents "believe these pointers can help their children imitate Luke Skywalker," placing them at increased risk of blinding each other. A giant feature marveled at the 2,200 special effects shots in the movie and wondered—as everyone in the industry was wondering—whether cinema had just effectively gone digital. (In fact, less of the movie was constructed by computers than viewers suspected; the spaceship models were still real, and the world was years away from the debut of CGI Yoda.)

The movie's soundtrack was reviewed in the arts section: "the score's most delightful stretch is the bouncy undulating stroll associated with Jar Jar Binks, the Gungan with attitude," it enthused. At the other end of the emotional spectrum, John Williams's *Duel of the Fates* had already become the first classical work in MTV's music video rotation. It was bombastic, ominous, choral, and it would inspire the presence of apocalyptic choirs in Hollywood soundtracks for years to come. Williams's music, the oxygen of *Star Wars*, was still operating at peak flow.

The scene at the Coronet had been repeated across the country; every local news outfit had a reporter standing in front of the lines of lawn chairs and sleeping bags. Many had helicopters flying overhead. One Oregon station ran this shocking news: a local theater had only *four* fans camping outside.

In 1977, *Star Wars* had opened on 32 screens. In 1999, *The Phantom Menace* opened on 7,700. Fox spent around $50 million advertising it, which was actually a low figure for such a major movie; the media was doing its job for them. That helped, because Fox was only getting 7.5 percent of the ticket gross, less than a third of its regular percentage. And Lucas? It was widely believed that the movie was about to make him a billionaire.

Lucas may have already passed that milestone by this point, based purely on the merchandising deals. Hasbro paid $400 million for the rights to make toys based on the movie—and they weren't even exclusive rights. Lego had jumped into the *Star Wars* universe with the first licensing deal in the Danish toy giant's fifty-year history; this despite the fact that one of the company's vice presidents had declared two years earlier that Lego would license *Star Wars* "over my dead body." The CEO, himself a *Star Wars* fan, won his executives over by commissioning surveys of parents in the United States and Germany that revealed a vast majority would purchase Lego *Star Wars* sets if they were available. Sure enough, more than $2 billion worth of *Star Wars* Legos were sold in 1999 and 2000, helping to pull the company back into profitability. Toys "R" Us and FAO Schwartz held their first midnight openings—an event called "Midnight Madness"—in May 1999, at which all of these new toys were made available at once. (Even the Coronet line warriors turned up at the local store en masse.)

There were seventy-three other official *Star Wars* licensees. Not all of them were aimed at children. Yves Saint Laurent, for example, produced Queen Amidala makeup. Plenty more ideas were left on the table. The world would never see the "gurgling Gungan" squeezable plastic heads or rip-cord pod racer toys dreamed up by one agency for the Pepsi *Episode I* promotions. Even so, Steve

Sansweet called the resulting flow of merchandise "a flood of biblical propor-tions." Pepsi produced an incredible 8 billion cans of *Episode I* soda. Instead of a golden ticket, there were 250,000 gold-colored cans of Yoda-themed Pepsi: these were worth $20 if you mailed them in. A decade that had begun with *Star Wars* fans essentially in hiding would end with more *Star Wars* characters printed on aluminum cans than there were people on the planet.

Star Wars fan club membership reached its zenith around the time of the *Episode I* release. Dan Madsen was mailing two million copies a month of *"Star Wars" Insider*, the new name for the Lucasfilm Fan Club magazine. (For com-parison, he mailed five hundred thousand copies of *Star Trek Communicator* a month.) In April 1999, Madsen was also the instigator of the first *Star Wars* Celebration, a three-day event at the Air and Space Museum in Denver. It was the first licensed Lucasfilm gathering of fans, all of it intended to promote *Episode I*. Madsen and his tireless MC, Anthony Daniels, paved the way for twenty thousand fans from around the world to gather in Denver. There was a torrential downpour, and the vendor tents began leaking. Still, there they were, thousands of *Star Wars* addicts calling friends back home on chunky cell phones about the short extracts from the movie being screened.

Such previewed scenes from *Episode I* were the subject of intense decon-struction, as were the trailers. The first *Phantom Menace* trailer debuted on-line and was downloaded ten million times. That may not make it sound like a big deal in the age of YouTube, but in 1998, when less than a third of Amer-icans were online, nearly all of them on horrifically slow 56K connections, it was huge. Downloading a video could take hours. Meanwhile, hardcore fans would pay for *Meet Joe Black* and *The Waterboy* and then try to claim their money back before the movie started—because these were the movies before which the *Phantom Menace* trailer appeared. Theaters soon caught on and refused refunds. But for the fans desperate for the smallest crumb of detail, it was worth it for the stories you could tell yourself based on this imagery: a queen in council, a field full of droids, a shining city on a waterfall. The idea of *Star Wars* was back—and how.

Once the movie was out, many hard-core fans would need to see *Phantom Menace* a number of times. Casual viewers wanted to see it at least once just to find out for themselves what all the fuss was about. Workplace consultants Challenger, Gray & Christmas estimated that 2.2 million employees in the United States alone skipped work on May 19 to see it. Some bosses simply de-clared a *Star Wars* holiday. The movie grossed $28.5 million in ticket sales on opening day, a new record.

The negative reviews were already starting to arrive by that point, but it didn't seem to matter. *Time* and *Newsweek,* both of which had raved about the original *Star Wars,* gave *Phantom Menace* the thumbs-down. "The actors are wallpaper, the jokes are juvenile, there's no romance, and the dialogue lands with the thud of a computer-instruction manual," thundered Peter Travers in *Rolling Stone.* "Joyless, overly reverential and impenetrably plotted," concluded the *Washington Post. Variety* complained that the movie lacked any emotional pull, wonder, or awe. There were quite a few positive reviews, though, including one from the biggest name in criticism. Roger Ebert had been personally briefed by Lucas and was on the director's wavelength. "Dialogue isn't the point," he insisted. "These movies are about new things to look at."

At first, moviegoers seemed to agree with Ebert. Gallup released a *Phantom Menace* poll—in fact, Gallup released three *Phantom Menace* polls, because that's how big a deal the franchise was—taken between May 21 and June 19, 1999. In the first poll, 52 percent of people who saw the movie described it as "excellent"; by the third poll, that number had fallen to 33 percent. But most of the balance had shifted into the "good" category. The percentage of people describing the movie as "poor" never went above 6 percent—about the same as the percentage of respondents calling it "one of the greatest movies I've ever seen."

Negative reviews may have slowed ticket sales, but only in the sense that a pile of sandbags can slow a tsunami. Prerelease estimates put the opening weekend gross at between $100 million and $190 million; as it turned out, *Phantom* took a week to reach $134 million. But the film was raking in money all the same. "It's entirely critic-proof," said NPR film critic Elvis Mitchell, who wasn't a fan. "It doesn't matter if this movie is basically like an intergalactic version of C-Span. They're talking about treaties for two hours. No. People will go. They want to see it because they want to be part of the phenomenon."

Phantom Menace was the biggest movie of 1999 and, unadjusted for inflation, the biggest *Star Wars* movie ever. It grossed $431 million in the United States, but $552 million in the rest of the world—the first movie in the saga for which the foreign take beat the American. It made most of its money in countries where most of the audience were reading subtitles and didn't care about the delivery of the dialogue anyway. I spent a good part of *Star Wars* Celebration Europe in 2013 drinking with German fans who raved about how much they loved *Episode I.* Japan in particular went nuts for the film. The gross in that country alone—$110 million—almost equaled Lucas's entire budget.

For Lucas, who had never cared for critics, the international success of *Episode I* amounted to a vindication. He didn't much care for the Academy either, so the fact that *Phantom Menace* lost the 2000 visual effects Oscar to *The Matrix* would have been a minor annoyance. The box office didn't lie: he was on the right track—playing the right music, so to speak. *Episode I* was a visual spectacular; the dialogue didn't matter. If the actors were always going to be upstaged by the effects, why worry about the acting? Best to stick with the silent movie / symphony concept. It seemed to have worked so well, in fact, that Lucas wasted no time in putting it to work again—this time with even more gusto.

I n August 1999, some three months after the premiere of *Episode I*, Lucas and his kids returned from their European travels. In September, Lucas began to write *Episode II*. The moment was once again captured by Lucasfilm cameras. The footage they recorded belied McCallum's claim in May 1999 that Lucas was "about a quarter of the way through the script" of *Episode II* and would "have it done in September." This discrepancy would not have been the biggest deal, except for the fact that production on the new film was already in motion. The stage had been booked. Filming was due to start—in Australia this time, where tax breaks and tech-savvy workers had also attracted the makers of *The Matrix*—in June 2000. McCallum spent most of fall 1999 on planes to and from Sydney, racking up ninety thousand air miles in the process.

Lucas had spent three years writing and rewriting *Episode I*; he would now have to turn out a script for *Episode II* in a mere nine months. He sat down at the door desks in his writing tower, "started on page one, and working my way through a first draft as quickly as possible," he told author Jody Duncan. Then he "started right away on a second draft." This would apparently be the second of a record number of drafts—fourteen or fifteen—that Lucas wrote *before* he had the results typed up as a "rough draft." He then did another two or three before having it typed up again as a "second draft." We don't know how many penciled versions preceded the third draft. The next part of the chronology to be recorded in Lucasfilm lore is that the fourth draft was polished by *Young Indiana Jones* writer Jonathan Hale, who had finally gotten that long-awaited call from Lucasfilm. Lucas estimated he'd done twenty rewrites of *Episode I* over three years. For *Episode II*, it appears he wrote twenty rewrites in ten months, or a draft every six days, given that Lucas told Duncan he was only writing three days a week.

This wasn't writing so much as live jazz performance.

This time, Lucas seems to have been coping with the psychotic process of scriptwriting by caring less about the actual outcome. Maybe that was the only way anyone could have done it, given the tremendous burden of expectations from Planet Star Wars. From the scripts that have leaked out of this production, which was even more secretive than *Episode I*, it seems he was having his most fun writing *Star Wars* ever. He walked right up to the line of spoofing himself *Mad Magazine* style, and then he stepped over it. Lucas's joking initial title for *Star Wars Episode II*, which he stuck with for a number of drafts, was "Jar Jar's Great Adventure"—as if setting out to tweak older fanboys who were already fuming about the character. In early drafts, when Padmé gets Jar Jar to fill in for her in the Galactic Senate, Lucas played with the notion that the Gungan can speak proper English when necessary:

> PADMÉ: *Representative Binks, I know I can count on you.*
> JAR JAR: *Yousa betchen mesa bottums.*
> PADMÉ: *What??!!*
> JAR JAR: *(coughs, recovers) Oh, pardone-ay, Senator. I mean, I am honored to accept this heavy burden. I take on this responsibility with deep humility tinged with an overwhelming pride.*

The joke would disappear from later drafts. Jar Jar emerged as a dangerous dupe of Chancellor Palpatine, proposing emergency war powers to the senate. Lucas was bending over backwards to find the most vital reason for Jar Jar to be in *Star Wars* in the first place. You think Jar Jar ruined the galaxy far, far away? Turns out he literally did.

There's more evidence for an increasingly carefree touch on the part of the Creator. Obi-Wan Kenobi encounters a drug dealer in a bar hawking "death sticks"; in his script, Lucas named the character "Elian Sleazebaggano." When Yoda encounters the separatist leader and secret Sith lord Count Dooku— another so-dumb-it's-hilarious name—Lucas not only changed his mind about whether Yoda ever wielded a lightsaber, he'd insisted to Kasdan during the *Return of the Jedi* roundtable that the little green guy didn't fight—but in describing Yoda's style, he started to sound like an announcer on an old-time radio serial:

> YODA attacks! He flies forward. COUNT DOOKU is forced to retreat. Words are insufficient to describe the range and skill of Yoda's speed and swordplay. His lightsaber is a humming blur of light.
> Count Dooku's lightsaber is sent cartwheeling from his hand. He staggers back, gasping and spent, against the control panel. YODA

jumps onto DOOKU'S shoulders, and is about to drive the lightsaber
into the top of the Count's head.

YODA: The end for you, Count, this is.

COUNT DOOKU: . . . Not yet . . .

It seemed Lucas had forgotten all Campbell-esque pretensions and was simply riffing on a theme of *Flash Gordon*. ("Words are insufficient to describe . . ."
could also be translated as "ILM, insert fight sequence here.") He admitted
as much himself. "This was much more like a movie from the 1930s than any
of the others had been," Lucas said, "with a slightly over-the-top, poetic style."
The title itself, *Attack of the Clones*, couldn't have been more *Buck Rogers*. Ewan
McGregor's reaction, when he was told the title on the red carpet at another
movie premiere: "Is that it? That's a terrible, terrible title."

And if there were plot holes? Then there were plot holes; there were more
than enough of them in the 1930s too. Lucas tap-danced past plot problems
like Guido Anselmi, the fictional filmmaker in Fellini's *8 ½*, another director
caught up in making a strange movie about rocket ships. Since Lucas was so
familiar with his material after so many drafts, he assumed the audience would
easily see through the mystery that Obi-Wan spends much of the movie trying
to solve—who ordered up thousands of Clone troopers, the proto-Stormtroopers who were to arrive just in time to save the Jedi from the separatists on the
planet of Geonosis? The truth behind their mysterious maker seemed gapingly
obvious to the Creator. "I was always worried in Episode II that I was giving away too much," he reflected in 2005, "in terms of people asking questions
about 'Where did the clones really come from?'"

Indeed, there was no mystery for anyone paying attention. Jango Fett, the
bounty hunter who provides the DNA on which the Clones (and his son, Boba)
are based, tells Obi-Wan he was recruited not by a long-lost Jedi master, as Obi-
Wan believed, but by "a man called Tyranus." Later on, the audience is told that
Darth Tyranus is Count Dooku's Sith name. Though the fact that the Clone
troopers would betray the Jedi was supposed to remain a mystery until the third
movie, it's an outcome hiding in plain sight. Obi-Wan, surprisingly incurious
about the whole Tyranus thing, now appears to be as much of a dupe as Jar Jar.

It could have been worse. The name of the lost Jedi master who supposedly
ordered the army was originally rendered as "Sido-dyas"—not a whole world
away from "Sidious," Palpatine's Sith name. Lucas evidently felt this was just
a little too obvious for the audience, and that it made the Jedi into even more
obvious dupes. But there was one typing error in a printed-up draft of the script

in which this never-seen character became "Sifo-Dyas." Lucas liked that. The name stuck, the Expanded Universe did the rest of the work, and today Jedi Master Sifo-Dyas is a full-fledged character with a lengthy *Wookieepedia* entry. (Spoiler alert: he was murdered by Count Dooku and his blood inserted into the cyborg Sith soldier General Grievous.)

Then there was the romance between Anakin and Padmé, which lurches on for scene after painful scene. From the start of the *Episode II* process, Lucas knew he was trying to write an old-fashioned romance. He expressed concern that the young boys in his target audience would roll their eyes at its flowery nature. But that's not actually what we ended up with. The love scenes, in the eyes of most viewers, are more flummery than flowery. Here's a taste of the young couple's supposedly flirtatious banter—and this from the *final* draft:

> ANAKIN: *Well, tell me, did you dream of power and politics when you were a little girl?*
>
> PADMÉ: *(laughing) No! That was the last thing I thought of, but the more history I studied, the more I realized how much good politicians could do. After school, I became a Senatorial advisor with such a passion that, before I knew it, I was elected Queen. For the most part it was because of my conviction that reform was possible. I wasn't the youngest Queen ever elected, but now that I think back on it, I'm not sure I was old enough. I'm not sure I was ready.*
>
> ANAKIN: *The people you served thought you did a good job. I heard they tried to amend the Constitution so you could stay in office.*
>
> PADMÉ: *Popular rule is not democracy, Annie. It gives the people what they want, not what they need. And, truthfully, I was relieved when my two terms were up. So were my parents. They worried about me during the blockade and couldn't wait for it all to be over. Actually, I was hoping to have a family by now. . . . My sisters have the most amazing, wonderful kids. . . . So when the Queen asked me to serve as Senator, I couldn't refuse her.*
>
> ANAKIN: *I agree! I think the Republic needs you. . . . I'm glad you chose to serve. I feel things are going to happen in our generation that will change the galaxy in profound ways.*
>
> PADMÉ: *I think so too.*

It would be hard to call this romance—harder still to call it a kids' movie. It's barely even intergalactic C-SPAN. It might be nearer the mark to call it "well-intentioned didactic dullness." It reminds us of Luke Starkiller in the second draft of *The Star Wars*, delivering pages of explanation to his younger brothers about the history of the gangsters in the Galactic Senate. Lucas, no romance novelist he, originally had the couple marry in the middle of the movie rather than the end.

As many rewrites as the script for *Episode II* apparently went through, Lucas still didn't turn over a single typed draft to his staff during the entire preproduction process. This was a step beyond only giving actors the pages they needed; the entire movie was unknown to almost everyone involved until Lucas got on a plane to Australia for the beginning of the shoot. An army of designers was stuck creating planets and creatures without having any idea where they would fit, or how long they would be featured on the screen. Mc-Callum, the producer who never says no, was stuck trying to make a budget without being able to itemize everything he was budgeting for. Lucas was play-ing jazz: bouncing back and forth from the design team's artwork, gaining inspiration for the script from the rest of Lucasfilm rather than the other way around.

McCallum made light of the situation in an interview with *"Star Wars" In-sider* in January 2000: "Right now we don't need a script," he said. "It's better for [Lucas] to concentrate on the dialog and themes as he goes along, while we're working on the look." The script would be completed "whenever George hands it to me." McCallum compared *Episode II* to *Citizen Kane*, the script for which Orson Welles finished two days before filming began. "We're not putting any pressure on him," he added.

Even when Lucas handed over the typed version of the final script, it wasn't finished; that was when he had Jonathan Hales do his polish, working remotely from London. On set, Lucas went over Hales's quickly assembled draft, re-wrote it, and finally delivered it to the crew three days ahead of the first shot, not quite—but almost—matching Welles's record. Even after the shoot, Lucas wasn't satisfied with the script and tried to flesh out the character of Count Dooku by inserting dialogue making him Qui-Gon's former master.

The key actor for *Episode II*, Canadian unknown Hayden Christensen, had been cast for the role of the adolescent Anakin Skywalker without reading a word of the story. When he finally saw the script, the new Anakin blanched: "The dialogue was, well, I didn't know how I could make it convincing," he recalled in 2005. "Finally, I just said to myself, I am George's voice. This is his vision, and I'm here to fulfill it, and that's how we worked." (We're a long way from the days of "you can type this shit, George, but you can't say it.")

And so the shoot proceeded, from June to September 2000, with an army of artists and engineers attempting to fulfill Lucas's vision. He himself was most concerned with his latest technological milestone: creating the first movie shot entirely digitally. He had gone to Sony and Panasonic and urged them to create a camera that was up to the task; what came back was the Sony HDC-F900, a digital camera that took twenty-four high-definition shots a second. But ILM was given less than twenty-four hours to vet the camera before it left for Sydney, and was horrified at the shots that came back. The camera compressed its blue channel data to roughly a quarter of the regular red and green size—which would have been of minor concern had most of the movie not been shot against a blue screen. To all intents and purposes, Lucas might as well not have used the blue screen at all. Dozens of artists and image specialists had to apply hundreds of painstaking fixes to what they called "garbage." Yet to Lucas, visual effects existed in an opaque box. ILM staffers remember John Knoll, cocreator of Photoshop and the movie's visual effects supervisor, being frustrated about the limited number of times he could intercede with the Creator on digital matters, after which Knoll felt he would have to shut up for a few days.

After the hoopla of *Phantom Menace*, the *Attack of the Clones* release on May 16, 2002, was a relatively subdued affair, at least in the United States. It opened on roughly half the number of screens—3,161—with relatively little advertising and no fast-food tie-ins. Still, at first, *Episode II* did even better than its predecessor, scoring a four-day gross of $116 million—the same as the movie's budget. For the first time, a *Star Wars* movie was opening all around the world simultaneously, in more than seventy countries. Add a $67 million international opening weekend, and it became clear those merchandising deals hadn't been necessary anyway.

While some critics felt the movie was an improvement on *Phantom Menace*, most reviewed *Attack of the Clones* even more poorly than its predecessor. Based on the "top critics" section of the reviews website *Rotten Tomatoes*, *Clones* is the least well-reviewed of the first six episodes, with a 37 percent fresh rating. No one doubted the movie would make buckets of cash regardless, and the reviewers showed a kind of resignation in their despair. For the first time, *Star Wars* was compared unfavorably to the *Flash Gordon* serials. "The screenplay would make Buster Crabbe call for a rewrite," wrote Michael Atkinson in the *Village Voice*.

Figuring out where the Republic, the Federation, the Corporate Alliance, and the Trade Guilds begin and end is more than Lucas himself manages to do, and the endless exposition is such irritating gibberish that you're prone to ignore it and look out the windows as the digital planes sail by. When I was a kid in school, we called this "tedium." Today, it's a secular theophany.

Taken as five films—or six, in a year or so—this is hardly an epic (a word that implies moral, human, and social weight). It's a marathon of irrelevant preadolescent dreaming. One could maintain that Lucas's ongoing opus will eventually juice more consumers than any other cultural manifestation in the history of the race besides the Bible. At the very least, if a Jedi emissary were to examine mankind through its most widely perused texts, Lucas's massive fantasy would surely stand in the top five.

Stop the planet, I want to get off.

There were points of light in the critical darkness. The lightsaber battle between Dooku and CGI Yoda won praise for being unexpected and effective: you'll believe a small green guy can fly. Then there was the hellish ending: legions of Clones assembling under dark red light on Geonosis, the largest digital army ever seen on screen. In the years since the first trilogy, fans had assumed that those Clones we'd been hearing about, the Clone Wars that Lucas kept off-limits to other writers, were some kind of external invasion. As a title, *Attack of the Clones* enforced that misdirection. Now it turned out that the Clones were space soldiers, proto-Stormtroopers—and they fought on the side of the good guys. "I was wonderfully blindsided by the reveal in *Clones*," says author Timothy Zahn. "Well played, George, well played."

Again, poor reviews bounced right off Lucasfilm like it was Teflon. Riding high on another successful movie, the company spun off its theater sound division, THX, as a separate private company, in which Lucas held a minority stake. Lucasfilm was evolving in other ways, too; Lucas moved most divisions of his company into Red Rock Ranch, just down the road from Skywalker Ranch, because it was getting too big for Skywalker to contain. ILM maxed out at around 1,500 employees. Lucas signed a lease to build a new headquarters in San Francisco.

Lucas Books, meanwhile, was busily divvying up the Expanded Universe into specific eras spanning thousands of years: the Old Republic, Fall of the Republic, the Rebellion, the New Republic, the New Jedi Order. It was a smart way to diversify *Star Wars* holdings at a crucial moment. Not a fan of the prequels? You could still find something to love in these other areas of the galaxy's long history. The Old Republic era, a twenty-four-thousand-year period when Jedi and Sith were fighting epic battles in much greater numbers than in the prequels, proved particularly popular in spin-off media, such as the *Tales of the Jedi* comics, the award-winning 2003 role-playing game *Knights of the Old Republic*, and the massively multiplayer online game *The Old Republic*, which gained a million players within weeks of its launch.

Internal *Star Wars* history was further brought into line at Lucasfilm with the creation of the Holocron, a database that not only listed all the characters, planets, ships, and concepts in the series so far but stated what level of canon they were. The highest level was G-canon, which stands for George: the movies and anything Lucas was directly involved in. The lowest level was S-canon, which might as well stand for "stupid"—the *Holiday Special*, alongside anything else from the early days when Lucasfilm wasn't paying quite so close attention. Until 2002, the continuity rules of *Star Wars* were dictated by the internally famous "black binders," of which Lucas holds the original. Afterwards, it would all be digital, in a surprisingly mundane-looking SQL database, just like millions of other collections of corporate assets on computers around the world.

Lucasfilm employee Leland Chee created and manages the Holocron to this day. Officially, he is described as a continuity database administrator. Unofficially he is the bearer of what *Wired* magazine dubbed the "coolest job in the world." Chee was the one who had to work out small but vital matters such as how long it took the *Millennium Falcon* to travel from Hoth to Bespin. He typed in every one of the fifteen thousand Holocron entries so it had a consistent voice; he was the one who had to decide just how important every single *Star Wars* character ever seen on screen or mentioned in a book is, on a scale of 1 to 4. "Luke is obviously a 1," he says. "A background character who doesn't even have a name is a 4."

Chee wasn't a fan of either of the latest works of G-canon, *Episodes I* or *II*, when he set up the Holocron. It didn't matter. Creating enough internal consistency to protect the idea of *Star Wars*, preventing the universe from ever having to "reboot," was enough of a responsibility to humble even the most hardened first-generation *Star Wars* fan. The fan-edited online encyclopedia, *Wookieepedia*, didn't start up (as a splinter group of *Star Wars* fans who'd been editing entries on *Wikipedia* proper) until March 2005. Chee's Holocron would always have three years' head start—though *Wookieepedia* would always be way more wordy.

As Chee beavered away, the world was no less obsessed with codifying the language of *Star Wars*. On September 25, 2002, the terms "Jedi," "The Force," and "Dark Side" were officially entered into the *Oxford English Dictionary*. Meanwhile in Texas, an energy brokering company called Enron was busy

executing a secret plan to extort money from the state of California by artificially raising the cost of electricity; the plan was called Death Star. Enron
helped set it up through subsidiaries called JEDI, Obi-1 Holdings, Kenobe,
and Chewco. *Star Wars* was a cultural institution now. Everyone—even the bad
guys—loved the idea of it. Not even the worst *Star Wars* movie George Lucas
could contrive to make would change that.

The familiar cycle of the prequels was under way once more. *Episode III* had
gone into preproduction shortly before *Episode II* arrived in theaters, at
which point Lucas left for his now traditional family vacation. Returning in late
August 2002, he once again had roughly nine months to gestate the script before
filming started. Once again, he would keep his design team updated on the locations he was planning to use, while keeping them in the dark about the script
itself. It had worked once, as far as he was concerned, and it would work again.

Before he wrote it, Lucas declared *Episode III* would be "the most fun to do."
Finally, we'd see the Clone Wars themselves. We'd see Anakin and Obi-Wan
duel over volcanic lava, a scene Lucas had been ruminating on since 1977. And
we'd see the final transformation of Skywalker into Vader.

The new script should have come naturally. But for months, Lucas wrote
nothing. "I've been thinking about it," he said in November. He still hadn't
started by the first week in December 2002. "Take an aspirin," he suggested to
a frustrated McCallum.

"Aspirin?" the producer shot back. "I need to freebase!"

Lucas's problem: too many characters and concepts clamoring for his attention, more than the movie could possibly contain. Young Boba Fett's revenge
on Obi-Wan for killing his father would be fascinating, but not essential. Ditto
with seeing a 10-year-old Han Solo meeting Yoda on the Wookiee planet of
Kashyyyk—a concept that made it as far as a design sketch and a single line
of dialogue in the rough draft. (Young Han to the Jedi master: "I found part
of a transmitter droid near the east bay. I think it's still sending and receiving
signals.") Lucas was determined to shoehorn Peter Mayhew reprising his role as
Chewbacca into the prequel trilogy, however, even if only for a few seconds: he
wanted to show that Chewie had actually been a little short for a Wookiee all
along. Artoo and Threepio had to be in there too, simply because they needed
to be in all six movies. To give Padmé some purpose, he wanted to show her
founding the Rebel Alliance. He needed to show the Jedi at war with Clone
Troopers at their side and initially had the notion that we would see seven

battles simultaneously on seven different planets. He felt he ought to kill off an important Jedi during the course of the movie, he felt, but pretty much every major character still alive at the end of *Episode II* (Obi-Wan, Anakin, Yoda) survives into the classic trilogy in some form; he decided on Mace Windu. Samuel L. Jackson understood, but insisted on an important, grandiose death scene.

The ending Lucas wrote for *Episode III* somehow didn't match up with the beginning of *Episode IV*, so he had to "disassemble Episode III and rethink it." He would admit to author Marcus Hearn that he had "painted myself into a corner" with the script. His solution: focus on Anakin's fall to the Dark Side at the expense of just about everything and everyone else. Boba Fett: out. Padmé founding the Alliance: gone. Seven battles on seven planets: *sayonara.*

Lucas was so boxed in by the needs of the plot that he couldn't even stay consistent to his own G-level canon. In *Return of the Jedi* Princess Leia remembered her "real mother," that is, Padmé, being around, "kind but sad," when Leia was a very small child. But Lucas felt it would make things that much more dramatic if Padmé were to die while birthing her twins. The "kind but sad" interaction with Leia was reduced to a few seconds between heartbroken mother and child.

By the end of January 2003, Lucas eked out a fifty-five-page treatment for McCallum's eyes only. Its title, clearly mirroring and acquiring the abandoned word from the *Return of the Jedi* title: *Revenge of the Sith.* As with the rough drafts of *Attack of the Clones*, there was little here that would not make it into the final movie. Some differences: Anakin's vision of the future that drives him to the Dark Side involved Padmé "consumed by flames" in the rough draft, rather than dying in childbirth as he foresees it in the final film; she eventually dies "on the operating table," possibly by injuries inflicted by Anakin; in the script, Palpatine also makes clear to Anakin that he was able to manipulate his birth via the Force, causing the midi-chlorians to create him out of nothing. "You might say I'm your father," said Palpatine, in what was likely intended as an echo of Vader's most famous line in *Empire*. Anakin responded just the way Luke did: "That's impossible!"

The rise to power of the Nixon-like overlord, the transition from Senator Palpatine in *Episode I* to Chancellor Palpatine in *Episode II* to Emperor Palpatine in *Episode III*: this was a story Lucas had long been interested in telling in the prequels, and it would just about survive as a subplot. It was a pessimistic summary of his reading of history: "All democracies turn into dictatorships, but not by coup," he told *Time* before the launch of *Episode II*. "The people give their democracy to a dictator, whether it's Julius Caesar or Napoleon or Adolf Hitler. Ultimately, the general population goes along with the idea. What kinds of things push people and institutions in this direction? That's the issue I've been exploring: how did the Republic turn into the Empire? How does a good person go bad, and how does a democracy become a dictatorship?"

That exploration would reach its end in *Revenge of the Sith*, peppered as it was with more political references than any other movie in the saga. Fans assumed that the dark overtones of *Episode II* were influenced by the political situation at the time: in 2002, it was hard to see a movie that featured a Republic beset by terrorist bombings and war on distant planets, a Republic sliding into dictatorship via the granting of emergency war powers, and not think you were watching a specific commentary on George W. Bush's administration post–9/11. But that wasn't Lucas's intent: when he'd finished his script of the movie in March 2000, Bush wasn't even president.

Episode III, however, was written around the US-led invasion of Iraq in March 2003. In the Bay Area, protests against the Iraq War and Bush were as hard to avoid as Vietnam and Nixon were during the writing of *Star Wars*, especially for a self-confessed news junkie like Lucas. Suddenly, after Anakin Skywalker is first dubbed Darth Vader and confronts Obi-Wan, we find him using this line: "If you're not with me, you're my enemy." Few adult listeners at the time would fail to pick up a reference to Bush's line in his speech to Congress on September 20, 2001: "Either you are with us, or you are with the terrorists." Obi-Wan's response would have cheered the heart of every voter who felt some nuance was lost in Bush's black-and-white worldview: "Only a Sith deals in absolutes." Promoting the film later, Lucas would declare his hostility to Bush for the first time, publically comparing him to Nixon and Iraq to Vietnam. "I didn't think it would get this close," he told reporters at Cannes. The endless circle of politics, as Darth Vader might say, was now complete.

As he wrestled with condensing all of this into a script, Lucas was riding his deadline like never before. By March 2003, he'd written half of a first draft. At a production meeting, he described the same mental-block problems he'd had all those years ago. His enemies, he said, were "inertia. Procrastination. I sit there with that page in front of me, . . . I can be chained to my desk, and still not write it." He was forcing himself to finish five pages a day again. The script had come so easy in *Attack of the Clones*, when he had been jazz-riffing, loose and carefree. Now it was crunch time, his final *Star Wars* movie, the end of all loose ends, the arrival of Vader, and he might as well have been back in 1974.

On April 10, 2003, with twelve weeks to go before shooting, Lucas finished a 111-page first draft in pencil. What had the Creator decided this time? He had pulled back from Palpatine telling Anakin outright that he was his father. (Making Vader Luke's father, Leia his sister, and Threepio his sort-of brother was fine, but apparently making the Emperor Luke's sort-of grandfather was a familial step too far.) Instead Palpatine tells Anakin the story of another Sith Lord, Darth Plagueis, who was able to create life and end death, but was ultimately and ironically destroyed by his own apprentice (i.e., Palpatine himself). He added Palpatine hinting that Obi-Wan was "seeing a certain senator," playing on Anakin's jealousy over Padmé. When Anakin is revived in his Vader suit after his tragic duel with Obi-Wan, he asks Palpatine about Padmé and is told "she was killed by a Jedi." (In the movie this would become "you killed her," filling Vader with self-loathing rather than rage against the Jedi order.)

By early June, Lucas delivered a second draft of the script. In late June, four days before filming was to start in Australia, Lucas finished a quick third draft. Again, the shoot ended in September; this time it was notable for having no location shots whatsoever. Everything was green screen. At the suggestion of Coppola and the urging of McCallum, Lucas hired an acting and dialogue coach, Chris Neil, who was coincidentally the son of Coppola's brother-in-law. Natalie Portman raved about Neil. Unfortunately, Portman was increasingly difficult to deal with on set—some of the crew say she made several actresses playing her handmaidens, including Keira Knightley (age twelve in *The Phantom Menace*), cry in the previous prequels, allegedly for the crime of talking to her without permission. According to some Lucasfilm insiders, many of her lines were cut from *Revenge of the Sith* for that reason. She had little left to do but to be barefoot and pregnant with the Skywalker twins.

Lucas had one more character to squeeze into the lineup after the movie was shot. Though he would only appear on screen for seconds during the opera scene in which Palpatine tempts Anakin to the Dark Side, and he had never appeared in any of the other films to date, this character was key to the entire six-movie arc. His name was Baron Papanoida, a blue-skinned playwright who, according to *Wookieepedia*, built himself an entertainment empire on his home planet and liked to keep his past shrouded in mystery. The actor who played Papanoida was insistent that his daughter Katie be in the shot too. The actor's name: George Lucas.

One final redrafting happened in postproduction. Having assembled a rough cut of the film, many ILM staffers felt that Anakin didn't seem to have enough reason to turn to the Dark Side. Lucas screened the rough cut for Coppola and for Spielberg; "Steven confirmed that most of everything was working," he said. But the more he edited, the more Lucas changed his mind. He added another vision of Padmé dying in childbirth, making absolutely certain the audience would understand that this was the reason Anakin turned to the Dark Side. Originally, the reason Anakin saved Palpatine from Mace Windu's lightsaber and killed Windu himself was because Skywalker believed there was a Jedi conspiracy against Palpatine. Christensen and McDiarmid were called in one last time to reloop their dialogue: now Anakin killed Windu because Palpatine insisted he knew how to save Padmé.

This, then, became *Episode III*'s shock reveal, the equivalent of the Clone Wars fake-out: Anakin became Darth Vader out of a selfish kind of love. He wanted to hold onto his wife at all costs. Lucas compared the result to *Faust*. But the plot was so disrupted by this decision that Lucas had left what he called a couple of "sharp right turns" on the road to the Faustian bargain. Case in point: Anakin tells Windu that Palpatine is a Sith who should be arrested, moments before he decides to kill Windu. Another few minutes go by, and Anakin is knighted as Darth Vader and declares he will kill all the Jedi. A few minutes more, and he's slaughtering children offscreen at the Jedi Temple.

This, in the end, is perhaps the most mystifying decision in the entire prequel trilogy. Vader's long conversion to the Dark Side was the story Lucas supposedly wanted to tell. Fans once assumed this fall would be spread over three movies. In the end, the fall took place in fewer than ten confusing minutes.

Everywhere at ILM, it seemed, all of *Star Wars* was being fixed up and given a new coat of paint—not just *Episode III*, but the now-complete sextet. Lucas was preparing to release the original trilogy on DVD—the Special Edition version, of course, though it would lose that nomenclature. It would simply become *Star Wars Episodes IV, V,* and *VI*—with hundreds more scenes tweaked or tinkered with. It became clear that *Star Wars*, to Lucas, was no historical document. It was a race car to be constantly tuned up and decked out. The same was true of *THX 1138*: Lucas released a special edition of his first movie in 2004, a week before the *Star Wars* box sets. It featured all-new digital additions such as a machine that helps THX masturbate in front of the holograms and mutant monkeys attacking the protagonist just before his final escape.

By now Lucas had at his command an unprecedented bevy of digital artists, adept enough to do anything he wanted, including the difficult task of grafting actors' lip movements from one take onto another. He could move actors from one side of a set to the other after the fact. *The Star Wars* universe—the part that appeared on screen, at least—was his to manipulate. He would probably never have this chance again, with this many artists and this many actors under contract for pickup scenes. He replaced actor Sebastian Shaw as Anakin Skywalker's Force ghost at the end of *Return of the Jedi* with one played by Hayden Christensen. Sound designer Matthew Wood added his Jar Jar Binks–like Gungan voice to the end of *Jedi*, the last audible dialogue of the entire series, over a new scene of celebration on Naboo: "We'sah free!"

It might as well have been the Creator saying it. The saga was finally over. He had triumphed over fan angst; he had pivoted from a millionaire into a billionaire. He had broken records, reached milestones, proved everything he had set out to prove with digital cinema. Hampered by an inability to write dialogue, he had decided not to sweat it, and in the process he took *Star Wars* back to its schlock-filled *Flash Gordon* roots. He'd completed and polished a twelve-hour saga as he saw fit, and dropped in educational lessons about the fragility of democracy and the suffering that comes from attachment. Now it was time for the Creator to tell the diehard fans what some of them might have expected, and some were shocked by: there were to be no more movies.

Lucas dropped this news while attending the triennial *Star Wars* Celebration convention for the first time at Celebration III, held in Indianapolis in April 2005, just prior to the release of *Revenge of the Sith*. During a Q&A session, Lucas was asked about whether there would one day be an *Episode VII*, following on from *Return of the Jedi* this time. After all, Dale Pollock had written that he had seen treatments for *Episodes VII* through *IX* but was sworn to secrecy about their contents. Pollock remains quiet on this matter even now, except to say that he remembers being excited about them and thinking them the best possible movies—but for all we know, each "treatment" was no more than a few sentences long.

Indeed, Lucas's answer seems to suggest that's an overestimate. "To be very honest with you, I never ever thought of anything that happened beyond *Episode VI*," Lucas said. "It's the Darth Vader story. It starts with him being a young boy and it ends with him dying. The other books and everything kind of go off on their path, but I never ever really considered ever taking that particular story further." Another answer he gave at the same session seemed to almost beg the fans not to demand more of him: "*Star Wars* is something to enjoy, and take away what you can from it that maybe helps you in your lives," he said, "But don't let it take over your lives. You know, that's what they say about Trekkies.

Star Wars fan don't do that. The point of the movies is to get on with your lives. Take that challenge, leave your uncle's moisture farm, go out into the world and save the universe."

But as it soon turned out, neither Lucas nor the fans were done with *Star Wars* yet.

24.

BUILDING CHARACTER

As far as the hardest of the hard-core fans are concerned, the old Kenner slogan—"*Star Wars* is Forever"—is an article of faith. You'll hear them say it almost as often as the slightly more syrupy motto "*Star Wars* brings people together." All that energy fans bring to the franchise: they don't necessarily use it to get off their metaphorical Tatooine moisture farms the way Lucas wanted. If that's the metaphor you're looking for, then let's say they form a kind of moisture farm collective, move into the hovercar storage area of their homesteads, and start tinkering on these garage projects. They cluster on the Internet according to the nature of these projects. Do they save the universe this way? Not in the strictest definition. But they certainly build community.

We've already seen how Albin Johnson and the 501st legion made a community of space soldiers appear from nothing. At the fringes of the organization, the 501st bleeds into a couple of communities devoted to the only two characters who appeared in all six movies: R2-D2 and C-3PO. No prizes for guessing which one is more popular, but both droidly communities have managed to achieve a strange kind of symbiosis with Lucasfilm.

Take the story of Chris Bartlett, a Stormtrooper with the 501st who decided in 2001 he wanted to build a screen-realistic Threepio costume. This was an order of magnitude more difficult than a realistic Vader or Boba Fett or Stormtrooper. No one outside the walls of Lucasfilm had really managed it at that point. Bartlett, however, was determined: he was thin enough, he was bumbling enough, and dammit, he could be Threepio. He had acquired an old Disneyland Threepio costume from 1997, but the suit was too big, its head especially. It just didn't look like everyone's favorite protocol droid.

Bartlett worked with collectors who had life-size Threepio statues and a friend in a fiberglass shop. Over the years they put together a kind of Frankenstein Threepio that eventually came to resemble the real thing. Bartlett, a very slender man, was just the right shape to make it work. He had a microphone and amp installed in the suit and played the classic trilogy on DVDs in his car on his commute, trying to get Threepio's voice just right.

"I always thought, 'Wouldn't it be neat if someone at Lucasfilm saw the costume and wanted to use it for something?,'" Bartlett said. He never imagined it would happen until he sent a picture of the outfit—just gold spray-painted, not yet chromed—to a friend in Lucasfilm Licensing. Three months later, Bartlett sent the suit off to a shop in Southern California that could do the chrome plating—and got a call from the video games division LucasArts that same day, asking to borrow the costume. "Don't you have like fifteen of these?" he asked, incredulous. "We have four," came the reply, "and they're all in museums."

A call was made to the chrome shop to speed up the process from five weeks to one; such is the power of the Lucasfilm name. A week later, Bartlett found himself flown out to San Francisco, where he assembled the suit in a conference room at Lucasfilm's headquarters. Three hours later, unexpectedly, he found himself on a plane to Sydney, where he delivered a rather dry and technical speech about the video game *Star Wars Galaxies* in full Threepio regalia. He got a paycheck and a plane ticket to Australia; Lucas got its marketing messaging delivered by the best kind of fan express. "If a person was giving the speech, you'd lose half the audience," Bartlett says. "But if you see Threepio giving it, you pay attention."

Bartlett has been Lucasfilm's official event Threepio ever since; now a member of the Screen Actors Guild, he has even received training from Anthony Daniels himself. Bartlett has appeared in Disney Channel shows and Toyota and McDonald's commercials, presented Samuel L. Jackson with an award on the cable channel AMC, and most memorably was dispatched at the last minute to the White House in October 2009 to take part in a Halloween trick-or-treat event. After assembling his costume in the basement of the West Wing, Bartlett and Lucasfilm's official Chewbacca took the closet-sized elevator to the second floor. It stopped at the first, at which point the doors opened and the president of the United States appeared. "Can I get on with you guys?" he asked.

"Hello," said Bartlett in pitch-perfect voice via his amp, "I am C-3PO, human-cyborg relations."

"Wow, you guys look awesome," grinned Obama.

"Well," Bartlett remarked to Chewbacca, echoing Threepio's line on first meeting Lando, "he seems very friendly."

Obama proceeded to introduce "Threepio" to Michelle and the kids. Michelle, it turned out, had specifically asked for the droid. Bartlett looked around and noted that Obama's press secretary, Robert Gibbs, was dressed as Darth Vader; his son was Boba Fett. Once again, proof that an obsession with *Star Wars* had found its way to the most powerful office in the world.

Bartlett can barely wear the costume for longer than an hour. Moving across a room without overheating is a challenge, as is the supermodel diet he needs to fit into the suit. "It's the character you have to stay the most in shape for," he says. "I had to lose ten pounds between Christmas and my next Lucasfilm event. You can't have a paunch at all, because that's where it shows, in the middle. The wires start bulging." But it's worth it, he says, for that "momentary magical interaction."

The other group of droid enthusiasts is even more self-effacing and tenacious than Bartlett and his fellow masked character makers in the 501st. Like Lucas, they prefer life behind the scenes. For this reason, as well as for their choice of character (and the fact that they're never done tinkering), they would seem to be the branch of fandom closest to George Lucas's heart—which might help to explain why they were the first *Star Wars* fans to actually work behind the scenes on one of the movies.

I speak, of course, of the R2 Builders Club.

In a garage in American Canyon, California, Chris James is showing me a screen-perfect R2-D2 replica. It took him a decade to build. "He's mostly aluminum," says James, and the droid bleeps randomly. "Yes, Artoo," he says, absentmindedly, as if to a pet. James is a five-foot-three-inch Welshman with gleaming, bespectacled eyes, a cheery smile, and a long scraggly beard that blends into his torso; if Artoo were to take human form, he might look something like James.

James's creation is detailed as exactly, and exactingly, as any official Lucasfilm version. The difference is that James and his fellow builders have gone so far as to name every nook and cranny. "We call these things 'coin slots,'" James says, pointing to the slim holes down the droid's side; a larger indent at the bottom of the base unit is the "coin return." The tapering part at the bottom is the "skirt" and the "booster cover." The legs run on wheelchair motors connected to 12-volt batteries. "Most droids are 12-volt, like a car," James says. With this much power flowing through them, droids like James's Artoo have incredible stamina: "He can run up to ten hours, depending on how much he's driving around."

The car metaphor is especially appropriate—given the builder's reputatiaon on Planet *Star Wars*. Bonnie Burton, former Lucasfilm social media manager, calls the Artoos the muscle cars of *Star Wars* fandom. "They break down all the time like muscle cars," she says. Burton should know: a huge Artoo fan, she staged a wedding between herself and the diminutive droid at Celebration V in 2010. Darth Vader was the best man; Darth Maul the officiant. Maul asked Burton if she vowed to "take unnatural pride in your relationship in times of full battery charges, as well as times of loose wires and astromech malfunctions." Like the R2 builders, she said I do.*

Fan-built Artoos have long been more realistic than the Lucasfilm versions. James's Artoo can spin its head all the way around, which is something the movie Artoo could never manage. James takes the dome off to show me the Lazy Susan inside, mounted on ball bearings, and the slip ring that prevents the fiber optics in Artoo's head from getting tangled up. Decapitated, Artoo bleeps sadly.

The dome is replaced, and we continue the lesson in droid anatomy. This Artoo used to have a periscope that came out of the top of his dome until a kid broke it off at a Maker Faire. ("Goes with the territory," James shrugged; he repaired it some months after our meeting.) The droid's main eye is simply the "radar eye," while the one that glows red-blue underneath it is the Process State Indicator. The blinking colored lights are the "logics." The three nozzles on the top, which on the 1976 Artoo model were Bakelite reading lights from old airplanes, are the unit's "holoprojectors" or HPs. The R2 builders came up with many names, which have since been incorporated into official Lucasfilm literature.

"Would you like to see his hologram?" James asks. I nod: of course. James flips a switch on a tiny remote—a high-tech custom-built RC device that James 3D-printed—hidden in his pocket. Artoo's side opens, and out comes a car radio antenna with a rare see-through Princess Leia action figure dangling off the end. Artoo plays her message: "Help me, Obi-Wan Kenobi. You're my only hope." The hologram gag came from James's wife, Tammy, and was an idea he initially dismissed. "Now I get more bang for the buck on that thing than anything else in it," he says.

The R2 Builders Club was founded in 1999, around the time *Episode I* came out, by an Australian named Dave Everett. It grew out of a small group of builders on a popular website called the Replica Prop Forum. Other than a

---

* Lucas's only stipulation in allowing the "wedding" to go ahead: "She knows it's not real, right?"

hacker space Everett runs in Sydney, there is no physical clubhouse; this is basically an Internet club for introverts. The R2 builders now claim more than thirteen thousand members around the world, far more than the 501st. But the vast majority have not yet completed an astromech, as Artoo's breed of droid is known. Only 1,200 members are actively posting.

That's because building Artoo is like summiting the Everest of *Star Wars* fandom. It requires tremendous commitment and years of practice; but like Everest, increasingly, it is within reach. James has devoted ten years to his astromech so far, which is not unusual; nor is the $10,000 he estimates he has sunk into it. (It helps that James is a former Silicon Valley software engineer who retired from his job at Hewlett-Packard in 2012 at age forty-two.)

The most challenging aspect of building an astromech is that it is true DIY. Even within the Builders Club, there is no factory churning out astromech parts. "That's the bit people really don't understand," says Gerard Farjardo, a technician for General Motors who joined the Builder's Club twelve years ago and took that long just to make all the parts for his Artoo. "If you're buying parts [from other builders] and you try to put them together, they won't work. Next thing you know, you're out buying a grinder to try to get the screw holes to fit where they're supposed to." Club members may band together in a metal shop to build the dome, say—the most difficult part to construct and the part most likely to roll off your workbench and get a dent. (Luckily, dents and scratches help make a true *Star Wars*–like astromech. The Used Universe strikes again.)

Some of these Artoo builders had been working haphazardly on their hobby even before the Builders Club was founded in '99. James built his first Artoo unit out of wood, cardboard, and plastic around 1997. Others built astromechs out of plastic or resin parts. Everett has posted free plans that let you build a whole droid minus the dome out of a few sheets of styrene. Cost: $500. Paint it and it'll look pretty realistic. But once you've come that far, why not go the whole Artoo?

For years, the droid builders struggled to make their astromechs accurate. Lucasfilm wasn't shutting them down, but it didn't supply so much as a single measurement for them to use as a reference. Builders had to guess Artoo's dimensions based on production stills and screen images. One club member went to the Magic of Myth exhibit, a collaboration between Lucasfilm and the Smithsonian that toured the world from 1997 to 2003, carrying a camera with laser pointers strapped to both sides in a bid to accurately assess the size of an Artoo behind glass. Greater love hath no dork for his droid.

Everything changed in 2002, at the second *Star Wars* Celebration—the same one at which the 501st was providing security and winning over Lucasfilm. Don Bies, an ILM model maker who was in charge of the company's archive, brought one of its dozens of Artoos to the convention. Accidentally on purpose, Bies left the droid in the Builders Club room overnight. Members rushed in with tape measures. "This was the first time we got to touch an official Artoo unit," James says. The club still calls it the Uberdroid.

There remained the mystery of what color blue Artoo had been painted. That sounds like it would be easy to ascertain, but it is maddening: on screen, Artoo seems a slightly different shade of blue depending on what scene you watch. The paint has an odd translucent quality; in some set photographs, Artoo looks almost purple. It turns out that the builders of the original Artoos had used a protective blue dye that is commonly applied to aluminum before cutting the parts out of a sheet; the dye is supposed to be temporary, and gets darker the longer it stays on, hence the confusing color changes.

For *Episode II*, Bies had helped ILM come up with a new, permanent Artoo color. Again, he couldn't officially leak it to the R2 builders. "But hypothetically," Bies wrote on the Astromech message boards, "if I was going to paint one, here's what I'd order from House of Color." He then gave a very specific mix of paint colors. The builders started calling the suggested mixture "hypothetical blue."

What kind of person devotes a decade of hobby time to building a droid? In the Bay Area alone, James says, the club boasts an opera singer, a dentist, and a philosopher. "None of these people had any mechanical or electrical background," he says. "They all have a love of building Artoo." The vast majority are men, unsurprisingly, in their thirties and forties: just old enough to have seen the original movie when it came out and now old enough to have a house, usually a garage (one builder put his Artoo together on the dining room table for six months, to his wife's chagrin), and disposable income.

The goal is not necessarily to complete one. When I asked club member Grant McKinney when he was going to finish his droid, the answer was "hopefully never." There's always a new challenge, a new way to deck out your astromech. Right now, the Holy Grail of the Builders Club is something they call "3-2-3": the ability for a droid to go from three legs to two and then to three again, at the same speed as Artoo is seen to do in the movies. Without his third leg, as the crew of *Star Wars* found out to its chagrin, Artoo has a tendency to topple over.

There are other kinds of astromech droid. You may recall R5-D4, the red droid that Luke and Uncle Owen were going to buy from the Jawas until it blew its motivator. The builders have significantly expanded this repertoire; one 501st member who dresses as Darth Vader built an all-black Dark Side droid. When 501st founder Albin Johnson revealed that his daughter Katie had brain cancer, and she had asked for an astromech to watch over her, it was the R2 Builders Club that banded together to create one. Thus was born R2-KT, an all-pink droid. Katie got to see and embrace it in July 2010. She passed away the following month. R2-KT lived on, enshrined in the franchise in an episode of the *Star Wars* TV show, *The Clone Wars*.

But it is Artoo, the original astromech, who commands most of the club's time and attention. When builders take their Artoo units out in public, it's not hard to see why. "He's a celebrity wherever you go," says James of his droid. "You could have the best Vader or Fett or even a Wookiee, but when Artoo rolls in, everyone just flocks to him."

Why is that? Why on Earth would a monocular trashcan hold our interest and gain our sympathy? Ask any R2 builder, and they'll give you the same answer: it's the voice. Those expressive bleeps that Ben Burtt created out of his own synthesized baby talk have been transferred to mp3 files and stuck inside hundreds of astromechs: the sad chirp, the excited noise, the petulant whine, the high-pitched squeal. When timed exactly to his curious head movements, the way Lucas and Burtt made sure they were in the movies, the sounds give us the sense of a lovable animal—one that appears to appeal especially to women. (Not for nothing was Artoo portrayed in a Lucasfilm mockumentary written by Bies, called *Under the Dome*, as a rock star with a drinking problem and multiple girlfriends.)

I watched Artoo work the crowd at Barbot, a San Francisco event at which inventors compete to mix cocktails by machine. Artoo attracted more admirers than any robot bartender. James stood off to the side, remotely controlling the droid so it appeared to be interacting with the most curious members of the crowd—again, usually women. James's wife need not be concerned, however. To have his creation be the center of attention is the whole point. He's proud of how easily his prototype remote can go undetected, and happiest when someone is frantically looking around, trying to figure out who's controlling the droid. "With Artoo, you can play up and do cheeky things you'd never do for real," James says. "He's an extension of you. You do have this invisible connection."

The Artoo builders got the ultimate accolade at Celebration III, three short years after they first got their hands on the Uberdroid. Lucas and Rick McCallum came to visit the droid room at the convention; making conversation, they asked the builders how much each droid had cost them. Around $8,000 to $10,000, came the reply. The droid builders report that the Creator and his producer were a little surprised by that number; jaws hit the floor. ILM and its subcontractors had been charging Lucasfilm $80,000 per droid. "If we ever make another *Star Wars* movie," McCallum said, "you guys are hired."

Lucas has let it be known that Artoo is his favorite character. He's the one Lucas liked to imitate on set (one happy story from the desert shoot of *Return of the Jedi* was that Lucas pranked Anthony Daniels by standing in as Artoo, crawling alongside him on all fours and bleeping). Artoo is prominent in every movie; unlike Threepio, he arrives in *Episode I* fully formed. Also unlike Threepio, he doesn't get his mind wiped at the end of *Episode III*, which might explain why he's so willful on Tatooine in *Episode IV* about connecting with Obi-Wan and ensuring that his former master's son rescues his former master's daughter. Artoo saves the lives of every main character in both trilogies. Plot-wise, he never puts a tripod foot wrong—unlike Yoda or Obi-Wan or the entire Jedi order. When the droid showed up for his first day on the set of *Revenge of the Sith*, Lucas told animation director Rob Coleman his ultimate framing device: that the entire story of *Star Wars* is actually being recounted to the keeper of the Journal of the Whills—remember that?—a hundred years after the events of *Return of the Jedi* by none other than R2-D2.

So if there is one eternal truth to every *Star Wars* movie, it isn't that the Force will be with you, since the Force appears as likely as not to lead you down the dark path. It's that R2-D2 is the *man*. And evidently he has the potential to absorb more of your life than all the other characters put together.*

---

* The happy postscript to this chapter came while I was finishing this book. Lucasfilm announced that two British members of the R2 Builders Club, Lee Towersey and Oliver Steeples, would be elevated to the pantheon of *Star Wars* creators. Kathleen Kennedy, following in Lucas and McCallum's footsteps, got a tour of the R2 builders' area at Celebration Europe 2013. Said Steeples to Kennedy, half joking: if you need us for *Episode VII*, we're ready. Kathleen took him at his word. It made perfect financial sense and formed part of Lucasfilm's strategy of outreach to the hard-core fans.

And so it came to pass that Kennedy allowed herself to be photographed and tweeted next to an Artoo, J. J. Abrams, Towersey, and Steeples. A week later came the first confirmation of a character appearing in *Episode VII*: it was Artoo. Towersey and Steeples would put their own version of the Uberdroid, painted hypothetical blue, front and center in the saga.

25.

HOW I STOPPED WORRYING AND LEARNED TO LOVE THE PREQUELS

As much as activities like droid building and costume making brought *Star Wars* fans together in the 2000s, arguments over the quality of the prequel trilogy tore them apart. No one doubted that *Episodes I* through *III* were a giant experimental leap forward for digital filmmaking, or that they left a large imprint on our culture (even the term "prequel" itself was not in common currency until 1999). But nor did anyone doubt that the movies left a bad taste in millions of moviegoers' mouths. Over the decade since their release, the prequels have inspired a level of enmity that doesn't seem to be going away—because as much as Lucasfilm would like to believe the divide is a generational conflict, the truth of the matter is much more murky.

If you could pinpoint the moment this divide began, it would have to be May 19, 1999, shortly after midnight at screenings across America—specifically the second the crawl said "turmoil has engulfed the Galactic Republic," before the dull reason for that turmoil—taxation of trade routes—crossed the screen. It was, as we know from the *Idle Hands* story, a beautiful shining moment of fan unity. There's a reason why director Kyle Newman's 2007 movie *Fanboys*, which deals with a group of *Star Wars* nerds trying to steal an early print of *Phantom*

Menace from Skywalker Ranch in order to screen it for a dying friend, ends at this moment: our heroes, who still haven't seen *Episode I*, sitting in the theater on May 19 as the lights go down. One asks another, "What if it sucks?" Fade to black.

Newman is actually pro-prequel, but he wanted *Fanboys* to recall the positivity and goodwill of that now-fabled era between the Special Editions and the prequels. "People were getting back into it," he says of the *Star Wars* franchise. "There was an energy—it was bringing people back together." After that? "There's no denying something changed. Fandom divided." Sure, there had been debates over the Special Editions. Some fans weren't all that keen on *Return of the Jedi*. But the crisis that was about to descend on *Star Wars* fandom would make heated arguments over Ewoks look like a minor disagreement over the finer points of lightsaber coloring.

It wasn't just that some fans loved the prequels while others loathed them. There were those whose affections shifted one way or another, slowly over months or years, and there were those who were able to convince themselves of the movies' worth over time. Newman says that a sequel to *Fanboys*, if he were to film such a thing, would open after *Attack of the Clones* and mirror this splintering of *Star Wars* fandom. One of his characters, Hutch, would be angry about everything in the movie; another, Windows, would be the rationalizer, explaining away every questionable plot choice. The third lead, Eric, would play the arbitrator, which is where I sit in the debate: mildly disappointed but curious about whether the rationalizers can make me believe again.

The Hutches of the *Star Wars* fan world, by their nature, tend to have the loudest voices. You can see their reaction to the prequels by watching Simon Pegg—the British actor later to play Scotty in J. J. Abrams's *Star Trek*—in Pegg's 1999–2001 UK sitcom, *Spaced*. In imitation of the scene at the end of *Return of the Jedi*, in which Luke Skywalker burns Vader's corpse on a funeral pyre, Pegg's character burns his *Star Wars* collection in his backyard after seeing *Phantom Menace*. It was played as comedy, but Pegg, a lifelong passionate fan, had a similar reaction to the prequels. In 2010, he called Phantom Menace "a boring, turquid, confused mess of pretentious masquerading as children's entertainment."* In *Spaced*, Pegg wasn't really acting when he is seen yelling at a child in his comic book store who asks for a Jar Jar Binks doll: "You weren't there at the beginning! You don't know how good it was, how important! This is it for you, this jumped-up fireworks display of a toy advert!"

---

* Pegg also says Lucas offered him this advice at the London premiere of *Episode III*: "don't suddenly find yourself making the same film you made thirty years ago."

Ah yes, the kids. Newman's three characters are useful avatars for the different factions of adult *Star Wars* fandom, but children who love the prequels are an equally numerous, and constantly refreshed, group worth considering. Lucas is keenly aware of this fourth faction. The Creator has in fact simplistically suggested that the only divide in his fandom is along the lines of age. "We know we had a real honest-to-God generation gap with *Star Wars*," George Lucas said at Celebration V in 2010, in an interview on stage with Jon Stewart. "Everybody over forty loves [*Episodes*] *IV*, *V*, and *VI* and hates *I*, *II*, and *III*. Kids under thirty all love *I*, *II*, and *III*, and hate *IV*, *V*, and *VI*." This caused a commotion in the audience, such that Lucas was nearly shouted down. "If you're ten years old," he shouted back, "stand up and fight for your rights!"

But the demographics of *Star Wars* fandom were never as cut and dry as Lucas suggested. I know a ten-year-old who hates *Phantom Menace* but thinks *Return of the Jedi* and *Revenge of the Sith* are the greatest movies ever. Kids are like that, as Lucas surely knows—unpredictable and picky. They like or dislike movies in the rather more innocent way that Lucas once spoke of, the way you enjoy a sunset, and they tend to change their opinions dramatically as they get older. "It was a magnificent spectacle as a child," says Liz Lee, star of the MTV high school mockumentary *My Life as Liz*. "That's when CGI was still exciting."

Lee was eight years old at the time *Phantom Menace* came out; now she's twenty-one. She's still enough of a *Star Wars* fan to get a tattoo representing the Mandalorians, the warrior race who wear the armor of Boba and Jango Fett. "The older I get," she says, "the more I appreciate the original trilogy, and the more I start to resent the prequels. It's not like I'm angry about it, but my adult self isn't as into them."

Regardless of age, everyone's reaction to the movies is slightly different. Many fans love one of the prequels and hate two, or love two and hate one—as did Newman, who found nothing at all to like in *Attack of the Clones*.

Perhaps you've wondered, as I have, what to do with your uneasiness about the prequels. Perhaps you too have wondered if it is simply impossible to enjoy any new *Star Wars* movie if you're over twenty, or thirty, or forty. We won't really know until *Episode VII* repeats the experiment on a planetary scale. In the meantime, a bit of amateur therapy can help to ease the pain—and it begins with working through the five stages of *Star Wars* prequel grief.

The first stage of grief, of course, is denial: you can take the movies you don't like and simply declare they don't exist.

Remember Chris Giunta, the guy who got engaged right before the midnight screening of *The Phantom Menace* with a little help from Rick McCallum? Fast-forward fifteen years. Giunta is back in Maryland, in a house outfitted with a resin-cast bar that looks exactly like Han Solo frozen in carbonite, a screening room–quality home theater system, and an absolutely firm policy: no prequels, ever. "None of my three kids have seen the prequels or the Special Editions," he says. "I have the 1996 laser disc of the original trilogy, and that's all they've ever seen. The girls understand that there is other *Star Wars*, and that Daddy gets mad when it's brought up. My son is seven; he's got friends at school who watch the *Clone Wars* cartoons. He says, 'Dad, there are other *Star Wars* movies!' I say, 'No, they're not real *Star Wars* movies.'"

A less extreme version of the denial response is represented by something called Machete Order. Colorado programmer Rod Hilton came up with this on his blog *Absolutely No Machete Juggling* in November 2011—hence the name. To Hilton's surprise, Machete Order became an Internet phenomenon and was widely discussed online throughout 2012.

Machete Order was Hilton's response to the problem of what order to watch the saga in. After all, watching them in numerical order spoils the biggest surprise of the series—*Episode V*'s "I am your father"—because a new viewer would learn Luke's parentage in *Episode III*. But watch the classic trilogy before the prequel trilogy, and you're confronted with the elderly Emperor before the young Palpatine, so his character arc is spoiled too. (Not to mention Hayden Christensen's Force ghost at the end of the post-2004 version of *Return of the Jedi*: Who the heck, you might wonder, is that guy?)

Machete Order compromises by presenting the saga this way: *Episodes IV, V, II, III,* and finally *VI*. This essentially makes the prequels an extended flashback after the parental revelation. The question of whether Vader is telling the truth—and if so, how it happened—adds new tension to *Episodes II* and *III*. The identity of the Emperor is preserved. *Episode I* is omitted altogether, and its loss is not felt because "every character established in it is either killed or removed before it ends," says Hilton, "or established better in a later episode. Search your feelings, you know it to be true!"

Those who've tried *Star Wars* marathons the Hilton way report a welcome ominous feeling creeping in during the two remaining prequels. "With the Machete Order," raved the website *Den of Geek*, "the control of the Emperor over the universe feels absolute and tyrannical. His knowledge of the dark side of the force is insurmountable. The end of the Emperor is the greatest day for the universe in 30 years; it gives justification to the scale of the celebrations that follow."

Would George Lucas object to Machete Order? In one sense, yes: he stands by *Episode I*. But the creator certainly knows the power of reordering movies in the saga, because that's what he was intending to do all along with the prequels: to change your perspective on the classic trilogy. "Part of the fun for me was completely flipping upside down the dramatic track of the original movies," Lucas said. "If you watch it the way it was released, you get one kind of movie. If you watch I through VI, you get a completely different movie. It's extremely modern, almost interactive moviemaking. You take blocks and move them around and you come out with different emotional states."

Star Wars fans embraced the interactive possibilities of the series as far back as 2000, when a LA-based film editor called Mike J. Nichols put together a poorly trimmed-down version of *Episode I* called *The Phantom Edit*. It was twenty minutes shorter than the original. In Nichols's version, scenes flashed by at speeds that might give even Land of Zoom supereditor Lucas whiplash (if he ever watched it; Lucasfilm has stated the Creator has no interest in seeing any kind of bastardized version of his work). Much of Jar Jar's dialogue was removed, making the Gungan more of a Buster Keaton–style silent comedian. Ditto with Jake Lloyd's dialogue as nine-year-old Anakin.

The edit was distributed anonymously online; it was burned onto DVDs and passed around by hand. Lucasfilm stepped in when it heard that bootleggers— and some video stores—were starting to sell copies of the DVD, which crossed the line from enthusiastic fan edit to copyright violation. "We realized that these were fans having some fun with *Star Wars*, which we've never had a problem with," Lucasfilm spokeswoman Jeanne Cole said in June 2001. "But over the last 10 days, this thing has grown and taken on a life of its own—as things sometimes do when associated with *Star Wars*." Two weeks later, Nichols apologized and said that his "well-intentioned editing demonstration" had "escalated out of my control."*

The commercial bootlegging would fade away with increased bandwidth speeds and the rise of file-sharing sites—if you could download a high-definition version of something like *The Phantom Edit* for free, why would you pay a guy on the street for an inferior DVD copy? Indeed, Nichols was only the first in a long line of reeditors. These days you can find hundreds of versions of each *Star Wars* movie, the original included, fixing dialogue and removing all sorts of perceived errors. (One of the most intriguing, and impossible to find, was an edit of all three prequels into a single eighty-five-minute film by the TV

---

* Lucasfilm confirmed to me that Lucas has no interest in watching *The Phantom Edit*.

actor and film nerd Topher Grace; Grace only screened it as a "one-time thing," according to Newman, one of the few who got to see it.) Fan edits are a prime example of "Read/Write" culture as opposed to "Read-Only" culture, according to the theory outlined in Harvard law professor Lawrence Lessig's seminal book *Remix*. It seems somehow fitting—or terribly ironic—that a perfectionist director whose first student movie was a one-minute collage ripped from magazines should have his most famous work subjected to this twenty-first-century form of collage.

There's one more denial response worth mentioning: denial of the dialogue, or at least denial of its delivery. Emily Asher-Perrin at the science fiction blog *Tor.com* decided to take Lucas at his word when he called the prequels "silent films," and watched the entire prequel trilogy with the sound turned down and John Williams's soundtrack CD in the background. "It plays on a distinctly different emotional level," she concluded. "It made me feel I understood what Lucas was going for."

If you're baffled and upset at the idea that you might need to watch the prequels on mute in order to truly understand them, you're probably ready for the next stage of prequel grief. It's the one that leads to suffering and the Dark Side, if Yoda is to be believed: anger. And there is perhaps no better example of sustained, simmering anger at the prequels than that which can be found in the Mr. Plinkett reviews.

In 2009, a Milwaukee-based filmmaker called Mike Stoklasa produced a comprehensive, vehement, and maniacally obsessive video review of *Phantom Menace*. The review lasted seventy minutes, so Stoklasa chopped it up into seven ten-minute YouTube videos. As unpromising as that sounds—a review that's more than half the length of the movie?—the videos were promoted on Twitter by prominent geeks such as Simon Pegg and *Lost* showrunner Damon Lindelof, and subsequently seen by more than five million people. Stoklasa followed up with ninety-minute reviews of *Clones*, *Sith*, and dozens of other movies, also chopped up into digestible chunks. Stoklasa's YouTube channel, Red Letter Media, has now racked up more than forty-six million views, most of them from the prequel reviews.

What's the appeal? Stoklasa plays the jester, adopting a character (created by a friend) named Harry Plinkett, the never-seen narrator of the reviews. Plinkett, it emerges, is part film nerd, part serial killer, off his meds, and frequently off topic; he offers several times to mail pizza rolls to his viewers. Stoklasa draws on his Chicago film school education to skewer Lucas's approach: how *Episode I* and *II* lack a real protagonist; how much of Episode III employs the dull editing technique known as shot reverse shot. But by putting it in the Plinkett persona, he is simultaneously parodying the obsessive *Star Wars* fan. Perhaps the most ironic result of Plinkett's popularity: one fan decided to blog a rebuttal of everything in Stoklasa's prequel reviews, point by point. This screed, unintentionally Plinkett-like, ran to 108 pages.

Stoklasa intended to show that the Emperor wore no clothes. "I'm not convinced that George is this genius filmmaker that he's always been portrayed as being," he says. "I see him as a guy who had a neat idea to make a space adventure movie in the spirit of the old *Flash Gordon* serials. Modernize it a little, make it share a lot of visual elements with World War II, add some mythological elements and call it *Star Wars*. Then get a whole other bunch of people to make it work somehow. . . . He works best when other people take his ideas and work with them. When he writes and directs, it's disastrous."

Stoklasa makes this point elegantly in the most oft-cited section of his *Episode I* review, which has him asking four fans who've seen both the original trilogy and *Phantom Menace* to describe characters from each, without describing their appearance or profession. Han Solo is roguish, dashing, arrogant, a scoundrel, walks the line, has a good heart. Qui-Gon Jinn is . . . Well, Stoklasa's four panelists have a very hard time coming up with a description until one suggests: "stern?" Threepio is prissy, bumbling, cowardly, anal retentive; Padmé Amidala is . . . The fans cannot come up with a single description that doesn't mention her makeup, clothes, or royal position, and it seems to be a genuine revelation. "This is funny," says one. "I get it."

The most damning words in the Plinkett reviews, however, come from Lucas and McCallum themselves. Stoklasa has done his homework, clipping quotes from DVD extras and documentaries that show the director and producer at their most inane. "It's like poetry; it rhymes," Lucas is shown telling his staff of the script, repeatedly. "It's so dense; every single image has so much going on," says McCallum. Stoklasa plays this quote in the context of some of the prequels' profoundly confusing special effects shots, where it isn't entirely clear whom we're supposed to be following or why. Suddenly it seems McCallum is describing a movie full of sound and fury, signifying nothing.

The clips give us the best sense of the exhaustion, creatively and physically, that seemed to dominate the production of the prequels. He shows clips of Lucas slumped in his director's chair with a large Starbucks cup or surrounded by people whose facial expressions speak volumes. Lucas jokes about not having finished the scripts yet; his underlings smile, while their eyes display the terror of someone trapped on an eternal funhouse ride. To paraphrase something Lucas once said about his father: he is the boss, the one they fear.* We see the actors against green screen with two cameras, and every nonaction scene looks boringly similar: two actors walk slowly down a corridor or through a room, stop, turn to a window. (As if this isn't boring enough, Stoklasa points out, nearly all of the important discussions in *Sith* take place on couches: once you realize this sort of thing about the prequels, it is a hard thing to un-see.)

For all his anger, Stoklasa denies himself some of the easy jabs favored by prequel haters. He doesn't blame Hayden Christensen's performance as Anakin: "Even Sir Lawrence Oliver [*sic*] couldn't make this shit work," mumbles Plinkett. As for Jar Jar Binks? "You can make an argument that Jar Jar was the only thing you could understand clearly," Stoklasa says. "He had some kind of motivation and a character arc. He was annoying, yes, but ironically, he was the most realistic and understandable thing in *Phantom Menace*."

Stoklasa is a bête noire for prequel defenders, largely because every *Star Wars* story and forum now seems to contain comments from people who link to his videos rather than voice their own opinion. But underneath its twisted humor, his is a relatively reasoned and educated take. Other commentators have taken a far cruder approach. In 2005, a band called the Waffles wrote a song called "George Lucas Raped Our Childhood." Three years later, the creators of *South Park* went even closer to the bone in an episode in which Lucas is shown raping a Stormtrooper. Hell hath no viciousness like a *Star Wars* fan spurned.

When denial and anger have run their course, there's always bargaining. Since *Star Wars* fans are such a creative bunch, everyone disappointed by the prequels has shared this thought: *I could have done better.* Arguments over exactly how each prequel movie could have been made better have been raging in bedrooms, dorm rooms, and coffee shops for years. Monday-morning quarterbacking is fun, up to a point—but this is Monday through Sunday morning quarterbacking, and it doesn't look as if it's ever going to end.

The poster boy for bargaining over the prequels is Michael Barryte, a twenty-six-year-old YouTube star from Los Angeles. Like Stoklasa, Barryte is a film

---

* It was around this time, in the 2004 documentary *Empire of Dreams*, that Lucas started comparing his life story to that of Darth Vader's: a man trapped in the Lucasfilm machine.

school graduate—from UCLA, Coppola's alma mater—but he's younger and way more upbeat in his outlook. Barryte was a child actor on Nickelodeon when he was in high school and played the young Jerry Seinfeld in an HBO special; he still has the excitable voice and wide-eyed shotgun delivery of a children's TV presenter. When *Episode I* came out, Barryte was twelve—no bitter old fogey he. But there were things that soon grew to bother him and his friends about the movie, such as the fact that it really seemed as if it should have been Obi-Wan's story and that Darth Maul's death wasted a perfectly good villain. In 2012, Lucasfilm rereleased *The Phantom Menace*, this time in 3-D. Barryte, who ran what was then a minor movie-focused YouTube channel called Belated Media, wanted to do a video review that focused only on the elements he liked. "Plinkett is skewering and deconstruction, and it's remarkable," Barryte says. "But I didn't just want to pan the film. Nobody goes to a movie to be disappointed. I've been trying to skew more positive."

It turned out there simply weren't enough elements he liked to base a review on, though, so instead Barryte let his imagination roam through a slightly altered version of the movie. The resulting video is called "What If *Episode I* Were Good?" It took a year for it to go viral, but viral it went; it has now been seen more than two million times. Barryte's channel went from five thousand to a hundred thousand subscribers. His new fans began clamoring for a follow-up, "What If *Episode II* Were Good?," which Barryte, more of a movie fan than specifically a *Star Wars* fan, had never intended to make. In 2013, he relented. The result got another million views in the space of a week, and Barryte began to be bombarded with emails from fans with their own alternate script ideas. "I unknowingly swatted the biggest hornet's nest in fandom," he says. (He's still working on his *Episode III* video.)

Barryte's is an infectious alternate vision of *Episode I*—and unlike much of the Monday-morning quarterbacking, it is an elegant proposition with as few changes to the movie as possible. In Barryte's telling, Jar Jar Binks is removed altogether, though the Gungans remain. Obi-Wan is moved to the foreground, becoming the protagonist, but his master, Qui-Gon, is still present. Anakin is brought up in age, and Qui-Gon can simply sense the Force is strong with him, rather than testing him for midi-chlorians. Padmé flirts with Obi-Wan, who later saves her life—diverting him from the lightsaber battle with Darth Maul. Maul kills Qui-Gon and survives, setting up Obi-Wan to hunt Maul down in later movies. Yoda is largely absent from the Jedi Council, creating a sense of mystery around the character. Palpatine becomes a functionary who mediates between the Jedi Council and the Senate, a role that gives him more strings to pull. And that is pretty much it. Barryte speedily recounts the scenes that follow logically from these decisions, with plenty of jump-cuts and visual gags to keep us entertained as we walk through the land of Might Have Been.

But of course, the *Star Wars* that might have been wasn't. This is the ultimate problem with the bargaining stage of grief: at some point, the fantasy has to collapse, and we experience the pain of the prequels all over again. Everyone has their preferences; everyone carries their own version of *Star Wars* in their heads. Expanded Universe author Timothy Zahn hated the midi-chlorian concept of the Force: "I hope that it will be dropped," he said in 2000, in vain as it turned out (midi-chlorians were mentioned again in *Revenge of the Sith*). Even Kyle Newman, prequel defender, would have had one actor and one actor only play Anakin throughout the prequels.

The fictional Mr. Plinkett, at least, accepts the reality of what happened in the prequels. "Perhaps the worst thing about them is that they will be around forever," he says in deathly monotone at the very beginning of his *Phantom Menace* review. "They will never go away. They can never be undone."

All thinking *Star Wars* fans must at some point wrestle with the significant gap between the shining, perfect *idea* of *Star Wars* and its sometimes less than perfect execution. The most passionate fans are often the most perfectionist, so they wrestle with this problem a lot, and this can lead them to the penultimate stage of *Star Wars* grief: depression. Nobody can say how widespread a condition prequel depression is, but remember those Darth Vader YouTube parodies I mentioned back in Chapter 9? The most viewed of all is "The *Star Wars* That I Used to Know" (15 million views), a parody of Gotye's monster 2012 hit which feature Vader singing to George Lucas. ("No you didn't have to make them blow. . . . What happened to the *Star Wars* that I used to know.")

No fan wants this state of mind; it just descends on them—not so much like the Dark Side of the Force but more like the version of the Dark Side that Lucas conceived during the second draft of *Star Wars*: the Bogan Force. When you're struck with the Bogan as that early version of Han Solo was, you too have to drive it from your mind. Otherwise you find yourself in the garbage masher with a line of thought that might go something like this:

It's no use trying to love Star Wars *the way you once did. You can't go home again; you can't find the spirit of 1977 except in history books. We're know-it-alls now, as the Navajo Nation's Manny Wheeler put it. The Internet is filled with us. We're too ready to throw our peanuts from the gallery and loudly opine on the nearest social media soapbox about what we would do differently. No one can just enjoy a sunset, so no one can successfully tell an epic, nonironic story any more; we lose the ability to be enraptured as teenagers. We gave in to hate. We got the prequels we deserved. We should accept that this was just diverting doggerel for children; its Creator couldn't come up with enough new ideas, so made movies that rhymed with the predecessors. This is the fate of all creators and all creative endeavors: they get tired; they get repetitive. The whole Joseph Campbell monomyth thing was just a pretentious layer self-consciously applied by Lucas in the 1980s and agreed upon by a society that was so desperate for escapism, so enamored with newfangled special effects, that it placed three movies on a pedestal that nothing else could reach, when really they were on rickety foundations to begin with. The only solution is to give up on* Star Wars *altogether and commit ourselves. Let us sell the* Star Wars *figures in the attic. Let us put away childish things.*

If that's the way you're thinking by this point in the chapter, if you've hit rock bottom in prequel grief, then perhaps it's time for a come-to-Jesus moment—or a come-to-the-Force moment, if you prefer. Let me introduce you to a good old-fashioned revival preacher.

A cceptance is the hardest stage of the grieving process, but also the most crucial. Only by understanding the prequel movies the way they are—not the way they might have been—can fans hope to move on and find peace in their perception of the franchise.

I wanted to see the prequels the way defenders saw them. So I turned to Bryan Young, *Star Wars* blogger (at StarWars.com, among other places), podcaster, and one of the smartest and most reliable defenders of the prequels on the planet. When *Phantom Menace* came out, Young had just graduated high school and waited in line for thirty days at his theater in Utah. Unlike the rest of the guys in line, he actually worked at the theater and was able to see the movie seventy more times. His son was born immediately after *Clones*; Young named him Anakin.

A solid-looking guy with an utterly unflappable demeanor, Young moderated a few "Why We Love the Prequels" panels at conventions. And he has done what no one else, to my knowledge, has dared: one drunken night at a Celebration in 2012, he defended the prequels in person to Jake Lloyd, the actor who played Anakin Skywalker in *Episode I*. Lloyd quit acting after that movie; now, in his early twenties, he bears an unambiguous, sneering disdain for the film, for which he was hounded throughout high school and college. Young didn't exactly succeed in winning Lloyd over to the prequels; Lloyd simply disengaged when he found out the name of Young's son, and later unfriended him Facebook.

I sat down with Young for several hours and craft beers in his hometown, Salt Lake City, and told him I was going to play devil's advocate. I was going to hit him with every problem anyone ever had with the first three movies, every question I could come up with. He nodded stoically. "Dealing with prequel hate is my specialty," he said. Ladies and gentlemen: Bryan Young, *Star Wars* therapist.

To begin, then: the dialogue. It was uniformly dreadful throughout *Episodes I to III*, right? To my surprise, Young didn't disagree. "George Lucas is not a writer," he said simply, and of course the Creator himself has said as much. Then how, I asked, are we to take the dialogue—as an intentional, humorous pastiche of *Flash Gordon* and *Buck Rogers*? Young nodded sagely: "I have to take it that way if I'm going to enjoy the movies."

For the kind of fan who needs in-universe reasons for things, Young has one of those explanations for their stilted dialogue, too. These three films deal mostly with aristocrats and politicians, queens and senators, the high-falutin' Jedi Council. To hear how that kind of person talks in the original trilogy, listen to Princess Leia and Grand Moff Tarkin. "They do talk in that really stilted faux-Victorian style the prequels are permeated with," Young said. "Only there isn't a Han Solo character to come in and roll his eyes at everything and sound cool. That kind of character doesn't exist in the prequels because we're in a different world. You're dealing with royalty. In the classic trilogy, you're dealing with every farmboy and shitkicker in the galaxy."

Ah, but there was one prominent member of the unsophisticated class: Jar Jar Binks. Surely there was no defense for this prattling, insufferable addition to the *Star Wars* canon? Again, Young was disarming: he found Jar Jar "totally obnoxious" just like the rest of us. "It took me a while to come around to why he was in the story," he said. It wasn't until he was watching an episode of *Clone Wars* with his daughter, who was eight at the time, in which Jar Jar featured; she declared that *Star Wars* wasn't *Star Wars* without Jar Jar. "He's supposed to speak to the kids and be obnoxious to everybody else," Young explained. "He's obnoxious to all the other characters. The moral of the story is you have to put up with these annoying people sometimes. You still have to treat them with dignity and respect. Every life has value."

It's hard to argue with that defense of Jar Jar, and it certainly beats the argument I'd heard from Lucas on stage at Celebration—that contemporary viewers hated Threepio in the original movies just as much as they did Jar Jar in the prequels. (That's a false equivalence if ever I heard one.) Regarding Young contemplatively over our beers, I began to think Lucasfilm should hire him to go on the road and evangelize: an old-time prequel preacher.

As devil's advocate, it was time to take the gloves off. How about the casting of Hayden Christensen as Anakin in *Attack of the Clones*, I asked him? Surely Young didn't buy Anakin's painfully whiny attempts to romance Padmé in that movie? Turns out he did. "He isn't any more or less whiny than Mark Hamill in *Episode IV*," he said (and it wasn't hard to tell what line Young was thinking about: "But I was going to Tosche Station to pick up some power converters!"*).

Christensen acted appropriately for the situation he was in, Young believes. "Think about it: you're a celibate monk who doesn't know how to deal with a girl, and all of a sudden you're thrust into a situation with probably the most attractive woman in the galaxy. You're going to act like an idiot and talk even stupider. Can you remember the first thing you said to a girl as a teenager? Was it any better than 'I don't like sand, it's rough, coarse, irritating, and it gets everywhere'?"

I conceded that it was not.

When Young does take issue with the prequels, it tends to be over the kind of thing you only notice after you've watched each movie dozens of times—such as the few scenes in *Attack of the Clones* where Ewan McGregor, filmed in pickup months after the original shoot, wears a fake beard that's glued on like a toupee. Young doesn't see what I see in much of McGregor's performance: boredom and barely disguised contempt. Maybe, just maybe, that perception vanishes when you've watched these movies as many times as Young has. "Nostalgia and familiarity are two things people don't attach to the prequels," he said. "If they did, they'd like them more. Think about it: by the time *Episode I* came out, how many times had you seen *Episode IV*?"

I admitted that I'd worn out my dad's VHS tape of *Star Wars* back in 1983 and stopped counting after I'd seen it fifty times.

"There you go," Young said. "Part of the feeling of watching a *Star Wars* movie is knowing it inside and out. I saw *Episode I* seven times over that first weekend, and I guarantee I liked it more the seventh time than the first."

The more he watched the prequels, the more parallels between the trilogies Young found. He saw and heard that rhyming Lucas kept talking about, and he

---

* Even today, Hamill defends his delivery of this line as deliberately whiny—it was so that Luke Skywalker would have an arc that took him from willful teenager to mindful Jedi Knight.

liked it. Anakin's and Luke's journeys started to mirror each other. Both ignore their training in their second movie because of their emotional attachments, for example. When Young heard about Machete Order, he embraced it, but reinserted *Episode I*, and now enthuses about how much it enhances the rhyming. You see Anakin's fall in its entirety after *Empire Strikes Back*; then the first time you see Luke in *Return of the Jedi*, he's dressed all in black and choking pig guards in Jabba's Palace. You can't help but wonder: has he fallen like his father? "The prequels enhance the experience of the classic films so much it's disgusting," Young says.

We went on for hours like this. Young handled everything I threw at him. The fact that the dirty "Used Universe" style seems to vanish in the prequels, to the point where historically inept reviewers chided Lucas for shunning the grime of *Alien* or *Blade Runner*? That just makes it clear how much of a mess the Empire has made of the galaxy by the time we get to *Episode IV*. Midichlorians in the bloodstream? They just showed that the Jedi were spending way too much time studying, over-intellectualizing everything. Young came out with the responses so readily, so naturally, that it was clear he wasn't just rationalizing. He genuinely believes in the prequels, as do millions more—whether they feel comfortable admitting it in public or not.

I may never be able to watch *Episodes I–III* without wincing, or perhaps playing them on mute with John Williams in the background. But I have finally made my peace with them. The novelizations of each movie are helping in this process: in those, at least, there are no worries about wooden dialogue or poor acting. Legendary fantasy author Terry Brooks clearly enjoyed himself turning *Phantom Menace* into prose (he called it a "dream project"). Brooks's literary version of Jar Jar is a sympathetic exiled Gungan who just wants to make things right with his people. Matthew Woodring Stover's interpretation of *Revenge of the Sith* is a minor classic, much beloved by fans; it fleshes out much of Anakin's motivation that was missing from the movie. Other entries in the Expanded Universe also have the benefit of resolving flaws and absences in the prequels. That whole "Sifo-Dyas" plot hole is tied up in the 2005 novel *Labyrinth of Evil*. The "tragedy of Darth Plagueis," the story Palpatine tells Anakin at the opera in *Episode III* (but which he leaves tantalizingly sketchy), was fleshed out into novel form in 2012's *Darth Plagueis*.

In short, if you want to find a new angle on the prequels, they are there for the taking. You could, for example, consider the possibility that there were actually two ideas of *Star Wars*. One idea belonged to us, the audience, and it was of a believable universe of cheerable heroes and hissable villians, one that transfigured in the retelling into something darker, weightier, more mythological, more adult. We saw Sergio Leone in a desert landscape, when it was really only that desolate because the Creator didn't have the budget to properly populate it. And this was fine.

Then there was the other idea of *Star Wars*—the Creator's idea. It was always a little bit goofier, and a lot more stuffed with wacky aliens and Land-of-Zoom spaceships. It was *Flash Gordon* fan fiction intended for children and our inner children. And this too was fine. And if you just can't appreciate the prequel movies or rationalize them away, does that make you any less of a *Star Wars* fan? Certainly not—just so long as you're the live-and-let-live type. "*Star Wars* is a buffet," Young says. "Take what you want, and leave the rest for everyone else. You don't put your finger in the mashed potatoes if you don't like them."

If it helps, consider the prequels are as effectively one long shaggy dog story. Anakin Skywalker is supposed to "bring balance to the Force," the meaning of which seems blithely accepted by the Jedi Council but little explained. Yoda and company simply seem to believe that the prophecy means something good. But after the prequels, so far as we know, there are two Jedi left in the galaxy (Obi-Wan and Yoda) and two Sith (Palpatine and Vader). That's balance, right?*

The prequels thus become a fable with a moral, and the moral is: don't believe everything that's foretold. For example, don't believe a filmmaker who says there will never, ever be any more *Star Wars* movies, period.

---

* Lucas went even further, suggesting that "bringing balance to the Force" would only be achieved at the end of *Return of the Jedi*: "The prophecy was right," he said in 2005. "Anakin was the chosen one, and he does bring balance to the Force. He takes the ounce of good left in him and destroys the Emperor out of compassion for his son."

26.

USING THE UNIVERSE

The *Star Wars* saga seemed like it was just getting settled into its happy retirement on June 25, 2005, just over a month after the release of *Revenge
of the Sith*. It was another mild and foggy summer day in San Francisco. The
Coronet had not been able to show that last episode of the franchise it helped
birth; suffering from declining ticket sales, the theater had closed its doors for
the last time in March and would be razed two years later to make way for a
senior citizen center.

In the Presidio, walking distance from the Coronet, George Lucas welcomed
the press to the official opening ceremony for Lucasfilm's new $350 million
headquarters. Called the Letterman Digital Arts Center, it would bring together most of the company's disparate divisions: ILM would move down from
San Rafael, Lucasfilm's licensing and marketing arms would relocate from the
ranch, and the video game branch, LucasArts, would arrive from the overflow
ranch, Lucas's property next door to Skywalker, known as Big Rock.

The opening was celebrated with one of Lucasfilm's now-famous all-day
picnics. The picnics were Lucas at his most generous. Attendees—myself included—all collected meticulously crafted wooden picnic boxes inscribed with
the date and location; we got serenaded by Bonnie Raitt and Chris Isaak and
served by a ridiculously good-looking wait staff. A VIP audience ranging from
real politicians (Nancy Pelosi, Barbara Boxer) to fake politicians (Richard
Schiff, who played Toby on *The West Wing*) wandered the winding stone paths

of the seventeen-acre headquarters, taking in its view of the Palace of Fine Arts and the Golden Gate Bridge. Downtown San Francisco and the delights of the Marina district's Chestnut Street were a short drive and walk, respectively, to the east.

Such a dramatic relocation had been necessary, and not just because Skywalker, Big Rock, and the ILM facility in San Rafael were bursting at the seams. Coming to the city just felt healthier. "We spent a lot of years hidden away," said Micheline Chau, the former health care industry executive and accountant who became Lucasfilm president in 2003. "I'm not sure if it was good for the company as a whole."

Lucasfilm had long been proselytizing for digital movies, and what better place to do that than in the world capital of digital ideas? What Chau didn't say, however, was that without more *Star Wars* to make, the company would need to drum up business in order to maintain the same level of employees. Lucasfilm couldn't rely on the good will of a benign billionaire forever.

Lucas had used his earnings from the first *Star Wars* movie to build Skywalker Ranch on a 1,700-acre plot of land in a Marin County valley. A World War II hospital had been demolished to make way for the second great house that *Star Wars* built. Bodies had been found on the grounds, and stories of hauntings by the staff would lead Chau to pay for a company-wide exorcism late one night that involved sprinkling rice around supposedly haunted sections of the building. The site soon acquired a restaurant and cocktail bar called Dixie's, whose bartender—when I visited, at least—had a lightsaber tattooed on his middle finger. There was a superfast fiber-optic connection to Skywalker Ranch running through the state-of-the-art servers in the Letterman Center's basement, annihilating time and distance between the two ends of the Lucas empire. "The Ranch" would always be called just that, whereas Lucas and ILM employees (1,500 of whom were about to start moving to Letterman at the time of the opening picnic) would take to calling the new facility the Death Star. (When, in time, Disney took over Lucasfilm, and hundreds of these same employees were fired in rolling waves of layoffs, some of them would start to employ a darker nickname for the site: Mouseschwitz.)

Rising to address the crowd in one of Letterman's large, light atriums on the day of the opening ceremony, Lucas mumbled through some remarks. He noted how fitting it was that Letterman had been completed at the same time as *Revenge of the Sith*, because both had begun at the same time: three years earlier. *Sith* had been released five weeks earlier and was of course another unqualified success. In a year in which movie attendance was declining precipitously and there were no real blockbusters, *Episode III* ruled the roost. In six weeks in the United States alone it made $361,471,114, or more than three times' Lucas's budget. Fans had still camped out for tickets even though online ordering was widely available; the line had become a ritual in itself. In Seattle, one obsessive fan began camping out for *Episode III* tickets a record 139 days in advance.

In media interviews after his remarks, Lucas announced that he had sworn off making $100 million movies for good, with the air of a man who was taking his winnings and getting out of town. Oh, he'd always be connected to the realm of special effects thanks to ILM, which at the time was working on new movies from franchises like Harry Potter and *Pirates of the Caribbean*, as well as a certain flick about a lion, a witch, and a wardrobe. *Indiana Jones 4*, which Lucas was then writing for Spielberg, didn't count; he meant he'd sworn off $100 million *Star Wars* movies, not $100 million movies in general. "A lot of *Star Wars* is over," he said, "in terms of the features."

What was Lucas going to do next? Why, he said, he was going to "go off and write my own little experimental films." He concluded his press interviews, and off he walked into the corridors of the Death Star, adorned with a half dozen Darth Vader statues and a Jar Jar Binks in carbonite that had been presented to him by the 501st legion.

Experimental films? Right. In fact, as Lucas had announced back in April at Celebration III, Lucasfilm was already working on not one but two *Star Wars* TV series—one live action, one animated. In fact, the very building itself was intended to serve as a production facility for *Star Wars* TV shows (and, if one line of discussion panned out, a whole TV channel dedicated to the franchise). These new initiatives—and the ultimate fight for survival that developed between them—would represent a kind of battle for the soul of *Star Wars*.

Over the preceding years, especially after the delights of *Young Indiana Jones* and the agonies of the prequels, it had become apparent to Lucas that he was most comfortable as a TV kind of executive producer—a showrunner, basically, the kind that comes up with the overarching themes and directions of a fictional world and then allows a bunch of smart writers to flesh it out. This was how *Empire* and *Jedi* had been written; the prequels had lacked any such writers' room conviviality, and fans had given Lucas hell for it. No wonder he yearned to get back to a collaborative mode of filmmaking.

It had also been evident for years that animation was Lucas's first love and that he found actors hard to manage. "If there were a way to make movies without actors," Mark Hamill had suggested in the 1980s, "George Lucas would do it." By the 2000s, computer animation was indeed offering Lucas a way to make movies without the inconvenience of actors, at least in their corporeal form. So it is perhaps not surprising that the *Star Wars* live-action TV series would ultimately flounder, while the animated series—*The Clone Wars*—would go from strength to strength.

The success of *The Clone Wars* was by no means a sure thing. The live action series, developed under the working title of *Star Wars Underworld*, had a great deal of potential. Lucasfilm was in talks with ABC, mostly, but also at one point HBO, for the rights to screen it. Centered on the Galactic capital of Coruscant in the two decades between *Episode III* and *Episode IV*, it would focus on the seedy underbelly of the Empire: the gangsters, smugglers, and bounty hunters who had been so missed by mature audiences in the prequels. It would also tie into a computer game of the same name (a game that was later renamed *Star Wars 1313* and even later was shelved by Disney). Unconfirmed rumors suggest the series was to use Boba Fett as a recurring character. One ship we know was going to be featured in the show, according to design sketches: the *Millennium Falcon*.

Underworld went through many years of intensive concept design. Lucas kept a small team of artists on the third floor of Skywalker Ranch, directly above his office, with private back stairs so he could reach them at any time (polite to a fault, Lucas would always knock). Technically, they worked for another Lucasfilm subsidiary, JAK Enterprises, named for the first letters of Lucas' three kids. As one artist put it, George treated the third floor like his sketchpad.

Rick McCallum executive produced *Underworld* alongside Lucas. Both men described the show as dark, Western-like, "*Deadwood* in space." But it soon appeared to the artists that they had distinctly different ideas about what this meant. McCallum saw a largely indoor drama that could be made very cheaply. "But then George would come in and say, 'Let's add another speeder bike chase,'" said a member of the production team. Lucas apparently wanted the show to focus on what the citizens of the galaxy did for fun. There would be more drag-race-style pod races. The boy racer had never grown out of his need for speed.

It could have been worse. Lucas would tweak McCallum by suggesting that Jar Jar Binks join the cast. McCallum let loose with a string of expletives, according to witnesses. Lucas was joking, but then again, Jar Jar did appear in *The Clone Wars* animated show. With George, McCallum knew, you really had to push back hard on Jar Jar.

Lucas and McCallum conducted a global talent search. They reached out to writers such as Russell T. Davies, the Welsh showrunner who revived *Doctor Who* in 2005 (Davies was thrilled to be asked but too busy building his own little empire of science fiction TV shows). Rather than just set one writer to work on his own, the coproducers convened lavish multiday international writers' conferences at Skywalker Ranch; the assembled talent would laugh and chat and eat and drink, and returned home to write around a hundred scripts between them.

One of the leading writers in the Skywalker Ranch conference was Ronald D. Moore, the man who rebooted *Battlestar Galactica*. The original *Galactica*, in 1978, had angered Lucas because, he said at the time, it spoiled the potential market for a *Star Wars* TV show. Then along came the series again in 2004, darker and far better and enrapturing all of geekdom for the next five years—just as Lucas was attempting to fulfill the promise of *Star Wars* on TV. But Moore's presence made it clear that Lucas held no grudge. In fact, he and McCallum sought to emulate it as much as possible; the "sketchpad" on the third floor of Skywalker Ranch was assigned to watch *Battlestar Galactica* episodes to figure out how the show could look so good on less than $3 million an episode.

The trouble was, Lucas wasn't envisioning the sort of show that could be made on a shoestring. All those speeder bike chases and pod races added up. *Underworld* episodes were being priced out at roughly $11 million apiece—an original *Star Wars* every week. By 2009, *Underworld* was on the shelf, awaiting some form of future technology that could render galactic drag races more cheaply. "It would have been a great show," says Ronald D. Moore. "I'm disappointed I never got to see it happen." Then he casually revealed one of the characters involved: "I had the satisfaction of writing a few lines for Darth Vader."

The chances of *Underworld* ever being made faded away. Lucas would start plundering the show's art for use in *The Clone Wars*, from Season 2 onwards. Recycling ideas was a very Lucas-like trait, but some of the third-floor artists were upset. "We were building this show up, and it felt like bricks were being taken away," said one. But the artists had to be sanguine about it, he added: "George viewed our art as one big toy box. Anything he wanted to pull out in a particular situation was fine by him."

The Clone Wars had begun as a series of short cartoons in 2002. This version of the series had been made by Genndy Tartakovsky, an award-winning, Russian-born animator, for Cartoon Network. Intended as promotional material to gin up interest in *Episode III*, Tartakovsky's show had aired for three seasons, gaining four Emmys. Some viewers described it as the best *Star Wars* they'd ever seen. It offered stylized art and a relative lack of dialogue—never a bad idea as far as *Star Wars* is concerned. Mace Windu silently destroying an entire robot army with a lightsaber and a lot of Force: this alone was worth the cable subscription. Tartakovsky took General Grievous—a lightsaber-twirling cyborg he was required by Lucas to introduce because Grievous shows up in *Episode III*—and made him far more scary in Stormtrooper white, a cyborg ghost.

Lucas had big plans for the series. He wanted to fill in the gaps between *Episode II* and II. What better way to burnish the reputation of the prequels than with more context, more answers, more adventure, more *Star Wars*? Lucas had been dreaming about the details of *The Clone Wars* for years, and then, in *Episode III*, most of the conflict happened offscreen. He never got his seven battles on seven planets. So once that movie was done, Lucas decided to reboot the *Clone Wars* cartoon into a CGI animated series. "We can do better," he said.

Lucas saw *The Clone Wars* differently from Tartakovsky. He envisioned the show as more of a CGI version of *Thunderbirds*, a British-made, puppet-filled science fiction show from the 1960s, than as the kind of stylized serial that Tartakovsky had turned it into. He also wanted 3-D—which had turned a technological corner since the days of paper glasses. Lucas told Celebration III that *Clone Wars* would be made in this increasingly sophisticated format. Like Underworld, it was not to be.

With two TV shows in development, and scripts pouring in for both, Lucas had precious little time for the sort of personal filmmaking he had mentioned at the Letterman Center and all those times before. Yet the Creator still planned to go there—once the next thing was out of the way. "After the TV series, I'm going to do my own little movies," he told *Time* critic Richard Corliss in 2006. For the first time he specified what those little movies were: a way to go back to his future, back to plotless dystopian documentary fantasy. "Basically," he said, "you have to accept the fact that it's going to be the land of THX and worse."

By now, Lucas could hardly ignore the fact that he'd been procrastinating on making those personal movies since 1977. "I'm not saying I'm going to make these features fast," he added. That was just his style: "I ruminate a lot and sit around. I'm one of these guys that come back and paint a little and then go back and paint a little bit more and come back a month later and paint a little bit more. I don't do things particularly quickly. I do when there's money involved, because I just can't afford to spend the money."

There was money involved in *The Clone Wars*, which was the last remaining basket for Lucas to put his visual *Star Wars* eggs into. Having inked a deal with the Cartoon Network, he was committed to getting the show into syndication, which meant one hundred episodes or more. He needed someone he could trust to steer the ship. Someone he could mentor. A fan, perhaps?

Star Wars fans didn't come much more hard-core than Dave Filoni. For the premiere of *Revenge of the Sith*, Filoni had dressed up as Jedi Master Plo Koon, an obscure *Star Wars* character if ever there was one. (He was the guy with the weird perforated goggles and the breathing mask on the Jedi Council.) Filoni had reason to celebrate by the time he put on that costume: a writer for the animated show *Avatar: The Last Airbender*, and a former animator on *King of the Hill*, he got a call from Lucasfilm about the possibility of working on another animated show. "I talked a lot about *Star Wars* at work—a lot of people in animation talk about *Star Wars* at work," Filoni remembered three years later. "I wasn't even aware that this job was out there, but friends of mine in the animation industry who know I'm into *Star Wars* put me up for it." He thought the call a practical joke by his friends on *Spongebob Squarepants*. Luckily, he hung on long enough to hear that George *really* wanted to meet him.

Later at Skywalker Ranch, Filoni nervously sat down with the Creator and showed him a sketch of five characters: Asla, Sendak, Lunker (a Gungan who looked like a large Jar Jar), Cad, and Lupe. Filoni's idea was that these characters were a team of Jedi and smugglers inserted into the galactic underworld during the Clone Wars to investigate the black market. All they would need was a cool ship, something like the *Millennium Falcon*. *The Clone Wars* would be like original trilogy *Star Wars*, in which the fun came from the nobles rubbing shoulders with the scruffy nerf herders. Major characters from the prequel trilogy could cross paths with these new characters every so often. It would be a treat for fans to see Anakin and Obi-Wan and others, but they wouldn't be the focus of the show.

Lucas considered Filoni's idea, and shook his head. "No," he said, according to Filoni. "I like my own characters. I want to get Anakin and Obi-Wan in." But there was one thing Filoni's sketch had given George an idea for: "I want to give Anakin a padawan," he said, pointing at the sketch of Asla. "Let's take that girl there."

George Lucas had two daughters, and he harbored a strong belief that science fiction and fantasy could—and should—appeal to preteenage girls. And thus Asla was brought up in age and reborn as Ahsoka Tano, aka Snips, padawan learner to Jedi master Anakin Skywalker.

The first outing for Ahsoka, Anakin, and Obi-Wan turned out not to be on the TV screen at all. After a few years of production work, with the scripts for the first season of *The Clone Wars* completed, Lucas viewed some of the early footage. Though he had his notes—Filoni says his team was told it was taking *Star Wars* too reverentially—Lucas made an apparently spontaneous decision that the first four episodes should be released as a movie. His executives were concerned but not surprised. "Sometimes George works in strange ways," shrugged licensing chief Howard Roffman, who set off to find as many last-minute licensing partners as he could, so the movie would launch with at least some merchandising tie-ins.

The Clone Wars movie was announced in February 2008 and debuted that August. It held a number of firsts in the *Star Wars* universe. It was the first animated *Star Wars* movie and the first to be released without the Twentieth Century Fox fanfare. (The film was distributed by Warner Bros, which was part of the same parent corporation as the Cartoon Network; Lucas, who had once wanted an internship at Warner's animation department, was finally doing one better by releasing an animated movie with the studio.) At a running time of ninety-eight minutes, *Clone Wars* was also the first *Star Wars* movie to last less than two hours. It was the first in which John Williams didn't have direct involvement, although a world music version of his theme is used in the film (as it is in the *Clone Wars* series itself). It was the first *Star Wars* movie that *actually* cost $8.5 million, the official budget for the original film. It had the fewest number of products attached—a few Hasbro figures, a McDonald's Happy Meal. (Pepsi had a ten-year licensing deal with Lucasfilm. A Pepsi spokesperson said they weren't aware that *Clone Wars* was coming out.)

Clone Wars also holds the dubious distinction of most poorly reviewed *Star Wars* film ever. Lucas had ignored that old advice of Gene Roddenberry's, that TV shows invariably take a few episodes to warm up; now here was Ahsoka's tentative early attempts at witty banter with her new master, Anakin, thrust into the spotlight of the movie theater. Action sequences dominated the film, looking like plotless experiments in CGI—which is in fact what they were. *Entertainment Weekly* critic Owen Gleiberman bemoaned the fact that the *Star Wars* universe was so "obsessively-compulsively cluttered yet trivial that it's no longer escapism. . . . It's something you want to escape from." He branded Lucas "the enemy of fun." This was the same year Pixar released its used-universe masterpiece, *Wall-E*; critics looking for a glimmer of hope in *Clone Wars* couldn't even fall back on the notion that its CGI animation was state of the art. *Wall-E* seemed more *Star Wars*–like than this latest *Star Wars*. Even Roger Ebert, who had reliably supported Lucas throughout the prequel years, slammed "a deadening film that cuts corners on its animation and slumbers through a plot that a) makes us feel like we've seen it all before, and b) makes us wish we hadn't." The movie bears a hideous 18 percent rating on *Rotten Tomatoes* and made many annual "worst of the year" lists. A few critics threw the ultimate slur: it was even worse than the *Holiday Special*.

Looking back on it now, some cast members think Lucas probably didn't make the best decision of his life. "We weren't ready for prime time," says James Arnold Taylor, the voice of Obi-Wan throughout the series. "We were still working out the storytelling, the look and feel of the characters. . . . I'm not knocking it—I just feel we could have had a better start."

Did any of that matter for Lucasfilm's bottom line? Was *The Clone Wars* also the first dud movie in *Star Wars* history? Not in the slightest. *The Clone Wars* made $68.2 million at the box office, roughly eight times its budget. In terms of return on investment, that made it more successful than *Revenge of the Sith* and *Attack of the Clones*, and on a par with *Phantom Menace*. Once again, Lucas's strange ways had been vindicated at the box office. *Star Wars* moviegoing: it's an addiction, and millions of us are hooked.

All that remained was for Lucas to prove that *Clone Wars* could make it as a TV show. He had set the bar at syndication, which meant *Clone Wars* would have to last for roughly five seasons, or from 2008 until 2013—which was how long Cartoon Network had the option to screen it for. But the network could also pull the plug at any time.

The series started out strong. Its premiere was the highest rated in Cartoon Network history. Week to week, the first season averaged three million viewers. The reviews were uneven; critics hated that the early episodes featured some of the prequels' weakest players, such as the battle droids (the ones that keep saying "roger, roger," constantly misfire, and are easily sliced by lightsabers), which dominated the first few episodes, and loathed even more the return of Jar Jar Binks. But *The Clone Wars'* greatest strength was that it had a long list of characters to follow. Episodes tended to bunch together in story arcs: You might have a Binks arc for a few weeks, then an Ahsoka or Anakin arc, then a Yoda arc after that. The same quality that made it uneven also gave it longevity. The universe was roomy. Miss the Han Solo–style, smuggler *Star Wars* universe? Try the arcs featuring the feisty new pirate character, Hondo Ohnaka. Want more high fantasy with your *Star Wars?* Meet the mysterious magic-wielding Night Sisters. "We have stories for every type of fun," said Filoni.

Clone Wars paid homage to *Star Wars'* hokey, earnest TV-screened origins. It was the closest thing the TV world had seen to *Flash Gordon* serials in a long time. The episodes, about twenty-one minutes each without commercials, lasted roughly the same time as a *Flash Gordon*. Each *Clone Wars* show opened with a different homily in the blue-on-black "a long time ago in a galaxy far, far away" font. Instead of a roll-up, voice actor Tom Kane performed his best imitation of a 1940s newsreel announcer. Lucas had once said that the original trilogy was World War II and the prequels were more like the Great War, but the newsreel introduction made us feel like *this* was World War II—a good and worthy war, with the voice of the Republic pulling us all together in the great struggle against evil Dooku and his Separatists. The fact that the whole war was actually a Sith plot added a layer of irony that was, unfortunately, rarely examined in the show.

There were times when Lucas seemed to be mentoring Filoni, grooming him as a sort of successor, schooling him in World War II and Kurosawa. For one episode, "Landing at Point Rain," Lucas threw the script out and made Filoni cut together actual film footage from movies such as *The Longest Day, Tora! Tora! Tora!,* and *Battle of the Bulge.* Lucas pulled out his reels from back when he was cutting together dogfights for the original *Star Wars.* Filoni absorbed Lucas influences and shared them with the crew; he made sure that every one of his animators watched *Seven Samurai.* (The plot of the second season episode "Bounty Hunters," in which Anakin and Obi-Wan protect a planet of farmers, paid direct homage to the Kurosawa film.)

Lucas would barely talk to the *Clone Wars* artists but was having a whale of a time during meetings in the writers' room with Filoni and six other writers. Once a week, Lucas would come in with a few ideas—he tended to be the creative impetus behind the episodes of the show that focus entirely on the Clones. The series took a bunch of soldiers who were supposed to look and talk the same way (all modeled on the Maori actor Temuera Morrison, who played Jango Fett) and developed different personalities for them, such as Rex, Cody, Fives, and an older, wiser Clone named Gramps. After being presented with such an idea, the writers at the meeting were then free to debate whether it would actually work, but Lucas would want to hear the result. "He always wanted to be there to push us," said Filoni.

The show initially aired on Friday nights at 9 P.M., which won it a large adult audience. But as Filoni catered more and more to that audience, with darker scripts and better animation, viewership declined—from 3 million for series 1 to about 1.6 million for series 4. For series 5, Cartoon Network tried something that was either radical or suicidal—it moved *Clone Wars* to Saturday mornings at 9:30 A.M. Ratings barely moved. Still, the fifth season was number 1 in its time slot among boys age between nine and fourteen, which was and remains *Star Wars*' core demographic—despite attempts to bring in the girls with characters like Ahsoka (and her fellow padawan, Bariss Offee).

The scripts got darker still. Darth Maul returned from his bisection in *Phantom Menace*, his lower half a skittering mechanical spider. The show was approaching what some fans called a *M*A*S*H* problem—it had been running for longer than the three years the Clone Wars themselves were supposed to last, just as *M*A*S*H* was on TV for longer than the Korean War. But *Clone Wars* had the inherent advantage of being set in the *Star Wars* universe; remember, the original movie covers the course of three or four days at most. Three *years* might be enough to keep the show in business for a lifetime.

Season 5 ended on March 2, 2013, with the show's most shocking cliffhanger: Ahsoka, wrongly accused but exonerated of bombing the Jedi Temple, walks away from the Jedi order. Filoni talked confidently about tying up some more loose ends in the sixth season. One of the Clones would discover the terrifying truth about the forthcoming Order 66 that was to wipe out the Jedi. Yoda would go on a galactic voyage that would allow him to commune with the dead and learn the secret of how to become a Force ghost. The show had vaulted over the hundred-episode hurdle, but "we need 100 more just to finish what we're trying to do," Filoni told *"Star Wars" Insider*.

By that point, however, Filoni had a new boss who didn't like what she saw in the *Clone Wars*' bottom line. On March 11, the plug was unceremoniously pulled.

27.

HELLO DISNEY

In January 2012, George Lucas chose a maroon sofa in his animation studios at Skywalker Ranch, beneath two paintings of Padmé, as the place where he would tell the world he was retiring from *Star Wars*. "I'm moving away from the business, from the company, from all this kind of stuff," he explained to *New York Times* freelance reporter Bryan Curtis. Once again, he declared his intention to get back to making personal films. Reporters who'd been around the block a few times raised their eyebrows.

The ostensible subject of the interview was *Red Tails*, the Tuskegee Airmen biopic Lucas had been struggling to get released with a major studio for years. Naturally, Curtis wanted to know about the prospect for future *Star Wars* films. If Lucas could make a fifth *Indiana Jones*, which was supposedly in the works, why not a seventh *Star Wars*? Lucas's response was one of the most revealing emotional answers he'd ever given. Years of fan pushback on the prequels, it seems, years of Plinkett and his ilk had gotten to him—and his answer suggested he had been reading more online commentary than he would care to admit. "Why would I make any more when everybody yells at you all the time and says what a terrible person you are?" he blurted to Curtis. (Such online focus, from a man who often claimed to be content with Victorian technology, was also to be found in a later *BusinessWeek* interview: "With the Internet, it's gotten very vicious and personal. . . . You just say to yourself, why do I need to do this?")

Note what Lucas's answer wasn't. It wasn't that he hadn't even written the barest treatment for *Episode VII*, as he'd said back at Celebration III. As early as 1999, he'd told *Vanity Fair* that "I never had a story for the sequels." By 2008, he was not only ruling out a sequel trilogy from himself, but from his successors at Lucasfilm: "I've left pretty explicit instructions for there not to be any more features," he told *Total Film* magazine. "There will definitely be no Episodes VII-IX. That's because there isn't any story. I mean, I never thought of anything!" But by 2012, around the time he was announcing his retirement, Lucas was secretly at work on a new treatment—for *Star Wars Episode VII*.

Lucas hadn't ever needed to make more *Star Wars*, or indeed any at all. He could have made *Apocalypse Now* back in his salad days and won the approval of his friends. He could have handed the franchise over to Fox in 1977 as planned. He could have left it to the Expanded Universe after the first trilogy was completed. He could have stopped at the prequels. That advice he offered to Simon Pegg—don't get stuck making the same movie for thirty years— could have been applied to himself *even as he gave it*. He could have gone off and made personal movies, burning through his *Star Wars* money the way he said he would.

But Lucas had taken none of these off-ramps. He had kept on making more *Star Wars*. He started to describe *Star Wars* as something that was happening to him. "*Star Wars* obviously snuck up and grabbed me and threw me across the room and beat me against the wall," he told Jon Stewart in 2010. "It was a very slow process accepting the reality of what happened." He was hooked, as hooked as any R2 builder or 501st member or lightsaber choreographer. His creation had taken over his life, whether he liked it or not.

Of course, Lucas had a financial incentive to keep *Star Wars* going. Given how well every *Star Wars* movie in history had done, it would be hard for even the selfless Creator to not see them as personal piggy banks. Indeed, he briefly discussed the idea of a new *Star Wars* film with McCallum in the late 2000s, viewing a sequel as a way to fund the production of *Underworld*. There were plans to rerelease 3-D versions of all six movies which got as far as a 3-D re-release for *Episode I* in 2012. It earned a relatively disappointing $22 million during its opening weekend; the least a *Star Wars* release had made, ever. *Episode II* was converted into 3-D but never shown outside Celebration Europe. *The Clone Wars* wasn't enough. The video games weren't enough. The *Star Wars* machine was winding down. Lucas would have to either set about making *Episode VII* or accept that layoffs were inevitable.

Lucas loved the company; this is why he bore the burden of the *Star Wars* machine so willingly. This is why he still showed up for work at 7 AM, the way his father had. In more than one interview, he compared his situation to that of Darth Vader, trapped unwillingly by the inner workings of a technological Empire. The Empire was increasingly far-flung—most of the *Clone Wars* production took place in Singapore—and increasingly difficult to manage.

In particular the games division, LucasArts, was "quite a mess," in the words of Jim Ward, a marketing manager who took over LucasArts in 2004 and was asked to perform a top-to-bottom audit. The division's 150 game developers were spending too much time building software engines and not enough on the games themselves. The best titles were outsourced; the *Knights of the Old Republic* may be widely considered one of the top 100 video games of all time, but that was largely thanks to the Canadian company that designed and built it, BioWare. LucasArts was reduced to distribution and marketing.

Hal Barwood, after an epiphany on the set of Dragonslayer in 1981, had walked away from moviemaking and followed his passion for game design. He came to LucasArts in 1990, just in time to design *Indiana Jones and the Fate of Atlantis*, only the second time Lucas had allowed the company to develop a game based on his property (computer game graphics had reached a point where he was no longer embarrassed by them; besides, Atari still held the *Star Wars* license). The future had seemed bright.

But over the next decade, Barwood watched his division slide downhill, hampered in particular by an increasing reliance on *Star Wars* games. "The marketing department, if it didn't have *Star Wars* on it, they didn't know what to do," he says. The company had found critical, if not commercial success with smart, witty adventure games such as Monkey Island and Grim Fandango. But the lure of *Star Wars* lucre had been impossible to resist, and haphazard development had torn LucasArts apart. Barwood, who quit in 2003, had ten different bosses in thirteen years: "George would get rid of them, or they'd leave," he says. "Nobody ever took control."

Not until Jim Ward and his ruthless 2004 audit. An overhaul of LucasArts was promised; in the end it boiled down to firing more than half the staff when the team moved into the Presidio. In 2010, after Ward himself had been ousted, another third of LucasArts was laid off.

The remainder worked like crazy on *Star Wars* 1313, the companion game to the canceled TV show *Underworld*. While *Underworld* scripts sat on a shelf, *Star Wars* 1313 soldiered on as a role-playing game set in the same dark, gritty part of Coruscant. You played a bounty hunter, and the content of the game felt more mature, more like *Empire Strikes Back*. Perhaps this would be even better than *Knights of the Old Republic*; perhaps it would be the title that would win video game critics over to the notion that *Star Wars* games could be just as good as all that other content. But in 2012, just as LucasArts was preparing to show two years' worth of work on 1313, Lucas declared that he wanted to change it all around—he wanted the game to be about Boba Fett instead. This was a prime example, said one employee, of the fact that Lucas was "used to being able to change his mind" and "didn't really have a capacity for understanding how damaging and difficult to deal with" such casual mind-changing would become.

As he paddled around trying to keep Lucasfilm afloat on a shrinking pool of revenue, Lucas would have looked longingly at the success of Pixar, an ocean liner by comparison. Lucas still called Pixar "my company." Originally called the Lucas Computer Division, Pixar had essentially started off as a skunkworks operation, and Apple cofounder Steve Jobs had bought it in 1986, in a postdivorce fire sale. Lucas had been desperate to unload assets in order to hang onto Skywalker Ranch and sacrificed the computer division on the altar of that utopian dream. Jobs gave him $5 million—way less than Lucas had been asking, but at just the right time—and promised to invest another $5 million in the new company, soon to be dubbed Pixar after one of the computers it had been developing. It took a while, but Jobs was eventually convinced to turn the company around, from selling $125,000 computers and specialized software to creating animated movies with that software instead.

The man who persuaded him was John Lasseter, an animator who had been fired from Disney Studios in 1981—interestingly enough, after declaring it his ambition to bring "*Star Wars*-level quality to the art of animation." When one of Lasseter's animated shorts won an Oscar in 1988, Disney CEO Michael Eisner belatedly tried to hire Lasseter back. Lasseter turned him down and went on to direct *Toy Story* in 1995. Bob Iger, Eisner's successor, snapped up Lasseter and the results of Lasseter's work in 2006 for $7.6 billion as one of his first acts; the board let Eisner speak out against the sale, but ultimately overruled his stern objections. For Disney, ignoring Lasseter's *Star Wars*-based desire turned out to be one of its more costly mistakes. For Jobs, it led to a 1,520 percent return on the millions he'd given Lucas.

For Lucas, that had to sting—especially given his lifelong love of animation. But he also noticed that after Jobs sold Pixar, Disney treated it like the crown jewels. Everything about the company, from its culture to its intense collaborative storytelling meetings, was to be run just as it was under Jobs. Lasseter was to become Disney's chief creative officer, and Ed Catmull, whom Lucas had hired to start his computer division way back in 1979, would be the head of Disney animation. It had all the hallmarks of a reverse takeover. Meanwhile, Pixar headquarters in Emeryville, the former bakery whose architectural reconstruction Jobs had poured as much of himself into as Lucas had into Skywalker Ranch, remained effectively independent from the rest of the Mouse House. By 2011, Pixar had produced two of its three top-grossing movies of all time—*Toy Story 3* and *Up*—as part of the Disney family.

In August 2009, some three years after he bought Pixar, Disney CEO Iger made his second surprise acquisition: Marvel, maker of comic books Lucas had been reading since the 1960s, the company that admitted it had been saved from its tailspin in the late 1970s by the *Star Wars* comic. Despite losing the *Star Wars* license, Marvel had roared back in the late 1990s, when the company made the leap to the silver screen with the X-Men trilogy and *Spider Man*; now it was worth $4 billion to Disney. Once again, critics suspected it was overvalued (after all, the X-Men and Spider Man franchises were both licensed to other movie studios; Disney couldn't use them). Once again, the supposedly overvalued company was left to run its own business, and once again, it found a string of box office successes (most notably the Iron Man series and *The Avengers*, which became the third highest grossing movie in history). And once again, there was a prominent *Star Wars* influence: Kevin Feige, president of Marvel Studios, was obsessed with the original trilogy and had gone to USC specifically because it was Lucas's alma mater.

If Iger had intended for his acquisitions to get George Lucas's attention, he could have picked no two better companies to buy than Pixar and Marvel. These were companies Lucas loved—and one that he had birthed himself—and he could see that Iger was willing to let them retain their respective idiosyncrasies. Disney also was clearly on the hunt for powerful characters with deep ties to the now-dominant nerd culture; with the Marvel deal it had just bought a universe with five thousand of them. Lucasfilm had many thousands more than that in the Holocron.

Iger had known George Lucas since 1991, when Iger was head of ABC TV and commissioned *Young Indiana Jones*. Lucas turned sixty-five in 2009; the chances of him staying on at Lucasfilm for as long as Iger was contracted into his job—until 2015—were slim. By then Lucas would be seventy-one. From the outside, he already seemed uninterested in running the *Star Wars* hit machine any more, at least not beyond a single animated TV show.

And there was something else Iger knew about Lucas. After all these years, George had fallen in love again, and he'd fallen hard. Her name was Mellody

Hobson; she was the chair of DreamWorks Animation, president of a $9 billion Chicago investment firm, and a friend of the Obamas. Lucas met her at a business conference in 2006. While very little is known about their relationship— least of all which conference that was—Lucas has indicated that they began dating around 2008. By 2009, Lucas let her meet the artists on the third floor at Skywalker Ranch. She burst in gleefully: "Hello boys, it's take your girlfriend to work day."

But before Lucas popped the question to Mellody, he would have to decide what to do with the advances of a most persuasive suitor of his own: the Walt Disney Corporation.

ger popped the question to Lucas on May 20, 2011. Lucas had just turned sixty-seven a week earlier.

The two men had come together at Disney World to inaugurate the second version of Star Tours. Lucas had decided to change everything about the ride, to make it new. Prior to 2011, the ride had been set during *Return of the Jedi* and called the Endor Express; you could call this upgraded version the Everywhere Express. The simulator could offer segments in eleven locations in the *Star Wars* universe, which in random combination would lead, Disney boasted, to fifty-four distinct *Star Wars* experiences. It was set between *Episodes III* and *IV* and thus would now feature characters, scenes, and planets from the prequel trilogy. The cultural shift in what constituted *Star Wars* was assured at Disney, with which Lucasfilm had been working on the ride since 2006.

Lucas and Iger had a packed schedule ahead of them that day. They had to appear at the opening ceremony for the ride, which was to be a scripted spectacular. Here's how it would go down: Emcee Anthony Daniels, alongside Chris Bartlett—contractually unacknowledged inside his Threepio costume— would welcome visitors. Stormtroopers would then invade the set, clearing the way for Darth Vader. Two Jedi would be seen on the screen racing through Disney World to save everybody from the Empire, lightsabers drawn to draw the blaster fire, faces covered in robe hoods. The screen Jedi would appear to run up to the doors of the stage. "Reveal yourselves, Jedi," Vader would say, and out would come Iger and Lucas, brandishing lightsabers. "Prepare to meet your Maker," Iger would tell Vader, indicating Lucas. Pause for audience laughter.

Vader would insist Iger and Lucas didn't have the power necessary to remove the energy shield he'd placed around Disney World. "Don't worry," Lucas was to say, his only scripted words in this whole unusual bit. "Artoo will know what to do."

With their lines securely in their heads, Iger and Lucas met for breakfast at the Hollywood Brown Derby, a complete replica of a famous old Tinseltown landmark restaurant. If one was trying to woo George Lucas, where else would one take him but a replica restaurant that evoked nostalgia, glory days, the glitter of movie history past? Iger did everything but get down on one knee with an R2-D2 wedding ring.

The men were dining alone; one of the perks of running Disney is you get to close down restaurants in theme parks and eat in them at will. Lucas ordered the omelet, Iger the parfait. Then, with the wait staff out of earshot, the Disney boss turned to business. Would Lucas ever consider selling his company?

Lucas played it cool. (Pay attention, would-be fiancés with cold feet.) "I'm not ready to pursue that now," Lucas said. "But when I am, I'd love to talk."

The seed planted, the pair headed out for the morning's festivities. When the big reveal came and the Jedi team strolled on stage, Lucas held his lightsaber casually, one hand in his jeans pocket. Iger held his two-handed with stiff shoulders, as if cradling something very fragile.

What was Lucas waiting for? Star Tours was complete. *Clone Wars* was chugging along under the watchful eye of Filoni. There was no other major *Star Wars* production on Lucasfilm's plate.

But that was precisely the problem. Lucas didn't just want to hand over his intellectual property to Disney—or any other investor, for that matter—with only a skeleton crew to keep the franchise running. Because Paramount owned the rights to distribute the Indiana Jones movies, that series was considered "revenue neutral" to the lawyers. *Star Wars* was pretty much the only asset Lucasfilm had. Even after all these years, the company was really still the Star Wars Corporation.

No, if Lucas was going to sell Lucasfilm, it would be the spiffiest Special Edition–style Lucasfilm it could possibly be. It was time to change everything around and make it new, one last time.

Step 1: secure a successor. Lucas said he "ruminated on it endlessly" until the answer occurred to him: Kathleen Kennedy, Spielberg's long-time production partner and one of the most accomplished producers in Hollywood. There was no other candidate. "Why didn't I see this before?" Lucas would recall thinking. "She's always been standing right there in front of me." The two met for lunch in New York; after catching up on family and friends, Lucas told her he was "moving pretty aggressively" to retire. Would she be willing to take the reins at Lucasfilm—and to potentially help him hand it over to another company?

Kennedy didn't need much time, if any, to think about it. "Once I realized what he'd said, I answered pretty quickly," she says. "I kind of surprised myself." She'd never seen herself running a studio. She already ran a successful production company with her husband, Frank Marshall: Amblin Entertainment, which they had cofounded with Spielberg and through which they had produced his movies *ET: The Extraterrestrial*, *Jurassic Park*, and *Lincoln*, along with a host of other films by directors like Martin Scorsese and J. J. Abrams. Amblin had produced a lot of movies with Disney and its subsidiaries, too. Kennedy accepted on the spot: it would "afford me the ability to take my skills and be part of something bigger," she said. New *Star Wars* movies were "something bigger" than every blockbuster motion picture she'd been involved in thus far.

Step 2 for Lucas: pop the old ship back into hyperspace. "I've got to build this company up so it functions without me," Lucas later said he thought at the time, "and we need to do something to make it attractive." And one surefire way to doll up Lucasfilm would be to get a few more *Star Wars* films into the rotation.

Lucas had stated explicitly that *Episodes VII, VIII,* and *IX* were not to be made. He'd never really thought of any stories for them. But how hard would it be to whip up a few more little space things? So one evening, casually, on the phone to his son, Jett, during dinner, Lucas revealed he was writing again. That's good, said Jett, who knew his father was happiest when he had his head in a creative project. Your personal movies, right? No, said Lucas. More *Star Wars*. "Wait," said Jett. "Back up. What?" Even the Creator's son believed *Star Wars* movies were over.

Lucas called the old gang: Hamill, Ford, and Fisher. Negotiations commenced. Fisher, who had been told to lose ten pounds to play Leia in 1976, agreed to lose thirty-five pounds to play her this time around. *Empire* and *Jedi* screenwriter Lawrence Kasdan, who had refused to help Lucas rewrite *Episode I*, was brought on board as a consultant, although he was not initially slated to cowrite *Episode VII*. Lucas wanted a younger screenwriter: Michael Arndt. He had independent movie bona fides; Arndt was so aggressively independent, in fact, that he had been fired as the writer of his first movie, *Little Miss Sunshine*, which he had sold to Fox Searchlight. (He was later rehired.) Lucas had to admire Arndt's tenacity and the award-winning mix of drama and comedy it had yielded—not to mention the fact that the last scene of the movie was written just weeks before the premiere. Clearly, this was a man after Lucas's heart.

Arndt had also been the main writer on the top-grossing Pixar movie of all time, *Toy Story 3*. He was a known quantity at Disney.

By June 2012, Lucas was finally willing to take the next step. Kennedy was announced as cochair of Lucasfilm on June 1. She had watched Lucas agonizing over whether he was ready. Now he was. He picked up the phone and called Iger.

Immediately, lawyers and accountants began combing Lucasfilm's property to assess its worth—and to make absolutely certain that Lucas actually owned everything he thought he owned in the *Star Wars* universe. Up to twenty lawyers at the LA office of Skadden Arps went through the surreal process of making files on 290 "primary characters" from the *Star Wars* universe, from Admiral Ackbar to the bounty hunter Zuckuss. It wasn't that anyone was seriously questioning whether Lucas owned the rights to these characters. But crackpot claims had been made over the years, and due diligence had to be done. The firm plugged away at it throughout July and August; they scrutinized chains of title dating all the way back to the days when United Artists or Universal could have bought into the franchise for a song but didn't.

The investigators quickly gave each character a code name, because the buzz in the office was already beginning. The head of the office, Brian McCarthy, had helped shepherd Disney's purchase of Pixar. This experience was different. "I was shocked by how many people knew the intricacies of whose father-in-law was married to whose sister," McCarthy told the *Hollywood Reporter*. Even after all these years, even in Hollywood, power players could still be shocked by how widely, intimately known the franchise had become.

At Disney, Iger confided to his direct reports that while they didn't have a deal yet, they were close. Nothing was to leak. "Trust became important," Iger said in 2013. Trust had always been important at Lucasfilm, which was used to the lockdown atmosphere. Indeed, the company was able to simultaneously work on new movies and the Disney deal, both in secret. Kennedy was running a small story development team. With notable exceptions, nobody was told of the impending deal—though staffers certainly had their suspicions. A hiring freeze and a marketing freeze were put in place by September 2012. "The writing was on the wall," said social media manager Bonnie Burton. "We were getting reorganized constantly. There was talk behind closed doors that was pretty loud. I kind of thought Disney was going to buy us, because the only other people who could afford Lucasfilm were, like, Sony or Microsoft."

Some Lucasfilm employees knew more than others. Leland Chee, keeper of the Holocron, first got curious when he was asked to come up with a definitive number of characters in his database. Brand communications manager Pablo

Hidalgo was told of the sale in advance: he'd just finished a mammoth book, *The Essential Reader's Guide*, which covered every *Star Wars* novel and short story ever published, and was now tasked with strange little assignments to explain *Star Wars* inellectual property. What he didn't know was that there was a whole lot of new intellectual property coming down the pike.

Then, on June 29, 2012, Hidalgo was brought into a meeting with his boss, Miles Perkins. Ostensibly, the meeting's purpose was to update the company's "messaging" to its fans. And why was messaging being updated?, Hidalgo wondered. "We're making seven, eight, and nine," Perkins said casually.

Hidalgo needed to sit down. He guessed his reaction was being gauged. And when it came, he says, his reaction was "something that's unprintable"— presumably spoken through a giant smile.

Star Wars was back from the dead. Again.

There was just one hitch. Lucas was refusing to give Iger any treatments for *Episodes VII, VIII,* and *IX* before the deal closed. They would be great; Disney would just have to trust him. Disney wanted to trust, but it also wanted to verify Lucas's assurances that the treatments were solid—or indeed that there were treatments in the works at all. The company easily could have dug up claims that Lucas had made on multiple occasions, one of them in front of thousands of people, about never having written any such treatments.

But Lucas was playing hardball. "Ultimately you have to say, 'Look, I know what I'm doing,'" he told *BusinessWeek*. "'Buying my stories is part of what the deal is.' I've worked at this for 40 years, and I've been pretty successful. I mean, I could have said, 'Fine, well, I'll just sell the company to somebody else.'"

Lucas didn't relent until he got, in writing, an agreement on the broad outlines of the deal. He was to get forty million shares of Disney stock and another $2 billion in cash. Even then, Lucas also had to have it in writing that the treatments he'd cobbled together could only be seen by three people at Disney—Bob Iger, new chair Alan Horn, and VP Kevin Mayer.

Iger's reaction to the treatments was muted. "We thought from a storytelling perspective they had a lot of potential," he told *BusinessWeek*. For a man well versed in marketing, that was either a deliberate underselling or the most damning faint praise in Disney history. Either way, it would have been hard to quit the deal at that point, with an agreement in writing and a full evaluation sweep going on at Lucasfilm. And it would be no skin off Lucas's back to turn round and sell the whole spruced-up company to someone else. Besides, even if the treatments were wretched, no *Star Wars* movie had ever failed to make a killing.

With the deal nearing, activity at both companies reached a fever pitch by October 2012. Bob Iger watched the six *Star Wars* movies back to back in a weekend and took notes. Kathleen Kennedy convinced Howard Roffman to come out of semiretirement and manage the coming explosion in licensing—it was, after all, always the consumer products division of Lucasfilm that minted the most money. Between October 11 and 14, during some tense phone calls from New York Comic-Con, Hidalgo learned that the sale was a go. He emailed *"Star Wars" Insider* to get it to hold its front cover. He couldn't tell them why—yet.

On Friday, October 19, 2012, George Lucas sat down to film what would be, in a way, his final feature as head of the company that bore his name. This time he would not be behind the camera but in front of it, along with Kathleen Kennedy. His aim was to officially pass the torch but also to get ahead of the story—and to remove all need to do TV interviews about the announcement by shooting an extensive conversation with the principals involved, a conversation he would then give freely to the world. It was to be one last triumph of media management for Lucasfilm before its landscape changed forever.

Lynne Hale, Lucasfilm's PR chief, would oddly play an uncredited role in the interview, asking smiling questions in the style of a TV anchor. The whole thing was to be edited down to about half an hour and released in five short episodes on YouTube.

As the camera rolled, Lucas talked about the media giant to which he was selling his company almost like it was a nuclear bunker. Disney was "the steadiest of all the studios," he said, a place where the *Star Wars* legacy could survive for generations. He praised the company for "nurturing a brand, licensing, that whole package of keeping them on a steady footing." It was almost like Isaac Asimov's classic science fiction series Foundation, a favorite of Lucas's, in which a visionary plots out the thousand-year future of his civilization. Lucas foresaw Kennedy picking her own successor, still backed by the strength of the Mouse House. "Ultimately," said Lucas, "when it's the end of the world and we're all going to die, the last thing to go will be Disney."

Like Obi-Wan telling Luke that what he'd been told about Darth Vader was true from a certain point of view, Lucas found a loophole in his earlier claims that there would be no more *Star Wars* movies. "I always said I wasn't going to do any more, and that's true, because I'm not going to do them," he said. (Those "explicit instructions" he'd mentioned in 2008 had apparently gone by the wayside.) "That doesn't mean I'm unwilling to turn it over to Kathleen to do more." The loophole, apparently, was the exact size and shape of one of the best producers in the business.

And where would Lucas be in this picture? An adviser, "my Yoda on my shoulder," in Kennedy's phrase. The "keeper of the flame" of *Star Wars*. The old Jedi in a cave whom the warrior turns to when her question is too important and all other options have been exhausted. Would this mean that Lucas was to still be, in some shadowy way, in charge of the *Star Wars* saga? Ponder how many of the events of *The Empire Strikes Back* and *Return of the Jedi* could be said to be Yoda's doing, and there you'll have your answer. (Not a lot—just the training that led to the key moment.)

Lucas, fascinated by education, is uniquely suited to the task of mentoring younger directors. It was what he had done for Dave Filoni on *The Clone Wars*; it was what he would do again, in far more of an advisory capacity, for J. J. Abrams. Kennedy would recruit Abrams away from the *Star Trek* franchise in January 2013 with four simple words: "Please do *Star Wars*." Abrams, the once and future *Star Wars* nerd, pulled strings at Paramount so he could comply. Later in 2013, Jett Lucas would reveal that his father was talking to Abrams "all the time."

That doesn't make Abrams the next Richard Marquand. He's more strong-willed and far more experienced than the Welsh director, for one thing, and for another, Lucas has genuine reason to want to step back gracefully into the shadows, back behind the scenes at last, and to sit, quite literally, in the back row. Perhaps the most touching moment in the PR film comes when the old Jedi reveals the great price of his mastery: he never had a chance to see his epic the way most of us did. "The one thing I missed in life is that I never got to see *Star Wars*," he said. "I never got that moment when I walked into a theater and was blown away, because I already knew it was nothing but heartache and problems." George James Sr., Navajo Code Talker, and George Lucas Jr. had something in common, then: neither of them had ever really seen this classic film.

After the New York Stock Exchange closed on Tuesday, October 30, 2012, this announcement was pushed out on Disney's website: "Disney to Acquire Lucasfilm Ltd." It offered a few obligatory paragraphs of hyperbole, and the rest was written in standard press-release-ese. "Acquisition continues Disney's strategic focus on creating and monetizing the world's best branded content," read the subhead. The galaxy far, far away became just another piece of branded content, belonging to the world's largest media company.

The price was exactly $4.05 billion as of that day's Disney share price. The terms of the deal were half stock, half cash. $2 billion in a virtual suitcase and forty million Disney share certificates, all of it handed to Lucasfilm Ltd.'s one and only shareholder, George Walton Lucas Jr., son of a stationery store owner. $4.05 billion: *Star Wars* was not worth as much as the $7 billion for Pixar, then, and only a hair's breadth more than the price paid for Marvel. $4.05 billion is more than the GDP of Fiji. And yet it may seem a somewhat deflating number to appraise this property at, given the $30 billion of revenue *Star Wars* generated in its first thirty-five years.

Like Lucasfilm, Disney had made a video, and it got its version out first. Iger had prepared a speech for the film, after which Lucas responded to offscreen questions. In the video, Iger pointed out that his $4.05 billion was paying for seventeen thousand characters (the number Leland Chee had determined resided in the Holocron)—though he neglected to say that the vast majority of them were minor characters in novels.

Iger also sought to reassure investors about the wisdom of dropping such a hefty sum on a single company by soothingly mentioning his other new crown jewels: ILM and Skywalker Sound. On a conference call the day of the announcement, he played up the smart financial aspects of the deal. Those forty million shares he had granted Lucas? Iger would be issuing them anew and intended to buy back that many shares before the new *Star Wars* arrived in 2015. He didn't mention that Disney had had $4.4 billion sitting in the bank and investors demanding they do something with it. Only $2 billion of that had gone to Lucas in cash; the rest was delivered in stock. Disney still had the capacity to swallow another Lucasfilm whole.

Investors weren't so sure about the whole deal. Disney stock fell amid heavy trading the day after the announcement, to $47 a share. In the immediate aftermath of the news there seemed to be a certain sense of dazed dismay in the mainstream media and in *Star Wars* fandom. "I felt a great disturbance in the Twittersphere," I tweeted at the time, "as if a million childhoods suddenly cried out and were silenced." But it didn't take long for me to realize I was wrong: the deal made sense, even for fans. There would be more *Star Wars*, funded by some very deep pockets. Look at how Disney treated Pixar and Marvel: reverentially. Look at who would be directing the next movies: not the director of the prequels. I wrote "*Star Wars* Just Got a New Lease on Life," the first positive op-ed piece published in the deal's wake. The next day, it was shared twenty thousand times on Facebook alone; it seemed I wasn't the only fan to feel a mounting sense of excitement once they weighed everything up.

Lucas, unusually for him, was more upbeat than that. He even cracked a smile. In his interview, the Creator emphasized that he'd been a big fan of Disney "from when I was born." He offered his final rationalization for abandoning his hopes of making more experimental films: "I couldn't drag my company into that." (A company that, by the way, was like a "mini-Disney . . . constructed similarly.") "Disney is my retirement fund," he said dryly. Which was something of an understatement: Lucas was now the second-largest private shareholder of Disney stock after Steve Jobs's widow, Laurene Powell Jobs. The kid who got to go to Disneyland on day 2 in 1955, who had revered Uncle Scrooge, who wanted Disney to back *Star Wars* in the first place, who had kept two Mickey Mouse bookends on his desk all these years, now owned 2 percent of the company.

The retirement fund would continue to rise and fall for the next two months, as Disney was buffeted by uncertainties in the market. But in January 2013, as Wall Street learned that J. J. Abrams was about to be announced as *Episode VII* director, the company's stock began a remarkable rise. On May 14, 2013—Lucas's sixty-ninth birthday—Disney stock would hit a high of 67.67. The present for the man who had everything? Stock that was worth $840 million more than when he first received it.

It was an end of an era, to be sure—but *Star Wars* was living on, and not just in the bank account of its Creator. In the PR video that Disney had released around the time of the acquisition announcement, Lucas talked about the future of *Star Wars* films. He casually referred to episodes *VII*, *VIII*, and *IX* collectively as "the end of the trilogy"—by which he presumably meant the trilogy of trilogies, which hadn't really existed until he'd finally decided to send over some treatments. "And other films also," he added—as usual, casually dropping a twist into the whole narrative at the last minute and, as usual, choosing wonderfully wooden words. This was the first mention of stand-alone *Star Wars* movies that would hit screens in the years between episodes.

"We have a large group of ideas and characters and books and all kinds of things," said the Creator. "We could go on making *Star Wars* for the next hundred years."

CONCLUSION: ACROSS THE UNIVERSE

If George Lucas is right about how many stories there are left to tell in the *Star Wars* universe—and he hasn't been proved wrong on that score yet—future generations of fans will still be lining up outside cineplexes to see the adventures of future Solos and Skywalkers in 2115. If we're going according to Disney's current schedule, that'll be *Episode LXXXVII*. For all we know, it will be screened as a giant IMAX hologram.

Sound ridiculous? Maybe it is. Then again, there was a time—forty years ago—when the very notion of space fantasy movies sounded ridiculous. And *Star Wars* still has plenty of new worlds to conquer. It's not just that the franchise and its acolytes are embracing whole new languages like Navajo. They're also continuing to expand into countries around the world that were not swamped by the original wave of *Star Wars* mania.

Take Turkey. Until very recently, it was a lonely thing to be a fan of Yildiz Savaslari—that is, *Star Wars* in Turkish. But Ates Cetin, born in 1983, was hooked from the moment he watched a dubbed version of *The Empire Strikes Back* on TV as a kid during the late 1980s. He began looking for ways he could play in this universe he had just discovered.

Sure, the original trilogy had screened at theaters around Turkey. But so did *Dünyayı Kurtaran Adam* (*The Man Who Saved the World*), an adventure film from 1982 that liberally plundered Lucasfilm's cinematic property for special effects scenes. The *Millennium Falcon* and the Death Star were reused. No one in the country seemed to notice, or much care. Today, the movie is commonly known as "Turkish *Star Wars*" and is a cult favorite; back then, it was panned and vanished without trace. "I've seen it a few times," says Cetin, "and I still don't understand the plot."

Star Wars merchandise was scarce back in the 1980s in Turkey. All you could find were the infamous Uzay bootleg action figures, the ones that thought they could get around copyright by changing one letter around in the names of their "Starswar" line. (Steve Sansweet cherishes his Uzay "stormtroper" and "C-PO" figures; the 501st Legion has built a costume of the Uzay "Blue Star" snowtrooper.)

The real Lucasfilm-licensed toys started to enter the country in 1997, in time for the Special Editions. But not everyone was buying. In 1999, Cetin saw reports from America about the long lines outside theaters showing *The Phantom Menace*, and was subsequently dismayed when only one or two people showed up in the entire theater for opening day in Istanbul. The small crowds were to be repeated for the rest of the prequels. Turks, it seemed, just didn't take to the idea of *Star Wars* the way people had in other countries.

The day *Revenge of the Sith* came out in 2005, a collector friend dressed up as a Stormtrooper and loaned Cetin a Darth Vader costume; they walked around Taksim Square, the most crowded and famous public area in Istanbul, testing the waters, trying to gauge reactions. Darth Vader, it turned out, was practically anonymous, even here in the cultural center of one of Europe's largest cities. "Only a few of them recognized the character," Cetin says. "Most of them thought I was Shredder, from the Teenage Mutant Ninja Turtles, or Robocop, or a fireman. One old lady called me 'the man from the mountains'; the meaning remains a mystery."

The police, meanwhile, were more apprehensive of the Dark Lord. Cetin had to hastily explain to an officer that he was in a stage play, and he seemed on the edge of being arrested, on suspicion of being suspicious, when his friend bundled him into a cab.

Cetin speaks softly, but he has a quiet persistence about him. In 2008, he founded a Turkish outpost of the 501st Legion; in 2011 he cofounded Turkey's own Rebel Legion. He watched Adidas launch *Star Wars*–themed shoes and jacketsin the country; he welcomed *The Clone Wars* to Turkish TV screens. Friends started playing the latest *Star Wars* video games. Facebook arrived, and brought *Star Wars* memes with it. Cetin noted that humor columns in newspapers began to make *Star Wars* references. Slowly but surely, something was changing.

Fast forward to July 2013, when Taksim Square was the center of a very different kind of police action. Citizens started gathering after police had tear-gassed a peaceful protest against the demolition of a local park, which was supposed to make way for a shopping center in the style of an Ottoman-era army barracks. Cetin decided he'd join the protests, dressed once again in the full Vader costume. His message: "even the most evil film character is on the side of the people."

Of course, if the Vader costume had been provocative last time, this time Cetin would really be risking arrest. But he couldn't resist. At the last minute he left his lightsaber at home and carried the Turkish flag instead; perhaps that would endear this mystery figure to the crowds. It turned out he didn't need it. In just eight years, *Star Wars* had gone from being a largely unknown, bootlegged curiosity to common cultural meme. "From [ages] seven to seventy, they all called 'Darth Vader,'" Cetin told me. "'Go Vader! Go get them! Show them!' After a few such cheers, you almost feel like you are really Darth Vader." To his astonishment, wherever he walked, the protestors started to follow—humming the Imperial March.

Star Wars is an increasingly global phenomenon, perhaps the first mythos all cultures can get behind without hesitation. Even its film sets have become shrines. In 2011, a small group of largely European fans discovered that the Lars homestead, that single white dome-like dwelling where we first meet Luke Skywalker in the first ever *Star Wars* film, was moldering away in the desert in Tunisia. On Facebook, the fans asked for $10,000 in donations to restore the building to film quality with plaster and paint; they promptly raised $11,700. The permits from the Tunisian government took a little longer, but the team completed the job in a few weeks. Tears streamed down their cheeks as they screened a video of the restoration effort at *Star Wars* Celebration Europe, to a packed house and rapturous applause.

Japan is probably the most *Star Wars*–crazed country in the Eastern hemisphere, if not the world. It was home to the "George Lucas Super Live Adventure," a bizarre and largely *Star Wars*–based arena show that toured the country in 1993. This is the country where you can watch Darth Vader hawking Pacific League baseball, Nissan cars, and Panasonic electronics. You can visit Nakano Broadway, a six-floor mall in the heart of Tokyo, and find rare *Star Wars* toys and trinkets for sale on every floor. When George Lucas came to open the original Star Tours at Tokyo Disneyland in 1989, he was chased around the park by hordes of Japanese schoolgirls. Then forty-five, he joked that he wished he were twenty years younger. Schoolgirls (and the occasional boy, but mostly schoolgirls) are still there, lining up in greater numbers for the new Star Tours, which I found to be the most popular exhibit in Tokyo Disneyland. As they line up, Threepio welcomes them to the ride in Japanese, once again sounding prissy and girlish in a foreign language.

South Korea was relatively unaffected by *Star Wars*, so much so that Harvard academic Dong-Won Kim presented a paper looking into the reasons why *Episodes I* through *III* had been seen by (gasp) fewer than two million Koreans. Even in Seoul, however, you can watch Darth Vader in ads for Korea Telecom or catch a performance of Stormtroopers filming a video—a K-pop hit by a group called the Wonder Girls. I found a shop in the heart of the Hongdae district formerly called *Star Wars* Coffee (tagline: "May the froth be with you"). It still sold knock-off artwork of Warhol-style Darth Vaders, and vast canvases of classic trilogy characters arranged around the table in the style of the Last Supper.

The list goes on and on. Visiting the island of St. Maarten in the Bahamas? You'll want to stop in at the Yoda Guy Movie Exhibit, run by one of the creature shop artists who worked under Stuart Freeborn on *The Empire Strikes Back*; it's one of cruise line Royal Caribbean's most popular destinations on the island. In Australia, a man named Paul French did a charity walk across the entire Outback, 2,500 miles from Perth to Sydney, in a skin-chafing Stormtrooper costume. Why a Stormtrooper? Because, French said, it would "create a bit more attention." He raised $100,000.

Such anecdotes are amusing in isolation, but together they speak volumes about the incredible reach and power of the shared culture that is *Star Wars*, a universal language of tropes and characters that sparks instant attention everywhere it goes. The language was born in 1977 and received significant upgrades in 1980 and 1983. It appeared to die out, but marinated in millions of memories until 1997, when the world was shocked to discover how many of us still spoke it, and a new generation of speakers started chattering excitedly. Another branch of the language opened up in 1999, a dialect that plenty of speakers vowed they would never speak but that entered the lexicon anyway. In 2002 and 2005, the latest language upgrades were delivered around the world simultaneously. By 2014, the steady buzz of anticipation for the next addition to the mother tongue had become a roar heard around the world. We all speak Star Wars now.

Perhaps the only humans on Earth who seem relatively unenthusiastic about the prospect of more *Star Wars* are those focused on getting off the planet.

The Creator has long been a strong advocate of real, as well as fictional, outer space missions. He grew up in the dawn of space exploration and eagerly followed the progress of Apollo missions in the 1960s. Armstrong landed on the moon shortly before Lucas started filming *THX 1138*. The *Viking 1* lander touched down on Mars in July 1976, less than a week after Lucas wrapped shooting on *Star Wars*. Later that year, it was erroneously reported that *Viking* had found traces of organic life in Martian soil. Hal Barwood remembers Lucas coming to his house one day during the editing of the first movie and being very excited about the news. "He thought it was a good omen for *Star Wars*," Barwood recalls.

The moment it became clear that the film was a huge hit, Lucas started talking about how it might influence the space program. "I'm hoping that if the film accomplishes anything, it takes some ten-year-old kid and turns him on so much to outer space and the possibilities of romance and adventure," he told *Rolling Stone* in 1977. "Not so much an influence that would create more Wernher von Brauns or Einsteins, but infusing them into serious exploration of outer space and convincing them that it's important. Not for any rational reason, but a totally irrational and romantic reason."

"I would feel very good," he continued, "if someday they colonize Mars when I am 93 years old, and the leader of the first colony says: 'I really did it because I was hoping there would be a Wookiee up here.'"

Up until the end of his career, Lucas was expressing the same hopes for the effect that his creation would have on the international effort to explore outer space. In 2010, he told Jon Stewart, "My only hope is that the first guy who gets to Mars says 'I wanted to do this ever since I saw *Star Wars*.'" Lucas's most expressive, political version of this wish had come in 1981, when he waxed lyrical to *Starlog*:

> There were certain underlying ideas when I started: one was to tell a fairy tale, which is what it is—a fairy tale in space guise. The reason it's in a space guise is that I like the space program, and I'm very keen on having people accept the space program. We've grown up in what is the flowering, and maybe the apex, of the space program, and *Star Wars* was made during that time when everyone was saying, "what a waste of time and money." I was hoping, and still am hoping, that if 10 years from now it comes up for a vote that people will be a little more prone to saying "yes, this is important and we should do it". . . . If suddenly the space program gets a lot of money 15 years from now then I'll say "Gee, maybe I had something to do with that. . . ." But it's hard to tell at this point whether *Star Wars* will have any effect or not.

By the mid-2010s, the United States was leaning toward "not." We haven't exactly been tripping over ourselves to send humans to Mars, whether in search of Wookiees or otherwise. As a share of the federal total, NASA's budget has declined to less than 0.5 percent. The agency's emphasis for the past two decades has been on unmanned spaceflight. Barack Obama, lightsaber-wielding, Death Star petition–responding, Threepio-welcoming Jedi Knight, cut funding for a future manned Mars mission. Before that happened, NASA's administrator suggested the agency plans to send humans to Mars in 2037—which, coincidentally, is the year Lucas will turn ninety-three.

We may have to wait even longer than that to find out what inspired the first person on the Red Planet—but if any fictional universe is inspiring the folks at NASA at the moment, it is that of *Star Trek*, not *Star Wars*. "My whole love of space is from *Star Trek*," says Bobak Ferdowsi, also known as Mohawk Guy, flight director at the Jet Propulsion Laboratory. The engineer who helps control the Martian rover *Curiosity*, Ferdowsi told me he prefers *Trek* over *Wars*. "There's the hope that we're progressing toward that *Star Trek* future," he said in an earlier interview, "that maybe it will be less about individual countries and more about a global organization." He's not alone; you'll find many *Trek*-quoting fans at the laboratory, which has on occasion described itself as the nearest thing Earth has to the Starfleet of the *Trek* universe.

Call it the final revenge of *Star Trek* fans, who for decades have been struggling with their feelings about the rival "star" franchise. (The latest perceived slight: director J. J. Abrams, who rebooted the *Trek* franchise in 2010, upped and left it for *Star Wars* at the first opportunity.) *Trek*'s focus on rational exploration over galactic mysticism is a natural fit for NASA. Ferdowsi's fellow social media star, astronaut Chris Hadfield, is also a Trekker, as is astrophysicist and host of the *Cosmos* TV show Neil deGrasse Tyson. "I never got into *Star Wars*," Tyson said. "Maybe because they made no attempt to portray real physics. At all." Tyson's predecessor on *Cosmos*, the late, great Carl Sagan, also took issue with *Star Wars*. His son Nick Sagan told me he remembers watching the original movie on VHS with his dad, who loved *Flash Gordon*–style serial adventures, but let out a giant sigh after Han Solo made his boast about doing the Kessel Run in less than twelve parsecs. Both knew what was wrong with that statement: a parsec is distance, not time. "Dad," protested Nick, "it's just a movie."

"Yes," said Sagan, "but they can afford to get the science right."

So much for the space fantasy approach to inspiring the Einsteins of the future.

Still, America's space industry is not without its *Star Wars* homages, which mostly can be seen in the names of its space-bound systems. Take for example NASA's Commercial Crew and Cargo Program, dubbed C3PO. Chris Lewicki, the former flight director for NASA Mars rovers *Spirit* and *Opportunity*, is about to blast an even geekier, more obscure *Star Wars* reference into space. Lewicki's private space company Planetary Resources, which plans to mine space rocks for precious metals, is launching an asteroid-hunting telescope called the Arkyd in 2015. That's a name you'll only know if you're schooled in the Expanded Universe; Arkyd Industries was a major manufacturer of droids and spacecraft in the Old Republic; when conquered by the Empire, it made the probe droids that we see landing on Hoth at the very beginning of *The Empire Strikes Back*. "We've got lots of *Star Wars* lore built into the company," Lewicki told me. Unlike Tyson, Lewicki was at least kind of inspired the way Lucas intended: "*Star Wars* was my gateway drug to hard science fiction," he said.

The agency's (and an astronaut's) greatest homage to the franchise came on November 3, 2007. That's the day when the *Star Wars* theme was played in space for the first time, thirty years after it first thrilled audiences back on planet Earth. It was a wake-up call broadcast by NASA to the crew of shuttle mission STS-120, then in its twelfth day aboard the International Space Station. In particular, it was directed at Mission Specialist Scott Parazynski, a rare *Star Wars* fan among the few humans who've made it into orbit and beyond. (His son, whom he had named Luke, was ten years old at the time; he had been born around the time of the release of the Special Edition.) "That was a great, great way to wake up," Parazynski told Mission Control. Then, for his son, he performed the first known Darth Vader impression outside of planet Earth: "Luke, I am your father," he said. "Use the Force, Luke."

As if the scene couldn't get any geekier, the shuttle that had transported the crew to the International Space Station had been carrying a special *Star Wars* payload: the very lightsaber Mark Hamill had used in *Return of the Jedi*. Space Center Houston officials had come up with the idea to fly it, to commemorate the thirtieth anniversary of the original movie, and Lucas had readily agreed. The lightsaber had been delivered to NASA officials in a ceremony at Oakland Airport, with Peter Mayhew (the actor who played Chewbacca) handing it over. Flown from Oakland to Houston, the lightsaber was received by R2-D2 and Stormtroopers from the Texas 501st. Lucas was onsite, watching the shuttle launch that blasted his prop into space.

That was NASA's greatest staged homage to *Star Wars*—but another, less intentional one occurred some four years later, in 2011, when the agency's astronomers used the Kepler telescope to discover, for the first time, a planet orbiting two suns. Officially, the planet was designated Kepler 16(AB)-b. Unofficially, astronomers at NASA and around the world gave it another name: Tatooine. This was something of a victory for Lucas: when *Star Wars* first came out, astronomers had declared it highly unlikely that a planet like Luke Skywalker's could exist so close to two suns. In the two years after Tatooine was discovered, another nineteen double-star-system planets showed up. NASA was moved to offer an official apology to Lucasfilm. ILM's John Knoll, speaking on behalf of Lucas, accepted the apology: "The very existence of these discoveries cause us to dream bigger, to question our assumptions," he said. Or as Einstein put it, imagination is more important than knowledge. Sometimes, when you're just trying to make space fantasy, it turns out you can be accidentally ahead of the curve of science.

G eorge Lucas may have spent much of his career with his eyes fixed on the heavens, but in his post–*Star Wars* life he would be preoccupied with more terrestrial, prosaic battles.

On the domestic front, everything seemed blissful for Lucas in 2013—the closest a person can get, perhaps, to happily ever after. Retired at last, he wasted no time proposing in January to Mellody Hobson. They were married in June at Lucas's own never-never land, Skywalker Ranch. Lucas's friend Bill Moyers was the officiant. Friends remarked, as they had remarked for a number of years, how much slimmer and happier Lucas seemed since he'd been with Mellody, how much better dressed. The media were far from the gates of Skywalker, faked out by rumors that the wedding was going to take place in Chicago. Minimal press attention, an elite crowd, and a utopian setting: just the way Lucas likes it. And there was even happier news on the horizon. Melody and George were pregnant with a first biological child, Everest, via a surrogate. The world would not find this out until Everest was born in August. The following year, in May 2014, Lucas threw yet another Skywalker Ranch celebration, inviting far-flung friends such as Laddie and Fred Roos to celebrate his seventieth birthday.

But Lucas's first few years of retirement didn't go so well. This was especially true when it came to preserving and controlling his legacy. Sure, he built a nice park for his neighbors in San Anselmo, where he unveiled statues of Yoda and Indiana Jones, marking the icons that were created nearby. But his eyes were on the glittering prize of the Lucas Cultural Arts Museum. This was his legacy project: a vast and vastly expensive edifice in the Beaux Arts style, near the gold-domed Palace of the Legion of Honor, in the Presidio of San Francisco, it would make the San Francisco skyline look a little more like Naboo. It would be steps from the Disney Museum, where the life of the other creator to birth a globally admired mass entertainment was celebrated. The LCAM, as it was known, would contain all the storytelling art Lucas had been collecting, funding, and dreaming about since he was a child—Norman Rockwell and Maxfield Parrish jostling for space alongside Scrooge McDuck creator Carl Barks and exhibits on CGI.

But Lucas hadn't counted on a couple of roadblocks on the way to the LCAM. The first one was called the Presidio Trust. This body of local grandees were appointed by the president of the United States to manage the national park, and as part of the deal they had forged with Lucas back when he had moved Lucasfilm into the Presidio in 2005, the trust asked Lucas for a quid pro quo: that he would someday build a "world-class cultural institution" in the Presidio. When a retail chain called Sports Basement vacated a building down by the waterfront, in the shadow of the Golden Gate Bridge, it seemed a given that Lucas would take it over. This was prime real estate for a memorial to any global icon, let alone one who had taken San Francisco values—the US military is an evil technological empire; corporations and bankers will destroy the republic—and turned them into two trilogies of the most fantastic world-conquering legend in history.

But *Star Wars* itself was also a road block to the LCAM, in a way—and perhaps also to Lucas's dreams for his own legacy. Lucas once confessed to Disney's Bob Iger that he knew the first line of his obituary would read "George Lucas, creator of *Star Wars*," no matter what he did, even if he sold the company, and that he had come to terms with that. Try as he might, Lucas couldn't shake the impression among certain concerned citizens of San Francisco that what he was building was essentially a *Star Wars* museum—one they feared would instantly become the most popular destination in the city and bring half the population of the world driving and tramping through their parkland waterfront.

Despite the fact that Lucas had an agreement with the Presidio Trust to build the museum (not to mention a hand-picked board and millions in escrow waiting to pay for construction), the trust decided at the last moment to open the museum space up to a competition and extensive public debate. Nancy Bechtle, chair of the Trust, was a well-to-do, fourth-generation San Franciscan, the former chief financial officer of an international consulting giant, the president of the San Francisco Symphony, and a George W. Bush appointee. It's also fair to say that she was not a huge fan of *Star Wars*. Before he knew it, Lucas the billionaire—who was offering to fully fund the museum—found himself competing against a museum proposal from the National Park Service, which didn't have funding but helps manage the Presidio and has strong ties to Bechtle and the Trust.

Lucas pulled political levers as adeptly as Chancellor Palpatine. He got the support of San Francisco mayors, past and present; both California senators; a letter of support was signed by a hundred *Star Wars*–loving luminaries of Silicon Valley, from Facebook COO Sheryl Sandberg to Steve Jobs's widow. After conveying his displeasure to her on a number of occasions, Lucas even got Democratic leader and San Francisco congresswoman Nancy Pelosi to work the phones for the LCAM.

Bechtle wasn't moved by any of this, so Lucas next tried a carrot and stick approach. The stick came first, in the form of a *New York Times* interview in which Lucas declared that the Trust members "hate us" and that his opponents' proposals were "a jar of jargon"; he also threatened to move the LCAM project to Chicago, Mellody's hometown, where "Rahm"—Mayor Rahm Emanuel—was waiting to offer Lucas a space.

The carrot came a few days later, at the only Presidio Trust meeting Lucas attended. Clearly nervous—he was still, as his sister said, a "behind-the-scenes guy"—he spoke haltingly about how the Presidio was the birthplace of digital arts (along with Marin County, he added quickly), and thus would be well suited as the site of the museum. He apologized for using the word "hate," a word he said he told his children not to use. But he couldn't help himself needling the Trust over the broken deal. "Plus the idea [of LCAM] was to help fund the Presidio, to, you know, pay the bills here," he said in conclusion. "You never know, they might need the extra money." He sincerely wanted to inspire kids, to promote the digital arts, to celebrate the "shared myth" of storytelling, and to give his traveling *Star Wars* exhibits (of which there have been a good half dozen since 1993) a home near his home. But that was Lucas's closing argument for the museum: cold, hard cash.

After several meetings in which Presidio residents made their distaste for Lucas's proposal known, Bechtle announced that the Trust had reached a "unanimous" decision: the prized real estate would go to none of the competitors and would be turned into parkland instead. But the Trust still hoped Lucas would build a museum "somewhere in the park." Lucas was furious. He was subsequently offered a much smaller plot of land close to the Letterman Digital Arts Center, and at time of this writing he was investigating a spot for the museum on the lakefront in Chicago.

Lucas had overcome every obstacle in his life; he had survived a crash that should have killed him, and he'd completed every creative project he ever set his mind to. He'd broken free of Hollywood. He'd made himself a millionaire and then a billionaire. He'd invested himself and his money and his passion and his research into his *Flash Gordon* fan project, pursuing perfectionism relentlessly until it exploded in a light show that burned itself into billions of imaginations. He'd built an Empire out of the dreams that resulted, spun a century's worth of stories, tapped almost by accident into deep spiritual notions and mythologies, shattered our visual expectations, transformed the meaning of merchandise, and changed our perception of the universe forever.

He'd accomplished so much. But when it came to building a suitable temple to house his vast legacy, George Lucas's plans were interrupted by not-quite-so-rich-folks who didn't like new money—or at least, not the kind of new money that came from a popular space fantasy epic.

W hatever one thought of Lucas's epic, by 2014 it seemed to be never ending. The seventh episode in the trilogy was approaching, and Lucasfilm was maintaining an even greater, tighter, more maniacal level of secrecy than ever before. Not a detail about the film's contents, its cast, or even its shooting locations was to be leaked by anyone working on the production or even slightly affiliated with it. A Hasbro toy merchandising executive tweeted the fact of his visit to the set in Pinewood Studios 20 miles west of London in February 2014; he didn't give away a single detail, but weeks later his Twitter account was inexplicably deleted.

Star Wars movie productions had been secretive before, but this was something else. It took Lucasfilm until March 2014 to "reveal" that the movie would be set thirty years after *Return of the Jedi* and would star "a trio of new leads alongside some very familiar faces," and until May 2014 to confirm what Lucas had let slip in an interview more than a year earlier: that the familiar faces belonged to Mark Hamill, Carrie Fisher, and Harrison Ford, not to mention Anthony Daniels, Kenny Baker, and Peter Mayhew.

When the company couldn't entirely suppress negative details, they were expertly buried in a slew of positive news. For instance, screenwriter Michael Arndt left the project under mysterious circumstances, to be replaced by director Abrams and Lawrence Kasdan; rumor had it that Arndt didn't like spending a lot of screen time on three "very familiar faces" and wanted to get straight to the trio of new leads; Abrams and his boss, Kathleen Kennedy, felt that more homage was due to the old crew. Lucasfilm managed to deflect stories about Arndt's departure by announcing a significant number of the movie's behind-the-scenes big names: it wasn't just Kasdan helping to create *Episode VII* now, but also sound gurus Ben Burtt and Matthew Wood and composer John Williams, then eighty-one.

Social media rushed to fill the vacuum purposefully created by Lucasfilm. A thousand amateur artists posted their ideal *Episode VII* posters to Twitter and Facebook. So many popular tweets were posted speculating about the movie and its rumored stars that to cover them properly would require an entire other book.

But for the most part, what fans and commenters contributed were *Star Wars* jokes, reflecting once again the franchise's propensity for loving spoofs. Comedian, actor, and *Star Wars* nerd Seth Rogen tweeted that *Episode VII* should open with a line that suggested nothing at all had happened in the thirty years since *Jedi*: "Damn, those Ewoks can party. Now what?" Fellow comedian Patton Oswalt went Rogen one better. Appearing in an episode of *Parks and Recreation* on NBC, Oswalt was asked to ad-lib a filibuster for the show's town council meeting. What he came up with was over-the-top brilliance: an eight-minute rant filled with his nerdiest heart's desire about what should happen in *Episode VII*. It featured Wolverine and the other superheroes of the Marvel Universe, based on the principle that Marvel and *Star Wars* were both now owned by Disney. The Oswalt ad-lib barely featured in the episode, but it found new life online, with three million YouTube views to date. The Nerdist channel added another million views simply for producing an animation of Oswalt's storyline. Fans would likely burn down Disney HQ in Burbank if the company ever merged its franchises the way Oswalt was proposing, but they couldn't get enough of his idea of *Star Wars*.

Disney was, if anything, sealed up tighter than Lucasfilm when it came to details about the latest movie in the franchise. Several years out, Disney reps explained that this was a long-term and deliberate strategy: "We're just going to let *Episode VII* speak for itself," one told me.

Disney president Alan Horn, a recent transplant from Warner Brothers, spoke about *Star Wars Episode VII* for the first time at CinemaCon, the annual confab of theater owners in Las Vegas, on April 17, 2013. It was the fortieth anniversary of the day George Lucas had sat down to write the first full *Star Wars* treatment, though neither Horn nor Kathleen Kennedy was aware of that fact. That day *Star Wars* fans were busy laughing at the Oswalt video, which had been released that day, and also mourning the death of Richard LeParmentier, who had passed the previous night. Le Parmentier was a fixture on the convention circuit, an actor known worldwide for a single scene on the Death Star. His character, Admiral Motti, is Force-choked from across the room by Darth Vader. "Every time we find someone's lack of faith disturbing," Le Parmentier's family said in a statement, "we'll think of him."

The theater Horn spoke in might as well have been an homage to Motti's workplace. If there was a screening room aboard the Death Star, it would have looked like the Colosseum, the $95 million theater at Caesars Palace. Cavernous, in black and red, it boasts 4,298 seats, 120-foot ceilings, one of the largest indoor HD screens in the United States, and one of the largest stages in the world. While Horn addressed the CinemaCon attendees, red lights blinked just above the screen, which meant a system called PirateEye was scanning the audience and running the feed through algorithms aimed at detecting the outline of someone holding up a smartphone. An announcer told us—I was one of those being scanned—that security teams with night-vision goggles would be patrolling the crowd throughout the presentation. I hoped Disney had hired the 501st Legion to do this job, but it turned out the company doesn't have that kind of sense of humor when it comes to piracy.

Horn, who was mostly there to sell theater owners on the forthcoming (and future flop) *The Lone Ranger*, seemed relatively uninterested in talking about the *Star Wars* franchise. Fifteen minutes passed before he told a folksy story about visiting Lucasfilm HQ in the Presidio for the first time: "It's not uncommon for someone at the end of a meeting to say, 'May the Force Be With You.' Well, what do you say to that? I said, 'And also with you, my brother.'" A smattering of laughter came from the owner-filled audience—not quite the old cusses with their big cigars that Charley Lippincott remembered, but clearly the descendants of that bunch. Later, Horn mentioned that Disney was going to release one *Star Wars* movie each year, with spin-off movies coming in between the *Episodes*.* This was not news to anyone paying attention; Iger revealed that schedule when he bought Lucasfilm. But Horn was the first to use the words "every year." The pens of every journalist in the room started moving on notebooks. Stories were posted online within the hour.

The relationship between Horn and Kathleen Kennedy—his direct report—is still shrouded in mystery. But we do know that the release date of *Episode VII* was a bone of contention. That day in April 2013, Horn announced that *Episode VII* would be released in Summer 2015. But Kennedy wasn't so sure.

---

* Despite online rumors to the contrary, the spin-off movies would not be based around well-known *Star Wars* characters.

"We'll see," she said through gritted teeth on the red carpet at CinemaCon that night, when I asked her if that seemed likely. As it turned out, the date would be pushed back—to December 18, 2015.

The release date wouldn't be the only thing that Kennedy slashed. The LucasArts games division was laid off in its entirety in 2013, and its unfinished, highly anticipated game *Star Wars 1313* was banished to the same shelf where the *Underworld* TV show on which it was based also sat unproduced. *Clone Wars* was cancelled in 2013, the show's fans assuming that Disney didn't want a show that was screened on a rival subsidiary, Cartoon Network.

With every bout of bad news, fans laid the blame at Disney's doorstep—without considering the fact that Lucasfilm had a new and steely Hollywood-based boss named Kennedy; itwas no longer under the wing of a benign billionaire dispensing bags of cash to his passion projects. *Star Wars* simply didn't have the financial backing it once enjoyed. With a slew of new movies for which to budget and an expensive Hollywood director to fund, the budget of roughly $2 million per *Clone Wars* episode was simply not viable, given the ratings. In the end, the decision to cancel that series, at least, came down to money.

Kennedy wasn't down on the idea of televising *Star Wars*, though. She may have decimated the animation group, but she retained animation supervisor Dave Filoni and his key talent. She arranged for the remaining *Clone Wars* episodes to be polished and placed on Netflix. And Filoni's second animated TV series, which arose from the ashes of *Clone Wars*, looks to be simultaneously cheaper and *better* than its predecessor. *Star Wars Rebels*, Filoni's new show on the Disney XD Channel, is still under wraps as of this writing. ("Difficult to see," as Yoda says. "Always in motion is the future.") *Rebels* is set fourteen years after the events of *Episode III* and five years before the events of the original *Star Wars*. It stars a motley group of anti-Imperial youths on the planet Lothal, recently occupied by the Empire. Kanan Jarrus, voiced by Freddie Prinze Jr., stars as a moody renegade Jedi who escaped the Order 66 massacre; the crew of his ship *Ghost* consists of Ezra, Zeb, Sabine, Hera, and the grumpy astromech droid Chopper. There's a Jedi-hunting Inquisitor after Kanan, and it doesn't take a *Star Wars* genius to guess which tall, black-armored, masked man in a cape is the Inquisitor's boss.

This is ripe, virgin territory in the *Star Wars* Universe: the height of the Empire and the rise of the Rebel Alliance. It's the same period *Underworld* was supposed to cover. Not even the Expanded Universe touched this period much, a hangover from the fact that Lucas was reserving all the time in his galaxy prior to *Episode IV* for the prequels.

As if to signal the old-school, original-trilogy fans that it's safe to come back, Filoni based all his concept art for *Rebels* on the paintings and sketches of that prime posse member, the man without whom *Star Wars* would not have been made, Ralph McQuarrie. When Filoni revealed the first batch of concept art from *Rebels* at Celebration Europe in July 2013, he did so surrounded by a squadron of 501st Legion members dressed not as the Stormtroopers we know, exactly, but as the McQuarrie concept versions, back when the space soldiers carried laser swords. "Ralph's designs are as real a part of *Star Wars* as anything that existed on screen," gushed Filoni.

Kennedy sees the work of the writers and the artists to whom George Lucas has passed the torch—whether on *Rebels*, *Episode VII*, or the first of many spin-off movies—as inviolate, paramount, beyond the control of any corporate strategist or marketing executive. "Imagination drives innovation," Kennedy told fans in Germany in 2013, before drawing wild applause for suggesting that *Episode VII*'s special effects would use models and puppets as much as CGI. "We're going to use every single tool in the tool box to create the look of these movies," she said (and this was confirmed the following year, when Abrams filmed a charity video from the *Episode VII* set in Abu Dhabi; it was quite deliberately interrupted by a giant pupper that looked like it had wandered in from *Dark Crystal*.) Discussing how unnamed other big budget movies had lost their way, she added: "if you don't pay attention to the foundation of these stories—and spend the time you need to find unique stories, complicated stories—after a while, the audience gets tired."

Kennedy's most important contribution to the future of *Star Wars* was to found the Lucasfilm Story Group in 2012. This shadowy organization is led by Kiri Zooper Hart, a writer, producer, and veteran of the Ladd Company and Kathleen Kennedy's production outfit. It consists of Leland Chee, keeper of the Holocron, plus representatives of the licensing group, brand communications team, and business strategy department. Their main day-to-day task is to co-ordinate between all of this new *Star Wars* content bursting onto our screens and to lay down the law on what can and can't be done—in other words, to approximate Lucas's intentions in the absence of Lucas. More importantly, the Story Group moved agressively to retire the Expanded Universe.

No longer would the Holocron contain a confusing division between movie canon, TV canon, book and comic book canon, and the lowest form of content, S-canon. There would only be the Story Group's stamp of approval, and everything else would be rebranded "*Star Wars* Legends," effectively banished to the Universe of It Never Really Happened. In May 2014, the Story Group's decision was announced: nothing had the stamp of approval except the six movies, plus *The Clone Wars*. This was a power not even George Lucas dared wield: the power to cull everything that has ever been said or written about the galaxy far, far away into a single, coherent Lucasfilm-approved narrative. *Star Trek*, the Marvel and DC superhero universes: all of these long-running franchises have had moments when the sheer amount of content spun out of control and started to contradict itself. Their custodians were forced to start all over again in an alternate universe, in effect—the dreaded moment known to fans as a "reboot." What the Story Group did was more an extremely drastic series of amputations. *Star Wars* authors would have loved to not be considered part of the infected limb. In 2013, Timothy Zahn pointed out to me, rather hopefully, that all of his books fit in the years between *Episodes VI* and *VII*. They didn't have to be wiped out, he said, because they don't affect the future trajectory of the franchise. But Zahn fell into line soon enough, and was quoted in the Expanded Universe–killing announcement praising Lucasfilm for its vast canvas.

The power to determine what gets painted where on that canvas has in effect been handed to a *Star Wars* fan. He's probably the most knowledgeable leader of the Story Group, and his job is to know and help steer everything about the future content of the saga—every movie, every game, every TV show, every book. A scary-smart superfan who wrote the book on *Star Wars* books and effectively explained *Star Wars* intellectual property enough to satisfy Disney. A man who, if *Star Wars* is around a hundred years from now, may well be responsible for the fact. A guy who is living the fanboy dream: Pablo Hidalgo.

Pablo Hidalgo, thirty-nine, is original *Star Wars* generation. He claims to have been spurred into his career because he was belittled for not drawing TIE fighters right—at the age of four. Born in Chile and raised in Canada, Hidalgo read the 1979 *Star Wars* novel *Han Solo at Star's End* until the pages began to fall out. In the mid-1990s, he started writing for the *Star Wars* role-playing game. In 2000, he was snapped up by Lucasfilm as an Internet content developer and moved to California; within a year, he was managing editor of StarWars.com and much more besides. "He wrote more of the *Star Wars* encyclopedia than I did," admits Steve Sansweet. In 2011, Hidalgo became "brand communications manager"—in other words, Lucasfilm's explainer in chief, a rare example of a total nerd who speaks mainstream-ese.

Hidalgo was the guy Lucasfilm tapped to help explain the *Star Wars* franchise to Disney before they bought it. In a similar feat in August 2013 he gave an hour-long version of his presentation to Disney's fan conference, D23, at the airy Anaheim Convention Center steps from the original Disneyland. It's called "Crash Course in the Force."

First, addressing the *Star Wars* fans rather than the Disney fans in the audience, Hidalgo acknowledged that intense speculation had been raging over *Episode VII*. "I can reveal exclusively," he said, pausing for dramatic effect, "that that's not . . . what . . . this . . . panel's . . . about." He laughed. "Let's pause for all the bloggers to walk out of the room. If you've got your smartphone out, you can relax."

I was laughing until I noticed that a sizable number of people, maybe a hundred, were actually walking out.

This is Hidalgo, at once the consummate Lucasfilm insider and utterly savvy about today's social-media-networked, blogging-on-hyperspeed culture. His mind can encompass the seventeen thousand characters that appear in *Star Wars* novels; he wrote the comprehensive 2012 guide, *The Essential Reader's Guide to the "Star Wars" Universe*. He is known for documenting every appearance in Lucasfilm movies of an old sound effect from the 1950s favored by Ben Burtt called "the Wilhelm screen." But he can talk with ease and poke an affectionate kind of fun at fandom at the same time. The previous day at D23, when Bob Iger had told a crowd of thousands that he was "speechless . . . and am going to remain speechless" about everything Lucasfilm, his remark had been met with boos. Earlier that day, when Alan Horn had repeated his stump speech about visiting the Lucasfilm campus—"And also with you, my brother'"—some in the audience had laughed, but still Horn got booed, both in person and on Twitter, for moving on without discussing Lucasfilm product. "I'm sorry," he said. "I wish I could say more. It will come soon." Some major newspapers reported the boos as news; Disney's communications department flew into a rage.

Hidalgo's response to all this? Posting this dry tweet after his talk to a capacity three-thousand-person crowd: "Heads up. No *Star Wars* announcements scheduled for the California Dental Association Convention, 8/15-8/17." (Don't bother searching for the post; in February 2014, overwhelmed by how much of a time-suck it was, Hidalgo left Twitter and deleted his widely followed account.)

In his "Crash Course on the Force," Hidalgo admitted that there are numerous entry points for explaining what *Star Wars* is about. His way is not to introduce George Lucas, nor even to talk about *Episode IV*. "*Star Wars* is about Jedi Knights," he said, bringing pictures of multiple Jedi up on the big screen behind him. "Guardians of peace and justice. Also we"—there's a Freudian pronoun—"own one of the coolest weapons known to the galaxy, the lightsaber.

Any lightsabers here in the audience?" Hundreds of many-colored fluorescent sticks wave in the air.

Star Wars, Hidalgo added, is also about the conspiracy by Sith Lords to bring down the Jedi. He got audience members with red Sith lightsabers to wave theirs. "These are bad folks," he said. "Not team players." The Sith kept losing, he explained, because they kept fighting each other. So one of them decided it was just going to be a conspiracy of two, and they retreated into the shadows, finally brought down the Jedi, subverted democracy, and created the Galactic Empire. Someone cheered. "We've got a very sinister individual here applauding oppression and tyranny," laughed Hidalgo.

Star Wars is about the Rebellion against that Empire. It's about soldiers—"you can't have a war story without soldiers," Hidalgo said. "Then, there are the scoundrels." The audience erupted in cheers as Han Solo and Lando Calrissian appeared on the screen. "They could care less about intergalactic battles, Sith Lords, Jedi, whatever. They're just trying to survive and make a buck."

Then Hidalgo outlined the first six films—running through them not in the order in which they were released, but rather in the order of their internal chronology. "Let's start with *Episode I, Phantom Menace*," he said, which elicited disgruntled murmurs from the crowd. A picture of Jake Lloyd got Hidalgo his first proper boo. He pressed on, showing how Anakin's growing-up story contrasts with the fall of the Republic and ultimately causes it. Then he reached *Episode IV*, "which for many of us is also the first movie."

The audience cheered, with a palpable sense of relief. The folks I spoke to afterwards were uneasy with what Hidalgo was doing: putting the three weakest and most recent movies first, reordering the history of *Star Wars* as the public encountered it. In this, Hidalgo was simply following the guidelines laid down by the Creator of the franchise before his departure: *Star Wars* is a single twelve-hour saga that covers the tragedy of Darth Vader in chronological order.

Still, what Hidalgo said next is very telling and beautifully phrased; you might call it the best description of fandom's idea of *Star Wars* yet to emerge from Lucasfilm. "As *Star Wars* fans will tell you, it's not about what happens; it's how the stories are told, with exquisite detail and texture," he says. "It's set in a universe that's very convincing. You can believe it's real. It has a history. It's lived in. It's alive. It's a place you want to revisit again and again." Hidalgo went on to rhapsodize about the "mind-blowing visuals" and "kinetic high-speed action sequences, exquisitely edited," and stepped into Joseph Campbell territory by describing *Star Wars* "archetypes that reach back into our collective history as storytellers." But then he brought it all down to Earth:

It's not so deep and mythic that it's not accessible. It's about human characters, human emotions, human relationships. It's stuff we can relate to: friendship, camaraderie, love. *Star Wars* isn't afraid to have fun. In addition to telling deep stories and dark stories, it finds humor in character, and circumstance, and sometimes in the most unexpected places.

I mused on what Hidalgo had said as I walked back into the Anaheim sunshine past costumed Disney fans wearing Chewbacca-themed backpacks. I took pictures of a Sleeping Beauty arm in arm with a Princess Leia and noted more "Darth Mickey" caps than I'd seen that morning. I checked in on Facebook and Twitter, and saw more *Star Wars* products and memes filling my feeds than ever. I saw fan art with Darth Maul dressed as the Joker from Batman; I saw a photo of a *Star Wars*-themed crib with "I am a Jedi like my father before me" painted on the wall between two lightsabers. I saw BBC newsreaders dressed up as Boba Fett and a Stormtrooper to celebrate news of an open casting call for *Episode VII*. Planet Star Wars certainly isn't afraid to have fun.

Had Kathleen Kennedy done it, I wondered? Had she steered Lucas's Rebel Alliance of a company to safety, hidden in plain sight under the protection of a giant benign media Empire? Had she tapped exactly the right person, a fan who defined and defended the idea of *Star Wars* more precisely than its Creator could, to control the overarching structure of its future? Had that fan grasped the basic principles that would unite the fandom fractured by the prequels— words that spoke for all the *Star Wars* generations?

In the history of *Star Wars*, 2013 and 2014 will go down as landmark years. A new conductor was tapping her baton, calling for a moment of quiet and reflection before summoning up a new symphony with a new melody but familiar themes. Lucasfilm's silence during this spell, its distinct lack of content between *Clone Wars* and *Rebels*, was all part of a greater plan. Suspense and speculation have always been good offscreen complements to *Star Wars* movies. Only in 2014, fans weren't wondering how Han was going to get out of that carbonite or whether Luke really was Vader's son. We were wondering about every single last detail of the movie to come. It was a silence in which to contemplate the pure idea of *Star Wars*: the richness, the possibility, and the endless expanse of the universe itself.

The moment would come soon enough when the uncertainty wave collapsed, and we found out whether Schrodinger's Cat was alive or dead in its box. Kennedy's canniness, Hidalgo's knowledge, J. J. Abrams's experience: all of these could yet conspire to produce a turkey. Difficult choices about the directions of a limitless franchise would have to be revealed. When they were, a world of fans lay in wait, preparing to pick apart every detail. At least one *Star Wars* fan predicted stormy weather ahead. "It's a complicated cultural icon," George Lucas said in 2013, when asked about his advice for Kennedy and Abrams. "You're always going to be in trouble no matter what you do. So the best thing you can do is just plough forward and try to do the best story you can." In private, he urged Kennedy and Abrams to remember that the movies worked best when they were both aspirational and retained a sense of humor.

But we won't know for sure whether the franchise's new stewards have told that best of all possible stories, not until that glorious and terrifying day in 2015, when we've all filed, finally, into a packed theater, filled with excited murmuring and plastic lightsabers. The house lights will dim, and an electric cheer will go up. Some version of "When You Wish Upon a Star" will play, incongruously, over a Lucasfilm logo. The screen will go black. Then up will come ten familiar words in blue: "A Long Time Ago in a Galaxy Far, Far Away . . ." Then silence. Blackness again.

Then an orchestra will explode in B-flat major, and the largest logo you've ever seen will fill the entire screen. And no sooner has it appeared than it will immediately begin to recede, slipping away, pulling back into the stars as if daring you to give chase.

ACKNOWLEDGEMENTS

As the nerdiest of *Star Wars* fans know, the original full name of the Force—as written in the crucial penultimate drafts of the original movie—is The Force of Others. I am here to testify that the Force of Others is real. I was knocked over by its positive spirit repeatedly during the process of writing this book. I found it in the stars of the *Star Wars* firmament; in the highest echelons of fandom; in Lucasfilm, though Lucasfilm did not officially cooperate with this book; in friends old and new.

The Force of Others manifested itself in generosity, advice and various other kindnesses. It was to be found in Consetta Parker, Steve Sansweet, Anne Neuman, Jenna Busch, Dustin Sandoval, Aaron Muszalski, Michael Rubin, Hal Barwood, Rodney and Darlene Fong, Chris Argyropoulos, Lynne Hale, Lynda Benoit, Anita Li, Charlotte Hill, Chris James, Pablo Hidalgo, Edward Summer, Dale Pollock, Alan Dean Foster, Alain Bloch, Michael Heilemann, Chris Lewicki, Liz Lee, Don Glut, Kyle Newman, Dan Madsen, James Arnold Taylor, Ed daSilva, Peter Hartlaub, Charley Lippincott, Manuelito Wheeler, George James Sr., Christian Gossett, Derryl dePriest, Anthony Daniels, Billy Dee Williams, Jeremy Bulloch, Cole Horton, Bryan Young, Lou Aronica, Paul Bateman, Audrey Cooper, Albin Johnson, Mark Fordham, Christine Erickson, Todd Evans, Chris Giunta, John Jackson Miller, Shelly Shapiro, Timothy Zahn, Mark Boudreaux, Bobak Ferdowsi, Sasha and Nick Sagan, Howard Kazanjian, Fred Roos, Tracy Duncan, Terry McGovern, Bill & Zach Wookey, Jennifer Porter, Josh Quittner, Jessica Bruder, Dale Maharidge, David Picker, Patrick Read Johnson, Daniel Terdiman, Cherry Zonkowski, Seth Rosenblatt, Bonnie Burton, Michael Barryte, Michael Kaminski, Patti McCarthy, Alan

Ladd Jr. and Amanda Ladd Jones, Jack Sullivan, Matt Martin, Andrey Summers, Phil Tippett, Shanti Seigel, Walter Isaacson, Simon Pegg, Ronald D Moore, Mike Stackpole, Steve Silberman and Gary Kurtz. Alongside that list, I would like to raise a lightsaber in silent salute to various Lucas employees past and present who asked that their names not be used.

I would also like to thank David Perry, spokesperson for George Walton Lucas Jr. Mr. Lucas is a brilliant and profoundly protective man whose strong feelings on the subjects of privacy and biography were bound to make his cooperation with a book like this impossible. But David was gracious in passing every request for an interview on to the Lucas desk itself. More than this: David and his husband Alfredo have become dear friends.

This book would not exist without the initial prodding, cheerleading and hustling of Kathryn Beaumont Murphy. Katherine Flynn, my agent, helped steer it to a safe landing. Tim Bartlett is the reason the book landed at Basic when it had an abundance of suitors, and he will always have MFNF (most-favored non fan) status. Alex Littlefield was a keen and capable editor whose modifications took this book to point five past light speed; my thanks also for the patience of project manager Rachel King and the corrections of copy editor Beth Wright. Of course, any mistakes that remain after their meticulous reads are mine and not theirs.

Writing a book of this scale in less than two years would not have been possible without the support and indulgence of all my friends and colleagues at Mashable, in particular Lance Ulanoff, Emily Banks, Kate Sommers-Dawes, and Jim Roberts. On the home front, family and friends too numerous to mention were supportive and tolerant when I vanished into my writing cave for weeks at a time. But the Yavin throne room gold medal for support and tolerance goes to Jessica Wolfe Taylor—a Star Trek fan for whom *Star Wars* was just alright.

Finally the author would like to acknowledge that Mowgli is a padawan wise beyond his years, and that his frequent attempts to push my laptop out of my lap during the writing of this book were simply his way of getting me to let go my conscious self and reach out with my feelings.

May the Force of Others be with you, always.

Chris Taylor
Berkeley
June 2014

NOTES

INTRODUCTION: A NAVAJO HOPE

vii   **"When I heard the title:** George James Sr., author interview, July 3, 2013.

ix   **"We're know-it-alls now,":** Manuelito Wheeler, author interview, July 3, 2013.

x   **"I used to have to just ask:** Christine Erickson, author interview, September 16, 2013.

x   **"I've had people say:** Natalia Kochan, interview by Daniel Terdiman of CNET, May 4, 2013.

xii   **"I know it's out of order,":** Jamie Yamaguchi, interview by Daniel Terdiman of CNET, May 4, 2013.

xiii   **"I know the big reveal,":** Tami Fisher, interview by Daniel Terdiman of CNET, May 4, 2013.

xvi   **"I am the father:** *Total Film Magazine*, April 2008.

xvii   **"That's when I realized,":** Andrey Summers, author interview, February 13, 2014.

xvii   **"If you run into somebody:** Andrey Summers, "The Complex and Terrifying Reality of *Star Wars* Fandom," *Jive*, May 31, 2005.

xviii   **"The Navajo must be:** Anthony Daniels to the author in the corridor at *Star Wars* Celebration Europe II, July 25, 2013.

xx   **"We call for strength:** Thomas Deel, author interview, July 3, 2013.

xx   **"Good was trying:** Annette Bilgodui, author interview, July 3, 2013.

1. MARS WARS

2   **never heard of Verne's book:** H. G. Wells, *The First Men in the Moon* (London: Newnes, 1901), Chapter 3.

2   **show me the Cavorite!:** Basil Davenport, *Inquiry into Science Fiction* (New York: Longmans, Green, 1955), 7.

2   **"that place just over the hill":** Michael Pye and Lynda Myles, *The Movie Brats: How the Film Generation Took Over Hollywood* (New York: Holt, Rinehart, and Winston, 1979), 133.

3   **idea of a fantasy Mars was rescued:** See Richard A. Lupoff, *Master of Adventure: The Worlds of Edgar Rice Burroughs* (Lincoln: University of Nebraska Press, 2005), Chapter 3, for the argument that Barsoom descended directly from Arnold's book.

417

5   **"effervescent giddiness.":** Aljean Harmetz, "Burden of Dreams: George Lucas," *American Film*, June 1983.

7   **say, Buck?:** Patrick Lucanio and Gary Coville, *Smokin' Rockets: The Romance of Technology in American Film, Radio, and Television, 1945–1962* (Jefferson, NC: McFarland, 2002), 35.

10 **"When I went home in the evening:** Kinnard, Crnkovich, and Vitone, *Flash Gordon Serials*, 34.

2. THE LAND OF ZOOM

13 **"He's a behind the scenes guy:** "Is George Lucas Returning to His Modesto Roots?," *Modesto Bee*, November 4, 2012.

13 **"A nerd, but:** Modesto quotes from "For Many, Parade Is Drive Down Memory Lane," *Modesto Bee*, June 7, 2013.

14 **"impeccably polite and implacably distanced:** Peter Bart, "Godfather, Starfather Eye New Galaxies," *Variety*, July 27, 1998.

14 **"the small one,":** "George Lucas Talks to the *Bee*'s Marijke Rowland," video interview, June 7, 2013, http://www.modbee.com/2013/06/07/2752579/video-george-lucas-talks -to-the.html.

15 **The Gallo winery:** Ernest and Julio Gallo, with Bruce B. Henderson, *Ernest and Julio: Our Story* (New York: Times Books, 1994), 55.

16 **"on all the coffee tables":** Dale Pollock, *Skywalking: The Life and Films of George Lucas*, updated ed. (New York: Da Capo, 1999), 19.

16 **"I like to say *Star Wars*:** Cole Horton, author interview and talk at *Star Wars* Celebration Europe II, July 2013.

16 **"no matter where they go:** *Duck and Cover* description and quote from *Watch the Skies! Science Fiction, the 1950s and Us*, directed by Richard Schickel (Lorac Productions, 2005).

17 **"frightening" and said he was "always on the lookout:** Pollock, *Skywalking*, 15.

17 **$30,000:** John Baxter, *George Lucas: A Biography* (New York: HarperCollins, 1999).

18 **"I was in heaven,":** Pollock, *Skywalking*, 21.

18 **"His dad was stern,":** Patti McCarthy, author interview, April 19, 2014.

18 **the boy detested having to mow the lawn:** The lawnmower anecdote is in Pollock, *Skywalking*, 20.

18 **"My first mentor was my father,":** Lucas to Bill Moyers in *The Mythology of Star Wars*, PBS, 2000.

18 **only one God, but so many religions:** Lucas editorial in *Edutopia*, the magazine of the George Lucas educational foundation, July 1, 2003.

18 **"I liked to build things,":** Melece Casey, "George Lucas: Behind the Scenes with Modesto's Movie Mogul," *Stanislaus Magazine* (Summer 2013).

19 **pictures of "space soldiers.":** Samuel G. Freedman, "Taking a Lightsaber to Tired Old Teaching," *New York Times*, August 31, 2005.

19 **Once upon a time:** "Slow Poke" manuscript from Patti McCarthy, Department of Film Studies, University of the Pacific, Stockton, California.

19 **"He was bored with school:** McCarthy, author interview.

19 **"It was very critical to him:** Mel Cellini interviewed in *The Unauthorized "Star Wars" Story* (Visual Entertainment, 1999).

21 **"EC Comics had it all,":** Lucas, foreword to *The EC Archives: Weird Science*, vol. 1 (York, PA: Gemstone, 2006).

21 **"*Mad* took on all the big targets,":** Lucas, foreword to *Mad About "Star Wars,"* by Jonathan Bresman (New York: Del Rey, 2007).

22 **Edward Summer:** Edward Summer, author interview, June 24, 2013.

24 **Charley Lippincott:** Charley Lippincott, author interview, July 8, 2013.

24 **Howard Kazanjian:** Howard Kazanjian, author interview, September 10, 2013.

24 **Don Glut:** Don Glut, author interview, July 9, 2013.

24 **"The original Universal serial:** J. W. Rinzler, *The Making of "Star Wars": The Definitive Story Behind the Original Film: Based on the Lost Interviews from the Official Lucasfilm Archives* (New York: Ballantine Books, 2007), 93.

24 **The serial was the "real stand-out:** Alan Arnold, *Once Upon a Galaxy: A Journal of the Making of "Star Wars"* (New York: Ballantine Books, 1980) 220.

26 **Lucas picked up a 1955 copy of *Classics Illustrated*:** Summer, in *Star Wars Insider* 141, July 2013), 26.

26 **"He was really taken with it,":** Cellini, interview from *The Unauthorized "Star Wars" Story*.

26 **"stay in his room and draw:** Randall Kleiser, in "George Lucas: Creating an Empire," *Biography*, Arts & Entertainment Network, January 27, 2002.

3. PLASTIC SPACEMEN

27 *Star Wars* **was the last thing:** Albin Johnson details and quotes from author interview, October 11, 2013.

31 **"The big invasion:** Lucas at the Tournament of Roses Parade from *Star Wars: Star Warriors*, documentary (Los Angeles: Prometheus Entertainment for Lucasfilm, 2007).

32 **Mark Fordham was a sniper:** Mark Fordham details and quotes from author interview, October 9, 2013.

34 **"It kind of reflects the films,":** Suzy Stelling, author interview, July 27, 2013.

34 **I've heard guys say:** Ed Da Silva details and quotes from author interview, June 21, 2013.

36 **When I met Ainsworth:** Andrew Ainsworth details and quotes from author interviews, April 26 and September 2, 2013.

38 **"viewing events through his own:** Quote from Mr. Justice Mann and other details from transcript [2008] EWHC 1878 (Ch) Case No: HC06C03813, High Court of Justice of England and Wales (Chancery division).

38 **didn't stop Muir from taking to the Internet:** Brian Muir, forum posts, therpf.com, December 5, 2010, http://www.therpf.com/f45/original-anh-stormtrooper-helmet-armor-just-facts-102219.

39 **"actually doesn't matter":** Brian Muir, email exchange with author, September 2, 2013.

4. HYPERSPACE DRIVE

41 **drove around like cars:** Dale Pollock, *Skywalking: The Life and Films of George Lucas*, updated ed. (New York: Da Capo, 1999), 154.

41 **"dumb little car":** Pollock, *Skywalking*, 24.

41 **always jabbering about a story:** "George Lucas—Allen Grant," YouTube video, 1:13, July 13, 2012, http://www.youtube.com/watch?v=KMxhdiVQvow.

41 **lure local toughs:** John Baxter, *George Lucas: A Biography* (New York: HarperCollins, 1999), 33.

42 **quieter and more intense:** Mel Cellini interview from *Unauthorized "Star Wars" Story*.

43 **"It gave me this perspective on life:** "Oprah's Next Chapter," OWN, January 22, 2012.

43 **"no longer a lot of mythology:** John Seabrook, "Letter from Skywalker Ranch," *New Yorker*, January 6, 1997.

44 **an "echo" of Lipsett's film:** Steve Silberman, "Life After Darth," *Wired* 13, no. 5 (May 2005).

45 **Wexler said he would have gotten:** Michael Rubin, *Droidmaker: George Lucas and the Digital Revolution* (Gainesville, FL: Triad, 2006), 8.

45 **"It's supposed to be easier than P.E.,":** Lucas, interview with American Film Institute, 2004.

45 **"For God's sake, watch this kid.":** Pollock, *Skywalking*, 35.

45 **millionaire before I'm 30:** Pollock, *Skywalking*, 38.

46 **"I had this idea for doing a space adventure:** Kerry O'Quinn, *Starlog*, no. 47 (June 1981).

46 **"Conditions were crowded:** Howard Kazanjian, author interview, September 10, 2013.

46 **bearded and strange:** Melece Casey, "George Lucas: Behind the Scenes with Modesto's Movie Mogul," *Stanislaus Magazine* (Summer 2013).

46 **Don Glut:** Don Glut, author interview, July 9, 2013.

48 **stay in and draw star troopers:** Randall Kleiser, in "George Lucas: Creating an Empire," *Biography*, Arts & Entertainment Network, January 27, 2002.

48 **run circles around everyone else:** Pollock, *Skywalking*, 56.

50 **friends with the guy who made it:** Walter Murch, interview, *THX 1138*, Two-Disc Director's Cut Special Edition, DVD extras, directed by George Lucas (Warner Home Video, 2004).

51 **"too fascist,":** Pollock, *Skywalking*, 61.

51 **take any shit:** Pollock, *Skywalking*, 63.

51 **"That damn movie:** Kerry O'Quinn, "Star Wars Memories," *Starlog*, no. 127 (February 1988).

53 **"erosbods and clinicbods.":** "Trends: the Student Moviemakers," *Time* (February 1968).

53 **not of this earth:** Pollock, *Skywalking*, 69.

53 **"It's a chase film,":** Charley Lippincott, author interview, July 8, 2013.

54 **"As corny as it sounds,":** Kerry O'Quinn, "The George Lucas Saga," *Starlog*, nos. 48–50 (July–September 1981).

54 **cheap, behind the scenes documentaries:** Pollock, *Skywalking*, 70.

55 **"stinky kid.":** Stephen Farber, "George Lucas: The Stinky Kid Hits the Big Time," *Film Quarterly*, Spring 1974.

55 **"George broke the rules:** Kazanjian, author interview.

55 **Lucas was captured on documentary:** Lucas and Francis Ford Coppola TV interviews in "Indies," YouTube video, 2:05, December 19, 2011, http://www.youtube.com/watch?v=JhfY4LvpevI.

5. HOW TO BE A JEDI

57 **"There must be something independent:** Deleted scene quoted in J. W. Rinzler, *The Making of "Star Wars": The Definitive Story Behind the Original Film: Based on the Lost Interviews from the Official Lucasfilm Archives* (New York: Ballantine Books, 2007), 18.

57 **Lucas feared:** Dale Pollock, *Skywalking: The Life and Films of George Lucas*, updated ed. (New York: Da Capo, 1999), 224.

57 **"Knowing that the film was made:** Pollock, *Skywalking*, 288–289.

58 **"The more detail I went into":** Laurent Bouzereau, *"Star Wars": The Annotated Scripts* (New York: Ballantine Books, 1997), 35.

59 **"When I was 12:** Jennifer E. Porter, "'I Am a Jedi': *Star Wars* Fandom, Religious Belief, and the 2001 Census," chapter 6 in *Finding the Force of the "Star Wars" Franchise: Fans, Merchandise, & Critics*, ed. Matthew Wilhem Kapell and John Shelton Lawrence (New York: Peter Lang, 2006), 101.

59 **"The theme that emerges:** Jennifer Porter, author interview, March 6, 2014.

60 **In 1977, Frank Allnutt:** Frank Allnutt, *The Force of "Star Wars"* (Van Nuys, CA: Bible Voice, 1977).

60 **"I devoured that book:** Albin Johnson, author interview, October 11, 2013.

60 **trying to do God's bidding:** Pollock, *Skywalking*, 141.

61 **that's one way to describe it:** Orville Schell, "George Lucas: 'I'm a Cynic Who Has Hope for the Human Race,'" *New York Times*, March 21, 1999.

61 **"We are trying to encourage people:** New Zealand email quoted in Porter, "'I Am a Jedi,'" 97.

62 **"For a group to be included:** Hugh McGaw in emails to Australian writers Bernhard O'Leary and John Stevenson, April 9, 2001, https://groups.google.com/forum/#!msg /aus.bicycle/fOAEYGAZGMU/N_YklxE8P_EJ.

62 **Some seventy thousand Australians:** Census numbers in this section are from Porter, "'I Am a Jedi,'" and numerous news media.

63 **In 2006, Labor's Jamie Reed:** Carole M. Cusack, *Invented Religions: Imagination, Fiction and Faith* (Farnham, Surrey, UK: Ashgate, 2010), 127.

63 **the *Daily Mail* couldn't resist:** "Jedi Knights Demand Britain's Fourth Largest 'Religion' Receives Recognition," *Daily Mail* (London), November 16, 2006, http://www .dailymail.co.uk/news/article-416761/Jedi-Knights-demand-Britains-fourth-largest -religion-receives-recognition.html.

63 **"It states in our Jedi:** "Jedi Religion Founder Accuses Tesco of Discrimination over Rules on Hoods," *Guardian* (London), September 18, 2009.

63 **"All religions are true:** Joseph Campbell to Bill Moyers, *Joseph Campbell and the Power of Myth*, PBS, 1988.

64 **"There was an ideological power struggle":** Jennifer Porter, author interview, March 6, 2014.

64 **"All of it is rather crap:** Alain Bloch, author interviews, September 11–12, 2013.

67 **"I was just goofing around:** "10 Years Later, Star Wars Kid Speaks Out," *Macleans*, May 2013.

69 **Waxy.org got remorseful:** Donations listed at http://waxy.org/2003/05/finding _the_sta/.

71 **"It's certainly been true in my own life,":** Bouzereau, *Annotated Scripts*, 286.

71 **Here's something I learned:** Lucas, speech to the Academy of Achievement, July 3, 2008, http://vimeo.com/19153918.

6. BUCK ROGERS IN THE TWENTIETH CENTURY

73 **"I bleed on the page:** Larry Sturhan, "The Making of *American Graffiti*," *Filmmaker's Newsletter* (March 1974).

73 **$150 weekly checks:** Lucas's contract in the *Hollywood Reporter*, September 18, 2013, http://www.hollywoodreporter.com/heat-vision/early-george-lucas-contract -reveals-649370.

73 **"You can't write.":** Lucas quoting Francis Ford Coppola in interview with Jon Avnet, chair of the American Film Institute Board of Directors, 2004, http://www.afi.com /members/features/lucas.aspx.

74 **the script was as much as 70 percent:** Paul Scanlon, "The Force Behind Star Wars," *Rolling Stone*, August 1977.

74 **Mona Skager:** J. W. Rinzler, *The Making of "Star Wars": The Definitive Story Behind the Original Film: Based on the Lost Interviews from the Official Lucasfilm Archives* (New York: Ballantine Books, 2007), 2.

75 **"A Japanese film:** Marcus Hearn, *The Cinema of George Lucas* (New York: Harry N. Abrams, 2005).

75 **lifted verbatim from Richard Nixon's:** Lucas, commentary, *THX 1138*, Two-Disc Director's Cut Special Edition, DVD extras, directed by George Lucas (Warner Home Video, 2004).

76 **"It is probably the most beautiful location:** Pittsburgh-based developer Thomas Frouge quoted in John Hart, "Saved by Grit and Grace: Wild Legacy of the Marin Headlands," *Bay Nature*, July 1, 2003, http://baynature.org/articles/saved-by-grit-and-grace/.

79 **only movie I really enjoyed:** Dale Pollock, *Skywalking: The Life and Films of George Lucas*, updated ed. (New York: Da Capo, 1999), 92.

79 **"It's like a sci-fi scene.":** "The Stones at the Speedway," *Wall Street Journal*, November 16, 2010.

79 **"It's a kind of therapy":** Sturhan, "Making of *American Graffiti*."

80 **"For low budget pictures, that was perfect,":** Gary Kurtz, author interview, April 24, 2014.

80 **"We had these huge heads,":** Bill Wookey, author interview, April 10, 2014.

81 **"probably just dropped his name to be silly.":** Terry McGovern, author interview, March 23, 2014.

81 **masturbation or a masterpiece:** Peter Biskind, *Easy Riders, Raging Bulls: How the Sex -Drugs-and-Rock-'n'-Roll Generation Saved Hollywood* (New York: Simon & Schuster, 1998), 98.

82 **"But I mean, it hurts.":** Stephen Zito, "George Lucas Goes Far Out," *American Film*, April 1977.

82 **"Some talent, but too much 'art,'":** "Goings on About Town," *New Yorker*, October 7, 1972.

82 **"We need the money,":** Marc Norman, *What Happens Next: A History of American Screenwriting* (New York: Random House, 2008), 392.

82 **"Because it's a fairly straightforward action:** Kurtz, author interview.

83 **I'll just invent my own:** Lucas, Francis Ford Coppola, and Saul Zaentz in "A Long Time Ago: The Story of *Star Wars*," *BBC Omnibus*, season 33, episode 10, July 7, 1999.

83 **"*Flash Gordon* is like anything:** J. W. Rinzler, *The Making of "Star Wars": The Definitive Story Behind the Original Film: Based on the Lost Interviews from the Official Lucasfilm Archives* (New York: Ballantine Books, 2007), 4.

84 **"Why don't you do something warm?":** Scanlon, "The Force Behind Star Wars."

84 **"Those who know George Lucas:** Judy Stone, *San Francisco Chronicle*, May 23, 1971.

85 **"I've been toying with this idea:** Rinzler, *Making of "Star Wars,"* 5.

85 **"You can imagine how many meetings:** David Picker, author interview, January 7, 2014.

86 **"The discussion about [the title] was:** Kurtz, author interview.

86 **"The name, before it came out:** Patrick Read Johnson, author interview, September 11, 2013.

86 **no one else dared to go:** Lucas, interview with Gene Roddenberry Jr., in *Trek Nation*, directed by Scott Colthorp (Roddenberry Productions, 2010).

87 **wasn't action-oriented:** Lucas, interview with Roddenberry Jr., *Trek Nation*.

87 **"If I went to a strange planet:** Gene Roddenberry, "*Star Trek* Still Has Many Fans," Associated Press, March 14, 1972.

87 **"To not make a decision:** Rinzler, *Making of "Star Wars,"* 108.

88 **"A large technological empire:** Lucas notes quoted in Rinzler, *Making of "Star Wars,"* 17.

88 **a big, brassy, Cinemascope-style graphic:** Kurtz, author interview.

89 **second picture:** Document in Rinzler, *Making of "Star Wars,"* 6.

89 **"The way we solved that was by saying:** Kurtz, author interview.

90 **"The set was very wild, very loose,":** McGovern, author interview.

91 **"It sounded great to me,":** *Starlog*, #120 (July 1987): 42.

91 **"I need R2, D2.":** Pollock, *Skywalker*, 141.

92   **"whipping up this treatment:** Jean Valelly, "'The Empire Strikes Back,' and So Does George Lucas," *Rolling Stone*, June 12, 1980.

7. HOME FREE

94   **"That's kind of cool,":** Hal Barwood details and quotes from author interview, May 21, 2013.

95   **"Science fiction movies ran roughly:** Edward Summer, author interview, June 24, 2013.

95   **ounce of taste for crazy humor:** "Screen: Wonderful Trip in Space; 'Forbidden Planet' Is Out of This World," *New York Times*, May 4, 1956.

96   **Anthony Daniels, seeing his first:** Anthony Daniels on *Dermot O'Leary Show*, BBC Radio 2, March 21, 2009.

97   **"To see somebody actually do it:** Lucas quote in *Standing on the Shoulders of Kubrick: The Legacy of 2001*, Blu-Ray (Los Angeles: Warner Brothers, 2001).

97   **the Chilean director Alejandro Jodorowsky:** The story of Jodorowsky's *Dune* film attempt is from *Jodorowsky's "Dune,"* directed by Frank Pavich (Sony Pictures Classics, 2013).

99   **"The 1970s was a perfect storm:** Summer, author interview.

100   **"They're these angelic creatures:** Barwood, author interview.

8. MY LITTLE SPACE THING

102   **Lucas began by scribbling a list of names:** Names list and first two pages of treatment in J. W. Rinzler, *The Making of "Star Wars": The Definitive Story Behind the Original Film: Based on the Lost Interviews from the Official Lucasfilm Archives* (New York: Ballantine Books, 2007), 8.

103   **"totally unreleasable.":** John Baxter, *George Lucas: A Biography* (New York: HarperCollins, 1999), 138.

104   **Joseph Gelmis loved it:** Baxter, *George Lucas*, 147.

104   **he offers the faint praise:** Lucas, interview, *Hidden Fortress*, DVD extras (Criterion Collection, 2001).

105   **Lucas's second treatment:** Treatment text on scifiscripts.com, cross-checked with extracts in Laurent Bouzereau, *"Star Wars": The Annotated Scripts* (New York: Ballantine Books, 1997), and Rinzler, *Making of "Star Wars."*

107   **"Disney would have accepted:** Rinzler, *Making of "Star Wars,"* 12.

107   **"I understood completely,":** Alan Ladd Jr., author interview, March 26, 2014.

109   **tapping into the collective unconscious:** Rinzler, *Making of "Star Wars,"* 16.

110   **"a small independent country:** Rinzler, *Making of "Star Wars,"* 16.

110   **"I thought, 'well, why the hell:** Charles Platt, *Dream Makers: Science Fiction and Fantasy Writers at Work: Profiles* (London: Xanadu, 1986), 74.

111   **"*The Star Wars* is a mixture:** Lucas interview in *Chaplin* [Swedish Film Institute] (fall 1973).

111   **the first script of *The Star Wars*:** First draft on scifiscripts.com, cross-checked with extracts in Bouzereau, *"Star Wars,"* and Rinzler, *Making of "Star Wars."*

113   **"It was a universe nobody could understand:** Willard Huyck in Rinzler, *Making of "Star Wars,"* 25.

113   **"You beat your head against the wall:** Dale Pollock *Skywalking: The Life and Films of George Lucas*, updated ed. (New York: Da Capo, 1999), 142.

114   **"George approached me:** Hal Barwood, author interview, May 21, 2013.

114   **"You go crazy writing,":** Rinzler, *Making of "Star Wars,"* 26.

114   **a gold-embossed folder:** The folder is in Rinzler, *Making of "Star Wars,"* 27.

114   **"And in the time of greatest despair:** Second draft on scifiscripts.com, cross-checked with extracts in Bouzereau, *"Star Wars,"* and Rinzler, *Making of "Star Wars."*

115 **"That's not true,":** Gary Kurtz, author interview, April 24, 2014.

118 **"the first multi-million-dollar *Flash Gordon*:** Lucas to *Esquire*, quoted in Brian J. Robb, *A Brief Guide to "Star Wars": The Unauthorised Inside Story of George Lucas's Epic* (London: Constable & Robinson; Philadelphia: Running, 2012), e-book, Chapter 3.

118 **"That was definitely a finger-in-the-wind time.":** Kurtz, author interview.

119 **"The Star Wars corporation shall have:** Legal document quoted in Rinzler, *Making of "Star Wars,"* 25.

119 **absolute gobbledygook:** Baxter, *George Lucas*, 165.

120 **"Absolutely 100 percent not,":** Anthony Daniels, author interview, July 25, 2013.

120 **"ratty little guy":** According to McQuarrie understudy Paul Bateman, author interview, August 30, 2013.

120 **"fascist white uniform":** From the second draft, scene 18.

120 **"They were done as a substitute:** Rinzler, *Making of "Star Wars,"* 32.

121 **The third draft still opened:** Third draft on scifiscripts.com, cross-checked with extracts in Bouzereau, *"Star Wars,"* and Rinzler, *Making of "Star Wars."*

125 **"it really straightened some of them out,":** Rinzler, *Making of "Star Wars,"* 63.

125 **"more man against machine than anything else,":** Scanlon, "The Force Behind *Star Wars."*

126 **"the whole idea of *Star Wars* as a mythological thing,":** Kurtz, author interview.

126 **"*Star Wars* is a sort of compilation,":** Stephen Zito, "George Lucas Goes Far Out," *American Film*, April 1977.

127 **"She was fairly quiet about the whole thing,":** Ladd, author interview.

9. SPOOF WARS

128 **"He acts now like:** Charley Lippincott, author interview, July 8, 2013.

129 **"This is one of the first things:** Interview with Jon Stewart, *Star Wars* Celebration V, August 15, 2010.

129 **"I laughed all through:** Ken P., "An Interview with Mark Hamill," IGN.com, May 2004, http://www.ign.com/articles/2004/02/03/an-interview-with-mark-hamill?page=2.

130 **"That's a powerful aspect:** Albin Johnson, author interview, October 11, 2013.

130 **Sean Goodwin looked at them:** Sean Goodwin and Anjan Gupta, author interviews, April 3 and 5, 2013.

132 **the White House responded:** https://petitions.whitehouse.gov/response/isnt-petition -response-youre-looking.

134 **probably contracted to build the Death Star:** Lucas, *Star Wars, Episode II: Attack of the Clones*, DVD commentary (Twentieth Century Fox, 2005).

134 **"you'll laugh, you'll cry:** *"Hardware Wars:* The Movie, the Legend, the Household Appliances," *Salon*, May 21, 2002.

135 **"Special Oscars should be awarded:** Lucas letter to *Mad* quoted in Jonathan Bresman, *Mad About "Star Wars"* (New York: Del Rey/Ballantine Books, 2007), 32; Roffman quoted on 23.

136 **"It should have been made several years:** Roger Ebert, review of *Spaceballs*, *Chicago Sun-Times*, June 24, 1987, http://www.rogerebert.com/reviews/spaceballs-1987.

136 **"I couldn't do a serious piece,":** Kevin Rubio quoted in *Backyard Blockbusters*, directed by John E. Hudgens (Z-Team Productions, 2012).

137 **who sent Nussbaum an approving letter:** *George Lucas in Love*, directed by Joe Nussbaum (Mediatrip.com, 1999).

138 **"He's like the most evil guy:** Jack Sullivan, author interview, April 21, 2014.

140 **just *Robot Chicken* neutered:** Devin Faraci, "Seth Green, George Lucas, Pixar Piss on the Ashes of *Star Wars*," *Badass Digest*, August 24, 2012, http://badassdigest.com/2012 /08/24/seth-green-george-lucas-pixar-piss-on-the-ashes-of-star-wars/.

141 **"We didn't think it made any sense:** Seth Green, "Ask Me Anything," *Reddit*, September 17, 2013, http://www.reddit.com/r/IAmA/comments/1ml9cw/seth_green_here_actorproducer_writer_director/ccaba64.

141 **"somehow do a Jedi mind-meld":** President Barack Obama, White House press conference, March 1, 2013.

10. STAR WARS HAS A POSSE

142 **"I've loosened up a little bit,":** J. W. Rinzler, *The Making of "Star Wars": The Definitive Story Behind the Original Film: Based on the Lost Interviews from the Official Lucasfilm Archives* (New York: Ballantine Books, 2007), 97.

143 **very happy if you came up with ideas:** McQuarrie in *Star Wars Insider*, no. 50 (July/August 2000): 63.

143 **"like bubbles in champagne,":** McQuarrie as recalled by Paul Bateman, author interview, August 30, 2013.

143 **"If I had a hundred people:** Bateman, author interview.

144 **"We did have long discussions:** Gary Kurtz, author interview, April 24, 2014.

144 **"Immediately, I could see this:** Burtt details and quotes from interview with Pablo Hidalgo, *Star Wars* Celebration Europe II, July 26, 2013.

145 **"George just asked me to come along:** Fred Roos, author interview, February 27, 2013.

146 **Lucas offered Mifune:** Mika Mifune made her comments in a Japanese history quiz show called *Sekai Fushigi Hakken!*, quoted in "How Star Wars Might Have Had a Different Darth Vader," Kotaku.com, January 14, 2013.

147 **"Good God, it's science fiction!:** Alec Guinness diaries quoted in Piers Paul Read, *Alec Guinness: The Authorized Biography* (New York: Simon & Schuster, 2011), 503–504.

147 **20 hours a day:** Rinzler, *Making of "Star Wars,"* 106.

149 **"think of a flying saucer":** Laurent Bouzereau, *"Star Wars": The Annotated Scripts* (New York: Ballantine Books, 1997), 52.

149 **"I'm trying to make props:** Rinzler, *Making of "Star Wars,"* 97.

150 **"compromising left and right":** Rinzler, *Making of "Star Wars,"* 160.

151 **"there weren't a lot of people there:** Kurtz, author interview.

152 **"depressed" and "desperately unhappy.":** Rinzler, *Making of "Star Wars,"* 160.

152 **like a second home:** "George Lucas Praises British Film Industry at Windsor Castle Event," *Yahoo! News*, April 5, 2013, http://uk.movies.yahoo.com/george-lucas-praises-british-film-industry-windsor-castle-143700635.html.

152 **"80 percent of the crew:** Carr quoted in *The Making of "Star Wars: Return of the Jedi,"* ed. John Philip Peecher (New York: Ballantine Books, 1983), 12.

153 **"A bit late:** Guinness diaries quoted in Read, *Guinness*, 505.

153 **The dialogue changes came courtesy:** Huyck and Katz contributions to the script noted in Laurent Bouzereau, *"Star Wars": The Annotated Scripts* (New York: Ballantine Books, 1997), 5–120.

154 **"It's not what I want it to be.":** Rinzler, *Making of "Star Wars,"* 190.

154 **"George came back from *Star Wars*:** "Spielberg on Spielberg," Turner Classic Movies, 2007.

155 **"My life was collapsing:** Rinzler, *Making of "Star Wars,"* 218.

155 **"This is where you're shooting:** Rob Lowe, *Stories I Only Tell My Friends: An Autobiography* (New York: Henry Holt, 2011), 54.

155 **"The originals were a little too:** Phil Tippett, author interview, April 11, 2014.

156 **"No applause:** Viewing story according to Kurtz, author interview.

156 **"It wasn't particularly the movie:** Rinzler, *Making of "Star Wars,"* 224.

157 **"It's the *At Long Last Love*:** Peter Biskind, *Easy Riders, Raging Bulls: How the Sex-Drugs-and-Rock-'n'-Roll Generation Saved Hollywood* (New York: Simon & Schuster, 1998), 334.

157   **"It's kind of a bubble gum movie,"**: Edward Summer, author interview, June 24, 2013.

158   **"Thirty years in Los Angeles:** Quotes and details from Charley Lippincott, author interview, July 8, 2013.

159   **"I heard you're making a movie:** Don Glut, author interview, July 9, 2013.

159   **"I'm watching a movie in my head:** Alan Dean Foster, author interview, June 26, 2013.

162   **Gary Meyer:** Coronet story quoted in *"Star Wars* and the Coronet in 1977: An Oral History," *San Francisco Chronicle*, May 27, 2013.

11. THE FIRST REEL

164   **"*Star Wars:* Magic Ride,"**: John Wasserman, *San Francisco Chronicle*, May 25, 1977, 51.

165   **"If you hook the audience:** Peter Biskind, *Easy Riders, Raging Bulls: How the Sex-Drugs -and-Rock-'n'-Roll Generation Saved Hollywood* (New York: Simon & Schuster, 1998), 99.

166   **"Thank goodness:** Allen Ginsberg quoted by *Wired* journalist Steve Silberman, who was with him that day, to the author.

167   **Rice found herself at ILM:** Details from Suzy Rice, author interview, May 15, 2013.

168   **"war drums echoing:** Quoted in the script, per Laurent Bouzereau, *"Star Wars": The Annotated Scripts* (New York: Ballantine Books, 1997), 5.

169   **"chickened out":** Lucas quoted in *Seattle Times*, May 1980.

169   **"Fox wouldn't let me.":** Lucas, *Star Wars, Episode IV: A New Hope*, DVD commentary (Twentieth Century Fox, 2004).

169   **"We were toying with the idea of calling:** Gary Kurtz, author interview, April 24, 2014.

170   **"What's all this Force shit?:** De Palma quoted in J. W. Rinzler, *The Making of "Star Wars": The Definitive Story Behind the Original Film: Based on the Lost Interviews from the Official Lucasfilm Archives* (New York: Ballantine Books, 2007), 256.

170   **It is a period of civil wars in the galaxy:** Crawl text on scifiscripts.com, cross-checked with extracts in Laurent Bouzereau, *"Star Wars": The Annotated Scripts* (New York: Ballantine Books, 1997), and Rinzler, *Making of "Star Wars."*

172   **seven or eight hypotheses:** "The Den of Geek Interview: John Dykstra," *Den of Geek*, November 2, 2008, http://www.denofgeek.us/movies/13733/the-den-of-geek-interview -john-dykstra.

173   **"model!":** Rinzler, *Making of "Star Wars,"* 275.

175   **a seven-year-old in Philadelphia:** Philip Fierlinger, author interview, January 2013.

176   **"When Vader came out of the darkness:** Todd Evans, author interview, August 17, 2013.

176   **"it was an invitation:** Kurtz, author interview.

177   **"sort of knew":** Paul Scanlon, "The Wizard of Star Wars," *Rolling Stone*, August 25, 1977.

177   **"We see Carrie Fisher:** Hal Barwood, author interview, May 21, 2013.

178   **"When it was first released":** Lucas, *Episode IV*, commentary.

178   **"The whole thrust:** Rinzler, *Making of "Star Wars,"* 300.

178   **"*Star Wars* was a joke:** Jody Duncan, *"Star Wars" Mythmaking: Behind the Scenes of "Attack of the Clones"* (New York: Ballantine Books, 2002), 218.

179   **"Full marks for the creation:** Piers Paul Read, *Alec Guinness: The Authorized Biography* (New York: Simon & Schuster, 2011), 507.

179   **"You've vaporized the audience:** Biskind, *Easy Riders*, 334.

179   **"Who's the hero?":** Don Glut, author interview, July 9, 2013.

12. RELEASE

183   **"My father had this wonderful:** Christian Gossett, author interview, August 15, 2013.

184   **"Old people, young people:** Al Levine quoted in *San Francisco Chronicle*, June 3, 1977.

185 **"I was a *Star Trek* fan:** Dan Madsen, author interview, August 12, 2013.

185 **"two people arguing about:** Kerry O'Quinn, *Starlog*, no. 7 (August 1977).

185 **A cartoon published in a *Trek* zine:** *Star Trek* cartoon in "The Sehlat's Roar #5," *Spectrum*, no. 34 (1977), quoted in "Star Trek and Star Wars," *Fanlore*, January 12, 2014, http://fanlore.org/wiki/Star_Trek_and_Star_Wars.

186 **"We're working out a policy:** Craig Miller quoted in *Hyper Space*, no. 3 (1977).

186 **"The word has come down:** Maureen Garrett letter quoted in *Alderaan*, no. 15 (1981).

186 **"I really learned to watch it:** Charley Lippincott, author interview, July 8, 2013.

188 **"Hi, kid, are you famous yet?":** John Baxter, *George Lucas: A Biography* (New York: HarperCollins, 1999), 237.

189 **"We were dismissing the lines:** Gary Kurtz, author interview, April 24, 2014.

189 **"There could be a 21st Century Fox:** "Off the Screen," *People*, July 18, 1977.

190 **"*Star Wars* was like they struck gold,":** Alan Ladd Jr., author interview, March 26, 2014.

191 **"send money.":** Coppola telegram in Dale Pollock, *Skywalking: The Life and Films of George Lucas*, updated ed. (New York: Da Capo, 1999), 186.

191 **"twerp cinema.":** Coined by Coppola's friend Dennis Jakob, quoted in Peter Biskind, *Easy Riders, Raging Bulls: How the Sex-Drugs-and-Rock-'n'-Roll Generation Saved Hollywood* (New York: Simon & Schuster, 1998), 346.

192 **reinstate high adventure:** Janet Maslin, "How Old Movie Serials Inspired Lucas and Spielberg," *New York Times*, June 7, 1981.

193 **"I'm an introvert:** "Off the Screen."

193 **"They don't know exactly:** "Summer Blockbuster," *Star Wars Insider*, no. 140 (May/June 2013): 51.

193 **"more than anything else,":** J. W. Rinzler, *The Making of "Star Wars": The Definitive Story Behind the Original Film: Based on the Lost Interviews from the Official Lucasfilm Archives* (New York: Ballantine Books, 2007), 306.

193 **because he "cut corners":** Paul Scanlon, "The Force Behind Star Wars," *Rolling Stone*, August 1977.

13. THE ACCIDENTAL EMPIRE

196 **"*Star Wars*," Lucas mused:** J. W. Rinzler, *The Making of "Star Wars": The Definitive Story Behind the Original Film: Based on the Lost Interviews from the Official Lucasfilm Archives* (New York: Ballantine Books, 2007), 224.

197 **Sansweet is snarky and avuncular:** Steve Sansweet quotes from author tour and Steve Sansweet, "Introducing . . . Steve Sansweet," *Star Wars Blog*, July 2, 2012, http://starwarsblog.starwars.com/2012/07/02/introducing-steve-sansweet.

199 **"Basically I like to make things:** Quote and Cukor anecdote from Stephen Farber, "George Lucas: The Stinky Kid Hits the Big Time," *Film Quarterly*, Spring 1974.

199 **"followed from the general idea":** Claire Clouzot, "The Morning of the Magician," *Ecran*, September 15, 1977.

201 **"$50 and a handshake.":** Mark Boudreaux, author interview, September 22, 2013.

201 **"He thought he should have had:** Charley Lippincott, author interview, July 8, 2013.

201 **"Okay, we sold a piece:** Mark Boudreaux, author interview, September 22, 2013.

202 **"Where are the guns?":** Steve Sansweet, *"Star Wars": From Concept to Screen to Collectible* (San Francisco: Chronicle Books, 1992), 65.

202 **"If you do something I don't like:** Sansweet, *From Concept to Screen*, 123.

204 **"tacky pilgrim mementos:** Jennifer Porter, author interview, March 6, 2014.

205 **"About 75 percent of our fans:** Derryl dePriest, author interview, September 4, 2013.

207 **"I told George:** Carrie Fisher, *Wishful Drinking*, Berkeley Repertory Theatre, February 28, 2008.

14. HERE COME THE CLONES!

208 **"We used to play cops:** James Arnold Taylor, author interview, June 18, 2013.

209 **"It will be a separate story:** "The Day the Droids Invaded Hollywood," *Washington Post*, August 4, 1977.

209 **"either we make this deal:** Alan Ladd Jr., author interview, March 26, 2014.

210 **"I want *Star Wars* to be:** *Starlog*, no. 9 (October 1977).

211 **"showed there was twice as much:** Peter Biskind, *Easy Riders, Raging Bulls: How the Sex-Drugs-and-Rock-'n'-Roll Generation Saved Hollywood* (New York: Simon & Schuster, 1998), 344.

211 **"We're fucking being blown off:** Smith and Friedkin quoted in Biskind, *Easy Riders*, 337.

213 **"The only thing it cleaned up:** Steven Bach, *Final Cut: Dreams and Disaster in the Making of "Heaven's Gate"* (New York: New American Library, 1985), 68.

214 **"a talky melodrama:** Roger Ebert, review of *Black Hole*, *Chicago Sun-Times*, January 1, 1979.

214 **"I stole it from everybody.":** David McIntee, *Beautiful Monsters: The Unofficial and Unauthorized Guide to the Alien and Predator Movies* (Prestatyn, Denbighshire, UK: Telos, 2005), 19.

215 **"Hollywood is like a bunch of lemmings,":** Ladd, author interview.

215 **"They wanted to follow through:** Dan O'Bannon and David Giler quoted in Tom Shone, *Blockbuster: How Hollywood Learned to Stop Worrying and Love the Summer* (New York: Simon & Schuster, 2004), 86.

217 **"was to bring attention to our:** Barry Ira Geller, "The CIA, the Lord of Light Project, and Science Fiction Land," 2013, lordoflight.com/cia.html.

218 **"the ambassador and the young prince:** *The Making of "Tron,"* directed by Robert Meyer Burnett (Buena Vista Home Entertainment, 2002).

219 **"I told Dino:** Charley Lippincott, author interview, July 8, 2013.

221 **"*Star Wars* was fun:** Isaac Asimov, "Science Fiction Is More Than a Space Age Western," Knight-Ridder Newspapers, September 17, 1978.

221 **"Glen Larceny.":** Harlan Ellison, *The City on the Edge of Forever: The Original Teleplay That Became the Classic "Star Trek" Episode* (Clarkston, GA: White Wolf, 1996), endnote 1.

221 **"the most blatant rip-off ever:** "Small Screen Star Wars," *Time*, September 18, 1978, 98.

221 **"The characters are given more:** *Newsweek*, September 11, 1978.

222 **Outraged fans protested:** "Boy Kills Self After TV Show Is Cancelled," Associated Press, August 26, 1979.

222 **"raised genuine issues of material fact:** Twentieth Century Fox Film Corporation v. MCA, 715 F.2d 1327 (9th Cir. 1983), http://openjurist.org/715/f2d/1327/twentieth-century-fox-film-corporation-v-mca-inc.

223 **"Wookiees have litters.":** *Star Wars Insider*, no. 141 (July 2013): 39.

223 **"but we can't say that.":** Quoted by Lenny Ripps, as interviewed by Bonnie Burton and told to the author.

223 **"That's one of those things:** David Itzkoff, "Tale from the Dark Side," *Maxim* May 2002.

224 **"The only sound they make:** "The Han Solo Comedy Hour," *Vanity Fair* (December 2008).

225 **"In the long run, it wasn't necessary,":** Gary Kurtz, author interview, April 24, 2014.

15. HOW TO EXCEED IN SEQUELS

227 **"I created Darth Vader,":** Vernon Scott, "The Real Darth Vader Is Unmasked," *Daily Chronicle* (London), December 5, 1977, 18.

227 **"I was confronted with what:** "May the Sequel Be with You," *San Francisco Examiner,* July 24, 1978, 4.

229 **Prowse had no memory:** David Prowse, author interview, September 5, 2013.

229 **"vaguely" remembers "something:** Gary Kurtz, author interview, April 24, 2014.

229 **"had *inadvertently* leaked story points:** J. W. Rinzler, *The Making of "Star Wars: Return of the Jedi": The Definitive Story* (New York: Del Rey, 2013), 100, emphasis added.

231 **In November 1977, Lucas sat down:** Lucas-Brackett story conference quoted in Rinzler, *Making of "Empire": The Definitive Story* (New York: Del Rey, 2010), 23.

233 **"During pre-production on *Empire*:** Howard Kazanjian, author interview, September 10, 2013.

234 **"I felt very flattered,":** Kershner in Rinzler, *Making of "Empire,"* 36.

234 **"I think George had it in mind:** Kurtz, author interview.

234 **"What we're doing here, really:** *Raiders of the Lost Ark* story conference posted at http://maddogmovies.com/almost/scripts/raidersstoryconference1978.pdf.

234 **It contained some intriguing:** Brackett's draft posted in full at starwarz.com, cross-referenced against extracts posted in Rinzler, *Making of "Empire."*

235 **"I liked her a lot,":** Rinzler, *Making of "Empire,"* 70.

236 **"I found it much easier:** Alan Arnold, *Once Upon a Galaxy: A Journal of the Making of "Empire Strikes Back"* (New York: Ballantine Books, 1980), 144.

236 **the dialogue of the sequel's:** Lucas's second draft quoted in Rinzler, *Making of "Empire,"* 49.

237 **"When you're creating something:** *Star Wars,* Definitive Edition Laserdisc (Industrial Light & Magic, 1993).

237 **"The problem of the hero:** Joseph Campbell, *The Hero with a Thousand Faces* (New York: New World Library, 1949), 125.

238 **"Suddenly Dagobah is full of:** Michael Kaminski, *The Secret History of "Star Wars": The Art of Storytelling and the Making of a Modern Epic* (Kingston, Ontario: Legacy Books, 2008), e-book.

238 **"finger in the *Star Wars* pie,":** Don Glut, author interview, July 9, 2013.

240 **"I was desperate,":** Dale Pollock, *Skywalking: The Life and Films of George Lucas,* updated ed. (New York: Da Capo, 1999), 207.

240 **"challenged everything:** Ringler, *"Making of "Empire,"* 65.

243 **"I tried to rein Kersh in a bit,":** Kurtz, author interview.

244 **"after the success of *Star Wars*:** Arnold, *Once Upon a Galaxy,* 247.

244 **"I'll guarantee that":** Lucas to the Starlog Salutes *Star Wars* convention, 1987, as recorded in *Starlog* 127.

244 **"It turned out he hadn't,":** Spielberg in *Indiana Jones: Making the Trilogy* documentary on Indiana Jones Trilogy, DVD, 2003.

244 **"I'm willing to take a risk:** Arnold, *Once Upon a Galaxy,* 172.

245 **"I've caught him looking:** Arnold, *Once Upon a Galaxy,* 162.

245 **Ford: I think I should be:** Arnold, *Once Upon a Galaxy,* 139.

246 **"But more than a few":** Fisher admitted to doing cocaine on the set of *Empire Strikes Back* to the Associated Press in 2010.

247 **Williams: Don't hit me:** Arnold, *Once Upon a Galaxy,* 143.

247 **"I'd have to argue to do another take:** Phil Tippett, author interview, April 11, 2014.

248 **"You guys are ruining my picture,":** Pollock, *Skywalking,* 218.

248 **"He's lying.":** Rinzler, *Making of "Empire,"* 305.

249 **"It ends on a very bleak:** John Brosnan, film review, *Starburst,* no. 23 (May 1980).

250 **"I would take out my portable:** Rinzler, *Making of "Empire,"* 300.

250 **"Trying to license *Empire*:** Sansweet, *From Concept to Screen,* 123.

250 **"What matters at the moment:** Roger Angell, "The Current Cinema: Cheers and Whimpers," *New Yorker*, May 26, 1980.

250 *The Empire Strikes Back* **is about as personal:** Vincent Canby, "'The Empire Strikes Back' Strikes a Bland Note," *New York Times*, June 15, 1980.

251 **"*The Empire Strikes Back* is the only blockbuster:** Chuck Klosterman, *Sex, Drugs, and Cocoa Puffs: A Low Culture Manifesto* (New York: Scribner, 2003), 152.

251 **"If you guys did this:** Rinzler, *Making of "Empire,"* 334.

251 **"They have done it again,":** Dave Prowse, *Straight from the Force's Mouth: A Career Most Extraordinary* (Croydon, Surrey, UK: Filament, 2005), e-book entry for May 19, 1980.

16. BEING BOBA

252 **"It's not ownership:** Anthony Daniels, author interview, July 25, 2013.

252 **"Here we are enacting:** Carrie Fisher, "Letter to Leia," *BullettMedia*, January 4, 2013, http://bullettmedia.com/article/character-study-carrie-fisher-makes-peace-with-princess-leia.

253 **"No one's going to play Lando:** Billy Dee Williams, author interview, March 29, 2013.

253 **"It's a character that sticks:** Jeremy Bulloch, author interview, July 25, 2013.

17. END OF THE JEDI?

258 **"I don't want to upset your readers:** Kerry O'Quinn, "The George Lucas Saga," *Starlog*, nos. 48–50 (July–September 1981).

261 **"discussions with the marketing:** Gary Kurtz, author interview, April 24, 2014.

262 **"I had to come up with another hundred pages:** J. W. Rinzler, *The Making of "Star Wars: Return of the Jedi": The Definitive Story* (New York: Del Rey, 2013), 11.

263 **"I said 'oh come on,'":** Hamill to *Entertainment Weekly* at the Cape Town Film Festival on May 4, 2013.

263 **"In the next book, I want Luke to kiss:** J. W. Rinzler, *The Making of "Star Wars": The Definitive Story Behind the Original Film: Based on the Lost Interviews from the Official Lucasfilm Archives* (New York: Ballantine Books, 2007), 107.

263 **"It adds an odd frisson:** Alan Dean Foster, author interview, June 26, 2013.

263 **Blogger Michael Kaminski suggested:** Michael Kaminski, author interview, April 7, 2014.

264 **"I didn't want to be a Lucas:** Josef Krebs, "'The Empire Strikes Back' Director: Irvin Kershner," *Sound and Vision*, September 30, 2004.

264 **top of the list was David Lynch:** Rinzler, *Making of "Jedi,"* 41.

265 **"I wanted to get it out of my system:** "The Forces Behind Jedi," *People*, August 8, 1983.

265 **"the most exciting and grandiose:** "Secrecy Shrouds a Star Wars Serial," *New York Times*, July 11, 1982.

265 **"with Shakespeare in the next room":** *The Making of "Star Wars: Return of the Jedi,"* ed. John Philip Peecher (New York: Ballantine Books, 1983).

265 **The four of them talked about the story:** Story conference quoted in Rinzler, *Making of "Jedi,"* 64.

267 **"It's like Hitler's on his deathbed:** Foster, author interview.

268 **"I smile a lot:** "Secrecy Shrouds a Star Wars Serial."

269 **"You'll have to ask her.":** John Baxter, *George Lucas: A Biography* (New York: Harper-Collins, 1999), 333.

270 **"As open as I thought:** Dale Pollock, author interview, May 16, 2013.

270 **"You can't be sick,":** Rinzler, *Making of "Jedi,"* 260.

270 **"You can actually tell why:** Rinzler, *Making of "Jedi,"* 260.

270 **"It was a case of:** From unpublished Lucas interview with Michael Rubin, author of *Droidmaker: George Lucas and the Digital Revolution.*

18. BETWEEN THE WARS

273	**"was just about every page:** Dale Pollock, author interview, May 16, 2013.

274	**"pretty good editor.":** Peter Biskind, *Easy Riders, Raging Bulls: How the Sex-Drugs -and-Rock-'n'-Roll Generation Saved Hollywood* (New York: Simon & Schuster, 1998), 422.

275	**"I think people sometimes forget:** Dale Pollock, *Skywalking: The Life and Films of George Lucas,* updated ed. (New York: Da Capo, 1999), 240.

276	**"an inverted triangle:** Biskind, *Easy Riders,* 381.

277	**"The divorce kind of destroyed:** *60 Minutes,* March 28, 1999.

277	**"immediately electric":** Stephen Larsen and Robin Larsen, *Joseph Campbell: A Fire in the Mind: The Authorized Biography* (Rochester, VT: Inner Traditions, 2002), 542.

277	**"That was it,":** Larsen and Larsen, *Joseph Campbell,* 542.

278	**"You know, I thought real art:** Larsen and Larsen, *Joseph Campbell,* 543.

278	**"I was really thrilled,":** Joseph Campbell, *The Hero's Journey: Joseph Campbell on His Life and Work,* ed. Phil Cousineau (Boston: Element, 1999), 187.

278	**"Bring him out to the Ranch,":** Larsen and Larsen, *Joseph Campbell,* 544.

280	**"They said, 'Thank you very much, you guys:** Mark Boudreaux, author interview, September 22, 2013.

281	**"close some of the psychological wounds:** Gary Arnold, "Magical & Monstrous, the 'Star Wars' Finale Is a Triumph," *Washington Post,* May 22, 1983.

282	**Anthony Dolan says no *Star Wars* reference:** Frank Warner, "The Battle of the Evil Empire," *Morning Call* (Allentown, PA), March 5, 2000.

282	**"misleading Red scare tactics:** Lou Cannon, "President Seeks Futuristic Defense Against Missiles," *Washington Post,* March 24, 1983.

282	**"supersonic Edsel,":** Edward Kennedy, speech at the Brown University Commencement Forum, June 4, 1983, http://tedkennedy.org/ownwords/event/cold_war.

283	**"Darth Vader in America now,":** TASS quoted in "Soviet Critic Says Reagan like Darth Vader," United Press International, June 13, 1983.

283	**"*Star Wars,* your honor, is a fantasy,":** *Lucasfilm Ltd. v. High Frontier,* DC District Court, November 26, 1985.

283	**"I definitely got the feeling:** Dan Madsen, author interview, August 12, 2013.

284	**"It was not a great time:** Howard Roffman, "Interacting with *Star Wars,*" TEDxSoMa, YouTube video, 12:40, January 22, 2010, http://www.youtube.com/watch?v=KAb1 Dzkc8KU.

19. THE UNIVERSE EXPANDS

287	**"Make it work as a Sergio Leone:** Transcript published in *Star Wars Insider,* no. 145 (December 2013): 20.

287	**"the story of Chewbacca's second:** Alan Dean Foster, author interview, June 26, 2013.

288	**"We can't do these casually,":** Lou Aronica, author interview, August 15, 2013.

289	**"I'll never forget the day that Lucy:** Howard Roffman, foreword to *Star Wars: Heir to the Empire* by Timothy Zahn, 20th Anniversary Edition (New York: Ballantine Books, 2011), 1.

289	**initial print run of seventy thousand copies:** Timothy Zahn, author interview, August 16, 2013.

289	**"They didn't approach us:** Aronica, author interview.

290	**"I was a physicist,":** Zahn, author interview.

293	**"They shunt her to the side:** Tracy Duncan, author interview, January 28, 2014.

294	**"He told us we could kill anyone:** Shelly Shapiro, author interview, August 24, 2013.

295	**"It was guidance in the sense:** Foster, author interview.

20. RETURN OF THE WRITER

296 **"My oldest daughter was sick:** *Star Wars, Episode I: The Phantom Menace,* DVD extras (Twentieth Century Fox, 2001).

297 **"For every person who loves:** Laurent Bouzereau and Jody Duncan, *The Making of "Star Wars, Episode I: The Phantom Menace"* (New York: Del Rey, 1999), 149.

297 **"You just never know with these:** *The Beginning, Star Wars, Episode I,* DVD extras.

298 **"everyone had tears in their eyes,":** Marcus Hearn, *The Cinema of George Lucas* (New York: Harry N. Abrams, 2005), 174.

299 **"I could see George:** Hearn, *Cinema,* 172.

299 **"The great thing about Rick:** Hearn, *Cinema,* 201.

300 **"Part of the reason:** Lucas press conference transcribed by Sally Kline, in *George Lucas: Interviews,* ed. Sally Kline (Jackson: University Press of Mississippi, 1999), 181.

300 **"It would hopefully make me:** Lucas on *The Charlie Rose Show,* September 9, 2004.

300 **Lucas started writing about:** *Episode I* draft details from Michael Kaminski, "The Beginning: A Look at the Rough Draft of Episode I," *The Secret History of "Star Wars,"* November 10, 2007, http://secrethistoryofstarwars.com/thebeginning.html.

301 **"dyed-in-the-wool 99-percenter:** Bryan Curtis, "George Lucas Is Ready to Roll the Credits," *New York Times,* January 17, 2012.

301 **"I'm a very ardent:** Lucas to Charlie Rose, *CBS This Morning,* January 21, 2012.

306 **Lucas says he modeled this new comic relief:** According to Lucasfilm creature designer Terryl Whitlach at DragonCon, Atlanta, July 1, 1999, http://dailydragon.dragoncon.org /dc1999/jar-jars-mom-speaks/.

306 **"Rastafarian Stepin Fetchit,":** Joe Morgenstern, "Our Inner Child Meets Young Darth," *Wall Street Journal,* May 19, 1999.

306 **"How in the world could you take:** Lucas interview on *Newsnight,* BBC 2, July 14, 1999.

21. SPECIAL ADDITION

308 **"I used to be able to catch:** Arthur Penn dinner account from the diary of Pulitzer Prize–winning journalist Dale Maharidge, provided to the author.

310 **"It's like a screen door:** "The Force Is Still with Us," *Newsweek,* January 19, 1997.

310 **"If I had the money:** *The Making of "Star Wars: Return of the Jedi,"* ed. John Philip Peecher (New York: Ballantine Books, 1983), 89.

311 **"I thought it was a very virile:** *Making,* ed. Peecher, 89.

311 **"The thing was to create a real Jabba:** "Life After Darth," *Wired* 13, no. 5 (May 2005).

312 **"Those animals moving actually distract:** Kurtz to Ken P., IGN.com, November 11, 2002, http://www.ign.com/articles/2002/11/11/an-interview-with-gary-kurtz.

312 **"They're shit.":** Peter Hall, "Brilliant Effects Master Phil Tippett Sheds Some Light on George Lucas' 'Star Wars'-Tinkering Mind," *Movies.com,* September 1, 2011, http:// www.movies.com/movie-news/phil-tippett-star-wars/4324.

313 **"We hadn't sold very many VHS:** "Life After Darth."

314 **"Does a filmmaker have the right:** "Is George Lucas Tampering with History?," *Chicago Tribune,* January 19, 1997.

315 **"People who alter or destroy works of art:** "The Greatest Speech Against the Special Edition Was from George Lucas," *Saving "Star Wars,"* 2010, http://savestarwars .com/lucasspeechagainstspecialedition.html.

315 **"To me, it doesn't really exist:** "Lucas Talks as Original Trilogy Returns," Associated Press, September 15, 2004.

315 **Luckily, the 1977 negative:** Library of Congress information provided by Mike Mashon, Head of Moving Image Section, Motion Picture, Broadcasting, and Recorded Sound Division, Library of Congress, email to the author, September 3, 2013.

315 **"disappointed in myself"**: Spielberg quoted at *Raiders of the Lost Ark* thirtieth anniversary screening, Film.com, September 14, 2011.

315 **"I felt that so long as the originals:** "Dennis Muren: Interview," *Sci-Fi Online*, August 16, 2004, http://www.sci-fi-online.com/Interview/04-08-16_DennisMuren.htm.

315 **"six ways from Sunday"**: *Hollywood Reporter*, February 9, 2012.

316 **"I'm sorry you saw:** "Lucas Talks as Original Trilogy Returns."

317 **"a little bit too disco."**: *Making*, ed. Peecher, 109.

317 **"The success of that rerelease:** "Life After Darth."

317 **Ian McCaig had been asked:** Ian McCaig, interview with Pablo Hidalgo, *Star Wars Celebration Europe II*, July 27, 2013.

318 **"deeply in love"**: "A Long Time Ago: The Story of *Star Wars*," *BBC Omnibus*, season 33, episode 10, July 7, 1999.

318 **"Do you want to do *Star Wars*?'**: *The Beginning, Star Wars, Episode I: The Phantom Menace*, DVD extras (Twentieth Century Fox, 2001).

22. THE LINE

319 **by "Yoda"**: Laurent Bouzereau and Jody Duncan, *The Making of "Star Wars, Episode I: The Phantom Menace"* (New York: Del Rey, 1999), 76.

319 **"This isn't real,"**: McGregor in "A Long Time Ago: The Story of *Star Wars*," *BBC Omnibus*, season 33, episode 10, July 7, 1999.

320 **"I thought he should take:** *Eon Magazine*, September 1999, http://www.theforce.net /episode1/story/darabont_kasdan_on_helping_george_with_ep_i_ii_78815.asp.

320 **"write better dialogue"**: "Sky's the Limit," *Detroit Free Press*, May 19, 2005.

320 **"The film is going to come out:** *The Beginning, Star Wars, Episode I: The Phantom Menace*, DVD extras (Twentieth Century Fox, 2001).

321 **"Now he's so exalted,"**: "A Funny Thing Happened on the Way to Tosche Station: FFC Interviews Mark Hamill," *Film Freak Central*, March 19, 2013, http://www.filmfreak central.net/ffc/2013/03/mark-hamill-interview.html.

322 **"It's bold:** Quotes from Lucas and Ben Burtt from *The Beginning*.

323 **Chris Giunta moved from Maryland:** Story details and quotes from Chris Giunta, author interview, August 29, 2013.

323 **"Everybody had different motivations:** Shanti Seigel, author interview, April 23, 2014.

324 **"It was nightmarish at night,"**: Todd Evans, author interview, August 17, 2013.

23. THE PREQUELS CONQUER STAR WARS

328 **"believe these pointers can help:** "S.F. Gets Tough on Popular Laser Pointers," *San Francisco Chronicle*, May 19, 1999.

329 **"the score's most delightful:** Joshua Kosman, "Inspired Phantom Menace Soundtrack Recalls Movie Moments," *San Francisco Chronicle*, May 19, 1999.

329 **"over my dead body."**: David C. Robertson, *Brick by Brick: How Lego Rewrote the Rules of Innovation and Conquered the Global Toy Industry* (New York: Crown Business, 2013), 39.

330 **"a flood of biblical proportions."**: Steve Sansweet, "Star Wars: 1,000 Collectibles," Harry N. Abrams, 2009, 17.

331 **"The actors are wallpaper:** Peter Travers, "Star Wars, Episode I: The Phantom Menace," *Rolling Stone*, May 19, 1999.

331 **"Dialogue isn't the point,"**: Roger Ebert, "Star Wars, Episode I: The Phantom Menace," *Chicago Sun-Times*, May 17, 1999.

331 **Gallup released a *Phantom Menace* poll:** Press release, Gallup, June 25, 1999, http://www .gallup.com/poll/3757/public-gives-latest-star-wars-installment-positive-rave-reviews .aspx.

331 **"It's entirely critic-proof,"**: Elvis Mitchell, *PBS Newshour*, May 19, 1999.

332　**"about a quarter of the way:** *Star Wars Insider*, no. 45 (August/September 1999): 63.

332　**"started on page one:** Jody Duncan, *"Star Wars" Mythmaking: Behind the Scenes of "Attack of the Clones"* (New York: Ballantine Books, 2002), 13.

333　**"Jar Jar's Great Adventure":** Marcus Hearn, *The Cinema of George Lucas* (New York: Harry N. Abrams, 2005), 216.

333　**PADMÉ: Representative Binks:** Excerpts from draft scripts on http://starwarz.com/starkiller/episodeii.

334　**"This was much more like a movie:** Duncan, *Mythmaking*, 89.

334　**"Is that it?:** Lew Irwin, "'Attack of the Clones' Attacked," *Hollywood*, August 8, 2001, http://www.hollywood.com/news/brief/473238/attack-of-the-clones-attacked.

334　**"I was always worried:** Lucas, *Star Wars, Episode III: Revenge of the Sith*, DVD Commentary (Twentieth Century Fox, 2005).

336　**"Right now we don't need a script,":** *Star Wars Insider*, no. 48 (February/March 2000): 11.

336　**"The dialogue was, well:** "Sky's the Limit," *Detroit Free Press*, May 19, 2005.

337　**"The screenplay would make Buster Crabbe:** Michael Atkinson, "Reproductive Rites," *Village Voice*, May 14, 2002.

338　**"I was wonderfully blindsided:** Timothy Zahn, author interview, August 16, 2013.

339　**"coolest job in the world.":** *Wired*, August 2008.

339　**"Luke is obviously a 1,":** Leland Chee at *Star Wars* Celebration Europe II, July 26, 2013.

340　**"most fun to do.":** Gary Dretzka, "Lucas Strikes Back: 'Star Wars' Creator Defends Jar Jar and Says Plot Rules His Universe," *San Francisco Chronicle*, May 13, 2002.

340　**"I've been thinking about it,":** J. W. Rinzler, *The Making of "Star Wars: Revenge of the Sith"* (New York: Del Rey, 2005), 31.

341　**"disassemble Episode III:** Rinzler, *Making of "Revenge,"* 36.

341　**"painted myself into a corner":** Hearn, *Cinema*, 240.

341　**"All democracies turn:** Jess Cagle, "Yoda Strikes Back!" *Time*, April 29, 2002.

342　**"I didn't think it would get:** "Sith Invites Bush Comparisons," Associated Press, May 16, 2005.

342　**"inertia. Procrastination:** Rinzler, *Making of "Revenge,"* 47.

344　**"Steven confirmed that most:** Rinzler, *Making of "Revenge,"* 188.

344　**"sharp right turns":** Rinzler, *Making of "Revenge,"* 204.

345　**"To be very honest:** Lucas at *Star Wars* Celebration III, April 26, 2005.

24. BUILDING CHARACTER

347　**Take the story of Chris Bartlett:** Story details and quotes from Chris Bartlett, author interview, August 23, 2013.

349　**the R2 Builders Club:** Story details and quotes from Chris James, Grant McKinney, and Gerard Fardardo, author interview, September 15, 2013.

350　**"And they break down all the time:** Bonnie Burton, author interview, January 31, 2014.

25. HOW I STOPPED WORRYING AND LEARNED TO LOVE THE PREQUELS

356　**"People were getting back:** Kyle Newman, author interview, August 14, 2013.

356　**"You weren't there at the beginning!:** "Change," *Spaced*, series 2, episode 2, directed by Edgar Wright, March 2, 2001.

357　**"We know we had a real:** Interview with Jon Stewart, *Star Wars* Celebration V, August 15, 2010.

357　**"It was a magnificent:** Liz Lee, author interview, February 14, 2013.

358　**"None of my three kids:** Chris Giunta, author interview, August 29, 2013.

358   **Machete Order:** Rod Hilton, "Star Wars: Machete Order," *Absolutely No Machete Juggling,* http://static.nomachetejuggling.com/machete_order.html, accessed April 1, 2014.

358   **"With the Machete Order,":** "Would George Lucas Approve of the Star Wars Machete Order?," *Den of Geek,* April 3, 2012, http://www.denofgeek.us/movies/star-wars/18992/would-george-lucas-approve-of-the-star-wars-machete-order.

359   **"Part of the fun for me:** J. W. Rinzler, *The Making of "Star Wars, Revenge of the Sith"* (New York: Del Rey, 2005), 84.

359   **"We realized that these were fans:** "The Phantom Edit," *Salon,* November 5, 2001.

359   **"well-intentioned editing demonstration":** "The Phantom Edit."

360   **"It plays on a distinctly:** Emily Asher-Perrin, "Watching the Star Wars Prequels on Mute: An Experiment," Tor.com, January 16, 2013.

361   **"I'm not convinced that George:** Matt Wild, "The Audience Strikes Back: Mike Stoklasa's Very Detailed (and Very Late) Takedowns of *Star Wars,*" *A.V. Club Milwaukee,* April 13, 2010, http://archive.is/YgsWm.

363   **"Plinkett is skewering:** Michael Barryte, author interview, January 12, 2014.

366   **"Dealing with prequel hate:** Bryan Young, author interview, September 5, 2013.

26. USING THE UNIVERSE

371   **"We spent a lot of years:** "Lucas' New Headquarters Give Bay Area Film a Lift," *New York Times,* July 20, 2005.

372   **"A lot of *Star Wars* is over,":** author transcript of Lucas press conference, June 25, 2005.

373   **"If there were a way:** Dale Pollock, *Skywalking: The Life and Films of George Lucas,* updated ed. (New York: Da Capo, 1999), 178.

373   **"*Deadwood* in space.":** James Peaty, "Rick McCallum Interview: Dennis Potter, Star Wars TV series, George Lucas and Red Tails," *Den of Geek,* June 3, 2012, http://www.denofgeek.us/movies/rick-mccallum/21562/rick-mccallum-interview-dennis-potter-star-wars-tv-series-george-lucas-red-tails.

373   **"But then George would come in:** Anonymous Lucasfilm source.

374   **"We were building this show up:** Anonymous Lucasfilm source.

375   **"We can do better,":** Anonymous Lucasfilm source.

375   **"After the TV series:** Richard Corliss, "A Conversation with George Lucas," *Time,* March 14, 2006.

376   **"I talked a lot about *Star Wars*:** Steve Heisler, "Dave Filoni," *A.V. Club,* August 14, 2008, http://www.avclub.com/article/dave-filoni-14293.

377   **"No," he said:** Dave Filoni, *Star Wars* Celebration Europe II, July 26, 2013.

377   **"Sometimes George works:** "The Force Lives On, as Do the Toys," *New York Times,* July 1, 2008.

378   **"obsessively-compulsively cluttered:** Owen Gleiberman, *Entertainment Weekly,* August 14, 2008.

378   **"a deadening film that cuts corners:** Roger Ebert, *Chicago Sun-Times,* August 14, 2008.

378   **"We weren't ready for prime time,":** James Arnold Taylor, author interview, June 18, 2013.

380   **"He always wanted to be there:** Filoni at *Star Wars* Celebration Europe.

380   **"we need 100 more:** *Star Wars Insider,* no. 140 (May 2013): 20.

27. HELLO DISNEY

381   **"I'm moving away:** George Lucas Is Ready to Roll the Credits," *New York Times,* January 17, 2012.

381   **"With the Internet, it's gotten:** "How Disney Bought Lucasfilm—and Its Plans for 'Star Wars,'" *Bloomberg BusinessWeek,* March 7, 2013.

382   **"I never had a story:** David Kamp, "The Force Is Back," *Vanity Fair,* February 1999.

382 **"I've left pretty explicit instructions:** Matthew Leyland, "George Lucas," *Total Film*, April 2008.

382 **"*Star Wars* obviously snuck up:** Interview with Jon Stewart, *Star Wars* Celebration V, August 15, 2010.

383 **"quite a mess":** Rob Smith, *Rogue Leaders: The Story of LucasArts* (San Francisco: Chronicle Books, 2008), 176.

384 **"used to being able to change:** Jason Schreier, "How LucasArts Fell Apart," *Kotaku*, September 27, 2013, http://kotaku.com/how-lucasarts-fell-apart-1401731043.

384 **"*Star Wars*-level quality:** Walter Isaacson, *Steve Jobs* (New York: Simon & Schuster, 2011), 243.

386 **"Hello boys, it's take your girlfriend:** Anonymous source, Lucasfilm.

387 **"I'm not ready to pursue that now,":** "How Disney Bought Lucasfilm."

387 **"ruminated on it endlessly":** Quotes from Lucas and Kennedy from "George Lucas & Kathleen Kennedy Discuss Disney and the Future of Star Wars," YouTube video, October 30, 2012, https://www.youtube.com/watch?v=YyqlTi7lkhY.

388 **"afford me the ability:** Kathleen Kennedy, Celebration Europe II, July 27, 2013.

388 **"I've got to build this company:** "How Disney Bought Lucasfilm."

388 **"Wait," said Jett:** "Jett Lucas Interview: Star Wars Episodes 7, 8 & 9, New Cast Rumours & J. J. Abrams," *Flicks and the City*, YouTube video, 13:02, October 16, 2013, https://www.youtube.com/watch?v=lnr18AUym-0.

389 **"I was shocked by how:** "Power Lawyers: How Star Wars Nerds Sold Lucasfilm to Disney," *Hollywood Reporter*, May 31, 2013.

389 **"Trust became important,":** Iger to producer Brian Grazer, Newsmaker Luncheon, Los Angeles, January 23, 2013.

389 **"The writing was on the wall,":** Episode 6, *Full of Sith* podcast, January 27, 2013.

390 **"something that's unprintable":** "On the Brink of the Future," Starwars.com, October 30, 2013.

390 **"Ultimately you have to say:** "How Disney Bought Lucasfilm."

390 **"We thought from a storytelling:** "How Disney Bought Lucasfilm."

391 **"the steadiest of all the studios,":** "George Lucas & Kathleen Kennedy Discuss Disney."

393 **Disney had made a video:** "Disney to Acquire Lucasfilm," YouTube video, 5:39, October 30, 2012, https://www.youtube.com/watch?v=QIkqX5fG_tA.

CONCLUSION: ACROSS THE UNIVERSE

396 **"Only a few of them recognized:** Ates Cetin, author interview, August 26, 2013.

398 **"create a bit more attention.":** Paul French quoted in "The Empire Strides Back for Starlight," *Magnet* (Australia), March 21, 2012.

399 **"He thought it was a good omen:** Hal Barwood, author interview, May 21, 2013.

399 **"I'm hoping that if the film:** Paul Scanlon, "The Force Behind Star Wars," *Rolling Stone*, August 1977.

399 **"My only hope:** *Star Wars* Celebration V, August 15, 2010.

399 **"There were certain underlying ideas:** Kerry O'Quinn, *Starlog*, no. 47 (June 1981).

400 **"My whole love of space:** Bobak Ferdowsi, GeekExchange.com, May 28, 2013.

400 **"I never got into:** Will Wei, "Neil deGrasse Tyson Tells Us Why 'Star Trek' Is So Much Better Than 'Star Wars,'" *Business Insider*, May 14, 2013.

401 **"We've got lots of *Star Wars*:** Chris Lewicki, author interview, June 11, 2013.

401 **"That was a great, great way:** Parazynski in NASA transcript of shuttle mission STS-120, http://spaceflight.nasa.gov/gallery/audio/shuttle/sts-120/transcript/fd12.txt.

402   **"The very existence of these discoveries:** Quoted in Charles Q. Choi, "Planet Like 'Star Wars' Tatooine Discovered Orbiting 2 Suns," Space.com, September 15, 2011.

404   **Trust members "hate us":** "3 Vie to Build Culture Center in the Presidio," *New York Times*, September 15, 2013.

404   **"Plus the idea:** Lucas to Presidio Trust, recorded and transcribed by the author, September 23, 2013.

404   **"somewhere in the park.":** Craig Middleton, Presidio Trust, recorded and transcribed by the author, February 3, 2014.

406   **"We're just going to let:** Disney spokesperson to the author.

407   **"Every time we find someone's:** "*Star Wars* Actor Richard LeParmentier Dies at 66," Thompson Reuters, April 17, 2013.

407   **"It's not uncommon for someone:** Alan Horn, April 17, 2013, transcribed by the author.

409   **"Ralph's designs are as real:** Behind-the-scenes video shown at *Star Wars* Celebration Europe II, July 27, 2013.

409   **"Imagination drives innovation,":** Kathleen Kennedy, Celebration Europe II.

410   **"He wrote more of the *Star Wars*:** Steve Sansweet, appearance at Books Inc., Opera Plaza, San Francisco, October 5, 2010.

411   **"I can reveal exclusively,":** Pablo Hidalgo, recorded and transcribed by the author, August 10, 2013.

414   **"It's a complicated cultural icon,":** *Access Hollywood*, June 14, 2013.

INDEX